Rebound 1998

MODERN STUDIES IN PHILOSOPHY

THE PRE-SOCRATICS

MODERN STUDIES IN PHILOSOPHY is a series of anthologies presenting contemporary interpretations and evaluations of the works of major philosophers. The editors have selected articles designed to show the systematic structure of the thought of these philosophers, and to reveal the relevance of their views to the problems of current interest. These volumes are intended to be contributions to contemporary debates as well as to the history of philosophy; they not only trace the origins of many problems important to modern philosophy, but also introduce major philosophers as interlocutors in current discussions.

MODERN STUDIES IN PHILOSOPHY is prepared under the general editorship of Amélie Oksenberg Rorty, Livingston College, Rutgers University.

ALEXANDER P. D. MOURELATOS is Professor of Philosophy at The University of Texas at Austin. He received his B.A., M.A., and Ph.D. degrees from Yale University. He is the author of *The Route of Parmenides*, published by Yale University Press in 1970, and has been a contributor to journals of philosophy and classical philology.

MODERN STUDIES IN PHILOSOPHY

Amélie Oksenberg Rorty
General Editor

THE
PRE-SOCRATICS

A Collection of Critical Essays

Edited by

ALEXANDER P. D. MOURELATOS

ANCHOR BOOKS

Anchor Press / Doubleday
Garden City, New York

1974

Anchor Books edition: 1974
ISBN 0-385-05480-7
Library of Congress Catalog Card Number 73-11729

First Edition

Journal of the History of Philosophy, Inc. Reprinted from the *Journal of the History of Philosophy*, vol. 6, no. 2 (April, 1968), 111–32, by permission of the editor.

"Plato and Parmenides on the Timeless Present," by G. E. L. Owen, from *The Monist*, 50 (1966), 317–40. Reprinted with permission of the publisher, Open Court Publishing Company, La Salle, Illinois, and of the author.

"The Relation between the Two Parts of Parmenides' Poem," by Karl Reinhardt, from Karl Reinhardt, *Parmenides und die Geschichte der griechischen Philosophie* (Bonn: Friedrich Cohen, 1916; repr. Frankfurt a.M., Vittorio Klostermann, 1959), pp. 18–88 with omissions. Translated by Matthew R. Cosgrove with Alexander P. D. Mourelatos. Selection translated and printed here with the permission of the publisher, Vittorio Klostermann, and of the late Frau Elly Reinhardt.

"The Deceptive Words of Parmenides' 'Doxa,' " by Alexander P. D. Mourelatos. Copyright © 1970 by Yale University. From *The Route of Parmenides: A Study of Word, Image, and Argument in the Fragments* (New Haven, Conn.: Yale University Press, 1970), pp. 222–63; abridged and slightly revised in the present version. Reprinted with permission of Yale University Press.

"Zeno and Indivisible Magnitudes," by David J. Furley. Copyright © 1967 by Princeton University Press. From David J. Furley, *Two Studies in the Greek Atomists* (Princeton, N.J.: Princeton University Press, 1967), pp. 63–78. Reprinted here by permission of Princeton University Press.

"The Tradition about Zeno of Elea Re-Examined," by Friedrich Solmsen, from *Phronesis*, 16 (1971), 116–41. Reprinted with permission of the editor of *Phronesis* and of the author.

"Religion and Natural Philosophy in Empedocles' Doctrine of the Soul," by Charles H. Kahn. From the *Archiv für Geschichte der Philosophie*, 42, (1960), 3–35, with the revisions and "Retractationes" included in its reprinting in John P. Anton with George L. Kustas, eds., *Essays in Ancient Greek Philosophy* (Albany, N.Y.: State University of New York Press, 1971), pp. 3–38. The appendix, "Empedocles Among the Shamans" (*AGP*, pp. 30–35, and Anton, pp. 30–36), is omitted. Reprinted here with the permission of Walter de Gruyter & Co., Berlin, the State University of New York Press, and the author.

"The Physical Theory of Anaxagoras," by Gregory Vlastos, from *The Philosophical Review*, 59 (1950), 31–57, with additional notes and revisions supplied by the author. Reprinted with the permission of the editor of *The Philosophical Review* and of the author.

"Anaxagoras and the Concept of Matter before Aristotle," by G. B. Kerferd, from *Bulletin of the John Rylands Library*, 52 (1969), 129–43. Reprinted with the permission of the Governors of the John Rylands Library and of the author.

"The Atomists' Reply to the Eleatics," by David J. Furley. Copyright © by Princeton University Press. From David J. Furley, *Two Studies in the Greek Atomists* (Princeton, N.J.: Princeton University Press, 1967), pp. 79–103. Reprinted here by permission of Princeton University Press.

OTHER VOLUMES IN THE
MODERN STUDIES IN PHILOSOPHY
SERIES

Augustine
Bertrand Russell
Hegel
Hobbes and Rousseau
Kant
Kierkegaard
Leibniz
Nietzsche
Plato I
Plato II
Sartre
Spinoza
The Philosophy of Socrates
Wittgenstein

CONTENTS

PREFACE

This volume differs from others in the Modern Studies in Philosophy series in that it does not treat of a single philosopher or pair of philosophers, but of a historical period of nearly two centuries. The principle of unity appropriate to this volume will therefore be suggested not by the Platonic paradigm of a one-in-many but by the Wittgensteinian images of a rope of many strands and family resemblance.

Envisaging the rationale and function of this volume as essentially pedagogic, and keeping the needs of university students in mind, I set myself the following aims in selecting articles. First, the volume ought to introduce readers to the great scholars—both living and dead—in the field; and so it would be desirable to include articles by as many of the recognized masters as possible. Second, the offerings ought to constitute a spectrum of the major topics and approaches in the field. Third, the volume should include as much of a sampling of continental work not previously translated as is commensurate with the consideration that the readership will be largely English-speaking. Fourth, only those articles should be included that are primarily philosophical in approach or involve interaction of philosophical and philological approaches. Fifth, as many of the articles that are listed as "suggested reading" in the better textbooks on Greek philosophy and on the Pre-Socratics should be included. Sixth, it would be best to select those articles that speak to one another as they group themselves around well-defined controversies of interpretation.

These multiple aims are not necessarily in harmony, and an adjustment had to be worked out. Given the limitations of space, some of the choices were difficult; they may in the end appear arbitrary. Fortunately, this is not the only English-language source of reprints of important studies in the area. The earlier appearance (or, in one instance, the anticipated early appearance) of the following have made my job of selection more manageable, though also more challenging: The Bobbs-Merrill Reprint Series in Philosophy (PHIL-52 Cherniss, PHIL-114 Kahn, PHIL-238 Kahn); Wesley C. Salmon, ed., *Zeno's Paradoxes* (Indianapolis and New York, 1970); David J. Furley and R. E. Allen, eds., *Studies in Presocratic Philosophy: Vol. I, The Beginnings of Philosophy* (London, 1970), and *Vol. II, The Eleatics and the Pluralists* (forthcoming); The Bobbs-Merrill Reprint Series in History of Science (HS-21 Gomperz, HS-45 Lloyd, HS-71 Szabó). With the exception of Vlastos' article on Anaxagoras, which was strategically needed for the unity of Part VIII, none of the studies in this volume appear in one of the collections listed above.

Some of the best accounts on topics of Pre-Socratic philosophy are not in journal articles but in books. These also deserve to become more widely available. It is distinctive of the selection for this volume that one third of the studies appearing here originally appeared as parts of a book. In this case, too, duplication of items easily available in inexpensive editions has been avoided. This explains what would appear as conspicuous omissions—e.g. no chapter from John Burnet's *Early Greek Philosophy*, or Werner Jaeger's *The Theology of the Early Greek Philosophers*.

Two studies, Kahn on the Pythagoreans and Long on Empedocles, were written specially for this volume. Moreover, the studies by Fränkel on Xenophanes, Hölscher on Heraclitus, and Reinhardt on Parmenides, specially translated for this volume, have not till now been available in English.

Though the primary materials of Pre-Socratic philosophy are notoriously slim, there is so much variety in themes and philosophical styles that no single anthology of essays could do justice to all the individual thinkers or schools. Except for a brief treatment in one article, the Sophists, who would be best handled in conjunction with Socrates and the minor Socratics (as in vol. 3 of W. K. C. Guthrie's *A History of Greek Philosophy*), have been left outside this volume's scope. It also seemed to me proper to emphasize some philosophers at the expense of others if this would indeed more adequately serve the six aims I listed above. The strong emphasis of the volume on Heraclitus and Parmenides is commensurate with the prominence of these two central thinkers in the whole of the literature on the Pre-Socratics.

It is embarrassing to me as editor and unfortunate for the volume's readers that Democritus should be represented here by a single article. One might argue or plead that Democritus would be best covered in an account of the whole succession of the Atomist philosophers of antiquity—Leucippus, Democritus, Epicurus, Lucretius. But the honest truth, and what is more to the point, is that the early Atomists have been badly short-shrifted in the literature. When one compares the number of books and essays devoted to Anaximander, or to the Pythagoreans, or Heraclitus, or Parmenides, the relative paucity of work on the early Atomists is striking. (The excellent study by Vlastos, "Ethics and Physics in Democritus," will be reprinted in Furley and Allen, II.)

Most of the studies in this volume were originally written for an audience of specialists in Greek philosophy. I have, therefore, edited them so as to make them more accessible to students with little or no background in Greek or classical philology. Wherever possible, long Greek quotations have been omitted, and translations have been substituted if none were originally provided. Translations have also been furnished for short Greek quotations that originally had appeared untranslated. Discussions of philological detail that could not interest the philosophically oriented reader—in the original version mostly in footnotes but occasionally in the main text—have been omitted or abbreviated. Those that remain are of intrinsic interest. Translations of the Greek in these discussions would, of course, have been pointless or impossible; the nonspecialists can generally circumvent these sections without losing the thread of the main argument. Abbreviated references (except those to ancient authors) that have become standard among classicists have been expanded if they appear of potential interest to the nonclassicist. The more drastic of editorial alterations are indicated by letter footnotes (editor's) passim.

Both in order to make the volume's appearance less forbidding to the nonspecialist and in order to keep costs down, Greek text in the main body of the selections, if shorter than three or four words, generally appears transliterated. In the footnotes, however, which are obviously intended for a more limited audience, and where there would be serious visual interference between the italics of references and those of transliteration, Greek lettering is generally used. For some articles, where there is considerable crossover discussion between main body and footnotes, transliteration is used in the footnotes too, if the frequency of italics in references seemed low enough to permit this.

I have discussed different versions of the volume's contents and received valuable comments and suggestions from fellow scholars too numerous to mention here, and from several of the contributors to the volume. Their advice is very much appreciated. I specially thank David Furley for informing me of the contents of *Studies in Presocratic Philosophy* before its vol. 1 appeared and while vol. 2 was still at the planning stage. I also thank Professor Dr. Uvo Hölscher for checking the translation of the Reinhardt selection. The Introduction was much improved by ample critical comments on its penultimate draft offered by Edward N. Lee. An early narrowing of possible selections was achieved with the advice of graduate students in courses on the Pre-Socratics at The University of Texas at Austin in spring and fall 1971. One of these students, Mr. Jack Winkler, very kindly helped in the work of editing articles in 1971-72.

I express here my appreciation for grants from the University Research Institute of The University of Texas at Austin in summer and fall 1971 and in 1972-73 that made it possible for me to have the services of a student research assistant.

My greatest debt is to that assistant, Mr. Matthew R. Cosgrove. The translations of the German language articles are basically his work. He has been unstintingly, faithfully, and invaluably helpful through all phases of editing, from the initial sifting of possible selections through proofreading and preparation of the Indexes.

A. P. D. M.

ABBREVIATIONS

AGP	*Archiv für Geschichte der Philosophie*
AJP	*American Journal of Philology*
CP	*Classical Philology*
CQ	*The Classical Quarterly*
DK	Hermann Diels, *Die Fragmente der Vorsokratiker*, 6th ed. rev. W. Kranz, 3 vols., Berlin, 1952
Dox. Gr.	Hermann Diels, *Doxographi Graeci*, Berlin, 1879
EGP	John Burnet, *Early Greek Philosophy*, 4th ed., a reprint of the 3d ed., London, 1930 (earlier editions specifically indicated where cited)
Furley and Allen, I	David J. Furley and R. E. Allen, eds., *Studies in Presocratic Philosophy, Vol. I: The Beginnings of Philosophy*, London, 1970
Furley and Allen, II	David J. Furley and R. E. Allen, eds., *Studies in Presocratic Philosophy, Vol. II: The Eleatics and the Pluralists*, forthcoming
JHS	*The Journal of Hellenic Studies*
KR	G. S. Kirk and J. E. Raven, *The Presocratic Philosophers*, Cambridge, 1957
LSJ	H. G. Liddell and R. Scott, *A Greek-English Lexicon*, 9th ed. rev. H. S. Jones and R. McKenzie, Oxford, 1940
RE	Paulys *Realencyclopädie der classischen Altertumswissenschaft*, neue Bearbeitung von G. Wissowa et al., Stuttgart, 1893–73.
TAPA	*Transactions and Proceedings of the American Philological Association*

As is customary, references to the Pre-Socratics are in accordance with the numbering in DK: numbers preceded by the letter B refer to the B sections of DK (fragments considered authentic); numbers preceded by the letter A refer to the A sections (ancient testimonia). Where confusion might arise, the chapter number is prefixed to the A or B reference. Thus 22B8 or Heraclitus B8 both refer to fragment 8 of Heraclitus in DK. The letter B is often omitted in successive references to the same fragment; it is also omitted when the references appear in a table. Abbreviations for ancient authors are generally those of LSJ—with occasional expansion to facilitate recognition.

EDITOR'S INTRODUCTION

"Secondary literature" is virtually a term of derision among teachers and students of philosophy in today's university. Since there is so much of the original works of Plato and Aristotle, alone, to read—not to mention Plotinus, Augustine, Aquinas, or other "greats" in the Western tradition—and when these works are now available in good translations, more easily and widely than ever before, it seems pedagogically distracting or even stultifying to encourage the study of commentaries and interpretations. The policy is, on the face of it, sound: We certainly want to nurture independent thinkers, not scholastic *famuli* who parrot the lines of a textbook or the opinions of received authority. Indeed, heirs, as we all inevitably are, to the positivism, antihistoricism, and New Criticism of the thirties and forties, we are too tempted to equate "secondary literature" with "second-rate literature." But there are also dangers and pitfalls in the "great works" approach that are by now all too familiar. It is common for a student nurtured on "primary literature" to develop a habit of unstructured, uninformed, and subjective reading. He learns to envisage the classical source as his private imaginary counterpart, either friend or foe, engages it autistically in make-believe dialogue or shadow-fighting, discusses it in a conceptual vacuum, without reference to recognized issues, or cites it selectively to facilitate or advance his own opinions. What is not learned in this approach is the true art of philosophical interpretation and criticism, one that places itself under the constraints of a certain *status quaestionis* and problematic, and seeks to come to terms with alternative views already on record. The practitioner of the true art operates in a public forum of philosophical dialectic that encompasses not only the community of contemporary readers interested in a given subject but also a community of readers of like interests that spans the ages.

"When one thinks what would become of any modern philosopher

I

if he were only known through the polemics of his rivals, one can see
how admirable the pre-Socratics must have been, since through the
mist of malice spread by their enemies they still appear great." This
remark by Bertrand Russell,[1] who was an avowed admirer of the Pre-
Socratics, is perhaps hyperbolic or too charitable. But it serves to remind us of what is distinctive about the early philosophers of Greece.
There is, in their case, no such thing as primary literature. Even what
are known as "fragments," the texts laboriously culled by post-Renais-
sance scholars from what appear to be quotations in the works of later
authors, inherently carry the encrustation of traditions of interpretation.
Typically, they cannot be adequately restored or properly understood
without attention to the context of quotation from which they have
been retrieved. The difficulty is not simply one of establishing the accuracy of the quotation, or of eliciting maximum information from its
accompanying context about the full, original, pre-Socratic text; we
must also account for the ideological motives that resulted in the happy
accident of the preservation of *this* rather than of some *other* text—for
we cannot assume that what struck a later commentator as important
and worthy of quote was commensurately important for its original
author.

There is little danger that a student of the Pre-Socratics will be
tempted to use exclusively the "primary literature" approach. The one
edition that gives the fragments with no testimonia at all (Kathleen
Freeman's *Ancilla to the Pre-Socratic Philosophers*) can be read cover-
to-cover in half a day; but the student will be left only tantalized and
bewildered at the end of each chapter. To understand the Pre-Socratics
one must work through secondary literature. And since the task of
working through the secondary literature of antiquity is enormous and
calls for special expertise, the approach must be through modern secondary literature, in which the interpretations of antiquity are implicitly
contained or explicitly sifted and examined. Sooner or later the student
who attempts to work on the Pre-Socratics at a level that is minimally
responsible and intellectually rewarding must learn carefully to distinguish among, and take adequate note of: (a) philosophical problems
in their suprahistorical identity; (b) these same problems as they may or
must have arisen in a sixth- or fifth-century context; (c) these and related problems as they are reflected in contexts of later philosophy;
(d) the various formulations of these problems in the modern literature
of interpretation; (e) essentially exegetic and interpretive problems, i.e.

[1] *A History of Western Philosophy* (New York, 1945), p. 45.

questions regarding strictly the evidence in our ancient sources rather than the underlying philosophical problematic.

If one considers what sort of demands might be immediately felt by the student who proceeds strictly by the "great works" approach, one is immediately aware of a certain ironic reversal. Plato and Aristotle—singling them out again as examples—believed that philosophy could only be practiced under the constraints of public dialogue. But the engaged modern reader who concentrates on working through an omnibus edition of Plato or Aristotle is less likely to find himself required to practice moves of actual philosophical dialectic than the reader who plows through half a dozen different interpretations of an intriguing Pre-Socratic fragment.

The importance of studying the historical origins of philosophy, and of the Pre-Socratics in particular, is a noble and familiar theme. It has been handled forcefully and persuasively not only by the great scholar-historians of the period, such men as Burnet, Cornford, Heidel, Jaeger, Reinhardt, Tannery, Zeller—not to mention any of a number of scholars of comparable stature who are presently alive—but also by such philosopher-admirers of the Pre-Socratics as Francis Bacon, Bertrand Russell, and Sir Karl Popper, in the English tradition; or Hegel, Nietzsche, and Heidegger, in the continental tradition. What the preceding paragraphs have emphasized is something often overlooked: the *pedagogic* importance of the study of the Pre-Socratics. Although the original texts are scanty and fragmented, the fund of interpretive traditions is incomparably rich. No other field offers as inviting a challenge to the philosophical imagination, yet in as demanding an environment of evidential and interpretive controls. Standards of precision are high, methodological issues have often been aired, a repertoire of alternative interpretations is already on record, and there is a firmly established tradition of doing justice not only to the primary texts but to ancient and modern commentary as well. At least in the last one hundred years, discussion within the field has been remarkably continuous and cumulative, and progressively more sensitive to the nuances, levels, or strata, as well as the presuppositions and repercussions, of philosophic argument. Relatively to the corpus of Western philosophy, there is no *closer* reading, line of original for line of commentary on it, than the kind of reading the materials on the Pre-Socratics demand and have sustained.

The numbered introductory Sections that appear below give a brief preamble to each of the eight Parts of the present collection. The aims vary somewhat with the Part concerned. Generally, these introductory Sections suggest the principle of unity in a given Part, review the context of controversy to which each essay belongs, suggest a program of additional readings, indicate connections—wherever this is appropriate —with essays published in other Parts of the collection, or call the reader's attention to important themes discussed in the essays in a given Part that are not mentioned in the Part's heading.

The Selective Bibliography, which appears at the end of the volume, is intended as a supplement to these introductory Sections. The reader will find in the Bibliography not only fuller entries on items referred to by author and title in the eight Sections below, but also suggested readings on figures and topics of Pre-Socratic philosophy that are represented inadequately or not at all in this collection.

Even with attention to the occasional notices given below regarding themes that lie outside the stated scope of a given Part, the volume's coverage of individual figures, schools, or concepts is not adequately reflected in the eight headings; the Subject Index has been selectively designed so as to help the reader locate informative discussions of important topics beyond what appears in the Table of Contents.

I. Concept Studies

The beginnings of Greek philosophy are inextricably involved with the historical origins of major philosophical concepts and with the development of a vocabulary of reflective-critical thought in the Greek language. Although most of the studies in this volume are oriented toward particular figures or schools, the two essays in Part I explore the development of two concepts: the epistemological concept of mind (*nous*) and the ontological concepts of quality and change. In the literature on the Pre-Socratics, this genre of diachronic conceptual or semantic study includes a number of important contributions, on such key terms as *physis*, "nature," *alētheia*, "reality, truth," *logos*, "discourse, reason," *einai*, "to be," and others. A selective listing of such concept-studies appears in the Bibliography.

The concept of mind is so obviously fundamental that the essay by Kurt von Fritz, "*Nous*, *Noein*, and Their Derivatives in Pre-Socratic Philosophy (Excluding Anaxagoras)," also constitutes an excellent and useful survey of the whole of Pre-Socratic philosophy. The essay's sections on Xenophanes, Heraclitus, Parmenides, Zeno, Empedocles, and the Atomists may well be read as supplements to corresponding Parts of this anthology. Also included in von Fritz' essay are sections on Hesiod and Protagoras, who are not otherwise represented in the readings offered here. The separate study of *Nous* in Anaxagoras, promised by von Fritz in his opening paragraph and suggested by the exclusion specified in the essay's title, was published by him in 1964 in German.[2] The 1943 article, "*Noos*, and *Noein* in the Homeric Poems" (1943), on which von Fritz's account of *nous* in the Pre-Socratics builds, is especially recommended to students who wish to investigate more fully the prephilosophical paradigms of the Greek vocabulary of cognition.

Beyond its obvious usefulness as a concept study, W. A. HEIDEL'S "QUALITATIVE CHANGE IN PRE-SOCRATIC PHILOSOPHY," of which the first (general) section is reprinted in this Part, has been a contribution of major importance in its reconstruction of the earliest stages of Greek philosophy. Heidel's essay had revolutionary implications when it first appeared, in 1906; it remains profoundly suggestive to this date. The traditional reconstruction of the beginnings of Greek philosophy—a reconstruction that was uniquely dominant in the nineteenth century and that is ultimately traceable to Aristotle—runs like this. All Ionian philosophers conceived of reality as *one* in its underlying *archē* or substratum; as *many* in the modifications or alterations of that underlying substratum. They only differed among themselves in how they characterized that substratum: for Thales it was water; for Anaximander, the *Apeiron*; for Anaximenes, air; for Xenophanes, God; for Heraclitus, fire. W. A. Heidel pointed out that this reconstruction was unhistorical, for it projected Aristotle's sophisticated substance-attribute conception, and a related conception of change as qualitative alteration, onto the beginnings of Greek speculative thought. What Heidel proposed as the original conception was one of change as recomposition, which involves not qualities—abstractly conceived—but material constituents or ingredients. The importance of Heidel's article was increasingly felt through the early decades of this century. His work encouraged Harold Cherniss to rethink the whole question of Aristotle's testimony on Pre-Socratic philosophy,[3] and in our own day it has become a commonplace—at least among scholars writing in English—that the early Greek philosophers conceived of qualities concretely, as things or quasi-things.

But the implications of the rewriting of the history of early Greek

[2] See "Der ΝΟῪΣ des Anaxagoras."

[3] See *Aristotle's Criticism of Presocratic Philosophy*, pp. 50 and n. 203, 57 and n. 233, 60 and n. 246, 91 and n. 387, and passim.

philosophy that was started by Heidel's article have not yet been fully realized. For if Heidel was right, Greek philosophy did not start from a holistic vision of the world as a unitary reality—which is how the beginning is still characterized in many of the textbooks and in the prevailing continental interpretations—but from a view of the world as a totality of concrete and relatively discrete things.[4] This indeed accords much better with what we have learned from modern historians of Greek art and Greek literature about the proclivity of the preclassical Greek imagination to view things separately, in *parataxis*.[5]

II. Ionian Beginnings

Of the four Ionian philosophers before Heraclitus, it is in the case of two of them only that the evidence in our sources—slight and garbled as it is—is suggestive enough to give some support to interpretive hypotheses that are philosophically interesting—in terms of their implications for the dialectic of philosophical problems and concepts. Strictly historical questions may, in any event, be raised. Scholars have sought to ascertain, for example, what knowledge of mathematics or astronomy Thales is likely to have had; possible connections between early Ionian thought and Oriental cosmologies and myths have been investigated; and questions may be raised, and answered with a respectable degree of plausibility, about details of Anaximander and Anaximenes' astronomy, or about their supposed doctrine of a cosmogonic whirl. We can also explore in general terms what might be called the early Ionian world-view, extrapolating mostly from what Heraclitus, Parmenides, and their successors react *against*. But if we are to study specific figures, and propose to look for recognizably philosophical themes in the evidence concerning them; if, moreover, we require a context with some minimal conceptual articulation for these themes, only two subjects lend themselves to study: Anaximander of Miletus and Xenophanes of Colophon.

Running through the various modern discussions of Anaximander and Xenophanes, two distinct themes, respectively for each, stand out.

[4] See Mourelatos, "Heraclitus, Parmenides, and the Naïve Metaphysics of Things."

[5] See Perry, "The Early Greek Capacity for Viewing Things Separately"; Notopoulos, "Parataxis in Homer"; B. A. van Groningen, *La Composition littéraire archaïque grecque* (Amsterdam, 1958).

As will be seen in a moment, the two themes are remarkably complementary. For Anaximander, what stands out is the theme of normative explanation, i.e. an explanation in terms of "right necessity." This would count as an *a priori* sort of explanation, one that envisages a well-ordered universe. Anaximander's world is indeed a *kosmos*, a "seemly array," governed by uniform periodicity, the cosmic opposites balanced within it, the whole structured symmetrically, and in proportions that conform to an intelligible arithmetical formula. The formative importance of this theme, not only for the teleological metaphysics of Plato and Aristotle but also for the whole tradition of philosophical rationalism, is obvious. CHARLES H. KAHN's study, "ANAXIMANDER'S FRAGMENT: THE UNIVERSE GOVERNED BY LAW," is concerned with precisely this theme.

What stands out in the case of Xenophanes is a "rationalism" of a different sort: one that defines itself in opposition to mythology, to tradition, and to seductively fanciful explanation. This is the rationalism of critique and rebuttal—many of the preserved fragments of Xenophanes come from works the ancients called *Silloi*, "lampoons." Xenophanes is the enemy of obfuscation, the friend of clear-headed, empirically oriented naturalism. An interpretation of Xenophanes along these lines was first worked out by HERMANN FRÄNKEL in his "Xenophanesstudien" (1928). The essay "XENOPHANES' EMPIRICISM AND HIS CRITIQUE OF KNOWLEDGE," which appears in this Part, is a translated excerpt from that study.

These two themes represent complementary, even antithetical, tendencies in the original thrust of philosophic thought: on the one hand, the quest for an ultimately satisfying explanation; on the other, the demand that explanation be subject to the constraints of *historia*, knowledge not of theories but of facts and information *about* the familiar world of human experience.

An important thread of continuity in the development of early Greek philosophy deserves to be brought out more clearly than it appears in the studies by Kahn and Fränkel. Parmenides is heir to both types of Ionian rationalism. Although his quest for an ultimate insight—certified, in figurative terms, by such mythological powers as *Anankē*, "Necessity," *Moira*, "Fate," *Dikē*, "Justice," and *Peithō*, "Persuasion"— harks back to Anaximander, the method of refutation and *reductio* argument he developed might be viewed as a radicalizing of the Xenophanean spirit of critique. This connection between Parmenidean *elenchus* and Xenophanean *Silloi* is perhaps more important than the outward resemblance between Parmenides' *eon*, "real," and Xenophanes' "one god."

III. PYTHAGORAS AND PYTHAGOREANISM

Viewing Pythagoreanism as a philosophical attitude or tendency in Western thought, one could give a general characterization of it by listing seven doctrines (overlapping in part with doctrines of its cognate movement, Platonism): (a) The fundamental realities of the world are structural and mathematical. (b) These structures necessarily articulate themselves into a single system; both the individual structures and the system as a whole conform to a principle, in accordance with which, what is causally *prior* and more *fundamental* is identical with, or coentails, what is *normatively* better, what is aesthetically more *beautiful*, and what displays greater *simplicity* and/or regularity in its mathematical proportions or properties. (c) Structures in superficially dissimilar contexts can be isomorphic; indeed, there is a pervasive affinity or sympathy between the inanimate and the animate, between man's psyche and the whole cosmos. (d) This cosmic sympathy affords the possibility of moral improvement through a patterning of the individual psyche on the cosmos. (e) Beyond moral improvement, the cosmic sympathy affords the prospect of ascent to a trans-human level of existence, even to immortality, through a process of "purification"; correlatively, it poses the threat of descent into an *infra*-human level of existence. (f) The process of knowing or understanding is inherently mystical and is consummated only by the elite. (g) The study of mathematics is the indispensable basis for all intellectual and spiritual progress.

Given the allusiveness of this complex of ideas, the influence of Pythagoreanism has often been felt on the side of numerology, superstition, occultism, and mindless formalism. But at crucial junctures and in important contexts, its influence has also been salutary and productive. In the words of a historian of science, "The founders of modern science were thoroughly imbued with the Pythagorean spirit. This is particularly true of Copernicus and Kepler, and almost as true of Galilei and Newton."[6] Within the wider context of intellectual history, Pythagoreanism as a formative and creative force in the arts—especially music and architecture—can hardly be overestimated.

But while this general characterization of Pythagoreanism in the

[6] A. Wolf, *A History of Science, Technology and Philosophy in the 16th and 17th Centuries*, 2d ed. (New York, 1950), p. 4.

Western tradition is relatively easy, the question of the origins of Pythagoreanism in Pre-Socratic philosophy is frustratingly difficult. Pythagoras himself wrote nothing; the Pythagorean schools practiced a code of secrecy about their doctrines and observed a policy of reverence toward the founder that required the attribution of all new discoveries, e.g. in geometry, to Pythagoras. Information about fifth-century Pythagoreanism is scrappy and slight. There is one main exception, in the fragments of Philolaus; but the authenticity of this seemingly rich source is in doubt. The information is richer in fourth-century sources, especially Aristotle, but there one must face the vexing problem of distinguishing between what is genuinely Pythagorean and what is Platonic or Academic (or Platonized-Pythagorean). When material gets plentiful, in the sources of late antiquity, the problems are further compounded by the admixture of the ideas of Neo-Pythagoreanism (a revivalist movement that starts in the first century B.C. and draws heavily on Platonist, Aristotelian, and Stoic themes). Even at its fifth-century stage, and, before that, in its sixth-century origins, the moral-religious side of Pythagoreanism is hard to distinguish from Orphism, or from that wider cultural phenomenon E. R. Dodds has called the Archaic "guilt culture" and Greek "puritan psychology."[7]

CHARLES H. KAHN'S "PYTHAGOREAN PHILOSOPHY BEFORE PLATO," an essay specially written for this volume, reviews and interprets the evidence concerning Pythagoras and early Pythagoreanism. Kahn draws on the rich fund of scholarship on the subject produced in the past fifty years, and formulates the major issues against the background of sharply drawn controversy (a summary of which appears in his opening section and notes). Kahn's essay must therefore carry more authority in its attributions and nonattributions of doctrine to Pythagoras and to fifth-century Pythagoreans than the first selection in this Part, F. M. CORNFORD'S "MYSTICISM AND SCIENCE IN THE PYTHAGOREAN TRADITION," which was written in 1922.

Cornford's essay reflects an earlier, more confident and exuberant, phase of scholarship on the Pythagoreans, before Erich Frank's skepticism (see below, p. 161) forced a closer look at the evidence. Beyond this general limitation, the distinctive thesis of its second section (Pythagorean "number-atomism"), with its special application to the interpretation of Zeno, has been tellingly criticized in recent decades (see Section VI, below). Even so, the essay deserves to remain required reading in the literature on the Pre-Socratics. The hypothesis of Pythagorean

[7] *The Greeks and the Irrational*, chs. 2 and 5, esp. p. 149.

number-atomism affords an alternative in interpretations of Zeno that is philosophically important, even if (as now widely held) it is historically unsupported. More relevantly for readers of this Part, Cornford's lengthier section on "The Mystical System of Pythagoras" is a masterly exposition of what is generally known as Pythagoreanism—perhaps the best short introduction anywhere available. Clear and often elegant in its formulations, Cornford's essay is full of insights into conceptual connections, into the import of the philosophic problems raised by the Pre-Socratics, and into the subtle interaction between philosophical ideas and moral-religious yearnings.[8]

IV. HERACLITUS

From antiquity to the present, Heraclitus has been known to the world as the philosopher of flux. But readers of the fragments know that Heraclitus speaks no less eloquently and suggestively of permanence and unification. Without actually challenging the relative importance of flux over permanence in Heraclitus, John Burnet observed that flux "is not the most original feature of the system."[9] The traditional interpretation was more directly attacked by Karl Reinhardt. In 1916 he wrote: "The fundamental thought of Heraclitus is the precise opposite of the flux doctrine: permanence in change, constancy in alteration, 'the same' (*tauton*) in 'turn-over' (*metapiptein*), 'measure' (*metron*) in 'transformation' (*metaballein*), unity in division, eternity in perishability."[10] Few scholars were persuaded then, or are now persuaded, by the whole of Reinhardt's interpretation—he contended that Heraclitus wrote *after* Parmenides, and under Eleatic influence. But his brilliant 1916 book, as well as his subsequent contributions on Heraclitus, did encourage radical rethinking of the traditional interpretation. Influential support for a revisionary approach to Heraclitus—not always appreciated or acknowledged, and often not felt directly by philologically oriented scholars—has come from Martin Heidegger, who not only dismisses the flux interpretation as unhistorical, but also argues

[8] For other important studies on the Pythagoreans see: Burkert, *Lore and Science in Ancient Pythagoreanism*; Guthrie's book-length treatment in his *A History of Greek Philosophy*, vol. I, pp. 146–340; Heidel, "The Pythagoreans and Greek Mathematics"; and von Fritz, "The Discovery of Incommensurability by Hippasus of Metapontum."

[9] *EGP*, p. 146.

[10] *Parmenides und die Geschichte der griechischen Philosophie*, p. 207.

that "Heraclitus says the same as Parmenides."[11] The major recent statement of an interpretation that shifts emphasis from flux to permanence was by G. S. KIRK in the fifties—first in general terms in his "NATURAL CHANGE IN HERACLITUS," reprinted here, then in detail as part of his important book, *Heraclitus: The Cosmic Fragments* (1954), and later in the Heraclitus chapter of KR.[12]

One of the finest chapters of W. K. C. GUTHRIE's now three-volume *A History of Greek Philosophy* is the chapter on Heraclitus in vol. 1. It includes a forceful and balanced exposition, which is excerpted and reprinted here under the title, "FLUX AND LOGOS IN HERACLITUS." While sympathetic to the traditional interpretation, Guthrie gives detailed consideration to Kirk's counterarguments. Of special interest to readers of this selection will be Guthrie's discussion of the river-statement, in an appendix to the Heraclitus chapter (vol. 1, pp. 488–92).

Whether the emphasis in our reading of Heraclitus should be on permanence or flux may well remain an open issue. What is not, and could not be, contested is that he is also a philosopher of *harmonia*, in the Archaic sense of "aptly structured pattern," and that he is a prime example of a philosopher whose thought intimately interacts with his form of expression. A number of stylistic or conceptual patterns that mirror characteristically Heraclitean ontological structures have been noted: parallelism, paired contrasts, analogies, expansion schemes, cyclic schemes, rhythmical patterns, and the like. Most striking and fully developed is the pattern of the geometric mean, $A/B = B/C$, which is studied in HERMANN FRÄNKEL's "A THOUGHT PATTERN IN HERACLITUS," reprinted in this Part.

Underlying these essentially syntactic patterns are the pervasive se-

[11] *Introduction to Metaphysics*, p. 83, cf. p. 82; see also M. Heidegger and E. Fink, *Heraklit* (Frankfurt, 1970).

[12] Kirk's publications provoked Karl Popper to issue a spirited attack on philological interpretations of the Pre-Socratics in general and Kirk's denial of a Heraclitean flux doctrine in particular (see Popper, "Back to the Presocratics," esp. sec. x). An answer by Kirk (see "Popper on Science and the Presocratics") and a rejoinder by Popper (see "Kirk on Heraclitus, and on Fire as the Cause of Balance") followed. Outside this particular controversy, the issues raised by Kirk have been extensively mooted in reviews of his book. The most important of these is Vlastos' review-article, "On Heraclitus," in which, after a careful assessment of the authenticity of certain crucial fragments (including the disputed river-fragments), Vlastos defends the validity of the flux interpretation by examining Heraclitus against the background of Anaximander's and Anaximanes' thought.

mantic patterns of ambiguity, metaphor, paradox, and pregnant state-
ment, which are explored in the study, "PARADOX, SIMILE, AND GNOMIC
UTTERANCE IN HERACLITUS," by UVO HÖLSCHER that closes this Part.
Hölscher's piece is a selection from his book, *Anfängliches Fragen*
[Questioning at the Beginnings]; it appears here in English for the first
time.[18]

V. PARMENIDES

Developing their respective interpretations of Parmenides against the
background of problems in contemporary philosophical analysis, and
utilizing its techniques, MONTGOMERY FURTH in his "ELEMENTS OF ELEA-
TIC ONTOLOGY" and G. E. L. OWEN in his "PLATO AND PARMENIDES ON
THE TIMELESS PRESENT" give rigorous formulations of the argument in
the first part of Parmenides' cosmological poem, the part on "Truth,"
and of ontological claims made in it. As suggested by its title, Owen's
discussion ranges beyond Parmenides: It traces and explores a pattern
of philosophical dialectic concerning the conceptions of time and timelessness that extends from Parmenides through Melissus to the Plato
of *Timaeus* and *Sophist*. Owen's essay is thus also an example—unique
in this volume but effective—of the way in which interpretive work on
the Pre-Socratics can have profound implications for our understanding
of the great classical philosophers, in this instance Plato.[14]

The other two essays in this Part address themselves to the second
great theme in studies of Parmenides, the interpretation of "Doxa."
Most English and American students of Parmenides (including Owen
and Furth) have assumed that the "Doxa" is merely polemical, an
assumption that precludes that this part of the poem could throw any
light on the doctrine of "Truth." An alternative approach that has been

[18] For another perceptive discussion of symbolism and ambiguity in Heraclitus, see Kahn, "A New Look at Heraclitus," esp. pp. 3–9.

[14] Of potential interest to the reader, for both their similarities to, and
differences from, Furth's account of the "fused" sense of *esti* in Parmenides,
are the following: Calogero, *Studi sull' Eleatismo*, ch. 1; Owen, "Eleatic
Questions"; Kahn, "The Thesis of Parmenides"; Mourelatos, *The Route of
Parmenides*, ch. 2, also "Comment on 'The Thesis of Parmenides,'" and
"Heraclitus, Parmenides, and the Naïve Metaphysics of Things." For a
critical discussion of Owen's "Plato and Parmenides," see Schofield, "Did
Parmenides Discover Eternity?" For a discussion of Furth's article, see
Jones, "Parmenides' 'Way of Truth.'"

widely favored on the Continent finds a tighter relation between the poem's two parts. The "Doxa" is interpreted as a phenomenology directly espoused and endorsed by Parmenides: a doctrine expounding how the real is "necessarily" projected and falsified in appearances. This approach was developed by the brilliant German Hellenist KARL REINHARDT in his book, *Parmenides und die Geschichte der griechischen Philosophie* (1916). The study by Reinhardt printed here, "THE RELATION BETWEEN THE TWO PARTS OF PARMENIDES' POEM," is a selection, appearing here in translation for the first time, from that book. Reinhardt's interpretation was influential not only on specialists in Greek philosophy; it was congenially received and then creatively expounded by Martin Heidegger.[15] Philosophers outside the continental-phenomenological tradition, too, found Reinhardt's interpretation especially attractive.[16]

The essay by ALEXANDER P. D. MOURELATOS, "THE DECEPTIVE WORDS OF PARMENIDES' 'DOXA,'" seeks to reconcile the Anglo-American and continental approaches. It argues that the "Doxa" is neither polemic nor phenomenology; it is rather an "ironic" exposition of a cosmology, studiously designed to bring out both similarities and contrasts with Parmenides' own doctrine of "what-is." The "Doxa" thus serves as an important semantic commentary on the language used in "Truth."

VI. ZENO OF ELEA

There have been two major approaches to the interpretation of Zeno's paradoxes in this century. The first and older approach views Zeno primarily as a critic of fifth-century Pythagoreanism, in particular of a certain tendency to construe all magnitude, including space, time, and motion, as composed of discrete quanta or unit-points. (For this interpretation of Pythagoreanism, see essay by Cornford, below, esp. pp.

[15] See *Sein und Zeit*, H. 222–23 with note, or *Being and Time*, trans. John Macquarrie and Edward Robinson (New York, 1962), pp. 264–66, and p. 494 n. xxxix.

[16] See, e.g., Karl Popper, *Conjectures and Refutations* (London, 1963), pp. 11 and n. 5, 159 n. 5, 236 and n. 19. Important recent studies that draw significantly on Reinhardt's interpretation of "Doxa" are: Schwabl, "Sein und Doxa bei Parmenides"; Mansfeld, *Die Offenbarung des Parmenides und die menschliche Welt*, esp. ch. 3; and Hölscher, *Parmenides: Vom Wesen des Seienden*, pp. 102–24.

155–60). Originator of this approach was the French historian of science Paul Tannery.[17] The attractiveness of this approach is twofold: It makes it possible to construe Zeno's paradoxes as cogent *reductio* arguments; and it assigns Zeno an important role in the history of Greek mathematics, viz. that of the philosophical critic who, by challenging simplistic models of magnitude, forced Greek mathematicians to come to terms with such concepts as continuity, infinity, and division.

Unfortunately for this approach, there is no adequate independent evidence that there ever existed a Pythagorean system, or even a general tendency, of "number-atomism." Nor do our sources show any awareness of Zeno's supposed impact on Greek mathematics. And so, as criticism of the evidential inadequacies of the Tannery hypothesis mounted, a second approach has increasingly won adherents over the past thirty years, a return, in effect, to the conception of Zeno's philosophy that was standard before Tannery. Scholars adhering to this second approach view Zeno, more or less, as Plato presents him in the *Parmenides*: as the faithful Eleatic pupil who undertook to argue Parmenides' case indirectly by discrediting all versions of the concept of "the many."[18] Within this approach, assessments as to how clear-headed, how coherent, and how plausible Zeno's defense of Parmenides may be said to have been, have varied.[19]

The excerpt from DAVID FURLEY'S *Two Studies in the Greek Atomists* appearing in this Part under the title "ZENO AND INDIVISIBLE MAGNITUDES" gives—in line with this second, and now dominant approach— a clear and sensitive formulation of Zeno's arguments that does justice to Zeno's genius without straining the historical scholar's credulity.

[17] See *Pour l' Histoire de la science hellène*, ch. 10, and "Zénon et Cantor." Some of the important studies that adopted and developed, with varying modifications, Tannery's approach are: Burnet, *EGP*, pp. 310–20; Lee, *Zeno of Elea*; Cornford, *Plato and Parmenides*, pp. 53–62; Raven, *Pythagoreans and Eleatics*, pp. 43–77.

[18] The most important studies are: Calogero, *Studi sull' Eleatismo*, ch. 3; Booth, "Were Zeno's Arguments Directed Against the Pythagoreans?" and "Zeno's Paradoxes"; Owen, "Zeno and the Mathematicians"; Vlastos in the article "Zeno of Elea" in the *Encyclopedia of Philosophy*, also in his "A Note on Zeno's Arrow," and "Zeno's Race Course"; Furley, *Two Studies in the Greek Atomists*, pp. 63–78, reprinted below; and Stokes, *One and Many in Presocratic Philosophy*, pp. 175–217.

[19] Most generous and sympathetic is Owen; least so (i.e. most inclined to charge Zeno with paralogism, conceptual confusion, and equivocation) are Booth and Stokes.

Especially noteworthy is Furley's original interpretation of the Moving Rows paradox.

The article by FRIEDRICH SOLMSEN, "THE TRADITION ABOUT ZENO OF ELEA RE-EXAMINED," takes an entirely fresh approach. Solmsen challenges the very basis, in the ancient sources, of the view of Zeno as a faithful defender of Parmenides. The suggestion is that he may have been a far more independent spirit, not the charmed disciple portrayed in Plato's *Parmenides*, but more like the "Eleatic Palamedes" he is called in the *Phaedrus*—independent enough even to direct *reductio* arguments against "the one" as well as against "the many." This implies that, contrary to ancient and modern tradition, the Eleatics do not constitute a cohesive, ideologically monolithic school, but a grouping that is looser yet richer in the dialectical relations among its three members.

Quite apart from its well-argued rethinking of questions that have long been assumed settled, Solmsen's essay should be useful to readers of this collection for yet another reason. It offers a case study in the use of philological analysis toward the eliciting of doxographical testimony from ancient sources. Readers interested in methodological questions of source assessment (see Bibliography, section V) should note how elaborately guarded and controlled, how sensitive to the nuances of immediate text and to the import of surrounding context, the procedure of eliciting testimony must be. (For another fine example of this procedure, see Furley, "The Atomists' Reply to the Eleatics," below, pp. 504–26.)

VII. EMPEDOCLES

As implied by the title of A. A. LONG'S original article, "EMPEDOCLES' CYCLE IN THE 'SIXTIES," the decade of the 'sixties was a period of ferment and controversy in the study of Empedocles, specifically on the question of the reconstruction of stages in Empedocles' cosmology, the so-called "cosmic cycle." In soliciting this article specially for this anthology, the editor suggested to Dr. Long that he should write both as interpreter of this complicated controversy to the nonspecialist reader and as arbiter to the contenders. Fulfilling each of these assignments, Long explains the issues involved in the controversy and formulates points of agreement and points of difference among the major proponents of competing reconstructions; he also evaluates the evidential support and internal coherence of arguments propounded on each side. On that basis he then makes some positive proposals of his own.

The major issues are two: (1) How many stages does the cosmogony involve? Are we to assume that it has four stages, i.e. two contrary terminal stages, the Sphere (or the One) and total strife (or the absolutely disunited Many), with two contrary transition periods, increasing strife and increasing love, during both of which transitions compounds such as those in our world emerge? Or does it have two stages, i.e. the Sphere, and then a gradual overcoming by Love of a disruption or insurrection initiated by Strife? (2) In either case, are we to assume that the progression repeats itself—that it *is* a cycle—or that it occurs only once—that it is a linear progression? Details as to how scholarly opinions are arrayed on these issues will be found in Long's article (see esp. his introduction, pp. 397–400).

It is perhaps easy to appreciate the philosophical import of the second issue—it obviously bears on the question of the Greeks' conception of time and history. But one might judge the first question to be of merely antiquarian interest, and esoteric. To do so would be a mistake. The four-stage and two-stage interpretations respectively place Empedocles in two distinct contexts of early Greek thought. Choosing between them would correspondingly enhance the prominence of one of two alternative conceptions of reality. What the four-stage interpretation emphasizes is the theme of *isonomia*, equal balance between polar and distinct powers.[20] Empedocles' philosophical congeners would, accordingly, be Anaximander, Alcmaeon, and the Greek medical tradition. The two-stage interpretation, by contrast, emphasizes the superiority of Love over Strife. For it holds that although there once was, and may again be, a period of the complete sway of Love, there never was, nor will there ever be, a period of the complete sway of Strife. The two-stage interpretation has affinities not with egalitarian but with hierarchical conceptions of reality, such as those of the Pythagoreans, of Heraclitus, and of Plato. Indeed, assuming the two-stage interpretation, it would be fairly simple to show that Plato's conception of the One-Many relation closely parallels that of Empedocles. (The ancient Neoplatonists, who unhesitatingly espoused a version of the two-stage interpretation, were happy to trace in detail such a modeling of Plato on Empedocles.)

As Long points out in his conclusion, settlement of the cycle controversy would bear significantly on the other (perhaps *the* major) question of Empedocles interpretation: the relation between the poem "On Nature" and the "Purifications." The essay by CHARLES H. KAHN,

[20] Discussed in Vlastos' "Equality and Justice in Early Greek Cosmologies."

"RELIGION AND NATURAL PHILOSOPHY IN EMPEDOCLES' DOCTRINE OF THE SOUL," reprinted in this Part addresses itself to this question. Although much admired and widely cited, Kahn's essay reflects an earlier stage of the *status quaestionis*, before the cycle came to be earnestly mooted in the 'sixties. Readers should take note of Kahn's "*Retractationes*," pp. 454–56.[21]

VIII. ANAXAGORAS AND THE ATOMISTS

The grouping of Anaxagoras with the fifth-century Atomists in a single Part is not intended as arbitrary. It has long been recognized that all versions of fifth-century pluralism, including that of Empedocles, sought to reconcile the demands of Parmenidean logic with the manifest facts of experience. But while the Empedoclean "reconciliation" is, in the last analysis, question-begging, verbal, and ad hoc, the other two pluralist philosophies are self-consciously critical and strict in their adaptation of Eleatic ontology—so much so that one could legitimately call Anaxagoras' system a *qualitative Eleaticism*, and that of Leucippus and Democritus a *quantitative Eleaticism*. This great theme, of the rigorous yet critical application of the Parmenidean canons on a pluralist ontology, runs through the three essays reprinted in this Part.

The general thrust of Anaxagoras' ontology lies in this principle: There can be no "coming-to-be" and no "perishing" of qualitative reality in any transformation or transition from constituting parts to constituted wholes, and vice versa. Unfortunately, Anaxagoras states this principle too globally and—as it would seem—paradoxically in the formula, "There is a portion of everything in everything." When that formula is spelled out in the light of such information as we have on Anaxagoras' theory of matter, a variety of interpretations suggest themselves. The majority of interpreters have assumed that Anaxagoras envisages at least the underlying possibility (even if, in the original and perennial condition of "universal mixture" that possibility is never fully realized) of pure elemental things, out of which ordinary (i.e. "mixed") things are constituted. GREGORY VLASTOS' "THE PHYSICAL THEORY OF ANAXAGORAS" is one of the best formulations of this interpretation—originally developed by the French historian of science

[21] Other important articles on this topic are: H. S. Long, "The Unity of Empedocles' Thought," and A. A. Long, "Thinking and Sense Perception in Empedocles: Mysticism or Materialism."

Paul Tannery.[22] The list of what would count as elemental things in Anaxagoras has been variously drawn. Some scholars list only the "opposites" (the hot, the dry, etc.);[23] others include these, but add either all natural substances,[24] or all except the four Empedoclean elements (earth, water, air, and fire).[25]

In view, however, of important difficulties this majority interpretation has in accommodating some weighty ancient testimony, especially Aristotle's, several scholars have urged that the only philologically valid approach is to accept the paradoxical everything-in-everything formula at face value—without tempering it with a doctrine of elements. This approach is represented here with G. B. KERFERD'S article, "ANAXAGORAS AND THE CONCEPT OF MATTER BEFORE ARISTOTLE."[26]

The Atomists' adaptation of Parmenidean strictures on coming-to-be and perishing and on the contrast between the real and appearances is a topic that has been discussed widely and often. Not as much discussed is a question that brings the whole dialectic between Eleatics and Atomists into sharpest focus: Were the atoms of Leucippus and Democritus merely physical unsplittables or were they unsplittables in a stronger, logico-mathematical sense? It is to this question that the third essay in this Part, "THE ATOMISTS' REPLY TO THE ELEATICS," a chapter from DAVID FURLEY'S *Two Studies in the Greek Atomists*, is addressed.[27]

Like Solmsen's essay in Part VI, Furley's "Reply to the Eleatics" will repay close study by readers interested in methodological questions of

[22] See Tannery, *Science hellène*, ch. 12; Burnet, *EGP*, pp. 263–75; Cornford, "Anaxagoras' Theory of Matter," I and II; Peck, "Anaxagoras: Predication as a Problem in Physics," I and II; Raven, "The Basis of Anaxagoras' Cosmology," and ch. 15 in KR; and Strang, "The Physical Theory of Anaxagoras."

[23] So Tannery, Burnet, and Vlastos.

[24] So Raven and Strang.

[25] So Peck. Cornford's interpretation is unique: In his scheme the elements are the "seeds," or smallest particles of homogeneous natural substances (excluding the Empedoclean elements); and each of these particles is in turn indissolubly composed of portions of each of the "opposites."

[26] See also Mathewson, "Aristotle and Anaxagoras: An Examination of F. M. Cornford's Interpretation"; Stokes, "On Anaxagoras," I and II; Reesor, "The Meaning of Anaxagoras," and "The Problem of Anaxagoras."

[27] For other recent studies on this question, see: Guthrie, *A History of Greek Philosophy*, vol. 2, pp. 395–96, 503–07; Stokes, *One and Many in Presocratic Philosophy*, pp. 218–36.

assessing the sources of Pre-Socratic philosophy. The following outline of Furley's analytical procedure should be helpful both to those readers interested in the methodological question and to readers primarily interested in Furley's topic.

(1) Furley assumes that the Atomists had worked out refutations of certain crucial Eleatic arguments. (2) He identifies (independently of the Aristotelian contexts he proposes to analyze) certain arguments or argument-types as characteristically Eleatic. (3) He spots critical allusions to these arguments in certain contexts in Aristotle. Within each of these contexts he distinguishes: (a) that part of the statement that represents or evokes Aristotle's own refutation of the Eleatic argument(s) involved; from (b) that part of the statement that cites, or alludes to, refutation(s) of the Eleatic argument(s) by others. Under (b) it must be determined whether these others were Atomists. If so, and only then, Furley proceeds to sort out: (i) that part of the refutation that represents Aristotle's own contribution; from (ii) the extractable original version of the Atomist refutation.

The reader should note that there is a substantial discussion of another topic of Leucippus' and Democritus' philosophy, their epistemology, in an article in Part I of this volume, Kurt von Fritz' "*Nous, Noein*, and Their Derivatives in Pre-Socratic Philosophy."[28]

[28] See also: von Fritz, "Democritus' Theory of Vision" (an important study which, having appeared in.a set not widely available, appears not to be as fully known and utilized as it deserves); Weiss, "Democritus' Theory of Cognition"; and Taylor, "Pleasure, Knowledge and Sensation in Democritus." Vlastos' "Ethics and Physics in Democritus" includes a discussion of Democritus' theory of mind. On the Atomists in general, the chapter in Guthrie, *History*, vol. 2, pp. 382–507, is especially helpful.

I

CONCEPT STUDIES

1

NOUS, NOEIN, AND THEIR DERIVATIVES IN PRE-SOCRATIC PHILOSOPHY (EXCLUDING ANAXAGORAS)

Kurt von Fritz

In an earlier article[1] I tried to analyze the meaning or meanings of the words *noos* and *noein* in the Homeric poems, in preparation for an analysis of the importance of these terms in early Greek philosophy. The present article will attempt to cope with this second and somewhat more difficult problem, but to the exclusion of the *nous* of Anaxagoras, since this very complicated concept requires a separate investigation.[a] By way of an introduction it is perhaps expedient to repeat briefly the main results of the preceding article.

HOMER

The fundamental meaning of the word *noein* in Homer is "to realize or to understand a situation." Etymologically, the words *noos* and *noein* are most probably derived from a root meaning "to sniff" or "to smell." But in the stage of the semantic development represented by the Homeric poems, the concept of *noein* is more closely related to the sense of vision. A comparison with the words *idein* and *gignōskein* as used in Homer leads to the following results.

I. The use of the word *idein* has so wide a range that it can cover all the cases in which something comes to our knowledge through the sense of vision, including: (*a*) the case in which the object of vision remains indefinite, for instance, a green patch the shape of which cannot be

---

From *Classical Philology*, 40 (1945), 223–42; 41 (1946), 12–34. Reprinted by permission of The University of Chicago Press and of the author.

[1] "*Noos* and *Noein* in the Homeric Poems," *CP*, 38 (1943), 79–93.

[a] [See now Kurt von Fritz, "Der NOΥΣ des Anaxagoras," in *Archiv für Begriffsgeschichte*, 9 (1964), 87–102, repr. in *Grundprobleme der Geschichte der antiken Wissenschaft* (Berlin and New York, 1971), pp. 576–93.]

clearly distinguished; (b) the case in which a definite object is seen and identified; and (c) the case in which the importance of an object or of its action within a given situation is recognized.

II. The word *gignōskein* is used where case *a* is to be clearly distinguished from case *a*, that is, when stress is laid on the fact that a definite object is recognized and identified (especially after first having been seen as an indefinite shape and without being recognized).

III. The term *noein* distinguishes case *c* from the first two cases and is used mainly where recognition of an object leads to the realization of a situation, especially a situation of great emotional impact and importance.

From this fundamental meaning of *noos* and *noein* several derivative connotations have developed, which can already be observed in Homer.

1. Since the same situation may have a different "meaning" to persons of different character and circumstances of life, the notion develops that different persons or nations have different *nooi*.[2] As these different meanings of a situation evoke different reactions to it, and since these reactions are more or less typical of certain persons, *noos* sometimes implies the notion of a specific "attitude."

• 2. A dangerous situation, or a situation which otherwise deeply affects the individual realizing it, often immediately calls forth or suggests a plan to escape from, or to deal with, the situation. The visualization of this plan, which, so to speak, extends the development of the situation into the future, is then also considered a function of the *noos*, so that the terms *noos* and *noein* can acquire the meaning of "plan" or "planning."[3] With this derivative meaning of the words, a volitional element enters into the concepts of *noos* and *noein*, which originally designate a purely intellectual function. It is also pertinent to add that in Homer this intellectual function is not, as in Plato, opposed to and restraining of, but very often rather an immediate cause of, violent emotion.[4]

3. Another derivative of the original meaning remains in the purely intellectual field. Ordinarily the realization of a situation merely adds a further element to the recognition of an object or of its action, for instance, the realization of imminent danger or inescapable doom to the recognition of the approaching enemy as Achilles.[5] In other cases, how-

[2] "Homeric Poems," pp. 81 and 90.
[3] Ibid., pp. 86 and 90.
[4] Ibid., pp. 83 ff.
[5] See *Il*. 12.90 ff.

ever, the realization of the meaning of a situation is the immediate consequence of the correction of a previous, but inaccurate, "recognition"
—for instance, the realization that the person appearing in the shape of
an old woman is, in fact, the goddess Aphrodite.[6] In this case the second
and more correct identification of the object is not the result of a clearer
vision of its external form—which may still remain that of an old
woman[7]—but rather of a deeper insight into its real nature, which
seems to penetrate beyond its outward appearance. This deeper insight
itself is then also considered a function of the *noos*. Another example
of this is the case in which a person, for instance, suddenly realizes that
evil intentions are hidden behind a seemingly friendly attitude, etc.

4. In the cases described under 3, the implication is usually that the
noos which penetrates beyond the surface appearance discovers the real
truth about the matter. There can, then, be no different *nooi* in this
situation, but the *noos* in this case is obviously but one.[8] What is of still
greater importance, with this connotation of the term *noos*, the later
distinction, so important in Pre-Socratic philosophy, between a phenomenal world which we perceive with our senses but which may be
deceptive and a real world which may be discovered behind the phenomena seems in some way naïvely anticipated.

5. Still another extension of the meaning of *noos*, closely connected
with the cases described both under 2 and under 3, is the *noos* which
"makes far-off things present." [9] In this connection *noos* seems to designate the imagination by which we can visualize situations and objects
which are remote in space and time.[10]

[6] See *Il.* 3.386 ff., and the examples discussed in von Fritz, "Homeric
Poems," p. 89.

[7] Sometimes Homer describes this experience in a very strange fashion.
In *Il.* 3.386 ff. Aphrodite appears to Helen in the shape of an old woman.
But after a while Helen ἐνόησε the beautiful neck, the lovely breast, and the
shining eyes of the goddess and realizes who has been talking to her. Yet
Homer does not say with one word that the goddess has changed her shape
and is now appearing in her true form. It seems rather as if in some strange
fashion the real beauty of the goddess shines through, or can be recognized
through, her assumed appearance. In many other instances, however (*Od.*
I.322, 4.653, etc.), the god who appears in human shape and retains this
shape to the end is recognized as a god without any reference to visible
qualities that might reveal him as such.

[8] See von Fritz, "Homeric Poems," p. 90, and below, pp. 28 f.

[9] See von Fritz, "Homeric Poems," p. 91.

[10] This meaning of the word is especially well illustrated by the passage

6. On the negative side it is important to stress the fact that *noos* and *noein* in Homer never mean "reason" or "reasoning." [11] Nevertheless, it is possible to discover even in the Homeric poems traces of a development which later, though very slowly, resulted in an extension of the meaning of the terms in this direction. When a man who at first has been deceived by a seemingly friendly attitude begins to suspect that evil intentions may be hidden behind the friendly appearance, he does so on the basis of certain observations. Putting these observations together, he deduces, as we would say, that the appearance must be deceptive. A certain amount of reasoning, therefore, seems to enter into the process. Yet there is absolutely no passage in Homer in which this process of reasoning is so much as hinted at, when the terms *noos* or *noein* are used. On the contrary, the realization of the truth comes always as a sudden intuition: the truth is suddenly "seen." It is most essential for a full understanding of early Greek philosophical speculation to determine as exactly as possible how far the element of deductive reasoning is clearly and consciously distinguished from the "intuitive element" wherever a philosophical discovery or the realization of a philosophical truth is ascribed to the *noos*.

Hesiod

All the derivative meanings of the terms *noos* and *noein* listed can also be found in Hesiod, but their frequency in proportion to the cases in which the words have preserved their original meaning has become much greater. Apart from this, one can observe that in several respects a development already started in Homer is carried somewhat further still.

Il. 15.80 ff.: "Just as when the *noos* of a man who has seen many lands and thinks 'If I were only here or if I were only there' darts from one place to another, just as quickly Hera flew through the air." Here we have also the origin of the expression "with the quickness of thought," *mit Gedankenschnelle*, which can be found in most modern languages. Thought or *Gedanke* in this expression, just as *noos* in the passage of Homer, does not, of course, mean the process of thinking or reasoning, which may be very slow (as Lessing pointed out in his famous fragment *Faust*, when he made Faust reject the services of a devil who is only *as quick as thought*), but it means the flight of the imagination. Cf. also *Od.* 7.36: τῶν νέες ὠκεῖαι ὡς εἰ πτερὸν ἠὲ νόημα.

[11] See von Fritz, "Homeric Poems," p. 90.

1. The notion that different persons may have different *nooi* has been further developed in two opposite directions. On the one hand, the same person may have a different *noos* at different times.[12] On the other hand, *noos* now can designate not only a more or less permanent attitude,[13] as in Homer, but also a fixed moral character, so that the word is now often connected with adjectives expressing moral praise or blame.[14]

2. In some cases the volitional element which the concept sometimes contains in Homer is strengthened and also enters into new combinations with the intellectual element. One very interesting example of this can be found in the *Scutum*. It is a well-known fact that the language of this poem of an unknown author shows the influence of both Homer and Hesiod. Naturally, the combination of these two influences sometimes produces something new. In my earlier article I tried to show[15] that whenever *noos* in Homer approaches the meaning of "wish," there is a definite connection between the realization of a present situation and the vision of a desired future, including the visualization of a way in which this desired future state may be reached. This connection seems no longer to exist in *Scutum* 222, when it is said of Perseus that he "flew like *noēma*." The *noēma* in this expression is, of course, essentially the imagination by which far-off things are made present and the quickness of which in overcoming time and space is already a familiar concept in the Homeric poems.[16] But when Perseus flies around "like *noēma*," his body follows his imagination with the same quickness, which, of course, implies that he "wishes" to be in the place of which he thinks. "Thought" and "wish" have become indistinguishable in the complex notion of *noos*, but the original connection with the realization of a present situation is no longer felt.

This new combination of the intellectual and volitional elements in the concept of *noos* may have been facilitated by the fact that in the genuine works of Hesiod the volitional element in the meaning of the word had been further developed in a somewhat different direction. While in Homer *noos* never means clearly "deliberate attention," though in a few very

[12] See, e.g., *Erga* 483: ἄλλοτε δ' ἀλλοῖος Ζηνὸς νόος αἰγιόχοιο.

[13] Not only *noos* but also *noēma* is now used in the sense of "attitude" (cf. *Erga* 129).

[14] So in the typical expressions κακὸς νόος, νόος ἐσθλός, or κύνεος νόος in *Erga* 67.

[15] See "Homeric Poems," p. 82.

[16] See above, p. 25 and n. 10.

rare cases it seems to approach this meaning,[17] this connotation is now definitely established in the expression *noos atenēs*, "inexorable." [18]

3. Most interesting, however, is the further development of the concept of a *noos* which understands a complex situation and also penetrates below the surface appearance of things. The implication, characteristic of the concept in Homer, that this *noos* always sees the truth, is occasionally, though less frequently, made also in Hesiod.[19] It is probably on this basis that, in the *Scutum*,[20] *noos* can acquire the meaning of "cleverness," or "intelligence" in the sense of "high intelligence."

But in contrast to the idea that this "penetrating" and "understanding" *noos* always sees the truth, the notion is now developed that this *noos* can also be deceived. It is quite interesting to observe how this idea, which cannot be found anywhere in Homer, gradually evolves. First, there is the notion, quite familiar to Homer, that something can escape the *noos*[21] or that the *noos* can be stunned, dulled, or entirely taken away either by a physical blow or by passion or strong emotion.[22] All this, of course, is not in conflict with the notion that the *noos*, if and when it functions, invariably sees the truth. But the transition from a dulled to a deceived *noos* is very easy, and this transition is indubitably made in three passages in Hesiod.[23] But, easy as the transition seems, it creates, in fact, an entirely new concept; for now we have a *noos* which

[17] See von Fritz, "Homeric Poems," pp. 82, 87, and 91.

[18] *Theog.* 661.

[19] The best example is *Erga* 293 ff.: οὗτος μὲν πανάριστος ὃς αὐτὸς πάντα νοήσῃ, but cf. also *Erga* 89 and 261; *Theog.* 12; etc.

[20] *Scutum* 5 f.: νόον γε μὲν οὔ τις ἔριζε τάων ἃς θνηταὶ θνητοῖς τέκον εὐνηθεῖσαι: "no mortal woman rivaled her in regard to *noos*."

[21] E.g. *Erga* 105 or *Theog.* 613.

[22] E.g. *Theog.* 122; cf. also *Scutum* 144.

[23] When (*Erga* 323) Hesiod says that greed deceives the *noos* of men, it is obvious that the *noos* of the greedy man not only recognizes an object but realizes a situation and, in agreement with the notion of *noos* in Homer, conceives a plan to deal with, or to draw advantage from, the situation. At the same time, however, the *noos* conceives of the situation or of its plan as of something that will be conducive to something that is good for the person conceiving it, and in this respect the *noos* is deceived or deceives itself. This must be contrasted with the many cases in Homer (and Hesiod) in which it is the function of the *noos* to realize the true importance of a situation for the welfare of a person. Similar allusions to a *noos* that can be deceived are found in *Theog.* 537 and *Erga* 373.

still in a way is more penetrating than mere vision or recognition, since it is concerned not with the appearance of things but with the "real meaning" of a situation and the "true character and intentions" of the persons involved in it. Yet what the *noos* "sees" behind the surface appearance may be all wrong, because the *noos*, though still functioning with seeming lucidity, is deceived by greed or anger and therefore no longer functioning properly.

It is very interesting to observe how, in these cases, concepts which later were to play an important role in the beginnings of a philosophical theory of knowledge and a scientific psychology are already developed in a naïve way out of the problems and observations of everyday life and in connection with speculations which in a way may be called "philosophical" but which are certainly very remote from any conscious theory of knowledge or scientific psychology.

With the rise of philosophical speculation in the narrower sense, common language and philosophical terminology gradually begin to develop on different lines. Though it would be interesting to observe the interrelations which in the beginning are naturally still very close and never cease altogether, it seems preferable, for the sake of clarity, from now on to follow the two trends separately.

There also arises a new problem because of the nature of the tradition. In regard to Homer and Hesiod, the danger of being misled by late interpolations is not very great. But it is commonly known that a good many of the sayings attributed to the early Greek philosophers by Greek tradition are not authentic. The investigation, therefore, will have to proceed with great caution, and it will perhaps be useful to start with a rough outline of the different types of tradition and of the procedure which has to be followed in regard to them.

It is obvious that the analysis must be based mainly on those fragments which have come down to us in their original wording. Fortunately, the works of most of the early Greek philosophers are distinguished from the products of later periods not only by their contents but also by their style, their dialect, and, in not a few cases, by the meter. Even so, however, since the dialect of indubitably genuine works of the sixth and fifth centuries, as, for instance, the work of Herodotus, has not been preserved in its original purity, so that faulty dialect forms do not necessarily prove that a fragment is spurious, it is not always quite easy to distinguish between authentic pieces and later imitations.

As to the rest of the tradition, Aristotle and his disciple Theophrastus

can, on the whole, be relied upon to have used the original and genuine
works of the authors whom they quote, though Erich Frank[24] seems
to assume that in one case Aristotle was misled by a work of Speusippus, which the latter had either partly or wholly attributed to the Pythagorean Philolaus—a somewhat strange assumption, considering the
fact that Aristotle must have seen Speusippus almost daily in the Academy from the time that the latter was about thirty years of age to the
time that he was fifty. On the other hand, Aristotle habitually translates
the ideas of his predecessors into his own terminology, so that he can
rarely be used as an authority for their linguistic usage. Nevertheless,
his discussions of Pre-Socratic philosophy are not without importance
for the present analysis; for, especially where they can be compared with
fragments of the original works, they often make it possible to show
how the change of concepts and of the connotations of terms influenced
the interpretation of the philosophical systems and ideas of an earlier
period. All this, though to a slightly less degree, is also true of
Theophrastus.

Some of the later doxographers and ancient historians of philosophy,
though not, for instance, Sextus Empiricus, are less thorough in the
adaptation of early ideas to the concepts and language of their own
times. Yet their testimony can hardly ever be accepted without careful
scrutiny. On the other hand, the results of the first part of the analysis
starting from the indubitably genuine fragments can occasionally be
used to prove that a late author whose reliability is justly questioned on
general grounds must have had some access to genuine information,
since he uses the terms *noos*, *noein*, etc., in a sense which had been more
or less common in the sixth and fifth centuries but which had generally
disappeared from philosophical usage after the middle of the fourth century or even earlier. The same principle may also be applied in order to
find out how far later imitations of early philosophical works may
have made use of authentic models.

XENOPHANES

The first Greek thinker—for some modern scholars would not grant
him the name of a philosopher—who uses the word in fragments of
indubitable authenticity is Xenophanes, who, in all likelihood, was
born in 571 B.C. but lived to a very ripe old age and, according to his
own testimony, was still active as a poet when he was ninety-two years

[24] *Plato und die sogenannten Pythagoreer* (Halle, 1923), pp. 290 ff. and 331 ff.

old.[25] The most important fragment in regard to our problem is B24 (DK), where he says of God: οὖλος ὁρᾷ, οὖλος δὲ νοεῖ, οὖλος δέ τ' ἀκούει [All of him sees, all of him *noei*, all of him hears].

The place of this fragment within the general philosophy of Xeno-. phanes is easy to determine. He objects to the anthropomorphic ideas of God or the gods which were current at his time. God is no more like a human being than he is like a horse or an ox.[26] If he is to be God, he can have neither the shape nor the character and attitude of a mortal creature.[27] He cannot move around and be first in one place and then in another, but he is always present everywhere.[28] He must be all-powerful and hence only one.[29] For the same reason he must be unborn

[25] In B8 Xenophanes says that it is now sixty-seven years that he has carried his sorrow up and down the land of the Greeks and that it was twenty-five years after his birth that he began his wanderings. This shows that when he wrote these lines he was ninety-two years old. But it does not, of course, in itself give an absolute date. Diog. Laert. IX.20 places his *akmē*, a date that he generally derives from the famous work of Apollodorus, in the sixtieth Olympiad, i.e. 540 B.C. This is also the date of the foundation of Elea, which shows that Apollodorus, according to his custom, determined the *akmē* by a famous event in which Xenophanes had taken part. Since Apollodorus usually equates the *akmē* of a person roughly with the fortieth year of his life, Clem. Alex. (*Strom.* I.64) and Sext. Emp. (*Adv. Math.* I.257) cannot be correct when they say that Apollodorus placed the birth of Xenophanes in the fortieth Olympiad, i.e. 620 B.C. This would also be at variance with the statement of Timaeus (also quoted by Clement) that Xenophanes came to the court of Hieron of Syracuse. The error in Sextus and Clement is probably due to a confusion of the figures M and N.

Since Apollodorus' *akmē*-dates are usually only a rough approximation to the age of forty, it is not necessary to accept 580 as the date of Xenophanes' birth; and if he came to the court of Hieron, he was probably still somewhat younger. It seems, then, most likely that the beginning of his wanderings falls in the year which, in another fragment (B22), he claims to have been the decisive date in the life of coequal friends, namely, the year when "the Median came," i.e. 546 B.C. On the other hand, it seems quite impossible to consider him a disciple of Parmenides (born after 540), as Karl Reinhardt (*Parmenides und die Geschichte der griechischen Philosophie* [Bonn, 1916; repr. Frankfurt a.M.: V. Klostermann, 1959]) has done.

[26] B15 and B16.

[27] B11, B12, B14, and B23.

[28] B26.

[29] (Pseudo-)Aristotle *De Melisso Xenophane Gorgia* 3.2, p. 977a19 ff. The expression is πάντων κράτιστος, which in itself can also be translated "the

and uncreated.[30] In connection with these ideas the fundamental meaning of the fragment quoted is quite clear: God can have no special
organs of sensation or perception. He is all-seeing, all-hearing, and also
altogether *noōn*.

It is characteristic of the meaning of *noein* in this fragment that it is
so closely connected with the sensual perceptions of seeing and hearing.
Its place *between* the two is probably due to the meter. But the connection itself must have been quite natural to Xenophanes. It is, then, perhaps not without significance for the history of the word *noein* that none
of the later authors who refer to the content of the fragment, without
quoting it literally, has preserved this connection. Diog. Laert. ix.19
mentions seeing, hearing, and *noein* in this sequence, but in two separate
sentences and so that *noein* is connected with *phronēsis* rather than with
the senses.[31] All the others mention either only the senses[32] or only the

strongest or most powerful of all." But the context shows clearly that God is
said to be not only stronger than any other being individually, but all-powerful, at least in the sense that he is more powerful than all the rest of the world
together.

[30] Ibid. 3.1, p. 977a14 ff. On the basis of these passages in the pseudo-
Aristotelian treatise, Reinhardt (pp. 103 ff.) contends that Xenophanes must
have been a disciple of Parmenides because his form of reasoning shows the
influence of the latter. But it is extremely unlikely that Xenophanes could
have been the disciple of a man who must have been at least thirty-three years
younger (see above, n. 25). At most, one could assume a certain secondary
influence. But even this is hardly necessary. The form in which the author
of the treatise presents the ideas of Xenophanes is, of course, that of a later
age. But there is nothing in the arguments that he attributes to Xenophanes
that could not easily be retranslated into the comparatively simple form of
the literal fragments of Xenophanes' work; and these fragments show no
trace of the heavy and difficult language and argumentation of Parmenides
or Melissus or of the keen dialectic of Parmenides' other disciple, Zeno. The
fact that Xenophanes says of his God what Parmenides says of the *eon*,
namely, that it does not move but stays where it is, certainly does not prove
anything, since this follows from the omnipresence of God, which, as Reinhardt himself concedes, is an attribute of God in a great many monotheistic
religions.

[31] Ὅλον δὲ ὁρᾶν καὶ ὅλον ἀκούειν, μὴ μέντοι ἀναπνεῖν· σύμπαντά τε εἶναι νοῦν
καὶ φρόνησιν καὶ ἀΐδιον.

[32] Pseud.-Ar., op. cit., pp. 977a37 ff., 978a3 ff. and 12 f.; Pseud.-Plut.
Strom. 4; Hippol. *Refut.* I.14.2.

nous,[33] but not both. Sextus[34] finally explains the attribute *noeros*, which Timon of Phleius had given to the god of Xenophanes, by *logikos*. All this, if taken together, seems to prove beyond doubt that the concept of *noein* must have undergone a great change between Xenophanes and those Greek authors who wrote about him and whose works have come down to us.

In Xenophanes' mind there was obviously no such clash between the notions of sensual perception and of *noein* as must have been felt by those later Greek authors who refused to connect these notions with one another, or as we feel in Diels' translation of the fragment: "Die Gottheit ist ganz Auge, ganz Geist, ganz Ohr." But this means only that, at least in one very essential respect, Xenophanes' concept of *noos* is still the same as Homer's. For in Homer also the *noos* is very closely related to sensual perception.[35] This observation may, then, also help to interpret the fragment correctly. Xenophanes' point is clearly that God does not see or hear by means of special organs. At first sight, it might, then, seem as if the analogy required that human beings and animals, in contrast to God, have a special organ of *noos*, just as they have special organs of vision and audition. But there is no trace of a connection between the *noos* and a special bodily organ anywhere in Greek thought before the second half of the fifth century. The *noos* in Homer and elsewhere perceives by means of and through the organs of the senses. There is no reason to believe that Xenophanes thought otherwise. What he wishes to say is that the *noos* of God does not perceive the truth about events or situations and their character through the medium of special organs of vision, audition, etc.

The second fragment in which the concept of *noos* occurs is B25: ἀλλ' ἀπάνευθε πόνοιο νόου φρενὶ πάντα κραδαίνει [but without toil he shakes all things through the *phrēn* of his *noos*]. Again the main point is quite clear. God does not need any tools or organs to "shake" the world. That he wills something is sufficient to bring it about. But the expression "through the *phrēn* of his *noos*" is interesting. It is, of course, impossible within the present context to attempt a complete analysis of the difficult concept of *phrēn*. The word itself disappears almost completely after the first decades of the fourth century, except in direct imitations of Homer, and survives only in its derivatives, *phronein, phronēsis, sōphro-*

[33] Simpl. *Comm. in Arist. Phys.* XXII.22.9; Timon Phl. Fr. 60.
[34] Sextus Emp. *Pyrrh. Hyp.* I.225.
[35] See von Fritz, "Homeric Poems," pp. 88 ff.

synē, etc. Even more than *noos*, it originally can refer to emotional, volitional, and intellectual elements in the attitude of a person. But, contrary to *noos*, it is always connected with the potential or actual beginning of an action. Contrary to *thymos*, it never is used where a passion or emotion is blind. The intellectual element is always present. This intellectual element comes even more into the foreground in the derivatives, *phronein*, *phronēsis*, etc. But, unlike *noein*, etc., these derivatives also refer always to attitudes which reveal themselves exclusively in actions. The connection of *noēin* and *phrēn* occurs as early as Homer.[36] But in this case *noein* means "to plan." So the reference to potential action is also implied in this part of the expression. *Noos*, on the other hand, in contrast to *noein* and *noēma*, never means "plan" in Homer. There may perhaps be just a shade of this connotation in Xenophanes' bold expression. But it is more likely that the genitive *noou* is used to strengthen the intellectual element in *phrēn*, so that one may interpret thus: "He shakes the world by the active will (or impulse) proceeding from his all-pervading insight."

The third and last fragment containing a derivative of *noos*[37] says that God is totally different from mortal beings in shape and *noēma*. This does not add very much to what has been discussed so far. But a negative observation may perhaps be made. Neither in the literal nor in the indirect fragments of Xenophanes' works are the words *noos*, etc., ever used in regard to human beings. Perhaps this is not quite accidental. The fragment just quoted, of course, seems to imply that mortals also have *noēmata*, even though they are different from those of God. In other fragments,[38] however, Xenophanes expresses extreme skepticism concerning the capacity of human beings for true insight. Opinion and guesswork[39] is all that is granted to them. This may not preclude the presence of *noos* in mortals altogether, but it seems to indicate that, in Xenophanes' opinion, the *noos* in mortals was not only more restricted in scope than it was in God but also very rare. If this inference is correct, we find here the most important deviation from the Homeric

---

[36] *Il.* 9.600: "Do not plan [or contemplate (νόει)] such a thing [namely, to go home and let the ships of the Greeks be burned by the Trojans] in your φρένες," says Phoenix to Achilles.

[37] B23.

[38] B34, B35, B36.

[39] This seems a more correct translation of the word *dokos* than Diels' translation, *Wahn*, which falsely implies that the opinions of the mortals are always wrong, while Xenophanes says merely that they are always uncertain.

concept; for in Homer all people naturally have *noos*, even though of varying quality and degree. In any case, the notion that *noos* is something exceptional which only few people possess becomes very prevalent in the generation after Xenophanes, especially with Heraclitus, though it can already be found in the poems of Semonides of Amorgos. It is obvious that this implies a change in the character of the insight which is supposed to be the result of genuine *noein*.

HERACLITUS

Reinhardt has proved conclusively[40] that Parmenides does not refer to Heraclitus[41] in the famous passage on the error of the "two-headed mortals," as most scholars since Bernays had believed. But his attempt to prove that Heraclitus was considerably younger than Parmenides and strongly influenced by his philosophy[42] is not very conclusive. What he considers direct chronological evidence for his assumption can easily be explained in a different way;[43] and the passages which, in his opinion, prove Parmenides' influence on Heraclitus seem rather to show that there may have been some connection between Heraclitus' philosophy and the thought of Xenophanes, on the one hand, and Anaximander, on the other, but that he remained completely outside the philosophical development which was initiated by Parmenides.[44] Since Heraclitus had also singularly little influence on later philosophers before Socrates—except the so-called Heracliteans, who, as everybody now agrees, misunderstood him and, in a way, converted his doctrine into its very opposite—while Parmenides had the deepest influence on all Greek

[40] Op. cit., pp. 64 ff.

[41] B6.3 ff.

[42] Reinhardt, pp. 155 ff. and 221 ff.

[43] Reinhardt has two arguments of this kind. One is the passage in Plato's *Sophist*, in which Plato says that the "Ionic Muses," i.e. Heraclitus, tried to solve the Eleatic problem, which was first posed by Xenophanes "or even earlier"; the other is Heraclitus' reference to Hermodorus (B121), which in his opinion was possible only after the complete democratization of the government of Ephesus. But the first argument is obviously conclusive only if one accepts Reinhardt's theory that Xenophanes was a disciple of Parmenides (see above, nn. 25 and 30). As to the second argument, see H. Gomperz, "Heraclitus of Ephesus," in *Festschrift Theophilos Boreas* (Athens, 1939), vol. 2, pp. 48 ff.

[44] See Olof Gigon, *Untersuchungen zu Heraklit* (Leipzig, 1935), pp. 31 ff., 75 ff., and passim.

36   CONCEPT STUDIES

philosophers of the next century, including the Heracliteans, it seems
expedient to analyze Heraclitus' concept of *noos* first, regardless of the
purely chronological problem.

Again, there are only three extant literal fragments in which the word
noos occurs, but they are deeply significant. Two of these fragments[45]
clearly express the opinion that *noos* is something which but few people
possess. The first denies that Hesiod, Pythagoras, Xenophanes, and
Hecataeus had *noos* and adduces this alleged fact as proof to show that
"polymathy" is not conducive to *noos*. The second seems to refer to the
overwhelming majority of human beings in general and says that they
have neither *noos* nor *phrēn*, "for they listen to the minstrels in the
street and use the crowd as their teacher, not knowing that the many
are bad [or, rather, 'worthless'] and that only few are good [or rather,
'worth something']." B. Snell has shown[46] that *mathein* and its derivatives originally mean a knowledge, a skill, or also an attitude which is
acquired by training, by being brought up in certain ways, or by practical experiences—as, for instance, when a man "learns" to be cautious
or even "learns" to hate[47]—but that later they come to designate also
the knowledge of specific objects and groups of objects about which
very definite and unquestionable knowledge could be obtained. It is,
of course, in virtue of this second meaning that the word could be used
specifically for what we still call "mathematics." Snell very ingeniously
finds the connection between these two very different meanings in the
fact that in both cases the knowledge and its acquisition are "determined
by the object" rather than by the subject. The man who learns by (very
often unpleasant) experiences learns the hard way, and his knowledge
is determined by objects which he not only studies but with which he
often collides. The mathematician, on the other hand, may *search* for
the truth, but more than any other scholar, and certainly more than the
poet or the philosopher, who are the representatives of knowledge and
wisdom in the period of our study, he is bound by his object. There is
no room for different and subjective viewpoints.

It is obvious that the meaning of *-mathiē* in the first of the fragments
under discussion does not coincide completely with either of the two
meanings pointed out by Snell, but is somewhere in between. All the
persons whom Heraclitus mentions were men not so much of practical

[45] B40 and B104.
[46] Bruno Snell, *Die Ausdrücke für den Begriff des Wissens in der vorplatonischen Philosophie*, Philologische Untersuchungen, 29 (Berlin, 1924), pp. 72 ff.
[47] Cf. Pindar *Pyth.* 4.284; Aesch. *Prom.* 1068.

experience as of prominence in various fields of theoretical knowledge. Pythagoras may or may not have been a mathematician, but the other three certainly were not. What is common to all of them is an unusually broad and detailed knowledge in specific fields: Hecataeus in geography and historical legend, Hesiod also in historical legend and in mythology and earlier mythological speculation, Pythagoras through his interest in various sciences and pseudo-sciences, and Xenophanes through his travels and as a man who πολλῶν ἀνθρώπων ἴδεν ἄστεα καὶ νόον ἔγνω [saw the cities of many men and came to know their *noos*, *Od.* 1.3]. The "polymathy" of which Heraclitus speaks is then obviously this factual knowledge in various specific fields. *Noos*, in Heraclitus' opinion, is not acquired by the accumulation of such knowledge, but it must be sufficiently related to it for such a claim to have been made, whether openly or tacitly.

In the second fragment there is the same close connection between *noos* and *phrēn* as in B25 of Xenophanes.[48] It can be interpreted with the help of B112, where Heraclitus says that *phronein* is the greatest virtue and that wisdom consists in saying and doing the truth (understanding it according to nature).[49] Wisdom,[50] then, seems to have a theoretical and a practical side; and if one may assume that, in accordance with pre-Heraclitean usage,[51] *noos* and *phrēn* represent these two sides respectively, it is perhaps possible to conclude that the *noos* has something to do with *alēthea legein*, "to say true things." This inference, however, since the *noos* is not actually mentioned in the fragment as we have it, is not quite cogent unless confirmed by further evidence; and even if it is correct, it will still be necessary to find out with what kind of *alēthea* the *noos* is concerned.

By far the most important fragment is B114: ξὺν νόῳ λέγοντας ἰσχυρί-ζεσθαι χρὴ τῷ ξυνῷ πάντων, ὅκωσπερ νόμῳ πόλις, καὶ πολὺ ἰσχυροτέρως. τρέ-φονται γὰρ πάντες οἱ ἀνθρώπειοι νόμοι ὑπὸ ἑνὸς τοῦ θείου· κρατεῖ γὰρ τοσοῦτον ὁκόσον ἐθέλει καὶ ἐξαρκεῖ πᾶσι καὶ περιγίνεται. Since Heraclitus likes to play with words and to suggest some significance in their similarity,[52] the choice of the parallel forms *xyn nooi* and *xynōi* is hardly fortuitous and

---

[48] See above, p. 33.

[49] Some scholars (see Gigon, p. 101) have expressed doubts concerning both the meaning and the genuineness of the last three words (κατὰ φύσιν ἐπαΐοντας) of the fragment.

[50] For the history of the term *sophia*, see Snell, pp. 1 ff.

[51] See above, p. 33.

[52] See e.g. B1, B25, B47.

obviously stresses the inherent connection between the *noos* and the *xynon* or *koinon* (the "common"): "Those who speak with *noos* must base [what they say] upon[53] that which is common to all and everything, just as a political community is based on the law, and even more strongly. For all the human laws are nourished by the one divine law, etc." It seems evident, then, that the *xynon* on which any *noein* must be based is identical with the divine law which governs everything. For the law of the political community is brought in only as an analogy in a more restricted field, which is at the same time part of, and determined by, the larger and more comprehensive order.

The function attributed to the *noos* in this fragment obviously goes far beyond anything attributed to it in Homer or Hesiod; yet the early and the new concept are closely related. In both cases the *noos* is concerned not with isolated objects or even conditions but with something more complex, which it tries to understand in its meaning and importance. What Heraclitus claims is merely that it is not possible to "understand" anything of this kind properly unless the divine law which governs everything is part of the picture.

But in what way does the *noos* attain knowledge of, or insight into, this divine law? By reason, by intuition, or in what other way? Since the word *noos* and its derivatives do not occur in any other fragment beyond those already discussed, the answer must be found with the help of those passages which refer to the main object of the *noos*—the *xynon*. At first sight it may seem as if Heraclitus was contradicting himself continually concerning the relation of this object to human knowledge. He says again and again that people (*anthrōpoi*) do not understand or recognize this *xynon* even after having been told the truth about it.[54] Yet there is B113: ξυνόν ἐστι πᾶσι τὸ φρονέειν [the *phroneein* is common to all]. In B54 Heraclitus says that "the hidden (*aphanēs*) harmony is superior to the one that is obvious (*phaneras*)." Yet in B56 he says that it is "visible" or "obvious" (*phanera*) things about which most men are in error.[55] Finally, in B35 he says that philosophers must be "acquainted with many things," while in B40 he seemed to express the

---

[53] Literally, "must strengthen themselves, support themselves with, or rely on (cf. Lysias VI.35) that which is common, etc." But obviously one has to supplement "in regard to what they say." For this reason the translation given above seemed to express the meaning more clearly than a more literal translation would have done.

[54] B1, B2, B17, B19, B34, B40, B51, etc.

[55] The seeming contradiction between the two fragments results from the

opinion that to have seen or experienced many things, like Xenophanes, is not conducive to true insight.[56]

In none of these cases, however, is there a real contradiction, and the solution of the difficulty leads also to an answer to the main problem. If B113 is taken together with B2: τοῦ λόγου δ' ἐόντος ξυνοῦ ζώουσιν οἱ πολλοὶ ὡς ἰδίαν ἔχοντες φρόνησιν [while the *logos* is common, the many live as though they had a private *phronēsis* of their own], it becomes quite clear that "*phronein* is common to all" does not mean, as Diels and most earlier scholars understood, πάντες ἄνθρωποι φρονέουσι, "all men have *phronēsis*," but, as Gigon was the first to point out,[57] πᾶσι ταὐτὸ τὸ φρονέειν—or, in other words, there is only one way in which one can *phronein*. But since the term chosen is the same as in B114, it is also clear that the two fragments B113 and B114 belong closely together and that the one way of acting or behaving wisely, which is the same for all, is determined by insight into the *xynon* in the sense of the all-pervading divine law. Interpreted in this way, B113 clearly constitutes a link between B112 and B114 and confirms the interpretation of the first of these fragments given above.[58]

The seeming discrepancy between B54 and B56 is perhaps not entirely removed but is explained by B51, B8, B10, and B80. All these fragments (and many others) speak of discord, conflict, strife, which are really concord and harmony. B51 states that men see only the discord but not the harmony in it. The meaning of B54 is then quite clear: the hidden harmony in discord is stronger and more profound than the obvious harmony which everybody sees. But the second half of B51—"a backward-turning harmony, like that of a bow or a lyre"—shows that this "hidden" harmony is not hidden in the same sense as in some of the cases where *noein* is used in Homer,[59] as, for instance, when hostile intentions are hidden behind a friendly appearance or a god behind the appearance of a human being. For the harmony in the tension or "discord" of the bow must not and cannot be "inferred" in the

---

fact that in both cases Heraclitus obviously refers, if not to the *xynon* itself, at least to its most essential manifestations.

[56] See above, p. 36.

[57] Op. cit., p. 16. Gigon has also rightly pointed out that B116 ἀνθρώποισι πᾶσι μέτεστι γινώσκειν ἑαυτοὺς καὶ φρονέειν, which does not show the characteristic language and style of Heraclitus, is probably an erroneous paraphrase of B113.

[58] See above, p. 37.

[59] See von Fritz, "Homeric Poems," p. 89.

same way in which the hostile intentions or the presence of a god is inferred from something in the expression or attitude of the person concerned which does not quite agree with his or her apparent character or nature. It is, on the contrary, quite directly visible for him who is able to see it.[60] In this sense, then, it can be said that those who do not see the hidden harmony are unable to see "the obvious things (*ta phanera*)."

This interpretation is confirmed both in a positive and in a negative way by the other literal fragments. He who has *noos* can and will speak the truth.[61] But though his *logos* contains the truth, which is the same for all, people will not understand it, even though they listen to it.[62] It is hardly without significance that there is no fragment which admits as much as that anyone ever has or could have grasped the truth merely by hearing it. Instead, there is B101*a*, which says that the eyes are better witnesses than the ears. In other words, the *logos* contains the truth, but it can be understood only by him who "sees" it—of course, *with* his *noos* but *through* his eyes. It is still the same close relation between vision and intuition which we found in Homer,[63] even though on a different plane. This explains also B35 and B40. In order to realize the essential truth, a man must see or "witness"[64] many things. But it is not sufficient for the acquisition of true insight to have witnessed many things, much less to have heard or learned about them from others.

The main results of this part of the investigation can then be summed up very briefly. Heraclitus says in the most outspoken manner what Xenophanes merely seemed to imply: that *noos* is something which human beings but rarely possess. Its scope is wider, its object greater, the insight which it is its function to attain more profound, than in the Homeric poems. For its essential object is the divine law which governs everything, and even where the *noos* is concerned with an individual constellation or situation, this divine law must always be part of the

---

[60] It is perhaps interesting to observe how a modern Heraclitean, Kurt Riezler, in his beautiful book, *Traktat vom Schönen* (Frankfurt, 1935), is vitally concerned with the description and analysis, in the field of art, of this "hidden" harmony and beauty that is not hidden behind something, and cannot be inferred, but must be directly seen.

[61] B112 and B114.

[62] B1, B2, B34, etc.

[63] See von Fritz, "Homeric Poems," p. 88, and above, pp. 23 f.

[64] For the history of the terms *histōr*, *historeō*, and *historia*, see Snell, pp. 59 ff.

picture. At the same time, however, the *noos* in Heraclitus' philosophy is even farther removed from "reason" or "reasoning" than in Homer, for even that element of reasoning "by inference" which, though perhaps unconsciously, was inherent in some of the examples of *noos* in Homer[65] is now completely eliminated from the function of the *noos*.

The indirect tradition about Heraclitus, with the exception of one long passage in Sextus Empiricus,[66] does not contain any reference to *noos*, *noein*, or any of the numerous other words designating knowledge or the acquisition of knowledge which can be found in the literal fragments. The passage in Sextus, on the other hand, is an almost perfect example of that special kind of vagueness and muddled thinking which makes for easy reading and gives the superficial reader the impression that he understands everything perfectly, because everything is expressed in familiar terms and reduced to simple alternatives, though there is no earthly reason why there should not be more than two possibilities. So Sextus begins at once with the statement that man has two organs for the recognition of truth—*aisthēsis* and *logos*—and that Heraclitus considered *aisthēsis* as untrustworthy and made the *logos* the criterion of the truth. Then he gives the following further explanations. The *logos*, which, according to Heraclitus, is the criterion of truth, is not any kind of *logos* but the common and divine *logos*. By "inhaling" this *logos*, we become *noeroi* or acquire *nous*. But when we sleep, the *nous* in us becomes separated from the external world, since the passageways of the senses are closed, and remains connected with it only through respiration. In consequence, it loses the faculty of remembrance. When we waken, it resumes the connection with the external world through the senses and recovers the *logikē dynamis*, whatever that may mean.[67] Finally, since the common and divine *logos* is the criterion of truth, it follows that that which appears to all people in common (τὸ κοινῇ πᾶσι φαινόμενον) is trustworthy and that which occurs (*prospiptei*) only to an individual is not.

It is hardly worth while to unravel this terrible confusion step by step and to show up in detail Sextus' misinterpretations of Heraclitus, which, fortunately, according to his own testimony, are based almost entirely on passages of Heraclitus' work which we still have in their original wording. To characterize his ability as an interpreter of Heraclitus' thought it is perhaps sufficient to point out that he attributes the opinion

[65] See von Fritz, "Homeric Poems," p. 90, and above, p. 26.
[66] *Adv. Math.* VII.126 ff.
[67] See below, p. 43.

that that which "appears"[68] to all people alike is the truth to Heraclitus, who again and again affirms that the overwhelming majority of men are absolutely blind and do not understand the truth even when it is explained to them. For the rest we shall have to confine ourselves to an inquiry into the difference between Heraclitus' own concept of *noos* and Sextus' interpretation of it, which necessitates a brief discussion of the term *logos*, since Sextus makes such ample use of it in the passage quoted.

Heraclitus' concept of *noos* has been analyzed above. As to his concept of *logos*, almost all recent commentators are rightly agreed that in Heraclitus it is still nothing but the noun belonging to *legein*, "to say," and that he means by it simply what he is going to state. His *logos* is common because it is the truth and because the truth is common to all, not in the sense that all people know or understand it, which is far from being the case, but because there can be no different truths for different people. It is also common because it reveals the common law which governs everything. It reveals this law by pointing out its various manifestations. But it is understood only by those who, when it is pointed out to them, are able to "see" with their *noos* the law in these manifestations—and there are but few who are able to do this. Whether one believes in the divine law which he tries to point out or not, the concepts of the "obscure" Heraclitus are all perfectly clear and can be very exactly defined.

[68] *To phainomenon* in Sextus usually means the phenomenal world comprising everything that "appears" to us or is conceived as an object outside ourselves, though, in fact, it may have no correlate in an external world considered "real" and independent of the subject conceiving it or, as a subjective phenomenon, may have been evoked by a "real" object which is entirely different. According to the preceding passage in Sextus, it should then seem as if the *nous*, when deprived of the help of the senses, was producing phenomena which have no correlate in the "real" world, while the senses establish the relation to the latter. Yet, at the same time, it is the *nous* which participates in the *koinos logos*, and the latter is the criterion of truth, while the senses are considered unreliable. At most, if one tries to find any sense in the whole exposition, one might say that the *nous* (or the *logos*?), when a man is awake, has the function of finding out which "phenomena" appear to all men alike. But this still does not explain why the same *nous*, which is always in contact with the *koinos logos* through respiration, does the very opposite when separated from the senses and, nevertheless, is more trustworthy than the latter—quite apart from the fact that all this has certainly nothing to do with Heraclitus' philosophy as revealed by the literal fragments.

In contrast, the empiricist Sextus, whose arguments seem so clear and easy to many readers, has no clearly identifiable concept of either *logos* or *nous* at all. *Nous* with Sextus is either identified with *logos* or considered a manifestation of it. *Logos*, where Sextus speaks in his own name, is most often "logical reasoning" or the capacity of logical reasoning or some force or entity having this capacity, though it may also be the order of the universe or a force upholding this order, the latter concept, of course, being essentially Stoic. But where Sextus reports the views of other philosophers, *logos* becomes just the alternative to *aisthēsis*, whatever this alternative may be, and so loses all clearly identifiable meaning.[69] Yet it is highly illustrative of the change which the concept of *nous* had undergone between Heraclitus and Sextus that Sextus, in trying to explain Heraclitus' concept, begins by connecting it with a term the preponderant meaning of which is "reasoning" and ends by almost identifying it with "sensual perception."[70] Heraclitus' own concept of *noos*, as we have seen, was clearly distinguished from both but somewhat more nearly related to the latter than to the former.

PARMENIDES

The philosophy of Parmenides marks the most important turning-point both in the history of Pre-Socratic philosophy in general and in the development of the concept of *nous* in that early period. After Parmenides the form of the questions asked and the answers given, as well as the terms and concepts used in giving these answers, is completely changed. Yet, though without doubt all post-Parmenidean Greek philosophy is most profoundly influenced by Parmenides, it is rather doubtful whether the character of Parmenides' thought is not nearer to that of his predecessors than to that of his successors, whether they professed themselves his followers and disciples or criticized his philosophy.[71]

The first and fundamental question which has to be answered before

[69] Sextus had, of course, a perfect right to hold and express the opinion, shared by many modern philosophers, that sense perception pure and simple and logical reasoning are the only ways in which human beings can acquire knowledge. But the fact cannot very well be denied that other philosophers were of a different opinion, and it is neither quite fair to them nor conducive to clarity to interpret their philosophy as if they had thought in the same terms as the empiricists.

[70] See above, n. 68.

[71] See below, pp. 52 ff.

any further analysis of Parmenides' concepts of *noos* and *noein* can be undertaken is that of their relation to truth and error. Since, at least at first sight, the evidence in regard to this question seems plainly contradictory, it will perhaps be helpful to remember that, even before Parmenides, the concept of *noos* had been somewhat ambiguous in this respect. As early as Homer the notion could be found of a *noos* which discovers a truth that is hidden behind a deceptive appearance[72] and which, since the truth is but one, is the same wherever it is found. On the other hand, there was the notion of different *nooi* in different persons. But this does not mean that in some of these persons the *noos* was mistaken. Since it is the original function of the *noos* to realize a situation and its importance for the person realizing it, and since a foreigner, for instance, actually *is* something different for the Laestrygonians and for the Phaeacians, the *noos* can function quite properly in both cases, though what it sees in the same object is in each case quite different. In other words, the Laestrygonians and the Phaeacians live in a different order of things, the world has for them a different aspect, and therefore the truth for them is also different.[73] In the Ho-

[72] In this connection, another observation can be made which is of some importance for the further development of the concept of *noos* and *noein*. It would not be incorrect to say that when the *noos* discovers that the old woman is really not an old woman but the goddess Aphrodite, it recognizes an object —or corrects a faulty recognition of an object—and does not realize a situation, which supposedly was the function of the *noos*. Nevertheless, it is easy to see how it came about that *noein* rather than *gignōskein* was used in such cases. First, because the recognition of the true character of the person implies the immediate realization of a situation of great importance, which did not seem to exist as long as there seemed to be only a human being. Second, because *noein* in its original meaning is the third step leading from *idein* over *gnōnai* to an ever more complex awareness and because this is also the case in the example under consideration, though the object after the last step is still an individual person and not a situation. But though the transition is slight, it is not without importance, because it explains how, later, *noein* can have—at least seemingly—very concrete objects, as, for instance, the atoms of Democritus.

[73] Cf. the excellent analysis of the connection between the concepts of *dikē* and *alētheia* and their relation to the different norms that govern the lives of different individuals and groups of individuals, in Hermann Fränkel's "Parmenidesstudien," *Nachrichten von der Gesellschaft der Wissenschaften zu Göttingen, philologisch-historische Klasse*, 1930, pp. 166 ff. [repr. in trans. in Furley and Allen, II].

meric poems, furthermore, the *noos* can be dulled or blunted, but there
is no passage saying that it can be deceived, while seemingly functioning
properly, but the latter notion is developed in Hesiod. In Heraclitus
the notion of different *nooi* in different people, as well as the notion
that the *noos* can be deceived, is excluded, since with him it is the function of the *noos* to be aware of the law which governs the universe, and
this law is but one.[74]

The philosophy of Parmenides falls into two parts, one dealing with
alētheia, the other with *doxa*. K. Reinhardt in a most penetrating analysis[b] has shown conclusively that the second part is neither a description
of the actual beliefs and opinions of the "two-headed mortals" who live
in the world of *doxa* nor an attempt to give a better system of the world
of mere belief than most people have, but that it is fundamentally an
attempt to show how there can be a world of belief side by side with
truth and how it originates.

The term *noos* and its derivatives occur in both parts. Right in the
introduction, when the goddess says ἀλλὰ σὺ τῆσδ' ἀφ' ὁδοῦ διζήσιος εἶργε
νόημα[75] ("but you keep away your *noēma* from this way of inquiry"),
the implication clearly seems to be that the *noēma* can err but that it
can also find the truth. It is in perfect agreement with this conclusion
that in a great many passages[76] *noein* seems to lead to the truth, while
in some others[77] we find a *noos* which is obviously in error. This fact
in itself, of course, is not strange, as long as we translate *noos* with
"thought" and *noein* with "thinking," as most translators have done,
and understand this to mean "logical reasoning." For reasoning can be
correct or incorrect, can start from true or from false premises, and
therefore can lead to truth or error. But a very real difficulty, which has
never been solved and perhaps does not admit a perfect solution, is
created by the fact that in some instances Parmenides seems to assert
that *noos* and *noein* are always and necessarily connected with *einai* and
eon, "to be" and "what is," and therefore with the truth, which seems
to imply that the *noos* cannot err.

The most comprehensive passage which seems to contain this assertion is B8.34–37: ταὐτὸν δ' ἐστὶ νοεῖν τε καὶ οὕνεκέν ἐστι νόημα. οὐ γὰρ ἄνευ τοῦ

[74] Xenophanes seems to approach Heraclitus' concept of *noos* but is not
quite clear and consistent (cf. above, pp. 34 f.).

[b] [See selection repr. below, pp. 293–311.—Ed.]

[75] B1.33; cf. B7.2.

[76] B2.1; B5; B6.1; B8.34 ff. and 50.

[77] B6.5 f.; B16; cf. also B8.17.

ἐόντος, ἐν ᾧ πεφατισμένον ἐστίν, εὑρήσεις τὸ νοεῖν· οὐδὲν γὰρ ⟨ἢ⟩ ἔστιν ἢ ἔσται
ἄλλο πάρεξ τοῦ ἐόντος κτλ. Fränkel[78] and Calogero,[79] in contrast to most
other translators, have interpreted the first sentence to mean "to think
and the thought that it [the object of the thought] is, are the same
thing." In my review of Calogero's book I accepted this interpretation;[80]
but I am no longer quite sure that it is correct. It is true, as Fränkel
points out, that in the overwhelming majority of the cases in which the
word *houneka* occurs in Homer, it means either "because" or "that"
(the latter in content-clauses after *verba declarandi*) and that there is
only one case in the *Odyssey* in which it means "because of which."
But, in spite of this, it can hardly be denied that essentially and originally
houneka is *hou heneka* ("on account of which"). It acquires the meaning
of "because" at first after a preceding *toud' heneka* ("on account of
this").[81] This shows that in these cases it takes the place of ὅ or ὅτι
through relative attraction, to which the Greek language is so prone. It
retains the same meaning when the preceding *toud' heneka*, by which it
originally was produced, is dropped; and it acquires the meaning of
"that" following a *verbum declarandi* in the same way as ὅτι in Greek
or *quod* in late Latin (Fr. *que*; It. *che*). But its origin from *hou heneka* is
so apparent that it was always possible to revert to the original meaning.[82] In Parmenides the word *houneken* occurs only once outside the
passage discussed, but in this case it certainly means "because of
which" or "therefore" and *not* "because," as Fränkel (*loc. cit.*) asserts.
Parmenides has stated that the *eon* is immovable and remains in itself.
Then he goes on to say: "Thus (*gar*) powerful Necessity holds it in the
confines of a boundary that constrains it all around. *Houneken* it is not
right that what-is (*eon*) should be incomplete; for (*gar*) it is not in need,
etc."[83] It seems obvious that the first *gar* in this passage is illustrative
or explicative rather than causative. If, then, *houneken* in the second
sentence meant "because" rather than "hence," this would imply that
Parmenides wished to say that the *eon* must be immovable because it is

[78] Op. cit., pp. 186 f.

[79] Guido Calogero, *Studi sull' Eleatismo* (Rome, 1932), p. 11. [German
trans. by W. Raible: *Studien über den Eleatismus* (Darmstadt, 1970), with
Kurt von Fritz' review of the original publication (see next note) reprinted
as an Appendix, pp. 302–20].

[80] In *Gnomon*, 14 (1938), 97.

[81] See e.g. *Il.* 1.110 f.

[82] See e.g. Pindar *Pyth.* 9.96 (165).

[83] B8.30 ff.

finite, which would completely reverse the natural logical order, as well as the order which Parmenides has followed so far, always putting the more essential qualities of the *eon* ahead of its less essential qualities.

Because of this analogy and also because Fränkel's interpretation makes it necessary to assume a very forced order of words in B8.34, it seems very likely that in this passage also *houneken* means *hou heneka*. But the passages in Homer as well as Parm. B8.32 do show that in early Greek, including Parmenides, *heneka* does not, or not preponderately, mean "for the sake of," but "because of," designating not the *causa finalis* or purpose as in Attic Greek but the *causa efficiens* as well as the logical reason. Diels' translation, "des Gedankens Ziel," therefore, is also incorrect. What Parmenides means seems to be that *noein* and the cause or condition of *noein* are the same. This interpretation is in agreement with the sentence "for not without the *eon*, etc.," which follows and which clearly states that the *eon* is the *conditio sine qua non* of the *noein*.

There still remain the words ἐν ᾧ πεφατισμένον ἐστίν, which have not yet been explained. Fränkel[84] again resorts to the assumption of a very forced order of words, because he thinks that the relative clause quoted, if it is to make sense, must be connected with *noein* in the following line rather than with *tou eontos*, which precedes. Consequently, he translates the passage in this way: "For not without the *eon* will you find that in which it is revealed, namely, the *noein*." But it is hardly necessary to attribute to Parmenides such a grammatical tour de force. *Phatizein* means "to express," "to reveal," "to unfold" (especially in words). It seems clear, then, that the *noein* can no more express or unfold itself without the *eon*, that is, without an object, than the *eon* can be revealed or expressed without the *noein*;[85] for without an object the *noein* would be completely empty or, in Parmenides' terms, a *mē eon*, "what-is-not," itself. The meaning of the sentence is, therefore, obviously that there can be no *noein* without its object, the *eon*, in which it unfolds itself. B3—τὸ γὰρ αὐτὸ νοεῖν ἐστίν τε καὶ εἶναι—must then be interpreted in the same way.

Since, as this analysis has shown, Parmenides undoubtedly does say that there can be no *noein* without the *eon* and that both are inextricably connected, even identical, and since the *eon* does not only belong to but

[84] Op. cit., p. 190.

[85] See also Kurt Riezler, *Parmenides* (Frankfurt a. M., 1934), p. 70 [2d ed., ed. Hans-Georg Gadamer, in series Quellen der Philosophie, 12 (Frankfurt a. M., 1970)].

is the realm of truth, how is it possible that in other passages Parmenides speaks of a *planktos* ("led astray") *noos* which errs? Fränkel[86] explains the sentence ἀμηχανίη γὰρ ἐν αὐτῶν στήθεσιν ἰθύνει πλαγκτὸν νόον[87] as ironical and deliberately paradoxical and self-contradictory, connecting two terms, *ithynei* and *noos*, which point to "straight" or true insight with two other terms, *amēchaniē* and *planktos*, which indicate bewilderment and error. This interpretation contains some truth, but it is hardly sufficient. For the *noos* appears again as dependent on the κρᾶσις μελέων πολυπλάγκτων in another passage, which undoubtedly intends to give a serious explanation. This second passage gives the key to the problem. Men have the *noos* which corresponds to the mixture of their constitution—not, as Fränkel[88] rightly pointed out in contrast to earlier scholars, "of their organs"—and this constitution is called *polyplanktos* because it causes them to err. For the further interpretation we may for once make use of the indirect tradition, since Theophrastus obviously read a part of the poem which is now lost. He says[89] that the mixture is of warm and cold, light and dark, and that we recognize only that which is prevalent in ourselves, whereas the dead, according to Parmenides, are aware only of the cold, the dark, and the silent, but not of warmth and light. This must be taken together with B2, where the goddess asks Parmenides (and anyone who wishes to see the truth) to see with his *noos* that which is far off as firmly present. That is, we are mistaken when we see dark here and light there and feel the warmth at one time and cold at another; for the world is not really split into these contrasts.[90] It is all one everywhere and at any time: the *eon*. If

[86] Op. cit., p. 171.

[87] B6.5 f.

[88] Op. cit., pp. 172 f.

[89] Theophr. *De Sensu* 3; Parm. A46.3.

[90] An additional difficulty is created by the fact that Theophrastus says that insight or *noein* according to warmth and light is better than *noein* through cold and dark, but that there must also be a balance or symmetry between the two; for it is not easy to determine how the preference for one side of the contrast fits in with the postulated symmetry. This uncertainty has led to two different interpretations of the sentence τὸ γὰρ πλέον ἐστὶ νόημα, which concludes B16. Fränkel (p. 174) understands this to mean "More (light) means full insight into the truth." But even if *noēma* ("als vollzogener Akt," as Fränkel interprets; but cf. below, n. 95) could mean "full insight" immediately after Parmenides has spoken of a *noos* which errs, it seems unlikely that Parmenides would use a rather indefinite comparative to designate that kind of mixture which causes insight into the absolute truth. As Riezler (pp. 68 ff.)

this explanation is correct, it follows that even the *planktos noos* of the mortals cannot fail to be linked up inextricably with the *eon*. It could no more exist without the *eon* than the *noos* which sees the full truth. But it wanders and errs in splitting the one *eon* up into the many contrasting qualities, finding one here and the other there. In this it is all wrong and falls prey to *doxa*.

This interpretation does not solve the logical difficulty, since one may still ask how there can be such an uneven mixture of the contrasting elements in the structure or constitution of human beings if it does not exist in the *eon*, since this mixture which is the cause of the error of the mortals, it seems, must be real and objective. One may also ask how something as vague and unreal as *doxa* can exist at all if only the *eon* exists. It is doubtful whether these difficulties can ever be solved, at least in the realm of human logic.[91] But the interpretation given seems to come nearest to what Parmenides actually says.

It is perhaps not without interest to observe the relation between Parmenides' notion of *noos* and *noein* in regard to truth and error with the notions of his predecessors and contemporaries. The *noos* of Parmenides is even less concerned with the understanding of individual situations than that of Heraclitus. Like Heraclitus' *noos*, it is essentially concerned with the ultimate truth, which is but one. But since the *noos*, in spite of being linked inextricably with ultimate reality, nevertheless can err, there is also, just as in Homer, the possibility of different *nooi* in different people, according to the mixture of their structures or constitutions. Yet, contrary to Homer, it cannot be said that the reason for the difference in their *nooi* is that the truth itself is not the same for all of them. For it is the erring *noos* which is different in them. This implies, of course, that—as in Hesiod but not in Homer—the *noos* can be not only dulled but also, at least in some way, deceived. So all the notions of *noos* in regard to truth and error that could be found before Parmenides appear in his work. But they are no longer separated but have all of them become different aspects of one and the same indivisible concept, and in the process of this unification they have all of them been slightly changed.

All this, however, does not yet answer the question of the nature of

---

has pointed out, it is much more likely that we must understand: Whichever of the two sides of the contrast prevails (is more) determines what we imagine that we recognize (cf. also below, nn. 93 and 131).

[91] See also Riezler, pp. 76 ff.

the *noos* in Parmenides' thought. Theophrastus says[92] that Parmenides makes no distinction between sensual perception and *phronein;* and, since he himself in this passage seems not to differentiate between *phronein* and *noein*, his statement seems also to apply to *noos* and *noein*. This interpretation is by no means, like Sextus' misinterpretation of Heraclitus, due merely to an indiscriminate application of the over-simplified concepts of a later period to a philosophy to which they do not apply. At first sight it may seem as if it could be justified even on the basis of Homeric and generally pre-Parmenidean terminology. For if the *noos* of human beings is concerned with warmth and cold, with light and dark, etc., it seems that it is not its function to understand situations, like the *noos* in Homer, or to recognize definite, concrete objects, which in Homer is the function of *gignōskein*, but that the *noos* in Parmenides is on the same level with *idein, akouein*, etc., in Homer, since warmth and cold seem to be "sensual qualities." Yet there is a very essential difference. The *noos* in Parmenides "perceives"[93] not only sounds, or rather sound, but also silence, which can hardly be called a sensual quality; and in this connection it is certainly significant that Parmenides does not, like Democritus, who is really concerned with sensual qualities, speak of color[94] but of light and darkness. We have then to remember that the presumed sensual qualities of which Par-

[92] *De Sensu* 3; Parm. A46: τὸ γὰρ αἰσθάνεσθαι καὶ τὸ φρονεῖν ὡς ταὐτὸ λέγει; but cf. Aristotle *Metaph.* I.5.986b32.

[93] It is very difficult to render adequately in any modern language what Parmenides means by *noein*. When we say, "It was so quiet that one could hear the stillness," we feel that we use a metaphorical, almost paradoxical, expression. But Parmenides' point is just that this is quite wrong. Silence and darkness are as positive and real as sound or light. In fact, to the dead they are what light and sound are to us. We should not make this difference, which is merely a difference in name (cf. B8.53 ff., and B9.1 ff.).

Perhaps this makes it also possible to explain the seeming contradiction in Theophrastus' two statements: (1) that perception through warmth and light is purer than perception through cold and darkness; and (2) that the two perceptions should be symmetrical or equally balanced. For in the light of the passages quoted, it seems likely that, according to Parmenides, perception through warmth and light is pure *in us* (the living) because it makes us feel light and warmth as something positive, while our perception through cold and darkness is not pure because it makes us perceive cold and darkness as something negative. If we had a "symmetrical" or well-balanced perception, we would feel no such difference.

[94] B9 νόμῳ γλυκύ . . . νόμῳ χροιή, ἐτεῇ δὲ ἄτομα καὶ κενόν.

menides speaks are most closely related to the primary contrasts from which, in the philosophy of Anaximander, the world in which we live emerges. It is these primary world-creating contrasts which the *planktos noos* of human beings, even though erroneously, imagines it grasps. This shows that what Parmenides has in mind in the second part of his poem is by no means sense perception pure and simple but something much more nearly related to the "intuitive" *noos* of Heraclitus, though the concept has become much more complicated, since the *noos* in Parmenides can err. The same "intuitive" nature of the *noos* is also most clearly described in frag. B2—λεῦσσε δ' ὅμως ἀπεόντα νόῳ παρεόντα βεβαίως —which belongs to the first part of the poem and deals with a *noos* which does not err but is aware of the truth.

So far it might seem as if Parmenides' concept of *noos* was still essentially the same as that of his predecessors, including his contemporary Heraclitus. In fact, however, Parmenides brings in an entirely new and heterogeneous element. It is a rather remarkable fact that Heraclitus uses the particle *gar* only where he explains the ignorance of the common crowd. There is absolutely no *gar* or any other particle of the same sense in any of the passages in which he explains his own view of the truth. He or his *noos* sees or grasps the truth and sets it forth. There is neither need nor room for arguments. Homer and Hesiod, likewise, when using the term *noos*, never imply that someone comes to a conclusion concerning a situation so that the statement could be followed up with a sentence beginning with "for" or "because." A person realizes the situation. That is all. In contrast to this, Parmenides in the central part of his poem has a γάρ, an ἐπεί, οὖν, τοῦδ' εἵνεκα, οὕνεκα in almost every sentence. He argues, deduces, tries to prove the truth of his statements by logical reasoning. What is the relation of this reasoning to the *noos?*

The answer is given by those passages in which the goddess tells Parmenides which "road of inquiry" he should follow with his *noos* and from which roads he must keep away his *noēma*.[95] These roads, as the majority of the fragments clearly show, are roads or lines of discursive

[95] This passage seems also to prove that Parmenides does not use the word *noēma* strictly as a *nomen rei actae* or to designate *einen vollzogenen Akt*, as Fränkel contends (see above, n. 90). The meaning of the word as used here and, in fact, in most of the passages where it occurs in Parmenides is rare with nouns in -μα but has a perfect analogy in the use of the word ἅλμα in Euripides *Electra* 439, where Achilles is called κοῦφος ἅλμα ποδῶν and where the reference is certainly not to the completed act of jumping.

thinking, expressing itself in judgments, arguments, and conclusions. Since the *noos* is to follow one of the three possible roads of inquiry and to stay away from the others, there can be no doubt that discursive thinking is part of the function of the *noos*. Yet—and this is just as important—*noein* is not identical with a process of logical deduction pure and simple in the sense of formal logic, a process which through a syllogistic mechanism leads from any set of related premises to conclusions which follow with necessity from those premises, but also a process which in itself is completely unconcerned with, and indifferent to, the truth or untruth of the original premises. It is still the primary function of the *noos* to be in direct touch with ultimate reality. It reaches this ultimate reality not only at the end and as a result of the logical process, but in a way is in touch with it from the very beginning, since, as Parmenides again and again points out, there is no *noos* without the *eon*, in which it unfolds itself.[96] In so far as Parmenides' difficult thought can be explained, the logical process seems to have merely the function of clarifying and confirming what, in a way, has been in the *noos* from the very beginning and of cleansing it of all foreign elements.

So for Parmenides himself, what, for lack of a better word, may be called the intuitional element in the *noos* is still most important. Yet it was not through his "vision" but through the truly or seemingly compelling force of his logical reasoning that he acquired the dominating position in the philosophy of the following century. At the same time, his work marks the most decisive turning-point in the history of the terms *noos*, *noein*, etc.; for he was the first consciously to include logical reasoning in the functions of the *noos*.[97] The notion of *noos* underwent many other changes in the further history of Greek philosophy, but none as decisive as this. The intuitional element is still present in Plato's and Aristotle's concepts of *noos* and later again in that of the Neoplatonists. But the term never returned completely to its pre-Parmenidean meaning.

MELISSUS AND ZENO

In the fragments of the works of Parmenides' immediate disciples, Zeno and Melissus, neither the word *noos* nor any of its derivatives

[96] Though the element of reasoning in *noein* is here much further developed and much more conscious, the connection with the Homeric concept of *noein*, which means an intuitive understanding, which, however, may be the result of a process of reasoning, is not yet completely broken.

[97] See above, pp. 51 f.

occurs. Nevertheless, they must be discussed briefly because their philosophy was not without influence on the further development of the concept. Setting aside a few deviations from the doctrine of Parmenides which have no bearing on our problem, as, for instance, Melissus' contention that the *eon* was *apeiron*, "limitless," rather than *peperasmenon*, "limited," both Zeno and Melissus tried to support the fundamental tenets of their master by new arguments and to defend it against the contrary evidence provided by our senses. This latter part of their philosophical labors implies at least a shift of emphasis, as compared with Parmenides' own view of the problem, and gave the speculation about the ways in which we can find access to ultimate reality a new direction.

Theophrastus was probably wrong when he said that Parmenides considered *phronein* or *noein* and *aisthanesthai*, "to sense, perceive," one and the same thing. But it is significant that, in the decisive sections of his discussion of *doxa*, Parmenides does not refer to the senses as the cause of erroneous beliefs but speaks of the *noos planktos* of mortals. In the Introduction, it is true, the senses are mentioned,[98] when the goddess asks Parmenides not to ply—or to give free play to—"his unseeing eye and his buzzing ear." But the senses are described merely as unable to grasp the true reality. It is not altogether impossible that in the lost parts of the second half of the poem the senses were referred to again as having somehow contributed to the errors of mortals. But there can be no doubt that the decisive error is committed by the *noos*, if it errs, even though, and in some respects even because, it is the *noos* which has access to ultimate reality and is, in a way, in touch with it even when it errs.[99] The senses, in other words, even though they are not identified with the *noos*, are certainly not contrasted with the *noos* either, so as to be considered as the *cause* of error committed by the *noos*, but come in only in a secondary function.

The difference between Parmenides and his direct disciples in this respect can be most easily shown by an analysis of B8 of Melissus. In this fragment Melissus tries to prove that if those things which people consider as real, namely, water, fire, air, gold, iron, etc., are truly existent; if, furthermore, they are black and white,[100] dead and alive, etc., as people believe to be true; and if (in this respect) we see and hear

[98] Parm. B1.35 [=B7.4 in most editions.—Ed.]

[99] See above, pp. 51 f.

[100] It is also characteristic for the shift of emphasis in regard to sensual perception that Melissus speaks of white and black, while Parmenides speaks of light and darkness, of sound and stillness, etc. (see above, p. 50).

correctly, then each one of them must have the properties which "it" (that which is) seemed to have (according to the preceding demonstration), which means that they cannot change in any respect or be converted into something else but must remain forever what they are. But, he continues, in fact, what is warm seems to become cold; and what is cold, warm; the hard seems to become soft; and the soft, hard, etc.; and everything seems to be converted into something else according to what we see in every instance.[101] It follows, therefore, that we did not see correctly and that the appearance of a multiplicity of things was deceptive.

Melissus' argument is somewhat vague and certainly much less precise and cogent than that of Parmenides. But a few definite conclusions can be drawn. It is the senses which he accuses of the error which Parmenides attributes essentially to the *noos planktos*. The words *noos* and *noein* do not occur in any of the literal fragments of the work of Melissus. We can, therefore, not be absolutely sure that he used them at all or, if he did, in what sense. But it is clear that he tried to disprove the testimony of the senses by logical reasoning. It seems, furthermore, that he started from the testimony of the senses in order to show that this testimony, if followed out into its logical consequences, is self-contradictory.[102]

Even though Zeno in the literal fragments neither refers expressly to the senses nor mentions the *noos*, it is obvious that his purpose and methods in this respect are essentially the same; for the testimony of the sense of vision shows that Achilles, for instance, in order to reach the

[101] This seems to be the meaning of Melissus' words when he says: "We say that we see and hear and understand correctly. But it seems to us that the warm gets cold and the cold warm, etc."

[102] The gist of Melissus' argument, which is not very clearly expressed in the fragment, seems to be this: (1) The senses tell us that various things, like water, fire, gold, etc., exist and that they are warm or cold, living or dead, hard or soft, etc. (2) If this were true, it would follow that water cannot turn into earth, and that what is hard cannot become soft, since this would mean that in each case of this kind one thing turns into another or disappears (in the first case the water, in the second case the hard) and something else comes out of nothing (in the first case earth, in the second case the soft). But this is impossible, as demonstrated before, since whatever exists cannot have come out of nothing, or have turned into nothing. (3) Nevertheless, the senses tell us that water does turn into earth (stone) and that the hard becomes soft. (4) Hence the testimony of the senses is self-contradictory.

turtle must first reach the point from which the latter started and that the turtle moves constantly. It follows, then, that, while Achilles reaches the point which the turtle had reached when he reached its starting-point, the turtle must have traveled some further distance, and so on ad infinitum. Hence it follows that Achilles can never reach the turtle. Yet the testimony of the senses says also that Achilles not only reaches the turtle but passes it by. Even though the senses are not mentioned in the fragments, it seems obvious that with this argument Zeno, just like Melissus, tries to prove that the testimony of the senses is self-contradictory.

With these arguments and this method of proof, Zeno and Melissus took a further important step toward the distinction between sensual perception and logical reasoning, which was to have a great influence on the development of the concepts of *noos* and *noein*.

EMPEDOCLES

Among the non-Eleatic Pre-Socratic philosophers of the two generations following Parmenides, Empedocles occupies a special position in two respects which are most essential for the further history of the concepts of *noos* and *noein*, namely, in regard to the general character of his philosophical terminology and in regard to the "theory of knowledge" which is gradually evolving in this period. In most other respects he has much in common with some of the most outstanding philosophers of his time, notably with Anaxagoras, Leucippus, and Democritus. All these philosophers are profoundly influenced by Parmenides' reasoning. Yet all reject, in one way or another, his fundamental thesis of the absolute unity of that which is and his denial of motion, while they accept his doctrine that nothing can come out of nothing and that nothing can really perish. Empedocles and Anaxagoras, furthermore, accept Parmenides' verdict that the *mē on* can in no way exist, and therefore they deny the existence of an empty space, while Leucippus and Democritus start from the assumption that the *mē on* does, in a way, exist, namely, as the empty space, the *kenon*. All these philosophers, finally, agree that the testimony of our senses is not sufficient to make us grasp the true reality but that this testimony is not completely without value and that it is, at least to some extent, possible to grasp the truly real by means of a correction of the testimony of the senses, though the extent of this correction and the methods followed in accomplishing it vary greatly from one philosopher to another. Yet there are some fundamental differences between Empedocles and all the others.

In the first place, Empedocles, in contrast to Anaxagoras, Leucippus, and Democritus, still writes in verse and begins his philosophical poem with a "mythological" introduction.[103] This he has in common with Parmenides. Yet here, too, there is an essential difference. The poetic form of Parmenides' work is appropriate inasmuch as the truth, even though after much hard thinking, has come to him as a "revelation." But, apart from this, neither his thought itself nor its expression has been essentially affected by the poetic form. Where the content of the "revelation" which he passes on to his listeners or readers is concerned, his language is abstract and his terminology very precise. Empedocles, on the other hand, wrote a religious and somewhat mystical poem, the so-called "Purifications," and a philosophical and scientific one, which ancient writers, if they mention a title at all, usually quote as "On Nature," though this title can hardly be original. This latter poem may be called more "scientific" than the work of Parmenides, because it attempts to give not only a causal explanation of the origin and evolution of the universe in which we live but also a detailed analysis of various special physical phenomena, not infrequently based on "scientific" experiments.[104] Yet in spite of this and in spite of the fact that the mythological introduction is much less closely linked up with the rest of the poem than in the work of Parmenides, the poetical and the philosophical or scientific elements are much less completely and clearly separated in his work. This is true not only of the introduction of the somewhat anthropomorphic forces of Love and Strife as the main driving agents in the genesis of the universe but, above all, of his terminology; for, in contrast to Parmenides, he uses in the philosophical or scientific parts of his poem many Homeric terms which in his time were no longer used outside of poetry, or even of epic poetry, and he not infrequently seems to vary the expressions or terms he uses merely for

[103] There can be no doubt that in the first line of the poem in which Pausanias is addressed (B1), Empedocles speaks in his own name. In contrast to Parmenides, who attributes the philosophical part of his poem directly to the goddess who reveals the truth to him, Empedocles seems to be the speaker throughout his work. But the invocation of the Muse in B4 is not merely a poetic form, since Empedocles obviously claims divine inspiration for what he has to say (cf. B23.11, B2.9, etc.).

[104] Cf. A66, A67, A34, B100.

the sake of stylistic variety, even where the most essential concepts are concerned. This makes an analysis of his terminology a good deal more difficult. Yet if this peculiarity of Empedocles' style is taken into due consideration, it seems not impossible to arrive at definite and clear-cut results, which then may make it possible to determine more clearly the second main point of difference between him and his contemporaries, namely, in regard to the character of their "theory of knowledge."

The peculiarity of Empedocles' style and terminology stands out very clearly in the very first fragment of his main work in which the word *noos* occurs:

> στεινωποὶ μὲν γὰρ παλάμαι κατὰ γυῖα κέχυνται·
> πολλὰ δὲ δείλ᾽ ἔμπαια, τά τ᾽ ἀμβλύνουσι μερίμνας·
> παῦρον δὲ ζωῆς ἰδίου μέρος ἀθρήσαντες
> ὠκύμοροι καπνοῖο δίκην ἀρθέντες ἀπέπταν
> αὐτὸ μόνον πεισθέντες, ὅτῳ προσέκυρσεν ἕκαστος
> πάντοσ᾽ ἐλαυνόμενοι, τὸ δ᾽ ὅλον ⟨πᾶς⟩ εὔχεται εὑρεῖν·
> οὕτως οὔτ᾽ ἐπιδερκτὰ τάδ᾽ ἀνδράσιν οὔτ᾽ ἐπακουστὰ
> οὔτε νόῳ περιληπτά· σὺ δ᾽ οὖν, ἐπεὶ ὧδ᾽ ἐλιάσθης,
> πεύσεαι οὐ πλέον ἠὲ βροτείη μῆτις ὄρωρεν.[105]

The central statement in this passage is obviously that the life of human beings is too short and that everybody therefore believes only that which has come within the compass of his own very limited experience, while he thinks and boasts that he has found out the whole. In this way, Empedocles continues, men can neither see nor hear "this" (*tade*, which means, obviously: that which Empedocles is going to explain and which is the fundamental truth about the structure and evolution of the universe), nor can they encompass it with their *noos*.

In this passage the *noos* is mentioned along with seeing and hearing almost in the same way as in the famous fragment of Xenophanes.[106] It is differentiated from the senses, however, inasmuch as its function seems to be to encompass (*perilambanein*) something. The relation of the *noos* to the senses is further clarified by another fragment,[107] in which Empedocles' listener or reader is warned not to give more credence to his sense of vision (*opsis*) than to his ears, or to his ears more than to the "revelations" (*tranōmata*) of his tongue (which obviously means "to his sense of taste"), or to favor these as against any one of

[105] B2.
[106] Xenoph. B24; cf. above, pp. 31 f.
[107] B4.

the other organs (*guia*) in however many ways there is a pathway to *noein* (ὁπόσῃ πόρος ἔστι νοῆσαι). This fragment makes it still clearer that, just as in Homer and Xenophanes,[108] the *noos* in Empedocles' philosophy perceives, at least ordinarily,[109] through the organs of the senses. It also explains the *perilambanein* in the first fragment. The *noos* comprises (and makes use of) the testimony of all the senses. It is also its function to embrace in its comprehension the whole of the universe, but it is hampered in this task by the shortness of human life and the consequent insufficiency of experience. Finally, the *noos* seems to have the function of selection; for we are exhorted to admit to the *noos* that which is presented to us by the senses only in so far as it is clear.[110] But what kind of clarity is meant, whether merely the clearness of the vision and distinctiveness of sounds or a clear and integrated insight into the interrelation between the testimony of various senses, is not determined by the fragment. On the negative side one may, furthermore, say that so far it is certainly not necessary to assume that the meaning of "logical reasoning" is in any way implied in the term.

The further interpretation of the two fragments is made rather difficult by the fact, already mentioned, that they contain a good many terms which seem either completely or nearly synonymous, partly with one another, partly with terms which have already been discussed. On the side of sensual perception the analysis of these terms is comparatively easy. In the first line of the first fragment mentioned, Empedocles says that narrow *palamai* are spread over our body. *Palamē* originally means "the palm of the hand," then "the open hand," and finally "the hand" without special qualification. But when in the other fragment Empedocles tells his reader ἄθρει πάσῃ παλάμῃ[111] and then enumerates the various senses, *palamē* obviously is a general designation of all organs of sensual perception. The choice of the term seems to convey the idea that the senses somehow *grasp* their objects. The other term, *athrein*, means originally "to gaze at," "to look upon something with great attention." In the expression quoted, this term also is extended to cover all the senses and obviously is chosen to mark the intensity with which the senses are bent upon their objects. It is perhaps interesting to note that the two expressions which Empedocles uses to designate sensual perception in general are borrowed from the sense of vision and the

[108] See above, pp. 31 f.
[109] For possible exceptions see below, p. 61 f.
[110] B3(4).13 νόει δὲ ᾗ δῆλον ἕκαστον.
[111] B3(4).9.

sense of touch,[112] that is, from the most comprehensive of our senses and from that sense which seems most directly in touch with its objects.[113]

The remaining two relevant terms in the two fragments are *merimna* and *mētis*. The first of these words is supposed to be etymologically related to a word meaning "to remember," but in Homer it usually means "care," "solicitude," while the second one seems etymologically related to Lat. *metior*, "to measure," and in Homer usually means "foresight," "premeditation of the future," then also "wisdom" and the "skill" of an artist who works according to a clearly visualized mental image of the thing which he is going to create. But in Empedocles the meaning of both these words can hardly be distinguished from that of *noos*. The statement of B2.2, πολλὰ δὲ δειλ' ἔμπαια, τά τ' ἀμβλύνουσι μερίμνας [and many the miserable things that intrude, which blunt the *merimnai*], is repeated in B110.7. But there it is followed by a description of how the *merimnai*, if insignificant things intrude upon them, go away and "join their own family." "For everything," Empedocles continues, "has *phronēsis* and its share of *nōma* [= *noēma*]!" Obviously, then, the *merimnai* belong to the same *genna* or family as *phronēsis* and *noēma*. This is confirmed by the first part of the fragment. Here we are told what happens if the *prapides* (which is the same as *phrenes*) are firm and vigorous (*hadinai*), while the second half explains what happens when the *merimnai* are blunted (*amblynontai*). *Prapides* and *merimnai* therefore seem equivalent. At most, they may be distinguished on the analogy of *noos* and *noēma*, the *prapides* being the organ and its function, the *merimnai* the results of this function.

The case of *mētis* is only slightly different. *Mētiesthai* in B139 means "to think of or contemplate an action." But this is also the meaning of *noein* in B84.1. *Mētis* in B23 means the "skill of an artist," which, however, as pointed out above, is also a kind of foresight. In the two other passages in which the word occurs[114] it means "mental capacity" in general. Aristotle, when quoting the second one of these passages,[115] translates the word *mētis* by *phronēsis* and adduces another fragment from Empedocles, which contains about the same statement as B106

---

[112] For analogies in other Pre-Socratic philosophers see Kurt von Fritz, *Philosophie und sprachlicher Ausdruck bei Demokrit, Platon und Aristoteles* (New York, 1938; repr. Darmstadt, 1966), p. 22.

[113] Cf. also Emped. B133.

[114] B2.9 and B106.

[115] *Metaph.* IV.5.1009b18.

but uses the word *phrenes*. Since *mētis*, in the sense of "artistic skill" or "planning," seems merely a specialization of a larger concept, which can also be expressed by *noos*, the conclusion seems justified that *mētis*, *prapides*, *merimna*, *nous*, and their various derivatives in Empedocles—in contrast to Homer, where they are well differentiated—all refer essentially to the same function and its results.

If this is so, two further inferences concerning the *noos* can be drawn from these lines in B2 in which *merimnai* and *mētis* are mentioned. The *noos* can be dulled or blunted. This notion is familiar from Homer. But in Homer the *noos* is blunted by a physical blow, by sorcery, or by a strong passion. In Empedocles it is blunted because, or when, it is too much directed toward trivial things.[116] There is also the notion, encountered above in the works of Xenophanes, that the *noos* of human beings, even if not blunted, is limited in its comprehension.[117]

Apart from this, the analysis so far has shown that, together with their synonyms, the words *noos* and *noein* in Empedocles seem to designate mainly two things: (1) a mental capacity or function which selects, sifts,[118] corrects, and, above all, co-ordinates and interconnects the testimony of the various senses and (2) planning of an action and foresight. The second meaning is interesting mainly because it shows that Empedocles has taken over a well-known Homeric usage, which, as far as we can judge from the fragments, was not adopted by earlier philosophers, though it seems to have also affected Anaxagoras' concept of *nous*.[119] But since it does not occur in any passage which is of central importance for Empedocles' philosophy, it need not be further discussed.

The first meaning quoted seems to come near enough to the most frequent and probably most original meaning of the word in Homer: the *noos* which not merely recognizes an object but understands a situation in which many objects are correlated to one another and the *noos* which corrects a first, but erroneous, impression. There is, however, the important difference that in Empedocles the word *gignōskein* no longer has the same meaning or the same range of meaning as in

---

[116] B110.6 ff.

[117] B2.9 πεύσεαι οὐ πλέον ἠὲ βροτείη μῆτις ὄρωρεν.

[118] See B5.3; cf. also below, p. 65.

[119] I take Empedocles and Anaxagoras as contemporaries, though Anaxagoras may have been born somewhat, but hardly more than ten years, earlier than Empedocles. There is no indication that Empedocles' use of the word *noos* was in any way influenced by Anaxagoras' very peculiar concept.

Homer and that, therefore, a very essential part of the function of *gignōskein* in Homer is now attributed either to the senses or to the *noos*.[120] For this and other reasons the relation between the *noos* and the senses must be further analyzed.

According to B2, the senses are the "pores" through which the *noos* receives the raw material for its insight into the true nature of the world. This may even be taken in a material sense, considering the fact that in B105.3 the blood about the heart[121] is described as the seat of the *noos* and that, according to Theophrastus,[122] Empedocles explained sensual perception as due to effluences or *aporrhoai* from the objects which penetrate into the sensual organs; for it seems reasonable to assume that these effluences are transmitted from the organs of perception to the heart, where they are sifted.[123]

Yet there are some passages which indicate that the *noos* in certain circumstances can acquire insight without the help of the senses. So Empedocles says of God[124] that he has no head or limbs (hence, we must infer, no special organs of vision, hearing, etc., but only a *phrēn*,

[120] The word *gignōskein* occurs only twice in the extant fragments of the work of Empedocles (B4[5].3 and B89). In both cases it does not mean "to recognize or identify an object," as in Homer, but "to understand a statement." Snell (p. 28) has tried to show how this meaning could derive from the original one, by pointing out that in an early period the thought which is expressed in words could be conceived as an object which must be recognized. To put it in a somewhat different way, one might perhaps say that to understand the thought means to recognize and understand its object, whether this be a concrete thing or an event, and add that in the early period of Greek speculation the thought and its object are often hardly distinguished. That this is still true to some extent of Empedocles is perhaps illustrated by B110.2, where Empedocles exhorts his listener to *look upon* that which he has to tell him with a pure effort (that is, free from selfish cares) and straining (literally, "leaning on") his *prapides* to the utmost. But the word *gignōskein* in the extant fragments of the work of Empedocles is used only where a statement is understood or an object through a statement but never, as usually in Homer, where an object is recognized directly as it presents itself to the sense of vision or touch, etc.

[121] περικάρδιον αἷμα.

[122] See Emped. A86.7 (from Theophr. *De Sensu*).

[123] Cf. also B5.3, where the words of the Muse are sifted in the *splanchna*. to which the heart belongs. Though it is the meaning of the words which in this case is sifted by the *splanchna* as the seat of *noos*, the words as sounds must have reached the *splanchna* through the senses.

[124] B134.

which, as shown above, in Empedocles is the same as *noos* and which pervades the whole universe with its swift *phrontides*).[125] In another passage[126] Empedocles says that we cannot reach God with our eyes or grasp him with our hands, "which," he says, "is the main path of firm conviction leading to the *phrēn* of human beings." The implications of this passage are much less clear than those of the first passage. It clearly says that (ordinarily?) the *phrēn* or *noos* gets its most important raw material for true insight through the sense of vision and the sense of touch. If, on the other hand, the assumption is made that human beings can have some knowledge of God, the implication seems to be that this knowledge is acquired by the *noos* directly and without the help of the senses. But there is still the possibility that Empedocles means merely to say that we cannot reach God with our senses alone and directly but that we can grasp his nature somehow indirectly by looking at the world as it is presented to us by the senses. In a way this would come rather near to the Christian idea of knowing God through his works. But it would still be necessary to ask whether this knowledge is acquired by logical inference, that is, by drawing a conclusion from the effect to the cause, or in some other fashion.

A partial answer to this question is given by two other fragments. In B17.20 ff., Empedocles speaks of *Philotēs* or Love as one of the main great driving agents which keep the world in motion. Then he goes on to say: τὴν σὺ νόῳ δέρκευ, μηδ᾽ ὄμμασιν ἧσο τεθηπώς [Grasp her through your *noos*, and do not sit with eyes dazed]—a rather close parallel to the passage quoted before. But the way in which we acquire knowledge of Love is further described in B109: γαίῃ μὲν γὰρ γαῖαν ὀπώπαμεν, ὕδατι δ᾽ ὕδωρ, αἰθέρι δ᾽ αἰθέρα δῖον, ἀτὰρ πυρὶ πῦρ ἀίδηλον, στοργὴν δὲ στοργῇ, νεῖκος δέ τε νείκεϊ λυγρῷ. [For we see earth by means of earth, and water by means of water, and bright air by means of air, and also destructive fire by means of fire, and love by means of love, and hate by means of baneful hate.] This passage is of decisive importance not only for the interpretation of Empedocles but also for a full understanding of some of his great predecessors; for it shows clearly that in Empedocles' opinion the recognition of Love and the insight into its nature is not an indirect one and that it is not brought about by inference or logical

[125] This idea is in harmony with the statement in B110.10 that everything in the world is pervaded with *phronēsis* and *nōma*, and it is not necessarily at variance with the assumption that the *phronēsis* or *noos* of human beings is especially concentrated in the heart.

[126] B133.

reasoning but is as direct and immediate as the recognition (or perception?) of earth, fire, and water. Yet he has stated with equal clarity that Love is not seen or recognized by the senses. How, then, is it recognized? The context leaves no doubt as to Empedocles' answer to this question: "Because love and hatred are in ourselves, are part of ourselves," he would say, "we can recognize them directly, not only in other living beings, but also as cosmic forces, everywhere in the world." But, according to B109, this is also true of the perception of earth, water, "aether," and fire, though these elements seem to be perceived by the senses.[127] What, then, is the difference between the perception of the elements and the perception of hate and love? Why, if there is such a difference, as other fragments seem to indicate, is the same common principle that like is perceived by like applied to both kinds of perception? What, finally, is the origin of that common principle itself?

The principle that like is perceived by like is most easily understandable for us in its application to love and hate. When a person has a certain facial expression, speaks in a certain tone, assumes a certain posture, etc., we seem to feel directly that this person is filled with hatred, is angry, is sad, or is full of joy, etc. At present we are inclined to attribute this feeling to an unconscious inference from the fact that we ourselves have a similar expression or behave in a similar way when feeling a similar emotion. From the extreme behavioristic point of view this may even be an unwarranted inference. But the accuracy or inaccuracy of these modern views and interpretations has no bearing on the present question. What matters is merely that when we see the expression of hate or anger in another person we are not conscious of drawing an inference from his facial expression or his behavior to his feelings but have the impression that we perceive his emotion directly. Yet this "direct perception" of the emotions of a person is not in the same way linked up with a specific sensual organ as is the perception of light and darkness or of sound, since the anger or sadness of a person can be perceived in his voice as well as in his facial expression. It seems, therefore, not difficult to understand[128] why Empedocles attributes the "direct perception" of love and hate not to the senses but to the *noos*.

At the same time, it seems clear how this kind of "perception," if it is felt as such, can lead to the theory that like is perceived by like; for when we see an angry or sad person, we have not only the impression that we know *in abstracto* that this person is angry or sad, but, even if

[127] Cf. also Theophr. *De Sensu* 7.
[128] See also below, pp. 64 f.

we remain free from any contagion by his emotion, that there is something in us which responds to it and that, even while remaining calm, we have the feeling that we understand the mood or the emotion of the person in its individual quality because, at least potentially, it is also in ourselves.

In its application, therefore, to love and hate and also to other passions and emotions, the principle that like is perceived by like seems easy enough to understand. Nevertheless, one may very well ask the question whether this is really the origin of the principle (1) because its transference to the perception of water, fire, etc., seems very strange and (2)—and this seems an even more cogent objection—because the principle is obviously older than Empedocles and because his predecessors, as far as we know, did not apply it to the perception of love, hate, and other emotions.

Yet it is exactly here that the key to the whole problem is found. Among Empedocles' predecessors, both Heraclitus and Parmenides, especially the latter, make use of the principle. Yet they do not apply it to emotions but to light and darkness, warmth and cold, silence and sound, etc. On an earlier occasion[129] it was pointed out that to Parmenides these were not merely sensual qualities and that they are closely related to the primary contrasts from which, in the philosophy of Anaximander, the world in which we live emerges. It is now time to point out that they are also emotional qualities, or, in the terms of early Greek thought, more correctly, qualities or conditions of the soul. When we speak of warm love, cold hate, the darkness of sorrow, etc., we say that we speak in "metaphors." But these metaphors would not occur in practically all languages if the transference of these concepts from one field to the other was not natural to the human race, whatever the reason for it may be. To Empedocles' predecessors, however, this was not a transference of concepts but actually an identity of qualities, as Heraclitus' famous fragments[130] on the wet souls of drunkards and the dry fire of the soul of the wise man clearly indicate.

Once this is clearly understood, both the origin and the later development of the theory that like is perceived by like become quite intelligible. In fact, the origin of this theory can be much more easily explained on the basis of the earlier concept than on the basis of Empedocles' philosophy; for the presence of love can still be understood by a man who is full of hatred, but he is no longer able to feel its warmth, and it is a

[129] See above, p. 50.
[130] B117 and B118.

common experience that in the darkness of sorrow everything becomes dark. It is only because to us the warmth of love, the darkness of sorrow or ignorance,[131] etc., have become mere metaphors that we understand the principle more easily in its Empedoclean application to love and hate than in its application to light and darkness, warmth and cold, silence and noise, etc. Likewise, what appears to us as the transference of the principle that like is perceived by like from the field of emotional to the field of physical qualities is much more natural where emotional and physical qualities are conceived as identical than in the philosophy of Empedocles, in which the theory of love and hate as the driving forces in the physical world and the extension of the principle of perception by like qualities to the elements seem due to rather artificial analogies.

As a result, then, it can be said that *noos* in Empedocles has three meanings or, if the *noos* is considered a unit, that it has three functions: (1) It directly perceives love and hate both in other human beings and as driving forces in nature, and it does so either through the senses or in some cases, perhaps, without this intermediary; (2) it co-ordinates and integrates the testimony of the senses into an understanding of the whole;[132] and (3) it has also the function of planning and guiding the actions of human beings.[133]

The last of these meanings of *noos* and *noein* is obviously taken over directly from the ancient usage of the word which can already be found in Homer. It is not of very great significance in Empedocles' philosophy. The second meaning shows a great affinity to the old Homeric meaning "to realize a situation." But it is extended to comprise the understanding

[131] The fact that ignorance appears related to darkness, and knowledge to light, explains perhaps the discrepancy in Parmenides' theory of the acquisition of knowledge pointed out above (n. 90). Theophrastus can hardly be completely wrong when he says that, according to Parmenides, *noein* through warmth and light is better than *noein* through cold and dark; for in the introductory myth in Parmenides' work the discovery of the truth appears as a travel from darkness to light (B1.6–10). But the truth itself, which is revealed to Parmenides at the end of this travel, paradoxically consists in the insight that we are wrong when we divide the world into light, warmth, sound, on the one side, and darkness, cold, silence, on the other, considering one group as positive and the other as negative. For the assumption that dark, cold, etc., exist but are negative implies the assumption of the existence of a *mē on*, which is impossible.

[132] See above, pp. 60 f.

[133] Ibid.

of the world as a whole. In this respect it has a certain affinity to the concept of *noos* as found in Xenophanes and Heraclitus.[134]

It is the first of the three meanings which is historically and philosophically most interesting. It is not found in Homeric usage, yet is not quite remote from it either; for it is very often the mood of a person, his friendliness or unfriendliness, etc., which is the decisive factor in the meaning of a situation.[135] At the same time, one finds here the only affinity between Empedocles' and Parmenides' concepts of *noos;* for the direct perception of love and hate by the *noos,* according to the principle that like is perceived by like, is obviously influenced by Parmenides' theory concerning the origin of *doxa.*

This relation to Parmenides appears even closer if one supplements the evidence provided by the literal fragments with the testimony of Theophrastus,[136] who says that, according to Empedocles, the *noos* functions most properly in those persons in whom there is an equally balanced mixture of the elements; for if the mixture is not equally balanced, a person will be partly blind to the presence of those elements in the external world which are inadequately represented in the person himself.

On the negative side it is most important to notice that in the philosophy of Empedocles *noein* never has the meaning of "reasoning" and that, in his opinion, all knowledge seems to be acquired by some kind of direct perception, since even the co-ordination and integration of the testimony of the various senses in his philosophy seems due rather to some special faculty of the *noos* by which it directly perceives the interrelation between the various sensual data than to any kind of reasoning. This is also what Theophrastus obviously has in mind when he says[137] that in Empedocles' system *phronein*[138] and *aisthēsis* are either the same (*tauto*) or very similar (*paraplēsion*) to each other. In this respect, therefore, Empedocles has no share in the most important development in the history of the meaning of the terms *noos* and *noein,* which was initiated by Parmenides and carried further by his disciples, Melissus and Zeno.

While in this respect Empedocles seems to represent a pre-Parmeni-

[134] See above, pp. 34 and 40 f.
[135] See von Fritz, "Homeric Poems," pp. 88 ff.
[136] *De Sensu* 11.
[137] Ibid., 10.
[138] Concerning *phronein* as a synonym of *noein* in the language of Empedocles, cf. above, p. 59.

dean type of thought, there are other features in his philosophy which show him to have been a child of his time and by which he has contributed to the rise of a theory of knowledge which was of decisive importance for the later history of the terms *noos* and *noein*, namely, the clear distinction between the immaterial forces of love and hate and the material elements of fire, aether, water, and earth, and the more detailed criticism of sensual perception which is attributed to him by Theophrastus.[139]

PROTAGORAS

In the fragments of the works of those Pre-Socratic philosophers who have not yet been discussed, the terms *nous, noein,* etc., appear but rarely and—with the exception of some fragments of the work of Anaxagoras—not in a very significant context. Nevertheless, there can be no doubt that some of them had a decisive influence on the later history of these terms by promoting the further development of the antithesis between *aisthēsis* and *nous*, the first traces of which could already be discovered in the philosophy of Parmenides' disciples, Zeno and Melissus.[140] Most important in this respect are the atomism of Leucippus and Democritus and what is often called the "subjectivism" of Protagoras.

Protagoras' contribution is crystallized in the famous statement: πάντων χρημάτων μέτρον ἐστὶν ἄνθρωπος, τῶν μὲν ὄντων ὡς ἔστιν, τῶν δὲ οὐκ ὄντων ὡς οὐκ ἔστιν. [Man is the measure of all things: of things that are that (*or* "how") they are; of things that are not that (*or* "how") they are not.] It is obviously not possible within the framework of this study to discuss in detail all the various interpretations of this sentence which have been given in ancient and modern times.[141] But it will be sufficient for our purpose to determine its meaning as correctly as possible as far as it has a bearing on the problem under discussion.

Plato, who is the earliest author to quote the famous sentence,[142] indicates clearly that Protagoras illustrated his statement by pointing out that when a wind is blowing, one person may feel cold while an-

[139] *De Sensu* 7 ff.

[140] See above, pp. 52 f.

[141] For a detailed discussion of this controversy, see Eduard Zeller, *Die Philosophie der Griechen*, I. Teil, 2. Hälfte, 6th ed., ed. W. Nestle (Leipzig, 1920), pp. 1349 ff.

[142] *Theaet.* 151e ff.

other does not; and that in such a case there is no sense in contending
that the wind in itself is cold or, on the contrary, that it is not cold,
since obviously it is cold for one person and not cold for the other. So
far there can be hardly any doubt that Plato gives Protagoras' own
interpretation of his statement,[143] even though he may have slightly
changed the wording. But when he goes on to explain that "to be cold
for a person" means *to appear cold to a person* and then identifies this
appearance (*phantasia* from *phainesthai*) with sensual perception (*aisthēsis*), he is obviously drawing his own conclusions from Protagoras'
interpretation, so that it is no longer certain whether these conclusions
coincide exactly with Protagoras' own opinion

E. Kapp in an excellent discussion of Protagoras' principle[144] has
pointed out that the famous statement "Man is the measure, etc." is
essentially directed against those earlier philosophers who, like Xenophanes, Heraclitus, Parmenides, Zeno, Melissus, and Empedocles, asserted that the opinions of "men," that is, of people in general, are all
wrong and that the truth is entirely different;[145] and that Protagoras
tried to prove his point by showing in an individual case that it is quite
senseless to try to prove to a man who is shivering in the wind that the
wind is not cold.

The correctness of this interpretation is confirmed by the fact that it
permits the easy and complete solution of both of the main problems
which Protagoras' statement presents, which have been discussed by
scores of scholars without obtaining a definite result. The first of these
problems is whether *anthrōpos* in the sentence means "man" in general
or every single human individual. Kapp's interpretation shows clearly
that it means both; that is, that primarily it means "man" as an ordinary human being and his concept of the world in general and the

[143] Cf. ibid., 152b ἢ πεισόμεθα τῷ Πρωταγόρᾳ ὅτι τῷ μὲν ῥιγῶντι ψυχρόν,
τῷ δὲ μὴ οὔ.

[144] *Gnomon*, 12 (1936), 70 ff.

[145] This defense of the "natural" views of the "ordinary" or "common"
man against the claims of philosophers and scientists, by the way, is also a
characteristic of the works of some other Sophists of the fifth century. Antiphon's contention, for instance, that a tangent touched the circle in more than
one point belongs obviously in this category. Far from proving that the Greek
mathematicians of the fifth century "were not yet able to form the purely mathematical concept of a tangent," as some scholars believe, this contention of
Antiphon is an absolutely certain proof that at his time a tangent had been
defined as a straight line that touches a circle in only one point.

individual things in it, in contrast to the presumed superior truth which the philosopher claims to possess and which he contrasts with the error of the common crowd. But, in trying to prove his point, Protagoras uses the individual as an example, and his demonstration implies unquestionably that even the individual concepts and sensations of the individual, even if they differ from those of other individuals, are as indisputably true for this individual as the common notions of most human beings are true for the majority of the human race, whether they conflict with the ideas of the philosophers or not.

The second problem is whether *hōs* in *hōs estin* and *hōs ouk estin* means "that" or "how." Though Kapp has not discussed this problem, it is not difficult to show that his interpretation of Protagoras' statement as a whole makes a complete solution of the problem easy. There can be no doubt whatever that, in accordance with the prevailing linguistic usage of the time of Protagoras, and especially in reference to the preceding *ontōn* and *ouk ontōn*, *hōs estin* means "*that* they exist" and *hōs ouk estin* "*that* they do not exist." Yet when Protagoras illustrates his point by means of the qualities or, to use Aristotle's language, the *poiotētes*, of "warm" and "cold," it seems equally clear that *hōs* in both cases must mean "how," though in good Greek this would really be *hoia*. At this point, however, one has again to remember that in early Greek philosophy, that is, for the predecessors of Heraclitus and Parmenides, warm and cold were not *poiotētes*, much less purely sensual qualities, but rather the fundamental contrasts of which the universe consists,[146] and in this sense *chrēmata* or *onta*. Both Parmenides and Heraclitus had affirmed that "men" are wrong when they speak of these contrasts as of an ultimate reality, Heraclitus by affirming that what is cold or death or generally negative for us is warm and life and positive from another aspect, Parmenides by resolving all contrasts in the unity of that which is. If then, opposing this philosophy, Protagoras declares that it is senseless to tell human beings that they are mistaken in distinguishing cold and warm as they feel them and that, in fact, cold and warm are what they are for the people who feel them, it is clear that, from the point of view of the philosophy which he combats and therefore, primarily at least, also from the point of view of Protagoras, *hōs estin* and *hōs ouk estin* mean "*that* they exist" and "*that* they do not exist"; for it was the *existence* of warm and cold, either as contrasts in general or in a given individual case, which had been in dispute. Yet from the standpoint of a later philosophy for which warm and cold are

[146] See above, pp. 50 f.

transitory qualities or *poiotētes* of things which exist independently of these qualities, *hōs estin* and *hōs ouk estin* in Protagoras' statement inevitably acquire the meaning of "*how* they are" and "*how* they are not." Since Protagoras is on the border line between the earlier and the later philosophy[147] and since, by the very statement under discussion, he himself has greatly contributed to the development and clarification of this later philosophy,[148] those modern scholars who have contended that *hōs* means "how" are not quite wrong from the point of view of later philosophy, though their knowledge of the Greek language is not beyond reproach. But one has to see Protagoras in his exact historical situation in order to understand him fully.

If this is correct, it follows that Plato, when drawing his further conclusions mentioned above, had already given a one-sided interpretation of Protagoras' statement; for, though Protagoras illustrated his point by referring to what we would call the "sensations" of cold and warm, he undoubtedly meant to give his principle a much wider application.[149] What he meant to say was that the world and everything in the world is what it appears to be (*a*) to human beings in general and (*b*) to every individual. What it appears to be to an individual may change from time to time, and this change may be influenced by various things, among others by teaching, rhetoric, and indoctrination. But there is no sense in the contention that there exists a true world totally different from what most ordinary people feel the world to be, and even less sense in the assumption that this true world is accessible to human knowledge. This view seems also to have been the serious element in Gorgias' dialectical *tour de force*, when in his famous pamphlet, "On Nature or On Non-Being," he tried to prove (*a*) that nothing exists,

[147] This distinction between the "earlier" and the "later" philosophy is, of course, very crude and inadequate, since the "later" comprises views so utterly different as, for instance, Aristotle's distinction between *ousia* and *poion* and Democritus' view (see below, p. 79) that warm and cold, light and dark, bitter and sweet, etc., are the ways in which our sensual organs perceive the shapes of the atoms and the impact with which they strike the various parts of our body, or, perhaps more correctly, the subjective qualities into which our sensual organs translate the shape and impact of the atoms. What is common to the "later" philosophy, in the sense in which the word is taken here, is merely that warm and cold, etc., have become real or apparent qualities of something else and are no longer the ultimate constituents of the "real" world.

[148] See below, p. 76.

[149] See Kapp, p. 71.

(b) that if something existed it would not be accessible to our knowledge, and (c) that if someone did have such knowledge it would be impossible for him to communicate it to others.[150]

We have no evidence of any kind concerning the terminology which Protagoras may have used in trying to prove his principle. Specifically, we do not know whether he used the terms *noos* and *noein* at all, or even a synonymous term. On the other hand, it is unlikely that he used the terms *aisthēsis*, *aisthanesthai*, since in all the literal fragments of the works of the Pre-Socratics that have come down to us the various senses are always mentioned separately and are not brought together under the one designation *aisthēsis*.[151] Yet, in spite of all this, there can be no doubt whatever that, through the way in which he tried to prove his principle, Protagoras had a very great influence on the history of the terms *noos* and *noein*.

THE ATOMISTS

Protagoras had tried to prove his point by referring to the qualities of warm and cold. In pre-Parmenidean philosophy these qualities had been considered the fundamental objective contrasts of which the world consists. Parmenides and Heraclitus, however, though in different ways, had contended that these contrasts appear as contrasts only in the belief of "men," while in reality they are dissolved in a deeper unity. In Parmenides' philosophy both true insight and *doxa* are ultimately produced by the *noos*. But Parmenides' successors, Zeno and Melissus, had tried to confirm his conclusions by a criticism of the senses.[152] As far back as the Homeric poems we find the notion that the *noos* has a deeper insight than our eyes and ears.[153] The same notion seems also inherent in the

[150] For a further analysis of Gorgias' arguments and of his terminology, see below, pp. 83 f.

[151] It is perhaps interesting to observe that Democritus, when distinguishing sense perception from another and more penetrating kind of *gnōmē* (B11), still enumerates ὁρῆν, ἀκούειν, ὀδμᾶσθαι, etc., but speaks of the fifth sense as of ἐν τῇ ψαύσει αἰσθάνεσθαι. The reason is, of course, that one can say ἐπ' ἔλαττον ὁρᾶν, ἀκούειν, etc., but not ἐπ' ἔλαττον ψαύειν because ψαύειν fundamentally and originally designates the action of touching something or the fact that something comes in contact with something else, but not the sense or sensation of touch.

[152] See above, pp. 52 f.

[153] See von Fritz, "Homeric Poems," pp. 89.

philosophy of Xenophanes and of Heraclitus.[154] In Empedocles' philosophy, finally, the perception of love and hate which is possible only to the *noos* is contrasted with the perception of the elements and their qualities which occurs through the senses.[155] If all this is taken together, nothing seems more natural than that a philosopher who wished to defend the existence of a "real" world different from the world in which people in general believe should draw a sharp distinction between Protagoras' principle in its universal application to all human knowledge, on the one hand, and the special example by which he tried to prove it, on the other. Having made this distinction, he would then point out that what Protagoras had tried to show might well be true to some extent of the special field from which he had taken his example but not of knowledge in general. In view of the preceding development, it would also be natural to identify the field in which Protagoras' argument, within certain limitations,[156] does hold true with perception by or through the various senses, while the field to which it does not apply might be identified with acquisition of knowledge through *noein*.

As shown above, the restriction of the validity of Protagoras' principle to the field of *aisthēsis* is made the starting-point for the further discussion, and more or less taken as a matter of course, in Plato's *Theaetetus*. But the distinction on which this restriction is based is much older and, within our knowledge, is found clearly formulated for the first time in the philosophical system of Democritus.

The atomistic theory, which Democritus tried to develop into an all-comprising explanation of all phenomena, had originally been created by Leucippus as an attempt to solve the fundamental problem raised by the philosophy of Parmenides.[157] Parmenides' irresistible logic had resulted in a denial not only of all coming-to-be and passing-away but also of all motion. Yet the evidence for the existence of motion seemed so strong that a way out of this dilemma had to be found. Leucippus

[154] See above, pp. 34 f. and 40 f.

[155] See above, pp. 62 ff.

[156] As to the meaning of this qualification, see below, pp. 76 f.

[157] For a more detailed analysis of the philosophy of Leucippus and of its relation to Parmenides, see von Fritz, *Philos. und sprachl. Ausdruck bei Demokrit, Platon und Aristoteles*, pp. 12 ff. In the same book I have also tried to determine more exactly the essential difference between the character of the philosophies of Leucippus and Democritus and so implicitly to refute the contention of Erwin Rohde and other modern scholars that Leucippus had never lived, and that atomism was exclusively a creation of Democritus.

found the solution of the problem in the bold assumption that, contrary to the fundamental premise of Parmenides' conclusions, the *mē on*, the nothing, that which is not, in some way did exist, namely, as the empty space. As the opposite to this true nothing of empty space, that which "really (*kyriōs*) is" is filled space and nothing else. Since, besides the space-filling *on*, the *mē on* exists as empty space, the *on* can move within this *mē on*. But if "that which is" existed, so to speak, all in one lump, it would still not be possible to explain the enormous variety of motion which we observe and the everlasting change of the shape and appearance of the things with which we are surrounded. Therefore, the assumption is made that "that which is" exists in the form of innumerable extremely small particles. Each one of these particles has all the qualities of the Parmenidean *One*. It is uncreated, imperishable, indivisible (hence the name "atom"), and immovable within itself. But by coming together to form a compound, the particles cause this compound to come into being; by separating from one another, they cause the compound to be destroyed; by changing their array, they cause it to change its form and appearance. Finally, by retaining their relative position to one another and moving as a group with the same velocity in the same direction,[158] they cause the compound to move without changing its shape.[159] With this general solution of the problem Leucippus seems to have contented himself.[160]

Democritus set himself a much larger task. He accepted the fundamental principles of the philosophy of Leucippus. But, not content with having explained the possibility of change and motion, he wished to show the real cause and origin of the qualities which the things surrounding us appear to have, of weight, rigidity, resistance to pressure, but also of the "sensual qualities" of cold and warmth, the tastes,

[158] The other possibility, namely, that the atoms do not retain their relative position to one another individually but that those atoms that leave their relative position are replaced by others, so that the general form of the compound nevertheless remains the same, is only a variation within the same fundamental theory.

[159] The question of what sort of existence the compound has in distinction from the atoms and whether its apperception as a whole is merely a subjective product of our organs of knowledge must be omitted from the discussion, since we have no evidence concerning Leucippus' views on this problem, if he considered it at all.

[160] For a more detailed discussion, see von Fritz, *Philos. und sprachl. Ausdruck bei Demokrit, Platon und Aristoteles*, pp. 12 ff.

smells, colors, and sounds. What is more, he wanted to show not only *that* all these qualities, whether seeming or real, could be produced by the atoms whose only fundamental quality was to be space-filling (from which, since they did not fill all space, it followed that they also had shape) but also what particular kind of atoms or combinations of atoms was the basis or cause of every single one of these phenomena.[161]

An enterprise of such scope could hardly be undertaken without a close reflection upon, and analysis of, the ways in which knowledge is acquired. Democritus' approach to this problem was naturally conditioned by the theories of his older contemporaries, Protagoras, Empedocles, and, to some extent, Anaxagoras. It is, therefore, quite impossible to attain a full understanding of what may be called Democritus' theory of knowledge and of his contribution to the development of the concepts of *noos* and *noein* without constantly keeping in mind that he had to formulate his own solution in such a way as to set it off as clearly as possible against the solutions attempted by his contemporaries and predecessors.

The ancient tradition concerning Democritus' theory of knowledge appears at first sight hopelessly confused and contradictory. The most extensive literal fragment of the works of Democritus which deals with the problem[162] distinguishes between two types of *gnōmē*, a word which it is difficult to render in English, since, like the German word *Erkenntnis*, it means both knowledge as something which one has and the process of grasping the truth. The first kind of *gnōmē* is called "dark" and is identified with the five senses of vision, hearing, smell, taste, and touch. The second is called "genuine" and described as coming in where the senses are no longer able to go *epi leptoteron*, "toward what is more fine-grained." This is a clear distinction between sensual perception and another and superior organ of knowledge. But the nature of this superiority is expressed in somewhat ambiguous terms; for the true contrast to "genuine" would be "spurious" (*nothos*). In consequence, it remains uncertain whether Democritus means to say that the first *gnōmē* is false or merely that it is imperfect, though the *epi leptoteron* seems to support the second interpretation.

The second largest fragment[163] is a brief dialogue between the *phrēn*

---

[161] The enthusiastic spirit of investigation inherent in this vast program is also beautifully expressed in the words βούλεσθαι μᾶλλον μίαν εὑρεῖν αἰτιολογίαν ἢ τὴν Περσῶν οἱ βασιλείαν γενέσθαι (B118).

[162] B11 (with Diels' conjecture on sequel).

[163] B125; cf. also B9.

and the senses, in which the *phrēn* says: "by convention (*nomōi*) color, by convention the sweet, by convention the bitter; but in truth (*eteēi*) atoms and the void," while the senses answer: "wretched *phrēn*, while taking your evidence from us you still seek to overthrow us? Our downfall will be your overthrow!" Here, then, the second kind of *gnōmē* is called *phrēn*, a term which, though originally of a different connotation, had become more and more synonymous with *nous*.[164] *Nomōi*, which ordinarily is contrasted with *physei*, usually means "by convention," but it means also what is made by man in contrast to that which is produced by nature and, finally, what is valid only within the circle or group which abides by the convention, in contrast to that which is valid everywhere because it is in the nature of things. In the fragment quoted, however, again the opposite with which it is contrasted is not the usual one, but *eteēi*, an adverbial expression derived from *eteos*, which, in the earliest passages in which it occurs, means the truth of a statement, a prophecy, or the like.[165] There is, therefore, again the same ambiguity, due to the fact that the decisive terms do not appear with their usual opposites. But just as in the first fragment one of the two possible interpretations of the contrast is stressed by the further elaboration of the relation between the two kinds of *gnōmē*, so here again the answer of the *aisthēseis* seems to lead to the conclusion that the inferior *gnōmē* is not entirely false or spurious, as the contrast to *eteēi* and *gnēsiē* would suggest, but merely less clear and hence imperfect. This interpretation is confirmed by the tradition that Democritus praised the formula of Anaxagoras ὄψις τῶν ἀδήλων τὰ φαινόμενα;[166] for this statement seems to say[167] that the truth is hidden (*adēlon*) but that it can be "seen" in the *phainomena*, that is, in that which appears to the senses; from which one may conclude that in some way it is hidden in the *phainomena* and that hence the *phainomena* do contain the truth, though in an obscured form.

A difficulty, however, is created by a number of fragments which seem to show that Democritus was rather an agnostic. These fragments are the following: B6 "And by this rule it is necessary for man to realize that he is separated (*apēllaktai*) from reality (*eteēs*)"; B7 "And indeed this argument, too, proves that in truth we know nothing about any-

---

[164] See above, pp. 59 and 61.

[165] Cf. *Il*. 2.300; 15.53; 20.255; etc.

[166] Anaxagoras B21*a*; cf. Democritus A111.

[167] For the interpretation of Anaxagoras' formula see Hans Diller in *Hermes*, 67 (1932), 14–42, and Kapp's criticism, op. cit., p. 167.

thing, but opinion is an in-flowing upon each individual (ἐπιρυσμίη
ἑκάστοισιν ἡ δόξις)"; B8 "Though it will be clear that there is no way to
know the character of each thing"; B9 "But we do not in fact know
anything that is certain (*atrekes*), but something that shifts in accordance with the disposition of our body and of those things that enter it
and impinge upon it"; B10 "And that, in truth, we do not comprehend
what the character of each thing is or is not, has been shown in many
ways"; and, finally, Aristotle's statement[168] that Democritus had said
that "either nothing is true (*alēthes*), or the true is hidden, at least from
us (*adēlon*)."

The last of these statements has been brilliantly explained by Kapp,[169]
who showed that Aristotle, when quoting the statement in connection
with his discussion of Protagoras' famous principle,[170] did not mean
to say that Democritus agreed with Protagoras but rather that he used
the fundamental observation from which Protagoras started in order
to draw from it the opposite conclusion. Protagoras had said that all
phainomena are equally true. Democritus answers: Either nothing is
true, or the truth is not manifest to us. But to him this undoubtedly
meant that there *is* a truth which is not manifest, which means that it is
hidden and difficult to find. Otherwise, his whole atomistic system
would be without meaning. In this respect, therefore, Democritus returns to the old conviction of Heraclitus, Parmenides, Empedocles,
Anaxagoras, etc., all of whom had believed that there is an absolute
truth but that this truth is hidden (*adēlon*).

Part of the other fragments quoted can be explained on the same
principle. But some of them contain another element which is not covered by Kapp's explanation and which is of very great importance for
the problem of the relation of *aisthēsis* and *nous* or *phrēn* in Democritus' theory. His repeated statements that "man" is far removed from
truth or that we do not understand truly how everything is in reality,
"because opinion for everybody is what is formed[171] in his mind (by
the atoms which move in it or into it)," cannot, like similar statements
of Heraclitus, Parmenides, etc., simply mean that the common crowd is
ignorant, while the philosopher knows the truth. The older philosophers
never say "we" in a statement of this kind, and Democritus could not
assume that he alone was exempt from the common law that the atoms

[168] *Metaph.* IV.5.1009b11; cf. Dem. A112.

[169] Page 165.

[170] See above, pp. 67 f.

[171] Concerning the interpretation of the term *epirysmiē*, see Kapp, p. 163.

form in our organs of perception various shapes which are not always a true image of the real things outside ourselves.

Democritus' theory of sense perception, of which Theophrastus has left us a rather extensive report,[172] shows clearly that, in his opinion, one has to distinguish two aspects of the question.[173] There can, he believes, be no doubt that, in the "real" world, nothing exists but the atoms and the empty space between them and that the atoms, when penetrating into our organs of perception, evoke there those images which most of us erroneously believe to be true pictures of the "real" world outside ourselves. But while we are mistaken when we believe that colors, smells, tastes, etc., are qualities of the "real" things, we can, from the nature of these subjective sensations, draw definite conclusions not only concerning the shape and motion of the atoms causing them but also, to some extent, concerning the internal structure and composition of the compounds from which those atoms have emanated. So far, and in this sense, it can then truly be said that the hidden truth is nevertheless *in* the phenomena and that sensual perception gives an "obscured" picture, but still a picture, of the "real" world. But—and this is the second aspect of the question—while all this is true in general, it does not permit us to draw exact and reliable conclusions concerning the actual structure of any object with which we are confronted in any individual instance;[174] for a person might be lacking in those atoms or combinations of atoms which had to be affected for the subjective impression of certain colors, smells, etc., to arise. In this case the person's view of the surrounding world or objects would inevitably be defective and distorted. Or, on the other hand, images, seemingly of external objects, might arise when the organs are affected by atoms which had not come from the outside but had already existed in the person. This would be the case especially when such atoms, by chance, formed a compound similar in shape to well-known objects of the external world. In this case the conclusion from the image to the existence of a corresponding object outside the person would naturally be erroneous and unfounded. While, therefore, a certain and definite knowledge concerning the general structure of the external world is possible and also a

---

[172] *De Sensu* 49–82; cf. Dem. A135.

[173] It is, of course, not possible within this article to discuss Democritus' theory of sense-perception in detail. But the accuracy of most of the following statements can easily be checked by a perusal of Theophrastus' report (see the preceding note).

[174] This is the meaning of ἕκαστον in B8 and B10.

general knowledge concerning the structure of objects causing certain sensations, the specific conclusions concerning the presence and structure of specific objects at a given moment, which we are accustomed to draw, are always uncertain. This is the meaning of Democritus' "agnostic" statements.

The analysis given so far makes it possible to determine accurately the relation between *aisthēsis* and *noos* in Democritus' theory of knowledge. The identity of *phrēn*, as it appears in the dialogue between *phrēn* and *aisthēsis*,[175] with *noos* could be inferred from the general synonymity of the two terms in the philosophical writings of Democritus' period if it was not directly attested by B129.[176] It is also clear that the *phrēn* or *noos* gets the material for its knowledge from the senses, but clarifies and corrects what the senses offer it, and by doing so attains a knowledge of the finer, that is, atomic, structure of the external world, a knowledge of great accuracy as far as the general structure of this world is concerned but less accurate and reliable in the individual case.

How does the *noos* or *phrēn* achieve this? Kapp[177] formulates it this way: "Thought has no way of its own to the truth. The truth is in the *phainomena*. But thought is not content with the phenomena. It criticizes them and contents itself only after it has made something which satisfies thought and at the same time is in agreement with the phenomena." This is an admirable description of the process as envisaged by Democritus. But it is not quite sufficient for the present purpose, since we have also to know how the *noos* makes this something, even if, in trying to answer this question, we have to take the risk of going beyond Democritus' own awareness of what he was doing. There can be hardly any doubt that two very different elements are involved in the process. On the one hand, there are the abstract deductions from a priori concepts, which lead to the conclusion that there can be nothing but empty space and filled space and which, if the attempt is made to reconcile this result with the evidence of the phenomenal world, lead to the further assumption that the filled space exists in the form of innumerable very small indivisible and indestructible particles moving around in the empty space. On the other hand, there is the attempt to determine the shape and the character of the motion of the atoms which cause the various kinds of sensations. This attempt operates obviously with a different kind of "reasoning." If Democritus, for instance, af-

175 B9; see also above, p. 76.
176 Φρενὶ θεῖα νοῦνται.
177 Page 167.

firms[178] that the bitter taste is caused by small, smooth atoms with a rounded surface with bends (but not sharp corners) and then adds that for this reason the bitter taste has something sticky (*glischron*) and glue-like (*kollōdes*), one can reconstruct his process of thinking in about the following way: The bitter taste has a sticky or gluelike character. Hence it must be caused by atoms of which glue could consist. Glue is sticky. Hence the atoms must have such a shape that, though being absolutely rigid, they will easily cling together. Hence the bends in their surface which may fit into one another. But glue is also liquid. Hence the atoms must easily change their position in relation to one another, and therefore they must have rounded bends and a smooth surface.

What, then, does the mind do when going through this complicated process? First, the taste-sensation of bitter is replaced by the similar or correlated touch-sensation of stickiness.[179] The reason is obviously that this latter sensation, or rather the objects causing it, lend themselves more easily to an analysis in terms of "atomistic mechanics." Then the substances causing the touch-sensation of stickiness are studied. Both the sense of touch and the sense of vision indicate that "substances" causing the sensation of stickiness are either liquid or semiliquid and that, nevertheless, their parts stick together and also stick to other objects. Since a priori deductions have led to the conclusion that what appears as a "substance" to the senses is in reality a compound of very small particles which are absolutely space-filling and rigid and differ from one another only through their shape (and motion), the question is then asked what sort of solid and rigid particles of visible size, if put together, would have approximately the same properties (of clinging together and to other objects, yet changing their relative position to one another easily, as liquids do) which are characteristic of gluey substances. Since it is found that particles with a smooth surface and rounded bends come nearest to this requirement (for particles with sharp hooks, if interlaced, would hold together more rigidly, and spheric particles with a smooth surface would not hang together at all), the conclusion is drawn that the gluey substances and hence all substances of bitter taste consist of invisible particles of this shape.

The process, then, which leads to the reconstruction of a particular section of the real but invisible world of which we obtain an "obscure"

[178] A135.66.

[179] Possibly the reduction of bitterness to stickiness is partly due to the fact that gall was considered the bitter-tasting substance κατ᾽ ἐξοχήν and that gall is a sticky substance.

knowledge in sense-perception seems to include at least the following elements: (1) the presence of the most fundamental a priori concepts of "to be," "not to be," space, etc.; (2) deductions from analytical judgments based on these concepts and from the evidence of motion in the phenomenal world; (3) a study of the correlated testimony of the senses concerning specific objects; (4) various inferences on the basis of analogy; and (5) the search for models in the visible world which satisfy certain conditions derived from 1, 2, 3, and 4 and which, therefore, again by analogy, can be used for the determination of the shape of their assumed correlates in the invisible world. Whatever additional elements may enter the process, there can be hardly any doubt that the activity of the *phrēn* or *nous* in Democritus' philosophy[180] does not exclusively consist of inductive and deductive reasoning in the traditional sense but is much more complex. How far Democritus himself was conscious of, or reflected on, these various elements in his thinking we have no means of finding out. It is, however, sufficient for our purpose to ascertain their presence.

CONCLUSION

With this analysis of Democritus' concept of *nous* and *noein*, the main task of the present inquiry can be considered completed.[181] It remains to draw some general conclusions. If one tries to determine the main changes which the meaning of the terms *nous* and *noein* underwent in the course of the philosophical speculations of the Pre-Socratics, as compared with the meaning or meanings of the same terms in Homer and Hesiod, two facts stand out most clearly: (1) In contrast to early Greek usage in which the *noos*, whatever its special function in a given case may be, always has to do with specific situations, in Greek philosophy almost from the very beginning it becomes the main function of the *nous* to discover the "real" world or the "real" character of the

[180] Apart from the function of the *nous* in Democritus' theory of knowledge, *noos*, *noein*, and derivatives, like *anoēmōn*, appear also not infrequently in Democritus' ethical fragments. But the meaning there is mostly either "practical wisdom," which has its origin in the Homeric use of *phrenes*, or the wisdom that distinguished the wise man from the common crowd, a meaning that was developed in early Pre-Socratic philosophy. These passages, therefore, do not add anything strikingly new to the history of the term.

[181] A few odds and ends that still remain may better be taken up later, when the main results of the inquiry have been stated (see below, pp. 83 f.).

world as a whole, in contrast to the erroneous beliefs of most human beings. But what is new in this usage is not that the *nous* penetrates beyond surface appearances and discovers the real truth—for this was also one of the functions of the *noos* in Homer—but the belief that the world is altogether different from what people in general believe it to be. (2) In Homer and Hesiod, *idein*, which properly designates the sense of vision, can also be used for the recognition and identification of objects and even for the realization of a situation.[182] The use of the term *noein*, on the other hand, seems originally to have been limited to the latter case but was, even as early as Homer, extended to "planning" and to "the flight of the imagination."[183] Yet with all this, its field was still rather narrowly circumscribed. In Pre-Socratic philosophy, on the contrary, especially after Parmenides,[184] the part assigned to *idein* and the other senses is ever more narrowly defined, while at the same time the domain assigned to *nous* and *noein* is enormously enlarged. In the course of this process, *nous* becomes synonymous with *phrēn*, *mētis*, *merimna*, and, to some extent, with *gnōmē*,[185] *noein* with *phronein*, *mētiesthai*, and, to some extent, with *gignōskein*.[185] This means that, at the end of the process, *nous* and *noein* cover not only all the meanings which they had had in Homer but also all the meanings originally belonging to those other words[186] and, in addition, designate some further functions of the mind for which no specific terms existed in Homer and Hesiod because they were not specifically reflected upon. The most important additions of this latter kind are: (1) the intuition by which Heraclitus is aware of the hidden harmony behind the apparent contrasts and conflicts which to the common crowd mean ultimate reality;[187] (2) the logical deductions by which Parmenides arrives at his conclusions *and* the direct contact with ultimate reality which, in his philosophy, is

[182] See above, pp. 23 f.

[183] See above, pp. 26 f.

[184] Before Parmenides and in the philosophy of Parmenides himself, the narrowing-down of the concept of *idein* and of the functions ascribed to the other senses is foreshadowed by the fact that the senses play only a very minor role in the discussion of the origin of human knowledge and error (see above, pp. 52 f.).

[185] *Gnōmē*, while no longer distinguished from *nous* in the same way as *gignōskein* is from *noein* in Homer, is sometimes used by Democritus as the larger concept covering both sense-perception and *noein* (see above, p. 74).

[186] This is true even of the original meaning of *gnōmē* and *gignōskein*; for the extended meaning of these terms belongs to a later period.

[187] See above, p. 39.

characteristic of the *noos* even when it errs;[188] (3) in the philosophy of Empedocles, the direct perception of Love and Hate in the external world through the response which these emotional agents engender in ourselves;[189] and (4) the complicated processes by which Democritus tries to attain a picture of ultimate reality.[190] In the fourth century the philosophies of Plato and Aristotle were to make still further very important additions of this kind.

In spite of all this, the preceding analysis has shown that, as long as one concentrates on those fragments which have come down to us in their original wording, it is quite possible to determine with considerable accuracy what the terms *nous* and *noein* mean in every individual instance; for, though the early philosophers used the terms with many meanings, they always knew exactly what they had in mind. But it is also easy to see that the enormous variety of meanings covered by the same terms could hardly fail to create a good deal of confusion in the interpretation of early Greek philosophy by later authors, both ancient and modern; for the interpretations attempted by these later authors were naturally conditioned by the specific meanings which the terms *nous* and *noein* acquired in later philosophical systems. The problem was further complicated by the fact that Hellenistic philosophy replaced the contrast between *nous* and *aisthēsis*, which is characteristic of the latest stage of Pre-Socratic philosophy, by the contrast of *logos* and *aisthēsis*.

Since a complete history of the misinterpretations caused by this situation could easily fill a book and is therefore outside the scope of the present article, it must suffice to give two illustrations drawn from examples which have already been touched upon. In the philosophy of Theophrastus, who is influenced by Plato and Aristotle, the concept of *nous* had again been narrowed as against its widest extension in late fifth-century philosophy. Consequently, since Theophrastus, too, thinks in terms of the simple alternative *nous* and *aisthēsis*, the field of *aisthēsis* is enlarged and covers any perception or understanding of individual objects, qualities, or even events, in space and time, whether it be sense-perception in the narrower sense or not. Therefore, when he finds that Parmenides ascribes the error which divides reality into the contrasts of warm and cold, etc., to the *noos* and that Empedocles attributes the perception of love by love and hate by hate also to *phronein*, he naturally

188 See above, p. 51.
189 See above, pp. 64 f.
190 See above, pp. 79 f.

comes to the erroneous conclusion that these philosophers considered *aisthēsis* and *noein* or *phronein* as the same thing,[191] "or something very similar."[192] Yet if one refers everything to his frame of reference, his interpretation does not go completely astray, and can still contribute something to an understanding of the original thought of these philosophers. This is different with Sextus Empiricus, who stubbornly tries to uphold the identity of *logos* and *nous*, and, since this identification is quite impossible if one takes *logos* in the sense which it had acquired in Hellenistic philosophy and *nous* in its Pre-Socratic meanings, ends in utter confusion.[193]

During the last few decades the interpretation of Pre-Socratic philosophy has made very great progress. But it has not overcome the difficulty altogether. This difficulty can be overcome only by a careful analysis of the history of the terminology. The present article is intended to be a first attempt in this direction—an attempt, which, like all first attempts, is still very imperfect.

In conclusion it is perhaps permissible to make application of the results obtained to some special problems which have been omitted from the previous discussion. As pointed out above,[194] Gorgias' contention that nothing exists, etc.—if divested of its deliberately paradoxical form—is nothing but a confirmation of Protagoras' opinion that man is the measure of all things and that it makes no sense to speak of something which *really* exists and which yet is totally different from the world which we experience. If one interprets Gorgias' famous work in this way, his second point—that, if something existed, it would not be accessible to our knowledge—is merely a different way of formulating the essential meaning of his first contention. But there is one interesting deviation from Protagoras' argumentation. He does not, like Protagoras, use sense-perceptions as examples but *phronein*. He first shows that things which do not exist, for instance, a wagon driven across the sea or monsters like Scylla and Charybdis, are objects of *phronein*. Then he concludes that, since that which is an object of *phronein* does not exist, that which exists is not an object of *phronein*. If taken without any further qualification, this is an obvious logical fallacy; and since the Sophists liked to play with their arguments, the conclusion was in all likelihood intentionally expressed in this ambiguous form. But if taken

[191] *De Sensu* 3 and 10; see also above, pp. 50 f. and 66 f.
[192] *De Sensu* 10.
[193] See above, pp. 41 ff.
[194] See above, p. 70 and Gorgias B3.

as a counterargument against philosophers who, like Anaxagoras and Democritus, contended that Protagoras might to some extent be right in what he said about sensations like warm and cold but that the *phrēn* nevertheless did have access to the reality behind the phenomena, it raised a serious difficulty.

Democritus has obviously struggled with this difficulty. He tried to overcome it by the theory that even the illusions of a dazed or an insane man were caused by atoms which belong to the "real world," though in a given individual case we could never be quite sure whether the combinations of atoms which provoke a certain image in our mind had come from outside ourselves or had been formed in our intellectual organs or whether, if they came from bodies outside ourselves, these *bodies* had exactly the structure indicated by the images caused by the atoms emanating from them. Yet, he contended, it was always possible within certain limits to draw a conclusion from a sensation to the form of the *atoms* causing it.[195] On the linguistic side it is perhaps interesting to observe that Gorgias uses *phronein* in the sense of "to imagine." He could do so because in the philosophical terminology of his period the synonyms *noein* and *phronein* covered any intellectual function that was not sense-perception in the narrowest sense of the word.

While Gorgias' use of the term *phronein* would make it possible to determine with considerable accuracy the time in which he lived, even if we did not know it otherwise, the opposite is true of the most famous of all the sentences in which the word *nous* occurs—Epicharmus' νοῦς ὁρῇ καὶ νοῦς ἀκούει· τᾶλλα κωφὰ καὶ τυφλά [*Nous* sees and *nous* hears; all other (faculties) are deaf and blind].[196] Much has been written about his adherence to a specific philosophical system as revealed in this sentence. But the preceding analysis has shown that, disregarding the Sophists, Protagoras and Gorgias, there was not a philosopher from Xenophanes to Democritus who could not have endorsed it, though none of them would probably have done so without adding some further explanation. The sentence is also in harmony with the Homeric concept of *noos*. It goes beyond Homer only in so far as it requires some philosophical reflection. But that is all that can be said about it.

In another instance, however, a definite chronological conclusion of some interest *can* be drawn. An extract from a work of Alexander Polyhistor (who lived in the time of Sulla) in Diog. Laert. VIII.30 says that the Pythagoreans divided the human soul into three parts—*thymos*,

[195] See above, p. 77, and the fragment on *allophronein* (A101).

[196] B12.

nous, and *phrenes*—and contended that *thymos* and *nous* were also found in animals but *phrenes* only in human beings. This attribution of *nous* to animals is certainly impossible in any philosophy influenced by Platonic thought. But the division is also uninfluenced by the identification of *phronein* and *noein*,[197] which is characteristic of Greek philosophy in the second half of the fifth century, and by the distinction of *nous* and *aisthēsis*. It is, on the other hand, in perfect agreement with Homeric terminology; for an animal can certainly have *noos* in the sense of the ability to realize, for instance, the danger of a situation, while it may not be credited with rational action, which is the function of the *phrenes* in Homer. All this, together with the fact that the terms *phrēn* and *phrenes* disappear from Greek prose after the first half of the fourth century, shows that it is hardly possible to place the origin of the doctrine later than the first half of the fifth century. It follows that Alexander's account, even though some of its parts show the influence of later philosophical terminology, does contain elements of genuine early Pythagorean doctrine and is not so worthless as Zeller and many other scholars have assumed.

A fortiori, it follows that Pythagorean philosophy was not entirely the invention of early Platonists and late Greek mystics, as some scholars seem to believe.

[197] The last Pre-Socratic philosophers who, within our knowledge, distinguished clearly between *noos* and *phrēn* are Xenophanes and Heraclitus (see above, pp. 33 f. and 37). The complete synonymity of the two terms can be proved only for the second half of the fifth century.

2

QUALITATIVE CHANGE
IN PRE-SOCRATIC PHILOSOPHY

W. A. Heidel

Strange as it may seem, this important theme appears never to have been treated fully, though the literature of Greek philosophy, ancient and modern, abounds in definite references or vague allusions to it. The Greek terms applied to such change are the nouns *alloiōsis* or *heteroiōsis* and their cognates. The latter, though occurring only once in Aristotle,[1] is probably the older term. In general, *alloiōsis* is the word that stands for a definite conception; and hence in the following discussion it will be used alone, though the two nouns are essentially synonymous.

Broadly speaking, *alloiōsis* signifies change; more specifically, change of aspect or quality. In itself it predicates nothing of the mode or process by which a given object, of whatever description, ceases to have one character and takes on another. Oftentimes the writer who employs the term manifestly has no clear and distinct idea to express; and it is not impossible that certain of the earliest philosophers had given the subject no thought. But it is evident that in general *alloiōsis* is employed by the

Reprinted here are pp. 333–44 and p. 346 n. 28 of Heidel's article of this title in *Archiv für Geschichte der Philosophie*, 19 (1906), 333–79. Footnotes have been abridged.

[1] *Phys.* 217b26. The word occurs as early as Melissus. The verb ἀλλοιοῦν stands in Heraclitus B67 (Diels), but I incline to think it due to a later redaction, such as appears not infrequently in Heraclitus. Zeller would have us think that it stands in a verbatim citation of Anaxagoras by Aristotle *De Gen. et Corr.* 314a15. But see n. 110, below. Heraclitus uses μεταβάλλειν and μεταπίπτειν. The latter verb occurs also in Melissus. The verb ἀλλοιοῦται occurs in [Hippocr.] *De Victu* (see n. 79), but the date of this tractate is too uncertain to yield satisfactory evidence. [Notes 79 and 110, not reprinted here, will be found in the sequel of Heidel's article in the original published version.—Ed.]

later Greek writers on philosophy in the sense which it bears in Aristotle's works.

Plato, whose free coinage of philosophical terminology is well known, was apparently the first to use the word in a signification definite enough to entitle one to speak of it as a technical term. At all events, the manner in which he introduces the distinction between *phora* and *alloiōsis* suggests a conscious innovation.[2] But even he does not define the mode of effecting this kind of change, except in so far as the object is said to remain in the same place—which is indeed the point of distinction as against *phora*—and elsewhere he employs the term with a certain indefiniteness, except when he refers to change of character by recomposition.[3]

Aristotle, likewise, at times speaks rather vaguely of *alloiōsis*, as if it could denote any qualitative change whatsoever; generally, however, the word bears a well-defined meaning. He says that "it is found whenever, the sensible substrate remaining the same, the substance changes in respect of its qualities, which are either contrary or neutral." [4] He thus distinguishes *alloiōsis* from such changes as are effected by transformation, by addition, by subtraction, or by composition.[5]

---

[2] *Theaet*. 181b ff.: speaking of the flowing philosophers, he suggests that their dictum πάντα ῥεῖ embraces not only motion of translation (φορά) but also ἀλλοίωσις. Cf. *Parm*. 138b ff.: the passage relates ἀλλοίωσις to ποιεῖν and πάσχειν, and the tone is more dogmatic. In *Theaet*. 157b and *Parm*. 162b–164b ἀλλοίωσις is used (in quasi-Heraclitean terms) as equivalent to θάνατος; cf. also *Legg*. 894e. How Plato would have us think of ἀλλοίωσις in Heraclitus is clearly indicated in *Theaet*. 152d ff. See below, n. 16.

[3] *Rep*. 380e–381d: Plato uses the term of changes of form as well as of character. There is latent, however, the same reference to the Eleatic protest against multiplicity, implied in all change, as in *Parm*. 138b ff. *Rep*. 454c ἀλλοίωσις is indefinite, merely opposed to ὁμοίωσις. *Tim*. 45d: After appropriating Empedocles' theory of vision, as based on the interaction of like and like, Plato explains the failure of sight by night as due to ἀλλοίωσις of the fire emitted by the eye, caused by the unlikeness to it of the air devoid of fire. *Tim*. 82b ἀλλοιότητες are changes in character due to recomposition of the four (Empedoclean) elements. *Crat*. 418a refers to change of meaning in a word. *Phaedo* 78d ἀλλοίωσις is opposed to that which has only one character (μονοειδές). Cf. *Legg*. 648e, where deterioration is implied, as in *Rep*. 380e ff.

[4] *De Gen. et Corr*. 319b10.

[5] *Phys*. 190b5 "Generally things which come to be, come to be in different ways: (1) by change of shape, as a statue; (2) by addition, as things which grow; (3) by taking away, as the Hermes from the stone; (4) by putting together, as a house; (5) by alteration (ἀλλοιώσει), as things which 'turn'

This statement would seem to be sufficiently explicit. Nevertheless many difficulties arise when one inquires just what changes shall be regarded as involving *alloiōsis*. Thus one is not a little surprised to find that Aristotle so considered the process of rarefaction and condensation,[6] whereas we are accustomed to regard it as a purely quantitative change, the alteration being such as a given mass undergoes in occupying more or less space.[7]

In another passage[8] he speaks of this process as the source of all qualities that are subject to *alloiōsis*. Again, we are informed that increase[9] necessarily involves *alloiōsis*, and the same would seem to be

---

($\tau\rho\epsilon\pi\acute{o}\mu\epsilon\nu\alpha$) in respect of their material substance." [Trans. R. P. Hardie and R. K. Gaye. Heidel quotes the Greek.—Ed.] Thus $\dot{\alpha}\lambda\lambda o\acute{\iota}\omega\sigma\iota s$ is allotropy, to use a modern chemical term.

[6] This is evident from many passages. One will suffice: *Phys.* 246a6 $\dot{\alpha}\lambda\lambda o\iota o\upsilon$-$\mu\acute{\epsilon}\nu o\upsilon$ $\tau\iota\nu\acute{o}s$, $o\acute{\iota}o\nu$ $\tau\hat{\eta}s$ $\ddot{\upsilon}\lambda\eta s$ $\pi\upsilon\kappa\nu o\upsilon\mu\acute{\epsilon}\nu\eta s$ $\mathring{\eta}$ $\mu\alpha\nu o\upsilon\mu\acute{\epsilon}\nu\eta s$ $\mathring{\eta}$ $\theta\epsilon\rho\mu\alpha\iota\nu o\mu\acute{\epsilon}\nu\eta s$ $\mathring{\eta}$ $\psi\upsilon\chi o\mu\acute{\epsilon}\nu\eta s$. The kinds of change are significant; for with Anaximenes, and the early Greek thinkers generally, rarefying and warming, condensing and cooling, are synonymous. That the process was called "rarefaction and condensation" rather than "warming and cooling" shows what aspects of the phenomena most impressed these philosophers. With Aristotle the emphasis was clearly reversed.

[7] This point of view was indeed quite familiar to Aristotle himself: See *Cat.* 10a16 and *De Caelo* 299b7. The opposition of $\delta\acute{o}\xi\epsilon\iota\epsilon$ and $\acute{\epsilon}o\iota\kappa\epsilon$ in the first passage may be significant, if the former verb, as is frequently the case, alludes to traditional views, while the latter expresses Aristotle's own opinion. It would then appear that Aristotle believed he was reflecting the opinions of predecessors (see n. 6), in making the distinction between the rare and the dense qualitative, whereas he himself held it to be quantitative. I hope to make it probable that the $\phi\upsilon\sigma\iota\kappa o\acute{\iota}$ shared Aristotle's own view, and that their doctrine was misunderstood.

[8] *Phys.* 260b7. Here once more $\delta o\kappa o\hat{\upsilon}\sigma\iota\nu$ and $\lambda\acute{\epsilon}\gamma\epsilon\tau\alpha\iota$ indicate that Aristotle believes he is reflecting the philosophical tradition. The passage is interesting also for other reasons. It appears to state discursively what the early physiologers perceived naïvely, viewing the process as the natural sequel of the $\kappa\acute{\iota}\nu\eta\sigma\iota s$ $\dot{\alpha}\acute{\iota}\delta\iota o s$; for Aristotle is trying to prove that motion of translation is the original form of change, and that the original form of $\phi o\rho\acute{\alpha}$ is the circular, because (as returning upon itself) it is continuous. The ideas are ancient; cf. Alcmaeon's explanation of man's mortality (Arist. *Probl.* 916a33) and Heraclitus B103, with Diels' note on Parmenides B3.1 in *Parmenides Lehrgedicht* (Berlin, 1897), pp. 66 ff. In our passage Aristotle had in mind the notion of a $\delta\acute{\iota}\nu\eta$ almost universally held by the early philosophers.

[9] *Phys.* 260a29. I do not know whose opinion Aristotle here thinks to repro-

true of freezing and of crystallization in general, which we should regard as changes in form or structure.[10] The fact that *alloiōsis*, as conceived by Aristotle, thus manifestly involves notions which are not coincident with modern conceptions of qualitative change, makes it imperative to examine the records of the Pre-Socratics, to determine just what they may have had in mind in speaking of such alterations as we call qualitative. For we surely have no right to assume that they approached the problem with the same presuppositions as we of modern times.

In the ancient accounts there appear two modes of conceiving what takes place when an object alters its character. One of these is technically known as *alloiōsis*; the other is called *mixis* or *krasis*.[11] Of the first of these modes we have already spoken; but we need to consider it more narrowly, in order to discover whether its implications are such as to fit into Pre-Socratic thought.

The term *alloiōsis*, in the Aristotelian sense, implies a hard and fast definition of identity and difference, with the identity residing in an unchanging essence, while the differentiae relate to the nonessential or accidental. Of these two pairs of ideas, the first—viz. identity and difference—received a distinct formulation only in consequence of the Eleatic dialectic; the second pair—viz. essence and accident, or substance and attribute—is a product of logic, as it was developed by Plato and Aristotle on the foundations laid by Socrates in his quest for general and universally valid definitions.[12] That a conception of such complexity cannot

---

duce; but it is his familiar doctrine of nutrition by "assimilation." We here meet for the first time Aristotle's deep-rooted *preconception* that wherever there is a change from one state to its contrary, there is ἀλλοίωσις. This assumption vitiated the account of sense-perception in their predecessors as given by Aristotle and Theophrastus. The play of contraries in ἀλλοίωσις is recognized in the definition, above [p. 86].

[10] See Prantl, *Aristoteles Acht Bücher Physik* (Leipzig, 1854), p. 519 (*ad Phys.* 246a1 ff.). The difficulty, as regards Aristotle, is enhanced by the fact that he often speaks from what he assumes to be the point of view of his predecessors, whereas he is in many cases unconsciously importing his own conceptions into spheres quite alien to them. Some of these cases can be proven beyond a peradventure, namely in regard to the so-called minute philosophers; in other cases the proof is necessarily somewhat less exact.

[11] The Pre-Socratics do not appear to have distinguished between these terms as did Aristotle and the Stoics in later times.

[12] See Arist. *Met.* 1078b17 ff. The definitions of Democritus and the Py-

be reasonably sought among the Pre-Socratics need hardly be proven by further arguments.

But it may be objected that this conclusion proves nothing, as Aristotle in this instance, as in so many others, is only defining with undue precision a conception which in the minds of his predecessors was rather indefinite. The objection deserves consideration: but the real question is whether the mode of change, however vaguely conceived by the early philosophers, was actually in essential points like that which Aristotle called *alloiōsis*. The difficulty—I had almost said the impossibility—of conceiving such a process, except on the basis of the presuppositions above detailed, is such that I believe no one who squarely faces the question will answer it in the affirmative. This alternative once rejected, we must look to the mode known as *mixis*, unless, indeed, we are to suppose that the early Greeks may have had in mind nothing more definite than the mysterious "sea-changes," to which their marine divinities were in the mythology thought to be subject, or those equally miraculous transformations of the prodigies, such as the conversion of a cock into a hen. Only an utter want of evidence tending to establish a more rational view could justify one, it would seem, in having recourse to so unphilosophical and, for the Greek philosophers, so unlikely a conclusion.

Turning now to the rival conception—that of *mixis*—we may say that the term denotes all forms of composition, decomposition, and recomposition. There is, to be sure, a sense in which *mixis* implies the existence of elements unitary, homogeneous, and eternal, as the possible ingredients of composition. If this was the only sense in which the term could be fitly employed, they might be in the right who hold that this mode of change is not to be found before Empedocles and Anaxagoras;[13] for, in that case, the notion would involve the same definite view of unity (identity) and difference which we have seen to be necessarily involved in the conception of *alloiōsis*. And this definition was the outcome of the Eleatic dialectic concerning the One. It would be as unreasonable to seek such a view among the Ionians as it would be to

thagoreans were not based on this procedure. Indeed, all the definitions of concrete things known to us from the Pre-Socratics have regard, like those of Empedocles, to the composition of the substance: In other words, their definitions are chemical formulas.

[13] Parmenides (B8.54 ff. and B9) represents his elements (Light and Night) in the same terms as Empedocles his Love and Strife (B17.20) and his four elements (B17.27).

expect to find there Aristotle's own *mixis*, regarded as chemical combination involving *alloiōsis*.[14]

But, fortunately, these are not the only presuppositions on which *mixis* is possible. Indeed, the passages in which change of quality is attributed to *mixis* are almost as numerous as those in which it is explained by *alloiōsis*. The practice of altering the character of a thing by admixture of something else is so simple and so primitive that there is no difficulty about assuming it for any period of human history above that of the veriest brute savagery. No assumption as to ultimate elemental characters need be made: any pronounced character, even though it be itself the product of a previous mixture, will serve the ends of such composition.

It is in this sense that Plato represents Socrates as maintaining that all the philosophers, excepting Parmenides,[15] agree in deriving things from motion and composition.[16] As this position, which I regard as essentially true, differs widely from that held quite generally by historians of Greek thought, it may be in order to pause long enough to indicate in the most summary way the grounds for this belief.

The real issue here concerns two principal points. First, what were the historical antecedents of the molecular theory of matter? Second, just what was implied in the monism of the Ionians? Everything depends on the answers given to these questions.

First, then, as to the molecular constitution of things. To my mind, this theory is the outgrowth of the observation of those meteorological phenomena commonly called evaporation (*anathymiasis*) and precipitation. It is clear that the appearance of the sun "drawing water" early impressed the Greek thinkers. Theophrastus refers to this phenomenon to explain Thales' assumption that all is water.[17] From Anaximander

[14] See Joachim, "Aristotle's Conception of Chemical Combination," in *The Journal of Philology*, vol. 29, no. 57, pp. 72 ff.

[15] This refers, of course, to his denial of multiplicity and change in "Truth"; but is it not significant that in his "Opinions of Men" he made a large use of composition?

[16] *Theaet.* 152d. It will not do to except all of his predecessors with Parmenides. The "Opinions of Men" and Heraclitus sufficiently indicate the point of view. There is μίξις here, both of the vaguer sort, and of the more definite kind (represented by Empedocles), with fully defined elemental substances.

[17] Aet. I.3.1. It is clear that Theophrastus was merely amplifying Arist. *Met.* 983b18 ff., and referring the words αὐτὸ τὸ θερμὸν ἐκ τούτου γιγνόμενον καὶ τούτῳ ζῶν to the cosmic process of evaporation and the production and replenishment of fire from water by means of it.

onward every philosopher of importance made a large and growing use of this conception for the explanation of things. Now this familiar process of evaporation and precipitation contained in embryo the large operations of nature as they were gradually formulated in the course of time. First, it afforded an example of the diminution of one body and the enlargement of another by increments individually beyond human ken. It thus became the type of "effluences" of all sorts, and the upward course of the vapors and the downward return of the precipitates exemplified the way up and down. Here also we are to find the meaning of rarefaction and condensation, with their synonyms heating and cooling. By evaporation air and fire encroach upon water and earth, and by precipitation water and earth encroach upon air and fire. Thus one typical form of existence (element, if you please) "changes" into the other. These "elements" may mix either in this sublimated form or else in a more palpable form as when the sea drenches the sand on the shore, only to retire presently and leave it dry. It is a far cry from this simple conception to the elaborate theories of Empedocles or Democritus; but it is a case of "old instincts hardening to new beliefs," as Lowell says.

Our second question concerns the implications of monism as held by the Ionians. Historians ancient and modern seem unable to conceive of the change of one element into another except as necessarily involving *alloiōsis*. Aristotle of course took this view;[18] but this need not daunt us as he was manifestly drawing a logical inference rather than stating a certain fact supported by documentary evidence. It is not enough to show that such a conclusion must follow, unless one can likewise prove that both the premises were known and acknowledged by these early thinkers. Such proof has never been offered and it is hardly too much to say that it never will be offered. Besides, Aristotle's testimony here will appear even more discredited when it is seen that he tried, by the most inexcusable reinterpretation, to father upon Anaxagoras this same doctrine, in spite of the clearest evidence that the philosopher did not and could not entertain it.[19] Aristotle clearly discloses the grounds for his inference, viz. the assumption that the Ionians had strictly defined

---

[18] *De Gen. et Corr.* 314a8, 314b1.

[19] More will be said below [see sequel of Heidel's article in orig. publ. version.—Ed.] concerning this effort of Aristotle's to make a place for his favorite conception of ἀλλοίωσις in the systems of Anaxagoras, Empedocles, and Leucippus. Here it is enough to note that he is compelled to do violence to their definitely expressed opinions to do so.

the unity and self-identity of the elemental substance, the express condition of his doctrine of *alloiōsis*.[20] The attentive student of Greek thought can hardly fail to see that Aristotle is pressing too much the conception of unity as held by the Ionians. The thought that unity or identity excludes difference is the contribution of the Eleatics. Had Thales and Anaximenes had this notion, they would have denied change outright, as did Parmenides. The distinction between essence and attribute was not yet current.

Furthermore we are not to assume, as historians ancient and modern are prone to do, that the Ionians emphasized the same characteristics of the "elements" as first occur to our minds. For example: When Heraclitus and Democritus spoke of the soul as fire, did they think first of the heat of fire, or of some other property? Did Lucretius do justice to Heraclitus, when he urged the objection that, on his theory, the only differences effected in the elemental fire by its condensation or rarefaction would be expressible in degrees of temperature?[21] To ask such a question is to answer it. When Anaximenes and Heraclitus, to mention only two names, chose these terms to denominate the process of differentiation, they gave unmistakable tokens of their deliberate intention: which clearly was to regard all other differences in things as subordinate and incidental to variations in density. So much once granted, there would seem to be left no basis for the assumption of such *alloiōsis* as Aristotle thought to discover in these early systems.

Early as we find this conception emerging, I incline to think that the notion of difference consisting in the relative degree of density is not original, but that it is one of the first generalizations from the phenomena of evaporation and precipitation. It may be doubted whether this notion ever stood alone as the means of accounting for the varieties of concrete things, unless this holds true of the system of Diogenes of Apollonia. It is not necessary to descant on the historical significance of this conception, as leading directly to the ultimate assumption that the essential properties of things are the properties of mass. But, taken by itself, it does not account for the distinctive features of such systems, say, as those of Empedocles, Anaxagoras, and Leucippus, who attrib-

[20] See n. 17 and the definition of ἀλλοίωσις above [p. 86]. Cf. *Met.* 983b6, where, as the most casual reader will observe, Aristotle supposes Thales' "element" defined as precisely as Empedocles'. It need hardly be said that this supposition affords a weak foundation for a theory of changes.

[21] Lucretius I.650 ff.

uted differentiation to composition and relegated rarefaction and condensation to a markedly inferior position.

What are we to say of this thought that things change their characters by recomposition? Some would have us think that it was a theory contrived to meet the fatal objections of Parmenides to the doctrine of *alloiōsis*. My discussion of the question thus far must have shown that I cannot accept this view. It is common to say that the difficulties raised by the Eleatics in regard to the One and the Many in predication were in large measure due to the substantive character attributed to the copula. There is, no doubt, much truth in this contention; but it does not touch the heart of the matter. The difficulty, as I conceive it, is with the predicate even more than with the copula. In other words, the predicate, whether noun or adjective, was regarded as substantive. What is implied in this assumption?

The question at issue is, in the last analysis, whether primitive man conceived of qualities as abstract, or as material constituents or ingredients of things. The only phrase in Parmenides which relates to change of quality is διά τε χρόα φανὸν ἀμείβειν (B8.41). One has only to consider the meaning of *chrōs*, *chroia*, and *chrōma* (signifying the surface as much as the color) and the verbs that go with these nouns to express change—*diameibein*, *ameibein*, *allassein*—all of which suggest *exchange*, to see that color is no abstraction; as indeed it would be surprising if so remote a conception should be found to be original. When Shakespeare said "Youth's a stuff will not endure," he used an expression that is true to primitive notions, as we meet them in such statements as that in *Proverbs* 27, 22 "Though thou shouldest bray a fool in a mortar among wheat with a pestle, yet will not his foolishness depart from him." Here folly is evidently thought of as an admixture, like the soul according to Epicurus, a "body of fine parts which is scattered throughout the whole aggregate (*athroisma*)" (Diog. Laert. X.63). When, therefore, we find Empedocles, Anaxagoras, and the Atomists taking this view of qualities, it is certainly more reasonable to suppose that they are merely adapting an old notion to the needs of philosophy than to believe this a newly contrived hypothesis to meet the objections of Parmenides. The dialectic of the Eleatic did compel a revision of previous views; but this revision was in the nature of a clearer definition of the process and of a sharper formulation of the elemental characters, in accordance with the assumed nature of the truly "existent," as unchangeable and homogeneous, which terms are practically synonymous. . . .

It may not be out of place at this point[a] to suggest that the notion of qualities "inhering" in substances is probably a "survival" of the conception of a quality, viewed as a physical constituent, present in an *athroisma*. This is the meaning of *metechein* and *pareinai* in the Pre-Socratics; whereas in Plato *methexis* and *parousia* represent the doctrine of logical realism for which things *participate* in Ideas. The primitive notion of a thing is that it "contains" certain qualities, the point of view being purely physical. The logical, or psychological view, is that a quality is one of the "meanings" of a "thing," both "thing" and "meanings" being constructs growing out of certain interests directed to the realization of ends. On this view "inherence" is meaningless and constitutes no problem. But in the transition from the physical to the psychological conception of qualities and things, a blending of the two points of view took place. The general stock of like "stuff" of which a thing partakes in virtue of containing that quality is converted into an Idea, half abstract and half concrete; and at once there arises the problem of relating the thing, as concrete, with the Idea, as abstract, and of relating the Ideas among themselves. This problem was to be solved only by a complete abandonment of the physical point of view with its implications. Aristotle was as much under the spell of the old conception as was Plato: his importation of the distinction between potentiality and actuality raised a false issue and retarded the solution.

[a] [This last paragraph appears as footnote 28 (p. 346) in the original published version.—Ed.]

II

IONIAN BEGINNINGS

3

ANAXIMANDER'S FRAGMENT: THE UNIVERSE GOVERNED BY LAW

Charles H. Kahn

Anaximander . . . declared the Boundless to be principle and element of existing things, having been the first to introduce this very term of "principle"; he says that it is neither water nor any other of the so-called elements, but some different, boundless nature, from which all the heavens arise and the *kosmoi* within them; "out of those things whence is the generation for existing things, into these again does their destruction take place, according to what must needs be; for they make amends and give reparation to one another for their offense, according to the ordinance of time," speaking of them thus in rather poetical terms. It is clear that, having observed the change of the four elements into one another, he did not think fit to make any one of these the material substratum, but something else besides these. (Simplicius *Phys.* 24.13, after Theophrastus)[1]

According to Simplicius, the entities which make reparation to one another for their wrongdoing are the elements. Is there any good reason to reject this view?

The "elements" for Anaximander are the opposite powers of cold and heat, moisture and dryness, darkness and light, and also the main portions of the visible world, regarded as embodiments of these universal factors.[2] Now it was long ago pointed out that only such opposing

From Charles H. Kahn, *Anaximander and the Origins of Greek Cosmology* (New York: Columbia University Press, 1960), pp. 166, 178–93. The book is hereafter referred to as *AOGC*. Selection reprinted with the permission of Columbia University Press.

[1] DK 12A9; from Theophr. *Phys. Opin.* fr. 2, Hermann Diels, *Dox. Gr.*, p. 476.

[2] See *AOGC*, ch. 2.

forces could reasonably be said to inflict damage on one another, and
to make recompense "according to the ordinance of Time." [3] The
opposites indeed are inevitably and continually at war with one another, and the advantage of one is the disaster (*phthora*) of its rival.[4]
Nothing can be more in harmony with this vivid picture of cosmic
strife than to speak of the vanquished party as "offended," and of his
periodic triumph as "revenge" or "compensation."

Since the old cosmological texts are lost, it is above all from the
medical literature that we can illustrate such expressions. The doctors
regularly refer in this way to the internal struggle of forces in the body,
as well as to the action of external factors upon the microcosm. Thus
the verb *adikein* describes the effect of a morbid agent: "One should
continue to make use of the same modes of regimen, when they clearly
do no harm (*ouden adikeonta*) to the man's body" (*Nat. Hom.* 9; Jones,
Loeb ed. IV, 28). The excessive strength of any power is considered a
wrong (*hamartēma*) for which punishment is due;[5] hence one factor is
said to chastise another (*kolazein*), or to avenge its intemperance
(*timōrein*).[6] The wronged party is in this case not so much the weaker
element, as the healthy state of the whole body. The aggressor may be
conceived either as the hot or moist within the body, or as its cosmic
"ally." [7] Hence it is the spring which kills men in an epidemic, and the
summer which "benefits" them.[8] Plato's doctor in the *Symposium* is

[3] Burnet, *EGP*, pp. 53 f.; W. A. Heidel, "On Anaximander," *CP*, 7 (1912),
233 ff. Similarly F. M. Cornford, *Principium Sapientiae* (Cambridge, 1952),
p. 168; G. S. Kirk, "Some Problems in Anaximander," *CQ*, N.S. 5 (1955),
33 ff. (repr. in Furley and Allen, I, pp. 323–49).

[4] See *AOGC*, p. 130.

[5] For the ἁμάρτημα inflicted by hostile forces on the body, see Hippocr. *De
Hebd.* ch. 19.31.

[6] Wind and water inhaled in breathing cool the body, and thus serve as
retaliation (τιμωρίη) against congenital heat (Hippocr. *De Cord.* 3, Littré,
IX, 82). Since the lung is cold by nature, and further cooled by respiration,
its presence around the heart κολάζει τὴν ἀκρασίαν τοῦ θερμοῦ (ch. 5). The
thickness of the heart's wall serves as protection (φυλακή) against the strength
of this heat (ch. 6, Littré, IX, 84). The same kind of compensatory action
(τιμωρέων) is provided by the brain against moisture (*De Gland.* 10, Littré,
VIII, 564). The comparison between these passages and Anaximander's doctrine was first drawn by Heidel, "Hippocratea, I," in *Harvard Studies in
Classical Philology*, 25 (1914), 188 f.

[7] Cf. Hippocr. *De Hebd.* 19.21.

[8] Cf. Hippocr. *Epid.* III.15, Jones, Loeb ed. I, 254.

speaking the language of the medical textbooks when he refers to "the hot and cold, and dry and wet," which, when blended and harmonized with one another, bring a season of health and prosperity to men, animals, and plants, "and cause no offense" (*ouden ēdikēsen*). But when *hybris* reigns among the seasons of the year, these same powers

> destroy many things and are cause of harm (διέφθειρέν τε πολλὰ καὶ ἠδίκησεν). For plagues generally arise from such circumstances, and many other irregular diseases for beasts and for plants as well. And indeed frosts and hailstorms and plant blights come from the excessive and unruly lust of such things for one another. (*Symp.* 188a–b)

The doctors are, of course, concerned with the damage inflicted by these powers upon the human body. The fragment of Anaximander speaks instead of the wrong (*adikia*) perpetrated by the cosmic powers upon one another. His words suggest an exchange of crimes like that which Herodotus presents as the antecedent for the Persian War, in which Greeks and Orientals are alternative offenders against one another: "this was the beginning of the wrongs done (*adikēmatōn*) . . . after this the Greeks were guilty of the secondary wrongdoing (*adikiēs*)" (Hdt. 1.2.1). In such a context, the balance is restored when the wronged party retaliates in full ("now this was equal for equal"). The crime establishes a debt, which the guilty party must "pay"; hence the phrase for rendering compensation: διδόναι δίκην καὶ τίσιν.[9] In the fragment, the conditions of payment are fixed by the arbiter Time, and his law is a periodic pendulum of give and take.

In this second, unmistakably authentic portion of our text, there is no real ambiguity. In a general way the relevance of the first part also seems clear: it is in the alternate generation and corruption of things that both wrong and retaliation must be found. The phrase κατὰ τὸ χρεών may contain a secondary allusion to the idea of retribution as a debt, since *chreos*, *chreōs*, "debt," is of course from the same root. But the primary force of *chreōn* combines the ideas of right and of necessity: death succeeds to birth in the course of time, *because it should and must*. In Anaximander's phrase κατὰ τὸ χρεών we have the most impersonal Greek formula for Fate.

But what are the *onta* whose generation and destruction represent

[9] For δίκη as a debt due, cf. Aesch. *Ag.* 534: ὀφλὼν γὰρ ἁρπαγῆς τε καὶ κλοπῆς δίκην.

such a relentless treadmill of offense and compensation? It is here that the problems of a literal interpretation become acute. Most modern commentators assume that *ta onta* must be the individual things of the visible world: the men, animals, and plants whose waning occurs after a fixed period of growth, and whose death balances their birth. These may, of course, be said to return back "into those things from which they came to be," and the expression is classic in Greece from an early period. Xenophanes insists that all things arise from earth and all return there in the end (B27); he is probably thinking of the fate of mankind. That is certainly the case for Epicharmus: "Earth to earth, *pneuma* aloft" (B9)—a thought that finds many echoes in the fifth century.[10] The author of *De Natura Hominis* formulates the doctrine in general terms. The genesis of things, he says, can take place only from an equitable blending of elemental opposites:

> And it is necessary that they return each to its own nature when the man's body comes to an end: wet to wet, dry to dry, hot to hot, and cold to cold. Such is the nature of animals and of all other things; all come to be in the same way and end in the same way. For their nature is composed out of all the aforesaid things and ends, as was said, in the same thing whence each was composed (τελευτᾷ . . . ἐς τὸ αὐτὸ ὅθεν περ συνέστη ἕκαστον). (ch. 3; Jones, Loeb ed. IV, 10)

Clearly this gives us a possible sense for the "out of those . . . into these" of the fragment. But such an interpretation of *ta onta*, as individual beings such as men and animals, encounters a serious obstacle in the explanatory particle *gar*, "for," which follows. For the statement introduced by this word says nothing of particular, compound things, but refers instead to a reciprocal action of the elemental powers upon one another (*allēlois*). How can an exchange of offense and penalty between the elements explain why compound things are dissolved back into the materials of which they were composed? In this

---

[10] See Eur. Fr. 839.8–11, cited DK 59A112; paralleled by *Suppl.* 532–34 and by the famous inscription for those who fell at Potidaea: αἰθὴρ μὲμ φσυχὰς ὑπεδέχσατο, σώμ[ατα δὲ χθών] (M. N. Tod, *A Selection of Greek Historical Inscriptions*, 2d ed. [Oxford, 1946], No. 59=*I.G.* I².945). It is because of this return of like to like that, according to the "Orphic" gold plates, the dead arriving in Hades must say "I am child of Earth and of starry Heaven, but my race (γένος) is heavenly" (DK 1B17.6).

view, the apparent parallelism of the two clauses loses its *raison d'être*, as does the binding *gar*. We would have two independent propositions, and no clear logical link between them.[11]

One may, of course, imagine various devices for bridging the gap which this view opens up. We might assume, for example, that the excerpt of Theophrastus has suppressed one or more steps of the original reasoning which is represented in our text by the particle *gar:* Anaximander may have argued that the formation of individual things involves the temporary supremacy of one power over another, perhaps in the form of a debt to be paid back when the compound is resolved into its elements.[12] Yet even with a great deal of ingenuity, we will hardly succeed in explaining why the payment is then made, not by compound things back to their elements, but by the latter "to one another." Furthermore, the use of a pronoun such as αὐτά (in the phrase διδόναι γὰρ αὐτὰ δίκην καὶ τίσιν ἀλλήλοις) naturally leads us to suppose that the things which exchange wrong and reparation are the same as those whose generation and destruction has just been mentioned. Can this have been the original thought of Anaximander, distorted by the doxographical citation? [13]

Now there is another interpretation of the words *ta onta* which would permit us to understand the text in just this way, without any additional conjectures and without supposing the sense to have been altered by Simplicius or Theophrastus. Simplicius, we remember, thinks that the fragment refers to the transformation of elements into one another, and the idea of a seasonal (as well as of a cosmogonic) cycle

[11] This apparent irrelevance of the two clauses to one another is emphasized by J. B. McDiarmid, "Theophrastus on the Presocratic Causes," *Harvard Studies in Classical Philology*, 61 (1953), 97 (repr. in Furley and Allen, I, pp. 178–238).

[12] The loan of elements in the formation of the human body is alluded to by Plato *Tim.* 42e9 (cf. 41d3). The same metaphor seems to have been applied by Philolaus to the intake of air in breathing: πάλιν καθαπερεὶ χρέος ἐκπέμπει αὐτό (sc. τὸ ἐκτὸς πνεῦμα), *Anon. Lond.* XVIII.23; W. H. S. Jones, *The Medical Writings of Anonymus Londinensis* (Cambridge, 1947), p. 72.

[13] Thus Kirk suggests that the original assertion paraphrased by Theophrastus "might have been to the effect that each opposite changes into its own opposite and into no other, for example the hot is replaced by the cold and not by the wet or the soft" ("Some Problems," p. 35). I largely agree with Kirk as to what Anaximander said, but see no reason to believe that either Theophrastus or Simplicius interpreted his words in a different way.

of elemental change was familiar to the Milesians. It would be natural
for them to speak of the formation of moisture in the rainy season as
a birth of the wet out of the dry, just as the fiery element of summer is
born and nourished from the moist.[14] May not these very principles
be the *onta* which, in the process of elemental change, perish again
into the things from which they have arisen?

The expression *ta onta* is so general that it may just as well apply
to natural compounds as to the elements of which they are formed.
Strictly speaking, the text of the fragment is compatible with either
view. On the other hand, a glance at the oldest recorded usage of the
term in philosophical contexts will suggest that it refers to elemental
powers rather than to unique, individual bodies. In the fragment of
Diogenes, for example, τὰ ἐν τῷδε τῷ κόσμῳ ἐόντα νῦν are specified as
"earth and water and air and fire and the other things which are observed to exist in this *kosmos*" (B2). In the *De Natura Hominis*, the
parallel phrase πάντων τῶν ἐνεόντων ἐν τῷδε τῷ κόσμῳ follows directly upon
a mention of "the hot, and the cold, and the dry, and the wet" (ch. 7;
Jones, IV, 22). The "things which were all together" of Anaxagoras B1
are of course not the individual bodies of men and animals, but air,
aithēr, and the various powers and materials of things yet to be produced. For him also "the things in the one cosmos" are exemplified by
the hot and the cold (B8). Anaxagoras is the philosopher whom we
would expect Protagoras to attack, and it is probably in terms of such
physical elements that we must understand the latter's opening reference to "all things, those which are and those which are not" (B1).
When Plato propounds the Protagorean thesis in the *Theaetetus*, his
first example is precisely the difference between a hot and a cold wind.
So the pretended *onta* which Melissus is concerned to refute, and
"which men say to be true," are not individual things but "earth,
water, air, fire, iron, gold, the living and the dead, dark, bright, and
the rest," including hot and cold, hard and soft (B8).

It is therefore most probable that the expression *ta onta* in the fragment also refers to such elemental powers. It is they who are one another's source of generation, just as they are the mutual cause of death.
On the grammatical level, it is these opposing principles, and these
alone, which are implied by the neuter plural pronouns: ἐξ ὧν, εἰς
ταῦτα, αὐτά, ἀλλήλοις. The wet is generated from the dry, the light from
the darkness. But the birth of such a thing involves the death of its
reciprocal, and this loss must eventually be repaired by a backward

[14] See *AOGC*, p. 132.

swing of the pendulum. Thus it is that "from a single necessity all things are composed and nourished by one another." [15]

This compensation of death for birth is absolutely necessary; it takes place κατὰ τὸ χρεών. The following *gar* shows that this very inevitability is expressed again in the idea of *didonai dikēn*. The archaic view of *adikia* is just this, that one who is guilty will always pay the penalty. It is probably misleading to lay too much stress on the moral or eschatological aspect of "cosmic injustice" for Anaximander. If the dominion (*kratein*) of one party over another is described as a wrong, this need not imply a different, pre-mundane or post-mundane state of harmony such as is dreamt of by Empedocles. The victory of one element over another is *adikia* because the weaker party suffers, and because of the disastrous consequences which must ensue for the offender. The words and imagery of the fragment indicate above all that the exchange of birth and death is sure, remorseless, inescapable, like the justice which the gods send upon guilty men. It will come at last, when its hour is full. For Necessity enforces the ordinance which Time lays down.

According to the interpretation here proposed, the meaning of the two portions of the fragment is one and the same. The first member states the necessary return of mortal elements back into the opposite powers from which they are generated; the second clause explains this necessity as a just compensation for the damage done at birth. The elements feed one another by their own destruction, since what is life to one is death for its reciprocal. The first law of nature is a *lex talionis:* life for life.

Thus the fragment does not announce a last end of things, when the elemental powers will return into the Boundless from which they have arisen (despite the number of modern interpretations which presuppose this view). Neither does it contain a particular reference to the dissolution of men and animals back into the materials of which they are composed, although such an idea was frequently expressed by other Greek thinkers. This brief text of Anaximander most naturally refers simply to that continuous change of opposing forms or powers into one another which is the common theme of Heraclitus (B126, B88, etc.), Epicharmus (B2), Melissus (B8), and Plato (*Phaedo* 70d–72). The most significant case for a Milesian cosmologist was no doubt the interchange of the major elements. "It is death for water to become earth," says

[15] Hippocr. *Nat. Hom.* 7, Jones, Loeb ed. IV, 22. For the full context, see below p. 112.

Heraclitus, "but out of earth water arises" (B36); the death of fire is birth for air, and the death of air is birth for water (B76). "These live the death of those, and die their life" (B62, B77).

Anaximander must have seen this exchange transacted daily, in the alternation of light and darkness, of the fresh morning dew and the parched heat of noon. He must have recognized essentially the same process at work in the production of the fiery thunderbolt out of wind and cloud, themselves in turn produced from evaporating moisture. The downward return of quenched fire and condensing rain cloud will counteract the upward surge of dryness and heat, and thus preserve the balance of the whole. The waxing and waning of the moon's light fulfills in turn the lawful interchange of generation and corruption. If the celestial equilibrium was conceived by Anaximander as a stable sphere, it is the turning circle which best symbolizes this rhythm of elemental change. The image is preserved in our own terminology, which is in this respect still that of early Greece: "cycle" from *kyklos* (originally "wheel"), "period" from *periodos* ("revolution"). In the Ionian view, the predominant cycle is that of the sun, since it is in step with this yearly movement that the seasons of heat and coolness, drought and rainfall succeed one another, while the dominion of daylight gives way before the long winter nights.[16] In Greece, even the winds are generally "opposite according to the opposite seasons" (Arist. *Meteor.* 364a34). And the mortal seasons of youth and age, growth and decay, exemplify the same periodic law.[17]

It is possible that Anaximander projected this pattern upon a still more majestic screen, and spoke (like Plato and his followers) of a Magnus Annus, in which the great astronomical cycles are to be accompanied by catastrophic transformations on the earth. Like Xenoph-

[16] In Hippocr. *De Victu* 5 the "divine necessity" according to which all things come to pass is just such a rhythmic oscillation between maximum and minimum, illustrated by the periods of day and night, of the moon, and of the annual solar motion. And see *AOGC*, pp. 104–06.

[17] "Old age arises from the loss of heat" (Parm. A46a); "a man is hottest on the first of his days, coldest on the last" (Hippocr. *Nat. Hom.* 12, Jones, Loeb ed. IV, 36). This idea, according to which man's life is a reduced model of the cosmic year (ending at the winter solstice), is developed at length by the author of *De Victu* (ch. 33; Jones, Loeb ed. IV, 278), who adds the sequence wet, dry, and then wet again in increasing age (corresponding to the rains of both spring and fall).

In stating the general law of alternation between opposites, it is the seasonal changes that Plato mentions first (*Rep.* 563e9).

anes, Anaximander may have taught that the progressive drying-up of the sea would eventually be reversed, so that the earth will sink back into the element from which it has arisen.[18] This would constitute the necessary "reparation" required by the fragment for any type of excess. The periodic destruction of mankind by fire and flood, to which Plato more than once alludes, seems to form part of the symmetrical pattern of this sixth-century world view.[19]

Did Anaximander envisage an even greater cycle, in which the appearance of this differentiated universe out of the Boundless would itself be periodically balanced by the return of all things, including the elements, back into their original source? This doctrine is ascribed to Anaximander by some doxographers, but there is no definite statement to this effect in our most reliable sources.[20] On the other hand, it seems difficult to deny such a view to the Milesians, if their belief in an "eternal motion" is to be taken seriously.[21] A periodic destruction of the

[18] Xenoph. A33.5–6 (Hippolytus): "A mixture of earth with sea is taking place, and it will at length be dissolved by the moist . . . all men will be destroyed, when the earth collapses into the sea and becomes mud; then there will be a new beginning of generation; and this transformation occurs in all the κόσμοι." For the meaning of the last phrase, see *AOGC*, pp. 51 ff.

[19] The alternate destructions of human societies by fire and water are mentioned by Plato at *Tim.* 22c; frequent destructions in the past, particularly by floods, at *Laws* 677a; similar cycles of human and cosmic transformations at *Politicus* 269a.

Democritus was author of a work entitled "Great Year or *Astronomiē*"; very little is known of its contents. For the astronomical meaning of the τέλεος ἐνιαυτός, see *Tim.* 39d4, and Arist. Fr. 25, where the version of Censorinus 18 adds: *cuius anni hiemps summa est cataclysmus, quam nostri diluvionem vocant, aestas autem ecpyrosis, quod est mundi incendium.* The concept of the *ecpyrosis* may have received a new interpretation from the Stoics, but the cosmic summer and winter are obviously part of the original Great Year (cf. χειμών and καῦμα at *Tim.* 22e6). They represent the alternate victory of Hot and Cold, in the most monumental of all struggles regulated by "the ordinance of Time." Cf. B. L. van der Waerden, "Das Grosse Jahr und die ewige Wiederkehr," *Hermes*, 80 (1952), 129.

[20] The destruction of the world (or worlds) appears in DK A10, A14, A17; no mention of it occurs in Hippolytus (DK A11) or in the primary excerpt of Simplicius (DK A12).

[21] An "eternal motion" should imply that some change took place before the present world order began to arise, and that something else will follow its destruction (if any). The expression would not have been used if Anaximander, like Anaxagoras, had avoided any reference to events before the

world order might well follow from Anaximander's conception of symmetrical action and counter-action, continuing unhampered throughout endless time. But there is no place for this doctrine in the text of Anaximander's fragment, which does not mention the generation of things out of the *apeiron*. There is therefore no reason whatsoever to suppose that the destruction of the world is an "atonement" to be made for some kind of wrongdoing.

On the other hand, if a cycle of world formation and dissolution is not implied by this brief text, everything else we know about Anaximander's cosmology has its place here: astronomical cycles, the succession of the seasons, the phenomena of the atmosphere, the origin of dry land and living things, all converge in the element doctrine of the fragment. There is another idea which we may expect to find here, in view of our earlier discussion of Anaximander's theories, and that is the principle of geometric proportion. In order to see how Anaximander's mathematical conceptions are related to his statement in the fragment, we must consider some Aristotelian passages in which a similar view is described. It is not difficult to recognize the Milesian doctrine in Aristotle's reference to those who declare that there is "an infinite body, one and simple . . . besides the elements, out of which they generate the latter."

> For there are some who make the *apeiron* not air or water, but a thing of this sort, so that the other elements should not be destroyed by the one of them that is infinite. For they are characterized by opposition to one another; air, for instance, is cold, water is wet, fire is hot; if one of these were infinite, the others would now have perished. Hence, they say, the *apeiron* is something else, from which these things arise. (*Phys.* 204b22)

There is no reason to doubt the substantial accuracy here of Aristotle's report.[22] This argument against the infinity of any single element

---

commencement of our cosmic order, or implied that no changes took place during this time; cf. Arist. *Phys.* 250b24, where the view of Anaxagoras is cited as an example of μὴ ἀεὶ εἶναι κίνησιν.

[22] See Simpl. *Phys.* 479.32 ff., where the argument is expressly assigned to Anaximander. The doubts expressed in general terms by E. Zeller, *Die Philosophie der Griechen*, Part I, 5th ed. (Leipzig, 1892), p. 215, and developed in detail by Harold Cherniss, *Aristotle's Criticism of Presocratic Philosophy* (Baltimore, 1935), pp. 27 f., 367, do not seem cogent. As Gregory Vlastos has pointed out ("Equality and Justice in Early Greek Cosmologies," *CP*, 42

corresponds exactly to the view expressed by the fragment: if there were no limits assigned to the supremacy of one of the participants in cosmic strife, its victory would never be compensated by the statutory defeat. It is this same idea which Aristotle has just adapted in his own proof that no element can be infinite: "The opposites must always be in a relationship of equality"; for an infinite elemental body will always exceed and destroy one that is finite (*Phys.* 204b13–19). Much the same principle is invoked by him in the *Meteorologica* against those who believe that the entire celestial region is filled with fire and air (340a1 ff.). That cannot be, says Aristotle, for, in view of the relatively small dimensions of the earth in comparison with the whole heavens, fire and air "would then exceed by far the equality of a common proportion with regard to their fellow elements." [23] Aristotle is prepared to admit that there is more air than water in the universe, for he knows that water expands when evaporated. What he requires is therefore not a simple arithmetic correspondence, but an "equality of power"—a geometric relationship which joins different quantities in a single proportion, just as a fixed amount of water produces a corresponding amount of steam (340a16).

[1947], 168, n. 121 [repr. in Furley and Allen, I, pp. 56–91]), the balance between the elemental powers is not a new idea with Aristotle, but everywhere presupposed in the early medical literature (see *AOGC*, p. 132 n. 4). Furthermore, a clear indication that the reasoning given here is not an invention of Aristotle may be seen in his reference to air as cold. This anomaly with regard to Aristotle's own theory—according to which air is defined as hot-moist (*De Gen. et Corr.* 330b4)—has often perplexed the commentators, both ancient and modern. The riddle disappears if we remember that the ἀήρ was originally defined by his predecessors as cold in opposition to the fiery αἰθήρ. (In the scheme of Anaxagoras, for example, the ἀήρ is cold, damp, dense, and dark.) Aristotle seems to have borrowed these examples together with their argument.

Hence it is peculiarly appropriate that Aristotle should refute Anaximander's thesis by an adaptation of his own principle: "There is no such sensible body besides the so-called elements. *For all things are dissolved back into that out of which they are composed;* so that this body would then appear in addition to air and fire and earth and water; but nothing of the sort is to be seen" (*Phys.* 204b32, where the plural ἐξ ὧν of Anaximander has, of course, been replaced by the singular ἐξ οὗ).

[23] *Meteor.* 340a4. According to the pseudo-Aristotelian *De Mundo*, 396b34, the universe is preserved by such an agreement and balance of opposing forces.

Aristotle feels himself entirely justified in using this principle against his predecessors, for he is conscious of having taken it from them. He discusses elsewhere (*De Gen et Corr.* 333a18 ff.) the statement of Empedocles that the elements are "equal in every way": Love is "equal in length and breadth" to the others, just as Strife is their "equipoise at every point" (Emped. B17.19–27). For Empedocles as for Aristotle, this geometric equality between the elements is an expression of their equal power.[24] Such an equilibrium between opposing principles is no less important in the view of Anaxagoras, for whom "all things are always equal" (B5; cf. B3). To preserve this necessary balance, his *aēr* and *aithēr* must each be infinite, for they are the two greatest things in bulk (B1). The same is true of the two symmetrical forms which together fill the cosmic sphere of Parmenides. They too are opposite to one another, and "both equal" (B9.4). Although the form which this idea assumes for Anaxagoras and Empedocles may be due to the direct influence of Parmenides, the general principle is not new with him. For we also find it in the "measures" which regulate elemental transformation according to Heraclitus: when Fire in the turnings of its cycle (*tropai*) has become sea and then earth, once more "sea is poured out, and measured back into the same *logos* as before it became earth" (B31).[25] This *logos* of elemental exchange is precisely a geometric "equality of common proportion" such as that which Aristotle postulates in the *Meteorologica*. It guarantees that the fundamental order of the universe will persist unchanged, despite its periodic transformations. From the modern point of view, it represents the earliest formula for the conservation of both energy and matter, since at this period bulk (*megethos*) and power (*dynamis*) are conceived as the two faces of a single coin.

The old Ionic theory of the elements is thus characterized by the same geometric symmetry which prevails in Anaximander's celestial scheme. The equilibrium of the earth at the center of a spherical world is reflected in the mathematical proportion by which the elements are bound to one another. These parts belong together in a unified whole, a community whose balance of power is maintained by periodic re-

---

[24] See the distribution of τιμή and κρατεῖν between the elements in Emped. B17.28 f., correctly interpreted by Vlastos in "Equality and Justice," p. 159, as a dynamic equilibrium.

[25] It is because of these equal measures, by which Fire is exchanged for all things and all for Fire (Heracl. B90) that "the starting-point and the limit of the circle [of elemental transformations] are one and the same" (B103).

adjustments, in accordance with that general law of astronomical cycles which Anaximander conceived as an immutable *taxis* of Time.

This is, I suggest, the conception which lies at the root of the Greek view of the natural world as a *kosmos*, an admirably organized whole. The term *kosmos* is interpreted by Plato as implying "geometric equality," [26] and the word is bright with the combined radiance of the moral and aesthetic ideals of early Greece. No ancient author, it is true, tells us that Anaximander spoke of the world as a *kosmos*. But the new philosophic sense of this term is as familiar to Heraclitus and Parmenides as it is to Anaxagoras, Empedocles, and Diogenes.[27] It is difficult to see where such a widespread notion could have arisen, if not in sixth-century Miletus—the mother city from which, like so many colonies, all the philosophic schools of early Greece are sprung.

Precisely considered, the *kosmos* is a concrete arrangement of all things, defined not only by a spatial disposition of parts, but also by the temporal *taxis* within which opposing powers have their turn in office. It is the spatial aspect (in which the *kosmos*, identified with the *ouranos*, appears as a body whose limbs are the elements) which tends more and more to obscure the temporal order that prevailed in the earlier conception. Both ideas, however, are inextricably linked from the beginning to the end of Greek philosophy. The cosmos has not only an extended body, but also a lifetime (*aiōn*), whose phases are celestial cycles.[28]

[26] "The wise, Callicles, say that both heaven and earth and gods and men are held together by community and friendship, by orderliness (κοσμιότης) and temperance and justice (δικαιότης), and for this reason they call this whole universe an Order (κόσμος), my friend, not disorder (ἀκοσμία) nor license. . . . But you have not noticed that geometric equality has great power both among men and among gods; and you think one should practice excessive greed (πλεονεξία), for you neglect geometry" (*Gorg.* 508a).

[27] See *AOGC*, Appendix I, p. 219.

[28] This sense of αἰών, the world's lifetime, occurs in Arist. *De Caelo* 279a22–30 and 283b28 (for the idea, cf. 285a29, 286a9; similar uses of αἰών in Bonitz, *Index*, 23b19,21). The meaning is probably the same in Emped. B16. For reasons of his own, Plato has redefined αἰών as the timeless eternity of the Forms, while χρόνος is its moving image in the heavens (*Tim.* 37d); Aristotle's use of the word is closer to the original meaning. The etymological sense of αἰών was "vitality, vital force" (see E. Benveniste, "Expression indo-européenne de l'éternité," *Bulletin de la société de linguistique*, 38 [1937], 103). Hence it came to mean "duration of life, lifetime." The later sense of "eternity" is due to a philosophic reinterpretation of αἰών as equivalent to ἀεί ὤν. For the transitional use of the term for the everlasting life of the universe

Two Hippocratic texts may serve to illustrate this conception in the minds of men penetrated by Ionian science. The authors of the *De Natura Hominis* and the *De Victu* both employ the word *kosmos* for the universal order, and apply this notion in detail to the structure and function of men's bodies. It was no doubt towards the end of the fifth century that Polybus, the son-in-law of Hippocrates, wrote as follows:

> The body of man always possesses all of these [the four humors, characterized by the four primary opposites], but through the revolving seasons they become now greater than themselves, now lesser in turn, according to nature. For, just as every year has a share in all, in hot things as well as cold, in dry things as well as wet (for no one of these could endure for any length of time without all of the things present in this *kosmos;* but if any one of these were to cease, all would disappear; for from a single necessity all are composed and nourished by one another); just so, if any one of these components should cease in a man, the man would not be able to live. (*Nat. Hom.* 7, Jones, Loeb ed. IV, 20–22)

The year and the *kosmos* each constitute an organized body, from which no vital member may be removed without catastrophe. Writing perhaps a few years later[29] the author of the *De Victu* holds a similar

---

or cosmic god, see A.-J. Festugière, "Le Sens philosophique du mot αἰών," *La parola del passato*, 4 [1949], 172).

It is because Time (χρόνος), as the sequence of astronomical cycles, was also conceived as the vital motion of the universe that it could be "inhaled" from outside like a breath-soul (in the Pythagorean view, DK 58B30), and be identified by some with the heavenly sphere itself, as well as with its motion (*Phys.* 218b1). Compare *Tim.* 38e4, where the stars "produce Time," and 41e5, where they are "instruments of Time."

[29] The date of the *De Victu* has been much disputed. Most authors assign it to the end of the fifth century, but Werner Jaeger has put it in the middle of the fourth (*Paedeia*, trans. Gilbert Highet, vol. 3 [Oxford, 1945], 33 ff., with notes), and Kirk even sees Peripatetic influence here (*Heraclitus: The Cosmic Fragments* [Cambridge, 1954], pp. 27 ff.). Their arguments are scarcely decisive. In regard to questions of cosmology, there is no trace of any influence later than Empedocles and Archelaus. The author cannot have read the *Timaeus*, or even the *Phaedo*. In view of his otherwise receptive attitude to the ideas of his predecessors, this makes it difficult to believe that he is younger than Plato. Anyone who compares *De Victu* 69 with the description of Herodicus of Selymbria at *Republic* 406a-b and *Anon. Lond.* IX.20 ff. (Jones, *Medical Writings*, p. 48) will wonder whether there can have been

view of the interdependence of natural factors. A good doctor, he claims, "must be familiar with the risings and settings of the stars, that he may be competent to guard against the changes and excesses of food and drink, of winds, and of the *kosmos* as a whole, since it is from these [changes and excesses] that diseases arise among men" (ch. 2; Jones, Loeb ed. IV, 228). Such vicissitudes of nature, he says, are due to the alternate dominion not of four principles, but of two alone: fire and water.

> Each one rules and is ruled in turn, to the maximum and minimum of what is possible. For neither one is able to rule altogether. . . . If either were ever dominated, none of the things which now exist would be as it is now. But as things are, these [fire and water] will be the same forever, and will never cease either separately or together (ch. 3, Jones, Loeb ed. IV, 232).

For this author too the *kosmos* takes the form of a rhythmically repeated cycle, executed by a system in dynamic equilibrium.

Perhaps the most striking expression of this old view of cosmic order is to be found in a relatively late text. Diogenes Laertius quotes from Alexander Polyhistor a cosmology which the latter is said to have found in certain "Pythagorean notebooks" (*hypomnēmata*). We do not know who these Pythagoreans were, or when they lived.[30] But the doctrine that follows clearly reflects the same conceptions that prevail in the Hippocratic Corpus:

> Light and darkness, hot and cold, dry and wet obtain equal portions in the *kosmos;* it is from their dominance that arises summer,

---

two doctors of the same period with such a similar εὕρημα. It will hardly do to claim the author of the *De Victu* as a "pupil" of Herodicus (as does Jones, *Medical Writings*, p. 48), since this is precisely the point where the writer insists upon his originality (ch. 69; cf. ch. 2). The argument of J. Jütner (*Philostratos* [Leipzig, 1909], pp. 15 ff.), that the "biting scorn" for gymnastics in *De Victu* 24 could not come from a former trainer is one that cuts both ways. (Since this was written, the case for the earlier dating has been reargued by R. Joly, who doubts, however, the attribution to Herodicus. See his edition of *Du Régime* [Paris, "Les belles Lettres," 1967] and his *Recherches sur le traité pseudohippocratique* Du Régime [Paris-Liège 1961].)

[30] Diels followed M. Wellman, *Hermes*, 54 (1919), 225, in assigning the doctrine to a contemporary of Plato; Festugière has argued for a late fourth-century date in *Revue des études grecques*, 58 (1945), 1.

from that of the hot, and winter, from that of the cold.[31] But when
their portions are equalized, the year is at its finest; its flourishing
season, spring, is healthy, but its waning season, autumn, productive of disease. Indeed, the day itself has a flourishing period at
dawn, but wanes at evening, which is therefore the most unhealthy
hour. (D.L. VIII.26 = DK 58B1a)

The medical theory of these three texts is, as far as we know, the
creation of Alcmaeon and of the founders of the Hippocratic method.
But the cosmology on which it is based—and of which it is a faithful
reflection—is the common heritage of all Greek philosophers after the
sixth century. Its earliest expression is to be found in the fragment of
Anaximander.

There are other traces of this view in the extant philosophical fragments. Anaxagoras, for example, declares that Nous "has set all things
in good order" (B12). It is clear from the context that the chief instrument of this order is the cosmic revolution (perichōrēsis) performed
by the heavenly bodies, the source of a differentiated universe. Further
details concerning the "order" brought about by Nous have been lost,
but may to some extent be supplied from the doctrine of Diogenes.
Like Anaxagoras, he too praises the intelligence (noēsis) of his cosmic
principle, which "arranges all things" (B5), and in his case, we have
a text that states the concrete evidence of this ordering:

For it were not possible for all things to be so distributed (dedas-
thai) without intelligence, that there should be measures of all
things, of winter and summer, of night and day, of rainfall and
winds and clear weather. And if one is willing to reflect on other
things, he will find them also so disposed as to be the best possible. (B3)

For this fifth-century Ionian, as for the Milesians before him, it is the
seasonal regularity of celestial and meteorological processes which best
exhibits the organic structure of the universe.

Here, at the starting-point of Western science and philosophy, we
find the Order of Nature clearly conceived as an "ordinance of Time."

[31] The "emendation" of Cobet ⟨ξηροῦ δ' ἔαρ καὶ ὑγροῦ φθινόπωρον⟩ (which
is printed by Hicks in the Loeb Diogenes as part of the text) stands in flat
contradiction to the following words: spring and fall are not subject to the
domination of any power, but represent the "finest" time of the year because
of their balance.

This oldest formula of natural law thus emphasizes that same notion of periodicity which, in a much more elaborate form, plays such an important role in modern physical thought.[32] The early appearance of this idea is no cause for surprise; indeed the great periodic occurrences have never passed unnoticed. The cycle of the stars and seasons is the fundamental fact in any agricultural society, which must strive to establish some harmony between the works of man and the motions of the heavenly bodies. Such is the theme not only of Hesiod's poem, but of all ancient religions.

What is new in Anaximander's doctrine is neither the concern for seasonal repetition, nor the application of moral and legal concepts to the natural world. The idea that "man lived in a charmed circle of social law and custom, but the world around him at first seemed lawless," [33] is based upon a total misconception. The earliest civilizations had no notion of the distinction between Nature and Society which has become habitual to us. In Homer, for example, no boundary is recognized between human usage and the order of the universe. In front of man stands not Nature, but the power of the gods, and they intervene as easily in the natural world as in the life of men. Poseidon is lord of the sea, shaker of the earth, but he stands in battle next to the Greeks before Troy. Zeus is god of the storm, and was once the personified power of the sky itself, but when he casts his thunderbolt, it is to exact punishment from perjurers.[34] The Horae, who are the Seasons, and will become the astronomical Hours, have for sisters the Moirae, the "fated portions" of mankind. Their common mother is Themis ("lawful establishment"), and their names are Justice, Peace, and Good Distribution (*eunomiē*) (Hes. *Theog.* 901).

These ideas are from the beginning so intimately linked that, in lands where mythic speculation is highly developed, a single term for "law" normally applies to ritual, to morality, and to the natural order. Such, for instance, is the case for the Vedic concept of *r̥tá*, literally, "what is adjusted, fitted together" (from the root **ar-* also found in

[32] "The birth of modern physics depended upon the application of the abstract idea of periodicity to a variety of concrete instances" (A. N. Whitehead, *Science and the Modern World*, ch. 2). The achievement of the Greeks was, of course, just the reverse: to pass from the experience of concrete periods to the idea of one principle governing all transformations whatsoever.

[33] Burnet, *EGP*, p. 9. Similarly R. Hirzel, *Themis, Dike und Verwandtes* (Leipzig, 1907), pp. 386 f.

[34] See, e.g., Aristophanes *Nub.* 397.

Greek *arariskō*, *harmos*, *harmonia*). The word designates not only ritual correctness—like Latin *ritus*, from the same root—but moral order, and the regular arrangement by which the gods produce the dawn, the movement of the sun, and the yearly sequence of the seasons. The annual cycle itself is pictured as "a twelve-spoked wheel of *r̥tá* which turns unaging round the heaven." [35]

Such ancient conceptions show that it is not the assimilation of Nature and Society which philosophy was called upon to establish, but rather their separation from one another. These two ideas were first defined, by mutual contrast, as a result of the fifth-century controversies regarding *physis* and *nomos*.[36] But the concept of the world as a *kosmos* or well-ordered constitution of things dates from the earlier period, when the two realms were still counted as one. It was then easy and natural for Anaximander to transfer terms like *dikē*, *tisis*, and *taxis* from their social usage to a description of that larger community which includes not only man and living things on earth, but the heavenly bodies and the elemental powers as well. All philosophic terms have necessarily begun in this way, from a simpler, concrete usage with a human reference point. For example, the concept of a "cause," *aition*, is clearly a development from the idea of the "guilty one, he who is to blame," *aitios*. Language is older than science; and the new wine must be served in whatever bottles are on hand.

The importance of the imagery of cosmic strife in early Greek thought should make clear that the rational outlook on the world did not arise by mere negation, by the stripping away of some primitive veil of pictures in order to lay bare *the facts*. In the historical experience of Greece, Nature became permeable to the human intelligence only when the inscrutable personalities of mythic religion were replaced by well-

[35] Rigveda 1.164.11. On the conception of *r̥tá*, see A. Bergaigne, *Religion védique*, III, 210 ff.; H. Oldenberg, *Religion des Vedas*, pp. 195 ff. Compare the Egyptian and Babylonian points of view described in *The Intellectual Adventure of Ancient Man* (Chicago, 1946), and the conclusion of the Frankforts, p. 26: "The life of man and the function of the state are for mythopoeic thought imbedded in nature, and the natural processes are affected by the acts of man no less than man's life depends on his harmonious integration with nature. The experiencing of this unity with the utmost intensity was the greatest good ancient oriental religion could bestow. To conceive this integration in the form of intuitive imagery was the aim of the speculative thought of the ancient Near East."

[36] See the study of this antithesis by F. Heinimann, *Nomos und Physis* (Basel, 1945).

defined and regular powers. The linguistic stamp of the new mentality is a preference for neuter forms, in place of the "animate" masculines and feminines which are the stuff of myth. The Olympians have given way before "the boundless, the necessary, the encompassing, the hot, the opposites," all expressed by neuter forms in Greek. The strife of elemental forces is henceforth no unpredictable quarrel between capricious agents, but an orderly scheme in which defeat must follow aggression as inevitably as the night the day.

The philosophic achievement of Ionia was no doubt made possible by the astral and mathematical science accumulated in the age-old Mesopotamian tradition. It is indeed the principles of geometry and astronomy which define the new world view. But the unity and the rational clarity of this conception are as completely Greek as is the term "cosmos" by which it continues to be known.

4

XENOPHANES' EMPIRICISM
AND HIS CRITIQUE
OF KNOWLEDGE (B34)

Hermann Fränkel

If we take the word "philosophy" in its strictest sense, then of all that Xenophanes said and was concerned with (at least from what we know), only his doctrine of God and his critique of knowledge can be included under this heading. In all other aspects, this remarkable man appears expressly unphilosophical.[1]

Of course, Xenophanes, like the Ionian natural philosophers, did construct a world view, and in doing so he too bypassed the gods of popular belief. But the *physikoi* had gone beyond this; they wanted to see through the surface of nature, and believed they had discerned, behind the compellingly forceful appearances, the workings of a fundamental element, or fundamental substance, at once natural and supernatural in kind. Xenophanes, by contrast, seems rather to have striven to picture the world altogether simply; to make unnecessary every explanation of the world's construction and functioning that departed from the realm of naïve sensation. He stays as close as he can to the immediately given.

[1] As the context shows, *sophiē* in B2.12 does not signify the observant and interpretative wisdom of the philosopher (it is only much later that the word assumes this meaning), or the arts of the dialectician, but rather that cleverness of the unprejudiced, practical man that assists the state toward *eunomiē*, "good government," and *olbos*, "prosperity."

In the same frame of mind in which Hesiod, the farmer, made earth the foundation of his world (*Theog.* 117 ff.), Xenophanes, too, made his start from those parts of the world that are nearest to man, from its most familiar and palpable elements. He had the earth reach downward into the boundless; and so, as Aristotle aptly observes (DK 21A47), he no longer needed to assume some particular cause for its support. In similar fashion, he made the air's height unlimited in extent. There is in his scheme no vaulted distant heaven over men's heads (A33.3); nor is there some deep ocean or infernal bottom into which the earth's roots extend. In his view, the two massive bodies on whose mutual boundary we lead our lives[2] alone suffice to occupy the All to its full extent. Of course, the sea must be counted as earth, and with it, water also, which in his view originates exclusively from the sea (B30). Sea and land are locked in constant battle with one another, as Xenophanes concluded from empirical observations. Where land is now, there—according to the evidence of fossils—water was earlier. And so he came to believe that the sea periodically devours the earth along with everything that lives on it, and that living creatures are periodically formed anew from solid earth and flowing water (A32, 33; B27, 29, 33). Meteorological phenomena also develop from water; they do not originate in heaven—there *is* no such thing—but stem from the same surfaces over which we men walk and voyage. The wind (which according to the old conception hurls itself from above) and rain have their real source (according to Xenophanes) in the sea.[3] He has the sun, too, freshly constituted each day from evaporations that arise from below (A32, 33, 40),[4] and likewise for all the other stars. He similarly interpreted the rainbow, lightning, and St. Elmo's fire as cloud formations or as effects of clouds, i.e. as things that result from terrestrial (or, more precisely, oceanic) vapor (A38–40, 43–46). He fixed the paths of the sun and of the moon so close to the earth that he could assume each region of the earth to have its own sun and moon. He explained

---

[2] This is more or less Xenophanes' own formulation (B28).

[3] Cf. B30. The testimony Aetius gives, and which he tries to document by quoting B30 (A46), is actually refuted by that very fragment. It is of course correct that Xenophanes considered meteorological phenomena as effects of the sun's warmth (A1.19); he does not, however, place the emphasis on the sun as the presumable *arktikē aitia*, "first cause" (indeed, the sun itself is only a product of the sea), but rather on the sea as *pēgē*, "source."

[4] On this, see Hermann Diels, "Lukrezstudien. II.III," *Sitzungsberichte der Preussischen Akademie der Wissenschaften zu Berlin*, Jarhgang 1920, 2–18.

eclipses as resulting from a sudden slipping (?) of the sun[5] into other sectors of the earth (A41, 41a).[6]

This theory seems singularly primitive and arbitrary, even for the time of its proponent. It is badly thought out and paltry. Original ideas are lacking in it—apart from an element of bold and unhesitating empiricism that makes itself strongly felt.[7] What is new and alive in this peculiar system is only the blunt empiricism. This was the motivating force behind the creation of such a world picture, and the construction proclaims itself the offspring of a tendency. This world of ours is made to seem as familiar, intelligible, and present, as this-worldly and free from mystery as possible. All things and appearances are explained in terms of everyday experience, and the theory of nature seeks to avoid any fundamental expansion of our conceptual possibilities. If there is anything philosophical in it, it is only this principle of the world's worldliness.

We should not regard Xenophanes as having raised himself above the thought pattern of common human reality even when, with his theory of the world's shape, he went, more or less accidentally, beyond the mere description of things and processes. We do, admittedly, have one case where Xenophanes definitely goes beyond description, but that statement is most peculiar, and is worthy of note. The most austere and radical rationalism imaginable speaks in the remark "the sun is conducive to the genesis and preservation of the world and of living

[5] Is Xenophanes the author of the theory, utilized by Herodotus (II.24) and mentioned by Lucretius (V.637), according to which the shifting of the celestial bodies' paths with the change of the seasons is brought about by the seasonally prevailing winds? This theory could have reached Lucretius in the same way as did that concerning the daily formation of the sun (see the previous note). Lucretius refers to the analogy of clouds: The same must hold true for the sun and all the stars. According to Xenophanes, the stars are in fact clouds. That the daily path of the sun is straight and only seems to curve (A41a) is certainly concluded from the analogy of the clouds' courses (Eduard Zeller, *Die Philosophie der Griechen*, I. Teil, I. Hälfte, 6th ed., ed. W. Nestle [Leipzig, 1919], pp. 668 f.). On the question of the source for Herodotus' theory of the Nile's flood, see W. Theiler, *Zur Geschichte der teleologischen Naturbetrachtung bis auf Aristoteles* (Basel, 1925), p. 7.

[6] On this interpretation of Xenophanes' theory of nature, cf. Karl Reinhardt, *Parmenides und die Geschichte der griechischen Philosophie* (Bonn, 1916), pp. 144-50.

[7] Cf. Diels, op. cit., and "Über Xenophanes," *AGP*, 10 (1897), 530-35.

things, but the moon is superfluous [*parelkein*]." [8] In the same way Xenophanes raises again and again, in human affairs as well, the question of utility.[9]

Xenophanes was a man of the present, a practical-oriented, realistically minded man. He dared—a Greek of the sixth century!—to spurn legend, as the fiction of an earlier age (B1.22) that the present has outgrown. He was the first Greek to articulate, in most clear terms, the idea of progress.[10]

It was his belief in progress that nourished his relentless reformatory zeal. As a rhapsode at the banquets of men, this enemy of Homer presented his own sayings and admonitions; and he wanted to see his suggestions translated into action on the spot. He boldly fought the established aristocratic ideal[11] in order to replace it with a practical, social ideal. And still more courageously, he mocked the religion[12] and the cult[13] of his people.

Now, is it probable that this urbane, practical-minded realist, this intrepid fighter, this optimistic, fanatical reformer, this singer who knew how to enjoy the festive moment to its fullest and who also gave others directions and instructions on how to make the best use of it,[14]

[8] A42, hitherto oddly misinterpreted, as in Burnet, *EGP*, 2d ed. (London, 1908), p. 135 n. 4 [but see 4th ed. (London, 1930), p. 123 n. 4.—Ed.], and in Zeller-Nestle, p. 667 n. 2. The term *parelkein* is the commentator's formulation; in the time of Aetius the word normally has this meaning, and the context requires precisely this sense.

[9] B1.23 *chrēston* (from *chrēsthai!*); 2.19 ff.; 3.1 *anōpheleas* (cf. *WuF* p. 179).

[10] B18, with a sarcastic jibe at the traditional notion of culture as a divine gift. For *hypedeixan*, cf. Hdt. I.32.9: ὑποδέξας ὄλβον ὁ θεός.

[11] Cf. K. Ziegler in *Satura Viadrina altera:* Festschrift zum 50.-jährigen Bestehens des philologischen Vereins zu Breslau (Breslau, 1921), pp. 110–15.

[12] The monotheistic idea is alive in many ways in early Greece, from Homer on; but it usually is in a friendly coexistence with polytheism. Only in Xenophanes does the One God triumph, as their enemy and conqueror, over the host of the many individual figures.

[13] B17 also is certainly to be interpreted as irony, which fails to come across in Diels' translation ("spruce boughs" [*Fichtenmaien*]). Xenophanes seizes upon the lowest form of popular belief in order to make his scoffing most effective—the scoff being directed against the belief that pine branches are themselves *bakchoi*. In this way he has provided us with an interesting ethnological testimony, through the medium of the lexicographers who adduced his verse in their gloss.

[14] B1 (*chrē*, 13; *procheiroteron*, 16), 22 (*chrē*, 1).

this proud Ionian of the sixth century who for seven decades led a life of restless wandering because he would not submit to the servitude imposed by the Persians, this investigator and portrayer of reality who took delight in the gathering and contemplation of facts, this man whom Heraclitus (DK 22B40) set alongside Hecataeus as a *polymathēs*—is it probable that this Xenophanes was a skeptic, a tired doubter or a deft but unconvinced dialectician, and that he had no real confidence in the reality of the world of appearances?[15] Should we not rather expect to find a more or less robust empiricism in his philosophical theory as well?

In the lines of fragment 34, the relativist (B38) and critic attached an epistemological caveat to his own doctrine, as he sent it out into the world. This highly significant utterance, from which many conclusions have been drawn, is printed and translated by Diels[a] as follows:

> καὶ τὸ μὲν οὖν σαφὲς οὔτις ἀνὴρ γένετ᾽ οὐδέ τις ἔσται
> εἰδὼς ἀμφὶ θεῶν τε καὶ ἄσσα λέγω περὶ πάντων.
> εἰ γὰρ καὶ τὰ μάλιστα τύχοι τετελεσμένον εἰπών,
> αὐτὸς ὅμως οὐκ οἶδε· δόκος δ᾽ ἐπὶ πᾶσι τέτυκται.

And as to the truth, there never was nor will there be anyone who knew it with respect to the gods, and to all things whatsoever I speak of. For even if he should once accidentally speak of what is most fully actual [*das Allervollendetste*] he would not himself be aware of this. For only illusory opinion is assigned to all.

It seems to me that this text and this translation is untenable in more than one respect. Only Plutarch preserves the first line in the above form, while it is given by Sextus three times and by Diogenes Laertius once with ἴδεν[16] instead of γένετ᾽. This fact is enough to force us to the

---

[15] Reinhardt's zealous attempt (p. 151 f.) to fit into a total picture of Xenophanes Diels' interpretation of the so-called "skeptical" fragment demonstrates the insuperable difficulty of that task. Xenophanes' "very strong preference for reality in every respect: experience, observation, detail, reasonableness, expediency" (p. 144) cannot be united with a "delicate skepticism" in consequence of which "man can always only advise and express opinion."

[a] [Fränkel here refers to the 1st through 4th editions of *Die Fragmente der Vorsokratiker*. In the editions revised by Walther Kranz, 5th and subsequent (here and standardly "DK"), the text and translation given are revised along the lines here urged by Fränkel.—Ed.]

[16] With the etacistic variants *oiden* and *eiden*. The first of these would present a serious hazard were it not rendered innocuous by the metrical form of the text.

conclusion that here, as so often, Plutarch is quoting imprecisely, from memory. The peculiar *iden*, which we should also prefer as the *lectio difficilior*, was supplanted in his memory by a *geneto*, which was suggested to him for example by the similar lines of the *Odyssey*: 6.201, 16.437, 18.79. But for genuine Archaic style it would be impossible to separate *to saphes* from *eidos* through the insertion of so significant a complex as οὖτις ἀνὴρ γένετ' οὐδέ τις ἔσται, however harmless this construction would be in the classical period. Early paratactic style first introduces all those parts necessary to the grammatical structure before adding anything further.[17] Thus the grammatically dispensable phrase "about gods, etc." can certainly be added at the end,[18] but the grammatical object cannot remain suspended for so long before receiving its governing verb. We conclude, therefore, that Xenophanes spoke here, in an ancient and very Greek way, of "seeing" in order to designate a truly reliable knowledge.[19]

From this correction of the text follow considerable consequences. In the first place, in B36 we shall not take the words "all that reveals itself to the view of mortals" to refer to the stars, as Diels comes close to doing, but rather shall find in them reference to that realm that is accessible to human experience and investigation. In Xenophanes "viewing" and "self-showing" stand for "knowing reliably" and "being explorable," respectively.

But at the same time, the immediately following word *eidos* receives in our fragment a particular, sharply pointed meaning. It presents itself here as the perfect tense form corresponding to *iden*, "saw," and accordingly designates only a knowing rooted in vision, or at least in experience (for sight, the leader of the other senses, can of course also

[17] Wolfgang Krause, in "Die Entwicklung einer alten elliptischen Konstruktion in den indogermanischen Sprachen," *Zeitschrift für vergleichende Sprachforschung*, 52 (1924), 246, points to similar features. Cf. also Fränkel, *WuF*, p. 47 n. 1. (A thorough investigation would be desirable.) For this reason, in the case of Xenophanes fr. 1, one cannot follow Karsten, who employs G. Hermann's emendation *agathon* in line 24 in order to make the entire four-line period dependent on this word, which ends the period.

[18] Possibly the preceding context originally had already given *saphes* a concrete referent and content, which was then redescribed with "about the gods, etc."

[19] I need not go any further into this matter, since Bruno Snell, in *Die Ausdrücke für den Begriff des Wissens in der vorplatonischen Philosophie*, Philologische Untersuchungen, 29 (Berlin, 1924), p. 25, has incorporated my interpretation of this fragment into his corresponding discussion.

represent them). The extended meaning of the word, in which it may designate all knowing, however acquired, is not present.[20]

The same possibility should be considered for *oide* in the fourth line. How do matters stand in this case? Lines 3 and 4 have been understood, following Sextus (7.51), as follows:

κἂν γὰρ ἐκ τύχης ἐπιβάλλῃ τούτῳ, ὅμως οὐκ οἶδεν ὅτι ἐπιβέβληκεν αὐτῷ (ἀλλ' οἴεται καὶ δοκεῖ).

[For even if by chance he should happen to apprehend it, he would not be aware of the fact that he did apprehend it—he is, rather, in a state of belief or opinion.]

And Plato already understood them no differently:

ἢ εἰ καὶ ὅτι μάλιστα ἐντύχοις αὐτῷ, πῶς εἴσῃ ὅτι τοῦτό ἐστιν ὃ σὺ οὐκ ᾔδησθα;[21]

[Alternatively, if you should chance to come right up against it, how will you know it is this—the thing which you did not know?]

So we read in the *Meno* (80d).[22] This reading would suppose Xenophanes to have raised his critique to the second level, and moreover to have given this second level the peculiar twist: "even he who knows it best does not know that he knows it." Furthermore, if Xenophanes had really wanted to say that, he could not have written *gar*, "for." The skeptical conclusion moves rather in the opposite direction: Because one knows nothing certain about things, one cannot know whether one knows something. Third, we can hardly ascribe[23] to the

[20] In Gothic the word *weitwops*, which corresponds syllable for syllable to *eidōs*, means "witness." In Greek literature the reference of primary interest in this connection is *Iliad* 2.485 f., where a knowledge acquired through another's communication is expressly designated as not-*eidenai;* only through *pareinai* does one reach *eidenai*. On *oida* as "I am a witness" and corresponding derivations (including *historiē*) from the older and narrower meaning of *oida*, see the study by Snell mentioned in the previous note.

[21] The close connection between the two passages puts it beyond doubt that Plato has our passage in mind, although he does not give his question as a quotation and although this question is meant somewhat differently.

[22] Plato solves the *aporia* by assuming a "seeing"—cf. the *iden* of Xenophanes—prior to the present life (81c).

[23] With Sextus (7.52), who elaborates as follows: "Imagine a dark building that hides many treasures, and in it men who are seeking gold. It will happen that each of them lays hold on one of the objects to be found in the building,

ancient thinker Xenophanes the rather precious image of a man who utters the deepest truth and does not notice it—particularly since, as no one doubts, the saying applies first of all to his own didactic poem. Would it have—this is my fourth objection—any sense for the author to envisage the possibility that he himself may have stumbled upon the purest truth in the views expressed in his work and yet may have been totally unaware of the fact that he had succeeded in making so forceful a discovery?

It would seem that Plato's reading is a mistake; and the origin of the mistake is obvious. The linguistic usage of Plato's own time forced this interpretation upon him, because for him αὐτὸς οὐκ οἶδεν could only mean "he himself does not know it." The same holds for later authors. But when *oida* could still mean for Xenophanes "I know it reliably, through seeing"—i.e. from experience—then *autos oida* is "I know it from my own experience." With this Xenophanes' concept of knowing comes close to that of Ionian *historiē*, as practiced, for example, by Herodotus. Indeed, the word *historiē* comes from this *oida*. And in Herodotus' work we find the confirmation of our interpretation of *autos oiden*. In the opening of his history he relates various versions of the legendary conflicts between Hellenes and Asiatics. In each case the one people accuses the other of having initiated the conflict. Herodotus explains that for his own part he wishes to refrain from expressing an opinion. And then he continues (I.5.3): "But there is one person [viz. Croesus] about whom I myself know (τὸν δὲ οἶδα αὐτός) that he initiated acts of aggression against the Greeks." Here the realm of what can be reliably investigated,[24] and investigated by Herodotus himself, the realm of *historiē*, is set by the words *oida autos* in opposition to legend.[25]

---

and each will then believe he holds the gold in his hands. But none of them will be sure that he has found the gold, even if by chance he has in fact found it. Likewise the horde of philosophers came into this world, as though into a large house, to seek the truth, and whoever might have got a grasp on it will mistrust his success."

[24] Cf. Herodotus III.98.2 τῶν γὰρ ἡμεῖς ἴδμεν, τῶν καὶ πέρι ἀτρεκές τι λέγεται; III.115 ἔχω οὐκ ἀτρεκέως λέγειν, οὔτε γὰρ ἔγωγε ἐνδέκομαι κτλ. οὔτε . . . οἶδα . . . τοῦτο δὲ οὐδενὸς αὐτόπτεω γενομένου οὐ δύναμαι ἀκοῦσαι; IV.16.1 οὐδεὶς οἶδε ἀτρεκέως . . . οὐδενὸς γὰρ δὴ αὐτόπτεω εἰδέναι φαμένου δύναμαι πυθέσθαι.

[25] For *autos* (or *egō*) *oida*, "I know from (my own or reliably reported) witnessing," cf. further, e.g., *Od.* 1.216 f.; Hdt. II.23; Thrasymachus, DK 85B1 (at the end, *hoposa men* . . .).

Let us now turn to the third line. *Tetelesmenon* is frequently found in Homer, but not as "complete = perfect"; rather, as something (as the case may be) "carried out, realized," "actual." [26] Thus *tetelesmenon eipōn* is the same as the *to on eipōn* of later prose: "speaking the real, saying something which turns out to be true." [27] Did Xenophanes, when he made *tychoi* the governing verb, wish to designate this finding and uttering of the truth as something purely accidental? We need not assume this, for in Archaic language *tynchanō* more often means "I hit my mark" [28] than "it accidentally befalls me." [29] The word's connotation thus always includes the working of chance, but it by no means always excludes the sort of intention or volition which, sure of its purpose, methodically contrives the actually ensuing result, even if it cannot bring about this result with infallible certainty. Thus *tynchanō eipōn* means "I succeed in saying what is correct" in, for example, Sophocles *Philoctetes* 223: "What country or family might I correctly say (τύχοιμ' ἂν εἰπών) you come from?" [30] The expression is being employed here in Xenophanes as well, and moreover *tetelesmenon*, "the actual," is added to *eipōn* as the object.

Finally, let us consider the expression *ta malista*. *Mallon* and *malista* are less expressions of quantity than of value and preference. [31] Here one may appeal to such passages as Plato *Critias* 108d; Demosthenes 18.21; Hesiod *Works and Days* 700, where *ta malista* means "especially (this and none other)." Therefore, in the Xenophanes passage, it certainly [32] belongs together with *tychoi* and the latter's subject, [33] to which

[26] How the word is to be understood in *Iliad* 14.196 (= *Il.* 18.427, *Od.* 5.90) remains uncertain; perhaps "real" as opposed to "fantastic/impossible."

[27] It seems that Pindar means the opposite of *tetelesmenon eipōn* when he speaks in *Ol.* 2.86 f. of untalented poets' ἄκραντα γαρύ(ειν), in contrast to himself, who is πολλὰ εἰδὼς φυᾷ.

[28] E.g. *Il.* 16.609, 15.581.

[29] That *tychē* means "succeeding" is repeatedly emphasized by Wilamowitz.

[30] Cf. further Aeschylus *Ag.* 1233, *Ch.* 418.

[31] Cf. *mallon boulesthai;* the qualifying expression *mallon*, "rather"; *malista*, "quite right, yes indeed"; *hekaton malista*, "the number 100 comes closest to being correct, approximately 100."

[32] It is, however, also possible, with Plato, to assimilate *ta malista* to *ei kai:* "even if entirely, however much." The distinction is not great.

[33] As usual in the Archaic fashion this remans unexpressed (see *WuF*, p. 63 n. 2).

it is in fact also attached:[34] "he hits the mark most closely, he hits it better than others."

Many of the accepted renderings of individual words had to be corrected in the few verses above. Now comes the test: What have we gained toward understanding the whole fragment?

And what is precise[35] no man[36] has ever discerned, just as there never will be anyone who knows,[37] with respect to the gods, as well as to the totality of whatever things I maintain (in this work).[38] For even if someone should succeed above all others (or "entirely") in articulating what is really present (which is precisely what Xenophanes hopes to have accomplished in this very poem), still he has no knowledge from his own experience . . . .

The text has become quite simple and straightforward, even primitive, but by the same token more self-contained and more striking.

Xenophanes, we now see, confidently bases himself on experience, believing that it alone is reliable. Therefore the ambiguous last half-line can mean neither "for only illusory opinion is assigned to all," as Diels translates, nor ὅτι πάντα ἀκατάληπτά ἐστιν ["that all things are incomprehensible"], as the ancient skeptics would have it.[39] The word

---

[34] *Tetelesmenon* no more allows the addition than *to on* (*eipōn*) would.

[35] *saphes* unites the notion of completeness down to the points of detail, with that of reliable, faithful, and unadulterated apprehending (cf. e.g. Plato *Republic* 478c) and reporting of the object.

[36] "Man" is emphasized, as "the mortals" in B36 is emphasized. Xenophanes is speaking of the limitations of human experience.

[37] With the word "know" is meant here a genuine knowing on the basis of empirical observations.

[38] It is also possible to construe the end of the sentence differently: "as well as (with respect to) what I assert concerning all things." But in any case the preceding words ἀμφὶ θεῶν τε καὶ show that what is meant cannot be "everything that I assert is unascertainable" = "nothing of it is ascertainable," but rather "not everything is ascertainable." For the supersensible world of the gods, concerning which a mere man can make no reliable (i.e based on sense perceptions) assertions, cannot, with respect to the impossibility of investigation, be likened to *all* other things but only to *many* other things.

[39] See Zeller-Nestle, p. 672 n. 5 for the testimonia; further, DK 21A35 ἠπορηκότα περὶ πάντων.

dokos, which is found only in this passage,[40] has to mean "assumption = valid opinion." For it comes from *dekomai*, "receive, accept," and from this verb are also formed expressions such as the following: *dokei moi*, "I adopt an opinion (or 'an intention')"; *dokimos*, "acceptable, winning recognition";[41] *doxa*, "assumption, opinion" or "recognition, fame." [42] Both *epi* and *tetyktai* speak in favor of the interpretation of *pasi* as neuter, so that it corresponds to the neutral *pantōn* in line 2. And finally, it is natural to take *dokos de* as the opposite of *to men saphes*. This yields: (τὸ μὲν σαφὲς ἄνθρωπος οὐδεὶς γνοίη ἂν πάντων γε πραγμάτων πέρι· τὸ δὲ δοξάζειν ἔστιν ἐπὶ πᾶσιν. "(A reliable knowledge with respect to all of the objects spoken of here, particularly concerning the gods, is not possible for men;) but there are (valid) suppositions that can be made with reference to all things." [43] In just this way Xenophanes characterizes what he says in B35 not as "illusory opinion" but as "probable": ταῦτα δεδοξάσθω μὲν ἐοικότα τοῖς ἐτύμοισιν ["let these things be accepted as plausibly tending to what is true"].

Fragment 34 is to be interpreted similarly. The closely resembling postscripts in the quotations by Areius Didymus[44] and Varro[45] give a good indication of the wider context: "but God has a genuine knowledge even of transcendent things." That these lines originally stood at the opening of the book[46] is clear from their content and from the fact that the same preliminary question appears again and again in the opening of didactic· treatises. Alcmaeon follows Xenophanes extremely closely in the first sentence of his own work:[47]

[40] And as a gloss in Callimachus Fr. 224 (Pfeiffer): τῷ γ' ἐμῷ δόκῳ, explained as δόκησις καὶ ὑπόληψις (i.e. "in my opinion").

[41] The concept of "test" in this connection first arises with the derivative *dokimazein:* "to determine the acceptability, to subject one to a procedure of sanctioning." Thus, strictly speaking, *dokimōs* in Parmenides B1.32 may not be translated "in the sanctioned manner."

[42] We should have expected *δέγμα*—but perhaps δόγμα by assimilation to the other words?

[43] Burnet, too, takes the half-line not as an expression of resignation or doubt, but of hope and qualified trust: "but all are free to guess." The Platonic *orthē doxa*, in contrast to *epistēmē*, is remotely comparable.

[44] In Stobaeus II.1.17: ὡς ἄρα θεὸς μὲν οἶδε τὴν ἀλήθειαν, δόκος δ' ἐπὶ πᾶσι τέτυκται.

[45] In Augustine *De Civ. Dei* 7, 17: *Hominis est enim haec opinari, Dei scire*.

[46] Cf. Reinhardt, p. 118; he adduces Alcmaeon as well.

[47] DK 28B1.

Περὶ τῶν ἀφανέων, περὶ τῶν θνητῶν, σαφήνειαν μὲν θεοὶ ἔχοντι, ὡς δὲ ἀνθρώποις τεκμαίρεσθαι.

["Concerning nonevident things, concerning things mortal: the gods see clearly, but men (are only able to) conjecture."]

The conformity in expression and in content cannot be accidental; Xenophanes, the empiricist and critic, had delineated the scope of empirical science, and later thinkers learned this division from him. The author of *On Ancient Medicine* also follows him at the beginning of his treatise:[48]

οὐκ ἠξίουν αὐτὴν [scil. ἰητρικὴν] ἔγωγε καινῆς ὑποθέσιος δεῖσθαι, ὥσπερ τὰ ἀφανέα τε καὶ ἀπορεόμενα, περὶ ὧν ἀνάγκη, ἤν τις ἐπιχειρῇ τι λέγειν, ὑπο-θέσει χρῆσθαι, οἷον περὶ τῶν μετεώρων ἢ τῶν ὑπὸ γῆν· ἃ εἴ τις λέγοι καὶ γινώσκοι ὡς ἔχει, οὔτ' ἂν αὐτῷ τῷ λέγοντι οὔτε τοῖς ἀκούουσι δῆλα ἂν εἴη, εἴτε ἀληθέα ἐστὶν εἴτε μή· οὐ γὰρ ἔστι, πρὸς ὅ τι χρὴ ἀνενέγκαντα εἰδέναι τὸ σαφές.

[I considered that it (scil. medicine) has no need of a novel postu-late, as do insoluble mysteries, which necessarily require the use of a postulate, if an attempt be made to discuss them, for instance the mysteries of heaven and of the regions below. If anyone were to express his opinion about the condition of these, it would not be plain either to the speaker himself or to the audience whether the statements were true or not. For there is no test the application of which would bring certain knowledge.][b]

In another sense Heraclitus (B1) and Empedocles (B2 and B4)[49] answer the same question at similar points in their own writings; they too take their departure from the sharp distinction between the empirical and the superempirical.

[48] Professor Pohlenz has most kindly called my attention to this passage.

[b] [Hippocrates (Heiberg ed.) I, p. 36, 15 ff. (= W.H.S. Jones, *Philosophy and Medicine in Ancient Greece*, Bulletin of the History of Medicine, Supple-ment No. 8 [Baltimore, 1946], p. 50). Except for reading καινῆς (with Fränkel), instead of κενῆς, the translation is as in Jones, p. 65.—Ed.]

[49] On the unbroken connection of B2 with B4, cf. Hermann Fränkel, "Homerische Wörter," ΑΝΤΙΔΩΡΟΝ: Festschrift Jacob Wackernagel (Göt-tingen, 1923), pp. 276 ff. Varro, too, cites Xenophanes' cautious stance at the beginning of his third book about the gods—precisely that book in which he no longer reports on the belief confronting him and on religion, but rather attempts a philosophic reinterpretation.

By now we are in a position to grasp Xenophanes' critical-epistemological standpoint, and to relate his position on this problem to the rest of his philosophy, i.e. to his doctrine of God.

Xenophanes characterizes as certain and exhaustive (*saphes*) only that knowledge that is empirically grounded. He holds only *opsis*, "vision," and *historiē*, "direct acquaintance" (to use Herodotus' expressions),[50] as reliable. In contrast, *gnomē*, "opinion" or "supposition," does not, in his view, lead to genuine certainty. Nevertheless he made quite energetic use of it also. For example, the experience that every race of men forms its gods in its own likeness became for him a proof that God is not like a man at all, not in any respect. Even animals, if they had the necessary organs, would fashion and paint theriomorphic gods. And so all the mutually contradictory attributes of divinity derived from evidence furnished by this world cancel each other out. Thus rigorous empiricism became for Xenophanes a springboard toward knowledge of the transcendent in its own special nature. The absolute does not fit into human modes of representation precisely because they are especially adapted to the grasping of what is earthly. Xenophanes separates these two regions from one another plainly and fundamentally. He strips visible celestial phenomena of all divine aspects; he even denies these phenomena their dignity and permanence, as well as their celestial origin, just as, on the other hand, he refuses to recognize all possible comparison of his God with earthly bodies.[51] He denies too that divinity speaks to men in signs and oracles (A52). In this way he made the chasm between the here and the beyond unbridgeable.[52]

All this can be clearly understood as a preliminary stage of Parmenides' doctrine, the doctrine of two different worlds with two different principles of knowledge and of being. But Xenophanes stands firm and secure in his empiricism, regretting the fact that one cannot see into the supersensible world and may only venture into that world with conjectures. Parmenides, in contrast, proceeds in the opposite way, from the certainty of absolute being. From its vantage point he unmasks this world and interprets it as erroneous and merely apparent.

[50] The two terms are used together at II.99.1.

[51] That is, of course, a rather modern formulation. Xenophanes himself is satisfied to deny God important characteristics of corporeal natures (composition out of specific differentiated organs, locomotion) and in their place to ascribe to him certain holistic attributes and a purely spiritual activity.

[52] Cf. Reinhardt, pp. 116–18.

He too speaks of valid opinion (*dokounta, dokimōs,* B1.31 f.), but it rules over the empirical world and only over that. Its validity is qualified, and so in the strict sense the opinion is false. But the opinion nevertheless affords a necessary semblance of our familiar realm, which realm, in turn, possesses only a qualified reality. Just as full truth and full being are inextricably bound up with one another, so half truth and half being are paired together in the strict autonomy of what is *dokimon,* "plausibly valid." Xenophanes, as he separated the two regions, sensed behind and above this firmly and securely believed, this narrow, crudely mechanical world of coming-to-be (B29) and passing-away, a broader and higher world that enclosed the transcendent along with the immanent. By contrast, Parmenides condemned our world as an inferior and lower one, a world that cannot exist in the face of the absolute.

III

PYTHAGORAS
AND PYTHAGOREANISM

5

MYSTICISM AND SCIENCE
IN THE PYTHAGOREAN TRADITION

F. M. Cornford

The object of this paper is to show that, in the sixth and fifth centuries B.C., two different and radically opposed systems of thought were elaborated within the Pythagorean school. They may be called respectively the mystical system and the scientific. All current accounts of Pythagoreanism known to me attempt to combine the traits of both systems in one composite picture, which naturally fails to hold together. The confusion goes back to Aristotle, who usually speaks indiscriminately of "the Pythagoreans," though now and then the phrase "some Pythagoreans" indicates that he was aware of different currents within the school.

I shall try to show that the criterion enabling us to distinguish the two systems is furnished by the Eleatic criticism of Pythagoreanism, which can be used as one might use a mirror to see what was happening on the other side of a screen. The history of Pre-Socratic philosophy is divided, circa 500–490 B.C., into two chapters by Parmenides' polemic against any system which derives a manifold world from an original unity. The first chapter contains the two great sixth-century systems of the Milesians and of Pythagoras, both of which fall under Parmenides' condemnation. Parmenides, bred in the Pythagorean tradition, was primarily a critic of the school from which he was seceding. Thus we have a clue to what sixth-century Pythagoreanism must have been, if we ask what is the radical fault found by Parmenides in the system he is criticizing. It will appear that this fault is the attempt to combine a monistic inspiration with a dualistic system of Nature. Parmenides declared for uncompromising monism, and in consequence denied plurality and becoming, including change and motion. The second chapter contains

From *The Classical Quarterly*, 16 (1922), 137–50, and 17 (1923), 1–12. Portions of text omitted, and some footnotes abbreviated or omitted. Selection reprinted here by permission of The Clarendon Press, Oxford.

the fifth-century pluralist systems of Empedocles, Anaxagoras, and the Atomists, who sought in various ways to restore plurality, change, and motion without infringing the canons Parmenides was believed to have established. It is antecedently probable that some section of the Pythagorean school would attempt a similar answer. Now, in the generation after Parmenides, we find his pupil Zeno attacking a system which appears to be that answer. It is an inchoate form of Atomism—a doctrine that the real consists of an indefinite plurality of units or monads (indivisible points having position and magnitude), which can move in space, and of which bodies can be built up. Of this doctrine there is no trace in Parmenides; it belongs to the early fifth century. Zeno's criticisms, on the other hand, point to this doctrine, and to nothing else. It is not the later developed Atomism of Leucippus and Democritus, from which it differs in various respects. The monads, for instance, do not differ, like the atoms, in shape, but are all alike. I infer that the system in question is another pluralist system, the immediate ancestor of Atomism proper, constructed by the scientific wing of the Pythagorean school as a reply to Parmenides' critique.

Aristotle, when he speaks of "the Pythagoreans," refers sometimes to the original sixth-century system, sometimes to this later doctrine, and probably in his own mind did not clearly distinguish the two. Hence his testimonies, if taken all together, are inconsistent. Here we are told that sensible things "represent" or "embody" (*mimeisthai*) numbers; there, that sensible things or bodies actually *are* numbers, built up of indivisible monads. And so on. But, with the guidance of the Eleatic criticism and our knowledge of the religious antecedents of Pythagoras, we can sort out the testimonies and refer them to the two systems I have mentioned. We can, in a word, distinguish between (1) the original sixth-century system of Pythagoras, criticized by Parmenides—the mystical system—and (2) the fifth-century pluralism constructed to meet Parmenides' objections, and criticized in turn by Zeno—the scientific system, which may be called "Number-atomism." There is also (3) the

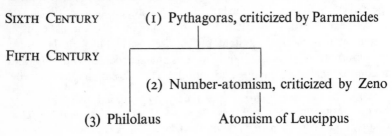

SIXTH CENTURY   (1) Pythagoras, criticized by Parmenides

FIFTH CENTURY

                              (2) Number-atomism, criticized by Zeno

        (3) Philolaus   Atomism of Leucippus

system of Philolaus, which belongs to the mystical side of the tradition, and seeks to accommodate the Empedoclean theory of elements. This may, for our present purpose, be neglected. The preceding diagram illustrates the development.

I. THE MYSTICAL SYSTEM OF PYTHAGORAS

We may start from a consideration of the type of society founded by Pythagoras. The beliefs of a religious community in its earliest stages are externalized in its rule of life, and of the Pythagorean fraternity we know enough to guide us. It was modeled on the mystical cult-society, to which admission was gained by initiation—that is, by purification followed by the revelation of truth. To the Pythagorean, "purification" partly consisted in the observance of ascetic rules of abstinence from certain kinds of food and dress, and partly was reinterpreted intellectually to mean the purification of the soul by *theōria*, the contemplation of the divine order of the world. "Revelation" consisted in certain truths delivered by the prophet-founder (αὐτὸς ἔφα), and progressively elaborated by his followers under his inspiration.[1]

The rise of mystical cult-societies or non-social religious groups seems to coincide with the breaking up, in the sixth century, of the old social units based on the theory or fact of blood-kinship. It had also psychological causes: there was a deepening and quickening of religious experience—the revival associated with the name of Orpheus. These two sets of phenomena lead to certain axioms in any philosophy that arises out of them. There is, moreover, among these axioms a latent contradiction: there is a tendency toward monism and a tendency toward dualism.

Take first the monistic tendency. In the old blood group the social bond, the sense of solidarity (*philia*), had formerly extended to the limits of the blood-kin (*philoi*); beyond were "strangers," if not enemies.

[1] The pious attribution of all discoveries to the Founder may be illustrated by a penetrating observation made in another connection by Auguste Bouché-Leclercq (*L'Astrologie grecque* [Paris, 1899], p. 51 n. 1). He speaks of "a psychological fact, amply demonstrated by the history of apocryphal literature: viz. that every doctrine that appeals to *faith* has an interest in making itself appear of great antiquity, and that those who develop such a doctrine are very careful not to offer their respective inventions as the products of their own genius. They escape from discussion by cloaking themselves with as enormous as possible a mass of unverifiable experiences and revelations."

There had also been a coextensive religious bond in the common worship of some peculiar set of divinities, heroes, or ancestors. The system is naturally polytheistic. The appearance of new religious groups, transcending the limits and ignoring the ties of kinship, is attended by consequences of great importance. On the social side, at least the seed is sown of the doctrine that all men are brothers; the sense of solidarity, set free from the old limits, can spread to include all mankind, and even beyond that to embrace all living things. *Philia* ceases to mean kinship in the ordinary sense, and begins to mean love. At the same time the social basis of polytheism is undermined. Either monotheism, in some form, must take its place, or at least the belief (essentially true) that the mystery gods worshipped by different groups, whether called Dionysus or Adonis or Attis, are really the same god—one form with many names. There emerges the axiom of monism: *All life is one and God is one*.[2]

On the other hand, there is a no less significant change in the psychology of the individual.[3] The old solidarity of the blood group had entailed that diffusion of responsibility for the actions of any one member among all the other members which still survives in the vendetta. When collective responsibility goes, individual responsibility is left. The guilt of any action must now attach personally to its author. It cannot be expiated by another, or by the blood group as a whole. The punishment must fall upon the individual, if not in this life, then in the next, or perhaps in a series of lives in this world. When the Pythagoreans reduced justice to the *lex talionis*, the effect was that it applied to the guilty person only, not to his family. The doctrine of transmigration completes the scheme of justice for the individual soul. The mere idea of reincarnation was no novelty. What is new in transmigration is the moral view that reincarnation expiates some original sin and that the individual soul persists, bearing its load of inalienable responsibility, through a round of lives, till, purified by suffering, it escapes for ever.

Thus, while God becomes one in the inclusive sense of monotheism—in religious terms, the Father,[4] not of this household, clan, or city, but of all mankind and of all living things—and his children become, on

[2] Cf. Sext. Emp. *M.* IX.127; Iamb. *VP* 108.

[3] Cf. Gustave Glotz, *La Solidarité de la famille dans le droit criminel en Grèce* (Paris, 1904), p. 587.

[4] The Pythagorean term was rather δεσπότης—the father and master of the household, or κύριος (Euxitheos *Athen.* IV.157c).

their side, one all-inclusive group, conversely the soul acquires a unity in the exclusive sense. The individual becomes a unit, an isolated atom, with a personal sense of sin and a need of personal salvation, compensated, however, by a new consciousness of the soul's dignity and value, expressed in the doctrine that by origin and nature it is divine. From God it came, and to God it will return.

But only on condition of becoming pure. So long as it is imprisoned in the bodily tomb, it is impure, tainted by the evil substance of the body. Psychologically—in terms of actual experience—this means that the soul is profoundly conscious of an internal conflict of good and evil, the war in the members. This conflict dominates religious experience. In philosophical expression, it gives rise to the axiom of dualism: *In the world, as in the soul, there is a real conflict of two opposite powers—good and evil, light and darkness.*

Both the axiom of monism and the axiom of dualism are implicit in the doctrine of transmigration, which was certainly taught by Pythagoras. All souls come from one divine source and circulate in a continuous series of all the forms of life. Each soul, involved in the conflict of good and evil, seeks escape from the purgatorial round of lives and deaths into a better world of unity and rest. Any philosophy that arises from a religion of this type is threatened with internal inconsistency. On the one hand, it will set the highest value on the idea of unity, and, at this stage and long afterwards, the notions of value and of reality coincide. Unity is good; reality must be one. On the other hand, Nature will be construed in terms of the inward conflict of good and evil, appearing in the external world as light and darkness. Light is the medium of truth and knowledge; it reveals the knowable aspect of Nature—the forms, surfaces, limits of objects that are confounded in the unlimited darkness of night. But it is hard to deny reality to the antagonistic power of darkness and evil. Hence the tendency to dualism —to recognize, not the One only, but two opposite principles.

Now, if we bring this preliminary inference to the test of the Eleatic criticism, it seems to be confirmed. The gist of Parmenides' doctrine is that we must choose between monism and dualism. If we assert that the real is one, we cannot logically maintain a dualistic system of Nature. And the particular form of dualism he attacks is the doctrine that in Nature there are two opposite "forms"—light and darkness—equally real. So far, then, it appears (1) that the religious experience which underlies the doctrine of transmigration would naturally give rise to a philosophy combining a monistic tendency with a dualistic; and (2) that the latent conflict of these two tendencies is the radical fault found by Parmenides in the Pythagoreanism of his time.

The reconstruction of Pythagoras' system may be approached through the analysis of certain pivotal conceptions which all admit to be characteristic of the Italian tradition. These are: the ideal of "becoming like God" and the notion of *mimēsis;* the correspondence of macrocosm and microcosm; the conception of harmony; the doctrine of numbers; the symbol known as the *tetractys.*

Aristoxenus[5] says of Pythagoras and his followers: "Every distinction they lay down as to what should be done or not done aims at communion (or converse, *homilia*) with the divine. This is their starting-point; their whole life is ordered with a view to following God, and it is the governing principle of their philosophy." This "following" or imitation of God was to end in a purification of the soul from the taint of its bodily prison-house so complete that there should be no need of any further reincarnation. Pythagoras was believed to have reached this threshold of divinity;[6] Empedocles later made the same claim for himself: "And I, among you an immortal god, no longer mortal," [7] echoed in the Orphic grave tablets, where the dead soul is addressed: "From a man thou hast become a god."

The means of rising to this condition was "philosophy," the contemplation of the cosmos in which God was contained or embodied. It was assumed, moreover, in sharp contradiction to orthodox Olympian religion, that there was no insuperable gulf between God and the soul, but a fundamental community of nature. The same order (*kosmos*) or structural principle is found on a large scale in the universe and on a small scale in individuals, i.e. those parts of the universe which are themselves wholes, namely living things. The living creature (soul and body) is the individual unit or microcosm; the world, or macrocosm, is likewise a living creature with a body and soul.[8] Individuals reproduce

[5] Iamb. *VP* 137 (= DK 58D2). Arius Didymus (?) ap. Stob. *Eth.* VI.3 Σωκράτης Πλάτων ταὐτὰ τῷ Πυθαγόρᾳ, τέλος ὁμοίωσιν θεοῦ.

[6] Aristotle Fr. 192 (Rose) τοῦ λογικοῦ ζῴου τὸ μέν ἐστι θεός, τὸ δὲ ἄνθρωπος, τὸ δὲ οἷον Πυθαγόρας.

[7] B112.4. Cf. B146, 147. "At the last they appear among mortal men as seers, singers, physicians, and leaders of men" (Empedocles was all these), "and then they spring up as gods highest in honor, sharing the hearth of the other immortals, free from human sorrows, from destiny, and from all harm."

[8] The expression "microcosm" first occurs in Democritus, B34 ἐν τῷ ἀν-

the whole in miniature; they are not mere fractions, but *analogous parts* of the whole which includes them.

This relation of the many analogous parts to the including whole is very important. It is implied in the term *mimēsis*, by which, as Aristotle remarks, the Pythagoreans meant the same relation that Plato called "participation" (*methexis*).[9] In Plato it is the relation of a number of similar individual things to the supersensible Idea whose nature is communicated to them. The things "participate" in that Idea, but in such a way that the whole Idea is represented in each, and yet not used up by any one. This meaning of *mimēsis* goes back to the original sense of the word. *Mimos* means an actor. A whole succession of actors may embody or reproduce a character, say Hamlet; but none of them is identical with Hamlet. Each represents the character, which yet is not used up by any one impersonator. The actor was, in the earliest times, the occasional vehicle of a divine or legendary spirit. In Dionysiac religion this relation subsists between the *thiasos* or group of worshippers and the god who takes possession of them (*katechein*). "Blessed," say the chorus in the *Bacchae*,[10] "is he whose soul *thiaseuetai*"—is merged in his group, when the whole group is possessed by one spirit, which, not being a fully developed, atomic personality, can alike penetrate the whole group and dwell in each of its members. At that stage "likeness to God" amounts to temporary identification. Induced by orgiastic means, by Bacchic ecstasy or Orphic sacramental feast, it is a foretaste of the final reunion. In Pythagoreanism the conception is toned down, Apollinized. The means is no longer ecstasy

θρώπῳ μικρῷ κόσμῳ ὄντι, but the conception is much older and akin to the astrological premise of a "sympathy" between the heavenly bodies and earthly life.

[9] *Metaph.* I.6.987b10. Otto Gilbert ("Aristoteles' Urteile über die pythagoreische Lehre," *AGP*, 22 [1909], 40 ff.) rightly urges that μίμησις, ὁμοίωμα, ὁμοιοῦν, etc., imply a relation between two *different* things, and holds that Pythagoras and his school (I should say, the Pythagoreans other than the "mathematicians" or number-atomists) did not identify numbers with things *in ihrer stofflichen Grundlage*. At *Metaph.* V.14.1020b4 Aristotle uses μίμημα for the plane or solid figure, which is the graphic "representation" of a number. In this case any number of similar figures can "represent" the same number.

[10] Eurip. *Ba.* 72. Cf. A. W. Verrall, *The Bacchants of Euripides and Other Essays* (Cambridge, 1910), p. 30, who translates "whose soul is congregationalized."

or sacrament, but *theōria*, intellectual contemplation of the universal order, whereby the microcosm comes to reproduce (*mimeisthai*) that order more perfectly and becomes *kosmios*, attuned to the celestial harmony.

From the analogy of macrocosm and microcosm certain cosmological premises follow. The One or All must be perfect (*teleion*) and limited. The Unlimited, the *apeiron* which Anaximander had called divine, cannot be reproduced in a miniature whole. To the Pythagorean it is an evil principle of disorder, the opposite of the good principle of Limit. Again, the derivation of the many from the One cannot be merely a splitting of the One into fragmentary parts. It must be such that the nature of the whole can be reproduced in each subordinate whole or analogous part.

The formula of that identical structure which is repeated in the universe and in its analogous parts is "harmony." This word meant, first, the "fitting together" or "adjustment" of parts in a complex whole; then, specially, the "tuning" of an instrument; and hence the "musical scale" which results therefrom. There was, from the first, the implication of a "right," or tuneful adjustment.

This conception adds to the notion of the mixture of opposites as it occurs in Ionian science, the notions of order, proportion, measure. Each mixture, resulting in a thing, conforms (or ought to conform) to a definite law which characterizes it and distinguishes it from another mixture of the same ingredients. The proportion comes to be regarded as the determining essence of the compound, in which its goodness and reality lie.

This doctrine that the goodness of a compound depends on exact numerical proportions is thus referred to by Aristotle: "One might raise the question what the virtue (*to eu*) is that things get from numbers because their composition can be expressed by a number, either by a simple proportion (*eulogistōi*) or by an odd number. For in fact honey-water is no more wholesome if it is mixed in the proportion of three times three, but it would do more good if it were in no particular proportion but well diluted than if it were numerically expressible but strong." [11] Though Aristotle's common sense rejects this theory in the

[11] *Metaph.* XIV.6 init. Alexander (ad loc.) explains: "Some Pythagoreans did not hesitate to say that the virtue or good (τὸ εὖ καὶ τὸ ἀγαθόν) in everything in this world results from numbers, when the mixture of ingredients is expressed by an even or an odd number, and most of all when the result is

case of the wholesomeness of honey-water, he suggests elsewhere a similar view in the case of colors. The multiplicity of colors, over and above black and white, may, he says, be due to differences in the proportion of their composition. The combination of black and white in the intermediate colors may be in the proportion 3:2 or 3:4 or according to other ratios. Other colors may be compounded in no commensurate proportion, and "colors may be analogous to concords (*symphōniais*). Thus, the colors compounded according to the simplest proportions (τὰ ἐν ἀριθμοῖς εὐλογίστοις χρώματα), exactly as in the case of concords, will appear to be the most pleasant colors, e.g. purple, crimson, and a few similar species. It is an exactly parallel reason that causes concords to be few in number" (i.e. the "simplest proportions" are few).[12]

Aristotle here applies to the explanation of the agreeableness of certain colors the Pythagorean doctrine that the virtue of a compound lies in the exact and simple numerical proportion of the ingredients. The analogy with concords points clearly to the original source of the theory, Pythagoras' discovery that the concordant intervals of the musical scale or harmony could be expressed exactly in the terms of the "simple" ratios, 1:2 (octave), 3:2 (fifth), and 4:3 (fourth), and that, if the smallest whole numbers having these ratios to one another (viz. 6:8:9:12) are taken, the internal terms are the means (arithmetic and harmonic) between the extremes. Thus was the principle of harmony revealed as an unseen and unheard principle of order and concord, identical with a system of numbers bound together by interlocking ratios. The system, moreover, is limited, both externally by the octave (for the scale ends, as we say, "on the same note" and begins again in endless recurrence), and internally by the means. The introduction of this system marks out the whole unlimited field of sound, which ranges indefinitely in opposite directions (high and low). The infinite variety

---

perfect and similar (τέλειον καὶ ὅμοιον) and obtained by multiplication, e.g. 3 × 3, not 3 + 3." Alexander wrongly interprets εὐλογίστῳ to mean ἀρτίῳ. The true meaning is clear from Arist. *De Sensu* 439b34: εὐλόγιστοι ἀριθμοί = "proportions where the division of one term by the other takes very little trouble" (G. R. T. Ross [Cambridge, 1906] ad loc.), i.e. the simplest proportions.

[12] *De Sensu* 439b21. Cf. Arist. *Pr.* XIX.35.920a27 ff.): The octave is the most beautiful concord because the terms of the ratio (1:2) are whole numbers, and the division leaves no remainder.

of quality in sound is reduced to order by the exact and simple law of ratio in quantity. The system so defined still contains the unlimited element in the blank intervals between the notes; but the unlimited is no longer an orderless continuum; it is confined within an order, a *kosmos*, by the imposition of Limit or Measure.

The mathematical genius of Pythagoras was capable of abstracting this complex of conceptions from the particular case of sound. It must have been by a flash of inspired insight that he saw in it a formula of universal application—the union of the two opposite principles of Limit and the Unlimited to form the Limited. To the microcosm it was immediately applied in the doctrine that the good state of the body (health, strength, beauty) is the proportioned mixture or temperament of the physical opposites, hot and cold, wet and dry, etc. This conception, stated by Alcmaeon,[13] a junior fellow-citizen of Pythagoras at Croton, persists throughout ancient medical theory.

There is no reason to doubt that the application to virtue, the health or good condition of the soul, is equally old. The distinction between soul and body was not so sharply drawn as to prevent the Pythagoreans from practicing psychotherapy. As they used charms for physical ailments, so they cured the sick soul by music and the recitation of poetry.[14] Protagoras in Plato's dialogue treats as a commonplace of educational theory the effect of music in producing *euharmostia*, "good temper," and *eurhythmia*, "good rhythmical order," in the soul, and its result, virtuous conduct.[15] This was not invented by Plato. The doctrine, indeed, only gave an exact and abstract expression to the popular notion that self-control (*sōphrosynē, kosmiotēs*) is moderation, the imposition of Limit or Measure upon turbulent passion that runs to excess—a notion that lay at the center of Greek morality. To say that virtue is *euharmostia* is only to restate this in terms suggested by the musical discovery of Pythagoras.

Does the doctrine that the soul itself is a harmony go back to Pythagoras himself? This is commonly denied on the ground that, if the soul is a harmony or *krasis*, "blending," of the bodily opposites, it cannot survive the dissolution of the body: the doctrine is inconsistent with transmigration or any form of survival.[16] This is, of course, the argu-

[13] Alcmaeon B4. Cf. Plato *Symp.* 186d.

[14] Iamb. *VP* 164.

[15] *Prt.* 326a. Cf. Eryximachus in *Symp.* 187d.

[16] Professor Burnet, who uses this argument, is hardly entitled to do so,

ment urged by Simmias in the *Phaedo* (85e and 92); but the inconsistency does not seem to have been perceived by Philolaus, whom the young Simmias had heard at Thebes. There is no doubt that Philolaus held both that the soul is, in some sense, a harmony and that it is immortal.[17] If Philolaus felt no inconsistency, it is still less likely that the earliest Pythagoreans would have been aware of any. It is probable that the objection was first raised by Plato; and his argument apparently was not accepted as conclusive, for Aristotle speaks of "soul = harmony" as an opinion that has been "handed down" (*paradedotai*) and that "commends itself to many minds as readily as any of those previously mentioned." [18] . . .

That the doctrine of the three parts of the soul goes back to Pythagoras himself we are told on the authority of Posidonius, who, as Professor Burnet says, was "not likely to have been mistaken on such a point." [19] Pythagoras must, indeed, have thought of the soul as in some sense divided into at least two parts. This follows from the central religious experience of the divided self, the internal warfare between good and evil, the Orphic double nature of man, the sense of sin combined with the consciousness of inward good and light taking part against inward evil and darkness. And with this must go also the possibility of internal reconciliation and concord, when the man, as Plato says, becomes φίλος ἑαυτῷ, "a friend to oneself," and εἷς ἐκ πολλῶν, "a one (man) out of many." If virtue is this concord (*symphōnia*) or peace of the soul gained by the mastery of passion and animal desire, what could be more natural to the Pythagorean mathematico-musical mode of thought than to conceive the soul itself as the

---

since he regards inconsistency between religious and scientific beliefs as normal in the Pre-Socratic philosophers (*EGP*, p. 295). Cf. p. 250: "All through this period there seems to have been a gulf between men's religious beliefs, if they had any, and their cosmological views."

[17] Cf. Erwin Rohde, *Psyche*, 2d ed., Freiburg i.B. (Leipzig and Tübingen, 1898), vol. 2, p. 169.

[18] *De Anima* I.4, init.

[19] John Burnet, *Plato's* Phaedo (Oxford, 1911), note on 68c, where the passages cited by Eduard Zeller (*Die Philosophie der Griechen*, vol. 1, 5th ed. [Leipzig, 1892], p. 447) are quoted. Professor Burnet also points out that the doctrine of the tripartite soul agrees with the Pythagorean apologue of the Three Lives, compared to the three classes of men who go to Olympia (1) θέας ἕνεκα, (2) to compete (δόξα), (3) to buy and sell (κέρδος), Iamb. *VP* 58.

harmonia, and the parts of the soul as the terms to be harmonized and brought into concord? . . .

I conclude, then, that there is good reason to regard "soul = harmony," thus interpreted, as an original Pythagorean doctrine. Indeed, if virtue is a *symphōnia*, I do not see how the soul can be anything but the *harmonia* which contains it. It was, moreover, because the human soul contained both the divine and the irrational parts that it could, if purified, become wholly divine, or, if still impure, sink into the lower forms of life. So far from contradicting transmigration, the doctrine of the tripartite soul, under the image of the charioteer and his horses, is seen in the *Phaedrus* as part of the scheme of transmigration. The sense given to "soul = harmony" by Simmias in the *Phaedo* is quite different. Not that it is necessarily incompatible with the other. It is possible to regard the soul both as the vital principle which, during earthly life, maintains a healthy balance of the opposite elements in the body, and also, in its other aspect, as a harmony of its own three parts, with its own peculiar concord, virtue. When disembodied, it would temporarily lose the former function, but would remain a harmony in the second sense, more or less well tuned according as it departs this life more or less "pure."

The fact is that in dealing with the doctrine of the soul in philosophies of the religious type, we are dealing with a thing that exists, as it were, upon two different planes—the spiritual plane and the natural. On the natural plane the soul acts as a vital principle, distinguishing organic living things from mere casual inorganic masses of matter. In that aspect it is conceived in Pythagorean mathematico-musical terms as a harmony or ratio, expressible in numbers. It is the element of proportion in an ordered compound. But on the spiritual plane, it is itself a compound of good and evil parts—of the element of limit, order, proportion, reason, and the disorderly unlimited element of irrational passion. So considered, it is a permanent immortal thing. The question how exactly this spiritual thing is related to the vital principle which distinguishes a living from a dead body is a question that might be put to any modern believer in immortality without the expectation of any very clear and precise answer.

The other argument urged in the *Phaedo* against "soul = harmony" seems to be fallacious. It is that, if you say that the soul is a harmony, you must not also say that virtue is a harmony, for then, in the virtuous soul, you would have a harmony of a harmony. The answer is simple:

"harmony" is ambiguous.[20] It may mean merely an adjustment, or a tuneful adjustment. A lyre that is out of tune (*anharmostei*)[21] is still adjusted, though wrongly. Virtue is not so much *harmonia* as *euharmostia;* vice is *anharmostia*. The virtuous soul is the well-tuned adjustment; the vicious, the ill-tuned. No doubt, a strictly logical and literal consideration will discover what seem to us to be obscurities and even contradictions in the conception. But the greater, in that case, the likelihood that it did not date from the end of the fifth century, when men were thinking much more clearly than they had a hundred years earlier.[22]

The reason for supposing that the doctrine "soul = harmony" goes back to Pythagoras is that it seems to follow from the correspondence of macrocosm and microcosm and to be required by the fundamental conception of the imitation of God, considered as the tuning of the soul into consonance with the celestial harmony, which alone will manifest *euharmostia* in perfection. "The whole Heaven is harmony and number." The macrocosm is a living creature with a soul, or principle of life, and a body. It is an easy inference that the soul of the world is a harmony or system of numbers (as it is described by the Pythagorean Timaeus in Plato)—that very harmony which is manifest to sense in the order of the heavenly bodies and is to be reproduced in the attunement of the individual soul.

We can now approach the interpretation of the famous symbol called the *tetractys* or "tetrad," which is a compendium of Pythagorean mysticism. The *tetractys* is itself a system of numbers. It symbolizes the "elements of number," which are the elements of all things. It contains the concordant ratios of the musical harmony. It might well be described in the Pythagorean oath as "containing the root and fountain of everflowing Nature." In one of the *akousmata* preserved in Iamblichus

[20] Hence the doctrine vacillated: Arist. *Pol.* 1340b17.

[21] Plato *Grg.* 482b.

[22] There is the same confusion and obscurity about the λόγος τῆς μίξεως of Empedocles, which Aristotle suggests that he identified with ἁρμονία καὶ ψυχή (*De Anima* I.4.408a13 ff.). I believe that Empedocles' physical doctrine of the nature of soul was consistent (to his mind) with transmigration. See *From Religion to Philosophy* (London, 1912), p. 239. Since the peculiar features of Empedocles' physical system can only be explained by the desire to accommodate his religious doctrines, the common view that the religion and science are incompatible must be rejected.

it is identified with the cosmic harmony.[23] It was also called *kosmos*, *ouranos, pan*.[24] Theon says it was held in honor because it contained the nature of the universe.[25]

The *tetractys*, also called the decad, consists of the first four integers $(1 + 2 + 3 + 4 = 10)$, represented in the old fashion by pebbles or

dots arranged in an equilateral triangle ⦙⦙ . It "represents all the

consonances," in the sense that these four numbers are those which occur as terms in the concordant ratios discovered by Pythagoras in the musical scale. It is "perfect," and "embraces the whole nature of number," because all nations count up to ten and then revert to one; all the other numbers are obtained by repetition of the decad.[26] Further, the component numbers symbolize the "elements of number."

"It is clear," says Aristotle,[27] "that the Pythagoreans regard number both as the matter of things and as their properties and states. The elements of number are the even and the odd, of which the even is unlimited, the odd limited. The One (or Unity) consists of both, for it is both odd and even. Number (proceeds) from the One, and numbers, as has been said, are the whole Heaven."

This obscure statement can be interpreted with the help of other authorities.

First, there is the identification of the Even with the Unlimited, the Odd with the Limited, or Limit.[28] Euclid's definitions of Even (Book VII, def. 6 "the number divisible in two [parts]") and Odd (def. 7 "the number not divisible in two [parts]") seem to be derived from the Pythagorean definitions given by Aristoxenus:[29] "among numbers,

---

[23] Iamb. *VP* 82 (= DK 58C4): τί ἐστι τὸ ἐν Δελφοῖς μαντεῖον; τετρακτύς, ὅπερ ἐστὶν ἡ ἁρμονία ἐν ᾗ αἱ Σειρῆνες.

[24] Plutarch *Isis et Osiris* 75.

[25] Theon. Smyrn. π. τετρακτύος 154 (ed. Dupuis).

[26] Arist. *Metaph.* I.5.986a8; Aet. I.3.8; Hippol. *Haer.* VI.23.

[27] *Metaph.* I.5.986a15.

[28] *Metaph.* I.5.990a8 has πέρας (not πεπερασμένον) and ἄπειρον as the equivalents of περιττόν and ἄρτιον. Πέρας (περαῖνον, Philolaus) is correct.

[29] DK 58B2; Diels compares Arist. *Metaph.* XIII.8.1083b28, q.v. For explanations and other definitions see T. L. Heath, *The Thirteen Books of Euclid's* Elements (Cambridge, 1908), vol. 2, p. 281. The curious and unique use of ἰσοσκελής = ἄρτιος and σκαληνός = περιττός in Plato *Euthyphro* 12d may be explained by the diagrams ·]·, :]:, :]:, etc., and ·]:, :]:, :]:, etc.,

even are those that are divisible in two equal (parts), odd those that are divisible in unequal (parts) and have a middle." Plutarch explains further: "Since even numbers start with 2, odd numbers with 3, and 5 is generated by the combination of these, 5 has rightly received honor as the first product of first principles, and has been named 'Marriage,' because the even is like the female, the odd like the male. For when numbers are divided into equal parts, the even is completely parted asunder, and leaves within itself as it were a receptive principle or space, whereas, when the odd is treated in the same manner, there is always left over a middle (*meson*), which is generative (*gonimon*)."[30] And again, "when numbers are equally divided, in the uneven number a unit is left over in the middle, while in the even there is left a masterless and numberless space, showing that it is defective and imperfect."[31]

Thus the Dyad, as the first even number, stands for the female receptive field, the void womb of unordered space, the evil principle of the Unlimited. The Triad is its opposite, the good principle of Limit, the male whose union with the Unlimited produces the Limited. As Aristotle says:[32] "The Universe and all things (in it) are limited or determined by three" (the Triad). The numbers 5 $(2 + 3)$ and 6 (2×3) are both symbols of the marriage of Even and Odd, Unlimited and Limit.

Such are the two opposite "elements of number" and of all things. In the Monad they are not yet differentiated; it "consists of both," is both odd and even, or, in mythical language, male and female (*arsenothēlys*), like the Orphic Phanes. The Monad, so conceived, is not the first in the series of numbers; indeed, it is not a number at all, but *archē* ("principle" or "origin") of number.[33] It is the original undifferentiated unity, from which emerge the two opposite principles Limit and Unlimited, the elements of number and of all things.

In this interpretation of the Monad in the *tetractys* I have taken the view that the Monad is prior to, and not a resultant or product of, the

---

which show even numbers when divided as "equal legged," odd numbers as having one leg longer than the other.

[30] *De E ap. Delphos*, 388A. On this subject see W. A. Heidel, "Πέρας and Ἄπειρον in the Pythagorean Philosophy," *AGP*, 14 (1901), 384–99.

[31] Plutarch (Diels, *Dox. Gr.*, 96) ap. Stob. *Ecl. Phys.* I.1.10, p. 22 (ed. C. Wachsmuth).

[32] Arist. *De Caelo* I.1.268a10.

[33] Aristoxenus ap. Stob. I.1 pr. 6. DK 58B2.

two opposite principles, Odd or Limit, and Even or Unlimited.[34] In favor of this view the position of the Monad at the head of the *tetractys* seems to be decisive. As Theon, discussing the properties of the numbers in the *tetractys*, says: "The Monad is the origin (*archē*) of all and the most dominant of all . . . and that from which all things issue forth (ἐξ ἧς πάντα), whereas it does not issue forth out of anything, being indivisible and potentially all things, unchangeable, never transcending (*exhistamenē*) its own nature in the process of multiplication" (i.e. $I^n = I$).[35] This view has also the advantage that it brings the Pythagorean scheme of thought into line with the other early systems, both mythical and scientific. The abstract formula which is common to the early cosmogonies is as follows: (1) There is an undifferentiated unity. (2) From this unity two opposite powers are separated out to form the world order. (3) The two opposites unite again to generate life. This formula is stated clearly by Melanippe the Wise (Eurip. Fr. 484 N²): "The tale is not mine; I had it from my mother: (1) that Heaven and Earth were once one form, and (2) when they had been sundered from one another, (3) they gave birth to all things and brought them up into the light, trees, and winged things, and creatures that the salt sea breeds, and the race of mortal men." [36] The same formula, stripped of the mythical imagery of sex, fits the cosmogony of Anaximander. He has (1) the primal undifferentiated *apeiron*, containing in complete fusion the opposites which are to be separated out of it;[37] (2) the separating out of these opposites in two pairs—first the Hot (fire) and the Cold (air), and later the Wet (water) and the Dry (earth)—to form the world order; (3) the reunion of the opposites (conceived, not as marriage, but under the alternative symbol of the warfare and agression of the opposite powers invading one another's provinces unjustly) to form those temporary combinations which are living things. The Pythagorean

[34] Hence in the above passage from Aristotle (*Metaph.* I.5.986a19) I translate τὸ δὲ ἓν ἐξ ἀμφοτέρων εἶναι τούτων "the One *consists* of both of these" (odd and even), not (with Ross, e.g.) "the I *proceeds* from both of these." Cf. Alexander on *Metaph.* 985b26, p. 30, 16 Bz.

[35] Ed. Jean Dupuis (Paris, 1892), p. 164.

[36] Cf. Appollonius Rhod. I.494. For the separation of Father Heaven and Mother Earth out of a primal unity and their subsequent marriage, see Edward B. Tylor, *Primitive Culture*, 4th ed. (London, 1903), vol. I, p. 325 (parallels from New Zealand, China, etc.), and Arthur Grimble, "Myths from the Gilbert Islands," *Folk-Lore*, 33 (1922), 91–112.

[37] So Aristotle, see *Phys.* I.4.187a20.

Monad similarly symbolizes the primal undifferentiated unity, from which the two opposite principles of Limit (physically, light or fire) and the Unlimited (space, air, "void") must, in some unexplained and inexplicable way, be derived. The union of the two opposites, as Plato explains in the *Philebus*, generates *to mikton*, "the mixed," when "the equal and the double and whatsoever puts an end to the mutual disagreement of the opposites, by introducing symmetry and concord, produce number" (25d).

The parallel with Anaximander suggests that, for the interpretation of the fourth number in the *tetractys*, we may use the identification of 4, as the first square number, with Justice.[38] In the third stage of the cosmogonical formula above stated, the combination of the sundered opposites to generate life is represented in mythical terms either as a marriage or as a warfare. In the Euripides fragment we have the immemorially ancient symbolism of the marriage of Heaven and Earth, mediated (in the Orphic cosmogony, as in Hesiod) by Eros or Phanes, and, in physical terms, by the rain, the seed of the Sky-father.[39] The marriage symbol is appropriate to the elemental forms arranged in concentric regions in the order of space. The two extreme elements, heavenly fire and earth, are united by the intermediate element, water or "air" (mist, etc.) or *to metaxy*, "the in between." The alternative symbol of warfare, on the other hand, fits the same elemental forms (Hot, Cold, etc.), conceived rather as the seasonal powers in the order of time, in which each prevails successively and yields in turn to its antagonist.[40] The principle of justice is preserved by this balanced alternation of advance and retreat. As Anaximander says, "Things pay to one another the penalty of their injustice according to the order of time" (BI). Now it can hardly be accidental that in the Pythagorean number-symbolism, after the undifferentiated Monad and the numbers 2 and 3 representing the opposites, female and male, the next two numbers, 4 and 5, symbolize Justice and Marriage. Justice, τὸ ἀντιπεπονθὸς ἄλλῳ, "reciprocal treatment," according to the law of Rhadamanthys,[41]

---

[38] Arist. *MM* I.1.1182a11, ἡ δικαιοσύνη ἀριθμὸς ἰσάκις ἴσος. This interpretation of 4 in the Decad occurs in a Paris MS. published by Armand Delatte, in his *Études sur la littérature pythagoricienne* (Paris, 1915), p. 167: ἡ τετρὰς δικαιοσύνη διὰ τὸ ἰσάκις ἴσον.

[39] Aeschylus *Danaids* 44 N².

[40] Cf. Empedocles B17.26, speaking of his elements; Alex. Polyhistor ap. Diog. Laert. VII.26 (Pythagorean doctrine).

[41] Arist. *EN* V.5.1132b21.

completes the tetrad, and assures that the opposite tensions of the contraries shall be held together in harmony.[42] It is easy to see why later authorities also identify the square number with *philia*.[43]

Such is the meaning of this extraordinary symbol, the *tetractys*, which both contains the elements of number and of all things, and, as "the fountain of everflowing Nature," symbolizes also the evolution of the many out of the One, the cosmogonical process. How was this process conceived?

We have hardly any information about the earliest Pythagorean cosmogony. Pythagoras was the discoverer of the world of mathematics, which was to be conceived later as a supersensible world of concepts related in an infinite system of eternal truths—a timeless world in which no change or process can occur, and which is unaffected by the existence, becoming, or perishing of any sensible thing. But Pythagoras was still far from realizing the nature of this new world of thought. To him numbers and their relations were not only invested with a halo of divine and mysterious properties, but were also implicated in the sensible world, serving as the substructure of reality within that world and occupying space. He could not yet distinguish clearly between a purely logical "process" such as the "generation" of a series, and an actual process in time such as the generation of the visible Heaven, which "is harmony and number." The cosmogonical process was thus confused with the generation of numbers from the One, and will appear to us as a transcription of this (really logical) process into physical terms. The physical system will be determined by the way in which the generation of numbers is conceived. It was at this point, I believe, that the two schools of Pythagoreans—the original sixth-century mystics and the fifth-century mathematicians—parted company. They took very different views of the nature of the Monad, and consequently of the generation of numbers and things.

We have seen how, in the primitive symbolism of the *tetractys*, the Monad was the divine, all-inclusive unity, containing both the opposites, male and female, Limit and Unlimited. According to the old cosmogonical scheme, from the undifferentiated unity emerge the two opposite principles, and these are recombined to generate determinate

---

[42] Cf. Plato's description of δικαιοσύνη in the *Republic*, 443c–e.

[43] Alex. on Arist. *Metaph.* 987a9 (p. 36, 18 Bz). The saying φιλότης ἰσότης is attributed to Pythagoras by Iamb. *VP* 162 and Porphyry *VP* 20 (probably following *Timaeus*; Delatte, p. 253).

(limited) things—the series of numbers and the things which represent or embody (*mimeisthai*) numbers. Thus any determinate thing will, like the Orphic soul, contain both principles, good and evil, light and darkness.

How this process was construed in physical terms is obscure. The Unlimited was evidently the unmeasured field of space, which, though called "the void," was filled by "air," the circumambient envelope of the limited Heaven, the breath of the living world. It is the primeval "Night" of the Orphics. The opposite principle of Limit is manifest to sense as light or fire. The product of the two principles is the cosmos or Heaven. As the unlimited range of musical sound is marked off by consonant numbers into the definite intervals of the musical scale, so the blank field of darkness is marked off by those boundary points of heavenly light, sun, moon, and planets, whose orbits (still conceived as material rings) are set at musical intervals to form the celestial harmony or scale, bridging and binding together the visible order from earth at the center to the outermost sphere of the fixed stars. How this majestic order was evolved we cannot say. There is no sign that the earliest Pythagoreanism went further.[44]

The geometrical character of Pythagorean arithmetic must, of course, not be forgotten. Indeed, we are told that Pythagoras identified geometry with science (*historia*) in general.[45] In the unlimited darkness of night all objects lose to the eye their colors and shapes; in the daily renewed creation of the dawn of light they resume their distinct forms, their surfaces and colors (*chroia* in Pythagorean language means both). Thus in the physical world, light, the vehicle of knowledge, acts as a limiting principle, which informs the blank darkness with bodies bounded by measurable planes and distinguished by all the varieties of color. A body is thus a visible thing in which two opposite principles meet—the Unlimited (darkness, "air," void, space) and Limit, identified with the colored surface (εἶδος, ἰδέα, μορφή, σχῆμα). True to its mathematical character, Pythagoreanism tends to conceive a sensible body as essentially a geometrical solid, whose surfaces are ultimately reducible

---

[44] Aristotle's obscure remark as to the Pythagorean κοσμοποιία (*Metaph.* XIV.3.1091a12) refers, I believe, to the later system of Number-atomism discussed below (see p. 157). At *Metaph.* I.8.990a8 Aristotle remarks that, though the Pythagoreans γεννῶσι τὸν οὐρανόν, they have no explanation how there is to be motion when only Limit and Unlimited or Odd and Even are posited.

[45] Iamb. *VP* 89.

to numbers and their relations. It is the mode of conception applied in Plato's *Timaeus* to the atoms of the four elements. In this way things "represent" numbers.

Now in this system of thought the most obscure and inexplicable moment is the evolution, out of the primal unity, of the two opposite principles, the elements of number and of all things.[46] The lucid and logical mind of Parmenides fastened upon this point. He accepted the premises (ultimately dictated by religious preconceptions) that Limit, Unity, Rest are good, and therefore attributes of the real. But, with a logic that seemed unanswerable, he exposed the latent contradiction in sixth-century Pythagoreanism, which had sought to combine these monistic premises with a dualistic system of Nature.[47] If the real is indeed one, Nature cannot be a battle-ground of two opposite powers, good and evil, light and darkness, equally real. If the One is at rest—motionless and immutable—it cannot become two, and then many; it must always be One. Plurality, becoming, motion, and change must be in some way unreal. We must choose between monism and dualism.

Parmenides' own choice is not that of a man of science, prepared to accept and explain the obvious facts presented by the natural world. His preference for unity, rest, limitation (perfection), can be ultimately explained only by the value, and consequent reality, ascribed to these conceptions as divine attributes. Rather than surrender these attributes, he is prepared to set all common sense at defiance. Hence it is in the Eleatic school that the distrust of the senses, so immensely important in later thought, first emerges. This doctrine was indeed latent in the other-wordliness of the Pythagorean type of religion, in the condemnation of the body as a dark prison hiding the light of truth from the soul. Like the appetites, the senses were regarded as bodily and inseparably connected with pleasure, which ascetic religion suspects and denounces. But the philosophic conclusion that the senses are false

---

[46] Later mysticism regards the emergence of the Dyad as an act of rebellious audacity: *Theol. Arith.* II.10 πρώτη γὰρ ἡ δυὰς διεχώρισεν αὐτὴν ἐκ τῆς μονάδος, ὅθεν καὶ τόλμα καλεῖται. So Plotinus, who in *Enn.* V.1.1 ascribes the fall of the soul to τόλμα. Proclus on Plato *Alc.* I 104e attributes this use of τόλμα to the Pythagoreans.

[47] Simplicius *Phys.* 181 (quoting Eudorus): "According to their highest teaching we must say that the Pythagoreans hold the One to be the principle of all things; according to a secondary teaching (δεύτερος λόγος) they hold that there are two principles of created things, the One and the nature opposed to it."

witnesses to the external reality they profess to show us was new. It was destined to lead, later on, to the skepticism of the Academy. Thus the first parent of skepticism was not science, but religion.

Here, however, we are not concerned with these developments, but only with the light thrown by Parmenides' criticism upon the character of the original Pythagorean system. The first part of his poem leaves the divine Monad incapable of generating a pair of opposites, and through them the world of appearances. The second part contains a cosmogony on the traditional lines, vitiated by its dualism. In neither part is there any trace of the pluralist system next to be considered. . . .

II. The Scientific System: Number-Atomism

The existence of such a doctrine in the generation after Parmenides is proved by the critical arguments of Zeno. Zeno did not, like Parmenides, attack the dualistic doctrine of two opposite forms, or the inconsistency of this doctrine with monistic premises. His criticism is directed solely against the pluralist view that a manifold world and motion, denied by Parmenides, can be restored by regarding the real as composed of a plurality of units or monads moving in space. He deduces the absurdity of the hypothesis "if the many are" in that sense. This is not the hypothesis of primitive Pythagoreanism, nor yet. the developed atomism of Leucippus. It appears to be an inchoate form of atomism, a reinterpretation of the doctrine of numbers, designed to obviate Parmenides' criticism.

Most of Aristotle's allusions to the doctrine of "the Pythagoreans" refer to this system. At *Metaph.* XIII.6.1080b16, for instance, he attributes to them the following theory. (1) There is only one kind of number—namely, mathematical number. (2) This number does not exist separately, but sensible substances are composed of it; indeed, the Pythagoreans construct the whole Heaven of numbers. (3) These numbers do not consist of abstract units, but the units are conceived as having spatial magnitude. (4) They are described as "indivisible magnitudes" (*atoma megethē*, 1083b13). (5) Things (*ta onta*) or bodies (*sōmata*) are identified with numbers composed of these indivisible magnitudes or monads; "at any rate, they apply their propositions to bodies as if they consisted of those numbers" (1083b12 ff.). (6) The Pythagoreans regarded numbers as generated—the process of generation being, of course, identical with the physical generation of the sensible world (1091a17 ff.).

My contention is that the theory here outlined is not merely not identical with the mystical doctrine reconstructed in the earlier part of this paper, but cannot be reconciled with it. It proceeds from a totally different conception of what is meant by the "monad," and of the way in which numbers are generated from it. In the old mystical system the Monad, standing at the head of the *tetractys*, was the primal all-inclusive unity, both male and female, from which the elements of number, Limit and Unlimited, proceeded before they reunited to generate numbers. Deprived of the mysterious power of generating plurality, this Monad becomes the One Being of Parmenides. It is obviously unique. Numbers cannot consist of a plurality of such units (*plēthos monadōn*) merely added together. Numbers are not obtained in that way, but by the union of the Limit and the Unlimited. But now this whole conception of the generation of numbers has been destroyed by Parmenides' logic. The "mathematicians" with a scientific turn of mind, indifferent to the obscure symbolism of the *tetractys* and to the religious premises of the founder's system, accept Parmenides' criticism of it. The Monad, the "beginning of number," is divested of its mystical properties. Let it be simply an indivisible unit. There is then nothing to prevent our supposing the existence of an indefinite plurality of such units, and saying that any number is simply a *plēthos monadōn*.

On this view, any number is a "finite plurality" or "collection of units." For the process by which numbers are generated we find the expressions "flow of quantity" (*chyma posotētos*) and "progression of multitude from a unit and retrogression of multitude ceasing at a unit." These are objective terms for the subjective processes of adding and subtracting. Thus Theon, after giving the second of the above definitions, proceeds: "A unit is a limiting quantity (*perainousa posotēs*)—a principle or element of numbers—which, when the multitude is diminished by subtraction (κατὰ τὴν ὑφαίρεσιν), is deprived of all number and takes an abiding position (μονήν) and rest. For the division (*tomē*) cannot proceed further; for even if we divide one sensible thing into parts, that which was one will become again a multitude or many, and, by subtraction of the parts, one by one, will end in unity. So the one, as one, is without parts and indivisible." We should say that any number can be obtained by adding one monad to another as often as is required; but the early Pythagorean mathematicians must have confused the generation of numbers with a real process that occurred in time and space, and was identical with the generation of the cosmos containing sensible bodies, which actually *were* numbers. This seems to follow clearly from the passage of Aristotle already quoted (1091a13 ff.), where he adds that it is impossible to doubt that the Pythagoreans believed in a generation of numbers, thereby committing the absurdity of holding a becoming of things which are really eternal. "For their language is clear when they say that when the one" (i.e. "the first unit having magnitude," 1080b20) "had been constructed, whether out of planes or of surface or of seed or of some (elements) they cannot describe, immediately the nearest part of the Unlimited began to be constrained and limited by the Limit. Since, however, they are describing the construction of the cosmos and mean what they say in a physical sense," their opinions, Aristotle concludes, need not be further examined here, but belong to physics.

It seems clear from this passage that the Pythagoreans had not yet reached the position of fully developed atomism, which postulates an indefinite plurality of atoms or monads as an ultimate and eternal fact. Such a plurality seems to be required if sensible bodies are to be built of monads or indivisible magnitudes, as they were in both systems. A body is a collection of monads, *systēma monadōn*, and so a number. But is there any sense in which one of the monads composing bodies— a "first unit"—can be regarded as prior to, or generating, the collection? For atomism, no; but the Pythagoreans confused the physical process with the so-called "processes" of arithmetical generation and geometrical construction. They had not faced the question which puzzled Socrates: how one and one can "become" two "by addition" (*dia prosthesin*), or how "division" (*schisis*) can be the cause of one becoming two (*Phaedo* 97a). Aristotle's mention of "seed" (*sperma*) suggests that their thought was governed by the analogy of the growth of the living body from its "seed" or "root": both terms are applied elsewhere to the monad as the principle of number.[48] If the cosmos is a living creature, naturally it also would grow from a seed. This growth is again confused with the generation of the solid by the "flowing" of the point into a line, of the line into a surface, of the surface into a solid. The first or minimum solid is the pyramid,[49] which is composed of four points having magnitude, and has four equal triangular faces. This could readily be identified with the atom of fire, the sensible manifestation of the principle of the Limit. So we reach Aristotle's alternative suggestion that the original unit was perhaps "constructed of planes or

[48] Plutarch ap. Stob. *Ecl.* I, pr. 2; Hermes ap. Stob. *Ecl.* I.10.15. Cf. also Arist. *Metaph.* XIV.5.1092a23–32; Theon, ed. Dupuis, p. 158.

[49] Speusippus *Theol. Arith.* p. 82 ff. (= DK 44A13).

surface." The doctrine, mentioned by Aristotle (*De Caelo* III.5.304a7), that Fire is the *only* element and has the pyramidal form must be Pythagorean,[50] though how it is related to Number-atomism we cannot say.

On the whole we are left with the impression of an atomistic type of cosmology struggling to free itself from mythical analogies and elementary confusions of thought. It is obvious that a theory of this kind would be immediately suggested by the practice of representing numbers by pebbles or counters arranged in geometrical patterns. The pebbles may stand for a sort of magnified atoms; the space or "field" (*chōra*) between them is analogous to the void. By adding unit to unit a solid body of any size and shape can be constructed. With this simple materialistic conception of a plurality of monads, the old mystical derivation of the world and its harmony from the divine Monad and the "elements of number" disappears, and with it go all the religious notions of the harmony of warring opposites, good and evil, the correspondence of macrocosm and microcosm, and the ideal of the imitation of God. The real is reduced to discrete quantity with the single purpose of restoring plurality and motion.

Aristotle himself draws attention to the two diverse ways of making numbers "the causes of substances and being," which, in my view, are characteristic of the two different schools of Pythagoreans. At *Metaph.* XV.5.1092b8, he remarks that "it has not been clearly distinguished in which of two ways numbers are the causes of substances and being—whether (1) it is as terms (*horoi*), as points are of spatial magnitudes (as Eurytus used to decide what was the number of what—e.g. of man or of horse—by representing the forms of living things with pebbles, as some people bring numbers into the figures of triangle or square). Or (2) is it that concord (*symphōnia*) is a ratio (*logos*) of numbers, and so is man and everything else?" As an example of the latter view he instances Empedocles' λόγος τῆς μίξεως, "mixture ratio," and objects that, on this view, it is the ratio itself (e.g. 3 parts of fire to 2 parts of earth) that is the essence, whereas the number is "matter." I believe that this second view is the original Pythagorean doctrine, according to which things *embody*

[50] There is no evidence for attributing more than πῦρ ἀρχή to Hippasus, though the story (countenanced by Heath, *A History of Greek Mathematics* [Oxford, 1921], vol. I, p. 160) connecting his name with the construction of a regular solid may be recalled. Simplicius ad loc. does not know to whom to attribute the doctrine mentioned by Aristotle.

or *represent* ($\mu\iota\mu\epsilon\hat{\iota}\tau\alpha\iota$) numbers, not *are* numbers; and the soul, as the essential reality, is a ratio or harmony, not a mere collection of monads. The other is the crude materialistic view of Number-atomism that things *are* numbers, and numbers consist of monads, which are the terms or boundary-stones (*horoi*) marking out the void "field" (*chōra*) in the geometrical patterns of numbers "figured" by pebbles.[51]

The doctrine that the soul is either a harmony or a "mixture ratio" is also foreign to this system. We should expect to find in it a materialistic conception of the soul approximating to the Atomists'. The soul can be nothing but a set of monads, and its chief function would be to cause motion. Now, among the philosophers who say that soul is primarily "a mover" (*to kinoun*), Aristotle mentions first the Atomists, with their soul consisting of spherical atoms or fire, and then remarks that certain Pythagoreans[52] held a doctrine which appears to mean the same thing— namely, that the soul is "the motes in the air," while others say it is that which moves these motes. It has been observed, he adds, that "the motes are constantly in motion even in a complete calm" (i.e. as if they had the power of self-motion, which he goes on to discuss as an attribute of soul). I suggest that this view is that of the Number-atomists. It is hard to see how it could possibly be combined with any doctrine of the nature of the soul resting on the old conception of the mixture or harmony of opposites. On the other hand, it could easily be connected with the fire-atom whose pyramidal shape, being "sharpest cutting" (*tmētikōtaton*), enables it to penetrate everywhere.[53]

I need not enter into Zeno's arguments against this view of reality. It is generally admitted that they are directed against "the Pythagoreans";[a] and Plato tells us that they were a counter-attack upon the

[51] The Pythagorean Ecphantus of Syracuse is said to have been the first who regarded the Pythagorean monads as bodily ($\sigma\omega\mu\alpha\tau\iota\kappa\dot{\alpha}s$) or as $\dot{\alpha}\delta\iota\alpha\acute{\iota}\rho\epsilon\tau\alpha$ $\sigma\dot{\omega}\mu\alpha\tau\alpha$ of which sensible things consist (Aet. I.3.19; Hippol. *Haer.* I.15). His date is unknown; but the testimony supports the view that this Number-atomism was no part of the original doctrine, and that the view that things are related to numbers by $\mu\acute{\iota}\mu\eta\sigma\iota s$ is older than the identification of bodies with numbers.

[52] Themistius observes that he does not know which Pythagoreans are meant (π. $\psi\upsilon\chi\hat{\eta}s$ I.2, p. 17, Spengel). The doctrine was evidently obsolete.

[53] Arist. *De Caelo* III.5.304a7; cf. *De Anima* 404a1 ff.: Democritus and Leucippus made soul consist of spherical atoms "because such shapes are most able to permeate everywhere."

[a] [This no longer "generally admitted." See above, pp. 13–15.—Ed.]

hypothesis "if the many are" as held by those who satirized Parmenides' argument and urged that it led to ridiculous contradictions.[54] This testimony exactly agrees with the view above advocated, that Number-atomism was the form of pluralism put forward by the Pythagorean mathematicians as a reply to Parmenides.

In trying to distinguish the two divergent schools of Pythagoreans I have naturally stressed the fundamental differences. I do not, of course, wish to imply that, for instance, the method of representing numbers by geometrical patterns was not practiced by Pythagoras. But it was the "mathematicians" who, so to say, took this method as giving a literal picture of the structure of reality, and so gave birth to Atomism, which in the series of philosophical systems stands in extreme contrast to the religious tradition continued by Philolaus and Plato.

[54] Plato *Parm.* 128c. The imaginary date of the dialogue is about 450 B.C. Zeno is "about 40 years old" (127b), and he speaks of his treatise as having been written "when he was young" (128d). This suggests a date about 470, which would be too early for an attack on Atomism proper.

6

PYTHAGOREAN PHILOSOPHY
BEFORE PLATO

Charles H. Kahn

The name of Pythagoras is not only the most famous, it is also the most controversial in the history of Greek thought before Socrates and Plato. Since antiquity it has been a name to conjure with: There is such a wealth of conflicting evidence concerning Pythagoras' teaching, but so much of this evidence is unreliable. In 1925 A. N. Whitehead could write, in reference to the function of mathematical ideas in abstract thought: "Pythagoras was the first man who had any grasp of the full sweep of this general principle. . . . He insisted on the importance of the utmost generality in reasoning, and he divined the importance of number as an aid to the construction of any representation of the conditions involved in the order of nature." [1] But just two years earlier Erich Frank had published a book in which he claimed that "all the discoveries attributed to Pythagoras himself or to his disciples by later writers were really the achievement of certain South Italian mathematicians of Plato's time (in the decades before and after 400 B.C.)," that these contemporaries of Plato are the "so-called Pythagoreans" referred to by Aristotle, and that this mathematical school must be sharply distinguished from the "genuine Pythagoreans who are attested in southern Italy since the sixth century as a religious sect similar to the Orphics." [2] The implication of this view is that, except in connection with religious doctrine concerning the soul, the name of Pythagoras should be struck out of the history of philosophy and replaced by the name of Archytas and other mathematicians of

This article was written specially for this volume and has not been previously published.

[1] *Science and the Modern World*, p. 41.
[2] E. Frank, *Plato und die sogenannten Pythagoreer* (Halle, 1923), p. vi.

Plato's time, whose scientific and philosophical work could not be characterized as Pythagorean in any important sense.

Between these two extremes the controversy continues to rage. Although most views are more moderate, a tendency in one direction or the other is generally clear. Thus W. K. C. Guthrie writes of Pythagoras, in 1962, that "his character as one of the most original thinkers in history, a founder of mathematical science and philosophical cosmology . . . must be assumed as the only reasonable explanation of the unique impression made by his name on subsequent thought." [3] But in a study published in the same year, which contains the most accurate, complete, and penetrating examination of the ancient evidence yet to appear, Walter Burkert concluded that "there is no direct testimony to be found for Pythagorean science and philosophy before Hippasus" in the middle of the fifth century,[4] whereas the cosmology of the Pythagoreans reported by Aristotle cannot be traced back beyond Philolaus in the last half of that century. For Pythagoras himself there remains only the role of the great wonder-worker and religious prophet, whose thought was essentially prescientific and whose reputation as a philosopher and scientist rests upon a misunderstanding.[5] On this view, the traditional picture of Pythagoras in the history of philosophy was produced by an ancient but unhistoric projection of later ideas back upon the venerable, well-nigh superhuman figure of the founder of the school.

My task here cannot be to settle this controversy but only to clarify the area of disagreement and to draw some tentative conclusions. There are in fact three distinct questions that can profitably be separated. In the first place, there is the question of historical evidence concerning Pythagoras and the earliest doctrines of the school. Second, there is the task of interpreting the only substantial body of information for Pythagorean philosophy that can be reliably dated before Plato: the testimony of Aristotle and the fragments of Philolaus. (As will be seen, I follow Burkert in regarding most of the fragments of

[3] W. K. C. Guthrie, *A History of Greek Philosophy*, Vol. I: *The Earlier Presocratics and the Pythagoreans* (Cambridge, 1962), p. 181.

[4] Walter Burkert, *Weisheit und Wissenschaft: Studien zu Pythagoras, Philolaus, und Platon* (Nürnberg, 1962), p. 202; now also in English translation, *Lore and Science in Ancient Pythagoreanism*, trans. by Edwin L. Minar, Jr. (Cambridge, Mass., 1972). All references hereafter are to the German edition.

[5] Burkert, ch. III and pp. 454-56.

Philolaus as authentic.) The central problem here is to determine the original Pythagorean content of the doctrine that Aristotle formulates as "things are numbers" or "things imitate numbers." Only when these first two tasks have been accomplished can we approach the most speculative question of all: How much of the Pythagorean doctrine of the late fifth century can we trace back to some earlier period of the school?[6]

I. THE EVIDENCE CONCERNING PYTHAGORAS

The fame of Pythagoras spread from one end of the Greek world to the other almost within his lifetime. In Ephesus on the coast of Asia Minor, Heraclitus knows him as a master of "inquiry" (*historiē*) and names him next to Hesiod as a celebrated polymath (B129 and B40; cf. B81). These remarks probably belong to the early years of the fifth century, when Pythagoras cannot have been long dead. Xenophanes of Colophon, like Pythagoras an Ionian who migrated to the West, carried with him or encountered in his travels an anecdote caricaturing Pythagoras and the belief in immortality, which he narrated in his

---

[6] This way of formulating the problem is designed to exclude any reconstruction of Pythagorean doctrine by what Guthrie (p. 171) has called "arguing *a priori* or from circumstantial evidence." Thus I reject without discussion Cornford's reconstruction of Pythagorean atomism and any similar attempt to guess what *unattested* Pythagorean doctrine Parmenides or Zeno may be reacting against. It is hard enough to satisfy minimal standards of historical rigor in discussing the Pythagoreans, without introducing arbitrary guesswork of this sort where no two students can come to the same conclusion on the basis of the same evidence. In fact, the direct testimony for Pythagorean doctrines is all too abundant. The task for serious scholarship is not to enrich these data by inventing new theories or unattested stages of development but to *sift* the evidence so as to determine which items are most worthy (or least unworthy) of belief. For an abundant bibliography see Burkert, pp. 457–67. Since Burkert's book and von Fritz's Pauly-Wissowa articles (*RE* vol. 24, 1963, "Pythagoras," coll. 171–29, "Pythagoreer," coll. 209–68), the most important study is that of J. A. Philip, *Pythagoras and Early Pythagoreanism* (Toronto, 1966). See also W. Burkert, "Orpheus und die Vorsokratiker: Bemerkungen zum Derveni-Papyrus und zur pythagoreischen Zahlenlehre," *Antike und Abendland*, 14 (1968), 93–114; and Jean Bollack, "La Cosmologie des Pythagoriciens dans Aristote, *Métaphysique* (A8)," *Les Études philosophiques* (1970), pp. 427–42.

verses (B7). Again, these verses can scarcely be dated later than the first decades of the fifth century.[7] We have a few other scattered references to Pythagoras in fifth-century literature, for example in Herodotus. His legendary status is clearly established by the beginning of the fourth century, when Isocrates in the *Busiris* (conjecturally dated around 390 B.C.) describes him as having visited Egypt and having been the first to introduce philosophy from there to the Greeks (*Busiris* 28). Plato and Aristotle, on the other hand, are much less informative. Plato mentions Pythagoras only once, as the famous founder of some unspecified type of training or education (*paideia*) and of a way of life that eminent men of Plato's own time still claim to practice (*Republic* 600b). In the extant works of Aristotle (excepting the inauthentic *Magna Moralia*) there are only two references to Pythagoras. At *Rhetoric* 1398b16 he is mentioned as having been held in honor by the citizens of Magna Graecia (in a list of wise men who received general honor, apparently borrowed from an early fourth-century work by Alcidamas, the pupil of Gorgias). The other reference is a much-disputed sentence in *Metaphysics* A (986a29): "Alcmaeon lived in the old age of Pythagoras." This sentence occurs at the end of Aristotle's account of Pythagorean philosophy, but it establishes no direct link between Pythagoras himself and any of the doctrines mentioned.[8]

This comparative silence of Plato and Aristotle can be explained in various ways. It may be due to ignorance of any philosophic doctrines that could be reliably ascribed to Pythagoras. But it may also be an expression of discreet respect for a figure who was held in almost religious esteem by some of Plato's friends in South Italy.[9] Or this reserve may merely reflect polite skepticism in the face of exaggerated claims for the wisdom and superhuman powers of the master from Samos. Whatever the explanation, the fact itself leaves us very much in the situation described by Porphyry (in a passage from a good source, probably from Aristotle's pupil Dicaearchus):

What Pythagoras said to his associates, there is no one who can

[7] Guthrie, p. 363, estimates Xenophanes' long lifetime as approximately 570–470 B.C.

[8] The mention of Pythagoras is missing in one of the best manuscripts of the *Metaphysics*, and has been bracketed by Ross and Jaeger as a later gloss. See *contra*, Guthrie, pp. 342 f.

[9] Many scholars have found a more significant but veiled allusion to Pythagoras at *Philebus* 16c, where Plato speaks of "some Prometheus" who brought the doctrine of Limit and Unlimited down to earth as a gift from gods to men.

tell for certain, since they observed a quite unusual silence. However, the doctrines which became most familiar to everyone were, first, that the soul is immortal and, next, that it changes into other kinds of animals; and, in addition, that everything which takes place at some time occurs again according to certain cycles, that there is nothing absolutely new, and that all living things should be considered as belonging to the same family. Pythagoras seems to have been the first to introduce these doctrines into Greece.[10]

There is no other good evidence for ascribing the doctrine of eternal recurrence to Pythagoras himself. But for the doctrine of transmigration the evidence is overwhelming, beginning with the fragment of Xenophanes already cited (B7), and including quotations from Ion of Chios (B4 DK), Empedocles (B129), and Herodotus (II.123 with IV.93–95). If there is anything about Pythagoras that we know with reasonable certainty, it is that he taught his disciples a new view of the human soul as deathless, hence divine, and capable of passing into other animal forms. This view provides the rationale both for a mystical view of human life and destiny and for a cult society practicing vegetarianism as a form of religious purification. There are important echoes of both ideas in fifth century literature, above all in some works of Pindar (*Olympian* II and Frr. 114, 116, 127 Bowra) and in the *Purifications* of Empedocles. There is no trace of either in Greece before the time of Pythagoras. It may be regarded as certain that ritual vegetarianism in some form and a religious view of the soul's destiny involving transmigration were part of the practice and teaching of the community founded by Pythagoras in Croton in the last third of the sixth century B.C.[11]

[10] Porphyry *Vita Pythagorae* 19, according to the text of DK 14A8a. The passage follows directly on a citation from Dicaearchus, but is omitted by Wehrli in his edition of Dicaearchus (see Fr. 33 in *Die Schule des Aristoteles*, I, p. 19). The doctrine of eternal recurrence was also ascribed to "the Pythagoreans" by Eudemus (Fr. 88 Wehrli = DK 58B34).

[11] I do not understand Philip's view (p. 24) "that there is no evidence for a religious or philosophical brotherhood (though there is for a political association)." When Plato says Pythagoras handed down "a Pythagorean way of life" that men still practiced in the fourth century, he is surely referring to a cult society based on ritual purity and including vegetarianism, not to a political association. The existence of such a society, with a distinctive ritual rule, is guaranteed by the mention of Pythagorean burial practice in Herodotus II.81 (on which see Burkert, pp. 103–05).

The question of Pythagoras' originality in this regard is more difficult. It hangs together with the notorious Orphic problem, which is
much too vexed for adequate discussion here. Many scholars have
supposed that Pythagoras derived his teaching and his vegetarian
practice from earlier cult societies associated with the name of Orpheus.
But the evidence for this is weak or nonexistent.[12] My own opinion,
which cannot be defended here, is briefly as follows. Pythagoras' doctrine of the soul was new to Greece; though it was not absolutely new,
since the very similar teaching of *karma* had been gradually developing
in India over the preceding centuries (where it was originally conceived
as a *secret* doctrine).[13] What connecting links there can have been
between Pythagoras and India I have not the slightest idea, but I very
much doubt that they were provided by Orpheus or by any books circulating under that name. The cult societies represented in the gold
tablets from Petelia and elsewhere, which also involved a mystic teaching on the soul's destiny, may or may not be independent of Pythagoras'
influence; they are not likely to have been the *source* of his doctrine.
In fifth-century Athens the legendary name of Orpheus was much more
widely known than the historical name of Pythagoras; hence Euripides
describes vegetarianism not as a Pythagorean way of life but as a life
"with Orpheus as master." [14] But my guess is that the wandering priests
who peddled purification rites and invoked the name of Orpheus as
author of their sacred poems owed a great deal more to Pythagoras
than he owed to the likes of them.[15] Whatever inspiration Pythagoras

---

[12] See Burkert, pp. 102 ff. and 109: "On the whole, the tradition gives more
grounds for speaking of Pythagoreanism than of Orphism in connection with
the doctrine of transmigration in Pindar, Herodotus, Plato, and above all
Empedocles."

[13] See the words of Yājñavalkya in Bṛhad-āraṇyaka Upaniṣad III.2.13: "'we
two alone shall know of this, this is not for us two (to speak of) in public.'
The two went away and deliberated. What they said was karman and what they
praised was karman"; in *The Principal Upaniṣads*, translated by S. Radhakris-
nan (London, 1953), p. 217. These older Upaniṣads probably belong in the
period 800–600 B.C., according to E. Frauwallner, *Geschichte der indischen
Philosophie*, Vol. I (Salzburg, 1953), p. 47.

[14] *Hippolytus*, 952–54. For commentary see I. A. Linforth, *The Arts of
Orpheus* (Berkeley, 1941), pp. 50–60.

[15] Thus I agree with ancient authors such as Ion of Chios and Epigenes,
who were inclined to suspect a Pythagorean origin for the books of "Orpheus." See Linforth, pp. 110–19 and 164, and Burkert, pp. 105–12. As far as
I can see, there is no real evidence for the existence of Orphic poetry before

may have received from the East or elsewhere, the doctrine of mystic purification associated with the cycle of transmigration has, in Pindar and Empedocles as later in Plato, a rigor and a speculative power that is the mark not of an anonymous folk religion but of a bold and original thinker.[16] I for one will accept the ancient view that Pythagoras was the first to introduce these teachings to the Greeks.

Still more controversial, however, is the question whether Pythagoras was more than a great religious teacher: Was he also a philosopher and the author of a world-view inspired by mathematics? Before reviewing the evidence on this point, we may take a brief look at the historical picture that has come down to us of Pythagoras' role as a teacher and a communal leader.

According to our most reliable (or least unreliable) sources, Pythagoras left his native Samos in about 532/1 B.C. as a man of mature years, who had presumably already worked out his own ideas before quitting Ionia. He settled in Magna Graecia (the instep of the Italian boot) in the Achaean city of Croton, which had recently suffered a disastrous defeat at the hand of its neighbors the Locrians. The founding of Pythagoras' brotherhood is closely connected with the moral and political revival of Croton after 530, culminating in the destruction of Croton's famous rival Sybaris in about 510. Shortly after this great military victory, Pythagoras is said to have left Croton and moved north to Metapontum, where he died. After the destruction of Sybaris, Croton was "the greatest power in south Italy for a long period," [17] and also the home of a famous medical tradition represented by the doctor-philosopher Alcmaeon and by Democedes, the court physician of Darius.[18] During this period of Croton's hegemony, the activity of the Pythagorean order spread throughout southern Italy. We can infer the

---

the fifth century. Clement's attribution of Orphic poems to Onomacritus (in the sixth century) seems to be a late confusion or invention, based upon the standard association of the names of Orpheus and Musaeus. It is only Musaeus whose "oracles" are involved in the original account of Onomacritus' forgery, in Herodotus VII.6.3.

[16] See my discussion of this point in "Religion and Natural Philosophy in Empedocles' Doctrine of the Soul," *AGP*, 42 (1960), 30–35 (= "Appendix: Empedocles among the Shamans"), repr. in John P. Anton with George L. Kustas, eds., *Essays in Ancient Greek Philosophy* (Albany, N.Y., 1971), 30–36.

[17] T. J. Dunbabin, *The Western Greeks* (Oxford, 1948), p. 369.

[18] For Alcmaeon see DK ch. 24; for Democedes see Hdt. III.125–37 and DK ch. 19. Compare Burkert, pp. 271–73.

importance of Pythagorean influence in the early fifth century from a
passage in Polybius that refers to the burning of "meeting houses
(*synedria*) of the Pythagoreans" throughout Magna Graecia at a period
that is not precisely indicated but that must lie toward the middle of
that century. There resulted, says Polybius, a general outbreak of
political disorder and civil strife "as was natural, since the leading men
in each city had thus unexpectedly perished." [19] We need not attempt
to reconstruct the political situation. The point is that (for Polybius
and his sources) an attack on the Pythagoreans in Magna Graecia in
the early or middle fifth century meant an attack on the principal men
in every city in the area.

How did Pythagoras, the newcomer from Ionia, establish an Italian
society of such importance? Our sources provide colorful accounts
both of the marvelous exploits of the man and of the new institutions
that he set up. Thus Aristotle (in his lost work *On the Pythagoreans*)
reported such feats as Pythagoras' biting to death a poisonous snake
in Etruria, his foretelling the future uprising against the Pythagoreans,
being addressed by a supernatural voice at the river Cosa, being seen
in Croton and Metapontum at the same time, and revealing his golden
thigh to spectators at the theater or at the games (Arist. Fr. 191 Rose).
Whatever historical events may lie behind these legends, it seems clear
that the personal impact of the man was quite extraordinary. (So much
is independently attested by the remarks of Heraclitus, Herodotus,
and Ion.) There seems to be no doubt that he used this powerful char-
isma to build a most unconventional social institution in Croton, with
a structure that was capable of being reproduced in other cities. A
rationalizing account of this establishment is given by Dicaearchus,
who says that Pythagoras so impressed the governing council of elders
"by his noble discourse" that they ordered him to address moral ex-
hortation and advice to the young men, then to do the same to groups
of schoolboys, and finally to the women, "for he also established an
assembly of women." [20] Other authors speak of a band of three hundred
young men, bound together by an oath, and of successive periods of
instruction and initiation. We can only guess at the relationship between the organization of civic groups and the observance of such
essentially private ritual practices as vegetarianism and the other purity
taboos with which the Pythagoreans regulated conduct at meals (salt

[19] Polybius II.39.2 = DK 14A16. For the probable date see Kurt von Fritz,
Pythagorean Politics in Southern Italy (New York, 1940), pp. 72–79.

[20] Porphyry *Vita Pythagorae* 18 = Dicaearchus Fr. 33 Wehrli.

must be on the table, bread is not to be broken, nothing that falls from the table is to be picked up), as well as conduct at sacrifices and in everyday life (not to step over a balance, not to stir the fire with a knife, not to sit on a bushel measure, and the like).[21]

We return now to the question: Did the teaching of Pythagoras go beyond these moral, ritual, and religious subjects? Did it contain any mathematical philosophy or any theory of the universe? A negative conclusion has been skillfully argued by Burkert, to whom I refer for a full discussion.[22] There is no place here for detailed counter argument. I can only report that I find myself unconvinced by the case for the denial. As Guthrie has remarked, in dealing with Pythagoras we cannot hope for anything stronger than probabilities. In regard to his philosophical ideas we must perhaps settle for even less. My own feeling is that, although the religious and charismatic influence of the man is what is best attested, the evidence as a whole points to something more. Heraclitus (B40) mentions Pythagoras after Hesiod and before Xenophanes and Hecataeus as four men famous for "the learning of many things" (polymathiē). Why should we assume that the learning of Pythagoras is here compared only with that of the Boeotian peasant who lived a century earlier, rather than with that of the two Ionian world-travelers who were his contemporaries? And when Heraclitus says that Pythagoras "practiced inquiry beyond all men and making a selection from these treatises contrived a wisdom for himself" (B129), why should we believe that the treatises (syngraphai) Heraclitus had in mind were only Orphic poems and the like?[23] Why not also the writings of Anaximander, Pherecydes, and whatever else there was in the new rational or rationalizing literature of Ionia? Since we now know that much of the specific content of Pythagorean mathematics goes back to Babylonian times, and since it is clear that later mathematicians like Archytas regarded themselves as Pythagoreans, why should we reject their implied claim that the Pythagorean mathematical tradition goes back to the founder of the school?

So far we have made no attempt to specify just which mathematical and philosophical ideas Pythagoras himself developed or communicated. But the burden of proof must surely fall on the claim that he

[21] See the material in Aristotle Frr. 195-97 Rose, and DK 58C.

[22] Burkert, ch. II, esp. pp. 142-50.

[23] So Burkert, pp. 107 and 143. This sense for syngraphai seems unnatural, and (as I have pointed out above, n. 15) there is no independent evidence for the existence of Orphic poetry in the sixth century.

communicated *none;* and I do not see how the evidence can support this burden. That this extraordinary Ionian, neighbor and contemporary of Anaximenes, must have dabbled in the new cosmology (as for example Xenophanes did) is quite likely on a priori grounds; and it seems explicitly confirmed a posteriori by the most natural reading of Heraclitus' words. But if this is so, then it is reasonable to suppose that some archaic elements in the later Pythagorean doctrine may go back to the founder. The harmony of the spheres, for example—which according to a later tradition only Pythagoras himself could hear—seems more likely as an invention of the superhuman prophet of archaic times than as a novel doctrine in the late fifth century.

We will return in Section III to the question of Pythagoras' own contribution. Let me say only that when I suggest that some mathematical philosophy or cosmology might reasonably be assigned to Pythagoras himself I do not have in mind a theory like Plato's *Timaeus*, or a stage of mathematics like that of Archytas, Theaetetus, and Eudoxus. The relevant level of sophistication is defined by the contemporary cosmologies of Miletus and, on the other hand, by the not very advanced mathematics presupposed in the fragments of Philolaus and in the Pythagorean doctrines reported by Aristotle. The history of early Pythagoreanism will be better understood if one bears in mind that the city of Miletus lay almost within sight of Pythagoras' native island of Samos, and was probably the first place a curious Samian would sail to in search of knowledge of the world. Miletus in the sixth century was famous for many things besides its learned philosopher-scientists, but it was also famous for them, as the legend of Thales demonstrates. The failure to take account of this well-nigh inevitable connection between Samos and Miletus seems to me to vitiate Burkert's portrait of Pythagoras as a great shaman. A charismatic religious figure he certainly was; but all the evidence (beginning with the word *historiē* in Heraclitus B129) suggests that he was also more than that. The testimony of Heraclitus confirms what we would anyway assume: that when Pythagoras left Ionia for the West about 530 B.C., he was fully acquainted with the natural philosophy of Miletus.[24]

II. Pythagorean Cosmology of the Fifth Century

In what follows I shall assume (with Burkert) that all the information in Aristotle concerning Pythagorean cosmology refers to a *single* theory,

[24] A similar conclusion is reached by Philip, pp. 69, 175 and passim.

with the exception of the table of opposites at *Metaphysics* A. 986a22 ff. This is methodologically the simplest hypothesis and also the safest, since Aristotle does not elsewhere clearly distinguish between different Pythagorean theories.[25] I assume also that Erich Frank's thesis has been refuted, according to which the philosophy of the "so-called Pythagoreans" (to give Frank's own tendentious translation of οἱ καλούμενοι Πυθαγόρειοι) is really the philosophy of fourth-century thinkers like Archytas, Speusippus, and Xenocrates. This thesis was always incredible, since it would require us to believe that Frank knew the chronology of the Pythagorean doctrines better than Aristotle did. Aristotle definitely places the Pythagorean doctrines before Plato, and "at the same time as or prior to" the other Pre-Socratics. (*Met.* 985b23, where the immediate chronological reference is to Leucippus and Democritus. Compare *Met.* 1078b21, where the priority of the Pythagoreans to Socrates and Democritus is even more unambiguously stated.) Frank's thesis has been finally laid to rest by Burkert's discussion, which shows that there is a radical contrast between Aristotle's account and the Platonizing doctrines assigned to Pythagoras (or Pythagoreans) by Speusippus, Xenocrates, Heraclides Ponticus, and nearly all later writers. These Platonizing versions are characterized by (1) the basic antithesis of Monad and Indeterminate Dyad, and (2) the generation of sensible bodies from numbers by way of the sequence point-line-plane-solid, where the point is defined as "a monad with position" or "a monad with magnitude," i.e. with extension or bulk. The presence or absence of these two doctrines serves as a kind of litmus paper test for Platonizing influence on "Pythagorean" philosophy. Neither of these doctrines is to be found in Aristotle's own account of the Pythagoreans (where there is no distinction between arithmetic monad and geometric point). Both are found, for example, in the "Pythagorean notebooks" excerpted by Alexander Polyhistor (Diogenes Laertius VIII.24 = DK58B1a). Such later versions of Pythagorean theory may, and normally will, incorporate pre-Platonic ideas. But this cannot be assumed in advance; it must be established, doctrine by

---

[25] However, simplicity and caution do not guarantee truth. In fact, Aristotle's sources were probably less homogeneous than I assume (see below, n. 29). But the evidence is simply not detailed enough for us to make the appropriate distinctions. My own guess is that Aristotle had oral information from visitors to Sicily and Magna Graecia and perhaps from Pythagoreans in Athens, as well as the treatise of Philolaus. Since we know of no other *written* work available to him, there was probably none of any real authority.

doctrine. The more trustworthy fragments of Philolaus and the report of Aristotle are our only *direct* sources for Pythagorean philosophy before Plato. And once the authenticity of some of Philolaus' fragments is recognized, they become the only *primary* source, the only source in which a Pythagorean speaks to us in his own terms. As a consequence of this fact, I shall treat Aristotle's second-hand report in the same way as we are accustomed to do in the case of other Pre-Socratics; that is, I shall use it to provide the framework and commentary for the literal quotations. My assumption, then, in what follows is that the fragments of Philolaus (at least B1–7) and the bulk of the information from Aristotle represent the same state of the doctrine. This means that the only pre-Platonic Pythagorean system for which we have serious documentation is the system of Philolaus. (In using this convenient phrase, I do not mean to beg any questions as to Philolaus' originality.) Where we have Philolaus' own words, they are of course the best possible evidence. But for much of the system we must rely upon the paraphrases of Aristotle and later doxographers.

Like other Pre-Socratics, the Pythagoreans present their theory as a cosmogony. According to Aristotle, the world begins to take shape when the primeval One or perhaps the primeval Limit breathes in some void from the unlimited air or *pneuma*, a void that separates and distinguishes the numbers (*Physics* 213b22–27). In another passage Aristotle says that after the original One was constituted "whether from a surface or a seed or from what they are at a loss to say, the nearest part of the Unlimited was drawn in and limited by the Limit" (*Met.* 1091a15). Aristotle's own words imply that his Pythagoreans gave no account of the formation of the primeval unit. One brief citation from Philolaus suggests (though it does not state) that the unit is composed of Limiting and Unlimited, like everything else in the world: "the first thing to be fitted together (or harmonized), the One, in the middle of the ⟨cosmic⟩ sphere, is called Hestia or Hearth" (B7; compare B1, quoted in the next paragraph). Another fragment speaks of number as having two forms, odd and even, "and a third from both mixed together, odd-and-even" (B5). Since, as Aristotle makes clear, the Pythagoreans coordinated odd with limit and even with unlimited, the reference here must be to the unit or the number one, conceived as lying outside the odd–even classification and as composed of both members of the primary pair of opposites.[26]

[26] Compare Arist. Fr. 199 Rose for the reason why the One is odd-and-even: "When added to an even number, one makes it odd; when added to an

As is clear from its location "in the middle of the sphere," the primitive One was conceived not as an abstract unit or number but as a unit with position or "a monad with magnitude" (*Met.* 1080b20). Thus there is no distinction between the arithmetic and geometric unit, nor between mathematical points and physical or sensible bodies: The same process that generates the numbers will generate geometric solids and the visible heavens. This is the point of view that Philolaus expresses: "The nature (of things) in the world-order is fitted together (or 'harmonized') from Unlimited and Limiting, both the world-order as a whole and everything within it" (B1). Philolaus alternates between saying that all things *are* "either limiting or unlimited or both limiting and unlimited" and saying that all things are fitted together *from* limiting and unlimited (B2; cf. B6). A similar variation can be traced in Aristotle's account, where the Pythagoreans are said on the one hand to hold "that the elements of numbers are the elements of all things," and on the other hand "that the heavens as a whole are *harmonia* and number" (*Met.* 986a1–21). What we have here is not two distinct theories but two ways of expressing the same thought, just as "all things are atoms and the void" is a more dramatic, paradoxical way of saying that all things are *composed* of atoms and void. The Pythagoreans seem also to have given this thought another, more epistemological turn: that number is what makes things knowable. "And all things which are known have number; for nothing can be understood or known without this" (Philolaus B4). This epistemic consideration functions perhaps as the motive, perhaps as the confirmation, for the basic cosmological claim: "The Being (*estō*) of things which is eternal and the nature ⟨of things⟩ itself admits divine but not human knowledge, except ⟨for the principle⟩ that nothing of the things that are and are known by us could have come to be if there was not as a basis the Being of those things from which the world-order has been composed, the Limiting and the Unlimited" (B6, text according to Burkert, p. 233). With the epistemic modesty that is customary in archaic thought, Philolaus does not claim full and adequate knowledge of the eternal Being or Reality (*estō*) that underlies the world-order; he insists only that this Being must include the principles of Limiting and Unlimited. (Notice the fundamental Eleatic distinction here between eternal Reality and the generated world-order. It is in this respect that a Py-

---

odd number, one makes it even; it could not do this if it did not share in both natures."

thagorean like Philolaus provides the natural link between Parmenides
and Plato. Plato may first have encountered Eleatic dualism in this
Pythagorean form, where mathematics studies the principles of eternal
Being insofar as they are manifest in the world-order.) These elemental
principles of number, the Limiting and the Unlimited, are required
both for the cognition and for the existence of the world as we know it.
It seems to be just such a fusion of epistemological and ontological
considerations that Aristotle has in mind when he reports that "the
Pythagoreans say that beings exist by imitation (*mimēsis*) of numbers"
(*Met.* 987b11).

I take it that the much-discussed term "imitation" is simply Aristotle's own expression for the point of view that he has attributed to
the Pythagoreans, namely that "they seemed to observe many resem-
blances (*homoiōmata*) in numbers to the things that are and come to be,
rather than in fire and earth and water," and that "other things appeared to be assimilated to numbers in their entire nature" (*Met.*
985b27–33). This is given by Aristotle as his own explanation for their
view that the elements of number are the elements of all the things
there are; it need *not* be an explanation that he found in a Pythagorean
text. Of course, the fact that Philolaus' fragments do not speak of things
imitating or resembling numbers does not prove that no other Pythagorean had done so. And Aristotle certainly seems to assign the
word *mimēsis* to the Pythagoreans. My point is that on such questions
of terminology Aristotle cannot be relied on for historical or philological accuracy. It is enough for him if he believes that he has given a
correct account of the internal logic of the theory under discussion.[27]

The notion that the world arises from the One or Limit breathing in

[27] The fact that neither *mimēsis* nor any comparable term for resemblance
appears in Philolaus' fragments tells against the view expressed, for example,
by J. E. Raven, "that the author of the fragments was dependent upon Aristotle rather than *vice versa*," (KR, p. 309). And it is not from Aristotle's account that the author of the fragments can have derived the epistemic formulation of B3 and B4 or the ontological dualism which opposes eternal Being to
generated cosmos in B6. Raven claims that these epistemic considerations
would be anachronistic in the fifth century (ibid, p. 311). But the parallel between what is real and what is knowable is at the center of Parmenides'
argument, as I have urged elsewhere (see "The Thesis of Parmenides,"
Review of Metaphysics, 22 [1969], 700–24). The language of B3, B4, and B6
shows only that Philolaus has been profoundly influenced by Parmenides,
that is to say, by the Eleatic fusion of epistemology and ontology. The language of B11 is another matter, but its authenticity is not assumed here.

void or breath from the surrounding Unlimited is paralleled in an interesting way by the biological theory ascribed to Philolaus by Aristotle's pupil Meno. "Immediately after birth the animal ⟨whose body is predominantly hot⟩ draws in the breath from outside, which is cold; and then it sends it back out as if paying a debt" (DK 44A27). The parallel to the cosmogony is not exact, but it does suggest an analogy between the birth of an organism and the formation of the cosmos that is typical of Pre-Socratic thought. The balance between the heat of the body and the cold life-breath from outside may represent another aspect of cosmic *harmonia*.[28] The connection between air, breath, and life is confirmed by Aristotle in a somewhat different form: "Some of the Pythagoreans say the *psyche* is the motes in the air, others say it is what moves these," i.e. air current or *pneuma*.[29]

The notion that the *psyche* is at home outside of the body and has a nature opposed to that of the body (as cold to hot) may reflect a basic Pythagorean dualism: The union of body and *psyche* is in some sense unnatural, and their separation at death can represent the release of the soul from a situation of misfortune.

To return to cosmogony. We saw that the cosmos arises from the One by breathing, like a newborn animal. In this context the notion that the unlimited void or air breathed in "separates the numbers"

[28] The doctrine that the *psyche* is a *harmonia* is assigned to Philolaus by a late source (DK 44A23; cf. B22), and it is easy to understand the attractiveness of such a view for a Pythagorean. (Compare the remark of Echecrates at *Phaedo* 88d and the statement of Aristotle at *Pol.* 1340b17: "There seems to be some kinship to musical harmonies and rhythms [in the human soul]; hence many wise men say the soul is a harmony or has a harmony.") But it is hard to establish any direct connection between Philolaus' biology, as known from Meno in the *Anonymus Londinensis*, and the theory of psycho-physical *harmonia* formulated in the *Phaedo*.

[29] *De Anima* 404a17. Here Aristotle distinguishes two Pythagorean views, neither of which need be that of Philolaus. Compare 410b28: "The doctrine in the poems called Orphic says that the *psyche* enters (the body of animals) from the universe as they breathe in, and it is carried by the winds." As we have seen (above, n. 15), there is some reason to suspect Pythagorean influence on Orphic poetry of the fifth century. Plato does not hesitate to make use of the "Orphic" idea that the body is the prison of the soul (*Cratylus* 400c7) within the Pythagorean framework of the *Phaedo*, where the discussion begins with a reference to Philolaus as in some sense the teacher of Simmias and Cebes. These interlocutors seem to have in mind a view of the *psyche* as liable to be dispersed into the air, like breath or wind (*Phaedo* 77d7–e2).

seems strange. Here we must abandon biology and pass to number theory. It was long ago pointed out by Burnet that we can understand this doctrine by reference to an archaic representation of the positive integers by dots or pebbles. The dots represent the unit or limiting principle; the space between them represents the unlimited void or breath that has been "drawn in and limited." The primeval One is thus conceived as intrinsically capable of self-repetition or reproduction, but it requires the complementary principle of empty space or "thin air" (*pneuma*) to sustain its plurality. We can see this from a picture of the first ten integers.[30]

We note that 4 gives the first square number, 6 the first oblong number, 10 is a triangle (though not the first one, since 3 and 6 can also be displayed as triangles). All numbers except the primes can be arranged either as square or as oblong. The even numbers are all rectangles with height 2; the odd numbers can be immediately distinguished by their irregular shape (as would be clear for 9 if it were rearranged with height 2). The number 10 was "thought to be perfect and to contain the whole power of number" (*Met.* 986a8), since it is the sum of the first four integers and displays the basic musical ratios 2:1, 3:2, and 4:3 as successive steps. Since the whole heavens must display the same perfection, but since there are only nine visible bodies (earth, moon, sun, the five planets, and the heaven of the fixed stars), "they invent a counter-earth to make ten" (*Met.* 986a11). This gives us the cosmic system ascribed by a later doxography to Philolaus, in which the earth

[30] The evidence for the use of pebbles in calculation in classical Greece is late, and it is sometimes doubted whether the figuration given here can go back to Pythagoras (see, e.g., Philip, p. 103). But the basic principle of representing the smaller integers as sums of unit-points (or unit-marks) requires no special system of *calculation;* and this is in fact the principle for forming the lower numerals in cuneiform and in Linear B, as also in the first three Roman numerals.

and all other bodies revolve about a central fire. Before discussing this scheme, we may consider Philolaus' own statement on harmony and proportion.

> Since the principles or origins (*archai*) ⟨namely, those from which the world order was formed, the limiting and unlimited, represented in numbers as the odd and even⟩ were not similar nor of the same kind, it would have been impossible for them to be set in order, if there had not supervened a fitting-together (*harmonia*). . . . It was necessary that they be fastened together by a *harmonia* such that by it they could be held in order. (Philolaus B6)

In giving his account of the *harmonia* by which the contrasting principles are to be disposed in a cosmos or world-order, Philolaus proceeds to describe the intervals of the octave or musical scale (for which his word is *harmonia*), and to explain its structure as based on the three ratios, 4:3, 3:2, and 2:1, that is to say, on the three ratios displayed in the tetractys or triangular number 10 figured above. It is clear that Philolaus regards these ratios as the fundamental principles of cosmic order.[31] The doctrine of a musical "harmony of the spheres" will thus emerge simply as an audible corollary to the basic Pythagorean thesis on the structure of the universe.

The discovery that the fundamental musical relations in the octave can be represented by simple numerical ratios is ascribed to Pythagoras himself in the later tradition, but there is no way to tell what the evidence was for such an ascription.[32] The discovery of the musical numbers must have been made prior to, or no later than, the doctrine of the music of the spheres, but this also cannot be firmly dated. An audible celestial harmony is of course presupposed in the sirens' song in Plato's Myth of Er (*Republic* X.617b). The doctrine is described in some detail by Aristotle, who rejects it (*De Caelo* 290b12–29 = DK 58B35). As we have seen, the doctrine follows almost trivially from Philolaus' conception of cosmic *harmonia*. But there is no indication anywhere that the doctrine was new with Philolaus.

Whatever its origin may be, there is no doubt of the central importance in Philolaus' scheme of the doctrine of cosmic music, understood

---

[31] This is clear, at any rate, unless one follows Diels in supposing that the two parts of B6 do not belong together. Philip (p. 127) seems to be misled on this point, since he finds no suggestion of the music of the spheres in Philolaus' fragments!

[32] See Guthrie's discussion, pp. 222–25.

as the claim that the simple ratios connecting in sequence the first four
integers (and displayed in the 10-triangle illustrated above) constitute
the basic structural principles of the universe. The more elaborate
theory of the decad given by Speusippus in his book *On Pythagorean
Numbers*, like other details ascribed to Philolaus in later writers, probably goes well beyond the fifth-century doctrine.[33] Still, there is no doubt
as to the pre-Platonic date of the basic conception. Even if one suspects
the authenticity of Philolaus' fragment 6, both the doctrine of celestial
harmonia and the cosmic importance of the number 10 are firmly
established in Aristotle's account of the Pythagoreans. And it is probably this view of the universe that is presupposed in Archytas' statement that astronomy, geometry, arithmetic, the theory of the (celestial?)
sphere, and music are all "sister studies." [34] It is also presupposed in
Plato's reference to the sages who believe that "heaven and earth and
gods and men are held together by community and friendship" based
upon "geometrical equality," i.e. proportion (*Gorgias* 508a). Now I
want to suggest that it is just this conception of cosmic music—of the
cosmos as a unity bound together by a *harmonia* expressed in simple
numerical ratios—that represents the fundamental and *explicit* doctrine of the Pythagoreans that Aristotle has reformulated in his own
terms as the claim that things resemble numbers, or that the elements
of numbers are the elements of everything there is. I mean that these
Aristotelian formulas are to be read as post-Platonic commentary and
paraphrase on the fifth-century view of Limiting, Unlimited, and
harmonia which we find expressed in the fragments of Philolaus. Here
as in the case of other Pre-Socratics, if we want to understand the doctrine in its own terms, we must rely on the original texts and not on
Aristotle's rewording.

The most important specific application of the theory of cosmic harmony is given in the celestial system which one doxography (Aëtius)
ascribes to Philolaus and which Aristotle attributes simply to "men of
Italy (i.e. Magna Graecia) called Pythagoreans." This is the scheme of
ten astral bodies circulating about a central fire known as "the hearth

[33] E.g. Proclus in DK 44A14; for Speusippus, A13.

[34] Archytas B1, echoed by Plato *Rep.* 530d, where the doctrine that music
and astronomy are sister sciences is expressly attributed to the Pythagoreans—
the only case of such an attribution in Plato. It is worth noting that the context in Archytas B1 represents this not as his personal doctrine but as part
of the correct view "concerning the nature of the universe" which has been
handed down by previous students of *ta mathēmata*.

of the universe" or "the home of Zeus." [35] The earth is not at the center but is one of the "stars" revolving about the center. We thus have the first attested break with a geocentric scheme since the Milesians began constructing geometric models for the heavens in the sixth century, and in this respect Philolaus represents one of the very few Greek precursors of Copernicus. The boldly speculative character of the system is also indicated by the introduction of an invisible "counter-earth" to bring the total number of revolving bodies up to ten. This preference for an abstract theory that goes beyond all observed phenomena provoked Aristotle's indignation; it might evoke more sympathy today from a mathematical astronomer.

Some details of the system are of interest. Counting outward from the central fire we have, in sequence: the orbits of the counter-earth, earth, moon, sun, the five planets, and finally the sphere of the fixed stars, which is composed of aitherial fire. The clear recognition of the five planets as a group seems to point to a date in the late fifth century, and it is not impossible that the system was Philolaus' own construction, though we really have no evidence for this. [36] The sun is conceived as a sort of magnifying glass, collecting light and heat from the aitherial fire and projecting it onto the earth. [37] Several other curious theories of this sort are attested for the middle and late fifth century. They represent unsuccessful attempts to generalize the discovery of the fact that the moon shines by reflected light. The circumstance that these particular attempts all failed should not prevent us from recognizing that the search for a wider application for an important new discovery was itself scientific in spirit.

How far Philolaus' system was inspired by scientific astronomy, how far it represents a mythical modeling of the world according to number mysticism, is a question that the evidence does not permit us to answer. And perhaps the alternatives are falsely posed. No doubt this speculative construction ranged far beyond the available astronomical evidence and far beyond any attempt to control speculation by careful observation. In this respect the cosmic system of Philolaus resembles that of Empedocles, Parmenides, and Anaximander. It is above all the Italian school that preserved the speculative audacity of the first great Milesian cosmology. But I for one would deny that the almost a priori use of

[35] So Aëtius in DK 44A16. In *De Caelo* 293b3 Aristotle gives the title as "guardpost (*phylakē*) of Zeus."

[36] See Guthrie, pp. 286–89; Burkert, p. 326.

[37] DK 44A19, with Burkert's commentary, pp. 320 f.

geometry and arithmetic in constructing simple (or not-so-simple) models for the heavens was incompatible either in principle or in historical fact with progress in scientific astronomy. One peculiar achievement of early Greek thought is precisely this union of science and philosophy in the creation of bold schemes based on clear and simple principles—in celestial models as in geometric proof.[38] Unlike his contemporaries Meton and Democritus, Philolaus does not belong to those who made an important contribution to observational astronomy or to accurate theory. But he (or whoever it was who invented the "system of Philolaus") deserves a place among the more imaginative theorizers of the fifth century. And just as the atomic theory of Leucippus and Democritus was recognized in the seventeenth century as a forerunner of the world-view of post-Galilean physics, so Copernicus himself could cite Philolaus as an ancient precedent to add respectability to his new cosmic scheme.[39]

III. SOME GUESSWORK ON THE HISTORY OF PYTHAGOREAN DOCTRINE BEFORE PHILOLAUS

We have not covered all the evidence from Aristotle and elsewhere concerning pre-Platonic Pythagorean doctrines. In particular, I have omitted the table of ten pairs of opposites given by Aristotle at *Met.* 986a22 ff. There are several reasons for not dwelling on this scheme. In the first place, Aristotle himself distinguishes the authors of this table from the other Pythagoreans whose views we have discussed. It is often supposed that the table of opposites belongs to an earlier stage of the doctrine, but Burkert has argued that the list reflects Academic influence and would belong to the fourth century.[40] I am not convinced of either view. But in any case the table is not self-explanatory, beyond the simple fact that the opposites are arranged systematically, so that one member of each pair is positive (right, male, light, good) one negative (left, female, dark, evil). What this tells us about the other pairs (limit–unlimited, odd–even, one–many, rest–motion, straight–

[38] I have argued this point elsewhere. See "On Early Greek Astronomy," *JHS*, 90 (1970), 110–16.

[39] Copernicus mentioned Philolaus twice. See the references in Burkert, p. 315 n. 1.

[40] Burkert, pp. 45 f. The most suspiciously Platonic pair is rest-motion, but this might only reflect Eleatic influence.

curved, square–oblong), and how the pairs are related to one another, are questions on which anyone can speculate for himself.

Another omission is more substantial, but it scarcely affects our theme. Archytas of Tarentum, the friend and contemporary of Plato, falls outside the period under discussion here. In any case, Archytas' importance lies primarily in the history of science, and specifically in mathematics, musical theory, and mechanics. Neither in technical astronomy nor in philosophical cosmology is there any clear evidence of an original contribution on his part.[41]

Before attempting to look back beyond Philolaus, we may mention the curious method of pebble arrangement that is ascribed to Eurytus by Aristotle and other authors, apparently on the authority of Archytas.[42] Eurytus is said to have been a pupil of Philolaus; if so, this procedure would belong to the *latest* phase of pre-Platonic Pythagoreanism. Eurytus represented the forms of animals and plants with pebbles "like those who present numbers in the form of triangle and square"; but Eurytus' presentation was more vivid. According to an Aristotelian commentator, Eurytus not only specified which number corresponds to a given thing—say, 250 for man and 360 for plant—but actually drew a mosaic picture of a man with 250 pebbles of several different colors! This may perhaps be regarded as a decadent, "realistic" version of the more ancient symbolic or expressive use of number patterns and ratios to signify concepts, as justice (understood as reciprocity or *lex talionis*) was represented as the number four: the first square, the product of a given number taken an equal number of times.[43] Similar number patterns were given for such concepts as soul and intellect (*nous*), opportunity (*kairos*), and marriage. Insofar as the older procedure is to be interpreted in the light of the views discussed in Section II, the ratios expressed in such number patterns must have been conceived as instances of the cosmic *harmonia* that binds together the nature of things, instances that were specifically appropriate to the

[41] Erich Frank's picture of Archytas as a great astronomer seems to rest largely on the vague praise of him in an ode of Horace (DK 47A3). More impressive is the argument to prove the infinite extension of the heavens by the thought-experiment of stretching out a cane beyond the limit of the world (47A24), no doubt the remote ancestor of the corresponding argument in Lucretius (I.968–83).

[42] DK 45A2–3, translated by Guthrie, pp. 273 f.

[43] Arist. *Magna Moralia* 1182a14 and *N.E.* 1132b21, quoted in DK 58B4.

concepts in question. This will be the original, symbolic meaning of the Pythagorean number-definitions that Aristotle has rendered in his formula that things "are" or "imitate" numbers: Both the unity and structure of the whole world and the specific nature of each thing are expressed by simple numerical ratios, and this is what makes them knowable. This is as far as we can go in recapturing the central doctrine of Pythagorean philosophy.

If we ask now, how much of this late fifth-century doctrine can be traced back to the early fifth century or to the lifetime of Pythagoras, we must recognize that any answer will and must be guesswork. The guesses may be more or less educated, more or less plausible. But there is simply not enough evidence, and what evidence we have is too ambiguous, for any one interpretation to claim a very high degree of probability. It is this recognition that distinguishes (or at least should distinguish) contemporary research on Pythagoras from the kind of bold and categorical pronouncement that I quoted from Whitehead at the beginning of this essay.

Having emphasized this caveat, I shall proceed to offer what I take to be the most plausible reading of the evidence. (For the sake of brevity and simplicity, I give my conclusions in rather dogmatic form.) Since we know of no Pythagorean cosmologist after Pythagoras himself and before Philolaus, the only question that is reasonable to ask is: How much of Philolaus' system could we plausibly trace back to Pythagoras? To answer this question is difficult enough. To answer any other is impossible. Evidence for intermediate phases in the development—for Pythagoreanism before and after Parmenides or before and after Zeno—is wholly lacking.[44] Even if such phases actually existed, there can be no hope of reconstructing them in the absence of evidence.

First of all, let me list the features in Philolaus' system that I would *not* trace back to any earlier stage of Pythagorean doctrine. These are, first, the specific astronomical detail of the cosmic model (including the five planets, the counter-earth, and the central fire) and, second, the biological detail of Philolaus' theory of three humors and the like (DK 44A27). Here the substantive content of Philolaus' doctrine fits

---

[44] The only exception is Hippasus of Metapontum, whom Aristotle and the doxography mention together with Heraclitus as making fire the cosmic principle. There is no other reliable information on Hippasus, and even his date is entirely uncertain, though the link to Heraclitus suggests that he lived well before Philolaus.

in well with the history of astronomy and biology in the last half of the fifth century, and although we have no way of assessing Philolaus' originality, I can see no reason to assign these doctrines to an earlier period. Much the same can be said for the Eleatic influence which is visible in the fragments: the ontological contrast of eternal Being and generated cosmos in B6 and probably the epistemological coloring of B3–4 as well. The explicit contrast between Being and cosmos is surely not older than Parmenides, and need not be traced back to any Pythagorean before Philolaus.

The case is quite different, however, with the specifically cosmic principles known from Aristotle and from the fragments, namely, the cosmogony of numbers and the cosmology of musical *harmonia*. By this I mean (1) the generation both of the numbers and of the cosmos from a primitive opposition of Limit (or Limiting) and Unlimited, and from a One that "breathes in" the void or *pneuma*, and (2) the explanation of cosmic unity in terms of *harmonia*, where the basic opposites to be harmonized are the Limiting-Unlimited, the *harmonia* itself conceived in terms of the three fundamental musical ratios (2:1, 3:2, 4:3). In both cases there is some reason to suppose that these doctrines were not new in the time of Philolaus, and some reason to believe that they were (or that they easily might have been) formulated in the time of Pythagoras.

(1) The failure to distinguish between the One as abstract unit, as a point with position, as a geometric solid, and as a physical body capable of breathing, is not a proof of early date, but it is surely compatible with one. The failure to distinguish between void and air is more significant (if Aristotle is correct on this point), since the corporeal nature of air had been established by Anaxagoras and Empedocles in the middle of the fifth century, at the latest. Even more suggestive is the notion of the One as breathing-in unlimited *pneuma* or "boundless air." In the first place, a good doxography reports for Xenophanes that his one great spherical god "sees as a whole and hears as a whole but does not breathe (*anapnein*); it is all *nous* and *phronēsis*" (Diogenes Laertius IX.19 = DK 21A1). Now the beginning and end of this excerpt gives a close paraphrase of extant fragments (B23–24). It would be strange indeed if "it does not breathe" were not the paraphrase of a lost verse. But what doctrine would Xenophanes be denying here, if not the Pythagorean view of a cosmic One that develops by breathing in *pneuma*? And if this doctrine was denied by Xenophanes, it is likely to have been asserted by the Master himself. Even if the doctrine that

Xenophanes has in mind is *not* a Pythagorean cosmogony, the denial at least shows that similar views had been or could be held at the end of the sixth century. And indeed, the concept of an unlimited or boundless breath is almost literally the principle of Anaximenes, who was Pythagoras' neighbor and contemporary. Furthermore, I have argued on different grounds that a kind of dialectical contrast of Limit–Unlimited can be traced back to Anaximander.[45] Even if this is doubted, both concepts are well attested for the sixth or early fifth century: the Unlimited in Milesian cosmology, the concept of Limit in the "Italian" ontology of Parmenides, where the term *peras* is closely associated with geometric shape.

(2) A kind of cosmic harmonia is alluded to by Heraclitus, who says "the obscure (unapparent) *harmoniē* is greater than that which is clear (apparent)" (B54). Emphasis on the early concrete sense of *harmonia* as "fitting-together" or "adjustment" has led many recent interpreters to ignore the fact that the term in Heraclitus must *also* have its musical sense of "attunement" or "scale." This is indicated by the *harmonia* of the lyre mentioned in B51 and by other evidence for Heraclitean reference to the fitting-together of disparate notes (B8 and B10). I am strongly inclined to see the "unapparent *harmoniē*" of B54—the harmony that is not accessible to most men—as an allusion to the Pythagorean doctrine of inaudible cosmic music. Of course, Heraclitus' own concept of *harmoniē* is not Pythagorean. But he exploits the Pythagorean notion of cosmic harmony, just as he exploits the Pythagorean doctrine of immortality and transmigration, for his own purposes. (Compare B25, B27, and above all, B62.) The concept of measure and proportion is central in Heraclitus' thought and utterance. He need not have got it from Pythagoras; both men may have taken it from Milesian cosmology.[46] Yet the juxtaposition of the *harmonia* concept and the *logos*-measure concept in Heraclitus strongly suggests that the similar juxtaposition in Pythagorean cosmology may well belong to the earliest period of the school. The doctrine of cosmic *harmonia* and the discovery of the musical ratios belong together. It is

[45] "Anaximander and the Arguments concerning the Apeiron at *Physics* 203b4–15," *Festschrift Ernst Kapp* (Hamburg, 1958), pp. 19–29.

[46] See *Anaximander and the Origins of Greek Cosmology* (New York, 1960), pp. 81, 84, 88, 96. It is noteworthy that the figures attested for Anaximander do *not* illustrate the musical ratios: The dimensions of the earth are 3:1; the dimensions of the celestial circles are 9, 18, and 27 (if Tannery's conjecture is accepted).

not easy to see why they should be dated later than Heraclitus. And the formulation of the *harmonia* doctrine in terms of Limit and Unlimited belongs more naturally in the period of Milesian cosmology than in any later stage of the philosophical development.

All of this evidence is circumstantial. Even if it is accepted as having some cumulative weight, it does not permit us to reconstruct the cosmology of Pythagoras. It does permit us to believe that the Pythagoreans were right in a general way in claiming that their philosophy goes back to the founder of the order. If doctrines (1) and (2) above are not original with Philolaus and his contemporaries, whom should we assign them to if not to Pythagoras himself? In other words, the general principles of Pythagorean cosmology known from Philolaus and Aristotle will, after all, be Pythagorean in the strict sense. As far as these general principles go, the philosophy of Philolaus is the philosophy of Pythagoras himself. If this proposition cannot be regarded as firmly established, it is surely more reasonable to believe this than to believe its denial. For there is some evidence in favor of this view, and there is no evidence against it.

IV

HERACLITUS

7

NATURAL CHANGE IN HERACLITUS

G. S. Kirk

The thought of Heraclitus of Ephesus is still often summarized as "All things are flowing," *panta rhei;* by which it is inferred that everything is in *constant* change. This summary goes back ultimately to Plato, who at *Cratylus* 402a wrote as follows: "Heraclitus says somewhere that everything is moving and nothing stays still, and likening things to the flow of a river he says that you could not step twice into the same river." Plato's interpretation was adopted by Aristotle, and through him by Theophrastus, whose "Opinions of the Physicists" became the basis of all later ancient accounts. In recent decades, however, some scholars have become skeptical about the accuracy of the Platonic-Aristotelian interpretation of Heraclitus' views on change; and with good cause, for the fact is that there is nothing in the extant fragments about the constant flux of all things, even though one would have expected the survival of some original support for a view so widely popularized in the fourth century. The assumption from this is that the constancy of change is not an idea which Heraclitus particularly stressed. What he undoubtedly did stress above all else was his discovery of the unity that subsists in apparent opposites: it is with failure to apprehend this unity that he so bitterly reproaches his fellow men. Plato bears witness to this theory as well as to the theory of change, and Aristotle mentions it repeatedly because he thought that Heraclitus was thereby denying the law of contradiction—which shows how little Aristotle appreciated the real application of Heraclitus' *grande idée*. Later Philo asserted categorically that Heraclitus' vaunted discovery was simply that if a unity is split opposites are revealed, and that opposites are really one; a discovery, Philo typically adds, which should really be credited to Moses.

From *Mind*, 60 (1951), 35–42. Reprinted with the permission of the editor of *Mind* and of the author.

How is it then, we may pertinently ask, that Plato gave such prominence to the idea of constant and universal change in Heraclitus?
Fortunately we possess a pair of certainly genuine fragments which are
in themselves capable of having misled Plato, who, it should be remembered, did not set out to be a historian of philosophy, and who
never took Heraclitus quite seriously in the dialogues. The more
important of these fragments, B12 in Diels' order, says: "Upon those
who step into the same rivers, different and different waters flow"
(ποταμοῖσι τοῖσιν αὐτοῖσιν ἐμβαίνουσιν ἕτερα καὶ ἕτερα ὕδατα ἐπιρρεῖ). The
following sentence, "and souls too are exhaled from moisture," must
be counted an irrelevant addition by the Stoic Cleanthes, to whom
ultimately the preservation of the fragment is due. The second fragment,
B91, consists simply of three pairs of verbs describing water in a river:
"Scatters–gathers; concentrates–disperses; approaches–departs" (σκί-
δνησι καὶ . . . συνάγει . . . συνίσταται καὶ ἀπολείπει καὶ πρόσεισι καὶ ἄπεισι)
—the rest being merely interpretation on Platonic lines by Plutarch.[1]

Now Karl Reinhardt has shown[2] that Heraclitus says nothing here
about *things being like* a river, but merely points to a certain aspect of
the behavior of rivers in general. Some think that B12 is no more than
another example, purely formal in type, of the coincidence of opposites
—in this case of "same" and "different": upon those who step into the
same rivers *different* waters flow. But this is to reduce its emphasis too
much, and there are serious objections against this interpretation: first,
the other Heraclitean examples of the coincidence of opposites are far
more concrete, less purely logical, than "same–other"; witness "summer–winter," "war–peace," "the young–the old," "the straight–the
crooked," "the way up–the way down"—for Heraclitus, these were not
abstractions as they are for us. Secondly, such examples in other
fragments are unmistakably framed as such: "the way up and the way
down is one and the same," and so on. Thirdly, the identification of
"same" and "other" would destroy all differentiation, while Heraclitus
was content that his unity should be an underlying one, an *aphanēs*

[1] The other commonly accepted river-fragment, B49a, consists of a later
paraphrase of B12 to which the un-Heraclitean deduction "we are and are
not" has been added. It has no value as evidence for Heraclitus.

[2] Most clearly in *Hermes*, 77 (1942), 18 f.; see also his *Parmenides und die
Geschichte der griechischen Philosophie* (Bonn, 1916), p. 177, where he touches
briefly on the implications of the river-image which are stressed below. He
does not, however, face the difficulty caused by his supposition that B12 comes
from a psychological context.

harmonia: he was not Parmenides. What these river-fragments *are* intended to show, I believe, is the regularity, the order, the *metron* or measure, which Heraclitus believed to underly and to control natural change in all its forms. The example of the river is intended to illustrate this *metron.* The repetition of the word "different," *hetera kai hetera,* well suggests the regularity of the onrush of waters, although it is no more than a suggestion; and the oppositions of B91, which in its original setting may have followed directly upon B12, express the reciprocity and quantitative balance much more unmistakably: "it scatters and gathers, concentrates and disperses, approaches and departs." The continued existence of the river as a whole, of the "same" river in Heraclitus' terms, depends upon the maintenance of this regularity in the movement of the waters past a fixed point, the *embainontes.* Of course the idea of the preservation of a kind of stability in change is there too, but it is subordinated to and dependent on the idea of *metron.* The river-fragments, then, seem to exemplify not the constancy of change—for there is no hint that all things resemble rivers —but the regularity of natural change in one particular manifestation.

Before this interpretation can be accepted (and it is pitted against that of Plato himself, a powerful authority, though I suspect that he may not have known as many of the actual sayings of Heraclitus as even we do) it must be compared with the evidence of the other extant fragments. Does the idea of measure in change appear prominently there? Indeed it does: in fact once the idea of *metron* is isolated it can be seen springing up everywhere. This of course is the trouble with Heraclitus; any idea which arouses the student's enthusiasm can do the same—that is why we have Heraclitus the Hegelian, and Heraclitus the Existentialist. However, consider the evidence. In B30 the cosmos is an everliving fire, kindling *in measures* and going out in measures (ἁπτόμενον μέτρα καὶ ἀποσβεννύμενον μέτρα). In B31 the sea is measured (*metreetai*) into the same proportion as applied to it before it became earth. In B90 fire is an exchange for all things and all things for fire as goods for gold and gold for goods. In B88 (of a group of opposites like summer–winter) "these things change places and are those, and those change places again and are these," where *metapesonta* implies a regular exchange. In B94 "the sun will not overstep his measures (*metra*); if he does, the Erinyes, agents of Dike, will find him out." In B51 that which tends apart also coincides: it is a *palintonos harmoniē,* a join which works in both directions like the string of a bow or a lyre; note that here too the tension must operate equally in each direction—the inward pull of the string must equal the outward pull of the arms of the instrument, otherwise the string is too loose or the whole instrument breaks. Akin to the idea of measure is that of plan and direction in the world, as in B41: wisdom is to know how all things are guided; and in B80: all things happen by strife and *necessity*. The concept of Logos supplements this whole picture; Logos for Heraclitus is the single formula or plan according to which all things happen (B1 . . . γινομένων πάντων κατὰ τὸν λόγον τόνδε); so also the use of *kosmos* in B30: "This *kosmos* no man or god made; it was, is, and shall be." Now *kosmos* for Heraclitus, in the early fifth century, must still have retained much of its basic meaning of "order," "regularity"; it cannot just mean "world" in our practical sense, and is perhaps best translated as "organism."

Two related questions may now be asked. First, if the river-fragments do not contain the idea of universal and constant change, how far was this idea held by Heraclitus? And secondly, why such insistence on *metron?* The answer to the first question is that the universality of change, though not its absolute constancy, was a commonplace of early Greek thought which Heraclitus cannot have avoided: change is going on everywhere, you only have to use your eyes. The Milesians did not think it necessary to give a formal explanation; probably they regarded all things as alive, and change is a property of life. Heraclitus had to be a little more explicit, because the unity which for him connected all natural existents depended on the inevitability of change, sooner or later, in every division of nature; while the somewhat different unity of the Milesians and their mythological forerunners depended upon a world-forming process out of a single source, a process which gradually slows down and in the final stages of which change is no longer indispensable to unity, but is taken for granted. Heraclitus' unification of apparent opposites depended in its clearest form upon an unfailing reciprocal movement between extremes: night succeeds day and day night, therefore night–day is a single continuum; so too with the other pairs of opposites; therefore, he concluded by an intolerable leap of the imagination, all things are one. If the succession fails the unity is destroyed, and with it the Logos which relates man to his surroundings and is therefore so important to understand. The reciprocity *must* continue, and it does so, says Heraclitus in metaphorical terms which are logically no advance on the reproductive imagery or the automatic assumption of his predecessors, because "war is common and strife is justice," because "war is the father and king of all," because "it rests by changing." It continues because things are an everliving fire and fire is creative, as in animal reproduction, and self-moving. But this is not to say, as will be seen later, that everything is flowing in the sense that it is changing at every instant. The answer to the second question, why there is such emphasis on *metron*, is not dissimilar: the unity which subsists in opposites depends not only on their alteration one into the other, but also on the quantitative regularity of this alteration. If the total amount of old age in the world begins greatly to exceed the total amount of youth, then the succession will eventually fail. If the total amount of heat and dryness in summer begins to outweigh the total amount of cold and wetness in winter, or vice versa, first the crops will fail and eventually the earth will be overcome by one of those catastrophes of fire or flood which are so often hinted at in Greek literature, and which belong perhaps to one of the earliest stages of primitive mythology, but which for Heraclitus at any rate were not more than theoretical contingencies. If the balance of processes is destroyed then the underlying unity of the cosmos fails, and this, for Heraclitus, was unthinkable. And this balance depends on *metron*.

This idea of *metron* was taken by Heraclitus primarily from the sphere of ethics and applied by him to the workings of nature in general, but most clearly to natural changes on the large scale; though we have seen that it underlies reciprocal change on any scale. For although Heraclitus had broken away from the old cosmogonical tradition, and although judging from the complaints of Theophrastus he did not devote much time to specific natural questions like What is a rainbow or What causes the flooding of the Nile, yet he could not and did not neglect to give some explanation of cosmology, the working of the world which men see around them. Indeed, if as he maintained there is a single Logos or formula of things, this Logos must explain meteorological and cosmological changes as well as the reciprocity between opposites in categories such as life–death and war–peace. Strangely enough, however, we do not find that Heraclitus used his discovery of the unity of opposites, in any obvious way at any rate, to explain cosmological phenomena. The cosmos (in the sense of an ordered whole) is a fire which turns into sea and into earth and then back again. This is a reciprocal and not a cyclical movement, but it is a reciprocal movement between three and not two members—that is, not between opposites—so that the simple logical unity that connects for example night and day does not apply here. Formally the only common factor between Heraclitus' account of meteorological-cosmological change and his account of change between opposites, which is implied to be the type into which all other kinds of change can be analyzed, is the idea of *metron*. In B31 we learn that the turnings of fire (*pyros tropai*) are as follows: first into sea, and half sea is turning to earth, half of it being replenished from fire; the portion that became earth eventually dissolves again and is measured into the same amount of sea as existed before it became earth. What is described here in these complicated and schematic terms is not, as Theophrastus thought, a world-forming or cosmogonical process; it is the constant weather-process by which the sun feeds on water evaporated from the sea, and precipitates it again as rain; part of the sea is drying up (for example Heraclitus' own Cayster river, which was silting badly; the fossils in Sicily, Paros, Malta, cited by Xenophanes; the legendary emergence from the sea of Rhodes and Delos), while an equal part of it is expanding (for example the submergence of the Strait of Messina, and the rise of new springs and rivers). As long as these large-scale natural processes remain in balance the unity of the cosmos is preserved, and the total amount of fire in all its forms remains the same. When he tried to explain how or why the *metra* were preserved, Heraclitus resorted to metaphor, as he did in the case of the source and motive of change. If the sun oversteps his measures[3] the Erinyes, traditional guardians of natural laws, will find him out. This resort to mythology and metaphor occurs at a certain point in all the Pre-Socratic accounts (and indeed in all philosophies) and is exemplified by the "penalty and retribution" of Anaximander and the "strong Necessity" with her fetters of Parmenides. It occurs as an attempt to *motivate* the structure or *metron* which has been observed in or deduced from phenomena.

In this large-scale sphere of meterological-cosmological change the process is clearly spasmodic; thus all sea is not always being evaporated, and parts of the earth may remain static for a time. If we look lower in the scale we see that there too, in Heraclitus' formulation, no necessity exists for a *constant* change in everything. Man, it is true, is in unceasing change: he is constantly growing older and as he does so the structure of his body alters. Thus a fragment which is ascribed to Epicharmus describes how a debtor excuses himself by saying that he is not the

---

[3] This probably means—for *hyperbēsetai* should be taken literally at this stage of the language—if he trespasses too far north or south on the path of the ecliptic, and so upsets the seasons: *metra* is still quantitative as always in Heraclitus, though in this case it would have the sense of "boundaries." It may just mean quantitative measures of fire, i.e. the sun must not become too large and hot.

same man as he who incurred the debt, his Logos has changed.[4] But when one descends still lower in the scale, to less animate objects like rocks and tables, it becomes exceedingly doubtful once more whether Heraclitus believed in *constant* change for everything. This would be hardly worth stressing were it not that one school of thought, of which Heidel was representative,[5] actually proposed a kind of molecular theory according to which this table, for example, is constantly changing by the *invisible* addition and subtraction of portions of fire, water, or earth, on a par somehow with the cosmological process. This unwarranted interpretation seems to stem from Aristotle, who in one passage (*Physics* IX.3.253b9) says, clearly of Heraclitus and his supporters: "And some say that all existing things without exception are in constant movement, but that *this escapes our perception*." It is most unlikely that Heraclitus ever held such a view. Contrary to what is often written of him, he believed strongly in the value of sense-perception providing that it is interpreted intelligently, with *phronēsis*, by souls which understand its language.[6] His criticism of men is based on the fact that the truth is there to be observed, it is common to all, but they cannot see it: apprehension of the Logos is no mystical process but the result of using eyes, ears, and common sense. Our observation tells us that this table is *not* changing at every instant, even if our experience concedes that it will eventually change. This eventuality is all that is necessary: just as the movement between war and peace, for example, was inevitable but nevertheless, in Heraclitus' day, spasmodic and not continuous, so objects may be held temporarily in stability by virtue of a *palintonos harmoniē;* the tendencies to turn into earth or fire may be equally balanced. Provided the total *metra* in the world are preserved, a large number of things may and do exist for a time without changing; but eventually the tension in one direction or the other will dominate and the material composing this table will return, perhaps deviously, to the fire from which it was originally extinguished.

The theory that all things are *constantly* changing was perhaps first explicitly formulated not by Heraclitus but as a manifest absurdity by

[4] The same idea, applied again to the human body, recurs in Plato: it is not, I suspect, a specifically Heraclitean invention, but a popular and traditional witticism or figure of speech.

[5] In his article "Qualitative Change in Pre-Socratic Philosophy," *AGP*, 19 (1905–06), 350 ff. [These pages not included in the excerpt from Heidel's article reprinted above, pp. 86–95.—Ed.]

[6] Cf. B55, 107, 101a; 17, 72.

the Eleatic Melissus.[7] He was trying to defend the paradoxical Eleatic idea of reality by attacking the validity of the senses, and wrote as follows: ". . . But to us the hot seems to become cold and the cold hot, and the hard soft and the soft hard . . . iron in spite of its hardness seems to be rubbed down by the finger through contact, and so also gold and stone and whatever else seems to be hard and fast; and earth and stone seem to come to be out of water; so the consequence is that we neither actually *see*, nor recognize things which *are*" (B8). Some of the oppositions here may be taken from Heraclitus, but I believe that the examples of iron, stone, and gold are an extension by Melissus himself, who had far more motive (though in a negative direction) for emphasizing the constancy and universality of natural change than Heraclitus ever had.

For Heraclitus then what we see in individual things is either the prospect or the actuality of quantitatively regulated change. What we see in the sum of things, changing and temporarily stable, is the single Logos which is a broader aspect of the *metron* which regulates all change. The concept of measure equals in importance, and surpasses in the consistency of its application, that other basic concept of War and Strife, of inevitable alteration. Both concepts are needed to make plausible the kind of unity which Heraclitus saw in opposites; both are needed to mediate between this unity and the other unity of Fire. In the river-fragments the concept of *metron* in change is the one which is stressed: to ignore this concept and build upon these fragments an anachronistic elaboration of the War–Strife concept, like the Platonic *panta rhei* interpretation, is to destroy that unified picture of the outside world which Heraclitus tried to present to obtuse mankind.

[7] This was suggested by E. Weerts, "Plato und der Heraklitismus," *Philologus*, Supplb. 23, 1 (1931).

8

FLUX AND *LOGOS* IN HERACLITUS

W. K. C. Guthrie

"War is father of all and king of all, and some he reveals as gods, others as men, some he makes slaves, others free" (B53). By calling War "father and king of all," Heraclitus deliberately recalls Homer's titles for Zeus, and so suggests that War, not Zeus, is the supreme god. It has been thought that here he has only in mind the limited, literal sense of war, though of course using it as an illustration of the universal conflict which for him constitutes the universe. This fits well with the statement that it makes some slaves and others free, but leaves the mention of gods and men more difficult to explain.[1] Whatever the reason, the statement does look as if it were confined to gods and men and their affairs. Apart from the second half of the fragment, the reminiscence of the Homeric Zeus, "Father of gods and men," suggests that the word "all" is masculine. But he may yet be thinking of war in its wider aspect, as creating opposition and tension between opposed classes everywhere, of which gods–men, slaves–free are only examples. In any case the general principle is stated in B80: "One must know that war is common, and justice strife, and that all things come about by way of strife and necessity." With this must be taken a passage from Aristotle (*Eudem. Eth.* 1235a25, DK 22A22) which runs: "And Heraclitus rebukes the poet who wrote 'Would that strife might perish from

From W. K. C. Guthrie, *A History of Greek Philosophy*, Vol. I: *The Earlier Presocratics and the Pythagoreans* (Cambridge: Cambridge University Press, 1962), pp. 446–53, 459–69. Selection reprinted here with the permission of Cambridge University Press and of the author. Vol. I of Guthrie's *History* hereafter referred to as *HGP*, I.

[1] See G. S. Kirk, *Heraclitus: The Cosmic Fragments* (Cambridge, 1954), pp. 246 ff. To read into this brief phrase a reference to the apotheosis of those killed in battle, even if Heraclitus believed in this, seems a little far-fetched.

among gods and men';[2] for there would be no melody without high and low, nor living creatures without male and female, which are opposites." Simplicius adds the comment, after the line from Homer, "For he [Heraclitus] says that everything would disappear." [3]

By saying that war is "common" Heraclitus immediately links it (more probably actually identifies it) with the Logos.[4] At the same time he gets in another covert attack on Homer, who had also called war "common." Homer's line[5] says that war strikes down all alike: "he that hath slain shall himself be slain." It is no respecter of persons, but deals its blows impartially all round. "Common" has a deeper meaning for Heraclitus, and by alluding to Homer's use of the same word he hints that its profundity had escaped him. War is common because the Logos that is the law of all becoming (B1) is a law of strife, of simultaneous opposite tensions. "That strife is universal follows from the assumption that whatever exists is in change with the added assumption that all change is strife." [6] In saying that justice (or right) is strife he probably shows himself aware also of Anaximander's teaching,[7] which branded the warfare of the opposites as a series of acts of injustice. On the contrary, retorts Heraclitus, it is the highest justice. Once again an erring predecessor is tacitly corrected.[8]

The kernel of Heraclitus' quarrel with other thinkers seems to lie in his revolt against their ideal of a peaceful and harmonious world. This was in particular the ideal of Pythagoras, of whom, it is relevant to remember, he speaks more than once with particular harshness.[9] For Pythagoras the best state was one in which opposite qualities were so

[2] Hom. *Il.* 18.107.

[3] For later versions of Heraclitus' rebuke, which omit the reference to high and low, male and female, see Kirk, p. 243.

[4] See *HGP*, I, p. 425.

[5] *Il.* 18.309 ξυνὸς 'Ενυάλιος καί τε κτανέοντα κατέκτα. The phrase was copied by Archilochus (Fr. 38 Diehl). Possibly this is one reason for the censure of Homer and Archilochus together in B42—that they could utter such words and yet remain ignorant of the true Logos.

[6] Gregory Vlastos, "On Heraclitus," *AJP*, 76 (1955), 357 [repr. in Furley and Allen, I, pp. 413–29].

[7] See *HGP*, I, pp. 76 ff.

[8] This possibility is strengthened by the addition of the words καὶ τὸ χρεών at the end of the fr., if (a) this is the correct text and (b) the words κατὰ τὸ χρεών in Anaximander's B1 genuinely belong to him.

[9] See *HGP*, I, p. 417.

blended by a law of proportion that their oppositions were neutralized and they produced, for example, euphony in music, health in the body, *kosmos*—order and beauty—in the universe as a whole. These states of peace between elements which had been at war, brought about by the imposition of limit (*peras*) on a chaotic *apeiron*, he and his followers called *good*. Their opposites—discord, disease, strife—were *evil*.[10].

Heraclitus rejects all these value judgments, which seem to him pusillanimous. "Rest and quiet? Leave them to the dead, where they belong" (Aët. 1.23.7, DK 22A6). Health, peace, rest, he says, are in themselves no more good than their opposites, and their goodness only appears when set against these opposites. The co-existence of what a Pythagorean would regard as good and bad states is necessary and right. "To God all things are good and fair and just" (B102). In fact it is all a matter of point of view, and good and bad are entirely relative notions. Sea-water is pure and good to fishes, foul and poisonous to men.

The Pythagoreans spoke as if the opposites exhibited no reluctance to be blended in a *harmonia*, but found rest[11] and, as one might say, contentment when they were contributing to a perfect *krasis*, as in a musical scale or a healthy body. But that is nonsense, says Heraclitus. By the very fact of being opposites, they must be pulling opposite ways, resisting all the time. Heat and cold, wet and dry, do not co-operate, they are mutually destructive. From their constant strife there may result a temporary *harmonia*, but equally well a disharmony like disease. The causal factors are the same in both cases. If there is a perfectly proportioned blend, it is only because the warring opposites have reached a state of equal tension or balance of power in which neither has the upper hand. Rest, cessation of effort, would mean the

[10] Some scholars will say that we know too little of the opinions of Pythagoras to make statements like this. That the ideas are Pythagorean they might admit, but would argue that we cannot know whether they were current before the late fifth century. However, unless we are going to deny any original ideas to Pythagoras himself (in which case it is a little difficult to account for his reputation), his teaching must have been on these lines. The full justification for attributing them to Pythagoras (or at least an early generation of his followers, contemporary with Heraclitus) is given in *HGP*, I, ch. 4. For a contrary view to that here given, see Kirk, pp. 218 f.

[11] In the Pythagorean table of opposites, "resting" (ἠρεμοῦν) is to be found on the "good" side, along with πέρας, φῶς, ἀγαθόν, etc.

opposite of *kosmos*, for it would result in the falling apart of the opposites, whose union in an "adjustment of opposite tensions"— locked, as it were, in an internecine struggle—is what keeps in being the world as we know it.

The doctrine that "harmony is of opposites" has already led to this conclusion, which Heraclitus drives home once again with a familiar illustration. A well-known drink or posset in Greece from Homer's time onwards was the *kykeōn*, made by taking a cup of wine and stirring into it barley and grated cheese. These of course would not dissolve, so that the mixture had to be kept in motion until the moment it was drunk. "The *kykeōn*," he said, "falls apart if it is not being stirred." [12] Kirk's comment on this fragment cannot be improved on: "The fragment is of greater importance than at first appears: it is the only direct quotation that asserts, even though only in an image" (but this was Heraclitus' declared way of announcing the most fundamental truths[13]), "the consequences of an interruption in the reciprocity of opposites." The illustration itself was not so entirely homely as it might seem, for in addition to other uses the *kykeōn* was drunk at the Eleusinian mysteries in commemoration of the myth of Demeter, who would accept no other refreshment during her sad search for the lost Persephone. This would give it a special significance in Heraclitus' eyes.[14]

One of his most famous sayings is: "You cannot step into the same river twice." [15] Plutarch (*Qu. Nat.* 912c) adds the explanation, which may have been given by Heraclitus himself: "for fresh waters are flowing on." Concerning the meaning of this parable our authorities are pretty well agreed. Plato (*Crat.* 402a) says that it is an allegory of "existing things" in general, and its lesson is "that everything moves on and nothing is at rest." That this was Heraclitus' belief he has already stated (401d), and in the *Theaetetus* (160d) he repeats that in the view

[12] B125. On the text see Kirk, pp. 255 f.

[13] See *HGP*, I, p. 414.

[14] Hom. *Hymn Dem.* 210; Clem. Al. *Protr.* 1.16 St.; M. Nilsson, *Geschichte der griechischen Religion*, vol. 1, 2d ed. (Munich, 1955), 622 f. For Heraclitus and the mysteries, see *HGP*, I, p. 425 n. 1.

[15] See *HGP*, I, Appendix, pp. 488 ff. The statement of the flux-doctrine which has become almost canonical in later ages, πάντα ῥεῖ, occurs in the ancient authorities only in Simplicius (*Phys.* 1313.11), and is unlikely to have been a saying of Heraclitus.

of "Homer and Heraclitus and all that crowd" all things move "like streams."[16] Plato, says Aristotle, while still a young man, became familiar with Cratylus and "the Heraclitean theories that all sensible things are for ever flowing";[17] and reflection on these theories led him to the conclusion that knowledge of the sensible world was impossible. Since he could not tolerate abandoning the possibility of knowledge altogether, this gave rise to the characteristically Platonic doctrine of transcendent Forms.

This Heraclitean doctrine of the flux of sensible things is mentioned more than once by Aristotle (e.g. *Metaph.* 1063a22, 35), but some of

[16] Plato was fond of calling Homer the ancestor of certain philosophical theories because he spoke of Oceanus and Tethys, gods of water, as parents of the gods and of all creatures (*Il.* 14.201, 246; see *Crat.* 402b, *Theaet.* loc. cit., 152e, 180c–d). Aristotle followed him (*Metaph.* I. 983b30), and neither of them can be supposed to have been very serious in this. Plato, as Ross remarks on the *Metaphysics* passage, "jestingly suggests that Heraclitus and his predecessors derived their philosophy from Homer, Hesiod, and Orpheus," and he adds that Aristotle himself admits that the suggestion has no great historical value. (This is an understatement. See also *HGP*, I, p. 56 n. 1.) The reference to Ὅμηρον καὶ Ἡράκλειτον καὶ πᾶν τὸ τοιοῦτον φῦλον suggests a similar levity, but the nature and frequency of Plato's allusions to the "flux" theory of Heraclitus and his followers are a guarantee of his sincerity. Admittedly he liked to make game of them for it (e.g. *Theaet.* 179e κατὰ τὰ συγγράμματα φέρονται; at 181a he calls the philosophers themselves οἱ ῥέοντες), but there was a basis for his jibes. Moreover we have the testimony of Aristotle that he took it seriously, and indeed that it was a formative influence on his own philosophy.

[17] *Metaph.* 987a32. Cratylus, Aristotle tells us (ibid., 1010a13), carried the views of Heraclitus to their logical extreme by correcting the sentence "You can't step into the same river twice" to "You can't step into it once." Between the instant when your foot touched the surface and the instant when it reached the bottom the river at that point had already changed. Cratylus was a Heraclitean heretic (one of τῶν φασκόντων ἡρακλειτίζειν, as Aristotle calls them) who was so carried away by the idea of uninterrupted change that in the end he thought it best not to speak (presumably because to make a statement about anything would give a spurious impression of permanence: by the time the statement was out of his mouth its object would have changed), but only waggled his finger! Although the continuous motion and change of sensible things *was* a dogma of Heraclitus, it was not the whole story. On Cratylus and the reliability of Aristotle's account, see D. J. Allan, "The Problem of Cratylus," *AJP*, 75 (1954), 271–84.

his remarks are vitiated by his mistaken assumption that Heraclitus' system was essentially Milesian, as he says in *De Caelo* 298b29:

> They [*scil.* the earliest natural philosophers] held that in general everything is in a state of becoming and flux, and that nothing is stable, but that there is one substance which persists, out of which all these things have evolved by natural transformations. This seems to have been the meaning both of Heraclitus of Ephesus and of many others.

(How Heraclitus would have wept to find himself included with the *polloi* after all that he had done to cut himself off!) In the *Physics* he says (253b9): "Some assert, not that some things are in motion and others not, but that *everything* is *always* moving, though this escapes our perception." Here we have the doctrine in its more strict and particular form, which we must refer (with Simplicius) to the Heracliteans, and, as Kirk says[18] to Heraclitus in particular. Trying to explain their meaning, Aristotle says it is like the argument (which he thinks fallacious) about a stone being worn away by drops of water or split by the roots of a plant. According to this argument, if we notice that over a period of months the drops have made a visible dint in the stone, it follows that each drop must have removed an infinitesimal fraction too small to be seen. It is plain from Aristotle's language, including his complaint that the thinkers in question "do not define the kind of motion they are talking about," that this illustration was not used by Heraclitus. Nevertheless it seems to represent just what he had in mind, although strictly speaking one must imagine a continuous stream of water flowing over the rock rather than separate drops. That the rock is changing every instant we cannot see with our eyes, but it is what their evidence suggests if we apply "minds that understand the language." To supplement their evidence we need that understanding (*noos*) which few men have but which is essential if the senses are not to lead us astray, for by itself the eyesight is deceptive (B107, 46, 40; and cf. B104). The continuous imperceptible change is a natural inference from the observation. Heraclitus did not use this simile, but he said the same thing by means of the image of the bow and lyre. The strung bow appears static to the eyes, but if the string should snap, that would be only the consequence of what the man whose mind was not "barbarian" would have known all the time: that its true condition had been a *continuous* putting forth of effort in contrary

[18] *Heraclitus*, p. 376.

directions, corresponding to the abrasive action of the water and the resistance offered by the hardness of the stone.[19]

The doctrine of the continuous change of physical things is closely linked with that of the identity of opposites, as it appears in particular

[19] I am truly sorry to adopt an interpretation which in the eyes of Kirk is "very far indeed from the truth" and "entirely contrary to what Heraclitus tells us in the fragments" (pp. 376 f.). "Our observation," he says, "tells us that this table or that rock are *not* changing at every instant; there is nothing in nature to persuade us that they are so changing; the very idea would be repulsive to Heraclitus." The fragments that he cites in support of this are B107, 55, 101a, and for comparison B17 and 72. B55 must, however, be read in the light of the important proviso in B107, and B17 and 72 seem to support the interpretation given here. The whole misunderstanding, Kirk thinks, arose from Plato's assertion that according to the Heracliteans "everything is undergoing every motion all the time," which he considers a disastrous misinterpretation.

To speak of "every motion" is no doubt to import distinctions that Heraclitus had not consciously made: Thinkers like him, says Aristotle, did not define the kind of motion they had in mind. But with that trivial qualification I believe that Plato was right. This would seem the place to say also that I believe not only that the flux doctrine was true for Heraclitus, but also that it occupied a central position in his thought: In short, that Plato, as knowledge of him would lead one to expect, had a pretty good insight into Heraclitus' mind, and did not go seriously astray even in the matter of emphasis.

I know that this will seem reactionary to more than one scholar for whom I have great respect. Bruno Snell for instance writes ("Die Sprache Heraklits," *Hermes*, 61 [1926], 376 [repr. in his *Gesammelte Schriften* (Göttingen, 1966)]; I translate): "Only now will it become quite clear how Heraclitus is misinterpreted when he is made the teacher of πάντα ῥεῖ." I can only say that it has not become clear to me. Of course πάντα ῥεῖ is not the whole of his message, but, as I hope to show, the other side of the picture is the confining of change within measures, not (at least in the sensible world) the exaltation of stability (for there is none) at the expense of change. "The dominating idea in Heraclitus is rest in change, not change in apparent stability." So Kirk, paraphrasing Reinhardt's view. But what Heraclitus says in B84a is that for this world change *is* rest, which, as I hope I have shown already, is something different.

To put it briefly, I find that from Plato onward all our authorities attribute to Heraclitus the doctrine ὡς ἁπάντων τῶν αἰσθητῶν ἀεὶ ῥεόντων. Those who take the *prima facie* improbable line that Plato grossly misunderstood him and every subsequent Greek interpreter meekly followed his lead, in spite of possessing either Heraclitus' book or at least a much more comprehensive collection of his sayings than we have, may be expected to produce incontrovertible evidence from the fragments that their conclusion is inescapa-

from B88. This is because the change is *cyclic*, from *a* to *b* and back to *a* again, and to Heraclitus' mind what could apparently change into something else and then back into what it was before must have been in a way the same all the time. He is drawing fresh conclusions from a common Greek conception on which the Milesians had already relied, the circularity of time, based on observation of the recurrence of seasonal changes year after year. Cold prevails over hot as summer gives way before winter, but nothing is more certain than that the hot will have its turn again in the following year. Anaximander spoke of the warfare and mutual "injustice" of the opposites, followed inevitably by reparation, and in Heraclitus it takes a new turn.[20] . . .

We must now grapple with Heraclitus' description of the process of change. To Theophrastus it was parallel to the Milesian scheme. He took the words "all things are an exchange for fire" to mean that fire was the *archē* or element (*stoicheion;* I am following the version of Diogenes Laertius IX.8), out of which other substances were formed, as in Anaximenes, by condensation and rarefaction. Since he immediately adds: "But he explains nothing clearly," we may feel justified in departing from this interpretation if we will. Diogenes Laertius does however reproduce some of Heraclitus' terminology, and we learn from him that the "way up and down," which Hippolytus tells us was "one and the same," was the name given by Heraclitus to the process of change.[21] Putting together these two references to the way up and down, we find them echoed by Plato in the words: "Everything is always flowing upwards and downwards." [22] In the light of other fragments

---

ble. But in fact the extant fragments offer no challenge to the universal ancient view.

[20] A reference, devoid of context, to "the seasons which produce all things" may be an indication that Heraclitus explicitly acknowledged the source of the general conception (see B100, discussed in detail by Kirk, pp. 294 ff.).

[21] καλεῖσθαι . . . τὴν μεταβολὴν ὁδὸν ἄνω κάτω. I see no good evidence to make us reject this statement as Kirk would have us do, though he says himself (p. 328) that "the specific physical application of these terms would not, it is true, be unsuitable."

[22] *Philebus* 43a (not assigned by name to Heraclitus, but impossible to attribute to anyone but him or his true followers). Kirk in his discussion of this sentence says that in its context it refers to changes of fortune, but this is not correct: The reference is purely general. I have given reasons already for trusting what Plato says about Heraclitus. The strongest is that from

(especially B51), and Plato's further testimony about the "stricter Muses" in *Soph*. 242d ("in drawing apart it is drawing together"), this must mean just what it says—not simply, as the prosaic and rational minds of some later Greeks thought, that some things are on the upward path while some are on the downward, but that *all* things are moving both upwards *and* downwards. It is not surprising that Aristotle accused Heraclitus of breaking the law of contradiction; or rather (since to his logical mind such a thing seemed impossible) said that some people supposed him to be doing so. "It is impossible for anyone to suppose that the same thing is and is not, as some people think Heraclitus said" (*Metaph*. 1005b23).[23]

The way up and down is that of the transformation of the various forms of matter, and presumably things made by their mixture, into one another. Heraclitus did not of course use the word "element" (*stoicheion*) of fire, but the way in which he expressed its primacy is also quoted by Diogenes, and more fully by Plutarch (B90): "All things are an exchange for fire and fire for all things, as goods for gold and gold for goods."[24] Once more he can only express himself by a simile, and hence to some degree imprecisely, but if he had wanted to describe fire as simply the basic substance which changed its shape or appearance in becoming earth or water he would have used a different comparison. (He could easily have said, for example, "as gold is fashioned into coins, necklaces, or cups.") In mercantile transactions the essential thing is parity of value: a certain quantity of gold will buy a certain quantity of goods. This is no doubt the primary thought, though he probably had in mind, as Kirk says, the single homogeneous character of gold (fire) as opposed to the manifold kinds of goods (physical things) for which it can be exchanged.

We need not expect Heraclitus' thought to be by our standards completely logical or self-consistent. From what we know of him that would be surprising. He seems to be saying that although in the cosmos as he sees it fire has a definite primacy, grounded in its divinity and perpetual life, yet it is not a permanent substratum which, in Aristotle's

---

Aristotle onward most writers do their best to make him into a rather conventional thinker, whereas Plato's remarks, casual though they are, give the clue to his originality; and that he was original stares us in the face from every fragment.

[23] Aristotle perhaps had in mind B49a: "We step and do not step into the same rivers, we are and are not," on which see *HGP*, I, Appendix, p. 490.

[24] On this fragment see Kirk, pp. 345-48.

later formulation, remains essentially the same though changing in its modifications. Such a permanent *physis* would contradict the law of flux, and introduce rest and stability into a world from which he thought they should be banished. There was law in the universe, but it was not a law of permanence, only a law of change, or, in something more like his own picturesque phraseology, the law of the jungle, since everything comes into being "by way of strife" and War is lord of all.

Fire was particularly well suited to embody this law. A flame may appear steady and unchanging, as in a candle, but it is constantly renewing itself by the destruction of the fuel, and giving off heat and sometimes smoke. The river-statement expresses the same truth, of apparent, or formal, stability coupled with continuous change of material.[25]

Heraclitus also expresses his conception of change by saying that each form of matter makes its appearance by the death of another (a natural result of the rule of War). This statement appears in the various forms of the suspected B76, and is repeated in B36, with "souls" substituted for the expected "fire." None of the Milesians spoke in this way of the death of the elements, although they contrasted the eternal nature of the *archē* with the arising and passing away of the transitory things which were formed by its modifications. Heraclitus was clearly groping after something different, though to say "groping" is to betray the modern demand for rational and intellectual justification. To himself he was one who had discovered the divinely-appointed truth, and was therefore divinely charged to proclaim it. He had not Aristotle's severe eye for the law of contradiction, and uttered his paradoxes with relish.

We know that fire was living and rational, and that there is consequently a parallel throughout the cycle of change between physical and psychical elements. When warm and dry the soul is at its most intelligent and vital. The encroachment of moisture brings a dimming of the flame of life, and these two threads—of the physical elements and of life—are twisted together in B36. Aristotle hits the mark (save

---

[25] It is interesting that Aristotle, in what sounds like a reminiscence of Heraclitus, links the flow of water and of flame together in a comparison expressive of continuous change within the limits of the same form and quantity: ἀεὶ γὰρ ἄλλο καὶ ἄλλο γίγνεται τούτων ἕκαστον [scil. air, fresh water, and fire], τὸ δ' εἶδος τοῦ πλήθους ἑκάστου τούτων μένει, καθάπερ τὸ τῶν ῥεόντων ὑδάτων καὶ τὸ τῆς φλογὸς ῥεῦμα, *Meteor.* 357b30 (Kirk, pp. 379 f.).

in his misconception of the *archē*) when he says that for Heraclitus the *archē* was not only fire, but *psychē*, and that he described *psychē* as an exhalation (*De An.* 405a25). This last word is prominent in later accounts of Heraclitus' physical theory, e.g. B12: "Souls are exhaled from moist things." [26] According to Diogenes, Heraclitus "reduces nearly everything to exhalation from the sea," and this, he says, is the upward way.[27] The sun, which Heraclitus believed to be quenched every night and renewed the next day (B6), and also the stars, consist of "bright exhalations" from the sea collected in certain "bowls" or cavities in the sky, where they turn to flame (D.L. IX.9). If we may trust this, it gives us some idea of the process involved in the "death and birth" of the elements mentioned in B36, which seems to be based (as in Anaximenes, and perhaps not independently) on a theoretical extension of the observed process of evaporation. On the one hand moist vapors are drawn up from the sea by the heat at the world's circumference, become dry and bright themselves and renew the heavenly bodies. On the other hand soul too arises out of moisture, and is fed in the same way by exhalations from the watery element.

B36 showed the double nature of the way, up as well as down. This entails that the death of anything, though it implies complete loss of its character as that thing—fire dies[28] and becomes mist or vapor, soul dies and turns into water—is nevertheless not complete extinction. Nothing is permanent, not even death. Everything must continue to move on the upward and downward path. Philo rightly comments on

[26] Whether Heraclitus used the word ἀναθυμίασις is doubtful. See Burnet, *EGP*, p. 151 n. 2 and Kirk, p. 274. Kirk thinks ἀτμίς a more probable word for him.

[27] Diogenes continues with a reference to the theory (expounded by Aristotle) of two kinds of exhalation, a bright one from the sea and a dark one from the land. Kirk (pp. 272 f.) suggests that Heraclitus' theory was of a single exhalation (from the sea), and that Aristotle was responsible for its expansion into a two-exhalation scheme. K. Deichgräber ("Bemerkungen zu Diogenes' Bericht über Herakleitos," *Philologus*, 93 [1938–39], 24 f.) supports the two exhalations for Heraclitus.

[28] Vlastos (p. 366) thinks that Heraclitus' choice of the word ἀείζωον (ever-living) rather than ἀθάνατον (deathless) in B30 was motivated by his belief that "the condition of life ever-lasting is not deathlessness but life endlessly renewed by death in a process where youth and age are 'the same' (B88)." If so, this illustrates once more the extreme difficulty of putting into words his novel conception of change.

B36: "What he calls death is not utter annihilation, but change into another element." [29]

One can understand a circular path of becoming on which fire changes to steam, then to water, then to earth, then back to fire through the same stages reversed; and soul pursues a parallel series of transformations manifested in sleep and death. Anaximenes took a not dissimilar view. But Heraclitus is obviously struggling to say something more, something harder. He ignores the law of contradiction, he insists that opposites are identical. The way up and down is one and the same, everything flows upwards and downwards *simultaneously*. This is why (B32) "the one wise thing," i.e. the Logos which is also fire, "is both unwilling and willing to be called Zen," a name which means both Zeus, the supreme god, and life; for life and death, Hades god of the dead and Dionysus god of life, are one and the same (B15). Another important statement of the law of change, a part of B31, may help here: "The turnings of fire are: first sea, and of the sea half is earth and half burning." [30] Sea is never *just* water, indeed there is no such *thing* as water. That would introduce rest (*stasis*) and contradict the law of flux and struggle. Water is only a momentary stage on the upward and downward path, and, by saying that sea is half earth and half a burning substance, Heraclitus seems to be telling us, in his Delphic manner,

[29] See *HGP*, I, p. 480 n. 1.

[30] Half earth and half πρηστήρ. This word has aroused much discussion. Burnet calls it "a hurricane accompanied by a fiery water-spout" (*EGP*, p. 149), referring to Hdt. VII.42 and Sen. *Q.N.* II.56 *igneus turbo*. Kirk considers this "absurd," and doubts whether Heraclitus would have chosen an uncommon phenomenon as a regular means of change between water and fire, or even a symbol of such change. He thinks it simply a synonym for fire, like κεραυνός in B64. On the other hand Heraclitus seems to have been interested in πρηστῆρες, and thought them worthy of an explanation ("ignition and quenching of clouds") alongside such common phenomena as thunder and lightning (Aëtius III.3.9, DK A14). Moreover, a man is more likely to be impressed by a rare phenomenon, and regard it as significant, if it happens to support his own views; and, as Diels saw, a waterspout accompanied by lightning ("Windhose mit elektrischer Entladung," and so LSJ) was ideal as ocular demonstration of the link binding fire and water in the process of reciprocal change (Hermann Diels, *Herakleitos von Ephesos*, 2d ed. [Berlin, 1909], p. 24; cf. Karl Reinhardt, *Parmenides und die Geschichte der griechischen Philosophie* [Bonn, 1916], p. 178 n. 1). In any case Heraclitus means that half the sea is reverting to fire.

that it is being transformed upward and downward at the same time, "drawn apart and drawn together."

In the light of this, B62 may be assumed to refer to this continuous transformation, a transformation of the physical bodies and of soul in one and the same process. It is quoted in various forms, but, assuming with Kirk[31] that Hippolytus' version is the most accurate, it runs: "Immortal mortals, mortal immortals (or 'Immortals are mortal, mortals are immortal'), living the death of the others and dying their life." It reads like an echo of B36. It has, however, been interpreted, both in ancient and in modern times, as implying the whole Pythagorean and Orphic doctrine of the soul as an immortal being for which this earthly life is a kind of death and the body a tomb, because it only enjoys full life when discarnate. Men may be described as mortal immortals, gods or *daimons* temporarily incarcerated in mortal bodies. . . .

We have not yet done justice to the presence of "measures" in the account of change. The reference in B30 to the measures in which the cosmic fire is kindled and extinguished is amplified by the second quotation made by Clement of Alexandria in the passage cited as B31. (Clement interprets both as descriptions of the formation of a cosmos in time and its subsequent destruction by fire; and their inappropriateness to such a conception inclines one still further to reject it.) "Earth is liquefied as sea, and is measured in the same proportion"—the word is *logos*—"as existed before it became earth." [32] The last sentence has been well explained by Vlastos. Any part of earth which becomes water retains throughout all its changes a pre-existing *logos*, it is measured in that *logos*. In other words, though it changes in appearance it is equivalent throughout in quantity or value, judged by an independent standard, which is that of fire; for all things are an exchange for fire, as goods for gold (B90). This "identifies fire as the thing that remains constant in all transformations and implies that *its* measure is the same or common measure in all things. . . . Each member of the whole series represents the same amount of fire, which is the common thing—*to xynon*—in all the different things that compose the series. . . . The

[31] Page 144.

[32] Accepting DK's text, with ⟨γῆ⟩ inserted before θάλασσα, on which see Kirk, pp. 331 f., Vlastos, p. 359 n. 46. Vlastos adopts a suggestion of Cherniss that the last three words of the fragment are a gloss (ibid., p. 360 n. 47).

invariance of *its* measures is what accounts for the observance of the
metron in all things, and fire is therefore that which 'governs' or 'steers
all things' (B41 and 64)." [33]

The idea of measure is introduced also in B94: "The sun will not
overstep his measures; otherwise the Erinyes, servants of Justice, will
find him out." "Measures" should be taken here in a general sense[34]
so that to overstep them means to deviate in any way from the normal
course. The sun is set to follow a measured path in the sky in a measured
time, giving out a measured amount of heat. If he were to depart from
it in any way (as for example in the myth of Phaethon, when he came too
near the earth), the cosmic balance would be upset, and this is never
allowed to happen.[35]

The emphasis laid in this account on Heraclitus' doctrine of flux
and contrary motions ("strife" or "warfare") has been disallowed by
Kirk, who writes[36] that "Heraclitus did *not* deny stability to the natural
world; on the contrary, his main purpose seems to be to assert such a
stability, which according to him underlies all change, and most notably
change between opposites. . . . Reinhardt is right in emphasizing
that there never was anything approaching a *Flusslehre* in Heraclitus
himself." [37] That the change was always contained within limits, the
battle swaying to and fro so that the global balance is always preserved,
is of course essential to the maintenance of the cosmos. Nevertheless
his main purpose seems to be to show that all stability in the world is
merely apparent, since if observed with understanding as well as with
the senses it proves to be only a resultant of unremitting strife and
tension. This is the tenor both of the fragments and of other testimony,
in particular that of Plato, whose remarks consort well with the fragments themselves. Perhaps the strongest evidence of all is the primacy
given to fire. Since it becomes all things, one might ask why one of the

[33] Vlastos, pp. 360–61.

[34] Cf. Kirk, p. 285.

[35] For the difficult B120, which Kirk connects with the measures of the sun,
see his pp. 289–93.

[36] Page 370.

[37] See Karl Reinhardt, "Heraklits' Lehre vom Feuer," *Hermes*, 77 (1942),
18 (repr. in Reinhardt's *Vermächtnis der Antike* [Göttingen, 1960], pp. 41–71).
The view expressed by Reinhardt was already contested by Nestle in Eduard
Zeller, *Die Philosophie der Griechen*, I. Teil, I. Hälfte, 7th ed., ed. Wilhelm
Nestle (Leipzig, 1923), 798 n.

others—water or earth—might not serve equally well as the standard of measurement and the ruling force. Heraclitus, who is seeking for poetical or religious as much as logical truth, gives a two-fold answer. First, as Aristotle said (*De An.* 405a5), fire is the most subtle element, which most nearly approaches the incorporeal, is itself in motion and imparts motion to other things. Secondly (a consequence of the first, as Aristotle knew), it is the same as *psyche*, the vehicle of life. "Heraclitus says the *arche* is soul, i.e. the exhalation out of which he composes other things. It is the least corporeal of substances and is in constant flux" (ibid., 25). For soul we may read fire.

In the identification of soul and fire he was perhaps at his least original. It was a popular Greek belief that *aither*, the substance which filled the upper heaven above the less pure *aer* about the earth and of which the celestial bodies were made, was alive and divine; and until the time of Aristotle, or a very little before him,[38] *aither* and fire had not been clearly distinguished. Moreover in the fifth century, and no doubt earlier, there was a widespread idea that the soul was immortal because it consisted of an imprisoned spark of *aither*, which at death would rejoin its like. Seeing that *aither* was believed to fill all the upper regions, it was not only the visibly fiery substance of the sun and stars, and this doubtless helped Heraclitus in his supposition that the "fire" of his own system was not flame but a hot dry vapor.[39]

An observation may be permissible on the wider significance of Heraclitus' doctrine of change. A fundamental distinction in speculation about the reality of things has always lain between those who see it in matter and those who see it in form. This distinction is very obvious in Greek thought, but is of course by no means confined to it. Now Heraclitus' statement about the river, that it is not the same river the second time you step into it, illustrates the culmination of materialist belief. We speak of a river as the same river from day to day, although we know that if we stand on its banks tomorrow we shall be looking at entirely different water from that which we see there today. Similarly we commonly regard our bodies as having continuity even though we may be told, and believe, that their material constituents are constantly

[38] See *HGP*, I, pp. 270 ff.

[39] *Aither* is divine in Aesch. *P.V.* 88 and Eur. Fr. 839 N. In Eur. Fr. 877 it is equated with Zeus. Cf. also other passages adduced by KR 200 n. 1. For the connection between soul and *aither* see Eur. *Hel.* 1014 ff., *Suppl.* 533 f., Fr. 971 (cf. W. K. C. Guthrie, *The Greeks and Their Gods* [London, 1950/54], pp. 262 f.).

changing and will have renewed themselves entirely within a period of seven years. Our justification for this habit of thought is that the form remains the same: the water or other matter as it comes in is poured, as it were, into the same mold, by which token we recognize it as having the same identity.

Through their mathematical studies, Pythagoras and his school achieved with remarkable suddenness a rational conception of the significance of form, and were much blamed by their successors for ignoring the material side. For them reality lay in form, for others in matter. Both views have persisted, and whatever may be their respective merits, in anything like a developed scheme of thought only those who see reality in form can find any permanence in the world. The logical outcome of materialism is the doctrine of uninterrupted flux, as Heraclitus had the intelligence to perceive and the courage to assert; for the matter of things is in fact always changing, and the only permanent thing is form, which can be expressed in the timeless language of mathematical equations.

The logical outcome of form-philosophy, on the other hand, is Platonism or something resembling it: a belief in absolutes, or "forms" of things, existing eternally in a region beyond the reach of space or time. On the nature of the physical world Plato agreed with Heraclitus. He makes the wise Diotima say to Socrates:

> Even during the period for which any living being is said to live and retain his identity—as a man, for example, is called the same man from boyhood to old age—he does not in fact retain the same attributes, although he is called the same person: he is always becoming a new being and undergoing a process of loss and reparation, which affects his hair, his flesh, his bones, his blood, and his whole body. And not only his body, but his soul as well. No man's character, habits, opinions, desires, pleasures, pains, and fears remain always the same: new ones come into existence and old ones disappear.[40]

In what way the flux of becoming was for Heraclitus limited or qualified by the existence of a permanent and stable reality is a question that needs further consideration.

Aristotle, as we know, represented Plato's doctrine of immutable forms as having been the outcome of, among other things, "the Heraclitean opinions that all sensible things are continually flowing and

[40] Plato *Symp.* 207d, trans. W. Hamilton.

there is no knowledge of them." Impressed by this, but unwilling to accept the impossibility of knowledge, Plato posited a permanent reality outside the physical world. It is usually assumed (a) that these opinions were Heraclitus' own (although Aristotle mentions Cratylus by name as Plato's informant), and (b) that although they are explicitly confined to the sensible world, this for Heraclitus constituted the total sum of reality.

Cratylus carried the consequences of the flux-doctrine to absurd lengths. Nevertheless we have seen evidence in the primacy of War and Strife, in the similes of the bow and lyre and elsewhere, that for Heraclitus the essence of wisdom lay in recognizing unceasing motion, unceasing struggle and effort in the exertion of contrary tensions, as necessary conditions for the continuance of the physical world-order. It seems accurate enough to describe this, with Plato, as a doctrine of the everlasting flux of physical things, and to illustrate it by the simile of the river into which one cannot step twice.

Over against this, however, stands the Logos, whose permanence Heraclitus emphasizes in B1 by the use of the word *is* or *exists*, in contrast to the changing phenomena which *become* according to its laws. Because of these laws, the order and balance (*kosmos*) of the world are also constant and everlasting (B30), though no particle of its internal components—earth, sea, or visible flame—is the same for two instants together. It is here that a would-be interpreter is most acutely embarrassed by the curious stage of thought represented by Heraclitus, which at this point is likely to have led him into what from our point of view is an illogical and inconsistent position. Spiritual and material forces are still united as aspects of one and the same entity, although in fact they are becoming so far distinguished as to demand complete separation. Hence the mysterious conception of a "rational fire," of a Logos, a law of limit, measure or proportion, which takes a physical form. In that aspect, as fire, it would seem to be itself subject to the all-pervading flux, yet in the eyes of Heraclitus there was a difference. It was in some way a standard by which all things were measured and evaluated (B90).[41] In its aspect as Logos, the same point is made by its appellation of "the common." [42]

[41] See *HGP*, I, pp. 460 ff.
[42] Ibid., pp. 425 f.

9

A THOUGHT PATTERN
IN HERACLITUS

Hermann Fränkel

The pattern is obvious in this saying:

> Man is stamped as infantile by divinity, just as the child is by man.
> (fr. 79)

For the sake of convenience, we call this pattern by the name of the geometrical mean and trànscribe it by formulae such as *God/man = man/boy*, or else $A/B = B/C$, using mathematical language rather loosely and disclaiming mathematical strictness. To ascertain the actual meaning and function of the pattern, we shall have to analyze the instances in which Heraclitus uses the scheme, starting from fr. 79.

There are three planes: the levels of God, man, and child (A, B, and C). The degree of perfection decreases, and the degree of imperfection increases, in equal measure in the transitions from A to B and from B to C ($A/B = B/C$). Or (and this will paraphrase more correctly what ·Heraclitus had in mind) we might speak of contrasts, and say that the contrast between perfection and imperfection is the same in both cases. Thus man, being the geometrical mean, may be called wise when compared to a boy, and childish when compared to God. He combines opposite qualities. It all depends on the standard by which he is judged. An adult man is perfect according to conventional conceptions but utterly defective according to philosophical truth.

Of the three elements A, B, and C, each has its characteristic function. The member C (child) is a known magnitude and its inferiority is unquestionable. For it was a truism for Heraclitus and his public that

From *American Journal of Philology*, 59 (1938), 309–37. Pages 309–13, 323–25, 330–32, and portions of other pages omitted. Selection reprinted here with the permission of the *American Journal of Philology*, The Johns Hopkins Press, and the author.

a child is a weak, foolish, and despicable being.[1] Referring to the indisputable defects of a child, Heraclitus makes the startling assertion that any respectable and dignified citizen, when viewed in the light of divinity, is by no means less miserable than an infant. B (man) is tantamount to C (child) when compared to A (God). Thus the term C (child) serves as predicate in the statement, and it indicates what specific quality or circumstance is ascribed to B and A: in this case, imperfection and perfection respectively.

It follows that the element C varies according to the predicate to be given the statement, or even to the shade of its meaning. Another saying of Heraclitus expressed the same idea of human imperfection in a more bitter and caustic way through the choice of a different term of reference. The saying is not preserved in its original wording, but its purport was that the most beautiful and wise of men, when compared to God, is like an ape (frr. 82 and 83). That which makes the ape appear so hideous, contemptible, and ridiculous is the fact that he seemingly tries to look like a man and to act and behave like a man. This is precisely the situation of man in reference to God. Humanity is a caricature of divinity.[2]

The pattern implies, as we have seen, the statement that the middle element B, when considered from a higher standpoint, is no better than its apparent opposite C. Thus Heraclitus can reduce the equation to a shorter form by simply asserting that B virtually amounts to its opposite C. Of this type are the statements in fr. 1 that ordinary people are equally uninformed before and after they have been told the truth; that they do not experience their own experiences; that even while awake they are like sleepers, unaware of what they had ever known before. All such assertions can easily be transformed into the complete scheme of the double proportion, e.g. the consciousness and alertness of ordinary people, eagerly pursuing their activities, is like unconscious

[1] It may be recalled that in the art of the period children are represented as miniature adults. The specific positive qualities of children were only discovered much later.

[2] The element B is put here in the superlative: "even the most beautiful and most wise of men." Heraclitus is fond of using the superlative in such statements and to show that even those who are commonly considered as supreme in reality are incompetent and ridiculous (frr. 56, 57; cf. fr. 124). For the comparison of ape and man cf. William C. McDermott, "The Ape in Greek Literature," *TAPA*, 66 (1935), 167.

and torpid sleep when compared to the state of a mind that has awakened to the contact with metaphysical reality. The opposites are said to be equivalent also in this fragment:

They that have no understanding, though hearing, are like (*eoikasi*)[3] the deaf. The expression "present but absent" is fitting for them. (fr. 34)

Those who hear the message and are present in a certain sense (viz. bodily) are virtually deaf and absent (viz. mentally) if they do not understand what has been said and fail to establish a contact with that metaphysical reality which surrounds them and which is the very essence of their existence. When we thus qualify the opposite notions, in order to make them compatible, by adding "bodily" and "mentally," we must be careful not to overlook that the two restrictions are on a different plane. It is mental comprehension alone that really matters. In statements of this type, Heraclitus does not mean to say that any predication can only be relative and therefore has to be properly qualified as to the conditions under which it is valid. The wording of fr. 79 shows how far Heraclitus was from advocating relativity as a universal and uniform principle. It is by no means to an equally limited degree correct to call ordinary man wise or foolish, for his claim to wisdom is based only on his superiority to complete foolishness, while the contrary verdict is passed on him by God's wisdom. Relative, and relatively real, is man's wisdom but his foolishness is absolutely true. When Heraclitus distinguishes two different factors making for contrary predications, he usually implies that only one of them is decisive and the other comparatively negligible and futile. In the following fragment he explicitly distinguishes between the bodily and the mental factors in perception, but at the same time he makes it clear that the final result depends on the soul:

Bad witnesses for men are eyes and ears of those that have barbarian souls. (fr. 107)

[3] Here, as in fr. 1, the notion "tantamount" is rather vaguely indicated by *eoikasi*. Heraclitus does not use technical language for the expression of his pattern. All the early Greek philosophers abstain from developing technical language. The specific meaning is not couched in specific terms or stereotyped schemes but it results by implication from an unlimited variety of expressions in current language and style, including instances, images, and other devices to guide the imagination. The philosophical ideas are intimated to the reader instead of being forced upon him with rigid and coercive strictness.

Many a time the opponents of Heraclitus will have recurred to common-sense experience in order to refute the lofty paradoxes of his creed.[4] But their experience, so Heraclitus points out, though they are proud of being civilized and enlightened Greeks, amounts to no more than the experience of primitive savages with an horizon confined to their base needs and menial interests.[5] The insight is a question not of sensual perception and superficial assimilation but of a deeper consciousness and thorough interpretation.[6]

In all the instances quoted so far it was always the element C (child, ape, sleeping, deaf, etc.) alone which varied, and with it the predicate of the statement. The term B constantly represented ordinary humanity, and the element A referred, in some sense or other, to God and the Absolute. The equation of the geometrical mean is a method of denouncing and humiliating humanity; it is equally a method for praising and extolling the divine. But there is one more gradation implied in the scheme. The term C (child, barbarian, etc.) is, as we have observed, a well known thing with notorious defects; the term B (ordinary man) happens to be a supposedly well known magnitude and a supposedly worthy subject, but the equation reveals that the common evaluation is erroneous and that the qualities of man are in actual fact the opposite of what was generally assumed. But then the term A (the Absolute) represents that which was unknown to mankind, not visualized by anyone, not worshipped or revered appropriately, until Heraclitus discovered its real essence and preached its gospel. God and True Reality are a something beyond the ken of inexperienced experience, senseless sensations, unreal realizations, and unwise wisdom; something beyond the competence of human imagination and description. The scheme of the geometrical mean thus becomes a device to express the inexpressible and to explain the inexplicable. The equation may be rewritten, on this view, with an x instead of an A: $x/B = B/C$. What is God? God is that compared to which the most perfect man will appear as an infant or as a hideous and ridiculous ape. What is divine

[4] Cf. the attitude of the half blind cave-dwellers in Plato's *Rep*. VII.516e toward those who see.

[5] Again we can form a double proportion: barbarian/Greek = Greek/the really enlightened.

[6] Perhaps the notion "barbarian" indicates rather the inability to understand Greek (or, figuratively, to understand the language of reality) than the lack of civilization and education. The difference is only slight, as in any case the fragment is concerned with the problem of interpretation.

clarity of mind and the insight of an illuminated soul, burning in a clear, unadulterated, fiery glow? It is a state in comparison to which ordinary consciousness is like sleep, and sober reasoning like the numbness of a drunken man, not knowing whither he goes, his soul being moist.[7]

Constantly upbraiding humanity, scolding and abusing it, Heraclitus tries to arouse it from its spiritual stupor and numbness and calls it to a new and unheard of awakeness and sobriety. He hates mysticism and ecstasy (frr. 14; 15), just as he despises vulgar intoxication, and yet he has a message that demands an almost superhuman effort of the mind to reach the state of illumination:

> Unless one hopes against hope, he will not find out that which is indiscoverable and inaccessible. (fr. 18)[8]

Instead of trying to enrapture his readers, to envelop them in a misty cloud of vague enthusiasm and whirl their minds upward to the beyond in a tornado of oratory, Heraclitus is content calmly to point out the direction in which the reasoning has to travel. Like the Delphian God who "does not tell nor hide but indicates" (fr. 93),[9] Heraclitus asks his readers to find the transcendental by the indirect means of extrapolation, through the device of the double proportion. The greatness of the

---

[7] I have combined fr. 1 (sleep) and fr. 118 ("Dry soul, wisest and best") with fr. 117: "A man when drunk is led by an immature child, not noticing whither he goes, his soul being moist." Fr. 117 is in itself an instance of the geometrical mean (man, drunk/child = child/man, sober; cf. Hermann Fränkel, "Heraclitus on the Notion of a Generation," *AJP*, 59 [1938], 90 f.). But I feel confident that this fragment, taken as a whole, in the original was only the one half of a double proportion, such as indicated in the text above. It is not likely that Heraclitus should have condescended, for its own sake, to a trivial denunciation of intoxication, or to a physiological proof of his thesis on the nature of the soul. And the words "not understanding whither he goes" are echoed, within a series of excerpts from Heraclitus, by Marcus Aurelius, 4.46.2: "he who forgets where his way leads him" (= fr. 71; cf. Seneca *Epist*. 98.10: *obliti quo eant*, scil. *ad mortem;* and Pindar *Nem*. 6.6 ff. in a context strongly influenced by Heraclitus), where the "way" is clearly metaphorical. It seems therefore that the "drunken man" was only an image used for exposing the state of man in general.

[8] In this instance, the combined opposites do not express incompetence but, on the contrary, the triumph of him who overcomes almost invincible obstacles.

[9] Cf. Bruno Snell, "Die Sprache Heraklits," *Hermes*, 61 (1926), 371.

metaphysical organization, the perfection of the hidden harmony which is far finer than the apparent one (frr. 123; 54), is indicated by him in this same way:

> The most perfectly organized universe is like a heap of garbage (*sarma*)[10] dumped at random—(scil. when compared to the less obvious organization behind and beyond the manifest regularity of sun, stars, and life[11]).

The obscure fr. 52 is perhaps taken from a similar context:

> Human existence is a child at a game, playing draughts; a child rules as king.

The course of nature, the sway of necessity, the codes of law and convention, or careful planning, or whatever else is controlling our lives, all this amounts to the willful moves of a child playing a game of arbitrary rules[12]—scil. when compared to the one divine law. This interpretation, however, is no more than a guess.

The notion of "the one divine law" which we tentatively supplied in the preceding fragment is to be found in this saying:

> One must speak in accordance with reason and by this means strengthen oneself (Ξὺν νόῳ λέγοντας ἰσχυρίζεσθαι χρή)[13] through that which is common to all, as a community (scil. is strong) through its law; and even more strongly (scil. does reason support those

---

[10] σάρμα is an excellent emendation by Diels for σάρξ.

[11] There is no means, as far as I can see, to have the quotation fit precisely and with strict logic into Theophrastus' own argument. The smoothest way, however, of coordinating the quotation with the rest of the context is to make Heraclitus say that the metaphysical system is even more perfect than the apparent organization, and to have Theophrastus use the quotation for indicating that it would be absurd if the fine organization of our visible universe were brought about by accident and fortuitous chance and not by correspondingly well organized definite principles.

[12] Cf. Plato *Laws* VII.803c–804b.

[13] It seems to me obvious that λέγοντας is also governed by χρή. Otherwise the participle would have been put in the future or the auxiliary μέλλω inserted, as in the Platonic reverberation of this sentence, *Rep.* VII.517c: δεῖ ταύτην (scil. τὴν τοῦ ἀγαθοῦ ἰδέαν) ἰδεῖν τὸν μέλλοντα ἐμφρόνως πράξειν ἢ ἰδίᾳ ἢ δημοσίᾳ. (That the preceding part of Plato's sentence also is indebted to Heraclitus can be inferred from its coincidence with Pindar *Isthm.* 5.1 ff.; cf. *Gnomon*, 6 (1930), 13.)

who are in keeping with it), for all human laws are fed (*trephontai*) by the one divine, for it prevails as much as it will and is sufficient for (and equal to) all of them and superabounding (superior).

Reason is, according to Heraclitus, not an achievement of the individual but a suprapersonal power; it is common and universal (fr. 2, etc.). Thus Heraclitus at first remarks that, as communities are strong as long as they act in conformity with their constitutional law (cf. fr. 44), so individual minds are strong when they comply with the common law of reason. But then, as in an afterthought, a new gradation is added in the scheme of the geometrical mean: The individual citizens/the common law of their social organization = all the individual community laws/the law of laws, the one divine law.[14]

Our analysis has ascertained that Heraclitus had a predilection for the thought pattern of the geometrical mean, and that this scheme helped him in the arduous task of approaching the conception of the transcendental. The essence of the pattern is[15] that mundane values, when compared to the paramount, are tantamount to their opposites, the non-values. This general idea is implied in various statements and expressed in various ways. There is no external uniformity. Heraclitus does not use stereotyped figures of speech, though the thought pattern seems to invite and provoke their application.[16] Nor does he clothe his thoughts in the distinctive but monotonous livery of technical language.[17] In the absence of any technical terms, there is no clue to indicate the field in which Heraclitus may have become acquainted with the scheme of the continued proportion before he applied it to metaphysics. Perhaps he had learned from the Pythagoreans about the harmonious contrasts in a succession of tones with equal intervals (i.e.

[14] This equation differs from all those analyzed before. No disparaging criticism is implied, for Heraclitus had no intention of depreciating the laws of man. This time positive and direct advice is given and the transcendental is extolled not by contrast alone but explicitly and directly.

[15] With the exception of fr. 114, cf. the preceding note.

[16] It is true that there is much in the style of Heraclitus to remind the reader of the *figurae orationis* as they were taught later by rhetoricians, but in the writing of Heraclitus the subject determines the expression and not the reverse. Cf. Eduard Norden, *Die antike Kunstprosa*, vol. 1 (Leipzig and Berlin, 1898), pp. 18 ff.; *Logos und Rhythmus* (Berlin, 1928), p. 23 [repr. in E. Norden, *Kleine Schriften* (Berlin, 1966), pp. 533–51].

[17] Cf. note 3, above, and Snell, p. 353.

equal proportions of string length) and about correspondent progressions in geometry and algebra.[18]

The function of the pattern is now, I hope, sufficiently well established to allow us to integrate and to interpret with its support another group of incomplete fragments.

Asses would prefer chaff (*syrmata*) to gold. (fr. 9)

The text suggests the equations: ass/ordinary man = ordinary man/ the discriminating philosopher, and correspondingly: refuse/gold = gold/real values. This interpretation is corroborated by the following two fragments.

If happiness lay in the pleasures of the body, we would call cattle happy when they find bitter vetch to feed on. (fr. 4)[19]

The best men prefer one thing to all other things, everlasting fame to things mortal; but the many are glutted in the way of cattle. (fr. 29)

The mass of humanity is degraded to the rank of their domestic animals, and their happiness to the delights of cattle and asses.[20] With archaic thoroughness, Heraclitus further and further exploits the conception of man owning animals, disposing of them freely and despising them profoundly, but not being aware that, measured against the standard of what he ought to be, he is by no means their superior. For it is an easy guess that when Heraclitus speaks of "revelling in filth" (fr. 13), he is denouncing the pleasures of the unenlightened. . . .

But the story of the geometrical mean in the philosophy of Heraclitus is not yet ended, for the extant tradition appears to yield yet other interesting instances.

[18] There are some references to music and musical harmony in the fragments (10 with testimonia; 51). Pythagoras is mentioned twice (frr. 40, 129). The usual derogatory tenor does not preclude indebtedness to the school (cf. U. von Wilamowitz-Moellendorff, *Der Glaube der Hellenen*, vol. 2 [Berlin, 1932], p. 188). It is less likely that Heraclitus should have invented the scheme of the continued proportion independently.

[19] It goes without saying that the original form of this saying was different from the text as given by Albertus Magnus. [Fränkel quotes the Latin; translation supplied here by the Editor.]

[20] Speaking of the fodder of asses (fr. 9), Heraclitus aptly uses the word σύρμα, "litter, refuse, chaff," just as he had compared the cosmos to σάρμα, "garbage" (fr. 124).

The scheme helps us better to understand the well known fragment

Strife is father of all things, and king of all things, and he appointed
some as gods and the others as men, he made some to become
slaves and the others to be free. (fr. 53)

Here again three levels are mentioned. Man (the ordinary free citizen)
holds the central position between the gods above and the slaves below
him. As slaves are ruled by (free) men, so man is controlled by his
heavenly lords: The gods/(free) men = free men/slaves. The power
behind both these relationships is the same creative and dominating
force of strife. The slaves have been thrown into their position through
the strife of warfare, and between gods and men there is not only the
contrast of opposite qualities (fr. 62) but also antagonism and strife as
expressed in Hesiod's and Aeschylus' representations of the Prometheus myth.

The following fragment is not concerned with man and god but with
some of nature's phenomena:

If the sun did not exist there would be night in spite of all the other
stars. (fr. 99)[21]

The fire of any star, of any αἰθόμενον πῦρ διαπρέπον νυκτί, cannot break
the spell of the night, nor can they all together with their combined
efforts; but the one sun outshines them all and turns night into day,
ἐν ἀμέρᾳ φαεννὸν ἄστρον ἐρήμας δι' αἰθέρος.[22] The glamor of all the stars,
brilliant though they are, amounts only to darkness and is called night
by comparison with that period in which the one sun illuminates the
world (darkness/brilliancy of the stars = brilliancy of the stars/light
of the sun).

Thus the sun is extolled as by far the greatest of all the fires in our
visible universe. But then again we read:

The width of sun: that of one human foot. (fr. 3)

[21] The wording is hardly authentic.

[22] I borrow expressions from the exordium of Pindar's first Olympian to
indicate that this passage, like others, shows the influence of Heraclitus. In
the exordium are implied the Heraclitean ideas of water being superior to the
varieties of the base element, and of fire equally surpassing water (see below,
pp. 224 ff.); of day and the one sun surpassing night and the many stars
(Heracl. fr. 99); of fire corresponding to gold (fr. 90); and of renown (as won
by an Olympian victory) corresponding to gold (frr. 29 + 9).

Lying down on your back and lifting one leg, you are able to blot the whole sun with one foot. The largest and most powerful of the heavenly bodies does not amount to more than that. This sounds exactly like many of the statements which we have analyzed. Even the greatest things of this world are contemptible—viz. when compared to divine things. The other half of the double proportion is missing. Can we hope to recover it?

In our extant tradition (A1.7) a reference to this fragment 3 is linked to another fragment (45), and we have been unwise in ignoring their connection. The other fragment supplies perfectly what is needed and makes an admirable complement:

> The boundaries of soul you will not find, wandering in whatever direction, so deep is the *logos* it possesses. (fr. 45)

The soul is the one thing in the world of man that can blend with the boundless *logos*, the all-embracing law of laws. Through insight and clear consciousness the soul can share in the supreme power of the *logos* and can intelligently and actively live the rules that govern the universe, instead of being unwittingly and passively controlled by them. The sun, on the other hand, is not more than an intermittent phenomenon, annihilated every night and produced anew on every morning.[23] The course it has to take is strictly prescribed to it and the police officers of Nature's justice enforce the heavenly traffic rules:

> Sun will not overstep its measures; if it does, the Erinyes, assistants of Justice, will find it out. (fr. 94)

While the *logos* in the soul may increase indefinitely (fr. 115), the extension of the sun is invariably determined by the size of the container in which the flaming masses are gathered. For the thing that man calls sun is not a real body, freely floating in the void, but a certain quantity of fiery exhalation rising from below during day time and intercepted by a bowl turned upside down. The sun is not so much an object as a transitory process, a fire kindled when the bowl rises, being sustained throughout the day by a steady flow of new material and extinguished as soon as the bowl sets at the horizon. That petty mechanical appliance, the bowl with what it holds, can be covered and blotted by one human foot (fr. 3). But—it is only a "but" we have to

---

[23] Fr. 6; Plato *Rep.* 498a with schol. Cf. Olof Gigon, *Untersuchungen zu Heraklit* (Leipzig, 1935), pp. 84 ff. Gigon is right in pointing out the similarity in the views of Xenophanes and Heraclitus. Cf. also fr. 16.

supply—the same foot, wandering in any direction, will never reach the end of a living soul. So deep is the *logos* it possesses (fr. 45).[24]

It can hardly be doubted that the thought pattern of the continued proportion was primarily used, if not invented, by Heraclitus in order to clarify the contrast between the mundane and divine. But we may well expect that so familiar a tool has served him for other purposes as well. One instance is his definition of a generation. A generation is passed, so he says, and one cycle of human nature completed, as soon as, after the lapse of thirty years, the begetter sees the begotten a begetter. The cycle closes when the equation *son/father* = *grandson/son* has been enacted, so that the central figure is endowed with both the opposite qualities, sonhood and fatherhood.[25]

There may be more instances in our extant tradition. But, if anywhere outside the sphere to which the scheme properly belongs, we shall first of all expect it to underly the theory of three[26] elements of nature. As fire for Heraclitus is either identical or cognate with the divine, it may well be that it takes the position of the divine (A) in the equation, with water and earth as the B and C elements respectively. . . .

After the time of Thales and the unknown authority behind Semonides of Amorgos[a] (he may be identical with Thales), the sea preserved its key position in the system of Anaximander (DK 12A27 and 30), fundamentally different though his views otherwise were, and to some degree also in what Xenophanes taught.[27] Sea held the central position

[24] It is not impossible that the three fragments 99 and 3 + 45 were connected in the original as indicated in our text above: The sun by far surpasses all other fires, but the sun itself is equally surpassed by the soul (fires/sun = sun/soul). The brilliancy of the sun is the "mother of our eyes" (Pind. *Paean* 9.2), but what are the eyes of the body when compared to the soul with the living and perceiving *logos* in it? The latter thought is expressed by Plutarch (*De Fortuna* 98c) in connection with Heraclitus, fr. 99; and on the other hand it is implied in Heraclitus, fr. 107. Seneca *Epist*. 88.13 may or may not be vaguely related.

[25] DK 22A19. For particulars, see *AJP*, 59 (1938), 89 ff.

[26] Gigon, pp. 99 ff., contends that Heraclitus assumed four, instead of three, elements. His arguments are not convincing. Cf. the review of Gigon by Harold Cherniss in *AJP*, 56 (1935), 415.

[a] [In a section immediately preceding but omitted here, Fränkel suggests that a cosmological scheme of two basic substances, earth and sea, is reflected in Semonides 7.21–42 (Diehl).—Ed.]

[27] Cf. DK 21A33.5–6; Gigon, p. 66.

among the three elements for Heraclitus likewise, and Clement says that sea, in his doctrine, is "the germ of creation" (fr. 31 testim.). This word may or may not correctly describe what Heraclitus meant but certainly it is sea from which both ways are open, the way upward through the rising fiery whirlwind to fire, and downward to earth:

> The conversions of fire: first sea; and of sea the one half earth and the other fiery whirlwind (*prēstēr*).—The sea disperses itself (*dia-cheetai*) and is measured into the same *logos* as before it became earth. (fr. 31)[b]

The second part seems to be incomplete and therefore somewhat obscure, but it can hardly be doubted that λόγος is used in a sense which at least comes very near to "correspondence" or "proportion," [28] and that the proportion, whatever the ratio may be, is meant to prevail in all the four upward and downward conversions: fire/sea = sea/earth. There is no lack of further corroboration for the equation. The middle term always combines opposite qualities, as we have seen in numerous instances, since its relations to the things above are the opposite of those to the things below it. This is precisely stated for the sea:

> Sea is purest water and foulest, to fish drinkable and life giving, to men undrinkable and destructive. (fr. 61)

In the sea all pollution collects, and yet its waters are used for ritual purification;[29] it is pure when compared to dirt, but foul when compared to purity. The sea is life for base animals with much earth in their constitution,[30] but it is death for higher life endowed with a soul of fire.[31]

Life and the soul of man is, in the view of Heraclitus, a process sus-

[b] [Fränkel quotes the Greek; translation supplied here by the Editor.]

[28] The idea of a ratio and fixed proportion in the relationships among the elements is likewise borne out by fr. 90.

[29] For particulars see *Philologus*, 87 (1932), 477.

[30] For the idea of prevalence of earth in base animals, see Plato *Timaeus* 92a–b, and cf. A. E. Taylor, *A Commentary on Plato's* Timaeus (Oxford, 1928), note on 92a4.

[31] Perhaps Heraclitus has also spoken of the sea as being mastered and dominated by the "fire" of storms, but overpowering and destroying in its turn the solid matter of ships (fr. 53 likewise implies the progression, Master/servant/servant's slave, above, p. 222). This idea is indicated, though not very clearly, in Nicander *Alexiph*. 172–76.

tained by continuous conversion of "water" into its opposite, "fire,"
i.e. through evaporation. Evaporation supplies the air for respiration
and thus supports consciousness and reasoning; evaporation likewise
brings about the assimilation of food (A15; A16.130).[32] The opposite
transformation, precipitation, is death for souls:

> It is death for souls to be turned into water, and for water to be
> turned into earth. But out of earth water is born, out of water soul.
> (fr. 36)

The two downward conversions are equivalent to a twofold death,
and the two upward transformations to a double birth, with water (it
is not "sea" this time) in the central position, where the ways of birth
and death meet.

We are now in a position to reach a conclusion. The old conception
of sea and earth as contrasting elements or bodies[33] possessing opposite
qualities still prevails in the system of Heraclitus, with a similar relationship between the partners. But then Heraclitus follows Anaximenes
in increasing the number of the elements and in assuming that they are
convertible into one another. Unlike Anaximenes, however, he con-

---

[32] In the early theories respiration and digestion are closely connected and
in fact identical. The action of "fire" (heat) which disintegrates and concocts
the food to prepare it for assimilation is thought to be both dependent on and
responsible for respiration by Plato in *Timaeus* 78e and 80d. The lungs, named
πλεύμονες for their function in respiration, are likewise supposed to be the
recipient of drink (Alcaeus Fr. 94 Diehl; Plato *Tim.* 70c and 91a).

[33] Our little survey has shown that the theory primarily referred less to the
substances water and earth than to the objects sea and land, the components
of the world in which we live. To the prehistory of the conception belong the
Homeric similes symbolizing powerful motion by the waves of the sea and
stubborn resistance by the stable cliff upon which the waves break. In some
of the similes storm takes the place of roaring sea, or storm is associated with
waves to symbolize the will of the leaders who stir the crowd (sea) and push
it into motion. Solon (Fr. 11 Diehl, cf. Werner Jaeger, "Solons Eunomie,"
Sitzungsberichte der preussischen Akadamie der Wissenschaften zu Berlin,
Philosophisch-historische Klasse, 1926, p. 81) uses the simile of sea and wind
in order to state that not the crowd (= sea) but the leaders (= storms) are
responsible for political unrest. This clever remark in some way preludes the
development from Thales (sea or water as motive power) to Anaximenes (air
as motive power). As a rule, the discoveries and theorems of Greek philosophy
are preceded by anticipation on the moral field.

siders the changes from one condition to the next not as slight and gradual transitions but as violent and dramatic transformations from opposite to opposite, and he restricts the number of elements to three. By this means they are made to coincide with the three states of matter (the solid, liquid, and gaseous), and at the same time to comply with the pattern of the geometrical mean. The contrast between dead inertia and vivid power exists twice in this configuration, with sea or water in the central position. This thesis explains the cosmos and the meteorological phenomena, but it holds good equally in everyday experience. Fire and heat, the substance of life, makes dead matter in the rigid state gain life and motion and melt; and again it makes half-dead matter in the heavy state of liquidity gain real life and energy, lose its weight, break its bonds, freely evaporate upward and become during the transition, *in statu nascendi*, conscious breath and living soul. Deprivation of fire and life, making things travel downward on one and the same path, has the opposite result.[34]

As soon as Empedocles had firmly established his four-element theory, the scheme of the geometrical mean was seemingly ruled out for ever from that province. But just at this late stage of the development it happened for the first time that the scheme was explicitly, as such, applied to the elements of nature. Plato in the *Timaeus* (31b ff.) deduces the Empedoclean system by starting from the extreme elements fire and earth, and then pointing out that an intermediate is necessary to bind the conflicting bodies to one another. He goes on to say that the binding element, in order to serve its purpose of mediation and harmonization, must be determined by the principle of the geometrical mean, for only through a geometrical progression can a complete cycle of mutual relations be brought about. But, as elements are tridimensional bodies, he infers that not one but two geometrical means have to be inserted between fire and earth. The final result is a sequence of four elements, determined by the double equation *fire/air = air/water = water/earth*. It has been assumed that either Plato

[34] This, however, is perhaps not the whole story. If we can trust our indirect evidence (A1.9–11), Heraclitus, in order to account for the phenomena of day and night and of the weather, introduced two kinds of evaporation, a bright and a dark one. This would involve a concession in the line of Anaximenes and not be consistent with the main thesis. But Cherniss, p. 415, is inclined to disbelieve the accounts of a double evaporation, and they are indeed open to several grave objections.

himself, or possibly Philolaus, introduced into cosmology the "Pythagorean" idea of the geometrical progression.[35] We now learn that
Heraclitus had done it long before, except for the mathematical strictness of expression. The difference in the number of elements is really
negligible. For every reader of the *Timaeus* will feel that the duplication
of the geometrical mean comes as somewhat surprising and uncon-
vincing.[36] The line of thought leads rather to three, instead of four,
elements, mutually related according to the simple pattern of the
geometrical mean. This is exactly what Heraclitus taught. With an
unimportant modification, Plato finally formulated with technical
precision a basic principle of Heraclitean thought.

The strong consistency in the grandiose system of Heraclitus im-
poses on the interpreter the duty of seeking the connections between
the parts of the doctrine, connections which in the original were either
expressed or tacitly implied. On the other hand, there is much to mislead our efforts. The power of Heraclitus' thought and style is so overwhelming that it is apt to carry away the imagination of his readers
(of those at least who do respond) beyond the limits of sober interpretation. Neither the ancient philosophers and physicians nor modern
scholars have escaped the danger of allowing their fancy to run riot
and Heraclitizing on their own account. The Stoics especially blended
with their own ideas the inspirations for which they were indebted to
the obscure philosopher. We have to use all the material and yet be
utterly suspicious of the views under which it is presented. Almost
every single statement in the indirect tradition, if it can be compared
with the original saying to which it refers, affords a striking proof of
limited ability, not to speak of limited will, to assimilate archaic thought
and reproduce it correctly. It is fortunate that we are able to settle
some of the problems by tracing back a certain pattern of Heraclitus'
original thought.

[35] Cf. Taylor, p. 98.

[36] Plato's argument that there is one geometrical mean for planes but two
for tridimensional bodies seems to be based on the theorems Eucl. *Elem.*
VIII.11 and 12 (cf. Eva Sachs, *Die fünf platonischen Körper: Zur Geschichte
der Mathematik und der Elementenlehre Platons und der Pythagoreer*, Philologische Untersuchungen, 24 [Berlin, 1917], p. 126 n. 1; substantially the same
explanation is given by Taylor, p. 96, but a different one by Kurt von Fritz,
RE XVII, 2268, s.v. Oinopides).

10

PARADOX, SIMILE, AND GNOMIC UTTERANCE IN HERACLITUS

Uvo Hölscher

Heraclitus fragment 93 seems to hint of a connection between the *logos* and paradox: "The lord whose oracle is at Delphi neither speaks nor conceals but gives a sign." In antiquity this sentence was taken to refer to the riddling style of Heraclitus;[1] his own method, it would seem, is explained here in terms of an implicit simile. The sense, accordingly, would be: "as the Delphic oracle, so I also . . . ." Heraclitus himself would have characterized his manner of speech as the style of an oracle.

The oracular character of Heraclitus' style has often been remarked upon. For the purposes of the present account it will suffice to bring out certain of its features. Generally speaking, it is the obscurity of his language that recalls the oracular. Now, the obscurity of oracles has various forms. In most oracles something is hinted at, and the hinting takes the form of metaphor. Kenning[a] is the dominant form in oracular language, from the "consumer of corn-ears" of the Odyssey[2] to the "mountain-drinkers" in Plutarch.[3] Metaphor may expand to a full simile, as, for example, when the oracle says of the mother of Cypselus:

From Uvo Hölscher, *Anfängliches Fragen: Studien zur frühen griechischen Philosophie* (Göttingen: Vandenhoeck & Ruprecht, 1968), pp. 136–41, 144–48, 149. Translated by Matthew R. Cosgrove with Alexander P. D. Mourelatos. Selection translated and printed here with the permission of the publisher, Vandenhoeck & Ruprecht, and the author.

[1] Lucian *Vit. Auct.* 14.

[a] [Kenning: an early German and Anglo-Saxon poetic figure, in which a metaphorical name stands in place of the common noun that is meant; e.g. "whale-acre" for "sea."—Ed.]

[2] *Od.* 11.128. ["Consumer of corn-ears" (*athērēloigos*): a kenning referring to the winnowing fan.—Ed.]

[3] Plutarch *De Pythiae Oraculis* 406e. ["Mountain-drinkers," i.e. "mountain-engorgers," a kenning referring to rivers.—Ed.]

"an eagle is pregnant in the mountains; it will bring forth a lion . . . ." [4]
While the image is all that is given here, the very lack of evident reference together with the incongruity of the biological combination reveals that we are dealing with a simile, which requires interpretation.
And so the warning ταῦτα φράζεσθε, "ponder this!" or φράζεο, "ponder!"
follows in the text of this as in that of many other oracles. That an
oracle is intrinsically a saying to be interpreted was something the
Greeks were fully aware of. One aspect of the contrast between the
barbarian Croesus and his Greek guest Solon is that Croesus is inclined to take an oracle in its initial and trivial meaning.[b] Yet it may
be just as intrinsic to an oracle that it should not be understood—
because it foretells the inevitable. Fatally ambiguous sayings, such as
that which told Hesiod the place of his death,[5] exemplify this.

It is common to all these forms that a surface meaning conceals another behind it, to which it nevertheless points. Like the solution to a
riddle, this hidden meaning must be sought out. "What does the god
mean, and what are we to make of this riddle?" wondered Socrates,
when Chaerephon brought to him from Delphi the saying of the oracle.[6]
Many oracles have the typical form of riddles, for example the saying
in which the Pythia hinted to the Spartans about the burial place of
Orestes.[7] Conversely, a riddle that closely resembles the tone of an
oracle is that of Simonides (Fr. 70 D).[c] Circumlocution belongs to the
oldest forms of both.

Closely related is another typical form of riddle, the paradox. It is
found in some form or other in almost every example collected in
Book 14 of the Greek Anthology. In oracles one finds it with almost
the same frequency. The "wooden walls" that would save Athens is a
paradox.[8] Especially favored is the paradoxical omen: "when the

[4] Herodotus V.92.

[b] [See Hdt. I.53–56, 86.—Ed.]

[5] Thucydides III.96; *Certamen Homeri et Hesiodi* 222 (= 322 in Loeb ed.
of Homerica).

[6] Plato *Ap.* 21b.

[7] Herodotus I.67.

[c] ["I say that he who is not willing to take upon himself the pains of the
contest of the cicada is to give a big meal to Epeios, son of Panopeus." Cf.
Pind. *Pyth.* 3.82, Aesch. *Prom.* 754. As the ancient scholion by Athenaeus
suggests, the meaning of the riddle is: He who does not take part in the musical rehearsal is to pay for a portion of food for the donkey called Epeios
(which carried the drinking water for Simonides' chorus).—Ed.]

[8] Herodotus VII.141.

female shall conquer the male . . . ." [9] Or the event itself is forecast in the form of a paradox: "Take the tip and you shall have the middle," hear the Aeginetans who wish to reconquer their home island.[10] Indeed, the oracle, reaching beyond the scope of common understanding, may pronounce its own nature as a paradox: "I perceive what is mute and hear what is speechless." [11]

The obscurity of Heraclitus' language can be similarly characterized. It is in the style of oracles that we find the pattern for those similes that do not have the explicit form of a simile: B22 "Gold-prospectors dig up much earth and find little gold"; B125 "The posset falls apart if it is not stirred"; B26 "Man kindles a light in the night";[12] B60 "The road to and from is one and the same." B16 "the never-going-under" is similar to kenning. The style reveals itself very clearly where it comes close to the form of a riddle: B34 "present, they are absent"; B49a "we step and do not step into the same rivers." Here too the riddle appears in the form of a paradox. And when Heraclitus speaks of his insight, he adopts a form as paradoxical as that of the Pythia, who hears the unhearable: "When one does not expect what is not to be expected . . . ." [13]

In B56 Heraclitus makes use of folk riddle: one that children are said to have posed to Homer after delousing themselves.[d] The anecdote is related by Heraclitus as a simile that refers, as he explicitly states, to "knowledge of visible things." Given this reference, the riddle signifies: In things the absent is present, the invisible visible. Nothing hinges on the *solution* of the riddle. The point, conveyed merely by the riddle form, is: Things, too, present a paradoxical, secret reality, which, at the same time, is manifest. Things themselves are a riddle to be solved—one has only to be able to read the cipher; that is, one must learn to understand the visible as a sign, as the self-proclaiming of the invisible. Homer did not grasp the obvious meaning of the

[9] Herodotus VI.77.

[10] Zenobius I.57.

[11] Herodotus I.47. See also Plutarch *De Defectu Oraculorum* 39: "A deaf man's hearing, a blind man's sight."

[12] See Hölscher, *Anfängliches Fragen* (Göttingen, 1968), pp. 150–56.

[13] On the interpretation of this fragment, see Karl Reinhardt, *Parmenides und die Geschichte der griechischen Philosophie* (Bonn, 1916; repr. Frankfurt a.M., 1959), p. 62 n. 2.

[d] ["What we saw and grasped, that we let go of; what we neither saw nor grasped, that we carry."—Ed.]

children's riddle. Men similarly fail to grasp the visible: "however many come upon it, they do not know it" (B17), because they lack the sense needed to grasp the visible as a *witness*. For "eyes and ears are bad *witnesses* for men, if they have muddled souls" (B107).

The preference for what can be seen, voiced by Heraclitus in B55, is thus not unqualified; his vision is not naïve and immediate, and has nothing to do with Xenophanes' homely empiricism.[14] The value of the visible is that it is a symbol and a simile that points to the invisible. And this invisible is none other than the "harmony" (B54), the coherence and unity of the opposites. B51 explicitly mentions it as that which is hidden to men. In the same fragment appear the similes of the lyre and the bow. Here simile is related to statement as the visible to the invisible. As visible things, lyre and bow point to the invisible harmony. The sun itself, highest and most conspicuous of visible things, points to something "that does *not* go under," to the invisible fire (B16). The sun is visibly what in a recondite way all things are, namely, fire. Fire is the all-encompassing cipher for the unity of all things, insofar as that unity is thought of as substance.

Not only the visible, the audible also—language—becomes symbol: the $\beta\iota\delta s$, "bow," of B48 (by its identity with $\beta\iota os$, "life") attests that "life" causes death, that each is bound up with the other—as B88 says without simile. Heraclitus takes the individual word, as he takes the individual thing, as a symbol. He dives into it, as it were, to discover in its meaning a countermeaning. Only with the isolating of the word does the clarifying paradox emerge. Etymologizing as such is alien to him: In contemplating the bow as a phenomenological totality, "death" is no more essential for him than "life"; as a whole, its "work" and its "name" taken together, the bow reveals to him the essential unity of life and death.

Yet another example of argument drawing on language, in this case on proverb, is B34: "The saying bears witness to them that, 'present, they are absent.'" Here the proverb is cited like a witness to a paradoxical state of affairs, as the name of the bow or the example of the lyre are cited—except that this gnomic saying already displays both the content and the form of Heraclitean statement.

The similes of Heraclitus are, therefore, no mere literary device; rather, what can be seen is for him a simile for what is hidden. Parmenides was able to deduce that the opposites are logical contradictories,

[14] For a different view, see Olof Gigon, *Untersuchungen zu Heraklit* (Leipzig, 1935), p. 113.

and in so doing developed the form of dialectical proof. For Heraclitus the paradox of the unity of opposites was something not to be proven, but to be grasped through intuition alone. B18 cautions us that insight into the paradox is not the acquired result of investigation; there is no "method of inquiry" (contrast Parmenides' ὁδὸς διζήσιος, "route of inquiry," with Heraclitus' ἄπορον, "impassable strait"); the paradox is not to be ferreted out, but presents itself "unexpectedly." In Heraclitus simile takes the place of proof. This function is perfectly clear in many fragments, for example in B51 and B67. It would not, however, be able to assume this role if it functioned merely as a model—which is how it functions in the Milesians (star-wheels, bellows, column-drum, felt cap) and in Empedocles (clepsydra, wind-lantern).[15] For Heraclitus, the thing one looks at is itself the riddle. It is difficult to decide whether sea-water (B61) is simile or phenomenon for him; the phenomenon *is* simile. His calling things *phanera*, "conspicuously clear," is pointedly suggestive. Things, properly understood, are manifestations of something hidden, of the invisible they present on their face— "what we did not catch, we bring" (B56): An "open secret," as Clement calls it, using the language of Heraclitean paradox.[16]

The visible is, accordingly, something in which the true essence, the *physis*, reveals and hides itself at once. Even B123 must be understood this way, for if "the true essence of things loves to hide itself," it is implied that essence is not something completely hidden and withdrawn. The concept of self-concealment is encountered again in B93 "The lord at Delphi neither speaks nor conceals . . . ." There is no implied contrast here between *physis*, which "conceals itself," and Apollo, who "does not conceal": The god proclaims in image and simile, just as the essence of what is proclaims itself in visible things. The form of proclamation, in the case of things as in the case of the Delphic oracle, is the riddle.

We now see that the oracle fragment does not merely allude to Heraclitus' style: It has a certain objective reference; it says something about how self-concealing *physis* is to be understood—as revealing itself in signs. It is, nevertheless, true that Heraclitus' own language is in large measure determined by the oracle's manner of speech. His language, too, must be one of paradox, simile, and riddle, precisely insofar as it seeks to proclaim the essence of what is. His speech is valid

[15] Cf. Walther Kranz, "Gleichnis und Vergleich in der frühgriechischen Philosophie," *Hermes*, 73 (1938), 99 ff.

[16] *Paedagogus* III.2.1.

statement, yet remains essentially not understood—as with the oracle, in both respects. So there is a significant analogy between the *physis* of things and Heraclitean style. The obscurity of the language of simile, even when it borders on affectation, is no willful, merely rhetorical obscurity, but corresponds to the riddle-like character of what is to be said. Heraclitus does not speak in metaphors, in order to obscure a state of affairs that in itself is clear; rather, for him as for the oracle, simile is the means of hinting at a state of affairs that lies hidden. His speech is paradoxical because his truth is paradoxical . . . .

Phenomena in Heraclitus have the status of a simile: They are significant; they have a meaning to which they point. This is brought out in the explicit comparisons: "a structure of opposed tensions *as* with the bow . . ." (B51); "exchange for fire *as* for gold . . ." (B90); "God is . . . he changes himself *as* . . ." (B67). But the fact that the phenomenon *is* a simile does not by itself imply the *employment* of similes as a stylistic device. The comparison form recalls the analogies employed by the Milesians. Once we make this connection, a crucial difference appears: The linguistic style of the Milesians would not have been much affected by their use of analogy; for Heraclitus, by contrast, comparison informs statement itself.

The effect of comparison may also be achieved without the use of "as": "We step and do not step into the same rivers—we are and are not" (B49a); "Man kindles a light in the night, when he has extinguished his eyes—the man alive kindles the dead man" (B26).[17] Image and what is meant are here simply juxtaposed, and it is precisely this form of simple parataxis that enhances the impression of depth meaning created by Heraclitus' style. The image becomes self-sufficient, and thus becomes a statement in its own right. Indeed, it is doubtful whether the normal pattern required an additional statement to furnish the image's reference. "The name of the bow is life, its work death": Heraclitus could hardly have continued "so also . . ."; the image had to speak for itself.

So it turns out that we often cannot tell what is properly image and what statement. "Doctors bring good and pain" (that is the sense of B58)—is Heraclitus discussing medicine? "Sea-water is healthy and unhealthy"—is the context that of physiology? "The road to and from

[17] What this fragment means is a separate question. Gigon, *Unters.*, p. 96, misses the simile-character of the first clause. See Hölscher, *Anf. Fragen*, pp. 150–56.

is one and the same"—is that a cosmological statement? When the image itself becomes statement, then the border between simile and reference disappears; the image takes on something of the quality of metaphor.

It was as metaphor that the quality of Heraclitus' style was felt by his immediate imitator, the author of the medical work *De Victu*. Whenever this author speaks in Heraclitean similes, he is actually referring to material interactions. Here the style is obscure because the author intends to be cryptic: He veils in metaphors or abstractions the medical facts to which he refers. In a similar vein, Theophrastus, too, assigned certain image-statements, which stood isolated in Heraclitus' text, to specific doctrines—with most drastic consequences in the case of the image of "the way up and down." It was precisely this isolation of the image-statement that eventually elicited the extravagances of metaphorical interpretation, which, after Theophrastus, came to dominate discussions of Heraclitus. From then on, a sentence such as "all animals are driven to pasture with a stick" (B11) could only be understood in metaphorical terms. For the Christian readers of Heraclitus this process of metaphorical interpretation eventually took over the entire text.

Is there a mark by which simile and doctrine may be distinguished? "The living and the dead are the same"—that is statement; "the way of the screw-press is straight and crooked"—that is simile. The criterion is the same as that formulated by Reinhardt for a different distinction: "What lies open to view, and what is paradox?" [18] The identity of manifest opposites, such as life and death, is the paradoxical doctrine. But where the unity of what is contradictory is perspicuously evident in a phenomenon, there it serves as *proof* of the doctrine: "We step and do not step into the same rivers . . . ." The image-statements of Heraclitus have more of the quality of example than of metaphor: in the example of the bather one sees that . . . ; in what doctors do to us we come to experience how . . . ; in the lyre it is clearly and palpably evident that . . . . All are concrete proofs, in which the coincidence of opposites is perspicuously evident. One must examine all of Heraclitus' statements keeping this character of perspicuity in mind.

[18] Karl Reinhardt, "Heraclitea," *Hermes*, 77 (1942), 244 (repr. in Karl Reinhardt, *Vermächtnis der Antike. Gesammelte Essays zur Philosophie und Geschichtsschreibung*, ed. Carl Becker [Göttingen, 1960], pp. 72–97; also in *Um die Begriffswelt der Vorsokratiker*, ed. H.-G. Gadamer, Wege der Forschung, 9 [Darmstadt, 1968], pp. 177–208).

Then it becomes obvious that the saying about sea-water is not a remark on the relativity of properties, the saying about doctors no invective against the art of healing; rather both these sayings point to manifest facts, both are similes.

The sayings that formulate doctrine are quite different. They do not explain and they do not argue; they seek paradox. Life and death, also youth and old age, are understood not as transformations of an identical entity, but as opposites, the nature of each consisting in the reversal of its complement. There is no formulation of doctrine, however, in a saying such as "Beginning and end are common in a circle's circumference" (B103): Its obviousness shows it to be a simile. It would be a mistake to ask what sort of circle or cycle Heraclitus has in mind; what he has in mind is the identity of beginning and end.

Let us finally consider the saying "The road to and from is one and the same" (B60). The obviousness peculiar to it is brought out in this translation.[e] If one were to take it to refer to the descent and ascent of the elements, or of the soul, then, to begin with, the right sequence, down to up, would have appeared reversed in this fragment. Moreover, the proposition, the soul and the elements undergo a re-transformation that is the reverse of the one they go through as they come to be, lacks—of all things—that contradictory and paradoxical quality indispensable for the expression of unity in Heraclitean statement. By contrast, the reference to the road, in its double aspect as a way to and a way from, makes obvious the unity of an essence constituted by opposites. In it the mystery of coincidence stands revealed.

It would now seem that the stylistic feature of isolation in statement, so prominent in Heraclitean similes, is not confined to their domain; it pervades the whole of his language. It is not necessary to adduce more examples; almost every sentence is a gnomic utterance; the general thrust of the language is toward gnomic utterance. The selectivity of the tradition may well have done much to reinforce this impression. Still, the effect on the Hippocratic *De Victu* and on Democritus proves that isolation in statement is an essential feature of Heraclitus' style.

As we compare Heraclitus with these two early imitators of his style, a certain distinction emerges. The Hippocratic writer, when introducing a simile patterned on Heraclitus, does not fail to add an explanation of its meaning. "Men saw wood: one pulls, another pushes.

---

[e] [The usual translation is "The road up and the road down are one and the same."—Ed.]

. . . So the *physis* of man: one thing pushes, another pulls. . . ." [f]
The language of the imitator is distinguished from that of the master
in that the simile is taken out of its linguistic isolation and inserted
into the context of an unfolding argument. His Heraclitisms stand out
because of their thought pattern and diction; what they cannot do is
to stand free of the text.

The gnome-pattern in Democritus, too, is an adaptation of the
Heraclitean form. To be sure, *Gnomae* collections have a tendency to
make aphorisms even out of statements that had no such function in
their original context. Democritus' own style is rather uncontracted;
it is so overly explicit that it verges on platitude. Yet he, too, appre-
ciates terse statement, modeled on that of his Ephesian predecessor,
whom he likes to quote. Simile and riddle are altogether lacking in
Democritean gnomae. Typical contents are: life experiences; anthropological judgments; rules of conduct—many of these strikingly astute.
Indeed, his gnomae are confined in subject matter to the moral-
anthropological domain—contrast the wide range of Heraclitean sayings. It is a pedagogical-didactic temperament that speaks in the sayings of Democritus. For him the fascinating aspect of gnome was its
character as maxim, its claim of universal validity. Consider B171:
ψυχὴ οἰκητήριον δαίμονος, "the dwelling place of fortune is the soul" (not
money). The contrast with Heraclitus B119, ἦθος ἀνθρώπῳ δαίμων, is
twofold. The Heraclitean statement is not a precept of practical
morality but an existential proposition: "For man, character is his
destiny." Moreover, for its validity as a remark, the statement counts
not so much on general endorsement by the community of right-
minded men, as the Democritean statement does, but rather more on
the fact of men's deafness. It is more threatening than edifying: The
soul's fate hangs on its merit . . . . Compare, too, Heraclitus B40
"much learning does not teach understanding" with Democritus B64
"even many men of much learning do not have understanding." Not
merely that the second statement had its teeth pulled out, the point is
that only in its Heraclitean form does the saying have the character of
an insight, one that throws light on human existence as a whole.
Similarly, μόροι μέζονες μέζονας μοίρας λαγχάνουσιν (B25)[g] becomes μέζονες
ὀρέξεις μέζονας ἐνδείας ποιεῦσιν, "the greater the desire, the greater the
needs" (B219). The latter gives no hint of the tone of prophetic power

[f] [DK 22C1(16).—Ed.]

[g] ["Greater deaths (or 'fates') are assigned greater fates (or 'portions')."—
Ed.]

and solemn promise, which Clement heard in the words of Heraclitus when he quoted B25. "The sun is new with each day" is Heraclitus' paradoxical doctrine (B6); "new with each day" (B158) is how Democritus, more edifyingly, describes the thoughts of men fresh at the workday's start. "Sea-water is the purest and the most sickening," says Heraclitus (B61); "deep water is useful in many respects, and then again bad, for one can drown in it," echoes Democritus (B172). The hidden-yet-manifest reality of contradiction is transformed into a relativity of properties. The Heraclitean saying clearly lacks the chief mark that all definitions of "gnome" or "maxim" tend to emphasize: the character of universality. It reflects, rather, a specific experience, which the saying turns into knowledge. In this respect it is close to proverb—consider: "Dogs bark at whomever they do not know" (B97). The essence of Heraclitean saying is not didactic, but assertive and apodictic.[19] A statement such as ἁρμονίη ἀφανὴς φανερῆς κρείττων (B54) offers this advantage over all Democritean sayings: one finds in it the knowledge through which the contradiction implicit in the world or in human existence is suddenly illuminated. All Heraclitean sayings are *discoveries:* insights that dawn upon the thoughtful soul like the solution to a riddle. The Heraclitean saying mirrors not only the riddle-form of his knowledge, but also the suddenness with which that knowledge presents itself. The revelatory character of Heraclitean truth has been justly emphasized. Hesiod and Parmenides experienced revelations, but the content of the revelation remained for them untouched by the *form* of the revelation. In Heraclitus it informs the manner of knowing itself; it becomes the inner form of his *logos*. It is what Goethe calls an "apperçu": the "sudden realization of what really underlies appearances." . . .

Thus Heraclitean utterance mirrors exactly the character of Heraclitus' knowledge: in its use of similes the hinting or signifying quality of phenomena; in its antithetical construction the paradoxical unity of contradiction; in its stylistic isolation the immediacy of "intuitive judgment" (to speak again in Goethe's terminology). Gnomic utterance is for him a necessary form.

[19] On gnome (*Spruch*) as a preliterary form, see André Jolles, *Einfache Formen* (Halle, 1929), pp. 163 ff. For ancient and modern definitions of "gnome," see Kurt von Fritz, *RE* Suppl. VI, and W. Spoerri, in *Der kleine Pauly*, s.v. *Gnome*.

V

PARMENIDES

11

ELEMENTS OF ELEATIC ONTOLOGY

Montgomery Furth

The task of an interpreter of Parmenides is to find the simplest, historically most plausible, and philosophically most comprehensible set of assumptions that imply (in a suitably loose sense) the doctrine of 'being' set out in Parmenides' poem.[1] In what follows I offer an interpretation that certainly is simple and that I think should be found comprehensible. Historically, only more cautious claims are possible, for several portions of the general view from which I 'deduce the poem' are not clearly stated in the poem itself; my explanation of this is that they are operating as *tacit* assumptions, and indeed that the poem is best thought of as an attempt to force these very assumptions to the surface for formulation and criticism—that the poem is a challenge. To be sure, there are dangers in pretending, as for dramatic purposes I shall, that ideas are definite and explicit which for Parmenides himself must have been tacit or vague—that Parmenides knew what he was doing as clearly as I represent him; I try to avoid them, but the risk must be taken. I even believe that not to take it, in the name of preserving his thought pure from anachronous contamination, actually prevents us from seeing the extent to which he, pioneer, was ahead of his time—the argument works both ways. So let me hedge my historical claim in this way: the view I shall discuss could have been an active—indeed a controlling—element of Eleaticism; to suppose that Parmenides held it not only explains the poem, but also helps explain the subsequent reactions to Eleaticism of Anaxagoras, Democritus, and

[1] This paper was prepared while the author was beneficiary of a Grant-in-Aid of Research from the American Council of Learned Societies, hereby gratefully acknowledged.

Plato (though there is not space to elaborate this here). In addition, it brings his thought astonishingly close to some contemporary philosophical preoccupations.

In the first of the following sections, I lay down some sketchy but necessary groundwork concerning the early Greek concept of 'being.' Then in Section 2 an interpretation is given of what I take to be the central Parmenidean doctrine, that 'it cannot be said that anything is not.' This section is the lengthiest and most involved, but it also contains all the moves that appear to be important. Of the remaining sections, Section 3 explains the principle: 'of what is, all that can be said is: *it is*,' Section 4 deals briefly with the remaining cosmology of "The Way of Truth," and Section 5 considers the question whether Parmenides himself believed the fantastic conclusions of his argument. There is a short postscript on a point of methodology.

1. A Word on ὄν

If we are to examine Parmenides' reasoning profitably, an indispensable preliminary is to establish at least a provisional reading for the Greek words translated "is" or "it is" (*esti*), "what is" or "being" (*on, to on*), "to be" (*einai*). For while it is evident enough that in his poem Parmenides purports to be delivering an insight of the utmost significance concerning *to eon* (as he calls it), still the construction which he puts upon the term and its cognates, and the understanding which he expects of his listener, are not so clear and have been topics of dispute.

Especially notable, and often noted, is the fact that Parmenides' discussion of 'being' shows no sign of the conceptual distinction considered elementary nowadays, between the "is" linking subject and predicate and the "is" of existence; and in fact it needs no documentation here that this distinction was not reflected in either ordinary or philosophical Greek idiom until, at least, a much later date than his, the word *esti* expressing both concepts. Also highly visible in the poem is the abundance of occurrences of *esti* used absolutely, unaccompanied by any predicate expression. As a result of this last, the poem can create in the contemporary reader the impression that *to eon* is being used to mean 'what is' in the existential sense only, to mean what *there* is; indeed some students of the poem conclude not only that Parmenides is unwittingly confining himself to the existential meaning, but even that his confusion on this score is responsible for his entire doctrine.[2]

[2] Thus Raven in KR, p. 270.

Such scant basis as there is for the latter idea will be adequately treated below;[3] but it is important to understand from the outset that the notion of 'being' studied by Parmenides and by early Greek philosophy in general, is not 'confined' to either of our two distinct concepts, that of existence and that of being something-or-other in the sense of having such-and-such properties (being a man, being green); rather, these notions are impacted or *fused* in the early Greek concept of being. A result is that a Greek inquiry *ti to on*, 'what is being?', frequently must be interpreted as concerned simultaneously with the concepts of being = existence and of 'being Φ' for variable Φ. To approach a Greek thinker, even as late as Aristotle,[4] without keeping this in mind is to risk serious misunderstanding of his concerns.

This fusion of the ideas of existence and of being-of-a-certain-sort does not merely show itself in the early use of the word *esti*, but seems to be part of a more general situation having other manifestations also; these have such close bearings on the interpretation of Parmenides that the matter should be explored a little further. First let us recall—what has often been pointed out—a tendency in ancient philosophy, (a) to take as the ideal or paradigm form of fact-stating assertion the ascription of a property to an object, and the further tendency (b) to take as the ideal or paradigm form of ascription of a property to an object the use of a subject-predicate sentence with subject and predicate linked by the copula.[5] In this way the predicative use of *esti* can come to be thought of as paradigmatic for asserting that anything at all *is the case*, or *obtains*. And once we see this we can discern a considerable variety of assimilations at points where nowadays it is customary to make distinctions; thus, a running together of

(1a) being-the case (*on*)	with	(1b) existence (*on*),
(2a) facts (*pragmata, tynchanonta*, etc.)	with	(2b) objects (*pragmata, tynchanonta*, etc.)
(3a) coming-to-be (the case) (*gignesthai*)	with	(3b) coming-to-be (= coming to exist) (*gignesthai*).

[3] Cf. footnote 34 below.

[4] Cf. Miss Anscombe, in G. E. M. Anscombe and P. T. Geach, *Three Philosophers* (Oxford, 1961), p. 22.

[5] Thus Aristotle remarks, as an earnest of the importance of the science of ὄν, that even sentences not containing ἐστι (ὁ ἄνθρωπος βαδίζει) can be taken as variants of ones that do (ὁ ἄνθρωπος βαδίζων ἐστίν, cf. *Metaph.* V.7.1017a27 ff.); whether this is true is of less significance here than the fact that Aristotle, on occasion at least, feels as if it ought to be true.

Parallel to the fusion of the notions of fact and object as items of the world, is a tendency at the semantical level to run together properties of sentences with properties of singular and general terms. Here the common element is an expression's 'corresponding (or failing to correspond) to something that is' in the two senses of "is"; thus *truth* for sentences, describing what is (the case), can tend to fuse with *applying to something* for singular and general terms, denoting something that is (= exists), and conversely falsehood for sentences tends to merge with failure to apply to anything for terms. In this case the assimilation is rather conceptual than fully visible in the vocabulary; for example, terms (*onomata*) that apply to or denote something are not for this reason[6] called "true" (*alēthē*); the fusion is evidenced when the notions are being *explained:* thus truth as 'saying, indicating in speech, that which is,' and falsehood as 'saying, indicating in speech, that which is not.' In these terms we can put the assimilation in this way:

(4a) saying, indicating in speech, that which is (= stating truly)	with	(4b) saying, indicating in speech, that which is (= designating something that exists),
(5a) saying, indicating in speech, that which is not (= stating falsely)	with	(5b) saying, indicating in speech, that which is not (= designating something that does not exist).

A final case, which need be no more than touched on here, is the assimilation of the propositional and the acquaintanceship senses of "know," the knowledge of knowing that the earth is round, versus the knowledge of knowing thyself. Here the assimilation at the level of vocabulary is partial but not total; ancient Greek stands somewhere between those languages, like modern French and German, in which the distinction is strongly marked in a differentiation of words, mis-choice of which is typically error (kennen-wissen, connaître-savoir), and those like modern English where the verbal differentiation (*know* vs. *wit*) has all but completely disappeared. For while the centers of gravity, so to speak, of *gignōskein* and *eidenai* seem to be respectively acquaintance (knowledge$_a$, let us say) and propositional (knowledge$_p$),

---

[6] Though Aristotle in the *Topics* speaks of their 'being true of something,' ἀληθεύεσθαι κατά τινος. The 'truth' of names to their bearers as mooted in the *Cratylus* is another issue.

there is nevertheless plenty of variation. Thus for *gignōskein* there is indeed *gnōthi sauton* and the numerous like, but a propositional use, *gignōskein hoti*, is common also. And for *eidenai*, though it comes to be commonly propositional (very often with *hōs*, *hoti*, or *ei*, and in Aristotle often used like *epistasthai*, 'to know [= know$_p$] scientifically'), still it also appears to retain its older flavor of having-seen, what is seen being thing (person, e.g.) or fact indifferently; compare its use in Homer's curious formulas for states of mind ("knew lawless things," etc.). And Adeimantus can say that we know (*ismen*) the gods only from the poets and tradition (*Republic* 365e2).

Thus the distinction between knowing$_a$ and knowing$_p$ is reflected to a degree in choice of words in Greek, although the reflection is somewhat shifting and uncertain. As evidence that there is nevertheless considerable fusion of the two concepts, however, one may recall the celebrated early *discussion* of 'knowledge'—one of the first occasions of its mention, as opposed to use—in *Republic* V (476–480), the passage which is supposed to establish the distinctness of the 'objects' of knowledge and opinion, *to gnōston* and *to doxaston*. The key to the passage is the employment of the principle 'what a man knows, must be,' a principle to which Socrates gains Glaucon's unhesitating assent in a famous exchange.[7] And Glaucon's assent is entirely reasonable; for the principle is none other than the fused form of the two theses, axiomatic for knowledge$_a$ and knowledge$_p$ on any account, that necessarily if something is known$_a$, then it exists, and that necessarily if something is known$_p$, then it is the case or obtains. Thus the truism which Glaucon accepts can be split thus:

(6a) Necessarily, what is known, is (= is the case),

(6b) Necessarily, what is known, is (= exists).

Now, as the ensuing discussion makes all too apparent, Socrates does not sufficiently distinguish between (on the one hand) the principles (6), which constitute part of the concept of knowledge itself on any theory, and (on the other) the extremely dubious principles (7):

(7a) What is known, is-necessarily (is necessarily the case, or a necessary truth),

(7b) What is known, is-necessarily (exists necessarily, or is a necessary existent).

For it is (7a) upon which he plays to obtain the desired contrast with (propositional) belief; belief being, as is agreed on all hands, such that

---

[7] ὁ γιγνώσκων γιγνώσκει τὶ ἢ οὐδέν; . . . — . . . γιγνώσκει τί:—Πότερον ὂν ἢ οὐκ ὄν;—Ὄν. πῶς γὰρ ἂν μὴ ὂν γέ τι γνωσθείη; (476e7–477a1).

(8a) It is not necessary that
what is believed, be (= be
the case).

Presumably, (8a) is as axiomatic for belief as (6a) is for knowledge$_p$; but given that (6a) is confused with (7a), it is not surprising that a similar confusion occurs between (8a) and

(9a) What is believed, is not-
necessarily (= is not necessarily the case, or is not a
necessary truth),

and that, contrasting (9a) with (7a), the conclusion is arrived at that what is known and what is believed (the 'objects' of knowledge and of belief) by their nature cannot be the same.

My interest here is not the modal fallacy involved in the transition from (6a) to (7a), or from (8a) to (9a), although I do think that, simple as it is, it is of some importance in encouraging (if not giving rise to) Plato's associations of 'what is known' with what is eternal, unchanging, of perfect and stable reality, and so on: in short, his idea that what can be known must be necessary existents and necessarily true propositions, like Forms and truths of mathematics, whereas what originally secures one's assent to the principle 'what a man knows, must be' seems to be the considerably more humdrum idea that what is known$_a$ must merely exist (6b), what is known$_p$ must merely be so (6a). Nor am I concerned with the additional startling consequence that, belief being confined by (9a) to contingent truths and falsehoods, necessary truths cannot be believed, only known, which on the surface squares badly with the philosopher-king arriving at knowledge about them from a state of right opinion; though in fact this probably is easily enough put right. What I do wish to point out is that the argument manifests throughout a fusion in the concept of knowledge that answers closely to that in the concept *on;* for it purports to establish (7a) and (7b) simultaneously, as (so to speak) a single proposition concerning a notion *to gnōston* in which 'known$_p$' and 'known$_a$' are combined.

The position becomes clearer still if we attend more closely to the notion of *doxa* with which the argument contrasts that of *gnōsis*. I have written above in terms of 'belief' in contrast with knowledge$_p$, since English (eked out with a subscript) affords us a compact formulation of the difference; but now let us ask ourselves, what for Plato stands to knowledge$_a$ as belief stands to knowledge$_p$? The answer seems to be something like: perception-by-the-senses together with formation-of-sensory-images-of-physical-objects; let us call it "sense-perceiving." It appears virtually certain that Plato would subscribe to the same contrast here as is explicitly used in the fallacious argument from the *Republic* as partially described above; that is, begin by putting the following quite reasonable condition on 'sense-perceiving,' differentiating it from knowledge$_a$ as characterized in (6b):

> (8b) It is not necessary that what is sense-perceived, be (= exist),

and proceed to infer from, or perhaps simply confuse with, (8b) the thesis

> (9b) What is sense-perceived, is not-necessarily (does not exist necessarily, is not a necessary existent),

which, however reasonable, has not been legitimately obtained by the methods employed. The point is that Plato (in this passage) is no more conscious of a distinction between the notions here rendered as 'believing' and 'sense-perceiving' than he is of a distinction between knowing$_p$ and knowing$_a$; both are covered by the general idea *doxazein*, so that one 'doxazises' contingent existents and states of affairs indifferently, just as (the argument would have it) necessary existents and states of affairs—and only these—are 'known.' Thus the fusion is really threefold, occurring in *to on*, in *to gnōston*, and in *to doxaston* as well.

Much remains to be said about the fused notion of being; but the foregoing may suffice as a sketch of what it is, and as making out that it, or something like it, occurs in early Greek thought. Its relevance to a contemporary assessment of Parmenides is of course great, in two ways. First, it explains the feeling commonly produced by his poem and already mentioned, that only one variety of 'being' is contemplated in his reasoning; the feeling is correct, but the single variety under study is not the existential but the fused. Second, it faces us with the question whether this assimilation on Parmenides' part is of any importance in obtaining his conclusions. I shall propose—in hopes that the sequel will bear me out—that the answer is roughly No, in much the same sense as would fit the argument from the *Republic* just considered. There we saw the fused notion employed, but the actual fault in the argument—the now-trite modal fallacy, converting *necessitas consequentiae* into *necessitas consequentis*—remained quite unaffected by our splitting each of the propositions (6)–(9) into two. Thus Plato could have reached the same conclusion in the same way even without the fusion of 'being'; and thus the fusion, critically important as it is, need not have played any role at all in the present connection.[8] To make the similar case for Parmenides, therefore, I shall depart from his own conceptions in the analogous way: instead of trying to carry out his reasoning (as I understand it) in the fused sense, I shall do so separately for the two senses, though with an effort to keep to an interpretation of these that is not too far from that which a fifth-century thinker might have had in mind. This has the drawback of failing to follow Parmenides as exactly as is possible for one to do today; but it has the merit of bringing out as clearly as possible exactly what is essential to his argument.

2. It Cannot Be Said That Anything Is Not

It is convenient to take as my starting point the fact that, as Parmenides several times stresses, he is floating a critique of 'ways (*or* roads) of enquiry,' *hodoi dizēsios* (B2.2, 6.3, 7.2);[9] these, he says, are three in number, and two of them, he argues, are impossible. The first (in the ordering of fragments 6, 7, and 8) is: [*it*] *is not* (*ouk estin*); the second is: [*it*] *both is and is not;* the third, and the sole survivor of the critique: [*it*] *is* (*estin*). Now it is easy to assume from the vast generality of the three 'ways' as described, that the type of 'enquiry,' *dizēsis*, which Parmenides has in mind, is of a very large kind indeed: some enormous *Seinsfrage* that would be expressed, *is it?* (answer, *it is*); or again, *what is?* (answer, *what is*). From here it will be but a short step to numbering Parmenides among the long line of speculative metaphysicians who have experienced no discomfort, and even some exhilaration, in discoursing about the idea of Being just in general, or of Being but being nothing in particular; there is a considerable tradition, not yet concluded it seems, of regarding Parmenides in this way. Alternatively, the implied vastness of the 'enquiry,' perhaps together with Aristotle's apparently automatic assumption that Parmenides is to be classified as a cosmologist, may suggest that the 'enquiry' is of the kind that would issue in 'physical opinions,' natural philosophy, in a more or less normal Pre-

[8] Need not, though the possibility will always remain that it did in fact.
[9] References of the form B *n.m* are to line *m* of fragment *n* in the text of Parmenides as given in DK.

Socratic sense; the final portion of the poem, or what is left of this, has encouraged some in this belief.

That Parmenides is not to be taken as a standard Pre-Socratic cosmologist I shall not argue here; as will appear below, I regard the cosmological conclusions of "The Way of Truth" (the universe is a single continuous solid mass; there is no change, plurality, motion; etc.) as remote corollaries of principles of a purely logical kind whose working is the real point of the poem; and as for the extent to which Parmenides himself should be judged to stand behind the world-view served up in "The Way of Seeming," I have nothing to add to Owen's discussion.[10] The *Seinsfrage* interpretation raises some more difficult questions; but discussion of contrasts between it and my own is best deferred until my own has been set out.

But it does not seem that we are *required* to understand 'enquiry' in any such general or elevated sense as the foregoing. By an 'enquiry' into 'what is' I shall understand Parmenides to mean *any investigation of 'what is' in the sense of what is so, or what is the case; any procedure aimed at ascertaining the facts*. It may be an enquiry whether a certain thing exists, or whether things of a certain kind exist, or whether a thing has a certain quality; nor need any restriction be placed on the subject matter—whatever Parmenides is saying will apply equally well to ascertaining whether there is animal life on Mars, or a rational root to a certain equation, or an amount of tribute that will satisfy the Persians, or whether Socrates is flying, or any broad-leaved plants are deciduous. I am not denying that among the matters included at the outset as potential topics of 'enquiry' there might be such large-bore specimens as whether there is change, or for that matter whether there is being (?); but it is not necessary to suppose this.

a) "Is" EXISTENTIAL. To see this more clearly, let us now invoke our decision to separate the existential and the predicative senses of *esti*, and let us therefore consider the idea of an 'enquiry' for the existential sense alone. I take Parmenides to be considering, then, the idea of any investigation, however commonplace or high-flown, abstract or em-

[10] G. E. L. Owen, "Eleatic Questions," *CQ*, N.S. 10 (1960), 84–102 [repr. in Furley and Allen, II]; in the present connection cf. 84–89. I should remark here that although the views presented in the present paper were formed before I belatedly encountered Owen's piece in 1965, I am indebted to it for valuable historical and textual lore, and for the opportunity it afforded me of sharpening my argument in various ways, occasionally by contrast. I cite particulars where possible below, but the reader is referred to it in general.

pirical, into a question of existence: anything from *Is there sand in this machine?* to *Is there a cause of the universe?*

I now introduce the idea of *a person's ontology*, understanding by this: what (the things which) that person believes to exist. Speaking in these terms, if Alphides believes that (say) lions, centaurs, and irrational numbers exist, and that ghosts and electrons do not, I shall say that lions, centaurs, and irrational numbers are in Alphides' ontology whereas ghosts and electrons are not. Thus Alphides' ontology will be distinguished from that of Betathon, who believes in the existence of lions and electrons but not in that of centaurs, irrational numbers, and ghosts. It will escape no one's notice that the notion of a person's ontology as I have described it is, to say the least, susceptible of further analysis; but I ask that the reader stifle temporarily his urge to ask whether, if *in fact* there do not exist any lions, centaurs or irrational numbers then Alphides' ontology is empty (whether Alphides knows it or not); still more to postpone pressing upon me even subtler points, e.g. occasioned by the confusions of Gammytas, who believes that equine solid-hoofed perissodactyl quadrupeds exist but that horses do not. Gammytas' type of case involves difficulties which even today are not clearly understood, and which are some distance from our present topic; and to rush in too rapidly on Alphides' type of case may have the undesirable effect of obscuring what I take to be a point being made by Parmenides.

So let us imagine Betathon, for example, telling Parmenides the results of his 'enquiry' so far into 'what is' in the sense of existence, of what *there* is; thus, as giving an account of what does and what does not fall within his ontology. The following dialogue ensues:

BETATHON: Lions are.	PARMENIDES: [silent]
BETATHON: Electrons are.	PARMENIDES: [silent]
BETATHON: Centaurs are not.	PARMENIDES: Thou canst not be acquainted with what is not, nor indicate it in speech.[11]

Several points should be observed about this little exchange, even before we watch its continuation. First, it is of the essence of Parmenides' procedure, as I understand it, that *he is not at this point putting forth an ontology of his own*, but is practising dialectical criticism upon that

[11] B2.7–8. γνοίης, "canst be acquainted with," seems to bear the sense of knowledge$_a$ here; cf. p. 244 above. On φράσαις, "indicate in speech," see LSJ s.v. φράζω, and footnote 27 below.

being put forth by Betathon; his own word for his argument is *elenchos* (B7.5), which we must assume means for him, as it presently was to mean for Socrates, the technique of refuting an opponent by reasoning from a premiss that the opponent accepts to a conclusion that he must regard as intolerable, such as an explicit self-contradiction or the negation of some proposition that (for whatever reason) he cannot deny, and thus forcing him to abandon the premiss. (This does not necessarily mean forcing him to assert the negation of that premiss, as will appear.) Secondly, what is related, Parmenides is not himself even putting any conditions upon potential candidates for 'what is,' such as that anything that *is* has to be corporeal (Burnet),[12] or has to be *one* (Cornford);[13] conditions of this general type will indeed emerge from the whole argument, but they are not assumed at the outset. Parmenides' only need is for his interlocutor to assert that anything at all 'is not.' Thirdly, and again related, the subject of the verbs *estin* and *ouk estin*, for which so zealous a search has been conducted since the nineteenth century, resulting in an amazing variety of improbable candidates,[14] is supplied not by Parmenides but at each round of the questioning by Betathon, whose ontology is what is under scrutiny at this stage. Fourthly, it is to be noted that Parmenides *so far* has no objections to "Lions are," despite its imputation of plurality.

The dialogue continues:

BETATHON: [expresses bafflement]	PARMENIDES: Either they (= centaurs) are, or they are not.[15] [If they are, then in saying they are not you speak falsely, a case of 'saying what is not' that we shall consider separately.][16] If they are not, then you speak of nothing,[17] for what is not, what does not exist, is the same as nothing. But this is utterly

[12] Burnet, *EGP*, pp. 178–80.

[13] F. M. Cornford, *Plato and Parmenides* (London, 1939), p. 29.

[14] A comprehensive survey up to 1962 is given by L. Tarán in *Parmenides: A Text with Translation, Commentary and Critical Essays* (Princeton, 1965), pp. 33–40.

[15] B2.2–5, 8.11, 8.16.

[16] Pages 262–63 below.

[17] B6.1–2, 8.10.

unintelligible ('inscrutable');[18]
thou shalt find no thought that
is not of what is (= something
that is), in relation to which it
is said (uttered);[19] what can be
thought or spoken of must
be;[20] what is not (= nothing) is
both unthinkable and unname-
able,[21] not being there to be
thought or named.

A few comments on this. First, it would be a mistake, I think, to snap
at the equation of 'what is not' and 'nothing'; for while Parmenides is
indeed making an assumption in this connection, which we shall
examine in due course, it is an extremely reasonable one; and seizing
triumphantly upon it now can divert attention from the assumption that
is questionable upon which the argument really turns. Let us use the
word "denotes" for general terms in the sense of Quine's term "is true
of." [22] Then the general term "centaur" may be said to denote something just in case centaurs are, and if centaurs are not, Parmenides is
reasonably claiming, then "centaur" does not denote anything, which
is to say that it denotes nothing. There is no way out of this by attempting to prevent the move to "nothing"; one's tendency to protest that,
'after all, the word "centaur" surely doesn't denote nothing at all' either
rests upon some unannounced equivocation on "denote," or else tacitly
supplies something that "centaur" *does* denote—perhaps, e.g. for the
character that Quine calls McX[23] or for a novice in his first encounter
with the point, an idea in his mind. It is this point that Parmenides has
absolutely clear; as he incessantly repeats: it is, or it is not; either
centaurs are, or they aren't. If you say they are, I will not object (yet).
If you say they are not, I reply that either they are, and you are wrong,
or they are not, and you speak of nothing. If you protest that you are

[18] B2.6.

[19] B8.34–36.

[20] B3, 6.1.

[21] B8.17.

[22] W. V. Quine, "Two Dogmas of Empiricism," in *From a Logical Point of
View* (Cambridge, Mass., 1953), p. 21. The phrase "multiple denotation" is
used by R. M. Martin to the same effect; see *Truth and Denotation* (Chicago,
1958), pp. 99 ff.

[23] Quine, "On What There Is," *From a Logical Point of View*, pp. 1 f.

speaking of something and you can specify it (for example, an idea in your mind), my response is to allow the move, but to point out that you have *changed the subject*, from the flesh-and-blood centaurs outside your ontology (which you said that there weren't) to an idea within it (which you say that there is; thus I do not object to it (yet)).[23a]

Parmenides reserves his choicest insults, however, for the respondent who believes that he can have it both ways: that centaurs are not, do not exist, yet are (there) to be thought or spoken of. If Betathon attempts this option, he is a 'know-nothing,' 'two-headed,' his 'wandering mind' directed by 'helplessness,' he is 'borne along, deaf, dumb and blind, gawping and goggling (*tethēpōs*),' together with the 'unjudging mobs' who go in for the philosophy of Heraclitus.[24] Strong language, but understandable, for this expedient, in its present form, is exactly what he calls it; it consists in saying that centaurs both are and are not— a contradiction.

Before considering what other expedients may be open to Betathon, however, let us complete this part of Parmenides' argument. The critique of Betathon's ontology will continue in the same way; anything which, according to Betathon's scheme of things, *is*, is accepted without comment; but in the way already described, Betathon is not allowed to say that anything is not, to *exclude* from his ontology. At no point does Parmenides venture any views of his own about what is (nor, of course, about what is not); the critique is confined to Betathon's views and is exclusively internal. It should also be clearly understood that if in some case Betathon elects to make the move that I had Parmenides call 'changing the subject,' the move that we moderns associate with McX, this is entirely a matter of his own volition; Parmenides himself does not harbor any such metaphysical view as McX's ('Pegasus must be, because it would otherwise be nonsense to say even that Pegasus is not')[25] which he would doubtless ridicule as Heraclitean nonsense. But if Betathon chooses to avoid speaking of what is not by speaking instead of something else that (he thinks) is, that is Betathon's affair (so long as he does not try to say of *it* that it is not).

The net result of this part of the critique, then, is that Betathon can

[23a] [Note added in this collection.] The move is allowed for the moment; though of course the 'idea in your mind,' if *of* something that is not, will shortly itself be challenged on the principles here developing. Cf. pp. 262–63 below.

[24] B6.4–9, 7.1–5.

[25] Quine, p. 2.

speak of what is in his ontology and cannot speak of what is outside it;
he cannot speak of what according to *him* is not. The other half of the
critique applies the same method to what, according to Betathon, *is*.[26]

BETATHON: Cows are.	PARMENIDES: Either they (= cows) are, or they are not. [If they are, then you pass, this round.] If they are not, then you speak of nothing, for what is not, what does not exist, is the same as nothing, etc.

The technique is the same, and Parmenides still has not committed
himself to any ontology at all. (This is very important; even at this point
Parmenides is claiming no privileged knowledge or infallible insights
into what *really* is: he is employing only the principle, 'either it is, or it
is not.') But the significance for Betathon is considerable, for now not
only are his statements of not-being (nonexistence), true and false,
ruled out as 'about nothing,' but his false statements of existence as well.
And so some part of his attempted recital of his ontology itself (unless
he is infallible)—which part it is being unknown to him (assuming he is
candid and honest, saying all of and only what he really believes)—is
babble, meaningless gesticulation at 'nothing.' Also, it seems that to ask
whether something is (exists) is meaningless if the answer is in fact
negative. Thus Betathon's situation is unenviable at best.

Then to what *is* Parmenides committed? From the arguments as set
out, we can see that his assumptions are quite economical. First, a
statement of the form Φ's *exist* is true if and only if there are Φ's, or
(roughly) the term Φ denotes something, i.e., pleonastically, something
that *is*. Secondly, as we today would put it, for any Φ, either Φ's are or
Φ's are not, *tertium non datur;* and in particular the disjunction is
exclusive. It is worth noticing that this second restriction, innocuous as

[26] Too much stress should not be laid upon which part of the critique precedes which in my presentation. The order I am using (Betathon's existential
ontology: [1] internal critique, [2] external critique; Betathon's predicative
ontology: [3] internal critique, [4] external critique) is adopted chiefly for
expository convenience and to serve certain purposes of emphasis, but is
otherwise without significance. Logically speaking, "It is all the same to me
where I start; for I will come back there again" (B5). It is actually best of all to
think of the critique as practised as a whole upon Betathon's entire ontology
simultaneously. The matter will recur in the Postscript below.

it appears to our modern eyes, actually is somewhat confining; for it not only rules out, by the exclusiveness of the disjunction (denying that both limbs can be true at once), the Heraclitean idea so scorned, but also is what short-circuits, by the wholly general *tertium non datur*, any possibility of distinguishing between the idea of a term's denoting what does not exist, and the idea of a term's denoting nothing. For example, were it not for the excluded third, one might be interested in considering the idea of Meinong and Quine's character Wyman, that the domain of individuals is a set of subsistent (alternatively, of possible) objects, that these are what is named by the singular and general terms of our language, and that some of these exist and the rest do not. This idea is nowadays widely regarded as silly, a view I do not share, for it is not clear to me that no acceptable formulation of it is possible; but in any event it is forbidden on Parmenides' assumptions, according to which a thing can exist only 'fully,' 'all the way' (*pampan*, B8.11) or not at all. Very likely he would consider Wyman a Heraclitean in disguise.

The third and controlling assumption, however, is also in a way the simplest. It is, put one way, that for singular and general terms, meaningfulness is identical with the having of denotation; put another way, that a singular or general term can possess meaning of just *one* kind, which Parmenides not unnaturally takes to be, that in reality which—if it exists—the term denotes.[27] It is owing to this assumption that the havoc wrought by Parmenides' single question (*Is it? Or is it not?*) is so great. Not because, if (say) Pegasus is not, then the name "Pegasus" denotes nothing, or (if we wish to speak in this way) Pegasus is nothing; for as we saw, on the entirely reasonable second assumption that is simply true and unblinkable. But because if a singular or general term lacks denotation, 'corresponds to (= denotes) nothing in reality,' then it is taken to be an empty name with no meaning at all. This assumption, I believe, is the real root of the matter, the source of the whole doctrine, to which everything else is ancillary. (Shortly I shall show how Parmenides derives from it [or might have done] all the rest of his fantastic

[27] Much importance has been (rightly) attached in several recent works to the pre-eminence for the early Greek view of language of the model of *spoken* as opposed to written communication. From this standpoint, the paradigm of meaning I fix upon above would be put in terms of, not the object(s) that a term denotes, but the object(s) that a person designates by the use of a term: to 'mean' something is to spear it with a spoken (winged?) word. Then to speak of what is not is to hurl a term at—what? It isn't there. Similarly for 'thinking of.' Cf. pp. 262–63 below.

theory of the world.) We should notice particularly its operation in the first part of the dialogue with Betathon, who, having attempted to say (let us assume, truly) that centaurs were not, is given only three choices:

(1) Stop trying to say that (Parmenides' preference),

(2) Continue to try to say that (and be pilloried for adverting to 'nothing,' and perhaps for being a Heraclitean as well),

(3) 'Change the subject' by claiming that the reference is to something that *is*, such as a mental idea (but then, of course, he will be told that centaurs are after all, if *that* is what he means by "centaur." As we saw, it's all the same to Parmenides; he only wishes to know whether according to Betathon it is or it isn't).

It is the third assumption that brands any attempt to import some further thing, distinct from the (nonexistent) denotation, that might be meant by a denotationless term, as 'changing the subject,' shifting to a new denotation.

Because of this, it is tempting to characterize Parmenides, on our interpretation of him, as a fanatical hyper-extensionalist who recognizes the denotation of expressions but who is refusing to think of them as possessing any further aspect or component of meaning such as, in Frege's language, 'sense,' distinct from the ordinarily intended denotation and also (what is not the same) not denoted by the expression. I believe that there is some truth in this idea but that as it is likely to be taken it does not hit the mark exactly. For in the notion current nowadays of an intensional component of meaning belonging to an expression over and above its denotation (if any), there are actually two ideas combined. One is that of a meaning distinct from the denotation, one which, so to speak, is guaranteed to belong to the expression if the expression has, in ordinary terms, any cognitive meaning at all. The other is the further condition, that the criterion for two expressions' having the *same* meaning in this over-and-above sense of "meaning" is stricter or narrower than that for their denoting the same denotation. This latter condition is what fits the intensional meaning of an expression to serve as its 'oblique' or 'indirect' denotation in Frege's famous analysis of certain failures of substitutivity of identity, which otherwise would appear to jeopardize Leibniz' law at the level of denotation within his theory. This is not the place to go into detail about that matter; without argument I shall say simply that I do not believe that the rather complicated issues involved there are issues for Parmenides, and that therefore the finer *discriminations* in meaning that are nowadays associated with the intensional level are largely irrelevant to Parmenides' problem.[28]

With that reservation, however, I believe that this characterization of Parmenides' problem is accurate; we might express the diagnosis by saying that he is, not exactly a hyper-extensionalist, but a hyper-denotationist (if that is any better). But it is important to observe that his hyper-denotationism is of such a kind that the mere assigning of meanings of a new type or level to each singular and general term would not automatically suffice to clear the matter up. For even if we do think of the general term "centaur" as carrying a further meaning than its (nonexistent) denotation, and even if we take the further step of ruling that this further meaning is the one that is to figure in the analysis of "centaurs are not," obviously we still have not gone far enough. Let the new meaning be, not the centaurs (which are not) but Centaur$_1$. What is being said of it, when we say that centaurs are not? That Centaur$_1$ is not? or that it is? After all, either it is or it is not. To regard the statement that 'centaurs are not' as having Centaur$_1$ as its real subject, without altering the interpretation of the original statement in any other way, merely results in the old dilemma that faced Betathon. The difficulty here encountered was a source of bedevilment to Plato, who could see on the one hand that if a Form was taken as performing the office here accorded to Centaur$_1$, statements of existence would have to be rendered, not as asserting that the *Form* existed, but as asserting that it was partaken-of or participated-in, this being a special type of property predicable only of Forms; but who, on the other hand, was not able to give an explicit accounting of this property, or to formulate in a clear and definite way the remainder of the reinterpretation required, although the *Sophist* appears to show that he attempted something of the kind.[29] At any rate, we see from this that Parmenides'

---

[28] "Largely," not quite "wholly." Suppose that the over-and-above component assigned to singular and general terms were assigned on a purely extensional basis, then denotationless terms would all be assigned the same. And no doubt Parmenides, if still in quarrelsome temper, might attempt to render embarrassing the consequence that (e.g.) "centaur" and "unicorn" meant the same in this sense of "meant." But the distinctively Parmenidean part of the problem would nevertheless have been broken, for such terms would, in this sense, still 'mean' something as opposed to nothing.

[29] I certainly do not mean to imply that the 'being' discussed in the *Sophist* is unequivocally existential; to the contrary, it apparently is a form of the

problem is no simple or childish difficulty, but involves several complex points of logical analysis; this last one, indeed, was not clearly perceived and decisively solved, so far as I know, until Frege did both in the late nineteenth century.[30]

Let us turn our attention to the predicative "is," and then see where we stand.

b) "Is" PREDICATIVE. Although, as I have said, it seems to me wrong to ascribe Parmenides' fantastic doctrine to his failure to distinguish between the predicative and the existential "is," it is also true, as I have also said, that he is very likely operating with a notion of being that fuses them. This means that, as a gesture toward historical verisimilitude, in trying to reproduce what his argument would have been for the predicative sense, or (so to speak) that longitudinal section of his actual argument that does apply to it, I should employ a model of what is done by the predicative "is" that does not diverge so greatly from the interpretation we have put upon the existential "is" as to preclude our finding any parallels at all. Actually, as I hope to show, what is important is not the fusion, but the fact that Parmenides makes the same three assumptions about the predicative that he makes about the existential; so, to reproduce his reasoning all we need is a model of predication that allows us to see that.

In fact, we have a superfluity of possible such models, each with fairly authentic ancient credentials. Here is one, its ancient credentials attested to by Professor Owen:

> Parmenides, though he certainly could not have drawn the necessary logical distinctions, might nevertheless fairly assume that, if one part of the world is white but not another, this can be formulated existentially as 'there is white, or a white thing, here but not there': the point may be confused but is not annulled by the use of *to leukon* to mean both the color and what has it.[31]

---

fused concept discussed above, different cases of which move into prominence at different points, as *we* can see, without being expressly marked off.

[30] It may be noted in passing that in Frege's writings from 1891 onward, after he had come to distinguish between sense and denotation, the part of his theory which handles this problem—namely, the hierarchy of 'concepts' (*Begriffe*) of first level, second level and so on—is entirely within the theory of denotation; thus we have here an example of the possibility imagined in the previous paragraph, of Parmenides' problem being met without the intensional level of meaning being invoked.

[31] Owen, p. 94 n.

Here is a related one, which I believe may actually play a considerable, though largely unannounced role in some early Socratic dialogues, the *Euthyphro* for one: that the predicative assertion '*a* is Φ' is true if there is in the object *a* a certain 'logical' *part*, which is the Φ part. (As if we could logically dissolve away the rest of the object—the complement of Φ within the object—like the flesh from the bones or the dross from the gold, and be left with a logical residue, *pure* Φ.) Without trying to settle here the complicated question of its role, if any, in the early Socratic dialogues, we can observe that the idea has to it a very characteristic late fifth-century feel or heft; if it was not actually an early Greek picture of predication, it perfectly well could have been, and this is the most we need.

Here is a third model: a predicative assertion '*a* is Φ' is true just in case there is, answering to it in reality, a certain *fact* such as the assertion asserts there to obtain (call it, e.g., *a's being* Φ). This idea, or one quite like it, flashes across the stage at *Sophist* 263.

It does not greatly matter which of these conceptions of predication we assume Parmenides to have in mind; they amount to the same in the respects that turn out to be relevant. The story that ensues can be quickly traced. Let our notion of 'a person's ontology' now be extended to include, not only what that person believes to exist, but what he believes to be the case in the sense of what properties he believes to belong to the objects he believes to exist. (But let us ignore the possibility of non-existence while considering this other sense of not-being.) Betathon is still explaining to Parmenides the outcome of his 'enquiry' into 'what is,' now in this other sense:

BETATHON: Lions are fierce.	PARMENIDES: [silent]
BETATHON: Zeno is a fool.	PARMENIDES: [silent, if restive]
BETATHON: Betathon is not flying.	PARMENIDES: Thou canst not be acquainted with what is not, nor indicate it in speech.[32]

The same points as before are to be noted. Briefly: (1) Parmenides is not putting forth an ontology of his own, but conducting an elenchus on Betathon. (2) Parmenides is not imposing any preconditions on 'what is' in this new sense, such as that only facts about the corporeal world will do, or the like; he is only (at this point) throwing out 'what is not,' i.e. what Betathon believes is not. (3) The subject of *estin* and *ouk*

---

[32] I retain the knowledge$_a$ rendering of γνοίης; cf. note 11. The corresponding knowledge$_p$ rendering will yield the same result.

estin, in this new sense, is still supplied by Betathon at each successive round, not by Parmenides. (4) No objection to plurality has been made so far; "Lions are fierce" is for the present allowed.

The dialogue continues:

BETATHON: [expresses baffle-ment]

PARMENIDES: Either this (= the fact of Betathon's flying, or the presence of flying in Betathon, or what you will) is, or it is not. [If it is, then you speak falsely; this we are still postponing.][33] If it is not, then you speak of nothing, for what is not, what does not obtain (etc.), is the same as nothing, etc.

Here, as previously for the existential case, I think we should not snap at the equation of 'what is not' and 'nothing'; this time, the point is the reasonable enough one that what is *not* the case simply is not to be found in reality, no more than what does not exist, and if it were, then it would be wrong to allude to it as something that was not.[34] Nor can we have it both ways, saying that Betathon's flying (or whatever) is not, yet is (there) to be 'said' (at)—the Heraclitean inconsistency again.

The elenchus proceeds as before, with Parmenides not contributing any ontology of his own, but instead rejecting every attempt by Betathon to place a fact outside of *his* ontology, to say that it does not according to him obtain. And as before, the internal critique is balanced by an

[33] Below, pp. 262–63.

[34] But it should be noted that, unexceptionable as the point may be, there also are alternative ways of putting it. Parmenides, his eyes on the point itself, interprets *this is not white* along the lines *white-here is not* or *no white thing here,* i.e. in terms of a formula whose truth is understood exclusively as in virtue of the world's *not* containing something, and in this way the previous strictures, or analogues to them, come into play. By the time of the *Sophist,* discussion has advanced to the point of alternative formulations being possible: where, for example, *this being not white* is a matter of its *being* (say) *blue,* the *Sophist* suggests that we understand the case as *this being other than white,* and the possibility of reconstructing these cases (even on a hyper-denotational basis, though the *Sophist* does not go so far) is revived. This seems to be the sole point at which Parmenides' use of the fused concept of being could be called relevant to his principal thesis.

external half, which is to knock out the false segments of what is in Betathon's ontology.

BETATHON: Cows are placid.

PARMENIDES: Either this is (so) or it is not. [If it is, then you pass, this round.] If it is not, then you speak of nothing, for what is not, what does not obtain in reality, is the same as nothing, etc.

Once again, Parmenides does not claim to be any better than Betathon at this level of ontologizing, does not attempt to correct him on points of fact or the like; the exterior critique employs only the principle 'either it is, or it is not.'

Where does this leave Betathon? We see that of all the innumerable statements that Betathon puts up as results of his 'enquiry' into everything that is, meaning both 'exists' and 'is Φ' for any Φ, statements of only one type survive the elenchus: statements that say, of something that *is* (in either sense) that it is (in that sense). Assuming him a good pupil, he apprehends this fact, does not try any longer to set any thing or fact outside his ontology by saying that it 'is not,' and recognizes that, at whatever points in his recital of what is within his ontology he has adverted to what in fact 'is not'—which points these are, be it noted yet again, Parmenides has not claimed to be able to tell him—he has gibbered meaninglessly, adverted to 'nothing.' Furthermore, it is plain enough that the elenchus just practised on Betathon can be practised on anyone, and the result will be the same, save for a single difference: viz., persons less well informed at the outset than Betathon, having fewer beliefs and/or a higher ratio of false ones, will emerge with a smaller residue at the end. An omniscient being, i.e. a being holding true beliefs about everything that 'is' (in both senses), would emerge with the largest residue, but he too could not say that anything *was not*, even if (precisely because) it was true; if the Devil is not, God himself cannot assure us. And since Parmenides is not at this point claiming special knowledge of his own, we can put his position in this way: *What is* (*everything that is*), *is*, he says, *and* (very emphatically) *that's all* (= nothing else!).

This attitude has interesting consequences which may be mentioned here. The notion of 'a person's ontology' with which we started—'what (the things which) that person believes to exist,' and 'what he believes to be the case in the sense of what properties he believes to belong to the objects he believes to exist'—is, as was pointed out at the outset, extremely crude, subject to all sorts of obvious objections which I have simply ignored.[35] One type of question was illustrated by the case of Alphides, who (let us suppose) holds beliefs about what is, in both senses, that are in fact totally erroneous; the question was whether his ontology is empty. We now see that by Parmenides' lights the answer is yes; for the cognitive relation of believing-to-be is being conceived as holding between a mind and the *object* which 'is' (if it does exist) or the *fact* which 'is' (if it does obtain), and thus it is that if it does not exist, or obtain, the relation holds between that mind and nothing whatever, no matter what Alphides may absurdly imagine. But we also see more than this. It is that for Parmenides, there is the totality of 'what is,' everything that exists and is the case, and a person's ontology is thought of *as being a subset of this;* for an omniscient being, the subset coincides with (is identical with) the entirety of 'what is'; at the opposite extreme, the subset constituted by the ontology of the omnignorant Alphides is the null set;[36] for most of the rest of us, as we like to think, the subset is somewhere between these extremes in size, although admittedly rather small. A person's ontology then proves to comprise that which he believes to be *and is*, for that which he believes to be and is not equals nothing. This is the explanation also of an asymmetry in the internal critique of Betathon's ontology, which we have postponed considering until now:[37] a difference in the treatment accorded Betathon's attempt to say that something 'is not,' according as he is (as we would put it) right or wrong. If he is right, then that thing indeed is not, so he speaks of nothing, et cetera. But if he is wrong, this is because that thing *is*. What are we to say of this? Not, I think, that he speaks of nothing, for in this case the thing (object, fact) is there to be spoken of, and Betathon's mistake seems to be of a different kind; its affinities are not with hallucination, but with blindness. For the same reason, to assume, just on general principles, that our account of 'saying of what is, that it is not' ought to be parallel to our account of 'saying of what is not, that

[35] Cf. pp. 249–51 above.

[36] Is it possible that this idea lies behind Socrates' strange notion—which otherwise I cannot interpret—voiced in the *Republic* argument discussed in Section I, that not only is 'what is' the 'object of knowledge,' but further, weirdly, 'what is not' is the 'object of ignorance' (477a)?

[37] Cf. pp. 252, 260 above.

it is,' and perhaps with this motivation to concoct supposititious *personae* like the not-being of the not-being of the thing in question, is not only to take a course which, as the history of metaphysics dismally attests, leads briskly into a bog of formidable proportions; it is also, in the name of the verbal parallel, to go against the grain of Parmenides' own principles. If something is which Betathon says is not, Betathon 'says what is not' in a sense to which, it seems to me, Parmenides has no more objection than does any sensible person; he sins, but he sins where man can do right—by speaking truly—; he does not unpardonably take the forbidden way, barred to the gods themselves, of speaking the unspeakable, of speaking where there can only be silence. There is a distinction between his papering over, concealing from himself, a fragment of reality, and his actively conniving at illusions behind which lie 'nothing'; and this distinction would be obscured by attempting to overcome the asymmetry in the internal critique. Besides, if we make 'saying of what is, that it is not' a species of 'speaking of nothing' on grounds of the not-being of the thing's not-being, this expedient will return to plague us as we belatedly reflect that in this sense 'saying of what is that it *is*' will be 'speaking of nothing' also; this indeed is part of that morass already mentioned, and like the rest of it better avoided.

Let us return from these general reflections to complete our case for the predicative sense of "is." I think it is evident that Parmenides is making three assumptions regarding this sense that parallel those that we distinguished for the existential. The first, roughly that '*a is* Φ' is true just in case *a* is Φ, we stated in three different ways at the outset of this part of the discussion. The second is that, given *a*, either *a* is Φ or it is not Φ (better, *a*'s being Φ either is the case or is not), *tertium non datur*, somewhat confining in the same manner as its existential sibling; it excludes subsistent but non-obtaining states of affairs for true negative (or false affirmative) predicative assertions to be about. Finally, he is assuming that truth stands to statements in general as (according to him) possession of denotation stands to singular and general terms: as 'being *of* something that is,' and that this is the only variety of meaning that a statement possesses; thus the meaning of a statement is identical with that in reality which—if it obtains—the statement describes. In this way the question *Is it? Or is it not?* becomes the same blunt instrument of assassination for the predicative use of "is" as for the existential.

What does seem important is that the three assumptions, *mutatis mutandis* for the senses of *esti*, are sufficient to generate an elenchus like that which I have ascribed to Parmenides; he needs no other 'premisses,' empirical or logical—only a respondent. On the other hand, they also appear to be necessary; I do not think any could be dropped without changing the outcome of the elenchus. And so it appears that they should be the focus of our attention. It may appear even more so when I show that Parmenides' *own* ontology and cosmology, upon which attention has traditionally focused, and which I take it is agreed to be absurd, can all be derived, without mistakes, from the standpoint at which we have now arrived.

3. Of What Is, All That Can Be Said Is: It Is

Socrates, according to tradition, used to extol the purgative powers of elenchus, the benefits of ridding oneself of falsehood and confusion; but Betathon could be forgiven for harboring mixed feelings about it at this point. "If that is purgative elenchus," we can imagine him saying, "it is much like being 'purged' of the use of both feet and one's dominant hand." And there is indeed much of what Betathon, like the rest of mortal mankind, used to think he could say that it proves now he cannot—say in the sense of meaningfully say. Namely, anything that is not, and that anything is not—a considerable amount.

But Betathon might on the other hand be cheered, at any rate consoled, by reflecting that after all a great many different things *are*, and can be said to *be*, that for all of Parmenides' strictures this is still a highly varied and interesting world. "I perceive now," he might reason to himself, "that the way of *is not* is impassable and no true way, and that the way of *is and is not* is preposterous; but there is still much to be done in the line of 'enquiry' into *what is*, which is still open; so let us get on with it."

In this spirit, he recommences his 'enquiry,' and we shall henceforth assume that as well as confining himself to reciting what he believes to *be*, he also is unvaryingly successful: naming and describing only what in fact is.

BETATHON: Trees are.	PARMENIDES: [silent]
BETATHON: Lizards are.	PARMENIDES: You're repeating yourself.

(Here, for the first time, I ascribe to the Parmenides of my dialogue a statement not identical with or closely related to a statement to be found in "The Way of Truth"; but the relation of the present line of thought to the text will shortly be apparent.) Betathon, not unnaturally, is baffled.

BETATHON: I said that something *different* was, the sec-
ond time.   PARMENIDES: How, 'different'?

BETATHON: Clearly, trees are
different from lizards. [He
puts into hyper-denota-
tional language the idea of
the classes' being disjoint.]   PARMENIDES: An example, please.

                                             PARMENIDES: [silent]
BETATHON: Henry, here, is a
lizard.

BETATHON: And is not a tree.   PARMENIDES: Thou canst not be
                                             acquainted with what is not,
                                             nor indicate it in speech.

Lest it be thought that the idea at work in this exchange is not to be found in the poem, let me hasten to dispel the impression. The two statements of 'what is' that are under discussion are existential; but the argument as I have given it turns on the impossibility of true predicative 'is not.' And suppose we interpret predicative 'is' in that classical fashion which we found in the paper by Professor Owen[38] (though the other interpretations we considered briefly would do also). Thus, one part of the world's being white but not another, is conceived existentially as 'there is white, or a white thing, here but not there.' We read in Parmenides,

Nor it is divided-off, since it all alike is,
Nor [is] anything more [*or* rather] here than there, as would ex-
clude its holding together,
Nor [is] anything more weakly . . .[39]

Owen argues[40] that the word translated "alike" in the first line of this passage has adverbial and not predicative force ("it all alike is," rather than "it is all alike"), and points out that this word is parallel to the phrase rendered "more" (or "rather") in the second line and that rendered "more weakly" in the third; these are good suggestions, with

[38] Cf. p. 258 above.
[39] B8.22–24.
[40] Owen, 92 ff.

which I gratefully agree. He also believes, however, that the *estin* in the passage acquires existential force and should be so accented (ἔστιν); and this matter seems to me more complicated, for (whatever the accentuation) I hear in the passage a paradigm exemplar of the fused concept of being. We are being told, for example, that there is no such thing as *white's* being more here than there because that would mean this being white (predicative = white being here) *and that not*. It is this principle that operates in the most recent exchange between Parmenides and Betathon; to say that trees are different from lizards requires (as an irreducible minimum) that we be able to entertain the possibility of something's being one and not the other, and this is what on Parmenidean principles we cannot do.

The particular example used obviously is quite arbitrary, and the point can be stated generally: given the is-not doctrine, Parmenides is in a position to claim that *the statement that something is asserts the same as the statement that [ostensibly] something else is*, because the attempted specification of the alleged difference is unintelligible. Nor is this conclusion confined to existential propositions like "lizards are"; the same reasoning shows that Betathon is 'repeating himself' when he follows, e.g., "Zeno is handsome" with, e.g., "Zeno is a biped"; for the two predicates involved are no better off than "tree" and "lizard." And so Betathon is at liberty, if he enjoys it, to continue mouthing statements like "trees are," "lizards are," etc., but the idea that he has actually asserted something different the second time from the first, or on any occasion from any other, is mere illusion, stemming from the single great illusion, the idea that what is not (something's not-existing, something's not-being-of-a-certain-sort) is intelligible, can be thought and spoken of, or worst of all, can be.

Thus far Parmenides, as I have represented him, has engaged in no ontologizing of his own; he has rather employed a certain set of dialectical methods upon that of Betathon, and by implication, of all men. But no one could suppose that Parmenides could get this far and the ontological significance of the foregoing still be lost on him. And so it proves; he states an ontology, the first 'really correct' one. It is very short. We know, now, that

> *Of what is, only one thing can be said,*

for we know that every true statement about what is necessarily says the same as every other; we are misled no longer by the various-sound-ing chatter that continues to assail our noise-filled ear. Perhaps guided by some such principle as

> *That of which only the same can be said is the same*,

we inevitably arrive at the conclusion

> *There is one thing, viz., what is.*

(Perhaps this conclusion should be stated, there is one thing *at most*. But I am inclined to think that the impossibility of stating an *empty* ontology would be for Parmenides a kind of ontological argument for the existence of *something*.) That last proposition, be it noted, is the first one that Parmenides has uttered in a language other than the dialectical metalanguage in which he interviews Betathon; his first first-order statement. But this statement differs *toto caelo* from any offered before about the nature of the world, since it is based, not on scattered and unreliable observations (moisture goes with living things, *ergo* everything is really water), but on an analysis, of the utmost generality, of the limits of the sayable, hence the thinkable. And now the statement, formerly the abbreviation for innumerable particular statements (as we used to distinguish them) about lions and lizards,

> *The only true thought is the thought that it is*,

becomes in its way a first-order statement also, the same as that last before displayed.

4. SOME COSMOLOGICAL COROLLARIES

Given what has gone before, derivation of the rest of Parmenides' view is fairly routine.

(a) There is no coming-to-be (B8.3, 6–21). If we split the fused notion of being, then there is no coming-to-exist, nor coming-to-be-Φ; for in neither case can one intelligibly describe the previous situation, when the thing in question did not exist, or was not Φ.

(b) There is no ceasing-to-be. Parallel reasoning.

(c) The universe (= what is) as a whole has no beginning or end. From (a) and (b).

(d) It is a single continuous solid mass (B4.1–4, 8.5–6, 22–33). For there is no 'being rather here than there' in the existential sense of 'being.' It is also wholly saturated with every property, since there is no 'being rather here than there' predicatively either.

(e) It is temporally continuous and indivisible also; "it will be" and "it was" (both existential and predicative) are merely further bad ways of pronouncing "it is."

(f) There is no change, e.g. of place or bright color (B8.37–41). Change is ceasing to be Φ and coming to be Ψ.

(g) It is spherical, or like a sphere (B8.42–49). The reason given is that otherwise it would 'be more' in one direction than another. This seems to be a quaint way of expressing (d). Owen is right, I think, not to take it as suggesting 'boundaries' and the traditional false contrast with Melissus.[41] A scandalous possibility is that it is a joke.

5. Did Parmenides Believe the Conclusions?

As to whether Parmenides himself actually accepted these conclusions, had satisfied himself that whatever anyone else might think, there was only one thing, plurality an illusion, motion an illusion, change an illusion—one can merely guess. My own groundless speculation is that he did, that his attitude toward his conclusion was belief in the sense that Hume's radical doubt was doubt, maintainable only (to his relief) in his study. Or, perhaps he believed it all the time, and was mad. No one knows, or needs to know; for it must be borne in mind that his procedure is elenctic, and his own ontology is corollary to this. And an elenchus may be practised on a respondent with either of two distinct motivations. One, Socratic, is to make him admit, and if possible believe, by reducing every alternative to self-contradiction, some proposition that at the outset he would have regarded as preposterous. (You cannot know what is right and not do it. Thus too, perhaps, there is no plurality, motion, change.) The other is to compel the respondent, by the very outlandishness of the conclusion, to begin searching for the tacit assumptions with which it was obtained. In the latter case, the elenchus functions as an instrument for forcing the assumptions to the surface. It is interesting to wonder whether Parmenides ever looked at his argument in this way; we know that the idea of regarding a piece of reasoning in such a spirit was familiar to Zeno, and we know that however Parmenides may have felt about the conclusions, they provided a sharp motivation to Anaxagoras, Democritus, and Plato to go about constructing a conceptual apparatus within which

[41] Ibid., 95 ff.

they could not be obtained. It was fitting, whether or not historical, for Plato[42] to have Parmenides himself assert that such an apparatus must be found, if the significance of all thought and discourse is to be upheld.

POSTSCRIPT: ON SAYING WHAT CANNOT BE SAID

Both in "The Way of Truth" and in my reconstruction of his argument, Parmenides makes constant use of expressions that on his own principles are meaningless—"is not," "nothing," etc.—in which fact some observers think to discern a difficulty. Must Parmenides assume that these nonsensical expressions have sense in order to prove that they do not?

It could be questioned whether this, if a difficulty, is a particularly serious one; but it is not necessary to do so, for resistance on this point is most likely to rest on a misapprehension of the role of these expressions in the argument. I have stressed throughout that Parmenides' basic procedure is elenctic; what this means in practice is illustrated by the dialogues with Betathon. In its general form, we imagine Betathon as reeling off his (ostensible) ontology, together with, at the outset, his meontology, his account of what he thinks is not, in the presence of Parmenides. Ideally, Parmenides should say nothing at all, but instead should administer some simple negative reinforcement—e.g. hitting Betathon over the head—each time Betathon 'says what is not'; and Betathon being assumed an apt pupil, he might be hoped in sufficient time to get the idea. But there are drawbacks to this in practice. In the first place, it could be expected to teach the lesson of the internal critique in fairly short order, causing Betathon to leave off giving his meontology, for he can tell when he is saying that something is not; but the external critique would be more difficult to convey, since Betathon might not understand why he was hit over the head on some occasions of 'saying what was' (as he thought) and not on others. Second, this way of regarding the matter does require universal ontological knowledge on Parmenides' part; presumably the elenchus should theoretically be regarded as conducted by God. Third, the procedure would take a very long time. And fourth, at the end only Betathon would have benefited, whereas the message is one that all mankind should understand.

For the first three of these practical reasons, Parmenides ekes out the bare elenchus (which uses only the negative-reinforcement device) with some heuristic explanation of the principles that lie behind it; thus when

[42] *Parm.* 135b.

Betathon first attempts to place centaurs in his meontology Parmenides issues a little lecture intended to 'bar' him from that 'way' *in general*, to get across the point that the 'way' as a whole is unthinkable; in so doing he uses empty names ("nothing," etc.) other than that used by Betathon ("centaur"); he does this without illusions, or supposing them meaningful, as a practical expedient in giving Betathon his drift. (*Betathon* may temporarily think them meaningful, in addition to his various other confusions; but this too is not required.) Likewise, to communicate the point of the external critique without being omniscient himself, he employs the principle 'either it is, or it is not' in the way we have examined, although it is not really a disjunction, a statement of alternatives.

For the fourth of these practical reasons, he embodies his principles, as modified for the first three reasons, in a poem that all mankind can read. Because a poem is one-dimensional, some parts must come before others; he takes advantage of this in laying out his doctrine, but goes out of his way to dispel the impression that the order is logical; "It is all the same to me," he says, "where I start; for I will come back there again" (B5). The same applies to his tactics with Betathon; pedagogical considerations guide his letting statements pass at first, in the internal critique, that will be challenged in the external critique; other orderings are possible, none pre-eminent. Basically the entire (ostensible) ontology is best thought of as examined simultaneously—in one instant stripped of negations, stripped of falsehoods, impacted together in a single "*it is*" and handed back (large or small according to his lights) to the respondent. No doubt that is God's way.

So it is not the doctrine itself that forces Parmenides to 'say what is not' in his own right, nor even the fact that he wishes to explain it; it is that he is anxious to explain it to *mortals*, short of life and shorter in patience, so that they will understand. Such is the price of prophecy.

12

PLATO AND PARMENIDES
ON THE TIMELESS PRESENT

G. E. L. Owen

I

Some statements couched in the present tense have no reference to time. They are, if you like, grammatically tensed but logically tenseless. Mathematical statements such as "twice two is four" or "there is a prime number between 125 and 128" are of this sort. So is the statement I have just made.[1] To ask in good faith whether there is still the prime number there used to be between 125 and 128 would be to show that one did not understand the use of such statements, and so would any attempt to answer the question. It is tempting to take another step and talk of such timeless statements as statements about timeless entities. If the number 4 neither continues nor ceases to be twice two, this is, surely, because the number 4 has no history of any kind, not even the being a day older today than yesterday. Other timeless statements might shake our confidence in this inference: "Clocks are devices for measuring time" is a timeless statement, but it is not about a class of timeless clocks. But, given a preoccupation with a favored set of examples and a stage of thought at which men did not distinguish the properties of statements from the properties of the things they are about, we can expect timeless entities to appear as the natural proxies of timeless statements.

Now the fact that a grammatical tense can be detached from its tense-

From *The Monist*, 50 (1966), 317–40. Reprinted with the permission of the publisher, Open Court Publishing Company, La Salle, Illinois, and of the author.

[1] This is a shortened version of a lecture given to the Philosophy Colloquium at Princeton University in January 1964. It seemed impracticable to try to remove all traces of the lecturing style or to strike out points which look forward to the argument of two other lectures given on the same occasion.

affiliations and put to a tenseless use is something that must be discovered at some time by somebody or some set of people. So far as I know it was discovered by the Greeks. It is commonly credited to one Greek in particular, a pioneer from whose arguments most subsequent Greek troubles over time were to flow: Parmenides the Eleatic. Sometimes it is suggested that Parmenides took a hint from his alleged mentors, the Pythagoreans. "We may assume" says one writer "that he knew of the timeless present in mathematical statements." [2] But what Aristotle tells us of Pythagorean mathematics is enough to undermine this assumption. According to him (esp. *Metaph.* 1091a12–22) they confused the construction of the series of natural numbers with the generation of the world. So Parmenides is our earliest candidate. His claim too has been disputed, and I shall try to clear up this dispute as I go, but not before I have done what I can to sharpen it and widen the issues at stake.

Parmenides seems to argue in the following way.[3] He begins, perplexingly enough, without specifying what the discussion is about, what the subject of his argument is. But the argument makes it clear that he does not want a specific subject on his hands: he wants to reason about whatever it is that can be a subject, whatever it is that can be talked and thought about. And he contends that if we have such a subject it must exist, since if it did not exist we should not have anything to talk about. (I think myself that he goes on to reinforce this argument with another and more interesting fallacy, but that is another story.) Then, having professedly proved the existence of his subject, he goes on to extract some other conclusions and occasionally to bolster them with independent arguments. He sets out his program with the meticulous accuracy that characterizes his whole procedure: "It exists without birth or death; whole, unique; and immovable; and perfect" (B8.3–4). And he goes on: "Nor was it ever nor will it be; for it is now, all together, single, continuous." The argument that he gives to support this—and we have no record of any other argument that he brought to bear on this point—is that the subject cannot have either a beginning or an end in time or indeed any temporal variation at all.

So the argument seems to be this. Let X be Parmenides' subject, viz.

[2] W. Kneale, "Time and Eternity in Theology," *Proceedings of the Aristotelian Society*, N.S. 61 (1960–61), 90.

[3] For this interpretation and the textual readings on which it is based see "Eleatic Questions," *CQ*, N.S. 10 (1960), 84–102 [repr. in Furley and Allen, II].

whatever we can talk or think about and so, derivatively, whatever there is. Then (i) X is unchanging: it does not begin or cease to exist and nothing happens to it. Consequently (ii) nothing can be said of it in the past or future tense, not even that it has gone on and will go on being the same thing. So stated, the argument is plainly incomplete: we need some further assumption to get us from (i) to (ii). And it seems clear what the simplest assumption would be for this purpose. It is that if X is to have a past distinct from its present, something must be true of that past which is not true of the present; and similarly with the future. Otherwise they could not be distinguished. And *ex hypothesi* this condition cannot be satisfied if nothing changes at all. We might put this, in a later idiom: times of which exactly the same things are true (at which the same states of affairs obtain, and which are not distinguished by their antecedents or sequels) are the same time. It is the identity of indiscernibles, with times and not objects for its arguments. But of course Parmenides could not say this. His assumption remains unstated. As such it need not come to anything more than the familiar readiness of the Greeks to picture the lapse of time as the parent and regulator and assessor of change.[4] When Aristotle came to argue that lapse of time is impossible without change he was the beneficiary of a century of discussion in which Parmenides' assumption had been pulled out and challenged.

So, on this interpretation of Parmenides, the force of the present tense in "X exists" does not depend on its family connection with other tenses of the verb. Those tenses have been scrapped, casualties of the argument. Just as Parmenides explodes the idea of nonexistence on the way to propounding an existential statement, so he discards the distinctions imported by other tenses and then produces a statement in the present tense. The sense of his existential claim does not seem to him to require any complementary and contrasting use to be found for denials of existence, and his use of the present tense does not depend on leaving any complementary and contrasting use to the other tenses. On one view of it, he has managed to detense the verb, and the way is open for Plato's more sophisticated use of the same device.

On one view of it. As I shall show you, there can be other views.

[4] See e.g. Charles H. Kahn, *Anaximander and the Origins of Greek Cosmology* (New York, 1960), pp. 170–71. If the variant οὐδ᾽ εἰ (better, with Coxon, οὐδὲ) χρόνος at 8.36 (Simpl. *In Phys.* 146.9) could be made plausible, it would entail a clarity on Parmenides' part about the issue discussed in this paper which I have thought better not to assume.

And to be fair I must advertise one of these views now, for it contradicts the conventional translation I have given of the essential lines in Parmenides. Hermann Fränkel, in a footnote added to the reprint of his *Parmenidesstudien*,[5] argues that the words ordinarily rendered "Nor was it ever nor will it be" call for a different rendering, and in particular that the word translated "ever" means rather "at one time but not another" or, in this context, "at some time in the past or future but not now." The whole clause then means "Nor is it the case that X existed at some time (*but not now*), or will exist at some time (*but not now*)." And thus Parmenides is arguing not for the timelessness but only for the temporal continuity of his subject. His denial comes merely to the claim that X not only existed at some past time but *also* exists now, and not only will exist at some future time but *also* exists now.

Now Fränkel's reasons for this suggestion are weak. Later it will be worthwhile trying to reinforce them. Two are linguistic, one is philosophical, and I shall not dwell on the linguistic reasons. So far as the Greek goes, it just is not the case that the phrase οὔ (or οὐδέ) ποτε, which I translated "*not* (or *nor*) *ever*," would ordinarily have the sense that Fränkel reads into it here.[6] It would *not* ordinarily mean "not *at some particular time by contrast with others*" (Fränkel gives no parallels for his sense): it would mean "not *at any time*." It is a joke to think that any Greek could claim οὔποτε ἦν κλέπτης οὐδ' ἔσομαι if by this he meant that he had not yet stopped being a thief and did not mean to give up the trade. (Given *t* as a time-variable, ποτέ is (∃*t*) . . . and οὔ ποτε is accordingly ∼ (∃*t*) . . . .) And Fränkel's second linguistic reason is no stronger. It is that he wants to emend the text elsewhere by importing a verb in the future tense; but even if all his assumptions about that other context were correct he would do better to bracket the doubtful verb as a gloss than tinker with the tense of it.[7] In any event, as we shall see, the occasional appearance of different tenses in Parmenides' argument is not ruled out by the interpretation that Fränkel would like to undermine. But I want to turn from these points of

[5] *Wege und Formen frügriechischen Denkens* (Munich, 1955), p. 191 n. 1 [repr. in Furley and Allen, II].

[6] Cf. W. K. C. Guthrie, *A History of Greek Philosophy*, vol. 2 (Cambridge, 1965), p. 30 n. 1. Of course Fränkel knows this, but feels compelled to evade it by the arguments I go on to consider.

[7] If Proclus' μίμνει is to be read in B8.29, the μένει of B8.30 is better read as an intrusive gloss which has displaced some other verb, e.g. πέλει.

scholarship and consider the substantial philosophical issue that is raised by Fränkel's final and only serious argument.

This argument is that Parmenides cannot have intended to deny himself the use of different tenses in framing his conclusion, for in his case it would be flatly self-refuting, logical suicide, to do so. For Parmenides expressly concludes, from his polemic against the possibility of change, that his subject *remains* the same (B8.29–30). And to say this is to say that it still is what it was, and will continue to be what it is. So if Parmenides had used this as a premise for rejecting all tense-distinctions, his conclusion would have disabled the premise on which it rested.

Now there are, on the face of it, other inconsistencies in what Parmenides says. He is ready, for instance, to use the language of motion in describing his immovable subject.[8] But this inconsistency is quite superficial: the jarring idioms can be neutralized without harming the argument. Fränkel seems to have his finger on a far more radical incoherence. The only surprising thing is that he assumes that this type of incoherence is foreign to Parmenides' argument, when other evidence makes it overwhelmingly clear that it lies at the heart of the reasoning. Let me explain this. Parmenides argues, you remember, that any denial of existence is nonsense: the nonexistent cannot be thought or spoken of (B2.7–8), denials of existence are "not sayable or thinkable" (B8.8–9). (More exactly, they are either self-refuting if they have a genuine subject or senseless if they have not.) Yet Parmenides sometimes puts this point by saying that there is no such thing as what is not (B8.46), that there is nothing except what there is (B8.36–7). He is driven to denying the existence of some kinds of thing— change and plurality *imprimis*—in order to maintain his thesis that nonexistence makes no sense. Nor would it help him to follow the more sophisticated path that seems to open at some moments in the argument (B8.38–41, 52–3; 9.1; 19.3) and recast these denials in the formal mode. He would still have to deny that there is anything for which such a word as "change" stands. Yet just this is what his own conclusion should disable him from doing.

So, to repeat that memorable image from Wittgenstein, Parmenides' argument is a ladder to be climbed up and thrown away. Such arguments are not, put it picturesquely, horizontal deductions; if they parade as deductions they are patently self-defeating. They are not even of the form of a *reductio ad absurdum*, for there is no more benefit

[8] See "Eleatic Questions," p. 96 n. 4.

in negating their premises than in asserting them. Gilbert Ryle has said something of such patterns of reasoning,[9] but I shall not generalize about them. They do not seem to form a genuine class, and I am sure that some of them are too substantial to be met by a call of contradiction. In particular I suspect Parmenides saw the oddity of his own argument. For instead of representing the denial of birth and death and change as final conclusions, corollaries to be drawn from the thesis that X exists, he is careful to call these *signs on the way* to that conclusion (B8.2–3). Destinations do not contain the signs that lead to them, and travelers at their destination have no use for the signs.

In sum, then: it is characteristic of Parmenides that he should argue from the impossibility of change to the untenability of time-distinctions and yet, on the way, represent his argument as implying the permanent immutability of his subject. For this is the twin of that reasoning which moves from rejecting the concept of nonexistence to simply asserting the existence of its subject, yet on the way represents the argument as denying the existence of change. Surely, we are inclined to say, if nonexistence is ruled out then there *is no such thing as* change? and then, equally surely, what there is must stay the same? Just these are the signposts, the intermediate rungs on Parmenides' ladder.

II

You will no doubt feel some unallayed qualms at this account. I promise to go looking for trouble directly. But first I want to strengthen my hand by noticing how such an interpretation throws light on some important moves made by Parmenides' near successors.

Anaxagoras is a notable example. He began his book with a sentence that is plainly framed as a flat contradiction of Parmenides on some major issues. Postulating a beginning of the physical world, he wrote: "All things were together, limitless both in number and in smallness." Parmenides had written "Nor was it ever nor will it be, since it is now, all of it together, single, continuous." "All of it together, single" is discarded for "All things together, limitless in number." "Continuous," which Parmenides understands (to Aristotle's indignation) as excluding divisibility into parts, is replaced by "limitless in smallness" which is shortly afterwards explained by the continuous divisibility of things. Even "together" takes on another sense; for part of Parmenides' argument was to deny not only temporal but spatial distinctions in the last

[9] *Philosophical Arguments* (Inaugural Lecture), Oxford, 1945.

analysis—to the mind, he says, distant things are present (B4); whereas Anaxagoras' collection of seeds takes up limitless space. And now all that is left in Anaxagoras' sentence is the verb in the past tense, "was"; and all that is left to be contradicted in the counterpart sentence in Parmenides is the phrase "nor was it ever nor will it be." Anaxagoras, I submit, must have read this phrase as disallowing the use of tenses other than the present.[10]

Thereafter he knocks home his point with a tattoo of tenses: "all such things as were yet to be, all such things as were but are no more, all that now are, all such as will be . . ." (B12). Similarly, it is just when Empedocles is insisting on the progress of time (even though a circular progress) that he goes out of his way to snub Parmenides (B17.26–29).

But the man whose position comes out in the sharpest relief is the later Eleatic, Melissus. That Melissus is given to improving on Parmenides where he thinks fit is common knowledge. Notice then how he introduces his thesis:

> It always was what it was and always will be. For if it had come into existence there would necessarily be nothing before it did so. Now if there had been nothing, there could not possibly have come anything out of nothing. . . . So since it did not come into existence it is and always was and always will be. (B1–2)

With the word "always" Melissus introduces others that found no place in Parmenides' verses: "limitless" (in connection with both time and space), "eternal," "the whole of time." So Melissus is quite clear on what has been proved if one shows that what there is has neither beginning nor end nor any kind of change. What has been proved is that it did exist, does exist, and will exist without change at all times in the past, present, and future. What else? Whatever is true of any of these times is true of them all. So Melissus is in effect denying, what we took Parmenides to be in effect maintaining, the identity of indiscernibles in its application to times.

---

[10] It might be thought that Anaxagoras just meant to introduce a past tense in a sense other than that in which, on Fränkel's view, Parmenides thought himself still entitled to it; i.e. Anaxagoras might be saying "This is how things were but are no longer." But this would be a mistake: Anaxagoras is at pains to insist that, so far as the state of affairs described in his opening sentence is concerned, matters are exactly the same now: "Just as in the beginning, so now, all things must be together" (B6).

If this is so, Melissus' deductions must be horizontal deductions. That is, the premises and intermediate steps must seem to him as solid and inalienable as the conclusions based on them. If the rejection of change shows that nothing new happened in the past or will happen in the future, then that *is* what it shows. And that this is Melissus' approach to the argument is clinched by his most remarkable departure from Parmenides' method. Namely, he wholly discards those arguments of Parmenides which hinge on the claim that some important expression has no sense, that what it purports to stand for cannot be "spoken or thought." The importance of this departure can hardly be overstressed (I cannot find that so far it has been stressed at all). For it was just that cry of "unthinkable, unsayable" that compelled Parmenides to treat his own arguments as stages to be passed and then dismissed, since those arguments were compelled to use the very expressions branded unusable. Melissus can make nothing of this. He consistently treats the denial of existence and the description of change and plurality as significant; demonstrably false, but never unthinkable. Just how this shapes his argument against any beginning of existence, and finally commits him to a plurality of indiscernible times, I shall try to show you shortly. But first I must point to the trouble which I warned you still lay in wait for our interpretation. There seems to be a reason for doubting whether we are entitled to this sharp contrast between Parmenides and his follower. On the main issue Parmenides may be less single-minded than I have depicted him, and it is time to call his consistency in question.

III

The trouble is uncovered by an argument that occurs a few lines later in Parmenides' poem. He goes on to maintain that what there is cannot have come into existence either from nothing or from something.[11] And he gives two reasons for saying that it cannot have come into existence from nothing. First, the antecedent state of affairs would be indescribable, for to describe it would be to deny the existence of anything at that time; and this denial is nonsense. Secondly, he says: "If it started from nothing, what (τi $\chi \rho \acute{e} o s$) could have made it spring up later rather than earlier?" This is the argument to which Aristotle refers when he says that the Eleatics ruled out all change because they

[11] I accept Reinhardt's emendation at B8.12 (cf. now Guthrie, pp. 28–29). But nothing in my present argument hangs on this.

were unable to answer the question, what started the change (*Metaph.* 984a29–b1). Let us look harder at it.

It is, as you will have seen, the argument that Kant repeats in the antithesis to his First Antinomy, and Moore discusses in his published lectures. "Assume the world had a beginning. Then that beginning must come after a time in which the thing did not exist, i.e. an empty time. But nothing can begin to exist in an empty time, for no part of such a time can be picked out from the rest as furnishing a condition of existence." Leibniz knew of the reasoning and discussed it in his third letter to Clarke. It is a very Greek pattern of argument. If the world starts from nothing, there can be no reason for it to start on Saturday rather than Thursday; and since it cannot start on both days there is no reason to suppose it started at all. Anaximander, asked why the earth stayed still in the middle of his universe, is credited with the reply that since the earth was symmetrically related to all the extremities of the universe there was no reason for it to move in any direction (*De Caelo* 295b10–16). He probably used the same reasoning in deciding that the regular circles of the heavenly bodies are not interrupted when they go below the horizon. Aristotle retailored the argument to rebut the possibility of motion in a vacuum; the Academy adapted it to show that, since no physical sample of equality has more right to serve as a standard sample than any other, the standard sample cannot be physical. And Leibniz found an excellent example in Archimedes' mechanics, and of course cited it as an illustration of his Principle of Sufficient Reason.

But there may be more to it than the Principle of Sufficient Reason We can give Parmenides' argument more or less of an edge according to our interpretation of the phrase ὕστερον ἢ πρόσθεν. It may mean just "later *or* earlier," and then the argument is: what reason is there for the world, if it comes from nothing, to start whenever it did (whether later or earlier)? But equally the phrase may mean "later *rather than* earlier," and then the argument is: what reason is there for the world to start at a given time t rather than some earlier time $t - n$? And, since the same question can be raised in turn for $t - n$ and for any earlier time whatever, we have a regress on our hands; and Parmenides will have furnished Zeno not only with a simple pattern of *reductio ad absurdum* but with a destructive sample of the infinite regress, his two chief weapons.

Elsewhere in his third letter to Clarke, Leibniz recognizes this regress version of the argument. Discussing the supposition that "God might have created the world several million years sooner," he says: "since God does nothing without reason, and since there is no reason assignable why He did not create the world sooner, it will follow either that He created nothing at all, or that He produced the world before any assignable time—which is to say that the world is eternal." In either version Leibniz would have none of the argument, for a reason which will have occurred to you already. The reason is that in all its versions the argument seems to assume the existence of absolute time, i.e. the existence of different times having all their properties, other than that of bare temporal order, in common. Yet surely this is just what Parmenides was supposed to be denying in his comment on "was" and "will be"? He seems now to be maintaining that if the world began at t it might equally have begun at $t - n$, and if at $t - n$ then at $t - nn$. But unless we borrow time from Newton and Melissus, what are we to make of this glib distinction between t and $t - n$ and $t - nn?$ It is not just that, as Kant puts it, no part of an empty time can be picked out from others as providing a sufficient condition for the world to start. It is that, on the view we took ourselves to have found in Parmenides, no part of an empty time (and generally no part of a time without events) can be picked out from others *at all*. It would be absurd to say that the beginning of things was to be brought forward by two days, or postponed sine die; and correspondingly absurd to ask why it should not be.

The suspicion that Parmenides is at least showing the cloven hoof here is reinforced by another consideration. As I said, he gives two arguments to show that what exists cannot come from nothing. Now it is this second argument that Melissus adapts to his own use. The first, which simply traded on the senselessness of all denials of existence, Melissus prudently and characteristically drops. It is the other, ready as it is to allow a use to the word "nothing" and hospitable as it is to absolute time-distinctions, that is father to Melissus' own reasoning: "If what comes first is nothing, there is no way in which that nothing can give rise to something."

Let us pick the bones of the argument a little cleaner. Of the assumptions that it brings into play one is a principle (P) which for our purposes can be formulated quite broadly, to the effect that if anything is the case there must be some sufficient reason why it should be so and not otherwise. This is neither challenged nor expressly adduced by proponents of the argument. The mischief starts when it is put to work with two other assumptions, namely

(I)   For any time t there is some time $t - n$ which is earlier than t, which taken together with P yields the corollary (c) that if any event occurs uniquely at t there is a sufficient reason for its not occurring at $t - n$; and

(II) There is an event, viz. the first event, which occurs uniquely at some time t but which *ex hypothesi* fails to satisfy the condition stated in (c).

Given a certain principle of explanation, then, propositions (I) and (II) cannot be jointly true. (Not that they are formally incompatible— this will be important later.) Leibniz accepts (II) and uses this as a lever to dislodge (I), and, with it, Newton's absolute time. Parmenides, on the other hand, is out to demolish (II). So, unless he is simply confused about the point of such arguments, he must surely accept (I). For the argument is a *reductio ad absurdum*, and where a *reductio* depends on a number of independent premises it can be used to destroy one of these only on the assumption that the others are true.

(I make no apology for picking at Parmenides' assumptions in this way. It is what his successors had to do in deciding what they must accept from him and what they could afford to reject. And Parmenides set the model for his successors in the care with which he uncovered the premises on which his own arguments hinged, and the care with which he marked those theorems which had been proved and which were now to serve as the basis of a further proof. To talk of confusion in his case is to judge him by the standards that he and Zeno invented.)

Certainly Parmenides may be confused. One thing, though, he cannot be confused over. He cannot have thought that he was entitled to Assumption (I) merely on the strength of that troublesome step in the argument which depicts the subject as going on without change, "standing fast, the same in the same place" (B8.29–30). For that step is inferred from the thesis that what exists can have no starts or stops; and this thesis in turn is established by means of the assumption we are discussing. In other words, Assumption (I) seems to be brought into play from the start of the reasoning. It is an independent premise, and as such it may naturally be supposed to represent Parmenides' own conviction. And if that is so, Parmenides is not a single-minded, and perhaps not any sort of, antagonist of temporal distinctions.

But we have gone too fast. We assumed that (I) and (II) must be logically independent assumptions. After all, Melissus was able to maintain (I) without (II); and Leibniz was able to maintain (II) without (I). So it did not occur to us that Parmenides could have assumed (I) merely because he took it to be naturally implied by the objectionable thesis (II). But this was a mistake.

It is far more likely that he did import Assumption (I) on just this ground—or even, if you prefer, that its connection with (II) would have seemed so obvious that the question of importing and justifying it did not arise. For, if we set aside Leibniz' special pleading, it does seem obvious that if the world started from nothing there must have been some time before it started. It does seem obvious that, if there is a time when X begins to exist, this can only be distinguished from other times when X exists by the fact that X exists at that time but not at any earlier time. And if there are puzzles in this—there are indeed, and they will catch up with us later—at any rate they are not Parmenides' present concern. He is refuting the suggestion that what exists started from nothing. He has just attacked it on the supposition that to say that nothing existed before that time makes no sense. Now, in the lines we are discussing, he attacks it on the more natural and charitable assumption that this does make sense. That is, he lets proposition (II) carry its conventional corollary (I). But this does not for a moment imply that he saw more sense in the corollary than in the hypothesis that seemed conventionally to entail it.

So the propositions that come into conflict in his *reductio ad absurdum* are just proposition (II) and that general principle of sufficient reason which lies unadvertised behind the argument. And it does not occur to him to jettison the latter. Perhaps it might have. When one recent writer pictures the first event as the "spontaneous decay of an elementary particle in a static universe" [12] he shows himself ready to abandon the principle, and this is not a recent liberty. Anaxagoras saw no need to satisfy Parmenides on this point when he described the beginning of this world from a static, characterless amalgam. In fact Parmenides' successors were generally content if they could meet his demand that there should never be a time at which there was simply nothing in existence. If they went on to picture a first event in a static (or otherwise timeless) world, they took no care to meet the query why it should have happened when it did. And in this their instinct, or their logic, may after all have been right.

Whether it was right is a question that I shall come back to. It does not lie on our way now. We were looking for signs of a cloven hoof,

[12] G. J. Whitrow, *The Natural Philosophy of Time* (London and Edinburgh, 1961), pp. 32–33.

signs that Parmenides was ready to admit time-distinctions even in a world without events. And we have not found those signs. Parmenides' traditional claim to have been the first to attack temporal distinctions stands firm. It is Parmenides that Plato is echoing when he says in the *Timaeus* (37e–38a):

> Days, nights, months, years . . . are all parts of time, and "was" and "will be" have come about as forms of time. We are wrong to apply them unthinkingly to what is eternal. Of this we say that it was and is and will be, but strictly only "is" belongs to it. "Was" and "will be" should be spoken of the process that goes on in time, for they are changes.

Indeed as soon as we attend to this echo we have another answer to an old objection. The difficulty was how to suppose that Parmenides meant to eliminate all talk of past and future, when he described his subject as remaining unchanged. The reply is that Plato knows of this conjunction, and has no objection to it at all. He is as ready here as in his other dialogues, and as ready as his mentor Parmenides, to describe his own eternal entities, the Forms, as staying firm (29b) and as continuing always in the same state (28a, 29a, 37d, 38a). Indeed it is this very description of them that he uses when he goes on to prohibit any use of the past or future tense in talking of them (38a). And Aristotle repeats the point with enthusiasm:

> Things that exist always are not, as such, in time; for they are not contained by time (sc. there is no time before and after they exist), and their existence is not measured by time. A proof of this is that none of them is affected by time; for none of them is in it (*Phys.* 221b3–7).

How Plato came to terms with the anomaly is something we have yet to discuss. Meantime there can be no question that when he came to recognize the essential tenselessness of those propositions that most interested him—the analyses of ethical and nonethical concepts, the theorems of mathematics, and many more—it was Parmenides' dictum that gave him his model of explanation.

It was, as we shall see, an unfortunate model.

IV

Look back for a moment. Even without the benefit of Zeno's contribution, the Eleatics had set their successors some rich problems about time. We have isolated two in chief: one is the question whether and on what terms to discard time-or-tense-distinctions, with its attendant debate on the possibility of indiscernible times. The other is the question how to talk of a first event in time. The first question was aired by the disagreement between Parmenides and Melissus. The second was still better canvassed, but the problem to which it leads—whether for every time there must be some earlier time—may not have come into the open before Plato. However, Democritus seems to have noticed it: he argued that not everything came into existence, and his counter-example was time (*Phys.* 251b15–17). And there is other evidence that the logic of time continued to exercise the men of that century. Antiphon is even credited with saying that time is not a substance but a concept or a measure (*Dox. Gr.* 318.22), but in this insight his name is linked with that of a Peripatetic philosopher of much later date who no doubt supplied the formula. Let us shift from this thin ice and watch Plato coming to grips with the Eleatic issues.

With Plato's attempt to describe a beginning of time I shall deal on a later occasion. It has had the lion's share of recent discussion and its twin-issue, the discarding of tenses, demands a hearing. Moreover Plato made the first issue pretty much his own; just now I want to discuss him in the context of an older debate.

When Plato says that the past and future tenses have no place in our talk about unchanging things he is taking his stand with Parmenides and against Melissus. When he prefaces this with the comment that "days, nights, years, are parts of time" he is calling attention to an oddity in Melissus' argument. Melissus had argued that something which is single and indivisible, as any Eleatic subject must be, could not have a body; for anything with a body has density (*pachos*), and consequently can be divided into parts; and anything with parts is no longer single and indivisible (B9). Therein he took himself to be complying with Parmenides' requirement that what exists must be indivisible—the requirement that all Zeno's arguments are ultimately designed to protect. But in admitting past and present and future into time or in letting similar distinctions into infinite space he felt secure: divisibility into parts comes only with density, for dense things can be broken or scattered, and then one meets with the gaps that vexed Parmenides or the infinitely elusive smallest parts that delighted Zeno. Differences in time and space, he thinks, are quite another thing. Plato corrects him: time has parts just as certainly as a block of wood, so his evasion is unsuccessful. And his correction of Melissus is deliberate, for in his own dialogue *Parmenides* he is prepared to show how Zeno's puzzles over divisibility arise in connection with time. This is another topic to be deferred for the present.

Now the use to which Plato puts Parmenides' device in the *Timaeus* is pretty widely agreed. When he says that "was" and "will be" are appropriate to our talk of the changing physical world, but that only "is" and "are" should be used in speaking of the timeless Forms, he is taken to have grasped the fact that such a statement as "Justice is a virtue" is temporally neutral or timeless, whereas such a statement as "The moon is a satellite of the earth" is not timeless but, at best, temporally general. He has seen that, while the second statement properly collects such questions as whether the moon will continue to satisfy the description tomorrow, and how long it has done so, and even how old it is, it is a false analogy to coin such questions about justice. Faced with Parmenides' admirable discovery of the tenseless proposition he applies this discovery to elucidate the logic of those propositions which preoccupy him as a philosopher.

Is this the right story? I am going to sow some doubts.

Look again at the device that he has taken over from Parmenides. Does Parmenides manage to isolate a use of the verb which is wholly independent of tense-affiliations? Certainly (let us take this now for granted) he wants to discard the past and future tenses—just as surely as he wants to discard denials of existence. But there are considerations which leave his move ambiguous. It is not just his use of those expressions for permanence and durability which Plato was ready to echo. It is that, while denying that his subject can be said to have existed ever in the past or to be going to exist in the future, Parmenides insists that it exists *now*. His treatment of time is too like his treatment of existence. He wants to maintain the existence of his subject and yet at the same time to allow no sense to denying its existence; and similarly he wants to maintain its existence in the present while admitting no use for the statement that it existed in the past or will do so in the future.

In a recent paper Professor Kneale suggested a connection between Parmenides' treatment of time and that puzzling piece of theological equipment, the eternal present that is enjoyed by God.[13] Augustine speaks easily of God's "everpresent eternity"; he tells his Maker "Your years neither go nor come, they stand all at once. . . . For you the present does not give place to tomorrow or follow after yesterday; your present day is eternity" (*Conf.* XI.13). Nor is this odd move pro-

[13] Note 2, above.

prietary to theology. Philosophy has thriven on attempts to leave some expression its familiar use while cutting it off from its family connections in the language. Think of the argument that any statement in the past tense must really be about the present or the future, because present or future evidence must constitute the whole ground for thinking it true or false. The manoeuvre fails, because to understand that some evidence is now available is to understand, inter alia, that it is false that that evidence was available but is so no longer. We reimport the past to mark out the sense of the present: without it we should have no right to the expressions "still," "now," "no longer."

Parmenides' isolation of one tense from its fellows suggests a view of language which underlies some puzzles in the *Theaetetus* and *Cratylus* and which Plato very effectively dismantles in the *Sophist*. It is not a device which promises to throw much light on those propositions about the concept of justice or the cardinal number five which interest Plato. Let us see what Plato made of it.

In the *Timaeus* Plato seems to be under its spell. He is apparently ready to drop the word "now" from timeless propositions, but he imports "always" in its place (38a). And there are other clues, almost too familiar to list. He is ready to use the same adjectives in describing both the timelessness of the Forms and the temporal progress of the physical world. He calls them both "everlasting," *aidion* (e.g. 29a, 40b). And he uses the noble word "eternal," *aiōnion*, first of the existence of the Forms and then, in the same breath, of time itself, viz. the regular motions of the astronomical clock (37d)—to the despair of Cornford, who insisted that eternity (*aiōn*) was the prerogative of the Forms, and wanted to emend the text in face of all the MSS and the ancient tradition.[14] But Cornford missed the argument. What Plato says is that the physical world cannot be *wholly or unqualifiedly* eternal (37d3–4: subsequently in 38b3 he coins the word διαιώνιος for this notion). And the idiom is the familiar language of the Theory of Forms. Plato means to recall those canonical arguments in the *Phaedo* and *Republic* which show that while things in this world can be beautiful or equal, large or single, they cannot be wholly or unqualifiedly so: in some other respect or relation they, unlike their respective Forms, will prove unequal or unbeautiful. Similarly with the eternity of the physical world. The movements of the planets, those movements which "define

[14] F. M. Cornford, *Plato's Cosmology* (London, 1937), p. 98 n. 1; "seems very plausible," Harold Cherniss, *Aristotle's Criticism of Plato and the Academy*, vol. I (Baltimore, 1944), p. 419 n. 350.

and preserve the numbers of time" (38c), are both stable and unstable: the pattern is stable, but it is a pattern of change. The Forms, on the other hand, are simply stable. But then why are we not allowed to credit them with a stable past and future? Melissus is obviously fretting to be back in the conversation. How does Plato keep him out?

By a very compressed argument. He says:

> That which is always unchangingly in the same state cannot be growing older or younger by the lapse of time. It cannot ever become so, it cannot have become so at present, it will not be so hereafter. And in general nothing can belong to it of all the things that the process of becoming attaches to the shifting things we perceive (38a).

So the argument seems to be this. To go on in time, and thus to collect a past and a future, is to grow older; but to grow older is to change; so what stays always the same cannot be staying so in time. Hence what stays always the same cannot collect a past or a future. Here, as you see, everything depends on what Plato means by "growing older." [15]

One thing that he does not mean is a change in the character of the subject, such as increasing decrepitude. For the description is meant equally to apply to the permanent furniture of the world, the stars and atoms. One thing that he may mean is the mere increase in age. This is suggested, both by his distinction between this and other characteristics of changing things, and by his claim that even to say of something that it "was and is and will be" is to report it as changing. Now if this is his meaning we can expect paradoxes. Certainly we, like the Greeks, talk of becoming (or growing) older as readily as of becoming hotter or happier. But we do not, and neither did they, ordinarily talk of mere progress in time as a kind of "change" (kinēsis, genesis). We expect to ask of any process of change how long it takes or how quickly it comes about, but the questions have no literal sense for our progress between different dates or ages. That progress is presupposed by, and not the subject of, our reports of change. Once reckon it among the familiar kinds of change, and the idea of complete stability finds itself curiously dispossessed. It cannot now, logically cannot, characterize anything that continues in time, yet the continuing in time is as essential to its logic as to that of change. What is left of it is a kind of logical torso

---

[15] "Growing older or younger" (cf. Parm.. 141a–d, 152a–e) called for separate discussion in a later lecture.

supported, as in the *Timaeus*, by a present tense without past or future connections.

And things are no different if Plato means something more than this by "growing older." For then he presumably means that to grow older is to have a history, in the sense that something is true of the subject at one time (something other than mere age) which is not true of it at another. But in Plato's view this is the case with all physical things. So again the idea of complete stability is dislodged from its hold on any temporal propositions save those couched in that degenerate tense, the eternal present. Later in the *Timaeus* Plato speaks of transient physical things as clinging precariously to existence, by contrast with the security of the Ideas. He is wrong. It is his stable Forms which cling precariously to their stability, by virtue of their tenuous and disreputable hold on time.

In sum, it is part of the originality of Plato to have grasped, or half-grasped, an important fact about certain kinds of statement, namely that they are tenseless whereas others are tensed. But he tries to bring this contrast under his familiar distinction between the changeless and the changing. So he saddles the familiar distinction with a piece of conceptual apparatus taken from Parmenides, a tense-form which retains enough of a present sense to be coupled with expressions for permanence and stability, yet which has severed its links with the future and the past. Armed with this device Plato is able to turn the distinction between tensed and tenseless statements into a more congenial distinction between timebound and timeless, changing and immutable, objects.

But at a price. The concept of stability has been stretched so that stability is no longer a function of time. And the interesting propositions, so far from staying tenseless, are restated in an artificial and degenerate tense-form. The theory for which we are asked to tolerate these anomalies will need to hold firm against scrutiny. But on scrutiny there seems to be something wrong at its roots.

V

What is wrong, I think, can be put very shortly. It is that to be tensed or tenseless is a property of statements and not of things, and that paradoxes come from confusing this distinction; just as they come from trying to manufacture necessary beings out of the logical necessity that attaches to certain statements. But how is the distinction to be

recognized? One way, a good way, is to notice that tenseless statements are not proprietary to one sort of subject and tensed statements
to another. And there seems to be evidence in another work of Plato
that he did notice this, and brought the point home by a valid argument. I want to end by discussing that evidence. It occurs in the *Sophist*,
in the criticism that the chief speaker brings against the so-called
"friends of the Forms." [16]

The argument hinges on some special concepts of action and change
which are brought into play a little earlier in the dialogue. An Eleatic
stranger sets out to examine the theories of other philosophers with a
view to extracting answers to a certain question. He wants to know,
namely, what kinds of thing they count as real, or what general criteria
they use in deciding that some kinds of thing exist and others do not.
(Existence, reality: the Greek does not distinguish them here, and we
need not.) After exposing the confusions of some earlier theorists he
turns to two other parties: the Giants, who say that the sole criterion
of reality is to be, or to have, a tangible physical body; and the Gods,
who are "friends of the Forms" and who say that the joint criteria of
reality are to be knowable and to be free from change. And he professes
to involve both of them in contradictions. The Giants are trapped by
the admission that there are souls (good material souls, of course),
and that souls can become wise and just. They are at once told that to
become just is to come into some relation with justice—it is for justice
to be possessed by, or to become present to, the soul (247a5–6). So
justice too must figure in the Giants' ontology, and no one would say
that justice had a physical body. On the strength of this move the
Eleatic proposes a more hospitable criterion of reality, to take care of
justice as well. It is that real things are things which are able *to do something to another thing, or to have something done to them*, however little
and however seldom (247d–e). This is the ambiguous formula on which
the later argument turns.

What does Plato mean by "doing something or having something
done to one"? The sole illustration he proffers is that justice can be
possessed by, or can become present to and again depart from, a soul
(247a5–9). Of course there is no suggestion that this activity makes any
difference to the nature of justice—it would be nonsense to suggest

[16] My account of this argument lies close to that given by J. M. E. Mo-
ravcsik in "Being and Meaning in the *Sophist*," *Acta Philosophica Fennica*,
14 (1962), 35–40 [repr. in The Bobbs-Merrill Reprint Series, Phil-138], which
should be consulted for its criticism of alternative views.

that the concept of justice is revised when that virtue enters, or comes to be exhibited by, Tom Jones. In fact the requirement to be met if X is to be said to do something to Y, or to have something done to it by Y, seems to come to no more than this: that there should be statements in which the name of X stands as subject to some active or passive verb, and the name of Y stands accordingly as object or in the instrumental case; and that these statements should be at some time (but not time-lessly) true. The class of verbs is undefined but wide. In particular it contains various expressions for the varying relations between justice and the just Mr. Jones.

Now turn to the Gods, the "friends of the Forms." Never mind whether they are Plato himself or, as some other friends of the Forms would like us to believe, a misguided minority in the Academy. They propose two criteria of reality, criteria that are severally necessary and jointly sufficient. What "really exists," they say, is (a) always unchanging and (b) accessible to, or known by, the mind alone (248a). The characteristics are familiar enough from Plato's other accounts of the Forms. And the Eleatic sets himself to show that these criteria are mutually incompatible. His argument falls into two stages, and the question to be decided is whether the first stage is the backbone of the case or merely something to be discarded when he gets to the second.

(A) He fastens first on the second criterion and the relationship that it postulates between the mind and reality. Surely, to know the Forms is either to do something to them or to have something done to oneself by them (248b2–8)? But suppose knowing is doing something; then for a Form to be known is for something to be done to it: and if something is done to it, it is changed. But if it is changed by being known, the criteria conflict (248d10–e4).

The argument sounds preposterous. It is absurd to suggest that if Tom Jones got his head clear on the nature of justice this morning, he was performing some occult operation on that virtue. And between the steps of the argument (248c1–d9) the Eleatic stranger allows that his opponents may well jib at this; they will probably refuse to say that knowing is any kind of *doing*. In face of this he moves on to a second stage in his attack.

(B) He turns his attention now to the first criterion, that of immu-tability. This is the criterion which had to be saved by saying that coming to know Y is not doing anything to Y. But the Eleatic argues that the cost of maintaining it is higher than its friends have realized. They will have to deny any reality to intelligence. For intelligence entails life, and life and intelligence are found in the soul; and it would be absurd to say that something with a living and intelligent soul is something that does not change. So, again, the criteria are in conflict (248e6–249b6).

Most readers of Plato, I suspect, feel some relief when they come to this second argument. They are very ready to believe that in producing (B) the Eleatic has quietly dropped (A). He is content now to point out that even for the friends of the Forms there must be one sort of changing thing in existence, viz. an intelligence going about its business; but he is not any longer pressing that deplorable point that in some sense the exercise of the intelligence must entail a change in its object. And there are two reasons for thinking that we have seen the last of (A). One is the sheer prima facie absurdity of saying that coming to know anything changes it. The second is that in the next few lines the Eleatic insists all over again that the objects of intelligence must be unchanging (249b8–c8).

But on a closer inspection these reasons lose their force. Bear in mind that the sort of change in question here is that which is implied by the vague notion of doing something or having something done to one. This, as we saw, covered the case in which justice came to be possessed by, or came to be present in, some soul. We had to explain it quite generally in terms of the active and passive uses of a very wide range of verbs. Now in this sense it seems beyond question that to say that Jones came to understand justice on his tenth birthday is to describe a case of doing something to something. But it does not in the least imply that the question "What is justice?" acquires a different answer once Jones has the Idea in view, nor that all the other generalizations by which I communicate my understanding of justice suddenly become reports of a transient state of affairs. Nor does it imply that my knowledge of justice is deficient if I do not know that it captured Jones' attention at lunch yesterday. In this respect the old requirement is absolute: justice must be immutable if there is to be any thinking about it. This is the point of the Eleatic's warning.

Still you may cavil at the suggestion that in having something done to it in this mild sense justice undergoes some change. But you have the answer by you. For if Plato can claim, as he does in the *Timaeus*, that even to have a history is to change, then to say that justice captured the attention of Jones yesterday is to report a change in the Form. For on such an account it is a sufficient condition of change that something should become true of the subject at some time that was not true before—even, for example, that some virtue came to be possessed, or understood, or manifested, or whatever.

If this is so, two points seem to follow. One is a point of detail: namely that, for all the objectors can show to the contrary, the argument (B) can be, as a first reading of the text would suggest, simply a reinforcing argument to (A). It is designed to cut away the chief reason for rejecting the conclusions of (A), namely the wish to cling to the first criterion and represent reality as unchanging.[17] The second point is more important for our purpose. It is that Plato will have recognized an important qualification to the claim that any statement about justice or a prime number is a tenseless statement, and recognized this as a corollary of his own theory. It does seem reasonable to say that, if "The number 3 is a prime number" is a tenseless statement about a number, "The number of congressmen now in jail is 3" is a tensed statement about that number. Both statements might appear in the records of a Pythagorean trying to establish the power and importance of 3. So I think that, so far as it goes, the claim is true. And I do not relish the thought of leaving Plato at this point wholly under the spell of Parmenides.

[17] This is certified, against some traditional misreadings of the passage, by the general conclusion in *Sophist* 249d: "Reality is all things that are unchanged and changed"—*not* "all things that are unchanged and some, viz. souls, that change."

13

THE RELATION BETWEEN
THE TWO PARTS OF PARMENIDES' POEM

Karl Reinhardt

Parmenides is by no means one of the *physikoi;* the core of his cosmogony is not at all what a first glance at its conventional shell might make
one expect. He often gives the appearance of a *physikos;* but it ultimately was not his purpose to explain the structure of the world in a
system which, while free from objections as much as possible, would
still be couched in terms of Ionian physics—rarefaction and condensation, the rising and ebbing of material constituents. He may have
relied upon this or that predecessor for physical details, but that was
incidental. What was essential, ingenious, and uniquely Parmenidean
was his version of primordial Chaos: a construct that made possible
the reduction of all the world's contents and special distinctions to
that ultimate distinction that would encompass all others in itself, the
contrast between light and darkness.

To understand this one would only need to take him at his word.
For he does expressly tell us that all things collectively and distribu-
tively are called light and darkness, and that these two are assigned,
in accordance with their respective powers, to all things (B9). Hence
the intertwined rings, hence the whole curious structure: It is meant

From Karl Reinhardt, *Parmenides und die Geschichte der griechischen Philosophie* (Bonn, Friedrich Cohen, 1916; repr. Frankfurt a.M., Vittorio Klostermann, 1959), hereafter *PGgP*, pp. 18–23, 29–32, 64–71, 74–82, 88, with
omissions as indicated. Translated by Matthew R. Cosgrove with Alexander
P. D. Mourelatos. Unless otherwise indicated, passages quoted from Greek
sources are translations of Greek text quoted but not rendered in German
in *PGgP*, and are intended to conform to interpretations therein given. Greek
text printed here is also supplied with translations even if no translation is
given in *PGgP*.

Selection translated and printed here with the permission of the publisher,
Vittorio Klostermann, and of the late Frau Elly Reinhardt.

to present a kind of prototype, which repeats itself throughout the entire cosmos and in each individual thing, in endless variation. What I see is composed of light and shadow; what I feel, of the loose and the firm. The principles are purely phenomenological. How startling it must have seemed in a milieu that included such radical *physikoi* as Anaximenes and Anaximander, to postulate light and darkness, that which is most external, superficial, and immaterial, as the essence and ultimate constitution of things. The principles, to repeat, are purely phenomenological, but these principles are treated as though they were physical substances. . . .

The same goddess who dispatches souls from the light into the dark, and from the dark again into the light,[a] is herself enthroned amidst light and darkness, and out of light and darkness has fashioned all things. Light is related to coming-to-be, to affirmation, to being; darkness, to passing-away, to negation, to nothingness. Coming-to-be-born and dying—here is exhibited the same opposition by virtue of which this entire world of *doxa* is reality for us mortals.

On the same fundamental thought rests the epistemology the essentials of which have been preserved for us by Theophrastus in *De Sensu* I (DK A46):

Parmenides did not give a general account, but said only that, there being two elements, knowledge is determined by the one that is preponderant. For if the hot or the cold should prevail, the thought will be, respectively, different; better and clearer, however, if it results from the hot—but even that thought needs some measure of balance.

However, when Theophrastus thinks it necessary to refer to the warm and the cold as the elements of sensory knowledge, he is possibly—indeed, probably—caught in the same basic mistake with regard to the principles of "Doxa" as was Aristotle. For they both unhesitatingly posit as elements the warm and the cold constituents familiar to them, while in the fragments themselves only fire and darkness, light and night, the light/thin and the heavy/firm appear as elemental opposites. . . . We do nothing inappropriate and unprecedented if instead of the warm and the cold we prefer to recognize light and darkness, or the thick and the thin, as elements of knowledge. That we have some right to do so is proven by the sequel to the text already cited from *De Sensu*:

a [Simpl. *Phys.* 39.18; cf. DK B13.—Ed.]

For he considers perceiving and thinking as the same. And he believes, accordingly, that memory and forgetfulness also come to
be produced from these [the hot and the cold] through mixture.
But if they should mix in equal parts, whether in that case there
will be thinking or not, and what the [body's] disposition will be,
that he failed to explain. Yet that he also thinks of perception as
produced through the opposite taken in itself, that is clear in those
lines in which he says that the dead [thing] does not perceive light
and the hot and sound, because of the absence of fire, but perceives
the cold and silence and the corresponding opposites. And he
generally believes that everything that exists has a measure of
knowledge.

There is, accordingly, contained in each thing, a non-entity and an
entity, an opposition by virtue of which it appears to us at once as light
and shadow. Now, since like is known only by like, our power of
knowing must also be mixed from the same opposites. The more parts
of fire and light are contained in this mixture, the more acutely the
spirit knows, and the better it holds what it has come to know firmly
in memory. For memory is something positive, forgetting something
negative; and as the one occurs through light, so the other through
darkness. It is no accident that *Lēthē* is, with *Thanatos* and *Gēras*, a
child of night. A corpse, in which the light is extinguished, still knows,
through the darkness that has prevailed in it. Yet it knows henceforth
only what is negative. It hears, sees, feels no more: that is, it sees only
the unseeable, darkness; it hears the unhearable, stillness; it feels the
unfeelable, the dead, the cold. As dying is a passing of the soul into
darkness and coming to be born an emerging into the light, the former
on its way to a negation, the latter to an affirmation, so also the ex-
tinguishing of knowledge is a transition from light to darkness, from
affirmation to negation. . . .

Whoever takes the trouble to understand Parmenides in all his bold-
ness as well as in his restraint, and at the same time in terms of his
historical situation, must first of all realize that the one great defect
from which the "Doxa" suffers in our eyes—namely, that it is unable
to take hold of the knowing subject and must turn for help to the things
themselves—was not very perceptible to Parmenides, and was perhaps
not perceived by him at all. He understood the proposition that like
can only be known by like so literally, so close to the level of visual
imagery, that he could not but think that the organ of perception and

its object were made up of the same constituents, and were even subject
to the same forms and laws. Thought processes in the soul appeared to
him not as corresponding with, but as exactly repeating the external
world. What was a law for thought had to have unqualified validity for
things also. If nature were shown contradicting the principle of non-
contradiction itself, then nature was *ipso facto* false and precisely not
existent: "For you could not come to know that which is not (for it is
not feasible), nor could you declare it; for it is the same to think and
to be" (B2.7–8, B3). Conversely, every character of the external world
led directly to a conclusion concerning human knowledge.

No matter how hard one looks, one will not find the slightest hint
of a separation between thinking and being (or representation and
appearance) in the fragments. Parmenides begins the "Doxa" by relating (B8.53) that men have agreed to designate a twofold form with
names, but he does not elaborate, as one would expect, on how they
fashioned their world-picture from both forms. Instead, the object of
their thought straightaway achieves an independent life: Dark and
light unite and produce the world; and to our surprise a cosmogony
springs from the epistemology. What had been no more than a name,
a convention, an *onoma*, enters into physical combinations, and finally
generates even man himself and his cognitive states. To our way of
thinking, that is certainly hard to take. Our only recourse, if we are to
grasp it, is to recite to ourselves once again the rule that was the life-
blood of Parmenidean conviction: "For it is the same to think and to
be" (B3). Because this world is composed throughout of light and
darkness, and is pervasively the same and then again not the same
(B8.58, B6.8), because contradiction is the essence of all *doxa*, this
entire world must be false, that is to say, subjective, or as the Greeks
would have said, it can only exist *nomōi*, "by convention," and not
physei, "in reality."

To be sure, this conclusion is not repeated in every sentence. Now
and then it even seems as though the critic and nay-sayer had let himself be carried along for a while on the broad stream of human opinions;
indeed, as though his critique were itself the repository of discoveries
in which he took pride. For since appearance by no means lacks all
reason and consistency, it can actually be explored. Yet its character
as appearance does not mitigate its contradicting the highest law of
thought, the sole guarantee of truth. This is said twice, briefly but
sharply, at decisive points: the beginning and the end of the second
part. Whether between these passages there were originally additional

reminders of the same fundamental idea, we do not know. The two that we do know are sufficiently complete. As though separated from the rest by a thick tallying stroke, at the conclusion of the whole stand the words that give the sum of all that has been said (B19):

> And so, according to appearances (*kata doxan*) these things came to be, and now are, and later than now will come to an end, having matured; and to these things did men attach a name, a mark to each.

In many ways our philosopher may have been in the same position as the Homeric poet who described the shield of Achilles. The Homeric author has so tenuous a hold on the image through which—as though through glass—he views the things themselves, their lives and fortunes, that he calls himself back, again and again, to the image in order not to become lost in the real. That Parmenides too was trying to grasp not the things themselves but an image, not *physis* but *nomos*—this could hardly be missed by a reflective reader. The conclusion that takes up again the introductory thought ("they came to agree to name two forms") can only be understood in this way: Men have made for themselves a law; the world is a convention, developed consistently on the basis of a sanctioned error. Recall lines 1.31–32 ὡς τὰ δοκοῦντα χρῆν δοκίμως εἶναι, "how appearances had to be valid." Beginning and end, sense and grammar—all this is best made coherent if we abandon the notions of hypothesis[b] and eristic. And who could better explain

---

[b] [An earlier section of this chapter in Reinhardt's book, omitted here, includes (pp. 25–26) the following important remarks, directed against the influential view of Zeller, Windelband, and others, that the "Doxa" is presented merely as a (counterfactual) hypothesis.—Ed.]

Parmenides does not speak at all hypothetically, but says—as apodictically as he could—that what he relates is the entire truth, the words of his goddess from whose lips no falsehood comes. How can Truth deliver an hypothesis? Actually, when the goddess begins to instruct her chosen pupil in the deluded thinking of mortals, bidding him hear the deceptive order of her words, I should think it ought to be quite clearly realized (even though the sequel might show this less clearly) that the falsehood resides not in her teaching but in what her teaching is about. She communicates the truth about a delusion; she shows how this delusion arose and why it had to arise. She advances no postulates, she sets no suppositions from which one would have to proceed. Rather she tells, as it were, of a primordial event, a kind of original sin of knowledge from which all the other errors of our ideas necessarily followed. And she explains why things must come to pass in this world with such a

what line 1.32 διὰ παντὸς πάντα περῶντα, "pervading all things through-out," means than Parmenides himself?

> But since everything was named Light and Night, and these two, in accordance with their respective powers (i.e. in accordance with their multiple meanings), reside in all things whatsoever, then everything is at the same time filled with Light and invisible Night, which are both equal (i.e. corresponding, parallel) to one another, since neither has a share in the other. (B9)[c]

We must not forget the conclusions of the first part; we must find our way into this thought-world far enough to sense that a thing which contains simultaneously two elements having nothing in common with each other, their mixture explaining the phenomenon that one and the same thing appears now this way, now another—that sort of thing is for this philosophy an impossibility, a ταὐτὸν καὶ οὐ ταὐτόν, "same and not the same." Fr. 9, we ought to realize, contains, indeed makes explicit, what is absolutely the most forceful contradiction possible for that philosophy. The explanation, ἐπεὶ οὐδετέρῳ μέτα μηδέν, "since neither has a share in the other," only then becomes at all intelligible when we understand light and dark not as material ingredients but as concepts. For it is the essential characteristic of this doctrine to make ingredients and concepts merge and overflow into one another constantly. This, after all, is the very first attempt at conceptual thought. We must, therefore, in thinking of the ingredients, keep in mind their meaning as concepts; just as in thinking of concepts we must keep in mind their character as ingredients. . . .

The opinion that the much-cited lines of Parmenides on the two-headed mortals, "who are carried along on their way at once deaf and blind, without judgment," is in fact only an all too thinly veiled, passionate attack on Heraclitus and his school, was first voiced by Jacob

---

consistency and obviousness: "I show you plainly this whole *eoikota diakosmon*" (B8.60). Once we have freed ourselves from the received interpretation of the "Doxa," we no longer need translate *eoikota* as "apparent" [*scheinbar*] —this would only be appropriate if it were contrasted to an *alēthē*, "real." We should instead understand that the goddess will unfold the *diakosmos* of mortals in all completeness and consistency in order to reveal all things to her chosen pupil.

[c] [The English renders Reinhardt's German translation, given in footnote. —Ed.]

Bernays.[1] This opinion gradually came to be regarded as so authoritative and compelling that, in the end, the whole interpretation of early Greek philosophy came to be conditioned and shaped by it. Bernays' observation must, indeed, if it really is correct, have the most far-ranging consequences. To begin with, it would seem that we have here a point from which the progress and the course of philosophy's development can be charted with documented precision. What is more, on this interpretation, the same lines seem to allow us a glimpse, through a crack, as it were, into the inner and true life of that age and its thought. Seeing through the solemn formality and self-satisfaction of the literary posture, we gaze at the unexpectedly agitated busy-work of a school. Here we see pupils traveling to this and that teacher; there we see teachers, admirably up to date, tearing apart one another's latest publications, disputing over this and that so vociferously that east and west resound with the echo of their words.[2] But however obvious or improbable all that may be in itself, the question remains: Was Bernays really right to take those lines completely out of their context, and to explain them—on the basis of what must have been an initial and very freshly formed impression—as invective?

We have already recognized[d] that the three "ways of inquiry" are the natural result of a standpoint which is posing a *single* question, and that the third way—that on which the two-headed mortals wander—belongs within the system just as essentially as do the other two. If anyone feels that the evidence from Gorgias' "On Non-Being" is not sufficient, perhaps he might more easily be persuaded by a text from the *Upanishads*, *Mândûkya-Kârikâ* 4, 83:

> "He is!" "Is not!" "Is and is not!"
> "He is not not!" Thinking him thus
> Inconstant, constant, twofold, nay-saying,
> His nature remains concealed to the fool.[3]

[1] *Gesammelte Abhandlungen*, ed. H. Usener (Berlin, 1885), vol. 1, p. 62.

[2] Emanuel Loew has no doubt gone the farthest in filling in the outlines of such a sketch: See "Parmenides und Heraklit im Wechselkampfe," *AGP*, N.S. 17 (1911), 343–69.

[d] [Relying on the parallel of Gorgias' treatise "On Non-Being" (see DK 82B3[67], cf. pseudo-Aristotle, *De Melisso, Xenoph. et Gorg.* 979a24–34), Reinhardt earlier argues, pp. 36–46, that Parmenides' "ways of inquiry" are three: (1) "Being is"; (2) "Being is not"; (3) "Being both is and is not."—Ed.]

[3] Cf. Paul Deussen, *Sechzig Upanishad's des Veda* (Leipzig, 1897), p. 602.

Or perhaps he can be convinced of the naturalness of that threefold logical division by Philolaus (B2):

> It is necessary that the things-that-are (*eonta*) should all be either limiting (*perainonta*), or unlimited (*apeira*), or both limiting and unlimited. But if they should be only unlimited, ⟨or only limiting⟩ [addition suppl. by Diels], they could not possibly be. For it is surely manifest (*phainetai*) that the things-that-are are constituted neither by a totality of the limiting nor by a totality of the unlimited. It is clear, therefore, that the world and all things in it have been put together from those limiting together with those unlimited.

I only hope that the reader will not draw the conclusion—which, admittedly, would be most welcome to many modern scholars—that this similarity too shows the Pythagorean influence under which Parmenides supposedly grew up. In fact, the proof-structure utilized by Philolaus is but a poor copy of the Eleatic original. In place of the highest logical opposition we find a geometrical distinction, that is to say, something that is no real opposition at all—the latter, according to the Pythagorean table of opposites, would have been the pair "unlimited and limited"—but rather a causal relation, the limiting and the limited.[4] (It is inconceivable to me how one can date so late and derivative a system in the sixth century, as though we were dealing not with speculative knowledge but with religious notions, where fixity from age to age is more plausibly to be expected.)

Now, if that threefold division was the foundation of Eleatic speculation, then the third part of it could not at the same time have served merely to counter an alien doctrine, least of all that of Heraclitus—for

---

[4] Hermann Diels, in the third edition of *Die Fragmente der Vorsokratiker*, observes (p. 309): "Limit (form) and unlimitedness (matter) are the principles of real, i.e. of visible things, which are grasped through number." I fail to see why it is not misleading to translate *perainonta* as "limited" [*Begrenztem*]. *perainein* intransitive, with *pros ti*, means "to border on something," but not "to be bordered or limited." Under *perainonta* Philolaus may have understood point, line, and surface; under *apeira*, line, surface, and space, insofar as these are infinite in themselves and can be made determinate in whatever way by point, line, and surface. If *ta perainonta* meant "the limited" then the proof περαίνοντα μόνον οὔ κα εἴη ("[if] . . . only limited, they could not possibly be") would be unintelligible, for the notion of merely limited spatial areas or bodies does not by itself contain any contradiction. [See, however, Kranz's translation of B2 and note on B1 in DK (fifth and following editions). —Ed.]

where in Heraclitus may we find any hint of the doctrine that being and non-being were *not* the same? The fact is that not a single word in Parmenides refers to anything alien, external, non-Eleatic. When we read of the mortals, *brotoi*, it must be remembered above all that it is not Parmenides but the goddess who speaks of all this, and that she talks about mortals no differently than the gods of epic poetry are wont to do: οἶον δή νυ θεοὺς βροτοὶ αἰτιόωνται, "Now look how mortals place the blame on the gods!" (*Od.* 1.32) She can therefore only have the totality of men in mind, not a special class of eccentrics. Furthermore, this is neither the only time nor the first time she uses the word. She employs it quite frequently—in B1.30, 8.39, 8.51, 19.3—and in so definite a way that it seems to do the work of a technical philosophical term. The truth and the mortals: These are the two poles on which her thoughts turn. And just as the word *alētheia*, insofar as all truth is transcendent, expresses also the concept of transcendence, for which there was as yet no other expression, so too "mortals" becomes in this proto-philosophy a closely circumscribed philosophical concept. It stands for the world in which we live, perceive, and feel—language still had no resources for referring to a "phenomenal world" either.

The mythological garb of the whole is far more than allegory; it is something altogether and fundamentally different from an empty pose or concession to poetic convenience. There is, strictly speaking, no "garb" at all, for there is nothing here that, having first been formulated abstractly, would then be given an artificially physical, if transparent, clothing. Rather, precisely the most abstract thoughts could only find their way to communication (in literary form, of course) through the ancient, mythological mode of expression; for the medium of language was still not adequate to the task of direct clarification. What words could possibly have sufficed to generate a conception of a region so lofty that from its vantage point the whole world of experience should vanish altogether into sheer nothingness? The vast chasm that lay between that transcendent realm and this world could only be compared to the distinction between god and man. If what had to be negated was nothing less than the world of man in its entirety, then it was—to say the least—no merely superfluous and trivial conceit to put the damning judgment into the mouth of a goddess. Viewed in this light, the form of religious revelation appears as the natural surface cover for this most radical of all philosophies; it follows the contours of all its parts easily and without constraint, and nowhere shows any incongruence or contradiction.

I am, of course, saying that myth forms *only* the external appearance; it is *only* being used—or if you will, misused—as an expressive medium, and therefore cannot have any impulse and life of its own. The various figures and images, considered as mythology, are unreal and shadowy for the simple reason that they are exclusively the expression of thoughts, and the thoughts in turn cannot achieve a powerful and living personification because they have been produced by the understanding alone, not out of emotional need. This is why one gets the impression of artificiality and coldness. What the reader familiar with genuine mythology will see in the poem will seem like frozen allegory. To the reader who comes from the opposite side, from later philosophy, the same features will appear as tedious adherence to an outmoded, hieratic form. Both impressions are false, because they are the result of alien standards. They do not take adequate notice of the constraints on archaic language, as well as that language's natural hostility toward emancipated thought. If one would only try to imagine the expression in archaic prose of what the poetic form actually accomplishes—and that is considerably more than what appears at first glance—the deduction of the sensory world, for example, is something Parmenides would hardly have risked giving in this form, *in propria persona*—then one would at least come to admire the economy, succinctness, and trenchancy of this "poem." One would also be much less disposed to take seriously the old question as to whether it might even be called poetry, according to the usual conception, and not rather prose. (With all due respect to Aristotle, I hope it will be forgiven if I consider his distinction in this case much too coarse to dispose of so difficult and unique a phenomenon.)

Let me now return to the "two-headed mortals." That this is not meant as a term of derision is shown by the other appellations with which it is coupled: "at once deaf and blind, dazed." It is hardly warranted to probe behind these words for a mood of petulance or antagonism.[e] In literature of not much later date the same words turn out to be common and fixed designations for purely sensory knowledge. As polemic they would have no parallel.[5] Why men who follow their senses are called "two-headed" is explained by the following:

  [e] [See Reinhardt, *PGgP*, p. 48.—Ed.]
  [5] Hermann Diels, *Parmenides' Lehrgedicht* (Berlin, 1897), p. 69, compares Heraclitus B34: "those who have heard without understanding are like deaf men"; but that is something quite different. There it is a question of the communication of a certain discourse; those to whom it is addressed do hear

> By whom to be and not to be are deemed (*nenomistai*) the same
> and not the same, and the path of them all is backward-turning.
> (B6.8–9)

The "who" and "they" here refer to the same "mortals" who appear
in B8.38; it would be arbitrary to drive a wedge between these two
texts:

> Therefore all will be a (mere) name—all such as mortals posited
> persuaded that they were true, coming to be and perishing, being
> and not being, changing place and exchanging bright surface.
> (B8.38–41)

The reference could only be to the totality of men. To the things
"deemed" correspond the things "posited": Men have made for themselves a *nomos*, a law, in saying "for us, being and non-being shall be
the same." And this law is in turn none other than what constitutes
the object of the entire second part, the "Doxa": "For they came to
agree to name two forms" (B8.53).

It is false, therefore, to say that the poem divides into two disjoint
parts. "Doxa" is inextricably connected with "Truth," and is continually contrasted with it. "Doxa" is nothing but the third way of
inquiry; the poet has done his utmost, and has spared nothing, to make
this connection evident. The opening of "Doxa" itself is but a more
precise exposition and confirmation of what he had previously suggested concerning the third way and its accord with the sensory world:

> For they came to agree to name *two* forms, of which it is not right
> to name the *one*—here is their error. They divided contrariwise
> (*tantia*) the two bodies, and separated their signs from one an-
> other: here the flame of ether-like fire, mild, most light, *altogether
> the same with itself but not the same with the other;* but they also
> set that other *by itself* (*kat' auto*) on the opposite side (*tantia*),
> lightless night, a thick and heavy stuff. (B8.53–59)[f]

Diels recognized that *tantia* is used adverbially here, just as *tanantia*
in Thucydides VII.79: *tanantia diastōmen*, "let us separate contrariwise." From this I conclude that *kata* is not to be taken with *tantia*,

---

it, but they are *like* the deaf. The two passages have utterly no relation to one
another.

  [f] [The English renders Reinhardt's German translation of the Greek text,
which he also quotes.—Ed.]

and that *auto* is not in apposition with the adverb; rather, *kat' auto* means "alone," "by itself." It seems to me that there is a gain in elegance for the whole sentence through this construction. Two forms are set in opposition to each other, each by itself. They are the two strongest, most thoroughly adverse opposites Parmenides was able to find in the world of sensory appearances: darkness and light. Each of these representations or ingredients—for he has no means to distinguish the one from the other—is, considered by itself, a *tauton*, "the same." It undergoes neither increase nor decrease in power; it is unified and undifferentiated. But insofar as it is an opposite, and only comes into existence at all by virtue of its complement, it is simultaneously an *ou tauton*, "not the same," i.e. it *is* and then again it *is not*. The error of this world-view is to posit two forms instead of one, but that is by no means to say that one of the two, e.g. light, would be closer to the true reality than darkness. The words "of which it is not right to name the *one*" are not meant to demand a decision from their hearer. For even light, in that moment in which it gets its name and becomes body, is removed from the realm of pure being and is banished to the same deceptive world of seeming to which its complement was banished. Both forms, as elements of our representations (*onomata*) and of our world, are at the same time most sharply distinct from one another and can never merge into one another. There exists, nonetheless, no thing in which both are not contained simultaneously *as a mixture*. The entire manifold of the world as we present it to ourselves depends solely upon countless variations of that mixture. That is the course of thought from B8 to B9. Behind this seemingly physical elaboration one can easily detect the familiar tripartite schema, which everywhere underlies the thought's construction: two opposites and, as a third, their mixture—"is"; "is not"; "both is and is not."

If from this vantage point we look back upon Parmenides' *chaos*, the structure of the material rings, then the last patch of obscurity which still seemed to pall that structure is illuminated: What we have here is nothing other than a transposing of the three logical categories into spatial ones—at both ends the two unmediated opposites, light and darkness, and in the middle their mixture. If the opposites present themselves duplicated, that is done purely for the sake of spatial symmetry. And when they manifest themselves as circles and rings rather than as strokes and lines, this is prompted by aesthetic need as much as by the familiar vision of the world-sphere. Parmenides surely preferred to think of his material ingredients bent back upon themselves rather than dissipating into infinity. Thus we come to realize that even the cosmogony has an origin that is more logical than physical. The contradiction between Parmenides the logician and Parmenides the physicist, which hitherto seemed to be undeniable, is completely and happily resolved through a more precise and comprehensive interpretation. . . .

Though it may sound paradoxical, I see no way to avoid the conclusion that the concept of mixture—the basis of all subsequent physical speculation—must have first grown in purely logical and metaphysical soil so that it could later be transplanted to the field of natural science. However little we know of Anaximander, it is clear that he did not think of his *apeiron* in terms of a mixture. If, as it would seem, he spoke of *apokriseis*, what he intended, surely, was not so much a separating-off and diverging of the different ingredients or material states from the unified, original stuff, but rather the spatial demarcation of different worlds within the infinite.

> And he says that that which is generative (*to . . . gonimon*) of hot and cold came to be separated off (*apokrithēnai*) from the eternal (*aidiou*) and that out of this (scil. the *gonimon*) a kind of sphere of flame came to grow (*periphyenai*) round the air surrounding the earth, like bark round a tree. (DK A10 = Plut. *Strom.* 2)

That is to say: As bark grows from the wood of the tree, so the ingredients grow from one another and from the infinite. The first to seek a more precise grasp and definition of the essence of change was Anaximenes, in his doctrine of rarefaction and condensation. In this he shared the view of Anaximander that the primordial material must have within itself an unlimited capacity for transformation.

It was against this assumption, which until then had served as the firm basis and secure warrant for all knowledge of nature, that Parmenides raised his voice. He, the great revolutionary, the uncompromising gainsayer to all speculation in the mode of the *physikoi*, became, nonetheless, a more fruitful influence on natural philosophy than any of its adherents. With his tendency toward extremism, and with the certainty which that unique weapon of his own discovery, his logic, provided, he explained: Things that are in opposition can never merge into one another; thick and thin are opposites, hence cannot be united in my thought, and the world is but the mirror of my thought. Therefore, when the same thing appears now thick and now thin, now hot and now cold, now bright and now again dark, that can only be possible by virtue of a parallel existence of the unchangeable opposites, or—to put it in material terms—through their mixture.

In this way Parmenides accomplishes the incredible: What had been thought of only as density states of one and the same material are themselves made into the original material and are equated with his two principal opposites, light and dark. There is here such scorn for the thought modes of *physikoi* as only the first logician could muster. But just as physical speculation immediately adopted the principle— formulated purely conceptually—of the imperishability of being, so also did it appropriate the notion of mixture and turned it to a new— or rather for the first time to its proper—purpose. For the fact is that the two thoughts have one origin, and were not to be brought together only by Empedocles. The visible marks and signposts of the path the concept of mixture traveled from then on may be seen in the constructions of precosmic states of mixture: the rings of Parmenides, the *Sphairos* of Empedocles, the *meigma* of Anaxagoras. As a natural philosopher would see them, i.e. considered as a mixture, the rings seem still extremely arbitrary and imperfect. The *Sphairos* satisfies the demands of physics better, insofar as it presents a single, uniform mass, and because the number of mixed ingredients has been raised from two to four. The *meigma* of Anaxagoras, finally, brings the original concept of mixture to its ultimate conclusion.

With the principle of mixture and the peculiar logic to which it owes its genesis is connected yet another great achievement, the theory of perception. We must briefly return to this theory and consider it from the new outlook we have acquired, so that we may gain a deeper insight into its origins from the doctrine of being. . . .

Among the "old physicists" not a single one can be named who, in the course of his thought, could have been struck by the problem of knowledge with even remotely the seriousness and forcefulness with which it struck Parmenides. "For the same is to think [or 'to know'] and to be": His whole philosophy rests on this one sentence. Just as truth coincides for him with logical, abstract thought, so corporeal opposition has its mirror image in the nature of human sensibility, for in both the same pre-established harmony reigns:

For depending on what the mixture of the much-erring organs is for a man at one time or another (ἑκάστοτ' ἔχει κρᾶσιν) such is the cognition that occurs to him. For it is just this that thinks: the disposition of the organs in men, in each and every one: that which prevails is the thinking.[g]

Coming from the goddess' lips, how studied is the emphasis on *human* knowledge! Note the deprecation expressed by the epithet *polyplanktōn:* "much-erring organs" (cf. *plakton noon,* B6.6, of the men who choose the third way, i.e. "Doxa"). Note finally, the brilliantly pointed expression of the closing phrase: "a little more or a little less in the mixture of the opposites, *that* is all their thought is, for each and every man (καὶ πᾶσιν καὶ παντί)." If someone should not feel in all this the calculated effect, the intentional contrast to that pure knowledge which was created from thought alone, I would not argue with him.

The two theories of knowledge presuppose each other, complement each other, and the system would be defective had not Parmenides derived sensory knowledge, too, from the same two elements from which the entire world of sensory appearance is derived. What is it that men call "knowing"? Answer: a relation between mixtures of opposites. Mixed opposites exist, however, not only in men alone, but in each thing with which the world of seeming dazzles us. Therefore—and here is yet another manifestation of that magnificent radicalism which is the distinctive mark of this philosophy—knowing is by no means the privileged possession of animals and men, a prerogative they have over other things: wherever in this world two similar mixtures collide, there too is knowing. We call a corpse dead, and deny it sensation, and yet it sees no more poorly than do the living. The only difference is that the proportion of its mixture is the reverse of that of living bodies. Thus it sees what we do not perceive: darkness. And as it is with the corpse so it is with all those things in this world which we consider dead. In other words, sensation is not something independent and discriminating, something in the nature of a judicial pronouncement. It is nothing but a consequence, an epiphenomenon: Where there are opposites, there too is sensation. Both, however, are merely an appearance, for both come to be through contradiction, and truth does not tolerate contradiction.

And so, finally, we face once again the same enigmatic question that seems to await us at the end of every interpretation: What is the mean-

[g] [Reinhardt quotes the Greek only. The English renders German translation furnished by Professor Uvo Hölscher, drawn by him from marginal notes in Reinhardt's copy of DK ad loc.—Ed.]

ing of the equation of body and concept? What sense can we make of the fact that Parmenides regards the bodily world as though it were the product of a single, and, what is more, erroneous abstract formula, as though that formula alone could suffice to conjure the world from nothingness, as though that formula could serve as core for the world to materialize and to be placed in space and in time around it? And what are we to make of the fact that bodies possess this marvelous capacity for evanescence, a capacity to become spirit and concept and to pass into a formula? What lies behind the fact that the formula, "same and not the same, being and not being" can suddenly assume the form of light and night and that all things of this world in turn, like those two primordial ingredients, can evaporate into mere names, into infinitely many names for the one ultimate "same and not the same, being and not being" that underlies every thing?

What we have said in answer to this question so far has only served to bring the unfamiliar closer to us, to encourage us not to reject the incredible out of hand—in short, so that we might come to understand the presuppositions from which such a thought might arise. This would hardly suffice to explain a philosophy or, to say the least, a system. To do this we should raise the question of purpose, of the meaning and function of every thought: Does it belong to the superstructure or to the foundation, to the supported or to the supporting parts? Is it there for the sake of the system, or is the system there for its sake?

Let us begin with the outer framework. At the beginning we come upon the three "ways." These are the fundamental insights; from these the whole sequel unfolds with a momentum of its own. It is only in this part of the poem that we get complete proofs; what comes later seems like a recital of consequences. Our introduction to the ways is followed by presentation of the goals or results toward which each way leads. For there can be no doubt that, strictly speaking, the "well-rounded truth" does not begin before B8.2: "and on it [the way] there are very many signposts." Just as "Truth" presents only the consequences to be encountered along the first way, so "Appearance" is intended to be nothing but what is reached along the third way. The second way is omitted as undiscoverable, *panapeuthēs*, because it leads to no result at all. Thus "Truth" and "Doxa" stand in the same relation to each other as do the first and third ways. Their relation is purely logical, though the two, in their subtle imaginative aspect, additionally and very aptly convey the poetic effect of contrasted foils.

Let us see to what extent the external form agrees with the assertions made in the two parts. In the case of "Truth," there is no reason to doubt that this part of the poem is—at least on the whole—precisely what it appears to be: a number of deductions, drawn out of the little word "being"; a content sought in order to fill that word's emptiness. This filling out is accomplished through a gathering together of such properties as seemed not to contradict the highly forbidding nature of the word "being."

The "Doxa" represents the opposite case: It is obviously something different from what it would appear to be, not a deduction but a thesis of identification. I have in mind such identifications the positing of which is motivated by the system—metaphysical coordinations, as one might call them, that reveal themselves with the suddenness of an insight. There is an element of adventure in identifications of this sort. For is not what happened, for example, to Schopenhauer with music or to Plato with the "state in the soul" an adventure?[h] The young Parmenides may long have labored in vain to capture the world and its real nature in his few logical distinctions. He shared with the young Plato this fate: With too strong an urge for knowledge, too strong a thirst for an explanation of the world, he had committed himself to a truth that was too narrow, a truth that had at first seemed incapable of development. And yet he could no longer retreat. So, like Plato, he became a revolutionary. Being is, non-being is not: This principle was for him the single certainty on which he could take his stand; only here did he still feel firm ground under his feet. The concept of being this principle yielded negated everything thought had previously pursued. Given the vision one has of the world, this monstrous negation must have seemed considerably more important than what little could be said about true reality. (And in fact "Doxa" turned out to be far more comprehensive than "Truth.") Thus negation required a proof, no less than did affirmation. Mere denial was not enough. However clearly the world's contradiction to the principle of being might have been exposed, this realization was not something on which serious thought could come to rest. Everything seemed focused on this one demand: to find a deduction of the one from the other, or, if that were impossible, to find a passage, to throw a bridge over the abyss that separated

[h] [Reinhardt is presumably referring here to Plato's doctrine that the soul is structurally identical with the state, and to Schopenhauer's view that music is structurally and fundamentally identical with the-world-as-will (see *The World as Will and Idea*, III.52).—Ed.]

the two realms. But where was the possibility, starting from being or non-being, to reach the world of appearances? The thought dawned on him: If non-being is superadded to being, how will the two be connected? He next thought of a formula to which all corporeality could be subjected, for every body is a "same and not the same, being and not being." Then, rashly, with the radicalism of all youthful logic, he took hold of the external form of the statement, construed subject and predicate as essentially identical, and turned their relationship around: "same and not the same" for him came to *be* the world of bodies.

One may find this derivation odd; still, the powerful labor of thought realized here ought not to be underestimated. The entire world is interpreted as a dualism; the opposition in all appearances is laid bare. Hitherto it had occurred to no one to doubt the unity of things. Together with this novel dualism the principle of the relativity of properties is articulated for the first time, formulated in terms of a mixture in the knowing subject and in things themselves. All experience is reduced to a single fundamental form, an ontological formula. How could one possibly say that Parmenides had renounced from the outset even any attempt to derive the world of appearances! The fact is that he staked everything he had on conquering this world, too, with his formula. Only when this project seemed to him to have succeeded could the feeling of a revelation take hold of him. Only then could he put his truth into the mouth of a goddess, *his* goddess, and make her the judge not only of eternally unchanging being but of the delusion of mortals as well. For it was only then that out of the formula a system had come into being. If, in spite of all this, the impossible could not become possible, if the relation between concept and thing could not be explained within the scope of the question he had posed, that was due to the problem itself, and not to some failure of his to think it through. Granted that an enormous leap was his only recourse for getting over this difficulty, was there ever an idealist who passed smoothly over the same question?

When being joins itself to non-being, the world of appearances is born. But where lies the cause of this conjunction? What is the origin of the plurality in which we live? How could illusion place itself side by side with truth? That was the last question of all and the most difficult. Parmenides' answer was and could be no more than a statement of fact: "For they came to agree to name two forms." At some point in the past, one became two; out of unity an opposition was fashioned, and men sanctioned the error. To our mind, the conception, and certainly the expression, could hardly be more inept or more puerile. And yet it represents an achievement of enormous consequence: We are at the cradle of the concepts *physis–nomos*. . . . It was Parmenides' epistemological relativism, proclaimed by him only with reference to the world of appearances, then transferred by Protagoras to *all* knowledge (the *homo mensura* fragment obviously takes its point of departure from the Eleatics)—it was this relativism that brought ethical relativism in its train. It was the epistemological *nomos* that gave the political *nomos* the stamp—unmistakable from then on—of an enlightenment doctrine, injecting into it the concept of convention and contract. From the political *nomos* this same concept spread to language, to religion, and to all manifestations of culture. Thus a development of two parallel and continuous strands led from the *doxa* or *nomos* of Parmenides to the last and most complete system in the tradition of Ionian science, the doctrine of Democritus: one strand to the *Mikros Diakosmos*;[6] the other, to atomistic epistemology. Conversely, the history of the concept of *nomos* confirms what could be concluded from Parmenides alone. His "Doxa," like his third way, is an image, an expression of the world as a representation by man. And that representation is itself scanned from a metaphysical summit, far from where the clamor of the schools might reach.

[6] See Reinhardt, "Hekataios von Abdera und Demokrit," *Hermes*, 47 (1912), 492–513. What is said there about Plato is thus not correct.

14

THE DECEPTIVE WORDS
OF PARMENIDES' "*DOXA*"

Alexander P. D. Mourelatos

It has long been noticed that the two parts of Parmenides' poem are connected both in contrast and by similarity. The contrast is clear: In the first part a monism, a tenseless a-historical account, a conception resulting from a radical *krisis* between "to be" and "not to be"; in the second part a dualism, a cosmogony, a doctrine of *krasis*, "mixture." But the similarities are also clear: The language of explanation and proof is heard in both parts; *Anankē*, "Constraint," has a role in both parts; there is a *krisis*, "decision, separation," in the "Doxa" as well; and there is enough resemblance between each of the two contraries and the *eon*, "what-is," to warrant the view that Parmenides' contraries anticipate the elements of the later Pre-Socratics; the language associated with Light and its cognate forms appears to show a certain affinity for *eon* or *alētheia*. The studies by Reinhardt,[1] Schwabl,[2] Deichgräber,[3] and more recently Mansfeld,[4] give a rich and cumulative

[1] Karl Reinhardt, *Parmenides und die Geschichte der griechischen Philosophie* (Bonn, 1916; repr. Frankfurt a. M., 1959), ch. I (see excerpt in translation, above, pp. 293–311).

[2] Hans Schwabl, "Sein und Doxa bei Parmenides," *Wiener Studien*, 70 (1957), 278–89; repr. w. revisions in Hans-Georg Gadamer, ed., *Um die Begriffswelt der Vorsokratiker*, Wege der Forschung, 9 (Darmstadt, 1968), pp. 391–422.

[3] Karl Deichgräber, *Parmenides' Auffahrt zur Göttin des Rechts: Untersuchungen zum Prooimion seines Lehrgedichts*, Akademie der Wissenschaften und der Literatur in Mainz: Abhandlungen der Geistes- und Sozialwissen-

record of these points of similarity and contrast. Following their lead, Guthrie has rightly emphasized the importance of this double connection for an interpretation of "Doxa." [5] To this fund of observations on the double relationship between the two parts I can make only minor additions. My aim in this study will be to show that two related concepts, drawn from the field of literary criticism, can serve to interpret faithfully both the facts of contrast and the facts of similarity. It will then appear that what is reflected in scholarly literature as controversy is actually a tension built into the argument and language of "Doxa," and that this tension is intrinsic to the philosophical message of this part of Parmenides' poem.

I have in mind the twin concepts of ambiguity and irony. It is actually surprising, considering that the goddess is impersonating a spokesman for mortal *doxai*, "opinions," and warns that her words are "deceptive," that these important analytical tools of the literary critic have been neglected in discussions of the second part of the poem. [6] Under "ambiguity" we should be prepared to allow any of the several types distinguished by modern literary critics, [7] although, as one would expect, only a smaller number can be illustrated in the rhetorical and poetic effects of the "Doxa." I will not pause over questions of classification here; the type will become clear in the analysis of individual passages. For "irony," consider Fowler's definition:

---

schaftlichen Klasse, Jahrgang 1958, No. 11 (Wiesbaden, 1959), 629–724.

[4] Jaap Mansfeld, *Die Offenbarung des Parmenides und die menschliche Welt* (Assen, 1964), ch. 3.

[5] W. K. C. Guthrie, *A History of Greek Philosophy*, Vol. II: *The Presocratic Tradition from Parmenides to Democritus* (Cambridge, 1965), pp. 71, 73. Cf. W. J. Verdenius, "Der Logosbegriff bei Heraklit und Parmenides, II," *Phronesis*, 12 (1967), 99–117. Leonardo Tarán, on the other hand, makes very little of this. He finds in the "Doxa" no more than a development of the consequences of "the minimal mistake of positing two things as real": See *Parmenides: A Text with Translation, Commentary, and Critical Essays* (Princeton, 1965), p. 231, cf. pp. 225–30.

[6] I note, however, that Charles H. Kahn has remarked: "The ambiguity of Parmenides' style is intentional" (*Anaximander and the Origins of Greek Cosmology* [New York, 1960], p. 227).

[7] See William Empson, *Seven Types of Ambiguity*, 3d ed. (New York, 1955), pp. v–vi; also William Bedell Stanford, *Ambiguity in Greek Literature: Studies in Theory and Practice* (Oxford, 1939), chs. 3, 4, and pp. 91–96.

Irony is a form of utterance that postulates a double audience, consisting of one party that hearing shall hear and shall not understand, and another party that, when more is meant than meets the ear, is aware both of that more and of the outsiders' incomprehension.[8]

The terms of this definition fit closely the situation in the "Doxa," where the goddess is speaking in the language appropriate to the audience of uncomprehending mortals (cf. B6.4 "mortals, who know nothing"), while addressing herself to the privileged Kouros, who has already heard the *elenchos*, "challenge," of B6–7 and the deductions of B8, and must, accordingly, be regarded as "a man who knows" (B1.3).[9] The ambiguity (cf. B6.5 "two-headed") which is the crucial fault in human *doxai* becomes transformed into dramatic irony on the lips of the goddess. But to forestall any doubts as to the propriety of these conceptual tools in a study of Parmenides, let me first cite a case in point.

Undoubtedly the most successful line of poetry in Parmenides, and possibly, to quote Jean Beaufret, "one of the most beautiful lines of poetry in the Greek language"[10] is the description of the moon in B14:

νυκτιφαὲς περὶ γαῖαν ἀλώμενον ἀλλότριον φῶς,

Shining in the night, wandering round about the earth, a foreign light.

The line involves a number of subtleties, both semantic and acoustic, but the ambiguity of the final phrase is of primary interest. Parmenides wants to tell us that there is some kind of unreality, inauthenticity, or falsehood about the moon. He prepares us by characterizing the moon by an adjective that combines the predicates of darkness and light. This mild oxymoron is then reinforced by words and sound-contrasts that underline the involvement of the moon in relationships of contrariety. The strongest contrast is between the two nouns at the end of each half: γαῖαν, "earth," against φῶς, "light."[11] And, of course, the word

---

[8] H. W. Fowler, *A Dictionary of Modern English Usage*, 2d ed. rev. E. Gowers (Oxford, 1965), s.v. "irony."

[9] Cf. Kahn, *Anaximander*, p. 227.

[10] *Le Poème de Parménide* (Paris, 1955), p. 8.

[11] But note also: the immobility of γαῖαν against the vagrancy in ἀλώμενον, "wandering"; the "down" of γαῖαν against the connotation of "above" in φῶς and in περί, "all over"; the hard consonants *kt*, *p*, *g*, of the first half,

ἀλώμενον, "wandering," is a signal of falsehood all by itself if one remembers the full connotation of "wandering" for Parmenides. But the final expression of this equivocal status of the moon is by an equivocal phrase. The combination ἀλλότριον φῶς, "a light not one's own," is instantly recognizable as an imitation of the Homeric formula ἀλλότριος φώς, "an alien man, a stranger" (φῶς, "light," and φώς, "man," are two entirely different words, with no etymological connection). By this extremely improbable pun Parmenides manages to say simultaneously: (a) "the moon is a light which is not its own"; (b) "the Face-in-the-Moon (cf. B10.4 kyklōpos, "round-eyed" or "round-faced" but also Cyclops, the mythological monster[12]) is a wandering stranger; (c) "the Face-in-the-Moon is not himself."

As poetry the line is both delightful and haunting;[13] as a device for stating the astronomical thesis, "the moon shines by reflection," it is surely a tour de force. At any rate, the line illustrates an effective use of ambiguity, precisely in the sense that has interested modern literary critics.

THE GODDESS AND HER DOUBLE AUDIENCE

Let me now turn to the question of the structure of ambiguity and irony in the text of Parmenides' "Doxa." The *elenchos*, "the challenge," that the goddess issued to mortal men in B6 and B7 is that they do not realize that their positive terms could be shown to make reference to unqualified negation. Her argument in B8 was designed to reveal this discrepancy between surface grammar and depth grammar.[14] This confrontation between intention and performance continues to some extent in the "Doxa," where many of the key terms appear to have been chosen so as to afford maximum contrast with "Truth." But,

---

against the soft *l*, *m*, *n*, *tr*, together with no less than five soothing *o*'s (three of them long) in the second half; the pitch of the two graves in the first half against the pitch of the acutes in the second.

[12] Cf. Plutarch *Moralia* 944b "the so-called face [of the moon] . . . has a grim and horrible aspect" (tr. Harold Cherniss; see his note *c*, ad loc., in the Loeb edition).

[13] A freer but poetically more sensitive translation will bring out something of the quality of the Greek: "Astray over earth, bright in darkness, its light also a wandering foreigner" (I am indebted for this translation to George Oppen).

[14] See *The Route*, p. 92 and chs. 4–5.

more typically, we find the reverse effect—not unmasking, but concealment. Everything is dressed up with a positive veneer, and this is what comes through to us as a similarity between the two parts. As long as we think of this as the goddess' own work, it is irony in the sense of dissemblance. But, of course, it is also the mortals who are speaking through her, and this reveals the tension and conflict in their collective mind. For they cannot help feeling the presence of the *eon*, "what-is": as a goal, as an intention, as an implicit commitment.[15] Yet the terms they use are ambiguous in every case. If pressed they turn back on themselves (cf. B6.9 *palintropos*): the *krisis*, "separation," turns out to be a *krasis*, "mixture, confusion," the *kosmos* a disorder—and so on.

Let me begin with an analysis of the warning statement at the transition from "Truth" to "Doxa":

> . . . listening to the deceptive (*apatēlon*) *kosmos* (order, form) of my words. (B8.52)

"Doxa" resembles "Truth," hence the deceptiveness. This is undoubtedly true, and the goddess indirectly repeats the warning in the closing line of B8:

> so that no mortal opinion may outstrip you (= may outwit you). (B8.61)

But the phrase "deceptive *kosmos*" may imply more than deceptive verisimilitude. The very combination of words conceals the tension of contrary ideas: To speak *kata kosmon* is to speak "truly, properly, and with due sense of relevance." Implicit in this tension between *kosmos*, "order," and *apatē*, "deception," is the warning, not merely that *doxai* are deceptive but further that the *arrangement* or the context in which the goddess' words appear may assign to them multiple or conflicting meanings.

Here we should remind ourselves of Hesiod's *etymoisin homoia*, "truth-resembling words" (*Th.* 27). The dissemblance may or may not involve equivocation in that context; but elsewhere Hesiod shows that the concept of equivocation is not beyond his ken:

Νείκεά τε Ψεύδεά τε Λόγους τ' Ἀμφιλλογίας τε,

Quarrels, and Lies, and Tales, and Double Talk. (*Th.* 229)[16]

[15] Ibid., ch. 7.
[16] For the text see M. L. West, *Hesiod: Theogony: Edited with Prolegomena and Commentary* (Oxford, 1966), ad loc. The sense "double-talk" is guaran-

Could it not be that the "deception," in the second part of Parmenides' poem is a case of *amphilogia*, "double-talk"?

Amphilogy as understood by Hesiod in this passage (or as practiced by Odysseus at the expense of Polyphemus, the Cyclops, in the "Noman"/"no man" episode of Odyssey IX) is deliberate and malicious. The mortals of Parmenides' poem practice amphilogy without knowing it, without malice, and at their own expense. And so when the goddess (who has seen through the amphilogy) becomes their spokesman, the impersonation takes on a dimension of irony. We can be sure that she will take every opportunity to play up the amphilogy in her advocacy of mortal *doxai*. She will, of course, stop short of explaining the amphilogy or correcting it because she has already done this in the deductions of B8. Again, insofar as we think of this as a stance by the goddess herself, it is irony in the classical sense of make-believe and sarcasm. But if we think of her words as something that mortals actually say, or might say, or subscribe to, this takes on the dimension of dramatic or Sophoclean irony. The author (Parmenides or the goddess) puts in the mouth of his heroes (mortals) words that have a sense contrary to, or quite other than, the sense intended or understood by the heroes themselves. And, to use the word "irony" in a third (more vague and colloquial) sense, here is the irony of the situation: Mortals practice amphilogy innocently, and thereby fall into error; the goddess practices amphilogy with full knowledge, and thereby reveals the truth.

Let me now resume using, instead of "amphilogy," the more familiar terms "equivocation" and "ambiguity." There is ambiguity in the goddess' general statement at the conclusion of B8:

This whole *eoikōs diakosmos* I declare to you. (8.60)

The noun *diakosmos* can be understood as "arrangement," "framework," "world-order." But there is also a suggestion of activity in the word—not an established *kosmos* but a *diakosmos*, an "order*ing*," a

---

teed by the decrescendo effect: 'Αμφιλλογίαι must be less drastic a form of hostility than Lies and Tales, which in turn are less drastic than an open Quarrel. The whole sequence is "Battles, and Clashes, and Murders, and Manslaughter, and Quarrels, and Lies, and Tales, and Double-Talk" (*Th.* 228–29). Cf. Stanford, *Ambiguity*, p. 116; and Clémence Ramnoux, *La Nuit et les enfants de la Nuit dans la tradition grecque* (Paris, 1959), pp. 72, 137, 171. Most translators give "Disputes" for 'Αμφιλλογίαι, which destroys the decrescendo and is simply redundant after Νεῖκος.

process in time, a cosmogony.[17] Moreover, there is a suggestion of thoroughness in the arrangement.[18] But this comes with a special nuance. In Homer the verb *diakosmeō* means primarily "to divide and marshal, muster, array." [19] The reference is usually to a battle formation. Early parallels for the noun *diakosmos* are few, and some are questionable. But in the solid parallel of Thucydides IV.93 the word means "battle-formation." To appreciate fully the effect in Parmenides' use of this word we should remind ourselves of the connotation of Parmenides' terms for contraries: *ta antia* (B8.55, 59) and *ta enantia* (cf. B12.5). Both *antios* and *enantios* are properly and primarily Homeric expressions for "one's opposite in battle." The terms preserve a hostile sense (confrontation, interception, an encounter between opposed or contrary-minded parties)[20] even outside contexts of war. Quite apart from the use of these words, the idea that the cosmic contraries are opposed in battle is familiar enough outside Parmenides,[21] but can also be illustrated from B18, which speaks of a "battle" between contrary "powers" and with "dire" consequences.[22] We can now see that Parmenides' *diakosmos* works in several ways: It makes us think of the marshaling of all contraries under Light and Night respectively;[23] it invites us to think of an impending battle; and, since the marshaling is in two, and of *antia*, there is a suggestion that the battle will be between these two formations. In short, by the choice of *diakosmos* the meaning of "order" in -*kosmos* is inverted into "segregation, division, cleavage, conflict." The *kosmos* of mortals is actually a battlefield.

A play of negative against positive meanings is also to be found in the participle *eoikōs*. Editors have debated whether the translation should be "fitting, appropriate, probable," or "seeming, apparent."

[17] Cf. Jula Kerschensteiner, *Kosmos: quellenkritische Untersuchungen zu den Vorsokratikern* (Munich, 1962), p. 122.

[18] Cf. Hans Diller, "Der vorphilosophische Gebrauch von ΚΟΣΜΟΣ und ΚΟΣΜΕΙΝ," *Festschrift Bruno Snell* (Munich, 1956), pp. 51–52.

[19] Cf. LSJ and R. J. Cunliffe, *A Lexicon of the Homeric Dialect* (London, 1924; repr. Norman, Oklahoma, 1963), s.v.; also Diller, ibid.

[20] See Cunliffe, s.vv. Cf. Kahn, *Anaximander*, p. 130.

[21] Cf. Kahn, *Anaximander*, pp. 109, 130 ff., 162 ff.; G. E. R. Lloyd, *Polarity and Analogy: Two Types of Argumentation in Early Greek Thought* (Cambridge, 1966), pp. 16 ff., 99.

[22] B18.4–6 *virtutes pugnent/ . . . dirae/ . . . vexabunt.*

[23] *Not* "the 'arrangement' or 'disposition' of all things, *according to the combination* of the two primary forms" (Kahn, *Anaximander*, p. 227, my italics).

Obviously both senses are present.[24] To the uninitiated mortals it means the first; to the goddess and the Kouros, the second. The same can be said for the concluding *kata doxan*, "according to what was deemed acceptable" (B19.1). Mortals would take this as the equivalent of *dokimōs*, "acceptably";[25] but "the man who knows" realizes that the reference is to "opinions in which there is no true fidelity" (B1.30).

THE RECORD OF CONTRASTS

Before we can properly document the use of ambiguity in the actual details of the "Doxa," we must have in front of us a record of the verbal and conceptual contrasts, between the two parts, for passages in which ambiguity does *not* play a significant role. The words and phrases from the "Doxa" which appear in the table below seem to have been chosen by Parmenides precisely because they bring to mind, without any equivocation, corresponding denials in "Truth."

TABLE (I) VERBAL AND CONCEPTUAL CONTRASTS BETWEEN "DOXA" AND "TRUTH"

(i)

8.54 μορφάς, "perceptible forms."

1.29 ἀληθείης ... ἦτορ, "the temper of truth."

(ii)

8.54 δύο, "two"; cf. 18.5 *nec faciant unam*, "and they do not make a unity," 18.6 *gemino*, "through a double."

8.5 f. ὁμοῦ πᾶν / ἕν, "altogether one," 8.22 οὐδὲ διαιρετόν, "nor divisible," 8.25 ξυνεχές, "cohesive."

(iii)

8.54 μορφὰς ... δύο (cf. the adjective δίμορφος, "of double form," in later Greek); cf. 18.2 *diverso ex sanguine*, "out of different blood."

8.4 μουνογενές, "of a single kind," 8.22 ὁμοῖον, "alike."

(iv)

8.55, 59 τἀντία, "the contraries," 9.4 ἴσων ἀμφοτέρων, "both equal," 9.2

8.29 ταὐτόν τ' ἐν ταὐτῷ ... καθ' ἑαυτό, "and the same and in the

---

[24] Cf. Guthrie, vol. 2, pp. 50 f. He translates "likely-seeming."

[25] Cf. B1.31–32 "how it would be right for things deemed acceptable (δοκοῦντα) to be acceptably (δοκίμως εἶναι)." On this see *The Route*, ch. 8.

κατὰ σφετέρας, "in accordance with their respective . . . ," 12.5 τό τ' ἐναντίον αὖτις, "and again the opposite"; cf. 14 ἀλλότριον, "not one's own."

same . . . by itself," 8.34 ταὐτόν, "and the same"; cf. 8.13 f. οὐδέ ποτ' ἐκ μὴ ἐόντος . . . γίγνεσθαί τι παρ' αὐτό, "nor that something should come to be from what-is-not along side it."

(v)

8.56, 58 τῇ μὲν . . . ἀτὰρ κἀκεῖνο, "here, on the one hand, . . . and again that other one," 9.2 ἐπὶ τοῖσί τε καὶ τοῖς, "on these and those," 12.1 στεινότεραι, "narrower in width (scil. bands)," 17 δεξιτεροῖσιν μὲν . . . λαιοῖσι δέ, "on the right . . . but on the left."

8.23 οὐδέ . . . τῇ, "nor here," 8.45 οὔτε τῇ ἢ τῇ, "nor here or there," 8.48 denial of τῇ . . . τῇ δ', "here . . . but there."

(vi)

8.57 μέγ' ἐλαφρόν, "greatly nimble."

8.23-4 οὐδέ τι . . . μᾶλλον . . . οὐδέ τι χειρότερον, "nor is it somewhat more nor somewhat less."

(vii)

9.1 πάντα φάος καὶ νὺξ ὀνόμασται, "all things have been called Light and Night," 9.2 τὰ κατὰ σφετέρας δυνάμεις ἐπὶ τοῖσί τε καὶ τοῖς [ὀνόμασται], "things in accordance with their respective powers have been spoken with reference to these and those," 19.3 τοῖς δ' ὄνομ' ἄνθρωποι κατέθεντ' ἐπίσημον ἑκάστῳ, "to these things men have laid down a name as an attached sign to each."

8.38 τῷ πάντ' ὀνόμασται, "with respect to it have all things been spoken";[26] cf. 8.35 ἐν ᾧ πεφατισμένον ἐστίν . . . τὸ νοεῖν, "on which (scil. the what-is) thinking depends having been declared." [27]

(viii)

9.2 δυνάμεις, "powers," 11.3 μένος, "force, vigor"; cf. 18.2, 4 virtus, -tes, "power(s)"; cf. 19.2 τραφέντα, "having matured."

8.4 τέλειον, 8.32 οὐκ ἀτελεύτητον, 8.42 τετελεσμένον, "complete, actualized, perfect"; cf. 8.33 οὐκ ἐπιδευές, "in no need."

---

[26] For the reading ὀνόμασται at B8.38, also translation, and interpretation of the line in its context, see ibid., pp. 180–85.

[27] Ibid., pp. 170–72.

(ix)

10.3 ὁππόθεν ἐξεγένοντο, "wherefrom they were born"; cf. 12.4 τόκου, "of birth," 18.1 *germina*, "seeds," 18.6 *nascentem*, 18.6 *semine*, "through seed."

8.6-7 τίνα γὰρ γένναν; ... / ... πόθεν ...; "what birth? from where?"

(x)

10.1-3 εἴσῃ ... ἔργ' ἀίδηλα, "you shall know devastating works," 10.4 ἔργα ... πεύσῃ περίφοιτα, "you shall learn wandering works."

1.28-9 πυθέσθαι / ἀληθείης εὐπειθέος ἀτρεμὲς ἦτορ, "to learn the unwavering temper of persuasive / compliant truth."

(xi)

10.4 περίφοιτα, "wandering," 10.6 ἄγουσα, "driving," 12.5 πέμπουσα ... μιγῆν, "dispatching to be mixed," 14 ἀλώμενον, "wandering," 16.1 πολυπλάγκτων, "much-strayed."

1.29 and 8.4 ἀτρεμές, "unwavering," 8.26 ἀκίνητον, "immobile," 8.29 κεῖται, "lies," 8.30 ἔμπεδον αὖθι μένει, "remains there firm," 8.41 denial of τόπον ἀλλάσσειν, "exchanging place"; cf. 7 and 8 attack of πλάνη, "wandering," of mortals.

(xii)

10.6 ἔνθεν ἔφυ, "wherefrom it came to be (grew)," 19.1 ἔφυ τάδε, "these came to be (arose)."

8.10 denial of ἀρξάμενον φῦν, "to come to be (grow) having started."

(xiii)

11.1-4 πῶς ... ἠδ' ἄστρων θερμὸν μένος ὡρμήθησαν / γίγνεσθαι, "how ... and the hot (also 'hot-headed') vigor of the stars were impelled to be born."

8.9-10 τί ... μιν χρέος ὦρσεν / ... φῦν; "what requirement might impel it to be born?" cf. 8.12 οὐδὲ ... ἐφήσει, "nor will incite," 8.14 denial of ἀνῆκε, "would encourage."

(xiv)

12.1-3 αἱ γὰρ ... / αἱ δ' ἐπὶ ταῖς ... μετὰ δὲ ... / ἐν δὲ μέσῳ τούτων ..., "the ones ... and those next to them ... and through them ... and in the middle ...."

8.44-5 μέσσοθεν ἰσοπαλὲς πάντῃ ... οὔτε τι μεῖζον / οὔτε τι βαιότερον, "from the middle equally extended every way ... neither bigger nor smaller"; cf. 8.47-9 and 8.23-4.

(xv)

12.3-4 δαίμων ... / ... μίξιος ἄρχει, "the goddess rules over mixing"; cf. 16.1 κρᾶσις, "blend, constitution,"

8.16 κέκριται ... ὥσπερ ἀνάγκη, "and it has been decided, as is the constraint"; cf. 8.15 κρίσις, "decision,

18.1 *miscent*, "they mix," 18.4 *per-mixto*, "in the mixing of," 18.5 *permixto*, "in the mixed."

disjunction," 7.5 κρῖναι, "decide, discern for yourself."

(xvi)

13 μητίσατο, "she devised" (scil. the goddess), 18.2–3 *informans . . . virtus / . . . bene condita corpora fingit*, "the shaping power moulds well-formed bodies," 18.4–5 *virtutes . . . faciant*, "the powers make"; cf. 8.39, 8.53 κατέθεντο, "they laid down (scil. the mortals)," 8.55 ἐκρίναντο, "they segregated," ἔθεντο, "they posited (scil. the mortals)."

8.15, 31 ἔχει, "she holds (scil. Justice, Constraint)," 8.31 ἐέργει, "bars, impedes (scil. the bond)," 8.37 Μοῖρ' ἐπέδησεν, "Fate shackled."

(xvii)

13 πρώτιστον, "first of all," 16.1 ἑκάστοτ', "at each moment," 18.1 *cum*, "when," 19.1–2 ἔφυ . . . καὶ νῦν ἔασι / καὶ μετέπειτ' ἀπὸ τοῦδε τελευτήσουσι τραφέντα, "came to be and now are and later than now will come to an end having matured."

8.9–10 τί . . . ὕστερον ἢ πρόσθεν, "why later rather than sooner?" 8.5 οὐδέ ποτ' ἦν οὐδ' ἔσται, ἐπεὶ νῦν ἔστιν, "nor *was* it ever, nor *will* it be for it *is* now," 8.20 εἰ γὰρ ἔγεντ', οὐκ ἔστ(ι) οὐδ' εἴ ποτε μέλλει ἔσεσθαι, "for if it *got* to be it *is* not—nor if it intends to be in the future."

Here is a parallel list of the ideas which are paired in opposition:

(i) perceptible appearance vs. inner being
(ii) duality vs. unity
(iii) heterogeneity vs. homogeneity
(iv) otherness vs. sameness
(v) axial differentiation vs. axial invariance
(vi) gradation and intensiveness vs. neutrality
(vii) putative naming vs. implicit or actual naming
(viii) potency vs. actuality
(ix) engendering vs. nonengendering
(x) activity, process vs. state
(xi) mobility vs. immobility
(xii) growth vs. no growth
(xiii) susceptibility vs. impassivity
(xiv) radial differentiation vs. radial invariance
(xv) mixing vs. sharp disjunction
(xvi) efficiency vs. containment and maintenance
(xvii) temporal differentiation vs. timelessness

Most of these are self-explanatory when read in their context in the poem. But some of the contrasts have received little or no attention from recent critics. It would be wrong for us to miss the contrast in rows (viii) and (xiii). We are more accustomed to associate the oppositions of potentiality versus actuality, or susceptibility versus impassivity with Aristotle. Yet Parmenides must have anticipated something of this, as we may gather from the variety of dynamic expressions which appear even in the few preserved fragments of "Doxa," in contrast to the emphasis on the character of *eon* as "fully realized ($\tau\acute{\epsilon}\lambda\epsilon\iota o\nu$ [or -$\epsilon\sigma\tau\acute{o}\nu$, -$\hat{\eta}\epsilon\nu$?] and $\tau\epsilon\tau\epsilon\lambda\epsilon\sigma\mu\acute{\epsilon}\nu o\nu$) in "Truth." [28] Rows (x) and (xvi) exemplify a related contrast. In the "Doxa" we learn of *erga*, "works, deeds," whereas in "Truth" we learned of a permanent state or condition. Correspondingly, the divine agency in "Doxa" plays an activist, creative, demiurgic role, whereas Justice and her congeners in "Truth" are pictured as girding, bracing, holding, and retaining the *eon*. This causality of containment is intended to be understood as internal to *eon*.[29] But the causality of "Doxa" is that of an external agent. Again, it would seem, what we have here prefigures the Aristotelian contrast between an efficient and a formal-final cause.[30] I suspect there is also some significance in (xiv), the contrast between the cosmic sphere of "Doxa" and the *sphaira* or "ball" with which the *eon* is compared in "Truth." [31] In the first part of the poem the *sphaira* functions as a symbol of the perfection, self-congruence, or actuality of *eon*. In the "Doxa," the cosmic sphere becomes the opposite: an encompassing framework for differentiation; a model of duality and mixing at a cosmic scale; and a field for the interaction between the contraries.

THE OXYMORA

Contrast as understood in the preceding section presupposes a sharp disjunction, and a denial of one of the disjuncts. At the other end from sharp disjunction we find cases in which contradictory elements are allowed to appear in a single word or phrase because one or both of

[28] Cf. Friedrich Solmsen, *Aristotle's System of the Physical World: A Comparison with His Predecessors*, Cornell Studies in Classical Philology, 33 (Ithaca, 1960), pp. 17–18, 277 and n. 9, 343 and n. 26; Deichgräber, p. 690; Kahn, *Anaximander*, p. 159.

[29] See *The Route*, ch. 6.

[30] Cf. Mansfeld, p. 164 and n. 3.

[31] Cf. Deichgräber, pp. 691 f.

the components has a saving ambiguity which can yield a positive construction of the whole unit. These are the cases in which ambiguity has broken out to the surface and is felt as an incipient paradox. We saw two relatively mild cases of this: *nyktiphaes*, "shining in the darkness"; and "the deceptive *kosmos* of words." Two more instances deserve special comment.

Beginning with the third edition (1912), the *Fragmente der Vorsokratiker* have included this one-word fragment (B15a):

Parmenides in his work of poetry called the earth *hydatorizon*, "rooted in water."

The sentence is a scholion in one of the MSS of St. Basil's *Homilies on the Hexameron*. It would be gratuitous to speculate as to how this conception relates to the cosmology of the "Doxa." But the adjective itself (attested nowhere else in the Greek corpus), taken as a semantic unit, is revealing: "Water-rooted" is a term coined in a mood of sarcasm. The popular idea that the earth had roots was meant to emphasize the rigid stability of the earth, called by Hesiod "the ever-sure foundation of all" (*Th.* 117).[32] As is well known, an alternative conception, articulated in early cosmologies, was that of the earth as floating on water.[33] It is plausible to assume that the use of the expression "rooted in water" by Parmenides involved a combined reference to these two conceptions, and that it was intended as an ironical comment on both. The adjective is a fit description for something like floating seaweed. It reminds us that to be rooted in water is to have lost one's roots. As Anaximander appears to have realized, the model of aquatic support leads to an infinite regress. So the image of floating seaweed points to rootlessness not in the trivial mechanical sense, but in a metaphysical sense which "the man who knows" will instantly recognize. But the adjective also works in the converse sense: it suggests that the idea of rooting *per se* will not explain support, that it too will lead to an infinite regress (cf. B8.7 "having grown from what?" 8.10 "to grow having started from nothing"). So to explain the stability of the earth by saying that it is "rooted" is as good as to say that it is "rooted in water." Either way, the adjective is an oxymoron. Mortals

[32] Cf. *Th.* 812 ἀστεμφής, ῥίζῃσι διηνεκέεσσιν ἀρηρώς, "immovable, growing out of unending roots." The conception of the "roots of earth and sea" (728) as growing out of the Underworld is also intended to convey the sense of stability. Cf. also Xenophanes A47 and B28.

[33] See KR, pp. 87–93.

will see in it no more than an innocent, if somewhat unusual, expression of a mechanical model of support which they favor and understand. But to the goddess and to the Kouros the term works as a signal of the incoherence of mortal opinions.

The strange word *aïdēla* of B10.3 seems to involve a similar effect. The full context reads:

the *aïdēla* works of the effulgent sun's pure torch [or, less probably, "of the sun's pure, effulgent torch"]. (B10.2–3)

The adjective *aïdēlos* can have the active sense "rendering unseen," even "destructive," or the passive sense "invisible, mysterious." [34] The Italian scholar Guazzoni Foà has made the suggestion that the word as used by Parmenides is "polysemous," involving a play both of the active sense against the passive, and of an ἀ- privative against an ἀ-intensive.[35] She explains the effect as follows: "That which is strongly luminous renders other things invisible (because it blinds), and because of its great splendor its own works cannot be seen." [36] This is an attractive interpretation, and it can be made stronger with two modifications: we need not exclude (as Guazzoni Foà does) the sense "destructive"; and we must determine the motivation for this play of multiple meanings.

The sun, especially the sun of southern Italy, can very well be a destructive force. It can scorch the land, and burn the skin, and give sunstroke. (The Phaethon story is a familiar archetype of the destructive power of the sun.[37]) So Parmenides' use of *aïdēlos* is indeed polysemous, and conveys at once the distinct senses of "so fiery as to be destructive," "so brilliant as to eclipse other stars," and "so bright as to be impossible to behold."

The rationale for the use of this multiply suggestive term can now be appreciated. In a nonphilosophical context the whole phrase, "You

[34] See *The Route*, pp. 237–39.

[35] Virginia Guazzoni Foà, "Per l'interpretazione di 'Αίδηλος nel Fr. 10 di Parmenide," *Giornale di metafisica*, 19 (1964), 558–69, 562.

[36] Ibid., p. 559. Cf. Guido Calogero, *Studi sull' eleatismo* (Rome, 1932), p. 52 n. 2: "if ἀίδηλος really means 'that which renders invisible' the allusion here could not be to anything other than the works of the sun insofar as it renders the other stars invisible with its appearance." (Calogero's book now also in German transl., *Studien über den Eleatismus* [Darmstadt, 1970].)

[37] Cf. Archilochus 63 (Diehl) "I hope the sun sears them (κατανανέει), piercing in its blaze (ὀξὺς ἐλλάμπων)"; also Empedocles B40 "sharp-shooting sun" (ἥλιος ὀξυβελής).

shall learn the *aïdēla* works of the sun's torch," would have passed simply as an appropriately evocative statement of the idea, "you shall learn the mysterious works of the Sun's holy light." It is, of course, this sense which saves B10.2–3 from being a mere contradiction. But in the context of the "Doxa" the tension between "the pure torch of the effulgent sun" and "*aïdēla* works" is not relieved. Mortals are welcome to take this as a poetically charged and pious statement. But the Kouros perceives the message in the incipient contradiction. The sun which the words "effulgent torch" describe as *megalodēlos* or *aridēlos*, "greatly evident, conspicuous," is also *aïdēlos*, "too bright to behold" and "too bright to allow anything else to be seen." Moreover, the light, which is "pure" and "gentle" is also so ominously powerful as to be a dazzling, scorching, flagrant peril. It is not just the incipient contradiction which points to the unreality of "the effulgent torch of the sun"; the very idea that the sun can be "*too* bright to . . ." or "*too* powerful not to . . ." reminds us of the contrast with the real, which admits of no "more or less," no grades or degrees. Unlike the sun, and unlike the antithetically ranged "powers" of "Doxa," the real cannot be assigned to a field or continuum of intensive qualification.

If this analysis is correct, then we have correspondence between the descriptions of the moon and the sun: The one "shines by night, with a light not its own"; the other outshines all stars by day, and is too bright to be seen directly (we can only look at reflections of its light).

The earth, the sun, and the moon are all given paradoxical descriptions—and *paradox* is what we should expect from the world of "Doxa." This use of paradox or of the oxymoron for a philosophic statement is better known from the fragments of Heraclitus. But it belongs with equal propriety to the second part of Parmenides' poem. The doctrine of the coincidence of opposites, celebrated by Heraclitus as an extraordinary insight achieved by the man of reason, is rejected by Parmenides much more decisively than it could have been by the adversaries Heraclitus had envisaged—the "many" whom he scorned. Parmenides claims he can show that the mortals' own view is unstable, and can easily lapse into Heracliteanism.[38] And so through the goddess

[38] Cf. Harold F. Cherniss, "The Characteristics and Effects of Presocratic Philosophy," *Journal of the History of Ideas*, 12 (1951), repr. in the Bobbs-Merrill Reprint Series (PHIL-52), p. 337: "Heraclitus had made explicit what was implicit in all the theories of a changing world . . . Parmenides saw this, that the opinions of all men were unconscious and unsystematic Heracliteanism."

he makes the mortals speak the very language which they find absurd and mystifying when it comes from Heraclitus.[39]

AMBIGUITY IN THE CONTRARIES

Unequivocal contrast and incipient contradiction or paradox are the two extremes in the tension between truth and mortal opinions in the second part of the poem. Most of the passages fall in between. They exploit concealed or deceptive ambiguity. This can be shown both for the attributes of the two cosmic contraries and for the governing principles and basic concepts of the "Doxa" as a whole. With regard to the contraries, the clearest and most direct way to present the data is again in the form of a table.

In the first column of Table (2), on pp. 328–29, I have collected the passages of "Doxa" that present the two contraries and their respective attributes. The order from (i) to (iv) under each of the A (Light) and B (Night) sections aims to capture the correspondence between descriptions of the two contraries. In the second column I collect from the first part of the poem (including the proem) passages which refer to the *eon* or to something closely associated with the *eon*. These are aligned with passages of the first column to which they show verbal affinity. Viewed in this alignment, they present cases of parallelism which would encourage us to think that one or both of the contraries in "Doxa" is modeled on the *eon* of "Truth." In the third column I collect passages from the first part which tend to suggest that the contrary described on the corresponding line in the first column has the status of "what-is-not." The third column contains, accordingly: (a) explicit or implicit references to "what-is-not," or to something closely associated with it; (b) references to the *eon* which sharply contrast with the description in the corresponding line of the first column. Generally speaking, the passages in the second column support a "good sense," i.e. association with the *eon*, and the passages in the third column a "bad sense," i.e. association with what-is-not, for the contraries respectively.

What is immediately striking about Table (2) is that Parmenides balances the descriptions that point up the positive aspects of Light with descriptions that do the same for Night. In fact, even though a

[39] I note three more instances of expressions with the force of an oxymoron: B10.4 ἔργα . . . περίφοιτα, "wandering works" (ἔργα has the connotation of accomplishment, which is negated by περίφοιτα); B8.57 μέγ' ἐλαφρόν, "greatly slight"; B10.6 ἄγουσ' ἐπέδησεν, "driving she shackled."

TABLE (2) AMBIGUITY IN THE ATTRIBUTES OF THE CONTRARIES

A. Light

Positive Associations	Negative Associations
1.10 the journey of the Heliades and the Kouros toward the light, "to-ward the light"; cf. 8.48 ἄσυλον, "inviolate."	8.21 γένεσις ... ἀπέσβεσται καὶ ... ὄλεθρος, "coming to be ... has been quenched ... and perishing" (coming-to-be and perishing are ablaze), 8.41 διά τε χρόα φανὸν ἀμείβειν, "exchanging bright surface."
(i) 8.56 φλογὸς ... πῦρ, "the blaze of fire," 9.1 φάος, 9.3 φάεος, "light"; cf. 10.2-3 καθαρᾶς εὐαγέος ἠελίου / λαμπάδος, "of the pure torch of the effulgent sun."	
(ii) 8.56 αἰθέριον:	
a. 1.13 the journey to αἰθέραι, "heavenly," gates.	
a. "heavenly" (contrary of ἐμβριθές).	
b. "bright-making" (contrary of ἀδαῆ).	
(iii) 8.57 ἤπιον ὄν:	
a. 8.29 ἀληθείης εὐπειθέος, "of persuasive / compliant truth," ἐόν (passim).	
a. "a mild, well-disposed, gentle being" (contrary of ἐμβριθές).	
b. Cf. 1.15 μαλακοῖσι λόγοισι / πεῖσαν, "through soft words they persuaded."	
b. "a well-speaking, sagacious being" (contrary would be νήπιον, but is actually ἀδαῆ).	
(iv) 8.57 ἐλαφρόν:	
a. "slight."	a. 8.26 μεγάλων ἐν πείρασι δεσμῶν, "in the confines of mighty (huge) fetters."
b. "nimble." Cf. 12.2 φλογὸς ἵεται αἶσα, "flame is discharged"; also 11.1-4, esp. θερμὸν μένος, "hot vigor," and ὡρμήθησαν, "were impelled."	b. immobility of ἐόν, attack on the wandering of mortals (passim).
c. "easy to bear."	c. 8.30-1 κρατερὴ γὰρ Ἀνάγκη / πείρατος ἐν δεσμοῖσιν ἔχει, τό μιν ἀμφὶς ἐέργει, "for mighty Con-

B. Night

(i) 8.59 νύκτα, "night."

(ii) 8.59 ἐμβριθές:
a. "heavy, ponderous, down-pressing," (contrary of αἰθέριον, as well as ἐλαφρόν).
b. "grievous, ill-disposed" (contrary of ἤπιον).

(iii) 8.59 ἀδαῆ:
a. "obscure" (contrary of αἰθέριον); cf. 9.3 ἀφάντου "obfuscating, invisible."

b. "ignorant" (contrary of ἤπιον, cf. νήπιος, "silly").[40]

(iv) 8.59 πυκινόν:
a. "thick, dense, of close texture."
b. "tight, well-fenced."
c. "shrewd, wise."

a. 8.29 κεῖται, "it lies"; cf. 8.30 ἔμπεδον αὖθι μένει, "remains there firm."
b. Cf. passage in A(iv)c, third column above.

a. 8.24 πᾶν ἔμπλεον ... ἐόντος, 8.25 ξυνεχές, "cohesive."
b. 8.31 ἀμφὶς ἐέργει, "bars it all around," and generally the language of a tight bond around ἐόν.
c. Cf. passage in B(iii)b, third column above.

1.9 the Heliades leave behind them the "house of Night."

a. 2.6 παναπευθέ(α) ... ἀταρπόν, "a path of no tidings," 2.7–8 οὔτε ... γνοίης ... οὔτε φράσαις, "you could not know it, nor could you point to it," 8.17 ἀνόητον ἀνώνυμον, "unknown and nameless" (all with reference to μὴ ἐόν).
b. 6.4 εἰδότες οὐδέν, "knowing nothing," 6.5 ff. ἀμηχανίη, "helplessness," etc. (all said of mortals).

[40] Cf. Mansfeld, p. 133 and n. 5; Mario Untersteiner, *Parmenide: Testimonianze e frammenti: Introduzione, traduzione e commento* (Florence, 1958), p. clxxiv n. 27. The latter accepts the opposition ἤπιος-[νήπιος] but translates ἤπιος as "utile."

priori the positive associations of Light are undeniable,[41] in the actual text of Parmenides' poem they are rather indirect, for they presuppose a parallelism between the language of light and revelation in the proem and the language of the *eon*. The positive associations of Night (grave, firm, full, tight), on the other hand, can be traced directly to the description of *eon* in B8. Notice also that it would be one-sided to stress the affinity of Light as illumination with the *eon*.[42] Parmenides' Light is also "fire," "color-play" (cf. B8.41), the bearer of "vigor" and "impulse" (cf. B11.3), and something which "bursts forth" (B12.1)—all of which are marks of unreality.

The table presents, further, the multiple meanings of the attributes of Light and Night. As we know from usage, the terms αἰθέριον (A[ii], first column) and ἤπιον (A[iii], first column), assigned by Parmenides to Light, each admit of two distinct meanings, a and b, either of which could be relevant in the context of "Doxa." Similarly admissible are the three meanings, a, b, and c, of the attribute ἐλαφρόν (A[iv], first column). Correspondingly for Night, usage suggests two relevant meanings, a and b, for the attribute ἐμβριθές (B[ii], left column), two, a and b, for ἀδαές (ἀδαῆ, B[iii], left column), and three, a, b, and c, for πυκινόν (B[iv], left column). Because of this multiplicity of meanings, the correspondence between the attributes is not one-to-one, and this results in multiple relations of contrariety. Thus αἰθέριον in the sense of "heavenly" is opposed to ἐμβριθές, "down-pressing," but in the sense "bright-making" to ἀδαές or ἄφαντον, "obscure." Allowing for some additional (but quite natural) differentiations of nuance or connotation (for example, drawing out the implicit meaning, "subtle, of thin texture" in αἰθέριον), the multiple relations of contrariety suggested by Parmenides' table of opposites are presented schematically in Table 2A, below p. 331.

Horizontal lines represent primary, slanted lines secondary contrariety. Note that if there were a clear semantic contrariety between ἐλαφρόν and ἀδαές-ἄφαντον the scheme would be perfectly one–three for each of the opposites. Because of these multiple relationships, represented by the crisscrossings, the Parmenidean table of contraries is felt as essentially a dualism of two *morphai*, "forms." And because of this essential dualism, positive or negative associations, or equivocity, in the case of one of the attributes is transferred to its other two cognates.

[41] See Lloyd, *Polarity*, pp. 42, 48, 80.

[42] Guthrie commits this error (vol. 2, pp. 55–57). But Mansfeld is more cautious: see esp. p. 139.

TABLE (2A) ONE-MANY CONTRARIETY OF THE ATTRIBUTES
OF LIGHT AND NIGHT

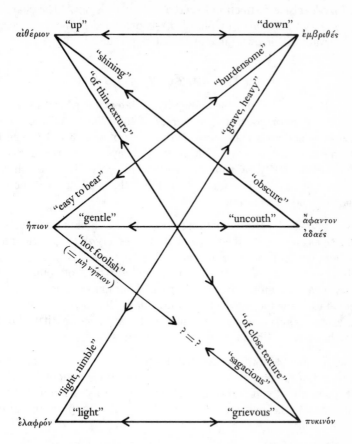

The result is that the whole of each side is felt as equivocally characterized as both positive (modeled on the *eon*) and negative (modeled on
a denial of the *eon*). Symptomatic of the ambivalence which affects
either side is the fact that ἤπιον and πυκινόν appear on opposite sides,
whereas both seem to have positive associations (see *A*[iii] and *B*[iv] in
Table [2], above, and note the equality sign interrupting the slanted line
between the two terms in Table [2A]).

Ambivalence, affecting some of the pairs, is not uncommon in
schemes of contrariety.[43] Parmenides, however, is not merely repro-

[43] See Lloyd, pp. 46, 62.

ducing a feature of traditional or current schemes for the sake of verisimilitude. He is reproducing *the* feature which prompted him to ask for a decisive distinction between "is" and "is not." The character of mortals as *dikranoi*, "two-headed," is projected in the ambivalence that pervades their own table of cosmic opposites.

B10: The Ambiguity of *Physis*

I now turn to examine the ambiguity in statements which involve the basic concepts or governing principles of the "Doxa." These are the passages which are usually recorded as cases of similarity between the "Doxa" as a whole and "Truth." It is always, of course, a case of deceptive similarity, a similarity-with-a-difference. B10 (which also features the oxymoron with *aïdēla*) shows this well and can be conveniently studied as a unit.

And you shall learn the nature (*physin*) of the shining sky, and all the signs (*sēmata*) in the sky; and the works (*erga*), too dazzling to behold (*aïdēla*), of the effulgent sun's pure torch, and wherefrom they arose (*exegenonto*); and the rambling works of roundfaced [*also* Cyclops] moon you shall learn, and her nature; and you shall come to know the heaven that holds things all around, wherefrom it arose (*ephy*), and how driving Constraint harnessed it to hold the bounds (or "bands," *peirata*) of the stars.

The fragment as a whole has the tone of the programmatic statements at the end of the proem. We get no fewer than three announcements of an explanation, "you shall learn" (B10.1, 10.4, 10.5). As noted first by Heinimann,[44] the passage involves a series of four pairs in parallel coordination:

A	B
1. the *physis* of the sky.	the signs in the sky.
2. wherefrom they arose.	the works of the sun's torch.
3. the *physis* of the moon.	the works of the moon.
4. wherefrom it arose (*ephy*).	how driving Constraint harnessed him to hold the bounds of the stars.

[44] Felix Heinimann, *Nomos und Physis: Herkunft und Bedeutung einer Antithese im griechischen Denken des 5. Jahrhunderts* (Basel, 1945, repr. 1965), pp. 90 f.

The patterning is indeed elaborate;[45] but I am concerned here only with the modulation of the term *physis*. On the left we have *physis* understood dynamically as growth; on the right ongoing processes or activities (*erga* or *sēmata*, the latter here, clearly, "portents, omens, signals for action"). Yet the three "you shall learn" also activate the sense of "nature" or "essence" in the three *phy-* words of column A,[46] and so in the column as a whole. The ambiguity is intrinsic to the passage,[47] and deliberate. "You shall learn the *physis* and the *works* of . . ." recalls the announcement of the argument of "Truth" in the proem: "you shall learn *alētheia* and its *ētor*, its temper" (cf. B1.29). But to the goddess and to the Kouros the two announcements are worlds apart: as far apart as timeless reality and temporal process. In effect, Parmenides is telling us that mortals turn the legitimate quest for *alētheia* into a misguided adventure after "origins" and "works." [48]

There is a similar effect in the phrase "how driving Constraint harnessed him." Naturally, this sounds like an echo of the statements involving Constraint and her congeners in "Truth." But note this difference: The Constraint of "Truth" was an agent of containment and maintenance; the phrase ἄγουσ᾽ ἐπέδησεν Ἀνάγκη, "driving Constraint harnessed," makes one think of a very different figure—an Ἀνάγκη who drives her victims from yokes or collars around their necks.[49]

---

[45] The φύσις of 1A and ἔφυ of 4A must represent the same concept, and this must also be true of φύσις in 3A and ἐξεγένοντο in 2A, both of which are paired with ἔργα in B: cf. Heinimann, pp. 90 f. On the other side, 4B clearly refers to works being performed by the sky. For σήματα in 1B, see *The Route*, p. 25 n. 40, and note that "signs in the sky" and "bands of stars" (cf. Aëtius in DK A37, and Tarán, pp. 240 ff.) are two alternative descriptions with the same reference. So in addition to being "portentous works" the signs in the sky are "wheeling works." Heinimann notes (pp. 90 f.) that the structure of the fragment is AB-BA-BA-AB, and notes an alteration of the form a-b-a-b (noun and verb expressions) under A against a pattern β-a-a-β (with ἔργα as the two a's) under B.

[46] Heinimann goes too far in saying that φύσις does *not* mean "Wesen" or "Natur" here (p. 91 n. 2). On the other hand, it is equally wrong to give one of these translations alone (so Tarán, p. 165; Guthrie, vol. 2, p. 60). In this case, as in others, the disagreement among scholars highlights and underscores an ambiguity that is built into the text.

[47] Cf. Mansfeld, p. 189.

[48] The φύσις of B16.1 is embedded in a similar context of ambiguity: See the discussion of B16, below.

[49] See the discussion of the phrase ἄγειν ἀνάγκῃ in Heinz Schreckenberg,

AMBIGUITY IN THE BASIC CONCEPTS OF "DOXA"

Bio is a good case in point of similarity-with-a-difference between
"Truth" and "Doxa." But, once again, the most direct way of presenting all the evidence is in the form of a table. Table (3) gives on the
left all the passages that show verbal resemblance (inviting a favorable
interpretation) with passages from "Truth," which appear on the right.
The key word, the one that marks the radical difference, may appear
either on the left or on the right or in both columns.

TABLE (3) SIMILARITIES-WITH-A-DIFFERENCE
BETWEEN "DOXA" AND "TRUTH"

(i)
8.55 ἐκρίναντο δέμας, "they distinguished with respect to body"; 8.56
ἔθεντο / χωρὶς ἀπ' ἀλλήλων, "they
posited apart of one another"; cf.
12.1 πυρὸς ἀκρήτοιο, "of unmixed
fire."

See above, Table (1), right column,
(xv).

(ii)
8.55 f. σήματ' ἔθεντο, "they posited
signs," 19.3 κατέθεντ' ἐπίσημον, "they
laid down as an attached sign"; cf.
9.1 f. τά τ' ἐν αἰθέρι . ∴ . σήματα, "the
signs in the aether."

8.2 ταύτῃ δ' ἐπὶ σήματ' ἔασι, "and on
it (scil. the route) there are signs."

(iii)
8.57 f. ἑωυτῷ πάντοσε τωὐτόν / τῷ δ'
ἑτέρῳ μὴ τωὐτόν, "in every way the
same with itself but not the same
with the other," 8.58 κατ' αὐτό, "in
itself."

See above, Table (1), right column,
(iv); cf. 8.36 f. οὐδὲν . . . ἄλλο πάρεξ
τοῦ ἐόντος, "nothing else except
what-is."

(iv)
8.60 διάκοσμον ἐοικότα, "a seeming
disposition" (see above, pp. 317 f.),

1.32 δοκίμως, "acceptably." [50]

Ananke: Untersuchungen zur Geschichte des Wortgebrauchs, Zetemata, 36
(Munich, 1964), ch. 1, and note the pictorial illustrations in the appendix
of his book.

[50] See *The Route*, ch. 8, esp. 197–205.

19.1 κατὰ δόξαν, "in accordance with what was deemed acceptable."

(v)
9.3 πᾶν πλέον ἐστὶν ὁμοῦ, "all is full together," 11.1 πλῆνται, "are filled"; cf. 16.4 τὸ γὰρ πλέον ἐστὶ νόημα, "for thought is the full."

8.4 οὖλον, "whole," 8.5 f. ὁμοῦ πᾶν / ἕν, "all of it together one," 8.6 συνεχές, "cohesive," 8.24 πᾶν δ' ἔμπλεόν ἐστιν ἐόντος, "and all of it is full of what-is"; cf. comparison with a sphere, and 8.25 ξυνεχὲς πᾶν, "all of it cohesive," 8.25 ἐὸν γὰρ ἐόντι πελάζει, "what-is consorts with what-is."

(vi)
9.4 ἴσων ἀμφοτέρων ἐπεὶ οὐδετέρῳ μέτα μηδέν, "both equal, since to neither does Nothing have a share."

8.22 πᾶν ἐστιν ὁμοῖον, "all of it is equal, alike," 8.46 f. οὔτε γὰρ οὐκ ἐόν ἐστι, τό κεν παύοι μιν ἱκνεῖσθαι / εἰς ὁμόν, "for there neither is what-is-not, which might prevent it from reaching the same [i.e. sameness]."

(vii)
10.1 ff. εἴσῃ . . . πεύσῃ . . . εἰδήσεις . . . ὥς, "you shall learn how," 11.1 πῶς, "how," 19.1 οὕτω, "in this manner."

1.28 πυθέσθαι, "to learn," 8.31 μαθήσεαι . . . ὥς, "you shall learn how," 2.3 ὅπως ἔστιν τε καὶ ὥς, "that / how it is and that / how"; cf. 2.5, 8.2, 8.9.

(viii)
10.1 ff. φύσιν . . . ἔργα, "the nature and works."

(See above, p. 333).

(ix)
10.7 πείρατ' ἄστρων, "the bands of the stars"; cf. implication of spherical universe in 10, 11, 12, and especially 11.2 f. ὄλυμπος ἔσχατος, "the outermost heaven."

8.26 ἐν πείρασι δεσμῶν, "in the bounds of fetters," 8.31 πείρατος, "of a bond," 8.42 πεῖρας πύματον, "an outermost boundary"; cf. comparison with a sphere.

(x)
12.3 δαίμων ἣ πάντα κυβερνᾷ, "a goddess piloting all things," 12.4 πάντη . . . ἄρχει, "she rules in every way."

Cf. the δαίμων and the Heliades as guides in the proem.

(xi)

12.4 στυγεροῖο τόκου, "of hateful, abominable birth."

8.21 τὼς γένεσις μὲν ἀπέσβεσται, "and so birth has been quenched."

(xii)

12.4 μίξιος ἄρχει πέμπουσ' ἄρσενι θῆλυ μιγῆν τό τ' ἐναντίον αὖτις, "she rules over mixing, dispatching the female to have intercourse with the male, and contrariwise."

8.25 ἐὸν γὰρ ἐόντι πελάζει, "for what-is consorts with what-is"; cf. 1.1 f. ὅσον τ' ἐπὶ θυμὸς ἱκάνοι / πέμπον, "conveyed me as far as heart might reach."

(xiii)

12.2 μετὰ δὲ . . . ἵεται αἶσα, "and through them a due portion is discharged";[51] cf. 18.3 temperiem servans, "maintaining proper proportion of mixture."

Cf. the character of what-is maintained by Dike-Themis-Moira, and 8.48 ἄσυλον, "inviolate."

(xiv)

13 Ἔρωτα, "Love"; cf. the goddess of intercourse in 12.

2.4 Πειθοῦς κέλευθος, "the route of Persuasion."

(xv)

16.2–4 τὸ γὰρ αὐτό / ἔστιν ὅπερ φρονέει μελέων φύσις ἀνθρώποισιν / καὶ πᾶσιν καὶ παντί· τὸ γὰρ πλέον ἐστὶ νόημα. "For it is the same that the nature of the limbs apprehends among men, both all and each. For thought is the full."

Cf. 3, 4, 8.34 ff. (See below, pp. 340 ff.)

(xvi)

19.1 καὶ νυν ἔασι, "and now are," 19.2 τελευτήσουσι, "will come to an end."

8.5 νῦν ἐστιν, "it is now," 8.32 οὐκ ἀτελεύτητον, "not incomplete."

In row (i) we find that the mortals practice a κρίσις, "separation," and a placing χωρίς, "apart." But unlike the radical κρίσις between "is" and "is not" of "Truth," which is a logical κρίσις, what we get here is a physical separation: not λόγῳ, "through reason," but δέμας, "with respect to body." Indeed, as we learn in B12 (cf. [x]–[xiii] in the table), the physical separation is perfect only at the outer limits of the universe. In (iii) we see that the κρίσις of "Doxa" is not between exhaustive or

---

[51] See Tarán, p. 237.

contradictory alternatives, but between contraries. The correct formula for reality is "in every way the same with itself and *not the same with anything else.*" In Greek the italicized clause would be μηδενὶ δὲ ἄλλῳ τωὐτόν. Instead, we get the weaker τῷ δ' ἐτέρῳ μὴ τωὐτόν, "not the same *with the other.*" The distinction is between *coordinate* entities, as we can see immediately from the pronouns which appear on the left in (i), (iii), and (vi). But the distinction between what-is and what-is-not is between entity and nonentity—a distinction *toto caelo.*[52]

The word σήματα, "signs" (see row [ii]), was used in "Truth" with reference to pointers to the bounds (*peirata*) of reality. In "Doxa" it is used with reference to the various manifestations of the dualism. But whereas in the first case the σήματα are pictured as lying "along the route" to the *eon*, so that our activity is limited to taking note of them, in "Doxa" the σήματα have been "posited," and "laid down," and superadded.

Especially interesting is the play with the idea of "fullness" as shown in (v). In "Truth" fullness appears as a corollary of the wholeness, simplicity, and indivisibility of what-is. The filling action is pictured as directed from the center out, as an overflow which has to be contained by "bounds." But in "Doxa" things get full in the manner in which one fills a container: from the outside. The fullness is induced by the action of the mixing goddess, as we see in row (xii). The same concept is thus given opposite interpretations in the two parts of the poem. In the first it functions as an expression of simplicity and unity; in the second as an expression of duality and confusion. This motif of fullness is developed further in B16. But this important fragment deserves, as I indicate in (xv), separate comment.

We already saw how Parmenides exploits the ambiguity of the term φύσις in B10. In (vii) I show the parallel ambiguity in the adverbs of manner. In "Truth" they are embedded in the context of the quest for reality; they serve to introduce the timeless "how" of the what-is.[53] This quest is still being felt in "Doxa," but it has been reduced to something more common and homely: the "how" expresses an historical or cosmogonical curiosity.

The proofs of B8 culminate in the comparison of what-is with a "well-rounded ball." [54] As we see in (ix), the comparison becomes

[52] For a fine discussion of this contrast, see Mansfeld, pp. 131 ff.; cf. *The Route*, ch. 3. Cf. also Lloyd, p. 23 and n. 1.

[53] See *The Route*, pp. 49–51, 70–73.

[54] Ibid., pp. 123–30.

reified in the "Doxa." The world is literally a gigantic physical sphere, or a nesting of rings: The "outermost boundary" has now become the shining "outermost heaven"; the "bands" or "bounds," which expressed the perfection or actuality of what-is, have now been projected as physical "bands" (the rings or wheels of the stars).

Fundamental to the doctrine of "Truth" is the idea of the quest (*dizēsis*), which brings with it the vocabulary of journey and guidance.[55] This quest is a relationship between two different orders or levels: mind and reality. In the passages to which (x) and (xii) refer we find again a "goddess" who "pilots" and "dispatches" (the same words are used which appeared in the first part). But her role is now mundane: She is no longer the mediator between the real and man, but a force that induces the wordly contraries to come together in mixture or intercourse. Moreover, whereas the real is "as far as heart might reach," the charges of the goddess in "Doxa" are pictured as reluctant partners. Since they are contraries, they would naturally tend to be apart, and the idea is reinforced by the phrase, "of abominable birth."

As shown in (xi), the adjective στυγερός, "abominable," carries double meaning. At the public and ordinary level it is understood immediately as a reference to the pains of childbirth, the unhappy consequence of a union of contraries.[56] But the goddess and the Kouros are aware of this as a reference to the flagrant impropriety of birth, which has to be "quenched." [57] Moreover, the pairing of "hateful birth" with μίξις, "intercourse," works like an oxymoron. "Intercourse" is something

[55] Ibid., ch. 2.

[56] Other associations may also be involved: childbirth was considered ritually impure (Erwin Rohde, *Psyche: The Cult of Souls and Belief in Immortality among the Greeks*, tr. W. B. Hillis [London, 1925], p. 295 and n. IX, 72); Hermann Fränkel finds in the adjective the expression of a negative attitude toward heterosexual love (*Dichtung und Philosophie des frühen Griechentums*, 2d ed. [Munich, 1962], p. 414 n. 32). But with the word being στυγερός (rather than something with the force of "unholy" or "impure") a more likely association is with the motif of hatred between generations, as we know it from Hesiod's *Theogony* (138, 155; cf. Paul Seligman, *The "Apeiron" of Anaximander: A Study in the Origin and Function of Metaphysical Ideas* [London, 1962], pp. 103 f.).

[57] But some editors would (once again) expunge the ambiguity by emending the text to read σμυγεροῖο (Theodor Bergk, *Kleine philologische Schriften*, ed. R. Peppmüller, 2 vols. (Halle, 1884–86), vol. 2, p. 82) or by simply giving the translation "painful" of σμυγερός without the benefit of emendation (so Untersteiner, p. 161; Tarán, p. 166).

philon, "lovable," or *philotēs*, "love," itself. That the goddess of mixture should preside over "abominable birth and intercourse" is a signal (like *nyktiphaes*, "shining in the night," B14) of the unreality of the whole process. Heraclitus would have declared openly, "pleasure is pain." But Parmenides' "mortals" express this more timidly, through a noncommittal "and," which allows the paradox to remain below the surface.

Indeed, the goddess of mixture is herself a projection of mortal indecisions. Mortals make a physical κρίσις, but the things they distinguish are not complete, self-contained entities. So they soon find themselves reversing the original decision by postulating a certain goddess as agent of mixing. B12 gives a physical model of this reversal. The outermost rings are pure fire; then come rings of night with just a "due portion" of fire showing through; but in the middle there is general (πάντῃ) mixture, under the goddess' prodding. Translated into logical terms: Mortals made a κρίσις, "separation," but not of contradictories, rather a half-hearted one of contraries, which lapses into Heracliteanism.

Also fundamental to the doctrine of "Truth" are the ideas of Justice and πίστις.[58] The real is *eupeithēs*: "faithful" and "compliant." [59] It is ἴσον, "equal," insofar as it is ὁμοῖον, "alike," or self-contained, self-congruent, and self-consistent. If one were to speak of the real as "just," the appropriate definition of this term would have to be obtained from Plato or from a rationalist—it fulfills its own appointed role. If we now look at the context in which these words appear, (vi) and (xiii), we find that the radical sameness of the *eon* has been translated into a democratic doctrine of *isonomia*, "equality in apportionment," in the "Doxa":[60] The contraries are described as "both equal"; fire is given a "due portion" in the mixed rings of the stars; and the Latin fragment (B18) mentions a *temperies* which is to be observed.

[58] See *The Route*, chs. 6, 7.

[59] Ibid., pp. 154–58.

[60] Gregory Vlastos has suggested that the justice of Parmenides' "Truth" is grounded in equality, understood as distributive ἰσονομία, but differing from the equality of the two forms in "Doxa" in that it obtains internally among the parts in the single whole of reality: see "Equality and Justice in Early Greek Cosmologies," *CP*, 42 (1947), pp. 162 ff. (the article is reprinted in Furley and Allen, I, pp. 42–55). But as the word "parts" betrays, "equality" is still too weak for Parmenides' "Truth." The sameness (ὁμοῖον, ἴσον) of which Parmenides speaks in "Truth" is reflexive rather than distributive (οἱ . . . ἴσον); it is nothing short of identity, unity, total integration.

We should recall here that Peitho is also a personification of Aphrodite. In (xiv) I have recorded a responsion which I find between the radical concept of Peitho in "Truth" [61] and the merely physical conception of Love or Eros in "Doxa." Indeed, it is interesting to note that the different aspects or faces of divine agency which appear in "Truth" have their secular counterpart in "Doxa." To the guiding *daimōn* (B1.3) corresponds a goddess who "dispatches" and "pilots" (B12); to Justice and Fate one who assigns "due portions" (B12.2); to Constraint a "driving Constraint" (B10.6); to Persuasion a goddess of Love, and Eros himself (B12, B13).

Finally, in the passages of row (xvi) we can see how two of the most important concepts in the proofs of B8 become trivialized in the "Doxa." The phrase "it now is" appears in B8.5 in a context which assigns it unmistakably the sense of tenseless reality; in B19.1 it expresses the historical present tense. Correspondingly, whereas the τελ- words of B8 convey the sense of actuality and perfection, the verb τελευτήσουσι in B19.2 has the more prosaic significance of "they will die."

It should be remembered that in all these cases the ambiguity achieves a number of effects. First, it shows us concretely that mortals are aware (if only subconsciously) of their commitment to reality. Second, the ambiguous character of the language shows why they are misled into thinking that they have reached truth. Third, it shows mortals as being indecisive, "two-headed," and ambivalent; they go only part of the way to reality, and then turn back. Finally, it serves as irony on the part of the goddess and Parmenides, at the expense of mortal *doxai*.

B16: "WANDERING" AND "FULLNESS"

Perhaps the most effective use of ambiguity is in B16. It is now generally agreed that the correct text is:

ὡς γὰρ ἑκάστοτ' ἔχει κρᾶσις μελέων πολυπλάγκτων,
τὼς νόος ἀνθρώποισι παρέστηκεν· τὸ γὰρ αὐτό
ἔστιν ὅπερ φρονέει μελέων φύσις ἀνθρώποισιν
καὶ πᾶσιν καὶ παντί· τὸ γὰρ πλέον ἐστὶ νόημα.[62]

[61] See *The Route*, pp. 146–63.
[62] So Tarán, pp. 168–70. Mansfeld keeps the accusative κρᾶσιν of the MSS. He then has to postulate νόος or "the goddess" (he favors the latter) as subject of ἔχει (pp. 175–85). With either subject ἔχει must carry an unusual sense. Tarán's solution is clearly preferable.

The simplest and most convincing syntactical construction of these
lines is the one given by Tarán.[63] He translates:

> For as at any time the mixture of the much wandering body is, so
> does mind come to men. For the same thing is that the nature of
> the body thinks in each and all men; for the full is thought.[64]

With most interpreters, Tarán reads the fragment as a physiological
theory of thought:

> In each and all men, what the constitution of the body thinks is the
> same, for the full is thought. The body, of the individual and of
> humanity as a whole, thinks the same, i.e. to pleon. That is, when-
> ever a given ratio of Light and Night is present in the body the same
> thought would result, since thought is the result of the whole mix-
> ture. Consequently, thought would be automatically determined
> by whatever is present in the body at any given moment.[65]

The poets had spoken of the mind of men as determined by what Zeus
sends from day to day, and Parmenides gave a naturalistic version of
this commonplace within the framework of "Doxa."

This is correct so far as it goes; but the Greek words have a background of associations which Tarán's analysis leaves unexplored. To
begin with, the ambiguity of τὸ πλέον should not be ignored. There has
been considerable discussion as to whether the relevant sense is "the
more" or "the full." But the idea of "the full," at least if we should
follow Tarán in connecting the latter with "ratio," cannot be isolated
from that of "*the more* relatively to *the less*," [66] and so a choice between these two senses is not to be pressed in the present case. It is
likely that the doctrine "thought is *to pleon*" derives whatever plausibility it had for Parmenides' audience not so much from philosophical
theorizing, but from familiar linguistic usage. In English we say "I
would rather . . ." (etymologically, "I would sooner," cf. French
plutôt). The corresponding Greek idiom uses *pleon*, "more," and can
serve to express an opinion or belief as well as a preference: πλέον ἔφερέ
οἱ γνώμη, "he inclined rather to the belief." [67] The view that the actual

---

[63] Cf. pp. 168–70, and 253–58.

[64] Ibid., p. 169.

[65] Ibid., p. 258.

[66] Tarán recognizes that his interpretation "does not nullify Theophrastus'
statement that thought would be different if what prevails is the hot (Fire or
Light) or the cold (Night)" (p. 258).

[67] Hdt. 8.100; cf. LSJ, s.v. πλείων, πλέον, II.2.

or final thought or preference is the one which "prevails" or "dominates" is built into the semantics of Greek, as well as in that of other
Indo-European languages, and Parmenides is exploiting the familiarity
of this view in saying "thought is *to pleon*." As I will show shortly,
some important associations of *pleon* = "the full," established in
linguistic usage, are also involved. But in the context of B16 these point
away from the commonplace toward a specifically Parmenidean doctrine. First let me focus on some of the other words in the fragment.

The adjective *polyplanktos*, "much tossed about" or "much led
astray," suggests immediately that there is more than physiological
psychology to the fragment. The word makes us think of the *plaktos
noos*, "distracted mind" (B6.6), of mortals,[68] and it activates the motif
of the Journey that is so distinctly dominant in the first part of the
poem. The effect is strengthened by the use of the word *melea*, "limbs,"
for the human frame (cf. "body" in the translation above). The combination "limbs much led astray" [69] has the emotive force of "weary
limbs of a luckless traveler." [70] Note further that the phrase *noos parestē-
ken*, "mind comes," is actually an instance of the idiom *paristasthai*, "to
come into one's head, to occur to one." [71] The idiom views thought as
a completely passive process,[72] something which happens or occurs.
This is the converse of Parmenides' own conception of thought as a

[68] Cf. Gregory Vlastos, "Parmenides' Theory of Knowledge," *TAPA*, 77
(1946), 69; Hermann Fränkel, *Wege und Formen frühgriechischen Denkens*
2d ed. (Munich, 1960), pp. 175 and 176 n. 3; Heribert Boeder, *Grund und
Gegenwart als Frageziel der frühgriechischen Philosophie* (The Hague, 1962),
pp. 128 ff.; also Reinhardt, p. 77 (above, pp. 306–07).

[69] It should be noted that μελέων πολυπλάγκτων taken by itself admits of
another translation as well, viz. "of the wretched (miserable, luckless) wander-
ers." In Homer the adjective μέλεος means "vain, useless, idle, empty" (see
Cunliffe, s.v.). But after Homer it appears with reference to men in the sense
given above, especially in tragedy: See LSJ, s.v., and cf. μελεοπαθής, μελεό-
πονος, and μελεόφρων. The word κρᾶσις in line 1 makes this translation of
μελέων unlikely. But the homonymous form might have been felt as a distant
echo, and this may account for Parmenides' choice of μέλεα for "limbs, body"
instead of the more common γυῖα.

[70] Recall that Odysseus is πολύπλαγκτος (*Od.* 17.511), that he is introduced
in the opening lines of the Odyssey as ὃς μάλα πολλά / πλάγχθη, and that
πολύτλας is one of his epithets.

[71] Cf. LSJ, s.v. παρίστημι, B, IV.

[72] Cf. Vlastos, "Parmenides' Theory," p. 69: "This extraordinary notion
of the corpse-like passivity of sense perception. . . ."

"quest," a directed search. Note finally that the syntax of the first two lines is that of the Homeric simile: "even as (hōs) . . . even so (tōs) . . . ." To notice this is to realize that the fragment does more than posit a causal dependence of the state of mind on the state of the body. It likens the occurrence of thought among men to the varying states (krasis hekastote) of "limbs much tossed about." Once again we hear that human thought is a planē, "wandering." But now we are also told that it is a krasis, a "confusion" or a "muddle," which amplifies the charges of "two-headed" and "hordes of no discernment" (B6).

What I have discussed so far are negative aspects of B16: They belong with the record of contrasts between "Truth" and the "Doxa." But the remarkable fact is that in the second and third sentences of the fragment there are also positive aspects. If the second sentence had been preserved in isolation, we would feel justified to place it in the context of "Truth." Tarán's translation is very revealing in this connection: "For the same *thing* is that the nature of the body thinks in each and all men." [73] If we hear of a certain "same thing" that is the object of thought of "the individual and of humanity as a whole," [74] can we resist the implication that this "same thing" is *to eon?* Of course, Parmenides did not say "same thing," but simply "same," and the correct paraphrase of the direct meaning is "same state" or "same condition." Still, there remains an uncanny similarity both in wording and in syntax between B16 and such lines as B3, B4, and B8.34 ff.

Indeed a number of scholars have stressed this affinity of B16 with statements concerning the relation of mind to reality, or with passages involving the idea of "fullness" in the first part of the poem.[75] But one can easily go too far in this direction. The similarities can seduce us into treating the epistemology and metaphysics of "Doxa" as the next best thing to the epistemology and metaphysics of "Truth"—against Parmenides' express warning to the contrary.[76] These similarities have

[73] Page 169 (italics mine).

[74] Tarán, p. 258.

[75] Cf. Fränkel, *Wege*, pp. 177 ff.; Deichgräber, p. 699; Untersteiner, pp. cxcix–ccx; Jean Bollack, "Sur deux Fragments de Parménide (4 et 16)," *Revue des études grecques*, 70 (1957), 66–71; J. H. M. M. Loenen, *Parmenides, Melissus, Gorgias: A Reinterpretation of Eleatic Philosophy* (Assen, 1959), pp. 50–60; Jackson P. Hershbell, "Parmenides' Way of Truth and B16," *Apeiron*, 4 (1970), no. 2, pp. 1–23.

[76] This is true, in varying degrees, of the interpretations by all of the authors mentioned in the preceding note. Bollack's account (which draws specifically

even nurtured the unorthodox thesis that B16 actually belongs to the first part.[77] At the other extreme, one may ignore these verbal echoes as only accidental, and then proceed to a physio-psychological interpretation of B16 without further comment.[78] But this would be to deny verbal features which are in no way esoteric, and which have repeatedly drawn the attention of modern readers.

In yet one more case, we find that what is reflected in modern scholarship as a controversy in interpretation is actually an ambiguity intrinsic to the text. B16 does three things: Openly and directly it gives a physiology of thought; indirectly it censures human thought as "wandering" and "confusion"; but it also gives subtle reminders of the proper relationship between mind and reality. What we hear is that the *physis* of the bodily frame for each and all men *phroneei* that very same thing, the what-is. This radical reorientation of the sentence as a whole is matched by a shift in the meaning of the two words I have left untranslated. The noun *physis* now assumes the meaning of "inner essence, inner reality." And the verb *phroneei* recovers its proper and global sense of "to mind," which combines intellect, volition, and affect. Deep inside, each and all men think and desire (cf. B2.2 "quest") the same thing.

But the most interesting shift appears in the final line, with *pleon*. As indicated in Table (3), row (v) (above, p. 335), the idea of fullness plays contrasting roles in the two parts of the poem. So when the goddess tells us "thought is the full" we think first of the full as a *krasis*, a mixture externally induced. Yet the language (see again Table [3]) rings with a radically different suggestion: "thought is the whole (cf. οὖλον), the all-together-one (cf. ὁμοῦ πᾶν ἕν), the cohesive (cf. συνεχές), the fullness of what-is (cf. ἔμπλεον ἐόντος), the consorting of what-is with what-is (cf. B8.25). Parmenides is, in effect, telling us that "thought is fulfillment." This idiom is no less natural in Greek than it is in English. The verb *pleroō*, "fill full of," can be used with reference to the realization

---

on the similarity between B4 and B16) goes furthest in reconciling "Doxa" with "Truth." He finds that τὸ πλέον in B16.4 refers to the "plénitude de ce qui est" (p. 69) and comments: "les hommes, dans l' univers de leurs propre opinions . . . peuvent faire l'expérience d'un être qui unit pensée et choses, qui est τὸ ἐόν et qui est τὸ πλέον, et devenir sensibles au reflet de l'Être" (pp. 70 f.). Also: "la pensée, à défaut de contempler la perfection de l'Être, peut saisir l'unité de ce qui est" (p. 71).

[77] Cf. Loenen, pp. 58–60; Hershbell, pp. 9–16.

[78] So Mansfeld, pp. 185–94; Tarán, pp. 253–63; Guthrie, vol. 2, pp. 67–70.

of what *thymos*, "spirit," wants;[79] it can also be used with reference to paying back a debt.[80] The adjective *plērēs* can also be used with reference to psychological fulfillment,[81] and it is well known that Plato (and others) projected this linguistic usage into a quasi-physiological theory.[82] The sense of "fulfillment, accomplishment" is well established for the verbs *ekplēroō*[83] and *ekpimplēmi*,[84] both of which mean literally "to fill up." Many of the contexts which are served by the *tel-* (accomplishment) words could also be served by one of the words with the root *plē-*.[85] Conversely, one of the familiar ways of expressing nonaccomplishment or nonrealization in Greek is through adjectives such as *chaunos*, "empty, gaping," [86] or *kenos*, "empty, void." [87] These uses of *chaunos* and *kenos* are especially interesting because they figure in the vocabulary of pessimistic anthropology of the sixth- and fifth-century lyric poets. However, all of the uses to which I have referred are recorded for the fifth century or earlier, and we may assume that they were familiar to Parmenides. Given this pattern of linguistic usage, *pleon* comes to be very close conceptually to *tetelesmenon*, "accomplished, perfect" (B8.42, cf. 8.4, 8.32). The phrase τὸ γὰρ πλέον ἐστὶ νόημα can also be understood as τὸ τετελεσμένον ἐστὶ νόημα, "thought is that which is realized." [87]

Let me review this analysis of B16 as a whole by presenting in sequence translations which capture the different aspects of the fragment. First the direct statement:

> For such as is the state of mixture at each moment of the much-wandering limbs, even such thoughts occur to men. For it is the same [condition] that the nature of the limbs apprehends among men, both all and each. For thought is "the full" [and "the more" and "the rather"].

[79] Cf. LSJ, s.v., I.2.

[80] Ibid., s.v., III.5.

[81] Ibid., s.v., I.3.

[82] Cf. *Gorg.* 493a ff., *Rep.* 585a ff.; cf. also Empedocles A95. The theory of *Phil.* 31b ff. and *Tim.* 64a ff. is more sophisticated.

[83] Cf. LSJ, s.v., I.4.

[84] Ibid., s.v., II and III.

[85] One may thus speak of the fulfillment (πλη-) or of the accomplishment (τελ-) of any of the following: μοῖρα, θυμός, a dream, the length of a year, a curse, sacred rites.

[86] Cf. LSJ, s.vv., II and I.2, respectively.

[87] Cf. Hershbell, p. 13.

Next the mocking statement of human thought as "wandering" and "confusion":

> For such as is the confoundment [or "the muddlement, mix-up, befuddlement"] at each moment of limbs much tossed about and led astray, even such thoughts come into the heads of men. For it is the same [confused complex] that the constitution of the limbs apprehends among men, both all and each. For thought is what preponderates [in the mixture].

And now the last two sentences with their radically different suggestion:

> For it is the same [thing, viz. "the what-is"] that the inner essence of the human frame apprehends, both for all mankind and in each man. For thought is what is fulfilled.

I am not saying, of course, that Parmenides intended that we should read the passage three times, each time attending to a different pattern of associations. Nor that he intended that we should choose among these three possibilities, or that he wanted to leave us puzzled. The correct and openly intended meaning is the one given in the first translation. But he chose his language deftly, so as to create something like counterpoint: a dominant theme, a second theme similar to the first but with a different tonality, and a third theme which is the reversal of the other two.

"DOXA" AS A STUDY IN DECEPTION

I am prepared to allow that not all of the cases of contrast, similarity, play, ambiguity, and irony explored in this study have an equal claim to being intentional. A good many may well be accidents. But, as it has often been argued, the notion of "accident" in literature is open-ended (as in ordinary life: a slip of the tongue is an accident, and yet it isn't). Certainly Parmenides did not consciously and programmatically design even a majority of the subtleties for which I have given evidence. He simply put himself in the frame of mind of a "deceptive ordering of words." Translated into mental directives this would be: (a) Speak in the manner which is directly intelligible to ordinary mortals. (b) Speak in a way that indicates the felt attractiveness of what-is. (c) Also choose words that point toward what-is-not. (d) Choose words that have a familiar-but-incoherent and an unfamiliar-but-illuminating meaning. (e) Choose words that are equivocal even at the ordinary level. (f) Speak as an ironist, so as to give the lie to the mortals' own beliefs. Something like this set of directives could have served as a controlling influence over his choice of vocabulary.

The primary contribution of the analysis in this chapter is, of course, to the old question of the relation between "Truth" and "Doxa." Why did Parmenides bother, after the proofs of B8, to append an exposition of "mortal opinions" that was actually longer than the first part? He did it as a case-study in self-deception, indecisiveness, and confusion. This does not contradict the usual reading of the "Doxa" as dialectical —in the sense of refutation. But it adds some depth to this view, and it accounts better for the detail and length of the exposition. Moreover, it tries to do justice to the many similarities between the two parts, but without mitigating the contrast between the "temper of *eupeithēs* truth" and "mortal opinions in which there is no true fidelity (*pistis*)."

There are three further implications. The first concerns Parmenides' status as a poet. He certainly did not compose the kind of poetry that the Romantics would have appreciated. Yet there is a rhetorical cleverness in his use of language. He can exploit pairings and contrasts, etymologies, associations, verbal conceits, and puns with at least as much relish, and often with as much success, as Heraclitus. Both men combine a philosopher's interest in literal, original, and paradigmatic meaning, with something of the poet's sensitivity to the psychological suggestiveness and acoustic associations of words. But whereas Heraclitus packs his observations into charged and luminous apothegms, Parmenides uses his keen sense for language to trace out implications at length, to project alternative and related models of his concepts, to establish multiple and systematic connections, and to detect and exploit ambiguity for the purpose of argument and refutation.

The second implication is of greater significance philosophically, for it concerns what might be called the "speculative" or "heuristic" use of ambiguity. As I have argued in this study, it is not enough to say that the "Doxa" is in a double relationship of contrast and similarity to "Truth"; we must also notice that the very words used in the table of contraries, or in expounding the basic assumptions and governing processes of "Doxa," carry double meaning. In short, there are multiple relations of *homonymy* between the two parts of the poem. What comes after the goddess' warning is a case-study in the deception which mortals unwittingly practice on themselves. And so, those who observe the warning and "pay heed" will get from the second part of the poem a semantic commentary on "Truth." Cast in the form of an epilogue to the poem as a whole, this commentary would read somewhat as follows:

We must make a *krisis*, a "decision," "separation," and "judgment" —but not in the sense in which mortals do so (B8.55–56). The what-is is "unborn and unperishing"—but it is so in a radical sense of "non-generable" and "nonperishable," not in any sense which might imply its being in time. The what-is is "whole" and "full"—but not in the sense of a physical *krasis* or *mixis*, "mixture" (B9.3, B12, B16). It is "immobile"—but not in the sense of ponderous earth. It is *tetelesmenon*, "realized, accomplished, perfect"—but not in the sense of "coming to an end" (cf. B19.2 *teleutēsousi*). It is "well-rounded"—but without implying a distinction between "outermost," "in-between," and "center" (B12.1–3). It is held by "bands" (*peirata*)—but not in the sense in which physical things or the sky are so held (cf. B10.5–7, B12, A37). It is within the "bounds" of Justice—but not for the purpose of preserving equality with its rivals (cf. B9.4). It submits to Constraint—but one that is internal, not a "driving Constraint" (B10.6). It submits to Persuasion—but not in the sense of Aphrodite or Eros, who bring opposites together (B12.4, B13, B18). Indeed, there is a "quest" for it—but not in the sense in which one of two opposites is impelled to join its counterpart, rather in the sense of a commitment, a relationship of *pistis*, trust and good faith, between our mind and reality.

Of course, Parmenides did not have this semantic vocabulary. His solution was to write a didactic poem in two parts. In the second part words occur in their familiar, ordinary meaning; but paradox and oxymoron are felt as incipient, and references to what-is-not are disguised all too thinly. In the first part there is logical consistency and rigor; but the words assume an unfamiliar and figurative sense.

The third implication is an historical corollary to the second. It assigns to Parmenides a role in the development of the concept of "systematic ambiguity," or "systematic equivocity." The suggestion will appear surprising at first blush, since the one author for whom this concept becomes central, Aristotle, repeatedly censures Parmenides for having failed to appreciate that "being is spoken of in many senses." [88] What Aristotle means, of course, is that there are no modes of reality or categorial distinctions within the domain of Parmenides' what-is. This is perfectly sound as an interpretation, so far as it goes. But note that Aristotle's criticism does not exclude equivocity of a different genre: one which is correctly understood not as *pros hen*

[88] Cf. *Phys.* I.185b20–30, *Metaph.* XIV.1089a1–15.

homonymy, or "focal meaning," [89] but as equivocity between different *levels* of knowledge. Homonymy is not only the Greek term for equivocation; it is also one of the words which express the relationship between particulars and Forms, images and originals, in Plato's metaphysics.[90] The sense in which a particular is F and the sense in which a Form is F are not the same. If we overlook this, we are caught in the paradoxes of the *Parmenides*. It is precisely because this implies transcendence or *chōrismos* that Aristotle was anxious to supplant the Platonic concept of *levels* of meaning with one of *focal organization*.

We seem to have an early model of this Platonic conception in the dialogic practice of Socrates, or (to speak in terms of the actual literary evidence), in the structure of the early, aporetic dialogues of Plato. Fallacy and equivocation in the context of these dialogues often point to an unstated but positive thesis. The disappointing conclusion at the end may even be identical verbally with a popular or traditional view criticized at the start. But the discerning listener or reader will notice that key terms have received (contextually) a fresh interpretation in the course of the argument, and that the lame conclusion may now serve as the homonymous vehicle of an important insight.[91]

It would now seem that this dialogic practice of Socrates was not the only source for Plato's conception of homonymous and graded levels of understanding. The goddess of Parmenides' poem was also one who had spoken as an ironist.

[89] Cf. *Metaph.* IV.1003a33 ff.; W. D. Ross, *Aristotle's* Metaphysics, 2 vols. (Oxford, 1953), vol. I, p. 256; G. E. L. Owen, "Logic and Metaphysics in Some Earlier Works of Aristotle," in *Aristotle and Plato in the Mid-Fourth Century*, ed. I. Düring and G. E. L. Owen (Göteborg, 1960), pp. 163–90.

[90] Cf. *Phaedo* 78e, *Parm.* 133d3, *Soph.* 234b, *Tim.* 52a.

[91] See Rosamond Kent Sprague, *Plato's Use of Fallacy: A Study of the* Euthydemus *and Some Other Dialogues* (London, 1962), pp. 80–87 and passim.

VI

ZENO OF ELEA

15

ZENO AND INDIVISIBLE MAGNITUDES

David J. Furley

Zeno's purpose[1] is explained to us by Plato. In the *Parmenides*[2] it is said that Zeno's writings were intended to support Parmenides against ridicule by showing that the consequences of believing in the existence of Many were still more ridiculous than those of believing only in One.

[1] I have learned most about Zeno from H. D. P. Lee, *Zeno of Elea* (Cambridge, 1936), Hermann Fränkel, "Zeno of Elea's Attacks on Plurality," *AJP*, 63 (1942), 1–25 and 193–206 (in German with revisions in Fränkel, *Wege und Formen frühgriechischen Denkens*, 3rd ed. [Munich, 1968], pp. 198–236; repr. in Furley and Allen, II, G. E. L. Owen, "Zeno and the Mathematicians," *Proceedings of the Aristotelian Society*, N.S. 58 (1957–58), 199–222 (repr. in Wesley C. Salmon, ed., *Zeno's Paradoxes* [Indianapolis and New York, 1970], pp. 139–63, and in Furley and Allen, II, and Gregory Vlastos, "Zeno," in Walter Kaufmann, ed., *Philosophic Classics: Thales to St. Thomas* (Englewood Cliffs, N.J., 1961), pp. 27–45. I accept Vlastos' interpretation of the argument against Plurality, and I agree with Owen about the overall tendency of Zeno's polemics. If anything new is added in this study, it is only in the interpretation of the Moving Rows paradox, and possibly in the assessment of Zeno's historical position. I am particularly grateful to Professor Vlastos for sending me his duplicated notes on Zeno.—My book, *Two Studies in the Greek Atomists*, from which this selection is excerpted, was written before I had seen Professor Friedrich Solmsen's article, "The Tradition about Zeno of Elea Re-Examined," *Phronesis*, 16 (1971), 116–41 [repr. below, pp. 368–93]. I still (1972) believe that Plato is essentially right about Zeno's purpose, but it would take long to defend this belief against Solmsen's skepticism.

[2] 128c = KR No. 365.

It is not always clear how the paradoxes that we hear of were supposed to serve this purpose; but in the following argument (Zeno B2 and 1) this is clear enough.

The argument (which for convenience I will call "Argument A") is preserved in disconnected pieces by Simplicius; it was reassembled convincingly by H. Fränkel and runs as follows (I use Fränkel's lettering of the sections of the argument):

If there are many things in existence:

(a) [Each of the many] has no magnitude, since each is the same as itself, and one. (Simplicius *Physics* 139.18–19)

(b) [Simplicius first summarizes this step in the following words: "If a thing has no magnitude or bulk (*pachos*) or mass, it would not exist." Then he gives the reasoning in full.] For if it were added to something else that does exist, it would make it no greater; for if it were of no magnitude, and were added, it could not contribute anything to magnitude. So it would follow that what was added was nothing. If when it is taken away the other thing is to be no smaller, and is to be no bigger when it is added, it is clear that what was added or taken away was nothing. (Ibid., 10–15)

(c) If it exists, each must necessarily have some magnitude and bulk; and one part of it must be distinct from another part. And the same story holds good for the outstanding part—it too will have magnitude and part of it will stand out. Indeed to say this once is to say it always, since no such part of it will be last or not related as one part to another part. (Ibid., 141.2–6)

(d) Hence if there are many things in existence, they must be both large and small—so small as to have no magnitude, and so large as to be infinite. (Ibid., 6–8)

For the detailed interpretation of this argument I must refer to the commentaries of Fränkel, Owen, and Vlastos.[a] In the present context I hope it will suffice if I offer a summary of Zeno's meaning, and a few comments on points of particular interest.

Zeno takes his opponents' premise, "many exist"—that is to say, what exists is not all one and indivisible, as the Eleatics said, but is divided up—and proves contradictory conclusions from it.

[a] [See above, n. 1.—Ed.]

First (a) he argues that if this division of what exists is carried through, each one of the resultant plurality can have no magnitude. His reasons for asserting this are given in brief by Simplicius, and I shall return to them in a moment.

(b) Now he takes up the conclusion of the first step, and deduces from it that each one of a plurality thus arrived at would not even exist, because if added to or subtracted from what exists it would make no difference to it. This step seems to follow only if it is assumed that what *is* must have magnitude; and it has sometimes been objected that this is an illegitimate assumption for Zeno to make at this point. But the assumption has been made initially by the opponents who have stated that what *is* can be divided up to make a plurality. Zeno's point is that if a thing is a part of some whole, it must be of the same nature as that whole. If the original whole was something that had parts and so had divisible magnitude, then the parts themselves must be of the same type. Hence the unit arrived at in (a), which has been shown to have no magnitude, cannot be a part of the original whole.

(c) Hence it follows that if the unit in question exists, it must have divisible magnitude and distinguishable parts. And the same is true of any one of these parts, and so on for ever.

(d) Hence the alleged unit has infinite magnitude, since it is composed of an infinite number of parts, each having magnitude—and it has already been shown that it must have *no* magnitude.

Simplicius' account of the first step (a) in this argument is unfortunately omitted from some of the editions most widely used; so it may be worth repeating the reasons for believing that it does in fact fill this position. After quoting step (b), he continues:

> Zeno says this, not by way of abolishing the One, but meaning that each of the many actually has "infinite" [reading ἄπειρον for ἀπείρων] magnitude, since there must always be something before the part that is taken, because of infinite divisibility; and this he shows after showing first [step (a)] that it has no magnitude since each of the many is the same as itself and one. (Simplicius *Physics* 139.16–19)

The reading ἄπειρον (proposed by H. Fränkel) seems to me almost certain. The manuscript text "each of the many and infinite" has no place in the argument. With the amended reading it becomes clear that Simplicius is merely summarizing step (c)—Zeno's attempt to prove that a divisible magnitude must have infinite magnitude. So in this passage Simplicius quotes (b), follows it with a summary of (c), and then says this was preceded by (a).

But (a) is still obscure in itself; Simplicius' very brief summary must be supplemented from elsewhere.

The combination of (a) and (b) puzzled the ancient commentators; Simplicius' comment in the passage just quoted, "not by way of abolishing the one," is a reflection of this. Taken together, they apparently prove that if there is a One it must have no magnitude, and therefore it must be non-existent; and this, it seemed, would demolish the Eleatic One as well as the opponents' plurality. Eudemus, apparently, knew a tale of Zeno himself saying that if someone would tell him what the One is, he would be able to speak about "things which exist" (i.e. a plurality). Eudemus commented that Zeno's doubt probably arose because every sensible object can be said to be "many," either by having different predicates or by division, and he would not allow that the point is a "one" at all—and Eudemus referred to step (b) in support of this last assertion. (In passing, it should be noted that Zeno was not necessarily talking about points; he was talking about any unit without magnitude, and there is no need to assume any special reference to geometry. It was Aristotle [*Metaphysics* III.4.1001b7] who mentioned the point and the monad in connection with this argument, and no doubt Eudemus followed him.) Eudemus himself apparently said that Zeno's argument "did away with" the One. But Alexander interpreted him as meaning that the argument attacked a plurality of real beings, rather than the One, "on the ground that there is no *one* among the existing things, and the many are a plurality composed of ones." [3]

What seems to emerge from all this is a Zenonian argument approximately as follows. To be one is not to be many. If a thing is divisible into parts, it is many, and therefore not one.[4] So each one of the alleged plurality (for a plurality is a collection of ones) must be indivisible and have no parts. But it is only by having the same kind of being as the whole that these alleged units have a claim to be parts of the whole: and that means that they ought to have divisible being. Hence these indivisible units cannot be parts of the whole. But the whole is, on the pluralists' hypothesis, "what exists." Hence these units cannot be parts of what exists.

[3] Eudemus quoted by Simplicius *Physics* 97.12 ff. and 99.10 ff. The passages are printed in DK 29A16 and 21.

[4] For this part of the argument, cf. Melissus B9, and Plato *Parmenides* 137c4–d3.

But if this, or something like it, was Zeno's argument, is it possible that it was not at once seen to be equally damaging to the Eleatic One as to the Ones of the opponents' plurality? The Eleatic One was certainly said to be one, and certainly had magnitude; yet this argument seems to require that the two properties are incompatible. Vlastos writes[5] of Zeno's assumption "that anything which does have size is at least logically divisible and has at least logically discriminable parts." Owen observes[6] that Zeno assumes without argument that the conjunction of size with theoretical indivisibility would be a contradiction. Are we to suppose, then, that Zeno overlooked the contradiction between this proposition and his own most cherished tenet? Such blindness or inconsistency seems as unlikely in Zeno as in Melissus, whom I have discussed elsewhere.[7] There must be some way of avoiding the contradiction.

It is probable *a priori* that Zeno took the same line as Melissus on this subject. There is evidence that Melissus believed in a One Being with magnitude but with no parts, and that the saving feature of *his* One Being was that it lacked bulk or solidity (*pachos*). There is a strong hint in the fragments of Zeno that he would have based his defense on the same ground; for the word *pachos* appears twice in significant positions in Argument A: it occurs in Simplicius' summary of step (b), and in his verbatim report of step (c). In each case the word is a gratuitous addition, unless it has the important function I want to assign to it; for on the usual view magnitude alone is significant, so that μέγεθος καὶ πάχος, "magnitude and bulk," must be a piece of unnecessary rhetoric.

Zeno's strategy, then, if I am right, was to attack the Pluralists on the ground that their "Beings," having "magnitude and bulk," could be shown to be both reducible to nothing and infinitely large. Eleatic Being would be exempt from this attack because it lacked bulk and therefore gave the divider no starting point for his division. The Pluralists' idea of Being included various kinds of qualitative differentiation, such as those attacked by Parmenides in the "Way of Truth" (B8, especially 22–25). The later Eleatics seem to use *sōma*, "body," and *pachos* as compendious expressions for this property of the Pluralists' Being. Such Being must always allow differentiation, and must always

[5] Page 29.
[6] Page 210.
[7] See Furley, *Two Studies*, p. 60. Others attribute both of the contradictory propositions to Zeno, apparently with no qualms (e.g. Raven in KR, p. 303).

be divisible into parts which have this same property; but the Eleatic Being allows no differentiation at all. (As I argue in another context,[b] the Atomists found an answer in the assertion of indivisible and undifferentiated units, making up a differentiated and divisible whole.)

So far I have concentrated on the first half of Zeno's antinomy in Argument A: his "proof" that the units of a plurality must have no magnitude and bulk and so cannot be numbered among the things that exist. Now I turn briefly to the second half, in which he argues that the units must have infinite magnitude.

Step (c) appears to prove that each of the many is infinitely *divisible*. But this is not the same as the conclusion ascribed to Zeno, that each is infinitely *large*. Hermann Fränkel observes that this conclusion is "an obvious fallacy," and he therefore tries to find a meaning for "so large as to be infinite" such that the phrase does not imply infinite extension, but only the lack of a limit (*peras*). Whenever we think we may have reached the surface of a thing, we observe that this surface can still be subdivided; we never reach the true surface, the limit; hence the object is "limitless" or infinite. Nevertheless, "the total extension, as the modern mathematicians express it, converges to a certain sum." F. Solmsen has proposed taking "large" and "infinite" to describe each of the many in relation to the decrease *ad infinitum* of its parts which the progressive division brings into existence.[8]

To adopt a solution like this would be to accuse the ancient commentators of a great misunderstanding; for they certainly thought Zeno meant infinitely large. But more seriously, it would also be to rob Zeno's objection of all its force, except the purely verbal success of forcing the Pluralists to use the word *apeiron* of their units. So long as they were not committed to infinite extension they might well be willing to make this concession.[9]

If we suppose that the commentators are right after all, and the argument is intended to show the infinite size of each unit produced by the division of a real thing, then clearly some premise has been omitted,

[b] [See below, pp. 504–26.—Ed.]

[8] Friedrich Solmsen, *Aristotle's System of the Physical World* (Ithaca, 1960), p. 172 n. 56.

[9] If Zeno's argument is regarded as an antinomy, it will not lose all its force, since there is still a contradiction between "of no magnitude" and "*apeiron* in this qualified sense." But its force as a dilemma will now be removed, since the Pluralists may now accept one of the alternatives.

either by Zeno or by the commentators, presumably on the ground that it is self-evident. The missing premise is one which Epicurus used in his argument for theoretical indivisibles (*Lett. to Hdt.* §57ᶜ): "When someone once says that there are infinite parts in something, however small they may be, it is impossible to see how this can still be finite in size."

Gregory Vlastos[10] has observed how very close together a false statement and a true statement can be on this subject. He contrasts the following two statements:

(1) The sum of an infinite number of terms, each of which has finite size, is infinitely large.

(2) The sum of an infinite number of terms, the smallest of which has finite size, is infinitely large.

The first of these is false; the second is true. Zeno's mistake is understandable enough. Aristotle was the first, so far as the records show, to understand the principle of the infinite convergent series. And even he did not explain it so well that mistakes were no longer possible, for he did not convince Epicurus,[d] and even Simplicius seems to assent to the first statement.[11]

Argument A, then, attacks the proposition that the Real might be divided up spatially into a plurality of real things, and that such a division might be completed. Zeno tried to prove that such things must be both without any magnitude and infinite in magnitude. Insofar as it is effective, the argument is a refutation of atomism, as well as other forms of pluralism. This is therefore an argument which Leucippus and Democritus had to evade or refute. How they did so will be explained in another context.[e]

Four famous arguments by Zeno are grouped together by Aristotle, our only authority, under the heading "arguments about motion." [12]

ᵉ [See Furley, *Two Studies*, ch. 1, discussion of the passage labeled C 1, pp. 9 and 14 f.—Ed.]

[10] "Zeno," in Kaufmann, *Classics*.

ᵈ [See Furley, *Two Studies*, ch. 1.—Ed.]

[11] Simplicius *Physics* 459.22; 462.3–5. See Furley, *Two Studies*, ch. 9, and "Aristotle and the Atomists on Infinity," in I. Düring, ed., *Naturphilosophie bei Aristoteles und Theophrast* (Heidelberg: Lothar Stiehm, 1969), pp. 85–96.

ᵉ [See below, pp. 504–26.—Ed.]

[12] *Physics* VI.9.239b9 ff. = DK 29A25 = KR No. 369.

This heading need not, however, be taken too seriously; it may well be Aristotle's own.[13] If it is possible to interpret these arguments as attacks on pluralism, such an interpretation should be preferred, if we are to follow the guidance of Plato about Zeno's purpose.[14]

The first paradox is the Dichotomy (sometimes called the Stadium).[15] It states that before you reach the end of the stadium you must reach a half-way mark, then the next half-way mark . . . and so on for ever, so that the end is never reached. (Alternatively, the argument may mean that you cannot even start, let alone finish, because you must first reach a half-way mark, before that, a mark half-way to *that* mark, . . . and so on. But this is for the moment unimportant.)

The Achilles paradox[16] points out that if the tortoise has a start on Achilles, Achilles can never catch up; for while Achilles covers the distance that initially separates them, the tortoise advances a little, and so on for ever.

Aristotle remarks that the Achilles paradox is the same as the Dichotomy, except that the former does not confine itself to division into halves. The point of both arguments, it might be said, is to draw a ridiculous conclusion from the supposition that divisibility goes on *ad infinitum*. This is the alternative to the concept of a division that can be completed. A question arises about the range of application of these paradoxes. Clearly they are parables in some sense: Zeno did not wish to make a point only about the stadium or only about Achilles and the tortoise (actually in the latter case Aristotle implies that Zeno used the terms "the quickest" and "the slowest"). I want to suggest that they were intended to be interpreted very generally indeed, as applicable to anything infinitely divisible in magnitude, and to any kind of division. There is confirmation of this suggestion in a passage from the pseudo-Aristotelian treatise *On Indivisible Lines* which deserves quotation. One of the arguments for the existence of indivisible lines runs as follows:

[13] It must be admitted, however, that although the heading "about motion" may be Aristotle's, the arguments must have been arranged in this order before *Physics* VI.9 was written; otherwise it would be hard to explain why Aristotle calls the Arrow argument the third (239b30), when he has already discussed it once by itself. Perhaps he could refer to a standard set of notes on Zeno: πρὸς τὰ Ζήνωνος is a title mentioned in the list of Aristotle's works in Diogenes Laertius (5.21.100).

[14] See above, p. 353.

[15] KR No. 370.

[16] KR No. 373.

According to Zeno's argument there must be a magnitude without parts, if it is impossible in a finite time to touch an infinite number of things one by one, and if it is necessary that anything that moves arrives at the half-way point first, and if there *is* a halfway point in everything that is not without parts. [The reference to the Dichotomy is clear enough.] But if something moving on a line touches an infinite number of things in a finite time, and something moving more rapidly traverses more than something slower in an equal time, and the motion of thought is most rapid, then thought could touch upon an infinite number of things one by one in a finite time; so if thought's touching one by one is the same thing as counting, it is possible to count an infinite number of things in a finite time. If this is impossible, there must be an indivisible line. (*On Indivisible lines* 968a18 ff.)

It is interesting, at least, that the movement of thought is the example chosen here. The choice would be explained if this were the common and perhaps the original way of interpreting the Dichotomy paradox.

Probably we have in these paradoxes of Zeno an early reference to what Epicurus calls *metabasis:*[17] that is, the process of "running over" or "scanning" an object mentally from side to side. When Epicurus says that we have to do away with infinite *metabasis*, he must have Zeno's arguments, or some repetition of them, in mind. Zeno would suggest to him that if the mind must touch upon an infinite number of divisions as it runs over an object, it can never reach the end of its task; moreover, according to the second part of Zeno's Argument A, the object itself must be infinitely large.

The third of the "arguments about motion" is called the Flying Arrow.[18] The text of this is doubtful. Roughly, the argument states that when a thing occupies a place equal to itself, it is at rest; but a flying arrow is always occupying a place equal to itself "now"—that is, at any given moment; so the flying arrow must be motionless. The point is that if the arrow is at rest at *every* moment in a stretch of time, then it is at rest throughout that stretch of time.

"It is easy to see," J. E. Raven writes,[19] "that this argument, unlike the two that precede it, treats time and space alike as composed of

---

[17] C 2 in the passage from Epicurus *Lett. to Hdt.* §57 discussed in Furley, *Two Studies*, pp. 9 f. and 16 f.

[18] KR No. 374.

[19] KR p. 295.

indivisible minima." I disagree. It certainly treats time as containing indivisible moments. But these moments cannot have any magnitude at all without destroying the plausibility of the arrow's being stationary, and hence they cannot be minima. On the nature of *space* I cannot see that it has anything to say at all. The point seems to be to draw a ridiculous conclusion from the mere fact of making distinctions in *time*. If you distinguish one moment of time from another, then Zeno will prove that at either of these moments, and then at all of them in a stretch of time, "the flying arrow is stationary." Since Parmenides was anxious to rule out temporal as well as spatial distinctions, Zeno's support would seem to be well enough directed.

The fourth of the arguments about motion will detain us longer, because it is the most misunderstood.[20] The Moving-Rows paradox (sometimes called "the Stadium") is reported by Aristotle, but perhaps most easily expounded with the help of Simplicius' diagram. The A's

represent four bodies of equal size, stationary; the B's are four bodies of this same size moving right, and the Γ's four equal bodies moving left at the same speed. The diagram represents the opening stage of the problem: at the end of the problem the leading B has passed the right A, and the leading Γ has passed the left A. At the end, says Aristotle,[21]

. . . it follows that the leading B and the leading Γ are at the end simultaneously, moving past each other. And it follows that this Γ has gone past all the B's, but the leading B has gone past half the A's; so that the time is half, since each is an equal time opposite each. And at the same time it follows that the B's have passed all the Γ's, since the leading Γ and the leading B will be simultaneously

[20] KR Nos. 375–76.

[21] I translate the text printed in KR, No. 375. For details of the various readings of the manuscripts, see W. D. Ross, *Aristotle's* Physics (Oxford, 1936), ad loc.

at their opposite ends, being the same time (says Zeno) opposite each of the B's as opposite each of the A's, since both lots are an equal time opposite the A's. (*Physics* VI.9.240a9 ff.)

This argument, according to Aristotle, was to prove that "half the time is equal to double." [22] As a matter of Greek idiom, this may mean either $t/2 = t$, or $t/2 = 2t$. It appears to be the latter that Aristotle has in mind. There is first the proof that "the time is half." "The time" is four time units (in our diagram)—the time taken by the leading Γ to pass all four B's. But in that time the leading B has passed only 2 A's. Therefore "the time is half, since each is an equal time opposite each" (the reasoning of this last clause will be discussed in a moment). If the proof were simply that $t = t/2$, it would now be completed—but Aristotle continues. H. D. P. Lee, in his very lucid and detailed exposition of this problem, argues for the interpretation $t = t/2$. I disagree with him without relish; but even though Aristotle did not say explicitly "so the time is double" at the end of it, it seems to me that he thought the second part was out to prove something new, since he made the second part *follow* his statement "the time is half."

Now it is generally agreed that this argument of Zeno's has no force at all *unless it is directed against a theory of indivisible magnitudes*. Once this condition is granted, it is clever and to the point; without it, it is puerile. Aristotle remarks,[23] "There is a mistake in supposing that to move past a stationary magnitude and an equal magnitude in motion takes an equal time." But suppose all these magnitudes are atoms, and there are also indivisible units of time. Then to move the distance of half an atom, or to take half a time unit, will be logically impossible. Then there would be a real problem in knowing how the leading B has moved past four Γ's, but only two A's.

This is an attractive idea, because Zeno is a popular hero, and we want to hear nothing but good of him. But there is no sign whatever in our texts that these units were supposed to be indivisible; the mere use of the word *onkos*, "body," certainly does not prove it, as some have argued. Moreover, it certainly did not occur to Aristotle that Zeno was speaking of indivisible units, even though he was well aware of the existence of such a theory in his own times, and also knew quite well

[22] *Physics* VI.9.240a1.
[23] *Physics* VI.9.240a2.

that it was open to objections similar to those allegedly brought against it here by Zeno.[24]

But it is not enough merely to say that Aristotle may be right after all. Did the argument never have any plausibility at all? If so, it would be unique among Zeno's paradoxes, all of which have a certain persuasiveness. N. B. Booth,[25] who rightly, I think, rejects the atomistic view of this argument, can only suggest that "the idea of relative motion . . . at a time when motion had hardly been thought of, . . . cannot have been at all easy." But this is quite inadequate: it is enough to remark that the author of the Achilles paradox must have done *some* thinking about relative motion. Before the atomistic interpretation is killed, we must find some other analysis of the paradox which gives it an appearance of plausibility. This can, I think, be done.

There is a clue to Zeno's probable meaning in Aristotle's text, though it is often obscured by tendentious translations and emendations. The first half of the argument, as set out by Aristotle, depends on the premise ἴσον γὰρ ἑκάτερόν ἐστι παρ᾽ ἕκαστον, and the second on the premise ἴσον χρόνον παρ᾽ ἕκαστον γιγνόμενον τῶν Β ὅσονπερ τῶν Α, ὥς φησι, διὰ τὸ ἀμφότερα ἴσον χρόνον παρὰ τὰ Α γίγνεσθαι.[26] Lee translates the first premise "since each takes an equal time in passing each body"; in the second (following Ross) he omits the first part, as far as ὥς φησι, as being a gloss, and translates "since both take an equal time in passing the A's." But the whole point, I think, lies in the use of a *static* vocabulary (ἐστι, γίγνεσθαι παρὰ ἕκαστον): the object "is opposite to," "lies against" the other—not "passes" the other. Zeno's argument was this. As the B's move past the A's, each B "is opposite to" each A for a certain time (call it *m*). Each Γ is also opposite to each A for the same time *m*, since the B's and the Γ's are moving at equal speeds. It follows that each Γ must be opposite to each B for the same time, *since they are both opposite to an* A *for this time*. Now the leading Γ passes all the B's in 4*m* (since it "is opposite to" each of the four for *m*): this Γ has been at it for 4*m*. Meanwhile, though, the leading B has passed only two A's; it has only been at it for 2*m*. So the time (4*m*) is half (2*m*); $t = t/2$. We have now proved that the time *t* is only 2*m*; but during this time the

[24] *Physics* VI.3.234a24 ff. The point is made by N. B. Booth, "Zeno's Paradoxes," *JHS*, 77 (1957), 195, and again by Vlastos, p. 43 n. 1.

[25] Booth, p. 194.

[26] I take it that the antecedent of this participle is τὸ πρῶτον Γ in the preceding clause.

leading B has passed all four Γ's—$4m$ again. So the time ($2m$) is double ($4m$); $t = 2t$.

The structure of this argument is reminiscent of the argument against plurality analyzed above. (There Zeno makes a case for thinking that units have no size: but in that case, they could not exist—so they must have size. But in that case they would be infinite.) The force of the argument, it seems to me, does not in any way depend on the indivisibility of the *onkoi*, or the indivisibility of units of time. It depends only on the idea that a length can be divided up into sections, such that to traverse the length is to "be opposite to" each section in turn for a period of time, and that time can be divided up into such periods.

It is not, of course, a cogent argument. The essential step is that since a B and a Γ are opposite to the same A for the same time, they must be opposite to each other for that time; and this is fallacious. But it seems to me to have enough plausibility to stand alongside some others of Zeno's arguments.

I hope this interpretation of the Moving Rows will prove acceptable. It allows full weight to be given (for the first time, I think) to all the words of Aristotle's report; it frees Aristotle from a charge of gross misunderstanding; and it does not depend on any special assumption about Zeno's opponents. The purpose of the paradox is to show an unacceptable consequence of making temporal distinctions—but clearly it has something to say about spatial distinctions as well.

If my analysis of Zeno's arguments is approximately correct, only one of the arguments is directed against a theory of indivisible magnitudes, and that is Argument A. I doubt if the nature of this argument requires us to believe that someone before Zeno must have held an atomistic theory. The argument, as we have seen, seems to form one of a set, dealing with the alternative possibilities that the Real may be completely divided and that it may be divided *ad infinitum*. These features seem to be more like the result of an attempt to be exhaustive than the result of aiming at particular targets. At least, it must be conceded that the existence of one argument in Zeno's philosophy which is directed against a completed division of the Real, is an inadequate foundation on which to rest the whole hypothesis of Pythagorean atomism.

But it is commonly stated that the Pythagoreans were not simply atomists but "unit-point-atomists"; that is, that they confused the geometrical point with the arithmetical unit and both with the physical atom[27] and that Zeno aimed to show up this confusion. The case against this view is put with great pungency by G. E. L. Owen. The Pythagoreans, he observes, are credited "with failing to distinguish physical bodies from geometrical solids, and with holding about these solids *both* that they are infinitely divisible *and* that they are divisible into atomic bits, which bits *both* have magnitude *and* have the properties of points without magnitude. Zeno's arguments cannot have been directed against such a theory unless his whole program was misconceived. For in order to provide his arguments with a target a theory had to be produced which housed every or nearly every incompatible view on the divisibility of bodies. But the direct refutation of such a theory would be to show the absurdity of holding any two or more of these views concurrently. What Zeno does is to distinguish each view and refute it in isolation. In brief, his arguments seem designed to close not some but all avenues of escape to anyone holding the unremarkable belief that there is more than one thing in existence." [28]

What avenues of escape were now left to the Pluralists? It is often supposed that one avenue was to accept the hypothesis that the Real is infinitely divisible. Thus it is usually assumed that Anaxagoras' theory of the infinite divisibility of matter was an answer to Zeno and the other Eleatics.[29] I doubt this. Zeno pointed out some of the difficulties in infinite divisibility: if the parts reached have any magnitude at all, the object must be infinitely large—but if they have no magnitude, they cannot contribute anything at all to the sum. It seems to me that Anaxagoras had no answer to this dilemma—I have argued elsewhere that even Aristotle had some difficulty in finding one.[30] And it does not seem reasonable that Anaxagoras should blandly take over from Zeno as a prop for his philosophy something that Zeno had shown to be riddled with holes.

So I prefer to think that Zeno was answering Anaxagoras. The chronology of the two philosophers is so vague that I doubt if any objections can be brought on that account. It is perhaps significant that the two scholars who have done most work recently on the subject of divisibility, Luria and Mau, both take Anaxagoras to be *before*

[27] KR, chs. 9 and 11.

[28] Owen, pp. 212–13.

[29] This is defended by J. E. Raven, "The Basis of Anaxagoras' Cosmology," *CQ*, N.S. 4 (1954), 124–37.

[30] See Furley, *Two Studies*, ch. 11, especially pp. 150 ff.

Zeno.[f] The evidence connecting Zeno and Anaxagoras is fairly convincing,[31] but so far as I can see there is no certain answer to the question which of the two was answering the other. But perhaps it is not necessary to decide this question here.

Two escape routes were in fact tried.[g] One was the assertion of a plurality of indivisible magnitudes; the other was Aristotle's theory of the infinite divisibility of matter—not now the naïve theory of Anaxagoras, but a theory hedged carefully around with qualifications.

[f] [See S. Luria, "Die Infinitesimallehre der antiken Atomisten," *Quellen und Studien zur Geschichte der Mathematik*, B 2 (1933), 106-85, and Jürgen Mau, *Zum Problem des Infinitesimalen bei den antiken Atomisten* (Berlin, 1954).—Ed.]

[31] KR, pp. 499-500.

[g] [See below, pp. 504-26.—Ed.]

16

THE TRADITION ABOUT ZENO
OF ELEA RE-EXAMINED

Friedrich Solmsen

This paper* makes no attempt to compete with the brilliant studies
through which in the last thirty years several scholars have advanced
our understanding of the evidence for Zeno of Elea and in particular
of the verbatim preserved fragments. In fact my intention is not to
replace theories by other theories but to create doubt about matters
that for some time have been taken for granted and to change confident
assumptions into hypotheses that would tolerate others besides them.

Accounts of Zeno's philosophy generally take as their starting point
some well known statements at the beginning of Plato's *Parmenides*.[1]
Given the paucity of reports bearing on his work as a whole, the information here vouchsafed about its content and purpose must seem
priceless. It also seems authoritative, the idea of examining it critically
almost sacrilegious. Zeno, we here read, wrote against those who
ridiculed the thesis of his master Parmenides that "all is one";[2] the
opponents tried to discredit this thesis by pointing out contradictions
and "ridiculous" consequences resulting from the Parmenidean "One."

From *Phronesis*, 16 (1971), 116–41. Reprinted with permission of the editor
of *Phronesis* and of the author.

* On earlier versions of this study, including one submitted to a meeting,
I have received valuable comments from more scholars than I can name. I
must however mention my obligations to Harold Cherniss, Alexander Mourelatos, and most of all to Gregory Vlastos, who twice sent me extensive critical
comments and suggestions, with the result that little has remained unchanged.
Acknowledgment in every particular point was impossible, and in spite of my
large debt the responsibility for the opinions expressed is entirely mine.—I
greatly regret that on many topics important in themselves, but peripheral
to my subject, I had to be briefer and more dogmatic than I like to be.

[1] *Parm.* 127d6–128e4, esp. 127e8–128b6.

[2] ἓν εἶναι τὸ πᾶν (128a8); ἓν ἔστιν (d1; cf. d6).

In return Zeno took the adversaries' position that "there are many" as basis for his reasoning, deducing from it in each of his arguments contradictions and other results even more "ridiculous" than what the opponents had found in Parmenides' theory.

It is easy to see why this testimony is so irresistible. Plato himself distinguishes between what is certain and what allows doubt and more than one explanation. Doubt is possible about certain accidental aspects (τῶν συμβεβηκότων τι, Zeno says, 128c5 f.), i.e. whether the ultimate convergence of the two treatises was meant to be obvious or to be concealed from the reader and also whether Zeno was anxious to build up a philosophical stature for himself or merely to help Parmenides against the detractors. Yet precisely because doubt is allowed on such items of secondary importance, the far more important statements concerning the subject matter, the method, and the objectives of Zeno's treatise seem immune to attack.

Scholars writing on Zeno have usually accepted Plato's testimony as a matter of course or with the most perfunctory justification.[3] A few have given reasons why the testimony deserves confidence, and no reason could be more attractive than the sensitive comments of Hermann Fränkel about Plato as being by his own individuality and temperament exceptionally qualified to appreciate the peculiar, rather wanton humor which Fränkel has found lurking in Zeno's sallies.[4] I should be loath to disagree with this argument, even if it did not form a part of what Gregory Vlastos at the time of its appearance justly called "easily the most important philological monograph published on the subject in several decades."[5] Still I am not the first to question the element of wantonness and trickery in Zeno's proofs,[6] and even if

[3] The only dissenter known to me is N. B. Booth, in *Phronesis*, 3 (1957), 1 ff. For other work (some of which will be cited later) it may here suffice to refer to W. K. C. Guthrie, *A History of Greek Philosophy*, vol. 2 (Cambridge, 1965), with its "Bibliographical note" on Zeno, pp. 85 ff., and e.g. for Vlastos' important contributions, to his article "Zeno" in *The Encyclopedia of Philosophy* (New York, 1967), with its bibliography.

[4] *AJP*, 63 (1942), 1–25, 193–206; repr. in Furley and Allen, II; revised in the German version (in *Wege und Formen frühgriechischen Denkens* [Munich, 1955], pp. 198–236, henceforth cited in parentheses); see esp. 202–06 (232–36).

[5] *Gnomon*, 31 (1959), 195, Review of Fränkel, *Wege und Formen* (henceforth cited as Rev. Fränkel).

[6] Vlastos, Rev. Fränkel, p. 197; Guthrie, p. 88 n. 2. Fränkel's approach remains significant because he has realized that without good reasons the passage in the *Parmenides* cannot be accepted as a historical report. Moreover

it were granted, one might wonder whether Plato's own humor is not normally more gentle and urbane (*asteion*)—the exuberance of the "youthful" *Protagoras* being an exception—and whether even a congenial sense of humor would guarantee the correct understanding of a philosophical endeavor. But it is perhaps more profitable to develop Fränkel's doubts "as to how much (Plato), or his readers for that matter, would be interested in problems of mere historicity." [7] For these doubts apply even farther than Fränkel may be inclined to think. Would Plato really wish to make sure that his readers had a correct knowledge of what Zeno's treatise intended and achieved? Had he carefully and with something approaching philological accuracy worked his way through all *hypotheseis* in the treatise and found out to his satisfaction what purpose they served? Does he now, to communicate this discovery to the readers, use the dramatic device of making Socrates ask whether his interpretation is correct and Zeno confirm that in substance it is? Why anyhow must this be more, or much more, than a dramatic device—especially if the device has a bearing on the later developments in the dialogue?

Actually we see how Socrates arrives at his view about Zeno's treatise. After making Zeno repeat something that he said in his treatise, he quite tentatively goes first one step and then another beyond the actual words, and while thus advancing *pedetemptim* asks at each stage: "is this what you mean?" (127e4; 128a1)[8] or "is this the purpose of your arguments" (127e8 f.)? Could it be made clearer that we are moving into the realm of "interpretation" (what may be less clear is where the report ends and where interpretation takes over)?[9]

---

in principle I should rather trust an argument based on congenial personalities than one which attributes to Plato historical and philological interests that are quite foreign to him. (Cf. F. M. Cornford, *Plato's Theory of Knowledge* [London, 1935], p. 31, and see below, p. 371).

[7] Page 205 (235).

[8] F. M. Cornford (*Plato and Parmenides* [London, 1939], p. 66) renders in the former passage λέγεις by "say," in the latter by "mean." For reasons connected with the subject of the next note I should prefer "mean" in both instances.

[9] While *Parm.* 127e1 ff. "that, if beings are many, it is necessary that they should be both like and unlike" was obviously one of Zeno's paradoxical conclusions, what follows in Plato beginning with the words τοῦτο δὲ δὴ ἀδύνατον has no parallel in the fragments and should not be included in a

And after all, if what Socrates and Zeno agree upon conveys to us the results of Plato's own painstaking analysis of Zeno—a piece of "historicity" quite unique in his oeuvre—would there not be the possibility that Plato is mistaken? Especially if he had to take so many steps beyond the actual wording of Zeno's treatise? Plato is not at all a historian of philosophy in our sense of the concept; we err, in his case as much as in Aristotle's, if we think of him as concerned with anything resembling our historical problems and employing anything approximating our historical methods.[10] What he says about philosophers of the past is determined by his own context and the specific philosophical question in which he happens to be engrossed. We shall find other instances of this.

It is indeed time to become more specific, and in the present case this is easy enough. For as we have seen, Plato's account of Zeno's treatise and its purpose is closely related to a corresponding account of Parmenides. The two summaries interlock, and if one of them is discredited, the other too, and so the thesis of an ultimate convergence between the two works is compromised. Now while we do not have enough first hand material to test Plato's suggestions about Zeno's treatise, the fragments of Parmenides allow us to form an independent judgment. Did Parmenides actually write his poem to prove what Socrates says he proved so "beautifully" (128b): ἓν εἶναι τὸ πᾶν, "that all is one," or differently worded, ἓν ἔστι, "the one *is*"? Is this really his thesis (or, as Plato says, *hypothesis*, 137b3)?

Fortunately no lengthy discussion of the problem is needed; for

---

collection of these, *pace* H. D. P. Lee (*Zeno of Elea* [Cambridge, 1936; repr. Amsterdam, 1967], pp. 20, 32; see however the reservations, p. 29), who incidentally omits the tell-tale δή. I agree with the judgment of Guido Calogero (*Studi sull' Eleatismo* [Rome, 1932], p. 108 n. 1; see ibid. for earlier discussions). Cornford (see note 8) seems to side with Lee.

[10] "As if any philosopher could ever understand his predecessors in this sense," scil. as Aristotle had been expected to understand Plato (Werner Jaeger, *Aristotle*, translated by Richard Robinson, 2d ed. [Oxford, 1948], p. 3). I am not aware of any instance to the contrary. Historical reconstruction of earlier systems has become so natural to us that we forget how exceptional it is. Having, like other historical studies, developed in the early 19th century (from roots in the Romantic and in Germany also in the Classical movement), it has been practiced by a few generations of scholars and may yet remain an "episode." Cf. nn. 6, 14, 18.

lately several scholars have stated firmly that Parmenides' subject is
not the *hen*, "one," but the *eon*, "being." [11] From the beginning, ἔστιν
ἢ οὐκ ἔστιν; "*is* it or *is* it not?" is the crucial choice for him, and in the
light of it we are bound to read the most informative fragment B8 as
setting up Being, not by any means One, in new and unheard of glory
(just as conversely the exalted status given to the *eon* in B8 throws light
back on the meaning of *esti*, favoring some of the currently advocated
interpretations rather than others). Moreover there is nothing in
Parmenides to support an identity of *eon* and *hen*, or to suggest for the
"oneness" of the *eon* a preferential status among its numerous predicates or *sēmata*, "signs." In truth the first and fundamental predicates
are *agenēton*, "ungenerated," and *anōlethron*, "imperishable" (B8.3);
of the others some are subsidiary to these, some additional. In whichever of these two groups *mounogenes*, "unique" (B8.4) is,[12] its status is
certainly no more exalted than that of *oulon*, "whole," *atremes*, "un-
shaking," *syneches*, "cohesive" (8.6), *akinēton*, "immobile" (8.26), *ouk*

---

[11] For what follows cf. Harold Cherniss, *Philosophical Review*, 59 (1950),
376; Leonardo Tarán, *Parmenides* (Princeton, 1965), pp. 188 ff., 269 ff., who
inter alia points out that Plato's misrepresentation was known to ancient
commentators. See further Alexander Mourelatos, *The Route of Parmenides*
(New Haven and London, 1970), pp. 130 ff., and Calogero, *Storia della logica
antica* I (Bari, 1967), pp. 172 ff. Cornford, *Plato and Parmenides*, p. 35 postulated "that which is one" as a "premiss for which Parmenides gives no
proof." His opinion has not enjoyed much favor and was refuted by G. E. L.
Owen, "Eleatic Questions," *CQ*, N.S. 10 (1960), 92 [repr. in Furley and Allen,
II], who finds in B8.22–25 the proof for ἕν, συνεχές of B8.6. Owen in turn is
criticized by Tarán, p. 107. In my opinion his theory carries more (or more
immediate) conviction for συνεχές.

[12] For my reading of 8.4 see "The 'Eleatic One' in Melissus," *Mededelingen
Nederlandse Akad.*, n.r. 32 (1969), 221 n. 1; for 8.6, Olof Gigon *Der Ursprung
der griechischen Philosophie von Hesiod bis Parmenides* (Basel, 1945), p. 261
The strongest argument for a prominent place of "the One" may be found in
8.53 where the positing of two μορφαί is the first and cardinal error of human
δόξαι. Here Parmenides does turn—not actually against pluralism but against
dualism, a significant difference, as has been pointed out to me (see now
Mourelatos, p. 132). Moreover the motivation need not be a particularly
strong attachment of Parmenides himself to monism but that the two "forms"
and the allied doctrine of "opposites" (τἀντία) struck him as the pervasive
error of earlier doctrines—and I think we understand why, although Uvo
Hölscher would not agree (see his *Anfängliches Fragen* [Göttingen, 1968],
pp. 9 ff., 111, 168 and passim).

epideues, "not in need" (8.33), and some others—*hen* in 8.6 should probably be connected with the immediately following *syneches*, i.e. as referring to intrinsic unity (compactness, homogeneity) rather than uniqueness. If we have to distinguish between more and less important predicates, the former would presumably be those supported by special arguments, i.e. in addition to the pair already mentioned *ou diaireton*, "not divisible" (= *syneches*, 8.22–25) and *isopales*, "equally balanced" (8.44–49). Plato himself refers in a different context to the repudiation of the *mē eon*, "non-being," as Parmenides' characteristic doctrine, and again elsewhere the Eleatics as a group uphold the One which "stands in itself." [13] We cannot here follow up these variations but may now say that by identifying Parmenides' thesis as "the One *is*" Plato has got his position out of focus. If we cannot accept Plato's testimony on this point, we must simultaneously dismiss his assertion that Parmenides in his affirmation of the "One" and Zeno in his refutation of the "many" are "saying the same" (128a6, b5).[14]

Yet perhaps Plato's testimony about Zeno's own treatise may still be salvaged from the shipwreck? For we do know three of his arguments against "the many" and it would be unreasonable to doubt that there were more. May Plato not have formed an entirely correct impression of Zeno's treatise and read the poem of Parmenides with Zeno's staunch hostility to pluralism in mind? Surely this is conceivable; yet as soon as we resort to such speculations, we find ourselves in the realm of possibilities and are no longer taking our stand, as students of Zeno have so far been convinced they did, on a definite unimpeachable testimony.

There would indeed be reasons for Zeno's preoccupation with "the many." Empedocles and Anaxagoras, whose systems he may have known, transferred some characteristics of Parmenides' Being to a

---

[13] See *Soph.* 237a4 ff., yet also 242d5 f.; *Theaet.* 180d8 ff. In the *Sophist* we see how in an examination of Parmenides' Being its relation to the One and other concepts becomes a problem (I cannot digress into this subject but refer to Cornford, *Plato's Theory of Knowledge*, p. 218; Tarán, p. 273).

[14] A few more examples may illustrate Plato's lack of concern with "historicity." If we had to rely for Heraclitus on Plato, we would be satisfied with ὅτι πάντα χωρεῖ καὶ οὐδὲν μένει (*Crat.* 402a) and ὡς τὸ ὂν πολλά τε καὶ ἕν ἐστι (*Soph.* 242e) as his doctrines. And *Legg.* 10.887a ff. would lead us to think of the Pre-Socratics in general as thoroughgoing materialists for whom everything happens τύχῃ and mechanically, intelligence or gods contributing nothing.

plurality of six or even infinite entities. To do so meant to give up monism, and the issue "one (*hen*) or many (*polla*)?" may very well have been particularly acute even among those who accepted Parmenides' canon (no becoming; no non-being) and other phases of his doctrine as well. If we consult the fragments of Melissus, we find *hen* again as one of the attributes of Being but may watch it advance to a leading position among them—and finally even emerge as *to hen*, "the One."[15] Although for Parmenides himself the "one" had not been central, his poem *could* yet be read as giving it a central position; οὖλον, ἕν, συνεχές, "whole, one, cohesive," the disapproval of *morphai dyo*, "two forms," and perhaps still other details known or unknown to us could be understood in this sense. Also whether or not Plato actually had information about people who ridiculed Parmenides' philosophy, it is intrinsically probable that "common sense" was most provoked by the idea of a monolithic Being which allowed no reality for the innumerable objects of human experience.[16] Yet even if Zeno defended the phases of Parmenides' philosophy that were under attack—or indeed defended Parmenides as he was understood at his time—it still is not true that he "said the same" as Parmenides, or that Parmenides' own thesis was the reality of the "One." Plato's testimony about their identical positions would need considerable qualifications to become acceptable. Some recent interpreters of the Eleatics seem prepared to make such qualifications but others do not, and what matters most for us, Plato himself does not make them.

We have tried to offer as good a case as we could for Zeno's opposition to "the many." Yet how far are we to go? Must really all of his arguments have been aimed at their refutation? Present-day students of Zeno are not quite unanimous; usually his arguments against motion and perhaps even one against space are set off from those directly aimed at plurality, while plurality yet remains the ultimate target for all.[17] We have already noticed to what extent Socrates relies on interpretation, and may still add the observation that he moves very fast, in fact by one big step, from one argument designed to disprove

[15] For details see my recent study cited above (note 12), pp. 221 ff., but with the modifications now made necessary by Mourelatos, pp. 132 f.

[16] It is probably no longer necessary to discuss the once popular opinion that the people in question were Pythagoreans holding a doctrine of number atomism. [See above, Cornford, pp. 155–60; contrast above, Furley, pp. 353–67.—Ed.]

[17] Raven's chapter on Zeno in KR, pp. 286 ff., may be taken as representative. For a very strict and stern view see Calogero, *Studi*, pp. 91 ff.

"the many" to "each of the arguments" in Zeno's treatise as having the same purpose (127e7–128a1). Other passages in Plato's dialogues where we find the gist of an earlier system "summed up" may warn us how treacherous such blanket statements are apt to be.[18] Must we really exert ourselves to interpret "A moving thing moves neither in the place in which it is nor in the place in which it is not" [19] as an argument against "the many"?

Instead of continuing to argue in terms of general probability, it is well to remember Plato's own strong and persistent interest in the problem of the "one and the many." From the *Euthyphro* or *Meno* to the *Laws* the relation between them remains for him a major philosophical problem; in a late dialogue it has earned the right to be called τῶν λόγων αὐτῶν ἀθάνατον καὶ ἀγήρων πάθος ἐν ἡμῖν (*Phil.* 15d7).[20] We need not dwell on these familiar matters, but should emphasize the importance of this perennial problem for the latter sections of the *Parmenides*. For whatever the philosophical purpose of the "hypotheses" concerning "the One and the many (or 'the other things,' *ta alla*)," [21] whose shifting mutual relations we follow with bewilderment in those sections, Plato must, when writing the first part of the *Parmenides*, have known how he would continue. We cannot imagine him as just drifting along without plan. Nor can we, accepting the conversation at its face value, naïvely suppose that Plato decided to investigate the relations between "the One" and "the many" because he found the former concept defended by Parmenides and the latter attacked by Zeno. For this

[18] See esp. the items of historical information in *Soph.* 242d f. For Empedocles the summary τότε μὲν ἓν εἶναι τὸ πᾶν καὶ φίλον ὑπ᾽ Ἀφροδίτης (e5) is in itself correct enough; yet who with this statement in mind would not be reluctant to believe that Aphrodite creates ἔθνεα μυρία θνητῶν (B35.16) or perfect and imperfect mixtures, like blood and flesh, bone, etc., if we found such matters reported in a late author and did not have Empedocles' own words in B96, 98?

[19] In the opinion of Gregory Vlastos (*Phronesis*, 11 [1966], 3 ff.) this proposition figured, roughly speaking, as a premise for the arrow paradox. He may indeed be right; if so, my question would apply to his entire reconstruction of the argument for this paradox.

[20] Cf. 14c–17a, and see further *inter alia* Euth. 6c ff., *Meno* 77a, *Rep.* 525d f., *Phaedr.* 249, 265c, *Theaet.* 179d ff. (183e ff.), *Legg.* 12.965b–966a.

[21] Plato for reasons on which it is easy to speculate found it advantageous to oppose most of the time τὰ ἄλλα rather than τὰ πολλά to τὸ ἕν, but the change—or rather, alternation—has no real significance (see e.g. 131e3–133a4, 136a4 ff., 137c4 f.).

theory (besides putting things on their head) is predicated on the wrong view of Parmenides' thesis and ignores Plato's own persistent concern with these relations. What fascinated Plato in Zeno and what the dialogue owes to him is obvious.[22] It is the method of pursuing a *hypothesis* into its consequences. Beyond this, we may readily admit that the *hypotheseis* dealing with "the many" attracted Plato particularly because "One" versus "many" were the one-sided positions whose limitations he meant to expose (just as in other dialogues of this period he shows "being" and "non-being," "motion" and "rest" to be inadequate or in need of one another).

Having built up his realm of true Being with the help of the Eleatic *eon*,[23] Plato would naturally turn to this "school" also for clarification of his own One or of the "One–many" relationship. Historically speaking, his debt to the Eleatic *eon* is larger, and not only because, as we have seen, his concern with "the One and the many" antedates his turn to the Eleatics and originated independently; also despite the immense strides that Plato made beyond Parmenides' ontology—by setting off the world of true Being from that of flux, by clarifying and developing the opposition between intelligibles and sensibles, truth and seeming, being and becoming—his discussion with the Eleatics continues to bear fruit while he examines "being and non-being." If he derived a comparable gain for his One, we are not aware of it.[24] Still if we were correct in

[22] Cherniss' brilliant paper "Parmenides and the *Parmenides* of Plato," *AJP*, 53 (1932), 122 ff., is to my mind the most convincing explanation of the ὑποθέσεις in the *Parmenides* and of their purpose. It also throws much light on Plato's attitude to Zeno.

[23] See my paper "Parmenides and the Description of Perfect Beauty in Plato's *Symposium*," *AJP*, 92 (1971), 62 ff.

[24] Of the Platonic triad ἀγαθόν, ὄν, and ἕν the first is wholly his own—unless we prefer to regard it as a legacy of the Socratic search—the second significantly indebted to the Eleatics, and the third, it would seem to me, only in its later stages related to aspects of Eleatic thought. Plato's original pre-occupation with the ἀγαθόν and moral values in general has left its imprint on his theory of the ἕν, perhaps also of the ὄν, or rather of the true ὄντα, the Forms whose quality of perfection has an axiological nuance different from Parmenides' τετελεσμένον (B8.42). See Plato himself, *Rep.* 509b. Even for τὸ ἀγαθόν as ἐπέκεινα τῆς οὐσίας (ibid.) the different provenience of the two concepts should be borne in mind, although it does not suffice to explain the meaning of this thought. See also H. J. Krämer, *Arete bei Plato und Aristoteles* (Heidelberg, 1959) pp. 143, 507 ff., 523 ff.

supposing that with the "second generation" Eleatics the alternative "One or many" had become an acute issue, we can easily understand Plato's wish to make contact with that stage of Eleatic thought.[25]

Bearing all of this in mind, we need not make great intellectual efforts to relate Zeno's paradoxes of movement and place to the refutation of "the many." That with the necessary ingenuity this may be done I should not deny—in fact it has been done; yet the prior question is whether ingenuity is well employed in such efforts (moreover, without entering upon details, I have an uneasy feeling that there is usually some recourse to anachronistically modern conceptions).

Still, even if the presentation of Parmenides as champion of the One is historically incorrect, if the "saying the same" (see above, p. 373) does not stand up under scrutiny, and if "the many" as target of Zeno's arguments throughout his treatise are open to serious doubt, may Plato not intuitively have arrived at the correct judgment of Zeno's over-all purpose? Once more the possibility must be admitted. How attractive it appears will be a matter of subjective reaction. It seems no more than fair to consider that in the *Parmenides* the statement of Zeno's purpose is closely linked to the problematic descriptions of his and Parmenides' philosophical positions, that Plato himself in the *Phaedrus* gives us a very different impression of Zeno's work,[26] and that one quality which almost certainly characterized this work—and which probably accounts for the divergent opinions about Zeno's intention— is a puzzling, tantalizing effect upon the reader, something elusive, as the *Parmenides* suggests ("something beyond us," in the words of Socrates, 128b5 f.). Of the difference between Plato's attitude to earlier thinkers and of someone imbued with the modern interest in history *per se* we have probably said enough, but it may be permissible to stress once more the advantage of establishing harmony between Parmenides and Zeno in a dialogue whose larger part was to combine the authority of the former with the methods of the latter. If we give due weight to

[25] For the "second generation" Eleatics see above, p. 373. We should perhaps make more effort than has been customary to compare and contrast the changing relation of ὄν and ἕν in Eleatic thought and a similar development in the Platonic Academy. To what extent Plato himself—especially the "esoteric" Plato—participated in this development is vigorously debated today. We do not go into the problem but have noted Plato's probing of the conceptual relation between ὄν and ἕν in the *Sophist* (above, n. 13).

[26] On *Phaedr*. 261d more will be said later (pp. 389 f., 392 f.).

these considerations, we shall hesitate to treat Plato's testimony in *Parm.* 127e–128e as the firm and solid basis on which all more specific interpretations of Zeno must rest.

What, then, was the actual relation between Zeno's thought and Parmenides? Several answers may be given but before we formulate them, some additional evidence must be analyzed.

For, it may be asked, is the testimony of the *Parmenides* not confirmed by other phases of the tradition about Zeno? There are reasons for taking this view, and we must examine whether they are as good as they look. Aristotle's treatises offer nothing pertinent,[27] nor does any other extant author prior to the fifth century A.D. provide a verbatim quotation. Proclus in his commentary on the *Parmenides* knows the number of Zeno's arguments to have been forty, whereas Elias puts the total figure at forty-five, asserting that all of them were designed to support the doctrine of Parmenides, forty by proving "that Being is one," the other five "that Being is immobile."[28] These testimonies hardly deserve more attention than they have received. We may immediately pass on to Simplicius whose commentary on Aristotle's *Physics* is by all odds our most important source of information for Zeno. Whether Simplicius had the entire treatise of Zeno at his disposal is a question on which I have nothing new to say.[28] Still besides presenting passages from it in the original wording, he also professes to know the content of the treatise and the intention in which it was written. This knowledge enables him more than once to pronounce on controversial issues. His comments on *Phys.* I.3.187a1 include his fullest statement on the general tenor of Zeno's work; therefore Diels many years after he had edited that part of Simplicius' commentary incorporated this statement among the "testimonia" in his *Fragmente der*

[27] See below, p. 382 on Zeno's ἀξίωμα in *Metaph.* III.4.

[28] Cf. DK 29A15.

[29] There is probably still more than a grain of truth in Wilamowitz' memorable words about Simplicius as the "brave Mann" who "in zwölfter Stunde . . . diese Bücher (scil. of Parmenides, Empedocles, Eudemus, etc.) aufschlug" which "seit Jahrhunderten ungelesen, immer noch in der Schulbibliothek lagen" and who saved the priceless fragments (*Die griechische Literatur des Altertums* in *Die Kultur der Gegenwart*, ed. P. Hinneberg, I 8, 3rd ed., 1911 and 1924, p. 283). Yet we can no longer consider 529 as the year in which the Academy was closed (see Alan Cameron's brilliant paper in *Proceedings of the Cambridge Philological Society*, N.S. 15 [1969], 7 ff.).

Vorsokratiker.[30] What Simplicius here says agrees with the *Parmenides*. It might seem to confirm Plato's testimony and clinch the case—if the agreement were not so complete that it is bound to engender suspicion. We place this passage of Simplicius as presented by Diels in the *Vorsokratiker* and *Parm.* 128c6–d6 side by side:

Zeno in Plato: ἔστι δὲ τό γε ἀληθὲς βοήθειά τις ταῦτα τὰ γράμματα τῷ Παρμενίδου λόγῳ πρὸς τοὺς ἐπιχειροῦντας αὐτὸν κωμῳδεῖν ὡς εἰ ἓν ἔστι, πολλὰ καὶ γελοῖα συμβαίνει πάσχειν τῷ λόγῳ καὶ ἐναντία αὐτῷ. ἀντιλέγει οὖν τοῦτο τὸ γράμμα πρὸς τοὺς τὰ πολλὰ λέγοντας καὶ ἀνταποδίδωσι ταὐτὰ καὶ πλείω, τοῦτο βουλόμενον δηλοῦν ὡς ἔτι γελοιότερα πάσχοι ἂν αὐτῶν ἡ ὑπόθεσις . . . .

[In truth, this treatise is a sort of support lent to Parmenides' argument against those who try to make fun of it in this way, that if the One is, the argument incurs many and ridiculous consequences, indeed some that are contradictories of it. So this trea-

Simpl. *In Phys.* 134.2 f.: (according to Aristotle some yield to Parmenides and) τῷ τοῦ Ζήνωνος (λόγῳ),[31] ὃς βοηθεῖν βουλόμενος τῷ Παρμενίδου λόγῳ πρὸς τοὺς ἐπιχειροῦντας αὐτὸν κωμῳδεῖν ὡς εἰ ἓν ἔστι, πολλὰ καὶ γελοῖα συμβαίνει λέγειν[32] τῷ λόγῳ καὶ ἐναντία αὐτῷ, δεικνὺς ὁ Ζήνων[33] ὡς ἔτι πάσχοι γελοιότερα ἂν αὐτῶν ἡ ὑπόθεσις . . . . (DK 29A23) [. . . to Zeno's argument, which, intending to lend support to Parmenides' argument against those who try to make fun of it in this way, that if the One is, the argument incurs the assertion of many and ridiculous consequences, indeed some that are contradictories of it, Zeno showing that their own

[30] DK 29A23 = Simpl. *In Phys.* 134.2–8.

[31] The meaning and context in Aristotle are barely relevant for us. Briefly, some thinkers posit a μὴ ὄν to save plurality and at the same time counter Zeno's demonstration of infinite divisibility by setting up "indivisibles." Simplicius believes Aristotle to have Xenocrates in mind; the modern interpreters recognize the position described as that of the atomists; see e.g. Cherniss, *Aristotle's Criticism of Presocratic Philosophy* (Baltimore, 1935), p. 75 n. 203; W. D. Ross, *Aristotle's Physics* (Oxford, 1936), p. 480 f.; David Furley, *Two Studies in the Greek Atomists* (Princeton, 1967), pp. 81 f. [repr. below, pp. 506 f.].

[32] πάσχειν Herm. Schöne (as reported by Diels). Whether or not he remembered the *Parmenides*, his suggestion acquires strong support from it.

[33] ὁ Ζήνων is syntactically offensive because ever since ὃς βοηθεῖν βουλόμενος the grammatical subject has been Zeno. We may yet leave the words in the text, hoping that it was Simplicius himself, not an interpolator, who put them there in the interest of clarity.

tise argues back against those who   hypothesis even incurs more ridic-
assert the many, and pays them   ulous . . . .]
back in full and then some, in-
tending to show this, that their
own hypothesis incurs even more
ridiculous . . . .]

(A few more clauses show the same relation between the texts.)

The agreement is so close that there can be only one opinion about
the relationship of the two passages, and we would form this opinion
even if Simplicius' own words did not guide us to it. For after the
passage which Diels included in the *Vorsokratiker* Simplicius continues:
"In Plato's *Parmenides* Zeno himself, through his speech, clearly
attests these things." [34] The Zeno of the Platonic *Parmenides* and the
historical Zeno were for Simplicius identical. Diels' failure to include
in A23 the sentence in which Simplicius names his source was a regrettable mistake. It is regrettable too that, as far as I can see, the omission
has not been pointed out by other scholars. [35] For it is most important
to know whence Simplicius derived his conviction about the content
and the objective of Zeno's treatise—and all the more important if this
source, for him an authority whose truth he would never question, has
now become a dubious historical testimony. For it is to Simplicius that
we owe almost all our verbatim quotations from Zeno's treatise. If we
know with what conviction—or to put it less politely, with what bias
and preconceived opinion—he approached Zeno, it becomes imperative
to examine whether this prejudice is reflected in the selection, the
presentation, the paraphrases, and the interpretation of the passages he
quotes. In fact the quotations themselves call for a close study, since
Simplicius may shorten or rearrange them.

We need not read much farther in Simplicius' commentary to realize
how determined he is to uphold the combined authority of "the divine
Plato" and "Zeno himself." While still dealing with the same passage

[34] The last two words probably mean: "(bearing witness) to the account."
—The next sentence in which Simplicius begins to explain Parmenides' λόγος
needs improvement: καὶ ὁ μὲν τοῦ Παρμενίδου λόγος ἐστὶν ὅτι πάντα ἓν [τὸ ὂν]
ἔστιν, εἴπερ τὸ ὂν ἓν σημαίνει. To Zeno Simplicius does not return before 138.3,
on which see below pp. 381 f.

[35] Even the fact that Simplicius in the previous sentences copies the *Parmenides* has been noticed only by Mario Untersteiner, *Zenone: Testimonianze
e frammenti* (Florence, 1963), p. 108. On Lee see below, n. 68.

of Aristotle's *Physics* (187a1), he reports: "Alexander says that the argument from dichotomy is Zeno's, who argued that if the One had magnitude and might be divided, Being would then be many and no longer one, Zeno thereby showing that the One is not among the being-things (ὅτι μηδὲν τῶν ὄντων ἐστὶ τὸ ἕν)" (138.3 ff.).

To judge from the last words, Alexander of Aphrodisias credited Zeno with intentions quite different from those which Simplicius knew from the *Parmenides*. He therefore protests: "It deserves consideration, to begin with, whether this saying, that 'the One is not among the being-things,' is authentically Zeno's, a man who, on the contrary, composed many an argument confuting the claim that 'many are' so that . . . the thesis that 'All things are One' would be confirmed, which is also what Parmenides intended" (138.18 ff.). We know the reason why Simplicius rebels against Alexander's opinion, just as we know how his certainty that Zeno wrote in support of Parmenides had originated.[36]

Yet Alexander is not alone in holding heretical opinions about Zeno's arguments. At 138.29 Simplicius suggests that Alexander owes his views about Zeno's "confuting" (*anairein*) of the "One" to Eudemus: "For here is what Eudemus in his *Physics*[37] says [after recognizing the problem whether there is a 'One']: 'They say that Zeno, too, asserted that if one could explain to him what the One is, he would be in a position to speak of the being-things. His puzzlement arose, it seems, from the fact that sensible things are each said to be many both in terms of the categories (*katēgorikōs*) and by division (*merismōi*). The (mathematical) point he regarded as nothing at all. For that which does not produce an increase when added nor a decrease when removed he did not consider as among the being-things.'" The last three sentences may need a few words of explanation, especially since LSJ does not provide the appropriate meaning of *katēgorikos*.[38] What Eudemus has in mind

---

[36] Simplicius' next point is that the passage in the *Physics* on which he is commenting would lose its meaning if Zeno wrote to prove the existence of "the many" and to disprove "the One." His reasoning would not permit conclusions about Zeno's treatise, even if his understanding of the *Physics* were still valid (see however above, n. 31).

[37] For Eudemus cf. Fritz Wehrli, *Die Schule des Aristoteles*, Heft 8, Fr. 37a with commentary.

[38] Lee's rendering: "called many categorically" (p. 15) makes no sense; yet his own fr. 8 (19.3 ff.) and the fuller version of Eudemus' comments in Simplicius 97.11–29 (see Wehrli loc. cit.) puts the connection of the adjective with Aristotle's categories beyond doubt. That Zeno did not think in terms

is that each sense-perceived object is "many" "in accordance with the categories." The same individual might be a human being (substance), fat or bald (quality), six feet tall (quantity), etc. With the next reason, divisibility, we are close to the historical Zeno. In the last of the three reasons the reference to the point need not detain us, since it goes back to a passage in Aristotle's *Metaphysics*[39] where it is an "interpretation" of Zeno's argument. But of this argument itself ("For that which . . . Being-Things," 139.2), for which Eudemus relies on Aristotle, Simplicius knows the original wording, and, as he cannot deny its authenticity, it causes him considerable embarrassment. For if it is really, as Eudemus maintains, directed against "the One" and puts "the One" out of existence, what becomes of Zeno's firm determination to write in support of Parmenides' "One"—or more precisely, what becomes of Simplicius' firm conviction that this was the objective of his treatise?

Finding himself put on the defensive, he begins a very involved manipulation, which has been called "confused" by one of his foremost students and "clumsy" by another,[40] and if Zeno was not himself confused, he certainly confuses the reader (I must ask mine for patience until I may clarify matters). First Simplicius makes a concession: "We should have expected it of Zeno to be proceeding in his argumentation as if to defend alternate sides, in the manner of an exercise (*gymnastikōs*) . . . and to be bringing forward arguments like these about the One in a stance of philosophical perplexity (*aporounta*)" (139.3–5). Soon however he turns to the attack and remembering the *Parmenides*, continues: "But in his book, which contains many arguments (*epicheirē-mata*),[41] he shows in detail that the man who asserts the many incurs the assertion of consequences contradictory of his thesis" (ibid., 5–7). Next he refers (without actually quoting the text) to one such *epi-*

---

of Aristotle's categories is obvious; cf. Paul Tannery, *Pour l'Histoire de la science hellène*, 2nd ed. (Paris, 1930), p. 261. Lee, instead of making this simple point, speculates about "fifth-century eristics" (p. 28).

[39] *Metaph.* III.4.1001b7–13 (part of DK 29A21; Lee fr. 4, p. 14). Cf. U. Schoebe, *Quaestiones Eudemeae* (Diss., Halle, 1931), p. 56. For Aristotle's own conception of στιγμή, which influences his interpretation of Zeno, see *Metaph.* V.6.1016b23 ff. (cf. Furley, pp. 47 f.).

[40] "Confusion," Fränkel, p. 17 ("verworren" . . . "Unklarheit," p. 214 n. 1); "clumsiness," Vlastos, Rev. Fränkel, p. 198 n. 1.

[41] Cf. Plato *Parm.* 127e11 (Simplicius uses ἐπιχείρημα instead of Plato's τεκμήριον, which would no longer be the right word). The γυμνασία motif also goes back to the *Parmenides* (135d–136a).

cheirēma which proves "the many" to be large as to be infinite in size and small as to be of no size.[42] It is in the course of this proof, he informs us, that the argument reported by Eudemus and used for such unwelcome purpose occurs. He next presents this argument as a whole, beginning with the conclusion, but first in his own words: "That which has no size, nor thickness (*pachos*), nor bulk (*onkos*) could not even *be*" (139.10). Now Zeno himself is allowed to speak: "For if it were to be added to another being-thing, he says, it would make it no larger; for since it is no size at all its addition cannot possibly contribute toward size. Accordingly, the thing being added turns out to be nothing. Moreover, if when one thing is subtracted the other turns out to be no smaller, just as it fails to increase when something is added, it is clear that what was added or what was subtracted were both nothing" (ibid., 11–15 = DK 29B2).

The full text of this painful argument having been presented, Simplicius once more feels the need of dispelling misunderstandings about Zeno's purpose. Zeno, he affirms, is not here doing away with the One (οὐχὶ τὸ ἓν ἀναιρῶν)[43] but says what we read "because (*hoti*) each of the many and infinite has size"[44] as a result of the infinite divisibility. This is a surprise, because in the light of his previous remark—and in view of his commitment to the testimony in the *Parmenides*—we should not expect Simplicius to accept any proposition about "the many" as Zeno's true opinion, but to treat it as one of two *enantia*, "opposites," attaching to "the many." However there follows in Simplicius a sentence which, though again somewhat puzzling, may be intended to set things right: "He proves this ('this' presumably = the size of the many and infinite) having previously proved that nothing has size because each of the many is identical with itself and one" (139.18 f.). "No size" would be the opposite of "size." Thus we should have the obligatory "opposites"

---

[42] 139.7–9; cf. DK 29B1 (to be discussed below, pp. 384 ff.).

[43] 139.16. I trust my report makes clear why this remark is in place. As we have seen, Alexander and Eudemus have credited Zeno with the intention of "confuting the One," and all that Simplicius here paraphrases, quotes, and explains is put forward with the idea of refuting them. Fränkel, p. 17 n. 42 (214 n. 1), sees "no connection" of the sentence with "what precedes or . . . follows"; we know his complaint about "confusion" and sympathize with it.

[44] μέγεθος ἔχει ἕκαστον τῶν πολλῶν καὶ ἀπείρων, ibid., 139.16 f. Fränkel's conjecture ἄπειρον has its attraction. However I reckon with no more than moderate accuracy in Simplicius' report, and have found it possible to make sense of his reasoning without the conjecture.

for "the many." Whether this actually is the function of the sentence in Zeno's context will be considered presently when we study his argument as a whole. One effect which the sentence certainly has is to leave the reader even more perplexed than he was beforehand. Still, Simplicius seems to have established to his own satisfaction that Zeno did not attack "the One." He has upheld the truth as enunciated by his authorities, even if in the process he has made a shambles of Zeno's reasoning. Someone having a clear case and straightforward arguments to support it would hardly proceed in so tortuous a fashion.

Fortunately, Simplicius quotes a good part of Zeno's argument again shortly afterwards (141.1 ff.), where, although he again has to prove a point, he does so without contortions of the kind we have just endured. Modern scholarship[45] has succeeded in reconstructing Zeno's argument and restoring, if not the complete text, yet the largest part of it. It will be necessary to look closely at what has thus been recovered, because we have by now reason for wondering how Zeno actually treated the "One" and "the many." How could the "One" have a key position in a proof that "nothing had size," and that what has no size is nothing? Here it would be most desirable to know Zeno's own words: yet the best we can offer is a tentative approximation. I agree except for minor items with the reconstructions of Fränkel and Furley (whom I follow in marking the steps of the argument as a, b, c, d):

(a) (What was obviously more than one step is reported by Simplicius thus) "That nothing has size (is shown[46] from the fact that) each of the many is the same as itself and one." This must be resolved into two propositions which as soon as they are formulated suggest that something is missing between them: a1) "Each of the many is the same as itself and one"; a2) "None of them has size" (139.18–19).[47]

(b) (Beginning again with Simplicius' words, "That which has no size, nor thickness, nor any bulk), if it were to be added to another being-thing, it would make it no larger; for since it is no size at all its addition cannot possibly contribute toward size. Accordingly, the thing

---

[45] I am particularly indebted to Fränkel, pp. 15 ff. (211 ff.), whose construction has been adopted by others. He gives credit to the achievements of Eduard Zeller, *Die Philosophie der Griechen* (citing the 6th ed. revised by W. Nestle [Leipzig, 1919], I. Teil, I. Hälfte, p. 752). See also Furley, p. 64 [repr. above, p. 354] and Calogero, *Studi*, p. 98 ff.

[46] Cf. προδείξας in 139.18 f., quoted above, p. 383.

[47] Fränkel paraphrases ἕκαστον τῶν πολλῶν by "the single units of which the One is composed," but to do so prejudges important questions.

being added turns out to be nothing. (lacuna?)[48] Moreover, if when one thing is subtracted the other turns out to be no smaller, just as it fails to increase when something is added, it is clear that what was added or what was subtracted were both nothing" (139.11–15). "(Hence) if Being should have no size, it would not be" (141.1 f.).

(c) "If it *is*, each must necessarily have some size and thickness; and one part of it must be distinct from another part. And the same holds for the outstanding part; it too will have size and part of it will stand out. Indeed to say this once is to say it always, since no such part of it will be last nor will it be related as one part to another part" (141.1–6).[49]

(d) "So if the many *are*, it is necessary that they should be both large and small—so small as not to have size, and so large as to be infinite" (141.6–8).

Although this reconstruction has some problematic aspects, we must ignore them if they have no bearing on our question. Does Zeno in the course of this reasoning discredit "the One" as well as "the many" and are both objectives of equal concern to him? Or is everything that he says (or appears to say) against the "One"—or "one"; this may now be left open—merely a stepping stone on the way to his true and only objective, the refutation of "the many"?

We may have to take the latter view if in the conclusion as formulated in (d) the words "so small as not to have size" rest on (a) rather than on (c). For if this is the case, the entire sequence (a)–(d) would deal with

---

[48] It would be strange if εἰ δὲ ἀπογενομένου κτλ. was not prepared at all, while the parallel thought μηδ' αὖ προσγενομένου . . . is so elaborately prepared. Cf. Zeller, vol. I, 5th ed. (Leipzig, 1892), p. 591 n. 2. How symmetrically the parallel arguments were worked out is of course not possible to say. Alternatively the argument for ἀπογίγνεσθαι may have come first, in which case Simplicius would only quote the second part of two parallel thoughts. Once more his report seems incomplete, and with all due respect for his integrity I do not exclude the possibility that what he omits would have created difficulties for his thesis. See below, pp. 387 ff.

[49] I do not discuss the content of this difficult piece whose understanding hinges largely on the meaning of τὸ προέχον. Our choice lies between the brilliant interpretation of Fränkel, pp. 193 ff. (233), who assumes progressively thinner outer layers of an object, and the simpler explanation given by Vlastos, Rev. Fränkel, p. 196, and illustrated by the diagram in his contribution on Zeno in W. Kaufmann's *Philosophic Classics: Thales to St. Thomas* (New York, 1961), p. 31. An infinite progress of the division materializes on either view, and on either ἄπειρα remains a problem.

"the many" and would prove "opposites" about them, namely (a) and
(b) that they are small and in the end nothing, (c) that they are large
and finally infinite, while (d) would pull these "opposites" together.

This opinion has been championed by Calogero, Fränkel, Vlastos,
Booth, and Furley,[50] a formidable array of authorities, in whose consensus it might be wise to acquiesce. Still, since the testimony of the
Parmenides does not have the same authority for us as it has for them
—and has for Simplicius—a new examination may have some excuse.

The champions of the theory now favored adduce, as far as I can see,
one principal reason against considering "so small as not to have size"
in (d) as based on (c), and one reason for considering these words as
based on (a). The "negative" reason stresses what Vlastos calls the
"logical gaffe" committed by Zeno if he went from (c) to (d). For if
the parts emerging successively in the process of the division become
smaller and smaller but no "last part" is ever reached, it clearly is illicit
to make the step from the constantly decreasing magnitudes to a nil
magnitude. This gaffe cannot be gainsaid; if Zeno proceeded from (c)
to both conclusions of (d), he is guilty of a serious logical error and
cannot be exonerated.

The reason supporting the connection of "so small as not to have
size" with (a) has far less force; for it rests on a dubious premise and is
open to various objections. Offhand "Nothing has size" (οὐδὲν ἔχει
μέγεθος), the last words of (a), would indeed seem to furnish the "not
to have size" (μὴ ἔχειν μέγεθος) of (d). The similarity in the language
might have the weight which scholars attach to it if we read (a) in Zeno's
own words. But we read it in Simplicius', and this faithful Platonist is
most anxious to make all arguments of Zeno prove that "the man who
asserts the many incurs the assertion of consequences contradictory of
his thesis" (139.6 f.). It would suit this purpose if the infinite division of
(c) proves only the presence of "size," whereas "no size" was proved in
the earliest part of the argument, scil. in (a). For if this were the case,
"contradictory consequences" about "the many" would not be confined

[50] Calogero, *Studi*, p. 98 ff.; Fränkel, pp. 23 (214) ff., esp. pp. 199 (228)
ff.; Vlastos (Rev. Fränkel), pp. 197 f.; Furley, p. 65 [repr. above, p. 355];
Booth, *JHS*, 77 (1957), 200. The alternative opinion, scil. that both parts
of (d) result from (c), was the obvious one to take as long as the entire argument from (a) to (d) had not yet been reconstructed. See esp. Tannery, p.
263; T. L. Heath, *A History of Greek Mathematics* (Oxford, 1921) vol. I,
p. 275.

to (c) and (d) but would materialize in the development of the entire argument.[51] Actually "Nothing has size" in (a) is not truly the same as "not to have size" in the conclusion.[52] . . .

Finally,[a] to return once more to the logic, anyone who tries to rescue Zeno from the mistake of passing illegitimately from "very small" to "nothing," runs the risk of saddling him with another. For if we must guess how he proved in (a) that nothing has size, we may wonder whether he relied on the indivisibility of the "One" or on its being unextended; yet he can hardly have used the proposition that "the One" is "small." [53] Actually, if Zeno—as seems to be agreed—having in (c) proved infinite divisibility and in some sense largeness, illogically and illegitimately moved from this position to infinite size in (d),[54] why should he not at the same time move illogically and illegitimately from small and ever smaller to "no size"?[55] The symmetry between the two mistakes has something to recommend itself; there is a certain—I am tempted to say "logical"—consistency in these parallel illogicalities.

[51] This may well be the impression with which the reader is left at 139.19 (unless he is too bewildered to have any impression at all). Vlastos, Rev. Fränkel, p. 198, interprets Simplicius correctly, i.e. as he presumably wished to be understood. Since Simplicius never quotes the text of (a) and what he tells us about it is incomplete (see above p. 384), there is room for suspicion.

[52] Fränkel, p. 17 n. 46 (214 n. 5), tries to correct this incongruity by changing (a) to οὐδὲν ἔχει μέγεθος τῶν πολλῶν ἐκ τοῦ ἕκαστον κτλ. and Furley, p. 64 [repr. above, p. 354], although not accepting Fränkel's text, accepts its meaning. Simplicius would have been pleased to find this wording in his copy of Zeno.

[a] [Two paragraphs of close philological examination of Simplicius' text, including footnotes numbered 53–56 in the original version, are omitted here. —Ed.]

[53] Cf. Fränkel, p. 200 (230). Vlastos, to give us an idea how Zeno may have arrived at "no size" in (a), makes use of Melissus B9 (in Kaufmann, p. 291). Except for feeling unsure about πάχος in Zeno before (c), I think he is on the right path.

[54] See the informative discussion of this problem in Furley, pp. 68 f. [repr. above, pp. 358 f.].

[55] If Zeno is the author of the argument reported by Aristotle De Gen. et Corr. I.2.316a14–b34, and more briefly by Simplicius In Phys. 139.24–140.6, he could envisage "infinite division" as ending in "points" or even "nothing." Zeno's authorship has recently been championed by Vlastos in The Encyclopedia of Philosophy, p. 371. Welcome as this would be, I adhere to my principle of relying only on verbatim quotations.

Stylistically, and in the structure of the argument, they are neatly balanced; in the first part of (d) Zeno is on safe grounds; after "and so large," he overstates his achievement in both directions.

Another disquieting aspect of the prevailing interpretation is that if (d) formulates the conclusion of the entire argument, the elaborate operations of (b) are completely ignored in it. Would Zeno be so careless about his brainchild?[56] In truth (b) is not gratuitous, as soon as we free ourselves from Plato's (and Simplicius') control. There was an ontological motif in the argument. "To be or not to be" became the issue in (b) and furnished the transition to (c).

It is impossible to exhaust the arguments that may be advanced for or against the one as well as the other interpretation. We have gone too deeply into details, which threaten to obscure the major considerations: whoever regards (a) as providing the basis for "no size" in (d) has delivered himself into the hands of Simplicius, and Simplicius, although doubtless a man of integrity and good will, could direct his good will toward a good purpose and adjust his integrity correspondingly. It would be in the highest degree surprising if he acquiesced in a view at variance with the testimony of the *Parmenides*, on which it is his habit to fall back.[57]

Moreover even if Zeno's entire argument, beginning in (a) and ending in (d), was directed against "the many," he clearly had no qualms about knocking out "the One" on the way. If Simplicius is correct in describing Zeno as "arguing on alternate sides, in the manner of an exercise" (139.3), the attack on "the many" would be *gymnasia*, "exercise," too, and if Simplicius for reasons by now well known to us does not take this view, we are yet free to form our own opinion. According to all reliable evidence, Zeno nowhere in his work tried to establish directly the reality of either "the One" or "the many." If he supported "the One," it was indirectly by showing the impossibility of positing "the many"; by now we may wonder whether he did not similarly in support of "the many" discredit "the One." Despite Simplicius' protests, it makes perfectly good sense if in our argument (a) and (b) have the function of "confuting the One," while (c) and (d) have the complementary of "confuting the many." Understood in this way, the

[56] Cf. Fränkel, pp. 24 f. (222, "übermütiges Spiel").

[57] *In Phys.* 99.7 ff., (102.28 ff.), 138.20 ff., 141.9 f. "It has often been said that the last pagan philosophers were just as dogmatic, just as dependent on authority as their Christian opponents, only . . . not the Bible but Plato, etc." (Cameron, p. 19).

entire argument would still be a case of eliciting "contraries" (τὰ ἐναντία)," but in an even more comprehensive manner, scil. by demolishing "the One," opening the way to "the many," and then demolishing these in turn.[58] Thus it would be a good illustration for what Plato says of Zeno in the *Phaedrus:* "speaking . . . so as to make the same things appear to his audience . . . one and many" (261d), and if we must be specific about the meaning of "the same things," the best candidate would in this instance be τὰ ὄντα, "the being-things." [59]

In the course of our study we have become acquainted with "testimonies" in which Zeno's purpose was understood as "demolishing the One." Still it would be unwise to play off statements of Eudemus and Alexander against the *Parmenides*; for neither of them gives the impression of first hand acquaintance with Zeno's text.[60] Nor should we linger over what Porphyry professes to know about actual proofs for the "One" in Zeno. Even Alcidamas' report, that "Zeno and Empedocles were students of Parmenides at the same time, then later . . . Zeno pursued philosophy independently (κατ' ἰδίαν φιλοσοφῆσαι)" (D.L. 8.56 = DK 31A1.56), may be discounted, although he bids fair to be our earliest witness. But even if we dismiss all that Alcidamas, Eudemus, and Alexander profess to know, including, hesitant though we may be, in this *massa perditionis* even Zeno's alleged remark, that "if one were to explain to him what the One is, etc.''—for it is after all introduced by a φασὶ λέγειν, "they say he argued" (Simpl. *In Phys.* 138.32), therefore "hearsay"—and if we also harden our heart against Plato's own testimony in the *Phaedrus*—perhaps on the ground that Plato refers to "impressions" (*phainesthai*) of the audience—there still remains the

[58] The refutation of the ἕν would, however, not take the form of proving ἐναντία for it; yet why should all of Zeno's arguments be cast in the same mold? A more serious point may be that in my interpretation εἰ πολλά ἐστιν in (d) may come as a surprise. The "many" would not be introduced but just emerge in (c).

[59] At 141.1 f. Simplicius "gives away" that Zeno's concern was with τὸ ὄν. See also n. 53. In τὰ αὐτὰ ὅμοια καὶ ἀνόμοια (*Phaedr.* 261d), τὰ αὐτά would be τὰ ὄντα regarded as πολλά (*Parm.* 127e). For the third illustration: μένοντα τ' αὖ καὶ φερόμενα, we may think of the arrow. Cf. also Isocr. 10.3: Ζήνωνα τὸν ταὐτὰ δυνατὰ καὶ πάλιν ἀδύνατα πειρώμενον ἀποφαίνειν.

[60] Lee's collection of testimonia especially under A (pp. 12 ff.) and B (14 ff.) includes arguments in Themistius and Philoponus purporting to be Zeno's; some refute the "many"; others actually argue for the "One." Since none of them show first hand acquaintance with Zeno's text, I do not think it safe to use them.

stumbling block of Zeno's own argument against the "One": Everything
that is identical with itself and one has no size . . . what has no size
. . . "would not even *be*." Surely if Zeno's listeners were nonplused by
his treatise, thought it "above themselves," and did not know what to
make of it, they are entitled to our sympathy. And perhaps those who
did not speculate about concealed ulterior objectives were wise.

Or were they just men of limited intelligence, failing to see what
would be obvious to any clear-headed person, scil. that there is a huge
difference between a "one" understood as a unit of "the many" (not
that we have any certainty about this), which may be added to or taken
away from another being-thing, and on the other side the sublime Parmenidean "One," a conception of an entirely different order, even if
there is little of this august "One" in Parmenides himself? Still he was
interpreted as the great champion of monism, of a "One" quite remote
from the small and insignificant "one" argued out of existence by Zeno
in a work designed to defeat the "many" and thereby to clear the
ground for the authentic Parmenidean "One." Again we come back to
the difficulty: how were the readers or, as we should rather with Plato
say, the hearers to realize the difference? Are contemporary students of
Zeno entitled to take this difference for granted and speak with complacent pity of the blundering, literal-minded Simplicius who "fails to
perceive that there are two senses of *to hen* in question and not only one.
There is *to hen* in the sense of the 'one being' of Parmenides, which
Zeno is certainly not attacking, and there is *to hen* in the sense of the
ultimate element from which plurality is made up, which is precisely
what Zeno is attacking." [61] Can we latter-day scholars really be so
"certain" about a distinction which, for all we can tell, escaped not only
Simplicius (although he had more of Zeno's text than we) but also
Eudemus and Alexander and perhaps some other post-Aristotelian
thinkers as well? In any case no ancient author ever points it out. And

[61] Lee, p. 26. Guthrie, p. 90, complains that Zeno "nowhere states the character of the unity in which he himself believes" (which is true and important,
but we after all do not have much of his text). Especially noteworthy is W. A.
Heidel, *AJP*, 61 (1940), 24 n. 51. Owen, *Proceedings of the Aristotelian Society*,
58 (1957), 199, takes a fundamental difference between Parmenides' "One"
and the "units" of plurality for granted. J. E. Raven in KR, p. 303, repeats
verbatim from *Pythagoreans and Eleatics* (Cambridge, 1948), p. 88, the astonishing assertion: "there is no mention in any of Zeno's actual fragments
of the Eleatic but only of the Pythagorean One," omitting only the word
"actual"; but actual or not, the fragments nowhere include a ἕν.

yet these men living in centuries when they had every reason to know about equivocity, enjoyed an advantage which was denied to Zeno's audience.[62] To make matters worse, absence of "size" is the reason why in (b) "Being" cannot "be"; and if it is to "be," "each" (scil. that *is*) must have "some size" as well as "thickness" according to (c); yet the presence or not of size and thickness in the Eleatic Being was in this generation an acute problem, even if when Zeno wrote his treatise Melissus had not yet come forward with his insistence on the former and rejection of the latter.[63] And yet we are asked to understand that it is not the Eleatic "One" which ceases to be if it has no size!

Whatever solution may be offered for all these troubles, it seems a poor method to ignore them and to hold on to the testimony of the *Parmenides*, as though it embodied gospel truth and evidence to the contrary were non-existent or easy to brush aside. If we are to interpret the fragments in Simplicius on the basis of that Platonic testimony, it would be fair to mention that for him what "Zeno himself says" in Plato is authentic and authoritative; yet as far as I am aware, no interpreter has seen fit to do so. There is no denying that Zeno moves within the orbit of Parmenidean concepts, arguing about Being, about limited and unlimited, about the divisible, and by implication about the continuum, about the "One" (of whatever description), against movement, against place, etc. If we miss topics like Non-Being, coming-to-be and passing-away, wholeness, differences of degree, relation of Being to thought, and other epistemological matters, the reason may lie in the inadequate material at our disposal or in circumstances unknown to us; in any case the absence of such topics need not influence our judgment. Since Zeno's hometown was Elea, it remains possible that he composed his treatise in the first place for a group of convinced Parmenideans or Eleatics, who realized that by making havoc of the ordinary world, especially by showing it to be full of inescapable contradictions, he was

[62] Vlastos in the *Encyclopedia*, p. 378, speaks of Zeno as "hampered by the poverty of his conceptual and semantic tools."

[63] See Melissus B3 and B9, and on the status of the question for him, Furley, p. 59. For Zeno too Furley has formulated the problem and asks (p. 66) why Zeno's arguments would not damage the Eleatic "One" as well. He bases his answer on $\pi\acute{\alpha}\chi o\varsigma$ as a "gratuitous addition" (comparing Mel. B9). But as Zeno's own words in (b) show, $\mu\acute{\epsilon}\gamma\epsilon\theta o\varsigma$ alone is crucial, and its absence fatal for the $\acute{\epsilon}\nu$, so that we have to ask again: why not for the Eleatic One also? Furley also relates the entire argument too exclusively to units resulting from a division and minimizes the ontological motif.

clearing the ground for a conception of an entirely different order
which remained untouched by the antimonies inherent in the realm of
human *doxai*, "opinions." As I emphasize, possibilities of the kind
must be admitted. Although Zeno would be the only thinker before the
founding of the Epicurean Garden who was content to put a powerful,
highly original mind at the service of another philosopher, a responsible
case would be welcome,[64] provided that possibilities are not presented
as the kind of certainties as which they have so long been treated. But
the "Plato must know what he says" type of argument would not be
good enough, even if we did not see with our own eyes how Plato
arrives at this alleged knowledge and if he did not "know" (*ismen*,
Phaedr. 261d6) something quite different elsewhere.[65]

What thesis other than the orthodox Eleatic could Zeno have tried
to defend by his curious, mutually contradictory, *hypotheseis*? Perhaps,
like Melissus, a modified version of the Eleatic theory. Some of our
observations might suggest an even more independent position, critical
alike of Parmenides' "One" and of the commonly accepted "many."
We should have the courage to admit this possibility. Still it is perhaps
best to remember our earlier remarks about the puzzling and tantalizing effect of his treatise. If Plato on one occasion puts him close to
Parmenides, as a defender of the "One," and on the other groups him
with rhetoricians like Gorgias as a man able to make contrary beliefs
plausible, we may wonder whether Socrates' questions in the *Parmen-*

[64] As a sample of the reasoning that could be advanced and as far as I
know pass unchallenged I quote from a book of deservedly high reputation.
Lee's first comment (p. 7) on Simpl. 134.2 ff. (see above, p. 379) is that "the
recurrence of the word κωμῳδεῖν makes it seem almost certain that Plato was
their source." How could it escape him that what recurs in Simplicius is far
more than this word, and that the immediately following sentence does make
certain what to him "seem(s) almost certain"? Next he remarks: "at any rate
it shows that they knew of no other tradition of the general tenor of Zeno's
work." Again one wonders how it could escape him that all quotations from
Zeno in Simplicius are intended to combat "other tradition(s) of the general
tenor of his work." Not surprisingly he concludes: "there seems to be no
reason for not accepting theirs and Plato's opinion."

[65] I have said nothing about *Parm.* 128b7–e4, where Zeno corrects Socrates
and tells the "true" (c6) story about the origin, intention, and publication of
his treatise. Scholars feel uneasy about the κλοπή motif (d7 f.). It is difficult
to imagine what Plato had in mind. Probably nothing very serious. Once more,
he was not a historian, and it is only for believers in historicity that the two
versions should be embarrassing.

ides do not prejudice the answer. To ask what Zeno "says" or "means" (*legeis*), what he "contends" (*diamachesthai*), for what he offers as many "proofs" as he has arguments, does suggest that Zeno was defending a doctrine. As we have seen, agreement between Parmenides and Zeno on a thesis suits Plato's purpose in that dialogue. Moreover we too are in the habit of associating a thinker with a position and we instinctively rebel against classing with Gorgias and Theodorus a man of so much greater acumen and originality. Nor do we actually need to go so far in that direction. Zeno, to judge from what we know, delights in intellectual experimentation, in the discovery and exploitation of new argumentative methods. Problems, dilemmas, paradoxes, equally defensible alternatives may have fascinated him more—and for their own sake—than a way out of the deadlock, a resolution, and positive "results." In the devising of new methods and argumentative techniques he remains a pioneer; here lies his main achievement. And a very great achievement it is, since it includes discoveries like the infinite divisibility, itself as infinite and inexhaustible in its implications as the ever smaller units which it produces. That for the application of his unique gift he found a fertile ground in the contemporary philosophical situation, or to be specific, in Parmenides' challenge to all earlier *doxai* would be natural even if Elea had not been his city, and even if critical reactions to Parmenides had not kept the issues alive.

He may well head the long line of those who professed themselves able to present two mutually contradictory *logoi* on every subject (even though we do not in every instance know his second answer, and he may indeed sometimes have thought one startling answer sufficient).

After twenty-four centuries and on the basis of our limited and on the whole one-sided information, it is precarious to be positive about his intention and motivation. And if the effect of this paper is to leave the reader wondering and baffled, perhaps even disturbed, it may be closer to Zeno's own intention than if it had finished with a positive, dogmatic theory about his "tenets."

VII

EMPEDOCLES

17

EMPEDOCLES' COSMIC CYCLE
IN THE 'SIXTIES

A. A. Long

In *The Presocratic Philosophers* (Cambridge, 1957) J. E. Raven wrote: "Empedocles, by his introduction of the cosmic cycle, has set himself a task which might well overtax even the most fertile imagination: he has imposed upon himself the necessity of describing a cosmogony and a world that are the exact reverse of the world we know and of the cosmogony that brought it into being. It cannot even be said that the cosmic cycle was unavoidable: it would surely have been a simpler undertaking to describe the emergence from the Sphere of a world in which the two motive forces, Love and Strife, instead of prevailing alternately, reached a stable equilibrium" (p. 348).

With these comments on Empedocles' theory of cosmogony and the evolution of life, Raven summed up an interpretation of Empedocles which was thoroughly orthodox at the time when he wrote.[1] Empedocles, it was held, posited a cyclical development of the universe consisting of four periods: (1) the rule of Love which unites all things in the form of a Sphere; (2) the progressive disruption of this unity by Strife; (3) the rule of Strife which separates all things; (4) the progressive reunification of all things by Love.[2] In stages 2 and 4, a world like

This article was written specially for this volume and has not been previously published.

[1] For a survey of interpretations of the cosmic cycle during the past hundred years, see D. O'Brien, *Empedocles' Cosmic Cycle: A Reconstruction from the Fragments and Secondary sources* (Cambridge, 1969), which includes an exhaustive annotated bibliography.

[2] In the next two pages I am drawing on remarks already expressed in my review of O'Brien in *JHS*, 90 (1970), 238–39. For further comments on traditional and recent interpretations, see Charles H. Kahn's review of Jean Bollack's *Empédocle*, vol. I (Paris, 1965), in *Gnomon*, 41 (1969), 442–44, and

ours arises; but the order of creation in 2, where the elements are being separated from a state of harmonious mixture, is the opposite of that in 4, where mixture and unity are being imposed on plurality.

The orthodoxy of this interpretation had the authority of Zeller, Burnet, and Bignone. In the mid-nineteenth century and later, some dissident voices were heard;[3] but they did not persuade most scholars to accept alternative explanations. During the last decade fundamental challenges have been sounded to the orthodox interpretation. What Raven (loc. cit.) calls "the necessity of describing a cosmogony and a world that are the exact reverse of the world we know" is held by some scholars to be a necessity imposed on the evidence, not required by it. The French scholar Jean Bollack, in a multivolume work on Empedocles, which is not yet complete (*Empédocle:* Vol. I, *Introduction à l' ancienne physique* [Paris, 1965]; Vols. II–III, *Les Origines* [Paris, 1969]), calls the difficulties raised by a double cosmogony and zoogony, and the conception of Empedocles' cosmic cycle from which they spring, "the false problem" (Vol. I, pp. 97 ff.). Bollack's first volume appeared in 1965, and in the same year Uvo Hölscher ("Weltzeiten und Lebens-zyklus," *Hermes*, 93 [1965], 7–33) and Friedrich Solmsen ("Love and Strife in Empedocles' Cosmology," *Phronesis*, 10 [1965], 109–48) also denied, from different perspectives, that alternate worlds of Love and Strife have a place in Empedocles' system. Adopting different attitudes toward the doxography, these three scholars claim that the evidence of the fragments and reliable secondary sources supports not a pair of oscillating worlds which contain the same events in reverse order, but a single linear development in which the impulse toward cosmogony is given by Strife, whereas Love acts as the creative power (of all things in Bollack, of living things in Hölscher and Solmsen).[4]

G. B. Kerferd's reviews of this work and the book by O'Brien, *Classical Review*, N.S. 17 (1967), 147 ff.; N.S. 21 (1971), 176 ff.

[3] Two scholars who argued long ago for a single world from Sphere to Sphere were Paul Tannery, "La Cosmogonie d' Empédocle," *Revue philoso-phique de la France et de l'étranger*, 24 (1887), 285–300, and H. von Arnim, "Die Weltperioden bei Empedokles," in *Festschrift Theodor Gomperz* (Wien, 1902), pp. 16–27.

[4] It is not appropriate to set the article by Edwin L. Minar, Jr., "Cosmic Periods in the Philosophy of Empedocles," *Phronesis*, 7 (1963), 127–45, along-side the works just mentioned, as O'Brien does, p. 160. Minar offers the strange suggestion that it is Strife's ascendancy, not Love's, which is expressed in the Sphere of fr. 27. But he also accepts, with O'Brien and other tradi-

Whether a new consensus will result from these radical studies it is too early to judge. But there are indications that the orthodox interpreters will not yield the ground easily. In 1969 D. O'Brien brought out a large book devoted to *Empedocles' Cosmic Cycle* (Cambridge, 1969), in which he interprets this theory "on the assumption that there were alternate worlds of increasing Love and increasing Strife within an endless alternation of the one and the many" (p. 156). In examining this assumption he rejects the new interpretations offered by Bollack, Hölscher, and Solmsen. His own explanation of the cycle contains several original features, yet O'Brien may be regarded as a proponent of orthodoxy by virtue of his acceptance of two worlds of mortal things from Sphere to Sphere, divided by a time of insignificant duration in which the elements are totally separated (in four concentric spheres). Actually, O'Brien did not write his book as an answer to the 1965 heretics: It was complete, as he notes (p. 160 n. 6), before their work appeared. But since O'Brien rewrote one chapter to take some account of their interpretations, his book provides a new challenge to those who reject the traditional views. In the second volume of his *A History of Greek Philosophy*, which was also published in 1965 (Cambridge), W. K. C. Guthrie accepts the main principles of O'Brien's interpretation, with which he was familiar from prepublication drafts of the latter's work.

Since the nature of Empedocles' cosmic cycle is being so hotly debated, it may be useful for someone who has not declared a definite opinion on either side to act as a provisional arbiter in evaluating the basic evidence and arguments which have been deployed. Clearly such an enterprise, if restricted to a medium-length paper, cannot take account of all the ancient evidence, much less the modern literature. But if the problem at issue is a valid one which admits of a solution, it should be possible even in limited space to clarify what is involved and express an opinion on the right kind of answer.

The problem, as I propose to discuss it, may be stated as follows: Did Empedocles advance a theory according to which the constituents of the universe (or reality) alternate between states of total mixture and total separation with two intervening periods in *each* of which a world like our own comes into being and ceases to be? By "world" I

---

tionalists, a zoogony (and cosmogony?) which proceed(s) in reverse order to events under Love. His article is not a rejection of the traditional thesis but a modification of some of its details.

mean the earth and heavens plus any living things or other bodies it may contain. I shall use the term "cosmos" to denote just the physical frame of the world, in abstraction from living things. Before approaching any modern interpretation it will be necessary to consider the crucial text from Empedocles himself. This requires a short introduction.

I

Empedocles' poem *On Nature* seems to have explained all sensible phenomena in terms of four "roots," called elements by Aristotle and later commentators: earth, air, fire, and water. These "roots," to which Empedocles assigns divine names (fr. 6), possess distinct properties of their own, and they are sentient and equal to one another.[5] (Empedocles does not specify the nature of this equality, but we may assume he means equal in respect of power and mass, at least.) The behavior of the four elements, as we may hereafter call them, is controlled by two powers, Love and Strife. Love's power is manifested by σύνοδος, bringing things together; and Strife possesses the reciprocal power to divide or separate things.[6] Both Love and Strife are probably equal, in the respects suggested, to each of the elements. But whereas Love is described as among them, Strife is "apart from them." [7] Owing to the actions of Love and Strife, the elements are subject to combination and separation.

Most of these statements are found in a continuous text, fr. 17 (= 31 Bollack, vol. II). But they do not occur in its first five lines. There Empedocles writes as follows:[8]

[5] They have their own "prerogatives" (τιμή), "character" (ἦθος), and "nature" (φύσις), fr. 17.28, 110.5. "All things have *phronēsis* and a share of thought," fr. 110.10. For the elements' equality and likeness of age, cf. fr. 17.27. See in general Guthrie, *A History of Greek Philosophy*, Vol. II, The *Presocratic Tradition from Parmenides to Democritus*, (Cambridge, 1965), pp. 138–59.

[6] Fr. 17.7–8 = 26.5–6.

[7] Fr. 17.19–20.

[8] This text and its sequel (lines 14–35) are a continuous quotation by Simplicius, *Phys.* 157.25 ff. (less line 9, see below n. 10) who introduces them with the sentence Ὁ δὲ Ἐμπεδοκλῆς τὸ ἓν καὶ τὰ πολλὰ τὰ πεπερασμένα καὶ τὴν κατὰ περίοδον ἀποκατάστασιν καὶ τὴν κατὰ σύγκρισιν καὶ διάκρισιν γένεσιν καὶ φθορὰν οὕτως ἐν τῷ πρώτῳ τῶν Φυσικῶν παραδίδωσι. The word ἀποκατάστασις, a Stoic technical term for the periodic "reconstitution" of the world, shows

I shall tell a double tale. At one time one grew to be alone out of many, and at another time it grew apart to be many out of one. Double is the birth of mortal things, and double their decline. For the coming together of all things both begets and destroys the one [viz. birth and decline]. And the other [viz. birth and decline], having been nurtured by things growing apart again, fled away.[9] And these things never cease from continuous exchange, at one

that Simplicius finds in the text a reference to a cosmic cycle in which the same events occur *in the same order* (i.e. not the two-world cycle asserted by traditional interpreters). I append an abridged apparatus criticus: 3 τοίη (bis) Karsten (cf. n. 9) 4 αὔξει Karsten 5 θρεφθεῖσα Panzerbieter: θρυφθεῖσα DF: δρυφθεῖσα E διέπτη Scaliger: ἀποδρύπτει Bollack: δρεπτή codd. 9 suppl. Diels

δίπλ' ἐρέω· τοτὲ μὲν γὰρ ἓν ηὐξήθη μόνον εἶναι
ἐκ πλεόνων, τοτὲ δ' αὖ διέφυ πλέον(α) ἐξ ἑνὸς εἶναι.
δοιὴ δὲ θνητῶν γένεσις, δοιὴ δ' ἀπόλειψις·
τὴν μὲν γὰρ πάντων σύνοδος τίκτει τ' ὀλέκει τε,
5 ἡ δὲ πάλιν διαφυομένων θρεφθεῖσα διέπτη.
καὶ ταῦτ' ἀλλάσσοντα διαμπερὲς οὐδαμὰ λήγει,
ἄλλοτε μὲν Φιλότητι συνερχόμεν(α) εἰς ἓν ἅπαντα,
ἄλλοτε δ' αὖ δίχ' ἕκαστα φορεύμενα Νείκεος ἔχθει.
⟨οὕτως ᾗ μὲν ἓν ἐκ πλεόνων μεμάθηκε φύεσθαι⟩
10 ἠδὲ πάλιν διαφύντος ἑνὸς πλέον(α) ἐκτελέθουσι,
τῇ μὲν γίγνονταί τε καὶ οὔ σφισιν ἔμπεδος αἰών·
ᾗ δὲ διαλλάσσοντα διαμπερὲς οὐδαμὰ λήγει,
ταύτῃ δ' αἰὲν ἔασιν ἀκίνητοι κατὰ κύκλον.

[9] The text and sense of this line are discussed below. My colleague Mr. A. H. Griffiths has shown me that the opening of this fragment, lines 3 ff., is a direct echo of Homer *Il.* 6.146 ff., a text which found many imitators. Hippolochus there asks Diomedes, "Why do you inquire about my lineage?" (τίη γενεὴν ἐρεείνεις;). Hippolochus goes on to compare the generation of foliage with that of men: οἵη περ φύλλων γενεή, τοίη δὲ καὶ ἀνδρῶν. This is clearly Empedocles' model in line 3 of fr. 17. In the development of the simile Hippolochus shows that the wind casts leaves to the ground and the burgeoning wood causes others to grow in the spring: ὡς ἀνδρῶν γενεὴ ἡ μὲν φύει ἡ δ' ἀπολήγει. It is difficult to know how precisely Empedocles is reproducing Homer's cycle of change here. To a Greek audience Empedocles' words could not fail to recall the cycle of birth and death which Homer describes. And we must assume that this is at least part of what Empedocles expresses here, though his δοιή introduces a complication which shows that the philosopher is using a commonplace notion to say something new and important.

time uniting all of them into one by means of Love, and at another
time carried apart again as individuals by the hostility of Strife.
So, insofar as one learned to grow from many, and many spring up
when the one grows apart again, in this respect they come into
being and have no lasting life; but insofar as they never cease from
continuous exchange, so far they are for ever, stable in their
revolution.

These lines seem to state a general law or principle of change. They
make no specific reference to the "four roots" or elements, but lay
down a law of alternation between one and many to which "all things"
are subject. "All things" is a vague term and at this stage we are only
entitled to say that it refers to the material, stuff, or constituents of
which "mortal things" are composed. Concerning "mortal things"
Empedocles becomes more precise in the verses which follow. Insofar
as one and many are alternating and mutually exclusive conditions, we
may perhaps say that one and many are transient or *mortal* conditions
of "all things." For Empedocles elsewhere asserts that the so-called
birth and death of mortals is only "mixture" and "separation of what
has been mixed" (fr. 8). What "the many" are we learn from the
sequel (lines 14 ff.), in which the first two lines of the fragment are
repeated and then followed by three lines which list as the reference of
ἐκ πλεόνων, "from many," and πλέον(α), "many," fire, water, earth, and
air, plus Love and Strife. But before naming these four elements,
Empedocles chooses to make assertions concerning what we may call
the consequences of the alternation between one and many. From this
alternation which governs all things we learn in lines 9–11 that in one
sense (τῇ μέν) "many" are generated and "have no lasting life." Because
on the other hand the interchange of one and many is an eternal
process, the subjects of this change are said to be "stable" or "motionless" (ἀκίνητοι) with respect to the "revolution" (κατὰ κύκλον), lines 12–13.

This contrast between rest and motion need not, I think, be examined
in our present context. The immediate problem is to establish the exact
meaning of δοιὴ γένεσις, "double birth," and δοιὴ ἀπόλειψις, "double
decline," in line 3. An important clue is provided by lines 9–11 cited
above.[10] These lines assert the "growth" (φύεσθαι) of "one from many"

[10] Line 9 of the Diels text, which I am following, is not found in Simplicius'
continuous quotation of fr. 17 in *Phys.* 157.25 ff. Bergk supplied it from line
8 of fr. 26, which Simplicius cites in an earlier section of his commentary,
Phys. 33.18 ff. This is almost certainly correct, for ᾗ μέν is needed to balance

and the "coming to be" (ἐκτελέθουσι) of "many from one." Both φύεσθαι and (ἐκ)τελέθειν are words which naturally apply to the growth or birth of animals, plants, etc. And according to the text this process takes place *both* as things unite into one *and* as they separate again into many. But Empedocles does not say that he means (only) the birth of plants, animals, etc. And there is good reason to suppose that this is too restricted a sense for θνητῶν, "mortal things," here. Toward the end of fr. 17 Empedocles writes that "all these things are equal and of like age in origin" (line 27). From the context it seems clear that he means the four elements plus Love and Strife. He goes on to say that they have different prerogatives and their own character; that they prevail in turn as time comes round. "And in addition to them," he says, "nothing else *comes to be* or *ceases to be;* for if they perished utterly, they would no longer exist" (lines 27–31).

It should be stressed that in fr. 17 Empedocles says nothing specific about "the world" or animals, plants, men, etc. Once, in parenthesis, he says of Love that "she is believed to be engendered in mortal limbs," but here and in the following lines about her name and her agency he is clearly talking in everyday language (lines 22–26). His subject-matter is the one and many: their alternation, and the identification of the many with the four elements plus Love and Strife. Fr. 26, cited above, which repeats many lines of fr. 17, begins as follows:

> And they prevail in their turn as time comes round, and perish into one another and grow according to the alternation of destiny. For there are just these things, but running through one another they become men and the tribes of other beasts, at one time coming together into one order (κόσμος) by Love, and at another time carried apart again as individuals by the hostility of Strife, until having grown together as one they become subordinate in the whole (εἰσόκεν ἓν συμφύντα τὸ πᾶν ὑπένερθε γένηται).

Here we are once again informed of the waxing and waning of the four elements plus Love and Strife. But Empedocles now also explains that in this process the six, or at least the four elements, become animals and men. "Running through one another" is an ambiguous expression,

---

ταύτῃ δέ (fr. 17.13). In view of the parallel lines in fr. 17 and fr. 26 it is possible that Bergk was too conservative in his supplement. If line 7 of fr. 26 as well as 8 is supplied to fr. 17, the two texts are identical from ἄλλοτε μὲν . . . κατὰ κύκλον. O'Brien, pp. 323 f., favors the restoration of both lines.

but it looks like a way of referring to the σύνοδος, "coming together," of fr. 17.

From these two fragments together, 17 and 26, the following conclusions seem to be firmly sanctioned by the text. What we would call the universe or the real is viewed by Empedocles as an alternation of one and many. The "one" is a condition of unity, "a single *kosmos*," but the many is a plurality of six entities, or classes of entity, which in some sense comes to be by separation from the one, and in some sense ceases to be by recombination into the one. The stuff of which these six entities consist is imperishable, but they only exist *as individual things* (ἕκαστα) when they are sundered from the one.[11] In being sundered from the one they "come to be" as distinguishable elements and antithetical powers, Love and Strife. In being united the elements give rise to animals and men, etc., and when fully "grown together" they cease once again to exist as individuals.

These remarks may now be applied to the analysis of fr. 17.3–5. After asserting the "double birth" and "double decline" of mortal

---

[11] I am trying to express here distinctions which Empedocles makes in fr. 17 and which seem to me fundamental to his notion of "element." Most modern scholars baldly assert that the elements are unchangeable and eternal, cf. Burnet, *EGP*, p. 230. From the remains of Empedocles' own words this statement is both true and false. The point cannot be argued at length here; fr. 17 speaks for itself. But although Aristotle was probably right in holding that Empedocles' elements are ἀμετάβλητα, i.e. do not change into one another (e.g. *De Gen. et Corr.* ˙333a31 ff.) as Aristotle himself held, Aristotle was probably also right in holding that the elements are in a sense generated from and destroyed into the one (ibid., 315a4 ff.). There is no inconsistency here. Empedocles could have held that fire is always fire as long as it remains unmixed with any other element. Fire does not change into, say, earth, but when bits of fire and earth are united by Love they constitute *a new* ἕν, "and perish into one another"; cf. O'Brien, pp. 314–16. I see no reason to assume from anything Empedocles says that what takes place in such mixture is not some kind of temporary fusion. Empedocles' basic categories in fr. 17 are one and many. He seems to envisage them as mutually exclusive and, if so, there is certainly a sense in which the elements are "mortal" according as they are united or separated. That is the only sense in which anything is "mortal" for Empedocles. Conversely, there is a sense in which compounds, in virtue of their constituents, persist after they have been separated. Plato was, I believe, expressing the fundamental sense of fr. 17 when he wrote: "the sum of things (τὸ πᾶν) is sometimes one and akin under Love and at other times many and at variance under Strife" (*Soph.* 242e–243a = DK 31A29).

things in line 3, Empedocles explains what he means in two antithetical clauses. These clauses are often taken to provide the key to the cosmic cycle, but if that is correct the key has proved difficult to turn and it does not yield readily to force. In fact, no interpretation can afford to rely too heavily upon this passage, for one and probably two words are corrupt at the end of line 5.[12] I shall accept the traditional emendations; but I shall reject the interpretation of line 5 which they have sometimes been held to support.

Line 4 does not present major problems: "the one" ($\tau\grave{\eta}\nu$ $\mu\acute{\epsilon}\nu$) is most easily taken as cognate object of "begets and destroys," i.e. "the one way of birth and decline." What brings this about is "the coming together of all things." "The other" ($\grave{\eta}$ $\delta\acute{\epsilon}$) therefore, with which line 5 begins, must refer to "the other way of birth and decline." I translate the whole line: "The other, having been nurtured by things growing apart again, fled away." "Nurtured" responds to "birth," and "fled away" to "decline." The parallels between both lines are very close, but two differences are noteworthy. First, in line 4 the verbs are present tense, and could refer to present time. "The other" of line 5 is something which *has been* nurtured and *has* fled away. This use of the aorist tense may have a generic rather than a temporal aspect; but I think the line is most naturally taken to refer to events which have preceded and will subsequently ($\pi\acute{a}\lambda\iota\nu$) follow those described in line 4. There is a second point of difference. In line 4 "coming together" governs both verbs, and it expresses an activity, elsewhere ascribed to Love, which may be on the increase and is certainly not declining. "Growing apart" ($\delta\iota\alpha\phi\upsilon o\mu\acute{\epsilon}\nu\omega\nu$) in line 5 goes with "having been nurtured," but it is by no means certain that what "fled away" did so because things *continued to grow apart*. Ceasing to grow apart (i.e. coming together) could be the reason why that way of birth and decline "fled away."

[12] "Having been nurtured" is the sense of Panzerbieter's emendation of the MSS. $\theta\rho\upsilon\phi\theta\epsilon\hat{\iota}\sigma a$ "having been shattered" to $\theta\rho\epsilon\phi\theta\epsilon\hat{\iota}\sigma(a)$. I see no reason for translating Scaliger's $\delta\iota\acute{\epsilon}\pi\tau\eta$ as if it were a timeless present. Empedocles discusses unification in line 4. Things "grow apart again," but this process must cease if unification is to recommence. If $\delta\iota\acute{\epsilon}\pi\tau\eta$ is given its natural reference to past time, $\grave{\alpha}\lambda\lambda\acute{a}\sigma\sigma o\nu\tau a$ in line 6 explains that the decline of separation is matched by the future development of unification and vice versa. $\delta\iota\acute{\epsilon}\pi\tau\eta$ does not mean "died" but "fled away," and should be compared for its sense and reference with $\grave{\epsilon}\xi\acute{\epsilon}\sigma\tau\eta\kappa\epsilon\nu$ and $\emph{\i}\sigma\tau\alpha\tau o$, fr. 35.10 and 36, the subject of which is Strife. Unification and separation are the manifestations of Love and Strife cited in fr. 17.7–8.

Ex hypothesi I assume the following scheme of movements to be represented in these two lines: *A* (line 4) moves from weakening Strife toward maximum Love; *B* (line 5) moves from maximum Strife to incipient Love. After *A* and before *B* is a stage *C*, not described here: the Sphere when all things are one and at rest (frr. 27–29).

An objection which may be raised against this scheme is its failure to locate a stage for the decline of Love and the growth of Strife. Quite so. Stage *C* must be followed by stage *D*: Love's loss of power to unite the Sphere and the development of Strife within it. At a precise moment Strife utterly shatters the Sphere, which brings the cycle to *B*. So we have this circular movement: *C-D-B-A*.

Confirmation for this scheme is provided by other fragments. According to fr. 30: "Great Strife, when he had been nurtured in the limbs, leapt to his office in the fulfillment of time." And the next fragment (31) reads: "for one by one all the limbs of the god (i.e. the Sphere) began to shake." I take these lines to refer to stage *D*. Strife is developing *within* the Sphere, and at the ordained moment he causes it to disintegrate by separating all its components. The consequences of this cataclysm are not described in the fragments, but we find an account of it in Plutarch which I shall discuss later. Let me anticipate the full discussion by asserting here that Strife causes a total fragmentation of the materials which Love had united, a melee of particles which are all divided from one another. How long this process lasts is unclear; but it represents the maximum of Strife's power. Love next begins to assert herself, and in fr. 35, where things are beginning to unite, Love is growing and Strife has begun to withdraw.

Such, in bare outline, is the cycle as I understand it. Further evidence and alternative proposals will be examined in the treatment of modern interpretations. To return to fr. 17: we are there told that "when one is divided, many spring to birth." The "many," as we have seen, are the four elements plus Love and Strife. The birth of these things, that is to say, their manifestation as individuals, is a "decline" of the "one," their earlier (and later) condition. The cause of this decline is the growth of Strife "within the limbs of the Sphere (or 'one')." The history of Strife and the history of the "many" are in some sense identical; and it is by no means unlikely that fr. 17.5 is deliberately worded to suggest the growth and decline of the "many" in language which mirrors the growth and withdrawal of Strife. Fr. 26.7 gives the firm prediction that separate things grow together into one and lose their autonomy. In other words, the decline of the "one" which produces the "many" is reversed by Love's reunification of all things.

Are we entitled to specify what comes to be by σύνοδος, "coming together"? In general terms the answer should be any particular compound and ultimately the unification of all things. Equally, what comes to be by "all things growing apart" and then passes away, as they start to unite, will most naturally refer to noncompounds, fragments of the totality of earth, air, fire, and water. If that is correct we should expect the creation of compound bodies in the world, whether living or inanimate in our sense, to be due to Love or unification, which ultimately destroys particular compounds by uniting them further into one. We should expect Strife or disunification to sift out the particular ingredients of the world prior to the formation of compounds and to account for the destruction of compounds prior to their complete reunification. For the creation of one set of mortal things—compound bodies—another set of mortal things—the fractured limbs of the Sphere or elemental particles—must combine with or "perish into one another." For the creation of new compounds the elements must be reborn, that is to say, must be made to desert previous compounds. Thus in fr. 110.8–9, the elements constituting a human body will desert it under certain conditions (ἢ σ' ἄφαρ ἐκλείψουσι, cf. ἀπόλειψις) out of a desire to travel to their own dear family (or origin), ποθέοντα φίλην ἐπὶ γένναν ἱκέσθαι. The association of ἐκλείψουσι and ἐπὶ γένναν ἱκέσθαι expresses the sense in which decline of the "one" is a genesis of the elements.

II

In offering this interpretation of fr. 17 I have tried to avoid all preconceptions about the cosmic cycle and to base my remarks solely on the text without reference to modern theories. More primary evidence would need to be considered in any comprehensive account of the subject, not to mention the opinions of the doxographers. But fr. 17 must be the starting point for any analysis of this controversy. It is the text of Empedocles on which the theory of a dual cosmogony and zoogony has been primarily held to rest. Thus O'Brien writes "we shall examine first fr. 17, where, if anywhere, Empedocles describes the succession of the one and the many, and where in particular, in lines 3–5, he describes alternate worlds of increasing Love and increasing Strife" (pp. 163 f.). Since O'Brien claims to find alternate worlds in these lines while Bollack, Solmsen, and Hölscher are out to deny their existence, I will attempt to summarize the main points adduced by both sides concerning this passage and to evaluate them with reference to my own understanding of it.

It is a serious deficiency in O'Brien's handling of fr. 17 that he fails to discuss the text as a whole. What he does, in considering the assumptions on which the hypothesis of alternate worlds is based, is to discuss lines 3–5. In the course of this, O'Brien makes a general assertion about fr. 17 which seems to me misleading, if not false. He writes that it "is concerned . . . with the generation and decay of mortal creatures as a whole" (p. 166). By "mortal creatures as a whole" O'Brien means here something like species or genera as distinct from individuals. I hope to have shown that fr. 17 is concerned with the alternation of one and many, the identification of the many as six specific entities, their properties and the sense in which they are both changeless *and* subject to generation and destruction. To be sure, reference to "mortal things" is made before we hear anything about the elements as such or about Love and Strife. But if, as I have argued, the elements themselves as well as O'Brien's "mortal creatures" are one reference of the term θνητῶν, that is a point of great importance in the understanding of these controversial lines.

According to O'Brien, "lines 3–5 tell us that *both* the process of increasing unification *and* the process of increasing separation bring forth, and then destroy, a world of mortal creatures" (p. 168). But Empedocles says nothing here about any *world*, whether of "mortal creatures" or the cosmos as a whole, including mortal creatures. Nor does he speak of "increasing unification" or "increasing separation." "Increasing unification" is a legitimate interpretation of πάντων σύνοδος, explaining as it does that "all things grow together into one" (fr. 17.1, 16; fr. 26.8) and the statement that unification is also a cause of destruction. But line 5 need not, and I would claim does not, posit "increasing separation" as a process by which birth *and* decline (of a world) occur. It is true that such an interpretation yields a symmetrical pattern of movement for both lines: *A*, growth of Love; *B*, growth of Strife. But the scheme I proposed above is equally symmetrical: *A*, incipient-maximum Love; *B*, maximum-declining Strife. No fragment of Empedocles makes reference to "increasing Strife" as a power responsible for the birth and destruction of "a world of mortal creatures." But, as I have indicated, there are fragments which refer to Strife's growth within the Sphere and his later withdrawal, at a time when mortal creatures are coming to be, under the growing influence of Love.

I conclude that O'Brien, in his discussion of fr. 17, gives no adequate arguments in favor of "alternate worlds of increasing Love and increasing Strife." He is right to claim that both unification and separation are processes from which "mortal things" arise. He is not justified to assume that "mortal things" means only "mortal creatures" in his sense, that the "mortal things" which arise by unification are of the same kind as those produced by separation, or that Empedocles makes explicit or implicit assertions here about *worlds* of Love and Strife.

Let us now consider Bollack's handling of this passage. (I should point out that Bollack's text and commentary were not available to O'Brien when he wrote.) Bollack observes that only "two movements are described" in fr. 17: "the reconstitution of the One by departure of the Many and the scattering of the One which recreates the Many. The πλείονα, the Plurality, are nothing else than the One dividing itself" (III, i, p. 51). Bollack then denies that Empedocles says anything here to justify the assumption of a cycle divided into four periods. But Bollack does allow that the alternation of one and many may be taken both as a description of an alternation between the Sphere and the world, and as "the most general expression of the polar orientations which animate becoming" (ibid.).

A little later, however, Bollack draws a sharp distinction between the alternation of one and many described in lines 1–2, and the "double birth" and "double decline" of mortal things, which is the subject of the next three lines. "Empedocles does not mean that there are two births (in two opposed worlds) but that in the world of things which have come to be (of θνητά), every birth is ambivalent, by contrast with becoming in its totality" (III, i, p. 52). Bollack ignores the fact that the one and the many are also "things which come to be." Empedocles may well have held that the birth of one thing implies the decline of something else and vice versa, but such an ambivalence does not establish a sufficient sense for "double" to make what it refers to quite independent of the cosmic alternation of one and many. In fact, the mention of "all things coming together" in line 4 proves it impossible to isolate the process by which (certain) mortal things are begotten and destroyed from that which constitutes the "one."

For line 5 Bollack proposes a text which removes any reference to "birth." On his reading, this line refers solely to the decline of mortal things, which Strife brings about by causing them to grow apart, a process in which Strife himself loses power. The text which is supposed to support this interpretation can hardly be defended as Greek.[13] That is unfortunate, for Bollack is right to invoke Strife's banishment, of which the fragments speak, in interpreting the end of the line; and it would suit his general concept of cosmogony in Empedocles to make Strife also responsible for the emergence of the elements, as I have suggested.[14]

Since Bollack defends an interpretation of line 5 based on a different text from that of Diels-Kranz and O'Brien, he does not provide an analysis of the "double birth" and "decline" which can properly be compared with O'Brien's. Bollack supposes that lines 3–5 refer to the creation and destruction of mortal things over a time-span which looks forward to Love's full development and back to the apogee of Strife. This analysis is, I believe, defensible on the traditional text, provided that θνητῶν be taken quite generally as a reference to anything (and in Empedocles "all things are sentient"), including the elements, which is subject to mixture and dissolution. The converse of this in Empedoclean metaphysics is that all things are in a sense "immortal." [15]

---

[13] δρυφθεῖσα is the reading of E in the Simplicius codd. which Bollack prefers to θρυφθεῖσα read by D and F, on the grounds that it is a Homeric word applied to the limbs of animals and men (*Il.* 16.324, 23.395, etc.). He argues that δρεπτή, the corrupt form which ends the line, suggests the same word and therefore reads ἀποδρύπτει. He then understands the whole line to mean: "l'autre, dispersant, se disperse, quand Ils se séparent à nouveau." This raises extreme difficulties of sense and grammar. δρυφθεῖσα should denote a time prior to ἀποδρύπτει, which is a *transitive* verb, but Bollack takes it to denote the "laceration" which ἀπόλειψις experiences in tearing other things apart; i.e. that Strife by dissipating himself loses power (III, i, p. 56).

[14] Bollack accepts, as I do, that Strife prepares for the cosmos by "disuniting the limbs of the god" (I, p. 31). For Bollack, however, these "particules" are not already elemental particles, as I should say, but what ultimately, under Love's unifying power, become elements (ibid., p. 41). For Empedocles' elements as particles, see J. Longrigg, "Roots," *Classical Review*, N.S., 17 (1967), 1–4.

[15] Cf. fr. 15 where Empedocles claims that existence is not confined to "what men call life," but extends beyond and before "they were composed as βροτοί." At fr. 35.14 "those things began to grow as mortal which previously learned to be immortal, to be mixed what previously (learned to be) unmixed, (ex)changing their movements." Here Empedocles is apparently saying that

Solmsen comments as follows on fr. 17: "We still find ourselves in the early section of the poem which introduces the elements and clarifies their nature. In vv. 1–13 Empedocles is particularly concerned with their relation to 'becoming' (γίγνεσθαι)"; and later: "the exploration of *genesis* as it affects the elements throws new light on the *genesis* of θνητά." [16] Solmsen's general position is that Love creates living things and Strife manufactures the physical frame of the cosmos. He is out to deny, that is to say, a cosmogony of Love and a zoogony of Strife. But it is doubtful whether this position, for which Solmsen makes out an interesting case, is wholly compatible with his interpretation of lines 3–5 of fr. 17.

Solmsen interprets these lines in much the same way as O'Brien. He reads them as a corollary of lines 1–2: "Developing the implications of vv. 1 f. he [Empedocles] realizes that on the way towards the ἕν there is not only *genesis* but also, when the process of unification reaches its logical end, destruction (of the compounds)." [17] So far I would agree. Solmsen continues: "Correspondingly in the process of διαφύεσθαι there is before the complete separation of the elements *genesis* of compounds, i.e. mortal beings." By "complete separation" Solmsen means a "cosmic pattern . . . of 'four concentric layers'," which he takes to be the construction of the cosmos by Strife (p. 117). Whether Empedocles envisaged such a condition of "complete separation" is not clear from the fragments (see p. 414 supra). On Solmsen's reading of fr. 17.5, Empedocles there describes increasing separation in which "*genesis* of compounds, i.e. mortal beings" will have occurred prior to the complete construction of the cosmos. What these compound "mortal beings" could be, placed between the Sphere and the cosmos, Solmsen does not say. (For O'Brien they are living organisms.) In fact, Solmsen understands the movements described in lines 4 and 5 similarly to those who claim from them support for a dual cosmogony and zoogony, which he denies.

Hölscher holds that the first part of fr. 17 refers neither to an alterna-

---

the elements come to be involved in genesis through the mixtures caused by Love. "They learned to be immortal" by avoiding mixture in the past, but the law of alternation between one and many rules out absolute immortality (i.e. permanent mixture or separation) for anything.

[16] *Phronesis*, 10 (1965), 138–40.

[17] Ibid., p. 140.

tion between the world and the Sphere nor to an alternation of "two organic worlds." [18] He takes it that two ways or processes of becoming are expressed by "things coming together" and "things growing apart." On this interpretation, fr. 17 is concerned, in its opening, with pointing out that "life" and "death" have a double aspect. "All life is nurtured from separation, all death creates a new formation" (p. 209). Hölscher supports this analysis by reference to a number of fragments which explain life and death in terms of mixture and separation (frr. 20, 9, 15, 8). One may accept what Hölscher says here and at the same time question his giving so restricted a sense to "things coming together" and "things growing apart." Empedocles speaks in the most general terms of an alternation between one and many at the beginning of this fragment, and it seems to me impossible to ban this from the interpretation of lines 3–5. The cosmic alternation between one and many is not a scholarly theory but a fact of Empedocles' system, firmly stated in our text and acknowledged by the doxographers. Nor is it incompatible in lines 3–5 with a parallel reference to the evolution of "mortal things." On the contrary, it is the alternation of one and many which provides the context of the birth and decline of mortal things. Alternating worlds are not implied by taking lines 3–5 to refer to the cosmic alternation of one and many as well as the birth and death of mortal things. These are two sides of the same medal; "one" is the *final* consequence of coming together, and "many" are the *immediate* consequence of growing apart.

III

The traditional interpretation seeks evidence from fr. 17 of a world created and destroyed by the work of Strife. In my judgment that evidence is not forthcoming. If there were independent evidence that Empedocles had such a theory, line 5 ("nurtured by things growing apart") might be read as a reference to it. But I believe that line is most convincingly taken as a veiled reference to the appearance and disappearance of the elements as separate, uncompounded entities. We must now consider what Empedocles has to say elsewhere about the origin of the world and living things. In fr. 21 Empedocles invites

[18] Hölscher's theories were originally set out in *Hermes*, 93 (1965), 7–33. The article has been reprinted, with some modifications and additions, in his book *Anfängliches Fragen* (Göttingen, 1968), pp. 173–212. References here are to the revised edition.

Pausanias to consider the sun, the air, the rain, and the earth. "In Strife," he writes, "they are all different in form and divided, but in Love they come together and desire one another. For from them sprang up all that was and is and will be, trees, men and women . . . for there are just these things, but running through one another they become different in appearance: so much does mixing change them."

The clear implication of this text is that the sun, air, earth, and water —the main cosmic masses which correspond with the four elements— each consist now of aggregates of like elements put *together by Love*.[19] Similarly, living things are compounds of the elements united by Love.[20] Under Strife there are neither cosmic masses nor living things since all the elements are ἄνδιχα, divided or apart. Fr. 22 also speaks of the sun, earth, heavens, and sea as being "all harmonious with their own parts, which are of a nature to wander from them among mortal things."[21]

[19] Empedocles can only mean that the sun, etc. which he invites Pausanias to consider are not "what all these things are in Strife." In Love (that is, now), the elements have united to form the cosmic masses, and mixture of the elements constituting these is responsible for all living things that ever exist (lines 9 ff.). O'Brien believes that the first lines of fr. 21 refer to the present world, as I do, but he identifies this with "the world of increasing Strife" (p. 175 n. 4). It is surely impossible for Empedocles to refer to "Strife's world" in lines 1–5 and then say in line 6 "In Strife they are all different and apart."

[20] Fr. 71 may go closely with fr. 21. In the later passage Empedocles speaks explicitly of "the mixture of water, earth, aether and sun from which sprang up the flesh and forms of all mortals which have *now* been begotten yoked together by Aphrodite." For the implications of "now," see Solmsen, pp. 112–13.

[21] O'Brien has a long discussion of this fragment, pp. 305–13. He rightly observes that lines 1–3 treat "the parts of each element considered in relation to themselves" and lines 4–9 treat "different elements considered in their relation to one another." "Within each half," he continues, "we are told first of joining together or mixing, and then of separation." In the second half joining together and separation are explicitly attributed to Love and Strife respectively. Is there any reason why these powers should perform a different role in the first half? Bollack, correctly in my opinion, says no (I, pp. 111, 181 f.; cf. Kahn, *Gnomon*, 41 [1969], 444). O'Brien, following Aristotle (*Met.* 985a21–29), supposes that Strife unites elements with their parts and Love causes them to wander. This is a gratuitous assumption which contradicts fr. 21 and the purely divisive power which Empedocles accords to Strife. The "limbs which wander" in fr. 20 do so because "they are severed by evil powers of Strife" and there is no reason to think that Love causes aggregates of like elements to "wander" in fr. 22.

In these two passages Empedocles implies that the heavenly bodies and the world as a whole are due to the mixture or harmonization of elemental particles.[22] He gives no grounds here for thinking that the generation of any compound, whether a cosmic mass or a living thing, is due to Strife.

For a detailed account of the state of things under Strife we are largely dependent upon a difficult passage of Plutarch (*De Facie Orbis Lunae* 12). There Plutarch warns his reader against tracing everything back to its natural place, and thereby setting up a theory of the dissolution of order (διάλυσιν κόσμου) and introducing Empedocles' Strife among things. Plutarch proceeds to describe the isolation from one another of heavy and light, earth and heat, etc. as "fearful disorder and disharmony," and in doing so he cites Empedocles fr. 27.1–2, two lines concerning the indiscernibility of sun, earth, and sea. Of these lines the first, along with 3 and 4 of the fragment, recurs in Simplicius' description of the Sphere (*Phys.* 1183.28 ff.). Plutarch evidently understands Empedocles to refer to a state of affairs in which the elements are all in their "natural places, unmixed with one another, unattracted to one another, and μονάδες, traveling their own motions," and he compares this to the condition of things in the *Timaeus* prior to the Demiurge's intervention. If Empedocles posited a phase of things which may be labeled "total Strife," this passage looks like a good candidate for it. Bollack and O'Brien agree that this is what Plutarch describes, and they also agree that the elements are separated by Strife in four concentric spheres (O'Brien, pp. 146–55; Bollack, I, pp. 165–69). But for O'Brien total Strife follows the creation and destruction of a world, whereas in Bollack it is a pre-cosmic condition to be followed by Love's creation of the world. Plutarch goes on to say that this was the state of things until desire came upon nature from Love, a phase which would follow here on either interpretation. But Plutarch's earlier reference to "the Giants and Titans of mythology" alongside Empedocles' Strife speaks strongly in favor of Bollack's linear development. Actually, Plutarch says nothing about concentric spheres. Are we to imagine them as solid masses of earth, water, etc.? If the elements are massed together in this way under Strife, why are they also indiscernible? Moreover, the description of them as μονάδες implies not isolated masses but isolated particles. I suggest that total Strife is to be viewed as a whirling mass of disunited elemental particles jostling against each

[22] Empedocles may have called the smallest fragments of elements θραύματα (θραύσματα), cf. DK A43 and Guthrie, *History*, II, pp. 149 ff.

other in their own regions (cf. Lucretius V.432–48, and the theories cited by O'Brien, pp. 146 ff.).

Unfortunately we have no fragments that explain what happens from the time when the Sphere is shattered up to the time when Love is in the center of the whirl, the situation described in fr. 35.[23] Perhaps, as O'Brien has argued (pp. 104 ff.), we are to think of Strife as disrupting the Sphere by pressing in from the circumference and forcing Love to the center. Love retaliates by causing unmixed things to come together, and Strife begins to withdraw. "Yet many remained unmixed alternating with those that were mixing, all that Strife still held back in suspense" (lines 8–9). The consequence of such mixtures is an outpouring of "countless tribes of mortal creatures" (line 16). Empedocles says nothing here about the formation of the cosmos. Solmsen identifies "the unmixed things still held aloft by Strife" with the cosmic masses (p. 111), but this is a doubtful inference. Strife may be presumed to have isolated the fragmented elements into different zones of the whirl, the heaviest at the center and the lightest at the circumference. But the stability characteristic of the earth, for example, is attributed by Empedocles to Love. He writes of earth (mingling with Hephaistos, rain, and aether to produce flesh and blood) "when it had been moored (ὁρμισθεῖσα) in the perfect harbours of Aphrodite."[24] "Having been moored" implies previous motion, and I would conjecture that as Love's power begins to grow she stabilizes as the cosmic masses a large number of the elemental fragments shattered by Strife.

However the cosmos came to be formed, we have no evidence from Empedocles' own words to conclude that it is subject to a double genesis, one by Love and the other by Strife. In all probability both powers contribute to it, Strife by sorting out the elements, Love by aggregating and mixing them.[25] So far as zoogony is concerned we are

[23] Simplicius refers the δίνη to the time of Love's ἐπικράτεια, De Caelo 530.22–26; cf. Bollack, I, pp. 168 f., 178.

[24] Fr. 98. The implications of this text have been overlooked. It is possible that Empedocles regarded earth as the first feature of the cosmos to be formed. This would suit O'Brien's view that Love's creative powers are first manifested in the center of the world, p. 119; cf. n. 25 below.

[25] Philo (De Prov. 2, p. 86 Aucher; = DK 31A49) reports "when aether had been separated, air and fire flew above, and the heaven was formed which revolved in the broadest area. But the fire which remained a little lower than the heaven *was aggregated into* the rays of the sun. The earth *running together into one*, having been compacted by a certain necessity, took up its clear place

on firmer ground. Solmsen has shown, with great clarity, that the production of living things and their organs is ascribed in our fragments only to Love, who mixes the elements.[26] There are no lines which speak of "tribes of mortals" coming to be by the separation of Strife, and I have already argued that fr. 17 is not convincingly construed to say that Strife brings living things, in the sense of animals and men, to birth.

O'Brien seeks evidence for a zoogony by Strife in the information recorded by Aetius of four stages in the development of animal life (V.19.5; = DK 31A72).[27] Aetius writes: "Empedocles says that the primary generations of animals and plants did not occur as complete wholes, but they consisted of parts disjoined, not grown together. The second generation was monstrous manifestations of united parts; the third generation was 'whole-natured forms'; and the fourth was produced no longer from like things, for instance fire and water, but by one another [i.e. sexual reproduction]." No reference is made by Aetius to Love and Strife, but I submit that an unprejudiced assessment of this passage will find in it a series of generations in which the higher is distinguished from the immediately lower by *increasing mixture*. To take only the last two, most controversial stages, sexual reproduction,

---

in the middle." Aetius (*Plac.* V.26.4; = DK 31A70) gives this summary: "Empedocles says that the first shoots of living things sprang from the earth, before the sun was spread around and day and night had been distinguished. And they embrace the principle of male and female owing to the symmetry of mixture." It is questionable whether O'Brien is right to call these passages "versions of Strife's cosmogony," p. 50 n. 1. In Philo Strife will certainly be responsible for separating out aether, etc. (cf. Eus. *Praep. Ev.* I.8.10 = DK 31A30), but "ignis . . . coacervatus" and "terra . . . in unum sedens" look like clear manifestations of Love's power. Aetius' "first shoots" feature "symmetry of mixture," a characteristic which no one could ascribe to Strife. If they exist prior to the sun, and day and night, that gives no necessary indication that we are in "the world of Strife." For it is an assumption, not confirmed by the fragments, that all "living things" are generated after the cosmos reaches its present condition.

[26] Pages 112–118. As he later remarks (p. 126), "it is Love whose activities are regularly characterised by συν- compounds, like συνέρχεσθαι, συμβαίνειν, whereas Neikos is associated with διαφύεσθαι and δίχα."

[27] While I disagree with O'Brien's division of the zoogonical stages into worlds of Love and Strife, his discussion of the evidence (pp. 196–236) sheds light on many points of detail.

the union of two compounds, is a higher level of mixture than the union of like parts by which the οὐλοφυῆ, "whole-natured forms," are produced. And as Minar points out, it is extremely unplausible to explain sexual reproduction as not the work of Love![28]

O'Brien argues that the separate animal parts described in fr. 57 belong to "the first stage of increasing Love" and at a later stage these are united into the "monstrous forms," which Aetius cites second and which are mentioned in frr. 60 and 61. But O'Brien tries to make the whole-natured forms of fr. 62 and men and women (Aetius' third and fourth generations) products of increasing Strife. O'Brien argues thus from the fact that the whole-natured forms are "dispatched by fire wishing to reach its like," or by κρινόμενον πῦρ, a fire which is "detached" or detaches itself. To O'Brien the word κρινόμενον and the principle of like being attracted to like are indubitable evidence of Strife's activity. If the whole-natured forms are the work of Strife, then men and women would be products of Strife since they are a later development of the whole-natured forms. There is, however, no textual evidence which proves that Empedocles believed the attraction of like to like to be the work of Strife. And Bollack has argued strongly that precisely the opposite is the case.[29] I believe Bollack is right about this, but at the very least, as Solmsen suggests (p. 134), the principle of like to like is neutral for deciding whether Strife is responsible for the productions of fr. 62. Nor again does the word κρινόμενον *prove* that we are in Strife's world. The fact which requires explanation is fire's capacity to rouse living things from the moist earth under its desire to unite with fire elsewhere. From fr. 73, a text not cited by O'Brien in this connection, we learn that "when Love had drenched earth with rainwater, busily fashioning forms, she gave them to swift fire to strengthen." This passage strongly suggests that the fire of fr. 62 is also engaged in the business of Love, a fact which would help to explain why fire "*longs* to join its like." In both contexts fire acts upon earth and water, and there is every reason to regard its "being detached" as an act of Love who makes fire an instrument of her creative powers.

None of O'Brien's further arguments about a zoogony of Strife seem

[28] "Cosmic Periods," 143; cf. Solmsen, p. 135.

[29] Pages 48–52, where Bollack rejects Aristotle's claim that Love is only responsible for uniting dissimilar things. Many modern scholars take Love to have this limited role and make Strife a power which unites like things: cf. O'Brien, pp. 312–13, Guthrie, *History*, II, p. 156; against this see C. W. Müller, *Gleiches zu Gleichem* (Wiesbaden, 1965), pp. 27–39.

to have any firm textual basis. Empedocles does not say that Strife ever creates living things, i.e. men, animals, and plants. But for him in a sense all things are alive. What we call organic life is viewed by Empedocles as a consequence of elemental particles uniting into temporary stable compounds. Love alone is responsible for the unification of many into one. But as Hölscher rightly stresses, Empedocles is redefining conventional notions of life, death, mortality, and immortality.[30] For Empedocles, continuity of existence is guaranteed by the cyclical interchange of one and many. Empedocles accepts from Parmenides that "what is" or "the whole" is subject neither to genesis nor destruction (frr. 11–14), but he does not extract from these premises a denial that "what is" can change. In Empedocles' system "what is" embraces one *and* many; these are the poles between which all things ceaselessly alternate. The alternation is both a cause of impermanence to the constituents of reality and an assertion of their continuity. If one considers the elements as the source and product of one and many, respectively, their existence is a phase with a beginning and an end. But as the ever-active partners in the exchange of one and many, they are steadfast in the cycle (i.e. if one considers their behavior over the whole alternation and not at specific periods, fr. 17.9–13, cf. lines 34–35).

IV

Empedocles' own fragments, even though they represent only a fraction of his original physical poem, provide enough evidence to show that he envisaged a cosmic cycle of the following basic form. The constituents of the world are subject to an endless alternation between a state of complete unity (the Sphere) and a state of complete fragmentation. Strife, who is absent from the Sphere during Love's time of total dominance, develops within it at an appointed time, and causes the Sphere to disintegrate. When the Sphere is shattered, the elements emerge from it as whirling fragmented entities, with Love herself perhaps divided among them. By "begetting" the elements Strife provides Love with the materials which that power needs for the construction of the cosmos and for zoogony. The desire for union within each elemental fragment or "limb" grows stronger, manifesting Love's gradual return to power. This is expressed in fr. 35. In the whirl, whose cause is unexpressed in our fragments, Love is present at the center.

[30] *Anfängliches Fragen*, pp. 207–12.

She "sucks," as we may infer from her presence in the whirl, elemental fragments together into one, thus creating cosmic and biological compounds. Strife is still active among things, though withdrawing, and we may suppose both powers to be at work simultaneously for a prolonged period, thus accounting for the cycle of "life" and "death," and change in general.[31] Subsequently all things will reunite into one as Love wins the victory over Strife.

This view of the cosmic cycle resembles most closely the scheme put forward by Bollack, and I am much indebted to his work. How far he is also right to regard generation and decay within the visible world as a microcosmic reconstitution and shattering of the Sphere is a large question which cannot be discussed here.[32] Bollack often writes as if the primary function of the cosmic cycle is to give a metaphysical explanation of life and change in general; and his interpretation is ambiguous concerning the return of the Sphere as a cosmic event.[33] Such an approach to Empedocles runs the risk of reading into him some of Simplicius' Neoplatonism, but traditional accounts can justly be accused of insensitivity to Empedocles' complex response to Parmenides.[34] Insofar as Solmsen and Hölscher argue for one cosmogony and zoogony, their views are compatible with Bollack's. But Hölscher gives no compelling reasons for denying the alternation between the Sphere and the world; and Solmsen, though he makes many excellent observations on Love's creative powers, assumes too readily that Strife alone creates the cosmos, and accepts, apparently like the Traditionalists, that compound mortal beings are generated in the process of separation. O'Brien does not succeed in proving his case for a dual cosmogony and zoogony, on the evidence of the fragments. But his book helps to establish beyond any doubt the eternal recurrence of the one and the many. If O'Brien is wrong to locate a world of "living things" in the phase which follows Strife's disruption of the Sphere and precedes Love's unification of things, his general understanding of the cycle, without this feature, is compatible in some respects with Bol-

[31] For Empedocles' theory of pores and effluences, and his use of mixture and separation to account for all kinds of change, cf. A. A. Long, *CQ*, N.S. 16 (1966), 256–76.

[32] Cf. *Empédocle*, I, pp. 34, 112, 116, 181 f.

[33] See Kahn, *Gnomon*, 41 (1969), 445. Ambiguity and imprecise language are unfortunate features of Bollack's important study of Empedocles.

[34] In making this charge I do not mean to include O'Brien, who gives a valuable discussion of Empedocles' reaction to Parmenides, pp. 239–49.

lack's. For both scholars agree that there is only one period of rest—the Sphere—and that Strife's total dominance is only a momentary phase in the movement of the many.[35]

<h1 style="text-align:center">V</h1>

Much of O'Brien's case for alternating worlds and the refutation of this theory by others turns on interpretations of the doxographers, especially Aristotle and Simplicius. In this paper it seemed best to concentrate attention on Empedocles' own statements, for these must be our first concern. But the doxographers were in a position to know more about Empedocles than we can ever recover. This said, one has to remember that neither Aristotle nor Simplicius is concerned with exegesis of Empedocles as such. Aristotle comments on and criticizes Empedocles in the light of his own concepts and categories. Simplicius is expounding Aristotle, and sometimes disagrees with his master over the latter's interpretation of Empedocles.

In general the comments of Simplicius raise fewer problems than those of Aristotle. Bollack, Hölscher, and Solmsen all accept Simplicius' analysis on certain crucial issues.[36] If this is justifiable, then the theory of a double cosmogony and zoogony loses still more credit since Simplicius consistently takes the cycle to be a single alternation between the Sphere and the world or many. Against this it is objected by O'Brien that Simplicius interprets Empedocles from the perspective of a Neoplatonist.[37] That is of course correct. But I believe that Simplicius makes it sufficiently clear when he is giving what he takes to be Empedocles' "real," i.e. Neoplatonic, meaning, and when he is interpreting the surface or literal meaning. I shall cite these two levels of interpretation in the following paragraphs and then exemplify Simplicius' self-consciousness concerning his Neoplatonic analysis.

Simplicius supposes that Empedocles "really" envisaged two eternal κόσμοι, one intelligible and the other sensible.[38] The former is represented by "the One" or "Sphere," and in it the four elements are predominantly unified by Love, though Strife also "plays some part in the

[35] See O'Brien, pp. 4-45, 55-103; Bollack, pp. 104-06, 127-36.

[36] Cf. Bollack, I, especially pp. 99-102; Hölscher, pp. 179-81; Solmsen, pp. 120-21.

[37] Pages 26-30, 99-101.

[38] *Phys.* 31.18-31; 160.22-161.20.

One." [39] The sensible cosmos is "this world," and in it the four elements are separated by Strife, though they are also at different times and among different things unified by Love.[40] Love and Strife are efficient causes of both worlds, but Love is the dominant cause in the intelligible and Strife the dominant cause of the sensible cosmos.[41] Hence the expressions "being unified by Love" (Sphere) and "separated by Strife" (this world).[42] The two worlds are related as being:becoming, or paradigm:copy.[43]

Where Simplicius is taking Empedocles literally he sees the cycle as an eternal alternation of the one (Sphere) and the many (four elements).[44] The one is a unification of the four elements by Love. The many is the physical world, a separation of the four elements by Strife.[45] In the physical world both unification and separation are manifest at different times among different things.[46] The creation of living things is due to Love.[47] The alternation of physical world and Sphere is an ἀλλοίωσις, "alteration," of the κόσμος, rather than two κόσμοι perishing and being born.[48] The world Strife brings to birth is always the same world.[49] The δίνη, "whirl," persists at the time of Love's dominance in this world.[50]

Simplicius' literal interpretation of the cosmic cycle is clear, and often confirmed by the fragments themselves. Bollack has been able to show that on many points it is correct. As he makes these different observations in different contexts, Simplicius states that "Empedocles expresses the double διακόσμησις enigmatically," i.e. the distinction between intelligible and physical worlds;[51] that Empedocles would be asserting the generation and destruction of motion "if one took him

[39] *Phys.* 159.8–10.

[40] *Phys.* 1124.2–9.

[41] *Phys.* 31.31–32.3.

[42] *Phys.* 1123.28–1124.3; *De Caelo* 294.10–13.

[43] *Phys.* 1123.26–28; *De Caelo* 140.25–30.

[44] *Phys.* 157.25–159.8; *De Caelo* 293.20–23. Cf. Aristotle *Met.* 984a9 ff.

[45] *Phys.* 154.6–14; 590.19–21.

[46] *Phys.* 1124.4–18; *De Caelo* 294.10–13.

[47] *Phys.* 33.3–4, 160.11–14; *De Caelo* 529.16–20.

[48] *De Caelo* 294.30–33; 307.14–308.4; 310.8–15. Cf. Aristotle *De Caelo* 280a11–23.

[49] *De Caelo* 293.20–23; 308.4–9.

[50] *De Caelo* 529.16–19.

[51] *Phys.* 160.22–26; *De Caelo* 140.25–30.

literally";[52] that he posits genesis of the ungenerated, separation of the unified (i.e. Sphere), and unification of the separated (i.e. physical world) in order to reveal the nature of things;[53] and that the "partial" dominance of Love and Strife is metaphorical.[54]

In order to establish the double cosmogony and zoogony it would be necessary to show that what I have called Simplicius' literal interpretation of the cosmic cycle is mistaken. If, as I have suggested, this interpretation is largely distinguishable from his Neoplatonic analysis, there is no reason to deny it serious consideration.

Aristotle's comments on the cosmic cycle have been much discussed during the last decade and assessed in different ways. Both O'Brien and Bollack claim the support of Aristotle for their interpretations. According to O'Brien, "Aristotle several times makes it clear that he understands Empedocles in terms of a cycle with an endless succession of the one and the many *and with alternate worlds of increasing Love and increasing Strife*." [55] For Bollack, on the other hand, Aristotle had a basically sound view of the cosmic cycle, which has been misinterpreted by those who attribute to him the words italicized in the last sentence.[56]

Although Aristotle says many strange and inconsistent things about Empedocles, one is reluctant to believe that his statements are so ambiguous that they can be taken as a whole to support both theories of the cycle. To simplify the problem somewhat I list below those relevant opinions which Aristotle expresses in the testimonia excerpted by Diels-Kranz.

Met. I.3.984a8 (DK A28): "Empedocles says that the four elements always persist and are not generated, but in respect of number and paucity they are combined into one and separated out of one." In this summary, which probably draws on fr. 17, Aristotle refers to the alternation, two-stage, of one and many.

Met. I.4.985a21 (DK A37): "For Empedocles Love often divides and Strife combines. For when all things are divided into the elements by

[52] *Phys.* 1121.17–21.

[53] *Phys.* 530.22–26.

[54] *Phys.* 530.12–17; 34.8–17.

[55] Page 169, my italics. The main texts cited by O'Brien are *Phys.* 250b26–252a32; *De Caelo* 279b14–17; 280a11–24; *Phys.* 187a10–26; *Met.* 985a21–29; *De Gen. et Corr.* 334a5–9; *De Caelo* 301a15–16. For the last four passages see below.

[56] I, pp. 102–06.

Strife, fire and each of the other elements are united into one. And when they come together again into one by Love their parts must once again be separated from each element." Nothing in Empedocles' own preserved fragments requires Aristotle's assertion that "Strife unites the elements into one." But though Aristotle may be wrong about this,[57] he gives no grounds for inferring a double cosmogony and zoogony here.

De Caelo III.2.301a14 (DK A42): "It is not reasonable to make genesis proceed from elements which are separate and moving. Therefore Empedocles passes over the genesis (scil. of the heavens) under Love. . . . For the cosmos is composed of separated elements. So it must come to be from a state of unity and mixture." Much has been made of this passage. O'Brien thinks it implies two cosmogonies, one by Strife and one by Love, though Empedocles failed to describe the latter (p. 176). Solmsen takes it to deny a cosmogony by Love (p. 124). Bollack gives, I think, the right explanation: Aristotle conflates the destruction of the Sphere with the formation of the cosmos (I, p. 56). The former is the work of Strife and could not be the work of Love. But Love combines what Strife disintegrates. Perhaps Empedocles did not describe Love's genesis of the heavens. He certainly, as O'Brien says, implies it. But Aristotle's criticism is not based on the claim that Empedocles provided for two cosmogonies and failed to describe one of them. Rather, Aristotle argues that Empedocles did attribute this genesis to Love but failed to describe it owing to the problem of starting the universe by an act of unification.

De Gen. et Corr. II.7.334a5 (DK A42): "At the same time Empedocles says that the cosmos is now under Strife similar to what it was previously under Love." From this sentence it has been inferred that we are in a world of increasing Strife, which manifests the same situation as a previous world of increasing Love. Now this inference is compatible with what Aristotle says here, but it is less certain that his remarks entitle one to draw it. Aristotle makes his observation within a critique of Empedocles' explanations of motion. As Cherniss points out, Aristotle's point is "if Love or Strife are causes of motion in Empedocles' system at different times, how could the world be in the same condition at different times, since Love and Strife are contraries?" [58] Cherniss also notes that Aristotle's objection depends on

[57] Bollack thinks he is (I, pp. 49–50).

[58] *Aristotle's Criticism of Presocratic Philosophy* (Baltimore, 1935), pp. 189–90.

the supposition that in either time mentioned only one of the two motor forces is at work, an assumption falsifiable from fr. 35 whether there is one world or two. Aristotle's "now" as evidence for the present condition of the world must also be set against Empedocles' own words in fr. 71, where forms fashioned by Aphrodite have "now" come into being. O'Brien remarks that elsewhere Aristotle (*De Caelo* 300b25–31; *De Gen. An.* 722b17–29) refers certain biological formations "under Love" to the past (pp. 172–75). But these texts say nothing which is incompatible with Love's influence now, for the formations mentioned were heads without necks, etc. The passage under discussion is concerned not with biology but with causes of motion. Love previously caused the elements to unite as the Sphere, and Strife separated them in initiating cosmogony. It is the latter event to which Aristotle may be alluding when he writes of the "cosmos now under Strife." [59] On the strength of fr. 17.12–13, Aristotle may have inferred that alternating movements of the elements do not alter the essential sameness of the cosmos; or, as he puts it elsewhere, that Empedocles has an eternal cosmos with "changing dispositions." [60] If one reads this passage in O'Brien's way as a reference to alternating worlds of increasing Love and Strife, one has to reckon with the fact that Aristotle never cites these worlds more explicitly than he does here. Alternating worlds are not implied by *Phys.* I.4.187a20 ff., where Aristotle's reference to περίοδος simply asserts a periodic reconstitution of one and many.

Research of the 'sixties has shown that interpretation of Empedocles' cosmic cycle in terms of alternating worlds of Love and Strife is open to very serious objections. I have tried in this paper to examine the problem as it arises from Empedocles' own text, and to show why I believe the simpler scheme of an alternation which proceeds in one direction, involving only one world, to be correct. It is possible to accept this scheme without subscribing to some of the more extreme arguments which have been used against the traditional interpretation. Apart from its coherence and evidential soundness, the two-stage linear cycle is more in line with the general current of Greek thought. There are clear

[59] Cf. Bollack, I, p. 104. Solmsen finds the source of Aristotle's assertion in Emped. fr. 26.5, and Hölscher cites fr. 16.

[60] *De Caelo* 280a11–23, cf. Solmsen, p. 131. O'Brien's argument (p. 173) that ἐπὶ τῆς φιλίας or φιλότητος in Aristotle should not carry quite different meanings is compatible with Aristotle's using it to refer both to biological formations "under Love" and to Love's formation of the Sphere.

points of resemblance between Anaximander's constitution of the world by the separation of opposites from the *apeiron* and Empedocles' elements which desert the Sphere under Strife. Anaximander may have posited a periodic destruction and re-creation of the world such as Empedocles introduced.[61] Balanced strife between opposites is fundamental to Heraclitus, and this looks back to Anaximander and forward to Empedocles. Heraclitus probably did not envisage a cycle in Empedocles' sense, but it is legitimate to compare his concept of the cosmos as an "ever-living fire, being kindled and quenched in measures" (fr. 30) with the waxing and waning of the elements in Empedocles through which the world comes to be and ceases to be. Two worlds created and destroyed by reverse processes have no place in this tradition, nor are they consistent with the philosophical economy of Empedocles' radical answer to Parmenides. Essentially Bollack is right to call the difficulties raised by Raven and other conservatives "the false problem."

The cosmic cycle will continue to justify vigorous discussion, but it has tended unfortunately to overshadow other issues. The major outstanding question, with which future studies of Empedocles must come to grips, is the relation of the physical to the religious poem. Much still remains to be established on the precise nature of the elements in Empedocles. If my suggestion concerning their relative genesis and decline in fr. 17 is acceptable, this may be a clue to understanding the "exile of the daimons" which Empedocles relates in the *Katharmoi*.[62]

[61] For the evidence and modern opinions, see Guthrie, *A History of Greek Philosophy* vol. I (Cambridge, 1962), pp. 106-15; Kahn, *Anaximander and the Origins of Greek Cosmology* (New York, 1960), pp. 46-53.

[62] I have not been able to take account of J. C. Luth, *Die Struktur des Wirklichen im empedokleischen System*, Monogr. zur philos. Forschung, 61 (Meisenheim, 1969). Work on this paper was begun at the Institute for Advanced Study, Princeton, of which I was privileged to be a member in 1970.

18

RELIGION AND NATURAL PHILOSOPHY
IN EMPEDOCLES' DOCTRINE
OF THE SOUL

Charles H. Kahn

Since Zeller's classic work, all students of Greek philosophy have recognized that the thought of Empedocles presents two quite distinct aspects. On the one hand, Empedocles is the author of a rational cosmology which explains all processes of the natural world in terms of the combination and separation of four elements under the opposing influence of the forces of Love and Hate. Yet in his poem of *Purifications* the same author appears like a figure from another world, an inspired seer who proclaims himself a god and exhorts all mankind to purify themselves by abstaining from meat, beans, and laurel leaves. This religious teaching is just as clearly dependent upon "Orphic" or Pythagorean mystery cults as his physical theory is upon the thought of Parmenides and the Ionian naturalists. Empedocles the philosopher of nature and Empedocles the prophet of transmigration are both intelligible when taken separately. Together, they seem to compose a split personality whose two sections are not united by any essential link.

In an historical context, of course, it is possible to interpret such a duality by reference to the ambiguous spiritual tendencies of the fifth century B.C., when rationalism and mysticism had not fully asserted their rival claims nor taken up the positions of clear-cut hostility which

From the *Archiv für Geschichte der Philosophie*, 42 (1960), 3–35, with the revisions and "Retractationes" included in its reprinting in John P. Anton with George L. Kustas, eds., *Essays in Ancient Greek Philosophy* (Albany, N.Y.: State University of New York Press, 1971), pp. 3–38. The appendix, "Empedocles Among the Shamans" (*AGP*, pp. 30–35, and Anton, pp. 30–36), is omitted. The paper was originally presented under the title "Panpsychism and Immortality in Empedocles" before the 1958 meeting of the Society for Ancient Greek Philosophy in Cincinnati, Ohio. Reprinted here with the permission of Walter de Gruyter & Co., Berlin, the State University of New York Press, and the author.

they often occupy in the modern world. And there are in fact significant precedents in early Greek thought for such a mixture of mystery religion with natural philosophy. Pythagoras himself seems to have borrowed the outlines of his cosmology from the Milesian physicists. We find elemental physics crossed with mystic immortality in the doctrine of Heraclitus that "we live the death of the gods and they live our death." [1] The metaphysics and the cosmology of Parmenides are cast in the form of a supernatural vision vouchsafed him on a journey to the realm of Light.

Yet even if the list of such intermarriages between philosophy and religion were considerably lengthened, it could not explain the relationship between the mystic and the rational elements in the thought of Empedocles. The problem, as Zeller put it, is that Empedocles' religious teachings "stand in no visible connection with the scientific principles" of his physics; the doctrine of transmigration and purification appear as "mere articles of faith, imperfectly appended to his philosophical scheme." [2] In fact to many scholars it has seemed that "the cosmological system of Empedocles leaves no room for an immortal soul, which is presupposed by the *Purifications*." [3] Such a radical disparity between the two aspects of Empedocles' thought led Jaeger to describe him as "a philosophical centaur, so to speak—a prodigious union of Ionian elemental physics and Orphic theology." [4]

[1] Heraclitus B77 and B62. All fragments are cited according to DK. The following works are cited below in the notes by the author's name alone: E. Bignone, *Empedocle* (Turin, 1916); H. Diels, "Über die Gedichte des Empedokles," *Sitzungsberichte der preussischen Akademie der Wissenschaften zu Berlin, Philosophisch-historische Klasse*, 1898, 396–415; U. v. Wilamowitz-Moellendorff, "Die Καθαρμοί des Empedokles," ibid., 1929, 626–61; W. Nestle, "Der Dualismus des Empedokles," *Philologus*, 65 (1906), 545–57.

[2] "[Die physicalischen Annahmen des Empedokles] erscheinen daher als Teile eines naturphilosophischen Systems, das . . . nach Einem Plan ausgeführt ist. Anders verhält es sich mit gewissen religiösen Lehren und Vorschriften, welche . . . mit den wissenschaftlichen Grundsätzen unseres Physikers in keiner sichtbaren Verbindung stehen. In diesen Sätzen können wir nur Glaubensartikel sehen, die zu seinem philosophischen System von anderer Seite her hinzukamen und demselben nur unvollkommen angegliedert wurden"; E. Zeller, *Die Philosophie der Griechen*, vol. I, 5th ed. (Leipzig, 1892), p. 806; cf. ibid., pp. 809–17 (= pp. 1001, 1004–16 in the 6th ed. by W. Nestle [Leipzig, 1920], who cites the earlier literature).

[3] Burnet, *EGP*, p. 250.

[4] *Paideia*, Engl. tr., 2nd ed. (New York, 1945), vol. I, p. 295, quoted with

Now this is a difficult prodigy for us to understand. If the contradiction between his philosophic and religious views is as flagrant as most modern authors have supposed, is it conceivable that Empedocles himself was unaware of that fact? Or that he found the situation a tolerable one? He cannot have consoled himself, like Averroes, by distinguishing between the conclusions of reason and the tenets of faith. The fifth century B.C. had only one standard of truth, and hence no notion of irrational faith: Empedocles makes use of the same term, *pistis*, for belief in his physical theories and in his religious doctrines.[5] If the religion of the *Purifications* is incompatible with the cosmology of the poem *On Nature*, we are left with an unmitigated contradiction between two views expressed by the same philosopher.

Diels and Wilamowitz thought they could avoid this antinomy by transferring all of the more obviously theological fragments to the religious poem, and interpreting the latter as the fruit of a spiritual conversion in Empedocles' old age. They made the most of the fact that Empedocles' political career seems to have ended in banishment and, since the *Purifications* speak of him traveling from city to city, these two scholars attributed that poem to the last period of his life, when he had perhaps become, as Matthew Arnold imagined him,

> . . . half mad,
> With exile and with brooding on his wrongs.

In their view, the two halves of the centaur belong to different periods in Empedocles' life: the rational materialism of the physical poem is later replaced by the religiosity of the *Purifications*.[6]

As far as psychological plausibility is concerned, this hypothesis of

---

approval by G. Vlastos, who comments: " 'Prodigious' is the right word for the union of physics and theology, as it is for the junction of immortal god and mortal flesh. The one is as much of a miracle as the other, and Empedocles doubtless devoutly believed it to be such. He left us no explanation of either, and it would be futile to try to supply it by rationalizing the theology of the mystic or mystifying the logic of the cosmologist"; *Philosophical Quarterly*, 2 (1952), 121.

[5] For $\pi i \sigma \tau \iota s$ see B3.10 and 13, B71.1, B114.3, and the other passages listed by Nestle (p. 548 n. 11), who also compares $\pi i \sigma \tau \iota s$ $\dot{a} \lambda \eta \theta \dot{\eta} s$ in Parmenides B1.30, B8.12 and 28; $\dot{a} \pi \iota \sigma \tau i \eta$ in Heraclitus B86.

[6] Diels, p. 406; Wilamowitz, pp. 655–56. For the exile see $\pi \epsilon \phi \epsilon \upsilon \gamma \dot{\omega} s$ in Diogenes Laertius VIII.52 and $\kappa \dot{a} \theta o \delta o s$, ibid., VIII.67. In B112 Empedocles describes himself as traveling from city to city, but his greeting $\chi a i \rho \epsilon \tau \epsilon$ to

a spiritual development for Empedocles is considerably more attractive than the usual view of his work as a mere juxtaposition of irreconcilable elements. Diels and Wilamowitz must be correct in recognizing the *Purifications* as the later of the two poems, and they may well be right in thinking that it reflects a change in Empedocles' vision of himself and his work.[7] But a difference in date and outlook between the two poems cannot possibly resolve the conflict between his philosophy and his religion, for the physical poem is also a religious work. Even if we were to follow Diels in assigning the theological fragments to the *Purifications* (although all the evidence is against this),[8] the poem *On Nature* would

---

the citizens of Acragas does not prove that he is actually writing from abroad. The contrary seems to be indicated by the phrase "I go about among you an immortal god" (Burnet); "Ich aber wandle jetzt als unsterblicher Gott . . . vor Euch" (Diels, in the early editions of the *Fragmente*).

[7] The chronological priority of the Περὶ Φύσεως was contested by J. Bidez, *La Biographie d'Empédocle* (Gand, 1894), pp. 160 ff., and more recently by W. Kranz, in *Hermes*, 70 (1935), 111-19, and in his *Empedokles* (Zurich, 1949). Kranz was answered by K. Reinhardt, "Empedokles, Orphiker und Physiker, "*CP*, 45 (1950), 172-77 [repr. in H.-G. Gadamer, ed., *Um die Begriffswelt der Vorsokratiker* (Darmstadt, 1968), pp. 497-511]. I agree on this point with Diels, Wilamowitz, and Reinhardt, but unfortunately I cannot accept what seems to be their most decisive argument: the second invocation of the Muse in B131 (εὐχομένῳ νῦν αὖτε παρίστασο, Καλλιόπεια). If this fragment came from the *Purifications* (as Diels' arrangement assumes), it would obviously constitute a backward reference to the physical poem, which begins with just such an invocation (B3-4). But for the true place of B131, see the next note.

[8] The λόγος ἀμφὶ θεῶν is introduced in B131 by the invocation of a Muse, of whom there is otherwise no trace in the *Purifications* but who appears of course in the proem of *On Nature*. Bignone observed that it would be natural for Empedocles to invoke the Muse once more (νῦν αὖτε) when entering upon the last portion of his work, and pointed out the similar invocation of Calliope by Lucretius at the beginning of his last book (VI.92). From B131 alone, then, we might conclude that there was a discussion of the gods to be found in the last section or "book" of the physical poem. Now Tzetzes actually quotes Empedocles' famous description of deity as a φρὴν ἱερή (B134) from "the third book of the Φυσικά": Ἐμπεδοκλῆς τῷ τρίτῳ τε τῶν Φυσικῶν δεικνύων τίς ἡ οὐσία τοῦ θεοῦ κατ' ἔπος οὕτω λέγει. For reasons of his own, Diels wished to dismiss this statement as a "Schwindelcitate" (despite the fact that Tzetzes also assigns fr. 6 to the first book—correctly), but Stein, Zeller, and Bignone drew the more natural conclusion that B131-34 must come from the end of

still not read like a tract of scientific rationalism. The proem of the work, and in particular fragment 3, brings us face to face with a religious poet whose verses breathe the spirit of mysterious, half-suppressed revelation:

> But, ye gods, turn away from my tongue the madness of those men,
> and from your holy lips pour forth a pure stream;
> and you, the much-wooed, fair-armed virgin Muse
> do I entreat, of what is lawful for creatures of a day to hear
> drive here your well-reined chariot from Piety's hall,
> nor will you be seduced by the blossoms of honor and fame
> to pluck them in men's sight, by daring to say more than is holy
> and then forsooth to throne on the heights of wisdom.

The invocation of Calliope, the muse of lovely verse,[9] may perhaps be interpreted as a literary convention devoid of religious significance—although the fact that her chariot is to come from the realm of Piety suggests rather more than that. But what are we to make of Empedocles' appeal to the gods to "turn away from my tongue the madness of those men,[10] and pour from your holy lips a pure stream"? Why does he ask

---

the physical poem. Bignone remarked that the repetition of verses from B29 in B134 can find numerous parallels *within* the poem *On Nature*, none between it and the *Purifications*; and that the attack on anthropomorphism which is contained in these verses is entirely at home in the physical work, while it would be less appropriate in the religious poem, which uses traditional imagery in addressing a popular audience (Bignone, pp. 477, 631–49). Furthermore, the use of the term κόσμος for "world" (B134.5) is much more likely to occur in a technical poem than in a popular work like the *Purifications*, which seems to avoid all philosophical complexities.

[9] For the Muse's name, see B131. Empedocles may have Bacchylides 5.176 in mind, where Calliope is similarly petitioned by the poet for a chariot of song. Other poetic chariots of the fifth century (without mention of a particular Muse) are cited by C. M. Bowra, *Problems in Greek Poetry* (Oxford, 1953), p. 42.

[10] Most scholars have assumed that the μανίη which fills Empedocles with such horror must be that of dogmatic philosophers like Parmenides, who deny both the evidence of the senses and the limitations of human knowledge. This interpretation can be traced back to Sextus Empiricus, who quotes these verses to illustrate Empedocles' theory of knowledge (VII.124, cited by DK in the introduction to B3). But to see how wrong Sextus can be, one need only

the Muse for inspiration only on those matters "which it is lawful for creatures of a day to hear"? The pious chariot of the Muse is "well-reined" (euēnion) because there will be limits to her revelation: she can be relied upon not to seek glory by "declaring more than is holy."

Like the poem of Parmenides, the physical work of Empedocles is thus presented in the form of a religious revelation. Unlike Parmenides, Empedocles insists upon the limited character of the revelation and also upon its esoteric quality: his teachings are entrusted to Pausanias alone, who is urged to keep them "mute within his breast." [11] The partial nature of the revelation makes one think of a preliminary initiation, which reserves the final disclosure for a later epopteia. In fact Empedocles adheres much more closely to the form and style of a religious revelation than does Parmenides. The poem begins and ends with an appeal for purity, and with an earnest denunciation of things impure.[12] The secret doctrine is credited with magic potency: the disciple will be able to cure old age, check or call back the winds, make rain or dry weather, and raise the dead to life.[13] Diels wished to read these promises as a scientific hope of mastering nature by the knowledge of its laws,

---

look at his exegesis of Parmenides' proem, where the "whirling wheels" of the chariot are interpreted as a cryptic reference to the ears (VII.112).

In view of the context provided by Empedocles' own verses, it is much more natural to understand the madness in question as that of impious men who disclose more than is "lawful for creatures of a day to hear" (B3.4–8; cf. B2.9). As far as bold dogmatism is concerned, Empedocles' account of the pre-cosmic Sphere can match anything in Parmenides.

Sextus and those who follow him have been led to their interpretation by the last five verses in B3 (not quoted above), which do indeed emphasize the prudent use of sense data. But they ignore the fact that this constitutes a separate topic, introduced by the formula ἀλλ' ἄγ' ἄθρει (cf. B17.14 and B20.8) and marked by the shift of interlocutors from the Muse back to Pausanias.

[11] B111.2, with B5.

[12] Compare καθαρὴ πηγή in B3 with καθαραὶ μελέται in B110.2, and πολλὰ δὲ δείλ' ἔμπαια in B2 with μυρία δειλά in B110.7. In the Purifications, δειλός is regularly used for the misery of those who violate the precepts of purification; see δειλὸν θνητῶν γένος (B124), δειλοί, πάνδειλοι (B141), etc.

[13] B111. The use of the future tense in this fragment (as in Parmenides B10) suggests that it appeared early in the poem, not at the end where Diels has placed it. The echoes of the proem in B110 probably indicate that these verses closed the entire work, which thus ends as it began with the opposition between purity and misery, true knowledge and dull perception.

but Empedocles' fifth-century rival in the practice of medicine, the Hippocratic author of *The Sacred Disease*, recognized the claim for what it was: a standard formula of sorcerers and medicine men, who proposed to treat epilepsy by charms (*epaoidai*) and purifications (*katharmoi*).[14] And it is precisely a "healing spell" of this kind which the crowds of sufferers expect to hear from Empedocles, as he tells us in his own poem of *Purifications*.[15]

It is not only the form and spirit of the physical poem which suggests a supernatural revelation, but the doctrinal content as well. The work probably concluded with a general discussion of the nature of the gods, and with the announcement of a divinity who can only be described as a "sacred and surpassing spirit (*phrēn*), darting through the whole world with his rapid thoughts." [16] Its cardinal doctrine is the power of a deity "whom no mortal man has discerned":

Fire and Water and Earth and the lofty zone of Air,
and baneful Strife apart from these, their match in every way,
and Love among them, equal in length and breadth;
her must you perceive with the mind, nor sit with dazed eyes,
she who is worshipped by mortals as instinct in their limbs,
by whom they think loving thoughts and perform deeds of union,
calling her by the name of Joy as well as Aphrodite;
her has no mortal man discerned whirling among the others;
but you shall hear the undeceptive march of my tale.[17]

The four elements had all been recognized in one form or another by the Ionians. The war between them is a central doctrine of Heraclitus. What Empedocles claims for himself is the discovery of Love and Attraction as a universal power in the physical world, on an equal footing with elemental Strife. His conception goes far beyond the poetic use of Aphrodite and Eros as symbols of the creative union of Heaven and Earth, and even beyond Parmenides' notion of the intercourse between elemental opposites, Fire and Night.[18] Since there are four unlike ele-

[14] *De Morbo Sacro* 4 (cf. ch. 2).

[15] B112.11: κλυεῖν εὐηκέα βάξιν.

[16] B134; for its place in the physical poem, see n. 8, above.

[17] B17.18–26.

[18] Cf. Hesiod *Theog.* 120; Aeschylus *Danaids* fr. 44; Parmenides B12–13. On the other hand, the role of Aphrodite in Euripides *Hippolytus* 447–50 shows the influence of Empedocles, as does that of Eros in the speech of Eryximachus in the *Symposium*.

ments in Empedocles' scheme, the idea of a union or harmony between them inevitably implies more than the sexual principle of an affinity between opposites. The best example of Love's work in forming natural compounds is the geometric proportion which unites the various ingredients of a mixture.[19] In this respect, every natural blend is an embodiment of *Philotēs* or *Harmoniē*.

Thus Empedocles' new divinity dominates the world of nature just as she dominates the poem in which this world is explained. When he comes to describe the fullest manifestation of this principle, Empedocles passes beyond the realm of generation and corruption to portray the perfect form of a universal Sphere within which, for a certain time, all the elements are periodically immobilized and transfigured under the absolute sway of Love.[20] Here, at the culminating moment of his cosmic poem, Empedocles presents us with a supramundane *theos*, the direct counterpart to Parmenides' revelation of the perfect Sphere of *to eon*, and the equivalent in early Greek thought of an apocalyptic vision.

There is, then, sufficient evidence of a religious orientation within Empedocles' poem *On Nature*. His cosmology is religious in the same sense that this term applies to the thought of Parmenides or Plato. The traditional view of it as atheistic or materialistic rests upon a confusion between the science of Empedocles and the science of the nineteenth century, or between the spirit of his poem and that of his great imitator Lucretius. There is no room for a "conversion" between the physical poem and the *Purifications*, for the author of *On Nature* is already a religious mystic who hints at his belief in immortality:

> A man wise in such matters will not surmise in his mind
> that when they are alive, in what men call life,
> then only do they exist and encounter good things and evil,
> but before mortals are composed and after they are dissolved,
> they are nothing at all.[21]

[19] See B96 and B98.

[20] B27–29; the sphere is called θεός in B31.

[21] B15:

> οὐκ ἂν ἀνὴρ τοιαῦτα σοφὸς φρεσὶ μαντεύσαιτο,
> ὡς ὄφρα μέν τε βιῶσι, τὸ δὴ βίοτον καλέουσι,
> τόφρα μὲν οὖν εἰσίν, καί σφιν πάρα δειλὰ καὶ ἐσθλά,
> πρὶν δὲ πάγεν τε βροτοὶ καὶ ⟨ἐπεὶ⟩ λύθεν, οὐδὲν ἄρ' εἰσιν.

Rohde, Bignone, and others have remarked the parallel between τὸ δὴ βίοτον καλέουσι and τίς δ' οἶδεν, εἰ τὸ ζῆν μέν ἐστι κατθανεῖν, τὸ κατθανεῖν δὲ ζῆν κάτω

We know from Pindar that a mysterious doctrine of punishment, purification, and rebirth, comparable to that which Empedocles presents in
the *Purifications*, had been taught in Acragas since the time of Theron.
Empedocles must have been familiar with this teaching when he composed the physical poem.[22] He is probably referring to it in the verses
just quoted, and it is not unreasonable to suppose that he has the same
mystic doctrine in mind when he insists upon secrecy concerning things
not "lawful for creatures of a day to hear."

If Empedocles believed in transmigration or in any form of immortality when he wrote the poem *On Nature*, all attempts to resolve the
conflict between his cosmology and his religion along developmental
lines are bound to fail. There is an obvious contrast between the religious attitude of the two poems, since one suppresses any direct reference to the doctrine which the other openly proclaims. And since the
more revealing of the two is also the more public, it is difficult to explain
this difference in terms of the audience to which they are addressed.
Empedocles' own attitude seems to have undergone a change, and we
must ask ourselves why. First, however, we must recognize the fact that
this change does not involve the rejection of his own cosmology. The
religious poem is as discreet on this subject as the physical work is mum
concerning the doctrine of the *Purifications*. But in neither case does
silence imply negation. Just as there are hints of the religious teaching
in the poem *On Nature*, a close reading of the *Purifications* will show
that they likewise presuppose Empedocles' cosmology.

The decisive moment of the physical poem is the disruption of the
divine Sphere by Strife, since from this event proceeds the formation of
the world as we know it. Turning to the *Purifications*, we see that this
rupture of primordial harmony is paralleled by the fall of a daimon—
that is, of a deified human soul—from its proper state of bliss into this

---

νομίζεται; Euripides Fr. 638; cf. Fr. 833; Plato *Gorgias* 492e. The phrase
σφιν πάρα δειλὰ καὶ ἐσθλά seems to echo the antithetic mystic formula for bliss
and suffering in the afterlife; cf. *Hymn to Demeter* 480–83, Pindar Fr. 121
(Bowra), Soph. Fr. 119. Plato *Phaedo* 63c5: εἶναί τι τοῖς τετελευτηκόσι καί,
ὥσπερ γε καὶ πάλαι λέγεται, πολὺ ἄμεινον τοῖς ἀγαθοῖς ἢ τοῖς κακοῖς.

[22] Pindar *Olymp.* II, esp. vv. 56 ff.; the esoteric nature of the doctrine is
hinted at in βέλη . . . φωνάεντα συνετοῖσιν. See also Pindar Frr. 114–16, 127
(Bowra). Both the connection of the Second Olympian with Acragas and the
close parallel between the favorable stages of reincarnation in Pindar Fr. 127
and Empedocles B146 suggest that Empedocles was familiar with this secret
doctrine "von Haus her" (Wilamowitz, p. 660).

"joyless place" of birth, suffering, and death. The parallel is easily remarked, for it is plainly indicated by Empedocles himself. He repeats the striking reference to "broad oaths," which seal the law of individual rebirth exactly as they ordained the physical period of the cosmos, and he tells us that the daimon fell because it "trusted in raving Strife." These formulas imply that the destiny of the human soul is grounded in the law of the universe, as revealed in the poem *On Nature*.[23]

It is therefore no trifling matter if, as many scholars have claimed, this physical cosmology is incompatible with the religious doctrine which Empedocles builds upon it. Is there or is there not a place in his physics for an immortal soul? This is the question to which some answer must be found. The chances of hitting upon the right answer will perhaps be greater if we first attempt to specify just what we mean by a "soul."

In modern usage, the term "soul" (and its various equivalents, such as *âme* and *Seele*) often refers to the conscious self in its broadest aspects—to the non-bodily reality of the whole person as seen from the inside. It may be "the essence or substance . . . of individual life, manifested in thinking, willing, and knowing," as *Webster's Dictionary* puts it. Now if the soul is understood in such a comprehensive sense, the doctrine of its immortality naturally implies the survival of the whole person in his full individuality. And in fact the identity between the immortal soul and the concrete human being is often emphasized by the belief that the soul will eventually be reunited with its original body in some spiritualized form.

Now if this is what we mean by an immortal soul, the modern critics are certainly correct in maintaining that such a view is excluded by the cosmology of Empedocles. But it may be fairly doubted whether Empedocles or any other Greek philosopher before Christian times ever maintained the doctrine of immortality in this form. The survival they contemplate is never that of the whole human being, but of one single element of our empirical self, one whose isolated existence after death involves a complete break with the conditions of human life. The most striking example of such a break is Aristotle's doctrine of the separable *nous*, which is eternally aware of intelligible realities but entirely un-

[23] Compare B115.2 and 14 with B30. For the concrete sense of πλατὺς ὅρκος, "a thick bond or enclosure," see J. Bollack, "Styx et serments," *Revue des études grecques*, 71 (1958), 1–35. The manner in which the *Purifications* thus alludes briefly to notions which have a fuller development in *On Nature* provides a good indication that the physical poem was composed first.

affected by—and hence without memory of—any specifically human experience. If we disregard the metaphysical complexity of Aristotle's doctrine, it may serve to typify the Greek view of what is implied in immortality. *Athanasia* means *homoiōsis theōi*, not the preservation of human nature but an assimilation to the divine. In the case of Plato too it may be doubted whether there is any significant personal individuality for the purified *psyche*, as defined by the last argument of the *Phaedo*. In the context of transmigration, above all, there can be nothing permanent or valuable in the human condition as such. It is only the last stage on a journey which begins with the vegetable and ends with the escape into unalloyed divinity. In this view, any reunion of the soul with an individual body can only signify a blot on its condition. What lives on is not the individual human personality,[24] in fact not the man at all, but the godlike element which was lodged within his breast.

In Greek philosophy, then, there is always an implicit distinction between the soul which survives—the immortal and therefore divine principle in man—and the soul in the broader sense, as the living totality of feeling, thought, and desire. Confusion between the two is naturally facilitated by the fact that *psyche* may designate either one. In the popular conception of an afterlife, this confusion was enhanced by the old tendency to imagine the spirits in Hades as phantoms of the men who had lived on earth. So Odysseus in the underworld can recognize the *psychai* of Ajax, Achilles, and Agamemnon.[25] But when we are dealing with a philosopher, we must be prepared to distinguish more rigorously between the divine psychic entity which lives on and the mortal complex in which it is embedded. This means, among other things, that we must

[24] Strictly speaking, a doctrine of personal immortality could scarcely be developed without a word for "person." The classical philosophers speak only of the survival of the ψυχή or νοῦς, which is not the same thing. A full study of the philosophical uses of πρόσωπον and *persona* would probably cast important light on the Hellenistic, Roman, and above all Judaeo-Christian origins of the concept of "personality." See the lexicographical survey of R. Hirzel, "Die Person," *Sitzungsberichte der Königlich Bayerischen Akademie der Wissenschaften zu München, Philosophisch-philologische und historische Klasse*, Jahrgang 1914, 10. Abhandlung.

[25] Only at this popular level can we speak of a Greek belief in personal immortality. Before a popular audience, Socrates alludes to the Homeric underworld and hopes to chat there with Orpheus and Agamemnon (*Apol.* 41a–c). But in the intimate seriousness of the *Phaedo* he expresses doubt as to whether he will really meet human beings in the other world, or only gods (63c).

separate the question of immortality from that of empirical thought or "consciousness."

In the case of Empedocles, there has been an unfortunate tendency to identify the two. Because he explains all phenomena of consciousness—all thought, feeling, and perception—by reference to the constitution of a mortal compound, most scholars have inferred that his physical theory excludes an immortal soul. How could there be good and evil for a man after death, if his "thought" (*noēma*) is dissolved at the same time as the physical compound of his body? To many it has seemed that one need only raise this question to show the incompatibility between Empedocles' natural philosophy and his religious beliefs.

Yet the question is not fairly posed unless we are prepared to distinguish between the deathless soul which transmigrates and the conscious mind or thought which is the function of a particular compound. And to do so, we must first look a bit more closely at the physical psychology of Empedocles.

In the matter of consciousness, the position of Empedocles may be defined as a rigorous panpsychism. In his view, which seems to be shared to some degree by most early Greek thinkers, the faculty of feeling, perception, and thought—*aisthanesthai, noein,* or *phronein*—does not constitute a prerogative of men, or even of men and animals, but is assumed to be distributed generally throughout the natural world. From this point of view, there is really no such thing as inanimate nature. The character of any object is conceived of as a vital urge that may be described in terms of thought and volition. This conception is analogous to the "animism" which is said to characterize the attitude of many primitive peoples in their dealings with nature. But the animism of Empedocles is scarcely primitive: it is explicitly formulated as a philosophic principle. He ends the poem *On Nature* with a warning to his friend Pausanias that the truths communicated must be carefully borne in mind, or else

> they will leave you all at once, when their time comes round,
> yearning after their fellows, to return to their own dear kind;
> for know that all things have intelligence and a share in thought.[26]

This statement implies a systematic parallelism between physical objects and mental conceptions. Not only does everything have a share in thought, but every thought is treated like a thing. Apparently Empedocles recognizes no radical distinction between the two, for the con-

[26] B110.6–10.

stituents of the physical world and of our perception of this world are described in the same terms:

> By earth we behold earth, by water water,
> by air bright air, by fire, ravaging fire,
> love by love and strife by gloomy strife.[27]
> For out of these are all things compounded and fitted together
> and with these do they think and feel pleasure and pain.[28]

The least we can say is that Empedocles posits a one-to-one correspondence between our conscious thought or mind and the physical composition of our bodies. It seems more likely that he simply identified the two. Love and Strife are described not only as dynamic principles of cohesion and dissolution, but also as physical masses on a par with Fire, Water, Earth, and Air.[29] So mind and body are homogeneous, and external sense objects act upon us by mingling their substance with the ingredients of our nature, that is, with our body and mind at once. Sensation and philosophic instruction are described in the same concrete manner. It is hard for the truth to reach us, for the passages of entry are narrow and clogged by "wretched impacts which dull men's thoughts." [30] It is these "wretched myriads" of oncoming sensations which distract us from the truth of Empedocles' words.[31] "For men's mind is increased according to what is present," i.e. what is physically present in their bodies; when our physical condition changes, the character of our thought and perception is altered.[32] Since learning, like sensation, is introduced from without, in order to be held fast it must be thoroughly integrated into the mixture of our own nature and character, our *physis* and *ēthos*.[33] If not, says Empedocles, it will hurry home to its own kind. The psychological fact of forgetting is understood as the escape of ingredients from a particular mixture.

Hence it is our physical composition or *physis* which accounts for—if it is not identical with—our psychic character (*ēthos*) and thought

[27] B109.

[28] B107.

[29] See B17.19–20.

[30] B2.2. Compare B114 and B133 for the difficulty truth has in reaching the mind (φρήν).

[31] B110.6–7.

[32] B106 and B108.

[33] B110.5.

(*noēma*).[34] This is clearly seen in Empedocles' reference to the central sensorium, which for him as for Aristotle is the heart:

> nurtured in the seas of the resurgent blood,
> there what men call thought is mainly to be found;
> for the thought of men is the blood about their heart.[35]

The heart-blood plays this privileged role because it is the substance in which the elements are most perfectly blended. But the same principle applies to the body taken as a whole, as well as to each one of its parts, as Theophrastus tells us in his summary of a lost section of the poem:

> Those in whom the elements are equally blended or nearly so, . . . are the most intelligent and most acute in sensation, and those closest to them are proportionately (acute and intelligent), while those with the opposite composition are the most foolish. . . . And those who have an equable blend in some one part are skillful with that part. Therefore some men are good orators, others craftsmen, because the (proper) blend in one case is in their hands, in the other case in their tongue; and the same is true of other capacities.[36]

As Aristotle saw, this view of Empedocles implies not so much a single "soul" as a multitude of mental units, one for each element (since each one perceives its corresponding object) and one for each part of the body (since each has its own blend or *physis*).[37] Our psychic nature taken as a whole is a compound of these elemental and organic "souls," just as our bodily nature is a compound of elements and of their mixture in the various parts. The psychic and somatic complexes are in fact one and the same. And since there is a fragment of mind or thought corresponding to every fragment of body, the panpsychism of Empedocles implies a kind of infinite divisibility of the "soul."

---

[34] Empedocles' doctrine is directly based on that of Parmenides (B16). Both philosophers represent, in a more rigorous way, the general fifth-century tendency to treat ψυχή as "the mental correlate of σῶμα" (E. R. Dodds, *The Greeks and the Irrational* [Berkeley, 1956], p. 138). But both philosophers avoid the ambiguous term ψυχή and speak more concretely of νόος, νοεῖν or φρήν, φρονεῖν (Empedocles uses the word ψυχή only once in the extant fragments, in the poetic sense of "life": B138).

[35] B105.

[36] Theophr. *De Sensu* 10–11 = Emped. A86.10-11. For the composition of the blood, see B98.

[37] See Arist. *De Anima* 404b11, 408a16.

It is this fragmentation of the empirical soul for Empedocles which must be borne in mind if his doctrine of immortality is to be made intelligible. On the one hand, our psychic nature at any given moment is obviously just as transitory as the physical mixture on which it is based. Not only does our mind in this sense not survive death, it does not survive any physical change whatsoever. The ratio of ingredients is altered by every bite of food, as well as every act of learning or forgetting. And the cohesion of the mixture is clearly terminated when the organism draws its last breath.

On the other hand, there can be no question of extinction, no utter destruction of psychic any more than of bodily reality. The necessary survival of the component parts of the soul is an inevitable consequence of the principle of Parmenides, which Empedocles has placed at the foundation of his cosmology. Nothing comes to be or perishes; there is only "mixture and the separation of what has been mixed." [38] Therefore death is as much an illusion in the psychic realm as in the physical. There is a continual formation and dissolution of individual compounds. But the elements of which a mind is composed are just as eternal as those of the body, for they are exactly the same.

A man wise in such matters will not surmise in his mind
that when they are alive, in what men call life,
then only do they exist and encounter good things and evil,
but before mortals are composed and after they are dissolved,
they are nothing at all. [39]

Fools: for they have no wits to reach long thoughts,
who imagine that something is generated which did not exist before,
or that anything dies away and is utterly destroyed. [40]

Whether we regard this as a religious belief or a philosophic doctrine, it clearly serves as the basis for Empedocles' whole physical system. In his view, the Parmenidean attack on generation and corruption had established the fundamental principle of permanence in nature—a principle that we may call either the conservation of matter or the conservation of mind, for the two are conceived as one.

Within the physical poem, therefore, immortality appears as the lot of every elemental ingredient in human nature. Since all of our members

[38] Emped. B8.
[39] B15 (quoted above, n. 21).
[40] B11.

are deathless, all are gods. Each one of them lives on as a psychic as well as a corporeal entity, liberated from the particular mixture "which men call life." Each one of them, then, might conceivably play the role of the transmigrating daimon. But whether all of them do, or, if not, which one does, and how it may be said to "encounter good things and evil"—to none of these questions do we find an answer in the physical poem.

Now when we turn to the *Purifications*, the combination and separation of the four elements drop out of sight. We can scarcely say that there is no trace of the elements in this poem, for they are certainly reflected in the four stages of the wandering daimon, who is cast from air (*aithēr*) to sea, from sea to earth, from earth to the blazing sun, and from the sun back to the air.[41] But nowhere in the poem is there any suggestion that these elements might constitute the nature of the fallen daimon. On the contrary, they only provide the scene within which the drama of his punishment and purification must be played out. The daimon himself is described simply as "a wandering exile from the gods," doomed

> for thrice ten thousand seasons to wander apart from the blest,
> growing into every form of mortal thing in the course of time,
> changing one for another the grievous paths of life.[42]

These various "forms of mortal things" and "grievous paths of life" correspond very well to the world of elemental transformation as it is described in the poem *On Nature*. It is a world in which the daimon is not at home. In another fragment the mortal form in which he is wrapped is described by Empedocles as an "alien garment of flesh."[43]

To say that the form of flesh is alien to the daimon is equivalent to denying that he is composed of earth, air, water, and fire, for these are precisely the constituents of flesh and blood.[44] Are we to conclude that this exiled spirit has come from a different, incorporeal world, of which the physical poem shows no trace? Do the blessed gods constitute a separate order of being, unrelated to, and incommensurable with, the natural cosmos that Empedocles has so elaborately described?[45] But

[41] B115.9–11.

[42] B115.6–8.

[43] B126.

[44] See B98.

[45] This is, in effect, the solution proposed by Nestle, following Erwin Rohde, *Psyche*, 2nd ed. (Freiburg i.B., 1898), vol. 2, p. 183. Bignone rightly protests

why then should he emphasize the parallel between the cycle of the daimon and the period of the world by his repeated reference to "broad oaths" and to the destructive role of Strife? And how are we to conceive the relationship between this divine stranger and the conscious "thought" (noēma) of the man whose supreme responsibility is precisely to purify the god within him? The hypothesis of an irreducible dualism between "nature" and "spirit" in Empedocles' thought may save it from the charge of contradiction, but it deprives it at the same time of any real claim to intelligibility.

Before resigning ourselves to such a desperate remedy, we must first consider the possibility of establishing a positive link between the psychology of the physical poem and the incarnate daimon of the Purifications. We have already noted the fact that, since all of the physical elements have a mental aspect and all are deathless, any of them might theoretically provide a seat for the wandering daimon. From the Purifications, however, it is clear that the banished god cannot be identified with the four corporeal elements. Empedocles is not referring to the vicissitudes of his bodily components in their previous combinations when he proclaims:

> I was once a lad and a lass,
> a bush, a bird, and a dumb fish of the sea.[46]

The punishment and purification of the daimon would be meaningless if he were doomed by his own nature to the eternal shuffling and reshuffling of natural compounds. The heterogeneous character of the

---

that such an absolute dualism runs counter to the whole spirit of Early Greek thought and, in particular, to the parallelism of mind and body for Empedocles; but I do not see that his own interpretation of the daimon is really different from Nestle's. (See Bignone, p. 11, n. 259–68.) Their conception of the daimon as an entity distinct from the physical elements and principles seems to me excluded by Empedocles' own words: καὶ πρὸς τοῖς οὔτ' ἄρ' τι ἐπιγίνεται οὐδ' ἀπολήγει. B17.30. And compare B23.8–10, where the "long-lived gods" are said to be composed, like men and women, from the physical principles alone. Bignone's interpretation of ὅσσα γε δῆλα "all beings, at least, which are manifest (but not the daimons)" does not fit the context. The point is not that there are some entities which are not manifest, but that of the infinite variety of apparent forms (θνητῶν ὅσσα γε δῆλα γεγάκασιν ἄσπετα) there are none which cannot be derived from these elements. The γε is therefore not restrictive but emphatic.

[46] B117.

daimon is confirmed not only by the description of his body as an "alien garment," but also by the attitude of Air, Sea, Earth, and Sun, who receive the exile only to cast him out again, since "they hate him one and all." [47] Still less is there any possibility of a positive link between the exiled god and the principle of Strife. The entire religious poem makes clear that Strife is the daimon's mortal enemy. It is Strife which has stained his godhead, as it is the elemental world in which he must be punished and purified. Hence, if the daimon corresponds to any principle in the physical poem, it can only be to the principle of Love. And most attempts to reconcile the doctrines of the two poems have in fact insisted upon a close connection, if not an outright identification, of the incarnate daimon and the physical principal of Love. [48]

The religious poem makes clear that there is some link between Love or "Aphrodite" and the godlike element in man. If it is a crime for the daimon to trust in Strife, then his true allegiance was to a different power: it must be Love who rules over the company of the blessed gods. This fact is not stated in any extant fragment of the *Purifications* but it seems to be implied, and one of the many lost verses may well have mentioned *Philotēs* or *Harmoniē* as sovereign of the pure daimons. [49] It is precisely because the daimon's homeland is a kingdom of Love that he can only appear as an exile in this world of elemental Strife, where the spirits of death and dissension have the upper hand:

> I wailed and I moaned when I saw the unfamiliar place
> where Bloodshed, Hate, and hordes of other Dooms,
> consuming Sickness, Rot, and running sores (?)
> swarm darkly over the meadow of Disaster. [50]

[47] B115.12.

[48] See F. M. Cornford, *From Religion to Philosophy* (London, 1912), pp. 234–42; and the same author in *The Cambridge Ancient History*, vol. 4 (Cambridge, 1926), pp. 563–69; H. S. Long, "The Unity of Empedocles' Thought," *AJP*, 70 (1949), 142–58; J. E. Raven in KR, pp. 348–61.

[49] There is a trace of this in B116, where Χάρις is said "to hate unbearable Ἀνάγκη." Ἀνάγκη is the principle which condemns the daimons (B115.1), and Χάρις must be another name for Love. Ἀνάγκη is hateful to her because it deprives her of her rightful subjects or "friends." So Hippolytus (in his commentary on B115) describes Φιλία as the good power which takes pity on the fallen souls and draws them together again.

[50] B118 and 121:

> κλαῦσά τε καὶ κώκυσα ἰδὼν ἀσυνήθεα χῶρον,
> ἔνθα Φόνος τε Κότος τε καὶ ἄλλων ἔθνεα Κηρῶν

The divided dominion of this world between the forces of Good and Evil, Love and Hate, is systematically illustrated in the poem by a catalogue of opposing divinities, each pair of which represents the contrast between a positive and a negative force: Waxing and Waning, Sleep and Waking, "charming Certitude and dark-eyed Confusion," "bloody Quarrel and seemly Concord." [51]

Now if it is bloodshed and quarrel which have polluted the daimon and driven him from the company of the blest, it is only amity and concord which may eventually restore him to grace. What he seeks is in fact to regain a life of harmony and fellowship, where he will be permitted to share the hearth and table of the other gods.[52] And the code of purification by which he may return to this community is itself based upon a universal law of kinship. Since all nature is animate, all nature is akin; and the abstinence from bloodshed and violence against all living things is, as it were, a matter of family affection.[53]

Thus the struggle between Love and Strife dominates Empedocles' message of salvation as well as his cosmological scheme. The dramatic theme of both poems is essentially a Manichean contest between the Spirit of Good and the Spirit of Evil—between the forces of unity,

---

αὐχμηραί τε Νόσοι καὶ Σήψιες ἔργα τε ῥευστά
Ἄτης ἀν λειμῶνα κατὰ σκότος ἠλάσκουσιν.

I follow Wilamowitz and Stein in assuming that ἀτερπέα χῶρον in Hierocles (B121.1) is merely a Homeric paraphrase of ἀσυνήθεα χῶρον in B118, so that the two fragments are really one. But Wilamowitz is certainly wrong in referring the meadow of Ἄτη to the underworld (p. 638). There is no place for the House of Hades in the cosmology of Empedocles: the true realm of death is this existence on earth "which men call life." It is described as a dark cave (B120) by contrast with the region of celestial light from which the daimon has come.

Note that Κότος here stands for Νεῖκος, exactly as in the physical poem (B21.7). Similarly Δῆρις in B122 and in B27a, contrasted with Ἁρμονίη in both cases.

[51] B122–23. Parmenides seems to have given a similar list of antithetic allegorical figures; see Ἔρως in Parm. B13, Bellum, Discordia, and Cupiditas, in A37.

[52] B147.

[53] B135–41. Compare the Pythagorean principle of universal kinship as stated in the Meno 81d1 (in connection with the doctrine of transmigration): τῆς φύσεως ἁπάσης συγγενοῦς οὔσης. In his citation of B128, Porphyry remarks that the recognition of this kinship prevented bloodshed in the Golden Age.

harmony, and life and those of multiplicity, discord, and death. In each case the pendulum of power swings back and forth between the two according to a periodic law confirmed by "broad oaths." And in each case the present history of the world represents a transition from the rule of Love to that of Strife. In the *Purifications*, Empedocles tells us of an earlier age when ardent affection (*philophrosynē*) prevailed among all living creatures, while bloodshed and violence were unknown:

> They did not have a god Ares nor Uproar
> nor Zeus the king nor Kronos nor Poseidon,
> but Cypris was their queen.[54]

This Golden Age in which Aphrodite reigned supreme forms an obvious parallel to the supernatural harmony of the cosmic Sphere, within which all elements were united in the sway of Love and there was "no dissension nor unseemly quarrel in its limbs." [55]

It is precisely this parallel between the roles of Love and Strife in the two poems that constitutes the real link between them, and the fundamental principle of unity in Empedocles' thought. He seems to be insisting that the same powers prevail in the destiny of the universe and in that of man. And just as the physical Sphere suggests a supernatural harmony, so the element of Love in mortal compounds seems to stand as a physical representative for the exiled daimon.

We may recall that *Philotēs* is the principle which gives unity and coherence to all natural compounds, and hence to Nature as a whole. Like her linear descendant, the Venus of Lucretius, Empedocles' Aphrodite represents a force of universal vitality and creativity. But she is more than that. As *Harmoniē*, the principle of geometric proportion, Love is responsible for the rational fitting-together of the elements and for the mental qualities which result from their symmetrical combination. We have seen that blood is the seat of intelligence because it forms a particularly smooth blend; that hands and tongue are skillful when their elements are of moderate size and proportionately mixed; that men are gifted with intelligence and keenness of perception to the extent that their components are properly blended. Hence, although the raw

---

[54] B128, together with B130. If we wish to place the Golden Age within the cosmic scheme of *On Nature*, it may fall very early in the present phase of the world cycle, when the Sphere has given way to individual creatures but Strife has not gained full mastery over Love. [See "Retractationes," below, for author's important recent qualification on this note.—Ed.]

[55] B27a.

materials of our thought and perception are to a large extent provided by Earth, Air, Water, and Fire, the decisive form or quality of these mental acts depends upon the excellence of the mixture, in other words, upon the presence of Love. For the element of Love is not merely one ingredient among the others. As the principle of unity and symmetry it implies the positive aspect of consciousness, the pattern of intelligence and sensitivity, as Strife signifies that of dullness and stupidity. Can there be any doubt as to which principle Empedocles would have chosen to represent himself—I mean, of course, his transmigrating, divine self?

Thus we are led to agree with Cornford and his followers in maintaining that the daimon or immortal "I" of the religious poem has a place in Empedocles' physical psychology only if it is embodied in the element of Love. Such a connection between Love and the daimon suggested by the role played by "Cypris" in the *Purifications*, is confirmed by the position of Aphrodite in the poem *On Nature*. The central proclamation of Love as a great cosmic power (in B17) may be compared to Anaxagoras' insistence upon the unique character of *nous*. This is Empedocles' own version of the great discovery of his age: the recognition of the Rational or Spiritual as a distinct and dominant element in Nature. Love cannot be seen by the eyes, but only by the mind (*nous*) or, more precisely, by the Love which is in us. For "by love we see love." [56] The element by which we communicate with this divine, creative force in the universe will fittingly stand for the divine principle embedded in man.

There is another sense in which a link between the daimon and Love is confirmed by the doctrine of the physical poem. Although all six elements are required to make up the concrete mind of the human being, it is only Love which may aspire to purification and release from the world of Strife. From the point of view of Empedocles' cosmogony, the principle of Love in man is a vestige of pre-mundane harmony, left behind in a world increasingly dominated by the hostile powers of diversity and strife. The loss of purity for this principle is represented by its admixture with other elements, in so far as they are distinguished by unlike, opposing qualities. Its release from pollution depends upon the abstinence from bloodshed, that is, from more Strife. Further obedience to this principle will, in Plato's phrase, fasten it to the flesh with new rivets. A life of purity and rationality, on the other hand, will

[56] B17.21. (cf. B133 for the incapacity of the senses to apprehend divinity). For the perception of Love by Love, see B109.

allow the Harmony within us to increase to the point where it will be ready for release. The closing verses of the physical poem seem to afford a glimpse into the mechanism of salvation. If the divinely inspired "pure stream" of truth succeeds in penetrating within the heart,[57] a man's share of wisdom will increase, for the intelligence grows by what it meets with.[58] Hence instruction augments the mind (*phrēn*), while deception destroys it.[59] If a man attends to Empedocles' doctrine with pure thoughts, the truth will actually increase within him, adding to his *ēthos* and *physis*. But if he is distracted by impure, erroneous concerns "which blunt men's thoughts," these truths will leave him after a certain time, "yearning for their fellows, to return to their own dear race." [60] They will return, of course, to where they have come from: the realm of Piety, the dwelling-place of the gods.[61] So, we may say, does the spirit of man, when its time of release is come. It hastens home to its fellows, back to its own dear kind.

If this hint has been properly interpreted, we see what the physical poem means by suggesting that men will experience good and evil after the dissolution of their mortal compounds.[62] Future happiness depends upon the extent to which a man's spirit—that is, his share of Love—returns to its own kind rather than to a condition dominated by Strife. Thus good fortune admits of degrees within the cycle of reincarnation. The purity and concentration of Love is presumably greater in a lion than in a laurel tree, as it is certainly greater in a man than in a beast, and in a wise man than in a fool. When a spirit like Empedocles has attained the ranks of the "seers and bards and physicians and princes among men on the earth," its complete liberation from the hostile elements is at hand.[63] When the final separation occurs, the pure spirit, no longer marked by any taint of its opposite, will experience the Good that answers to its own nature. The epistemology of Empedocles sug-

----

[57] B4.3: γνῶθι διατμισθέντος ἐνὶ σπλάγχνοισι λόγοιο (with Wilamowitz' correction for διατμηθέντος: διασσηθέντος Diels). The difficulty of ingress for truth is emphasized in B114 and B133.

[58] B106.

[59] B17.7; B23.9.

[60] B110.

[61] B3.1–5.

[62] B15 (above, n. 21).

[63] See B127 and B146, to be compared with Empedocles' own career in B117 and B112.

gests what blessedness must mean for the purified daimon. By love we know love.[64]

On this view, then, the two poems of Empedocles are fundamentally compatible with one another. His conjunction of natural philosophy and mystic religion is effected by his own notion of Love or *Harmoniē* as a complex reality, at once physical and spiritual, inherent in the symmetrical mixture of unlike components but capable of existing apart from them as an independent, imperishable entity. This is Empedocles' solution to the recurrent problems of the relationship between matter and life, body and spirit, between the animal and the god in man. Such problems do not lend themselves to final solution, and we had best not look for perfect consistency in Empedocles' view. Furthermore, there is no good reason to suppose that his two poems were conceived together as a single unit. The few clear links between them do not suggest an attempt to make their doctrines coincide point for point. On the contrary a number of years must have passed between the composition of the two works, and some of the discrepancies between them may be due to changes in Empedocles' way of looking at the subject. Above all, the poems are addressed to different audiences and speak on the whole different languages: in one case, the traditional imagery of Greek religion; in the other, the concepts and theories of fifth-century physics.

The two poems thus belong together in a loose unity, and any attempt to impose a systematic pattern upon them is bound to resort to artifice. Such is the case with Cornford's detailed interpretation, which assumes that the two works are simply alternative statements of one and the same theory. In that case the fall of the daimon must correspond exactly to the rupture of the Sphere, and his purification must culminate in a loss of separate existence, when (as Cornford claims) he is finally "merged with the other portions of Love in the unity of the Sphere. This is the physical transcription of the reunion of the soul with God." [65] But such a neat parallel between the two doctrines is not really to be found in the poems. Besides many minor difficulties,[66] the fusion of the

[64] B109.3. Cf. B17.23 τῇ τε φίλα φρονέουσι καὶ ἄρθμια ἔργα τελοῦσι. This would, I think, be Empedocles' answer to the question raised by Vlastos: how does the disembodied daimon get along without flesh and blood, the basis of thought? "How does he think the thoughts of love when he has nothing to think with?" (p. 121).

[65] *Cambridge Ancient History*, vol. 4, p. 569.

[66] For example, in the present world period Love must be passing out of the world as more Strife flows in: where does it go? If we identify the out-

elements in the physical Sphere does not correspond even in principle with the account of the daimons in the *Purifications*. Unlike his fellow believers in transmigration, the mystics of India, Empedocles does not imply that the purified spirit will lose itself in Deity as a drop of water loses itself in the sea. On this point the modern Orphic scholars tend to be slightly more "Orphic" than their ancient originals. If immortality in Empedocles' view cannot be defined as the personal survival of a particular human being, still less can it be identified with the escape from individuality as such. Empedocles is no more a Buddhist than he is a Christian. The terms he uses suggest the continued, harmonious co-existence of discrete individuals, very much like the celestial cavalcade of gods and spirits in the *Phaedrus*.[67] Neither the common hearths and feasting of the daimons nor the possibility that they may be guilty of perjury and bloodshed is compatible with the view that they are to be fused into a single Deity, as the elements seem to be fused within the cosmic Sphere. The fellowship of the daimons, like the breach of this fellowship, is Empedocles' symbol of a vision which cannot be translated into any other terms. It is his way of expressing the inner conviction of

---

going stream of Love with the purified daimons, their number will be complete when Strife has gained full mastery over the elemental universe. The reunion of the blessed will then coincide not with the complete unification of things by Love (i.e. not with the Sphere), but with their complete separation by Strife. [See "Retractationes," below, for author's important recent qualification on this note.—Ed.]

[67] This is of course no accident. The feasts and banquets of the gods at *Phaedrus* 247, in which the noblest human ψυχαί may also share, were probably inspired by the common hearths and tables of Empedocles B147. The *Phaedrus* passage is full of Empedoclean reminiscences (cf. τὰ μὲν θεῶν ὀχήματα ἰσορρόπως εὐήνια ὄντα at 247b with εὐήνιον ἄρμα in Emped. B3.5) and it is probably Empedocles (with Pindar) whom Plato has in mind when he begins his description of the blessed life (247c3).

It is more difficult to say whether the parallels between Empedocles and the mystic verses inscribed on South Italian burial plates are due to his influence on the cult poets or theirs on him. (The latter alternative is the more likely, but the tablets are not old enough to prove this.) In both cases salvation consists not in the loss of one's identity· but in becoming "a god instead of a mortal" and in dwelling with the other immortals or "heroes" after paying the penalty for unjust deeds. (See DK, under "Orpheus" IB17–20.)

There is an obvious parody of the mystic promise of bliss in Aristophanes' speech in the *Symposium*. Having lost their original condition because of ἀδικία, human beings must rely upon Eros to restore it (193d).

all mystics, that there dwells within us a fallen spirit or a portion of deity whose rightful place is elsewhere, in a realm of pure harmony and peace. Empedocles' physical doctrine of Love is an attempt to integrate this conviction within a systematic explanation of the natural world. In this context, the cosmic unity of the Sphere certainly has a religious significance, but it does not necessarily tell us anything about Empedocles' conception of the beatific life. What real connection there was between this unity and the company of the blessed daimons, we simply do not know.[68]

There is, then, no prospect of tying up all of Empedocles' ideas into a neat system, even if we are correct in interpreting Love as the embodiment of the daimon in Empedocles' physical psychology. But such an interpretation has at least the merit of explaining how the religion of purification can appear in the background of the physical poem, and how the natural cosmology can be presupposed at more than one point in the *Purifications*. In brief, it is only this connection between Love and the daimon which can save Empedocles from the unintelligible schizophrenia that characterizes him in most modern presentations.

It seems inconceivable that this reconciliation of his religion and his natural philosophy was not designed by Empedocles himself—that it is somehow an accident, or an invention of our modern ingenuity. Yet there is one serious objection to this solution, which seems to have prevented most scholars from accepting it: namely, the lack of explicit documentary evidence. There is no clear statement of this link between Love and the daimon in any extant fragment, and no ancient author ascribes such a view of the soul to Empedocles.[69] This poses a problem

[68] A similar problem is posed by the incorporeal $\phi\rho\dot{\eta}\nu$ $\dot{\iota}\epsilon\rho\dot{\eta}$ which flits with rapid thoughts through the whole $\kappa\dot{o}\sigma\mu o s$ (B134). The verses which introduce this divinity are almost identical with those used to describe the Sphere (B29). What are we to make of the parallel? It tempts us to identify this $\phi\rho\dot{\eta}\nu$ with Aphrodite, the power who dominates the Sphere (so Cornford and Bignone). But the quotation of Ammonius suggests that these verses apply either to Apollo (i.e. to the great Pythagorean god of knowledge and light) or to $\tau\dot{o}$ $\theta\epsilon\hat{\iota}o\nu$ in general. It may be that Empedocles' polytheism permitted him to envisage divinity—even supreme divinity—under a number of intimately related, but not interchangeable aspects: Love, $\phi\rho\dot{\eta}\nu$, and the Sphere.

[69] The only possible exception is a passage in Aristotle's *De Anima* (408a10–28), where Empedocles' doctrine of Love ($\phi\iota\lambda\dot{\iota}a$) is treated as rigorously parallel to the definition of the soul as a $\dot{a}\rho\mu o\nu\dot{\iota}a$ or blend of opposing elements. Aristotle's point is of course not that the $\dot{a}\rho\mu o\nu\dot{\iota}a$ doctrine belongs to

of methodology, a sort of scholarly *cas de conscience*. In order to make sense of our author, do we have the right to adopt an interpretation for which there is so little direct evidence in the texts?

I think that we do. One must not lose sight of the fact that the poems of Empedocles are not literary documents of the normal type. They are well-nigh unique examples of mystic poetry from the classic period, and accordingly they pose problems which a textual analysis alone is helpless to resolve. We cannot interpret the writings of Empedocles without taking into consideration factors that are neither literary nor philosophical. If it is true (as I think it is) that the whole work of Empedocles points to a link between the religious destiny of man and the cosmic principle of Love, we must ask whether he may have had some motive for not stating this connection fully and clearly in either poem. Perhaps an explanation can be found in the special character and intention of the two works.

The poem *On Nature* observes a discreet silence on all aspects of human destiny after death. It has therefore no motive to carry its psychological analysis beyond the point of mortal dissolution, and no occasion to mention the transmigrating ego, much less to identify it with any single element in the mixture. The *Purifications*, on the other hand, are addressed to a popular audience. Despite an occasional reminiscence of the physical work, the doctrine of transmigration and release is presented here as a self-contained whole, depending for its credibility not upon Empedocles' philosophical speculation but upon his personal authority as a god among men. The doctrine of physical mixture is never mentioned; Love and Strife appear only as general principles of Harmony and Violation, Purity and Taint. The ascent to blessedness is not described in abstract philosophical terms, but in the concrete formulae and imagery of religious poetry. Most of the citizens of Acragas to whom this message was directed would scarcely be concerned to reconcile it with a complex physical theory of which they may never have heard. The poem *On Nature* was after all an esoteric work. The few who were familiar with it would discover more than one unanswered question in the *Purifications*, and would naturally turn to the master himself for an explanation.

We must remember that the links between the philosophical system

---

Empedocles, but that it is philosophically of the same type. But see the next note.

and the doctrine of salvation are not indispensable for the popular diffusion of the latter. They are only required if one seeks a full understanding of all aspects of Empedocles' thought. Why should Empedocles put this understanding at the disposal of every chance comer? Why should he fully satisfy our curiosity? Is it the part of a prophet and a mystagogue to divulge all his secrets at once? On the contrary, we should rather expect him to keep a few things to himself, for private communication to his closest disciples.[70]

But if the physical poem was really an esoteric work while the *Purifications* were addressed to the general public, why does the doctrine of transmigration appear only in the latter? Why should all the citizens of Acragas hear of a matter which is not mentioned to the chosen disciple Pausanias? Here again we are asking a question which the texts do not answer. But they do suggest that the religious poem was composed at a later date, after some considerable change had taken place in Empedocles' conception of himself.[71] Now the gospel of purification must

[70] If Empedocles' view of the immortal soul as "Love" was in fact communicated in this way, we would have a solution to the strange mystery of the $\psi v \chi \dot{\eta} - \dot{\alpha} \rho \mu o v \acute{\iota} a$ doctrine, which first shows up in the *Phaedo* expounded by Simmias, a pupil of Philolaus, and is immediately accepted by the Pythagoreans of Phlius (*Phaedo* 86b–c, 88d; the origins of the doctrine are inconclusively discussed by Burnet, in his note on 86b6, and by R. Hackforth, *Plato's* Phaedo [Cambridge, 1955], pp. 101–03). There could be no more natural place for the influence of Empedocles than among the Pythagoreans of Southern Italy and their disciples in Greece. And $\dot{}A\rho\mu o v \acute{\iota} \eta$ is of course one of Empedocles' names for Love.

As presented by Plato and Aristotle, the $\dot{\alpha} \rho \mu o v \acute{\iota} a$ doctrine is no longer Empedoclean. Plato's argument turns precisely upon the fact that the "attunement" is a mere compound, incapable of existing apart from the elements of which it is composed. The theory has become practically identified with the medical conception of health as a harmony or equilibrium of diverse factors in the body. There was from the first a close link between this medical view (which can be traced as far back as Alcmaeon of Croton) and Empedocles' own theory. But if the $\psi v \chi \dot{\eta} - \dot{\alpha} \rho \mu o v \acute{\iota} a$ doctrine was really current among Pythagoreans, it must once have implied a more substantial kind of $\dot{\alpha} \rho \mu o v \acute{\iota} a$: a principle of harmony that was also capable of transmigrating. That is to say, it must originally have coincided with Empedocles' conception of $\Phi \iota \lambda \acute{o} \tau \eta s$.

[71] I do not believe that Empedocles refers to himself as a god in the physical poem. Such a reference is sometimes sought in B23.11 $\dot{\alpha} \lambda \lambda \dot{\alpha} \ \tau o \rho \hat{\omega} s \ \tau a \hat{v} \tau' \ \ddot{\iota} \sigma \theta \iota$, $\theta \epsilon o \hat{v} \ \pi a \rho \dot{\alpha} \ \mu \hat{v} \theta o v \ \dot{\alpha} \kappa o \acute{v} \sigma a s$. But the exact parallel to this formula is to be found in B4: $\dot{\omega} s \ \delta \dot{\epsilon} \ \pi a \rho' \ \dot{\eta} \mu \epsilon \tau \acute{\epsilon} \rho \eta s \ \kappa \acute{\epsilon} \lambda \epsilon \tau a \iota \ \pi \iota \sigma \tau \acute{\omega} \mu a \tau a \ M o \acute{v} \sigma \eta s, \ \gamma \nu \hat{\omega} \theta \iota$. Unlike his

originally have been communicated to him in some private cult, presumably Pythagorean, where it was guarded by a rule of silence. When he worked out his physical system, Empedocles seems to have been motivated in large measure by the desire to lay a rational foundation for these religious teachings, and we may guess that his friend Pausanias was also an initiate. The poem *On Nature* is in fact a kind of fifth-century *Timaeus*—a synthesis of the physical knowledge of the day, conceived within a religious framework. We have seen that the religious element appears in both proem and conclusion, in the insistence on immortality and the beneficent role of Love, in the vision of the Sphere and the culminating announcement of the *phrēn hierē*. But at the moment when he composed this poem, Empedocles still felt it was not "lawful" to publish the secrets of salvation—not even in an esoteric work. He describes the temptation to do so as an impious urge "to sit upon the heights of wisdom" and "cull the blossoms of fame and honor in the sight of men."

Now at the time of Empedocles' poem, the doctrine of transmigration as such was not much of a secret. It had been parodied by Xenophanes more than a generation before, and is mentioned by Herodotus with no noticeable air of secrecy.[72] But the religious meaning of the cycle and of the abstinence from flesh does not seem to have been made public before Empedocles, and by him only in the second poem. From the Pythagorean point of view, this must have been an act of heresy and sacrilege. A trace of the scandal it created seems to be preserved in the tradition, recorded by Timaeus and Neanthes, that Empedocles was expelled from the Pythagorean society for stealing and publishing sacred doctrines.[73] It is natural to connect this surprising change in Empedocles' attitude in the second poem with his proclamation there of his own divinity. No longer mortal, Empedocles is no longer bound by mortal rules. The doctrine of the god in human form, which had

---

religious message, Empedocles presents his physical doctrine not on his own authority but on that of the Muse. And the proclamation of his divinity in B112 strikes the reader as a piece of news.

[72] Xenophanes B7; Hdt. II.123. Such revelations may have prompted Empedocles' prayer to the gods to avert from his tongue "the madness of those men."

[73] Neanthes and Timaeus in Diogenes Laertius VIII.54–55 (= Felix Jacoby, *Die Fragmente der griechischen Historiker*, vol. 2 [Berlin, 1926], 84F26; vol. 3 [Leiden, 1950], 566F14).

reached him as a traditional teaching, has now become a fact of his own experience. The author of the *Purifications* can recall his previous incarnations and is assured of imminent release. He has thus gained such confidence in his immortal powers as "prophet, poet, doctor, and prince" that he can brave the Pythagorean injunction to silence, and can offer all men a chance to follow the way of salvation by which he himself has regained the status of divinity.

RETRACTATIONES (1971)

Looking back on this essay after some ten years, I still agree with the main features of the interpretation. However, recent studies in Empedocles have led me to revise my views on two questions which are at issue here, one tangentially and the second more essentially.

(1) I no longer believe in the four-phase reconstruction of Empedocles' cosmic cycle by Zeller and Burnet, which led me to describe the present world phase as a period of increasing strife. Jean Bollack's *Empédocle* I (Paris, 1965) has convinced me that there is only one (recurrent) world history for Empedocles, beginning with the total dissolution of the Sphere by Strife and characterized by the continuous recreation of partial unities under the increasing dominance of Love, until (in some future moment, which Empedocles hints at but does not describe) the universal harmony of the Sphere is reconstituted and the cycle begins anew.[1] Hence all references in my article to a present state of the world in which Strife has the upper hand, or is increasingly dominant, or in which Love is yielding to Strife, should be stricken from the record. This has the effect of nullifying my note 66. And it tends rather to strengthen the analogy between the cosmic history of the physical poem and the life history of the daimon in the *Purifications*: in both cases the pattern is one of perfect harmony yielding *at first* to a state of separation and alienation but gradually recovering its initial perfection. Insofar as the analogy holds, the Golden Age must correspond to the Sphere and not to any later moment (contra n. 54). But our knowledge of the *Purifications* is too incomplete to permit any confidence on this point.

---

[1] See my review of Bollack in *Gnomon*, 41 (1969), 439-47. For reconstructions of Empedocles' cosmogony which parallel that of Bollack on essential points, see the articles of Friedrich Solmsen, "Love and Strife in Empedocles' Cosmology," *Phronesis*, 10 (1965), 109-48, and Uvo Hölscher, "Weltzeiten und Lebenszyklus," *Hermes*, 93 (1965), 7-33 [repr. with additions in Hölscher, *Anfängliches Fragen* (Göttingen, 1968), pp. 173-212].

(2) Bollack's interpretation emphasizes that Love is not a separate element over and above the basic four but is *immanent* in them as their principle of unity, homogeneity, and mutual adjustment.[2] From this it follows that, for the physical poem at least, the purest condition of Love is not one of separation from the elements (for separation is the work of Strife) but of complete fusion with them in a perfectly homogeneous blend, where the elements cease to be distinct from one another—the condition realized in the Sphere. I am not sure how far this can apply to the daimon, but perhaps we may understand its "alien garment of flesh" as constituted not by the elements as such but by their *diversity and opposition to one another*. In its state of purity the daimon will have, or will be, an elemental body after all,[3] only not one composed of *distinct* elements. The hatred which the daimon encounters in the elemental zones will reflect the fact that he, like themselves, is estranged from perfect harmony. On this view, release from strife cannot mean physical separation from the elements but rather the attainment of a new (and original) state of freedom from elemental plurality and opposition. A judgment on details had best be suspended until we have Bollack's volume on the *Purifications*. In any case I would no longer speak of Love as "capable of existing apart" from the elements "as an independent entity." The essential methodological point, established for the first time in recent work on Empedocles, is that his popular poem *Purifications* must not be used as a key for the interpretation of the esoteric work *On Nature*, but conversely.

In response to a recent article by A. A. Long[4] which treats many of the problems discussed here but ends by denying the compatibility of the physical and religious doctrines, I would like to make clear in what sense I claim to have reconciled the two poems and the two sides of Empedocles' thought. I agree with Long[5] that there is no *clear* connection between the psychophysics of the poem *On Nature* and the doctrine of the transmigrating daimon. If the connection were clear, there would be less disagreement among interpreters. What I claim is, first, that the parallels and echoes between the two poems strongly suggest that Empedocles thought of their doctrines as compatible.

---

[2] Cf. Φιλότης ἐν τοῖσιν . . . μετὰ τοῖσιν ἑλισσομένην in B17.20–25, whereas Νεῖκος is δίχα τῶν, B17.19.

[3] Cf. φίλα γυῖα in B115.3.

[4] "Thinking and Sense-Perception in Empedocles: Mysticism or Materialism?" *CQ*, N.S. 16 (1966), 256–76.

[5] Page 275.

Hence it is the task of a sympathetic interpretation to discover what compatibility there might be. Secondly, I claim that *if* the two doctrines are compatible, then the daimon can only correspond to the principle of Love in living creatures: all other elemental constituents—insofar as they are *distinct* from Love and from one another—are excluded for the reasons given in my essay. That Empedocles *intended* the two doctrines to be compatible in this way is a legitimate inference from the fact that he has taken pains to link the two poems together by verbal echoes and by the common pattern of a conflict between Love and Strife. Whether they are *in fact* compatible is a different question altogether.

Perfect consistency in a mystic doctrine of the soul, or in any theory of mind, is a hard goal to reach. I would claim only that Empedocles has gone a long way in this direction. His theory is certainly not exempt from difficulties. One of the most acute concerns the doctrine of transmigration itself, regardless of its relation to the physical theory. This is the problem of individuation and identity: what makes a daimon one and the same as it passes from creature to creature? How can it preserve the memory of its previous incarnations? The fragments of the *Purifications* do not suggest that Empedocles ever faced up to this problem. But then, neither did Plato.

VIII

ANAXAGORAS AND THE ATOMISTS

19

THE PHYSICAL THEORY
OF ANAXAGORAS

Gregory Vlastos

No Pre-Socratic system has been studied more intensively than that of Anaxagoras, and none with better reason since by common consent it is one of the most brilliant products of the great age of Greek speculation. Tannery, Burnet, Giussani, Bailey, Cornford, Peck, and many

From *The Philosophical Review*, 59 (1950), 31–57, with additional notes and revisions supplied by the author. Reprinted with the permission of the editor of *The Philosophical Review* and of the author.

Author's Note: I regret that I have not yet had the opportunity to make the fresh study of the fragments which I would need to make if I were to attempt to revise this paper in the light of subsequent discussions of Anaxagoras. I have added a few additional comments in two new footnotes, 65a and 72a. In the course of these I refer to the following publications by author's name only: W. K. C. Guthrie, *A History of Greek Philosophy*, vol. 2 (Cambridge, 1965); R. Mathewson, "Aristotle and Anaxagoras: An Examination," *CQ*, N.S. 8 (1958), 67–81; C. Strang, "The Physical Theory of Anaxagoras," *AGP*, 45 (1963), 101–18.

I have made no substantive changes in the text, with one exception: I have eliminated references to "the infinitesimal" and even to "the infinitely small" in Anaxagoras. As I have since come to see (in the course of trying to thread my way through Zeno's paradoxes) the notion of "the infinitesimal" is a confused one, and even the expression "infinitely small" is misleading. There is some excuse for using the latter, since Anaxagoras himself said practically the same thing in such a phrase as τὸ σμικρὸν ἄπειρον ἦν. There is none whatever for using the former, for there is absolutely no basis in the fragments for thinking that Anaxagoras was guilty of the confusions epitomized by that term. In B3 he gives us an admirably precise statement of what he means ("of the small there is no smallest, but always a smaller"), and I have retained this wording wherever possible. I have also spoken of his "principle of continuity," an expression which ties his rejection of the existence of smallest others have labored to reconstruct it.[1] Many of the details have been clarified by their researches. But no consensus of belief has yet been reached on the main lines of the system. The extent of the disagreement is wider and sharper than one would ever guess from the complacent simplifications of the schoolbooks.[2] Cyril Bailey, who offered some years ago an original interpretation of the system, now concedes that "as yet no solution seems to have been reached which is both tenable in itself and will tally with the extant fragments." [3] The present reconstruction is offered in the hope that the problem, however formidable, is not insoluble.[4] It proceeds by way of a fresh examination of the relevant fragments, seeking to comprehend them first of all by comparison with contemporary doctrines, especially that of Empedocles. It is guided throughout by the conviction that Anaxagoras can be under-

---

quantities in B1 and B3 to his denial of discrete substances in B6 and B7.

For the rest, I should warn the reader that the solution I offer to the problem discussed in Section III is admittedly conjectural. I do not pretend that there is evidence that this was Anaxagoras' own solution to the problem. All I claim is that it is consistent with what I take to be the explicit assertions of his theory, falls well within the limits of possibility for a man of Anaxagoras' intellectual powers working with the logical and mathematical techniques available to him at the time, and constitutes a reasonable solution to the problem.

[1] P. Tannery, *Pour l'Histoire de la science hellène*, 2nd ed. (Paris, 1930); Burnet, *EGP*; C. Giussani, *Lucretius* (Turin, 1896), Book I, Excursus III, pp. 147 ff.; C. Bailey, *Greek Atomists and Epicurus* (Oxford, 1928), Appendix I; F. M. Cornford, "Anaxagoras' Theory of Matter," *CQ*, 24 (1930), 14 ff. and 83 ff.; A. L. Peck, "Anaxagoras and the Parts," *CQ*, 20 (1926), 57 ff.; "Anaxagoras: Predication as a Problem in Physics," *CQ*, 25 (1931), 27 ff. and 112 ff. To the first, second, fourth, and fifth of these and to the second of Peck's studies I shall refer hereafter by the author's name. All references to the fragments of the Pre-Socratics are as in H. Diels and W. Kranz, *Die Fragmente der Vorsokratiker*, 5th ed. (Berlin, 1934–37).

[2] The latest and best of the textbook accounts—K. Freeman, *Companion to the Pre-Socratic Philosophers* (Oxford, 1946)—follows Cornford's interpretation, but without so much as a mention of the major difficulty which besets this particular view.

[3] In his commentary on Lucretius (Oxford, 1947), vol. 2, p. 743. He is referring to the impasse between the two contradictory theories which will be discussed in Section III, below.

[4] I am indebted to Friedrich Solmsen and Max Black for some valuable suggestions which I have incorporated into this paper.

stood only in terms of his immediate philosophical heritage that defined the problems he tried to solve and equipped him with assumptions that are presupposed in his boldest innovations.

I. THE SEEDS

In the primordial mixture "there was much earth and an infinite multitude of seeds in no way resembling one another." [5] In all subsequent parts of the mixture[6] "there must be many things of all sorts and seeds of all things having all sorts of forms[7] and colors and savors." [8] In these lines we encounter the only new term that the surviving fragments of Anaxagoras introduce into the technical vocabulary of Greek cosmology.[9] His other technical terms—mixture, segregation, composition, and the rest—are strikingly traditional.[10] They go back to the

[5] B4, ad fin.

[6] Literally, "in all the things that are coming together (or combining)," ἐν πᾶσι τοῖς συγκρινομένοις. Cornford's alternative interpretation of this expression will be discussed in Section III, below.

[7] Burnet and others render this as "shapes." *Idea* may, but need not, mean "shape." It is as general as the English word "form," which need not refer at all to physical configuration. So, e.g., Democritus B11, "two forms (ἰδέαι) of knowledge." In the medical literature *idea* is used to denote the qualities or "powers" of a given thing; cf. the expression "form" (ἰδέα) and "power" (δύναμις) in *Nature of Man* 2.7–8 and 5.15–16 (*Hippocrates*, ed. W. H. S. Jones, vol. 4), and ἰδέας in ibid., 5.7. In the last of these it is perfectly clear that the *idea* of blood is its nature, i.e. the sum total of the specific properties by which blood is observably different from another substance, bile. The use of *idea* in Empedocles B35.17 and Diogenes B6 is equally general.

[8] B4, ad init.

[9] I say this without prejudice to the authenticity of *homoiomereia* as an Anaxagorean innovation, since the latter does not, of course, occur in the fragments (see below, Section II ad fin.). To these mentions of seeds in B4, we may add Arist. *De Caelo* 302b2, where Anaxagoras' seeds are "flesh, bone, and the like," and *De Gen. et Corr.* 314a28, where Anaxagoras is said to hold that earth, fire, water, air are "seed aggregates" (*panspermia*) of all the *homoiomerē*, "flesh, bone, and the like." Cherniss' alternative rendering of the latter passage (*Aristotle's Criticism of Pre-Socratic Philosophy* [Baltimore, 1935], p. 108 n. 444) is a perfectly possible one, but immaterial for my interpretation of Aristotle's account of Anaxagoras.

[10] I do not mean, of course, that Anaxagoras did not recast the meaning of these terms and will explain in due course how he did. I am only saying that none of them involves a terminological innovation. I may remark in passing

beginnings of Ionian physics; in all probability they are as old as
Anaximander.[11] But no one before Anaxagoras had ever used "seed"
as he did,[12] while after him the term became current in physical terminology. The atomists took it up. They speak of their atoms as seeds,[13]
and Aristotle refers to the primordial atomic mass in Leucippus and
Democritus as a "seed-aggregate," *panspermia*.[14] The innovation is so
radical that one may well sympathize with those commentators[15] who
refuse to believe that Anaxagoras could have really meant to stretch
the word so far beyond its ordinary sense, applying it to inorganic, as
well as organic, matter. But the context makes it perfectly clear that the

---

that Bailey's view (546 ff.) that σύμμιξις is employed in a radically different
sense from σύγκρισις has no foundation in the fragments, and is incompatible
with the juxtaposition of συμμίσγεται and ἀποκρίνεται in B17 (cf. B12) as
correlative contraries.

[11] Arist. *Phys.* 187a20–21; Simpl. *Phys.* 24.23–25. These are, of course,
paraphrases. But the terms ἀποκρινομένων and ἐκκρίνεσθαι are in all probability
Anaximander's own. What other words could he have used to express these
ideas?

[12] I am not ignoring such expressions as "seed of fire" in the poets (e.g. *Od.*
5.490; Pindar *Pyth.* 3.37). By obvious metaphor "seed" could be used for the
causal beginnings of any process, physical or social, as much as biological.
Thus σπέρμα καὶ ῥίζα is used in Demosthenes 25.48, and there is every reason
to think that this, like ἀρχὴ καὶ ῥίζα, πηγὴ καὶ ῥίζα, or ἀρχὴ καὶ πηγή, was
a fairly common expression. I am merely insisting, so far as we know,
Anaxagoras was the first cosmologist to use this term not in this vague and
general fashion, but as a precise and technical concept. I know of only one
exception to my statement, the use of "seed" in Aristotle's discussion of
Pythagorean doctrine in *Met.* 1091a16; but (a) this is not directly ascribed to
Pythagorean vocabulary, and (b) even if it were, there would be no evidence
for placing it in the earlier, pre-Anaxagorean phase of Pythagorean doctrine,
while (c) we know of no Pythagorean doctrine that would give a technical
meaning to this term.

[13] Epicurus *Ep.* I.38, 74, and 89. All three passages refer to "seeds" of all
things, including inanimate objects. So too in Lucretius I.59 et passim, *semina
rerum* has the same denotation as *materies*, *genitalia corpora*, *corpora prima*.
The Empedoclean *radices* is also borrowed by Lucretius for the same purpose
(II.203). See Bailey, *Greek Atomists and Epicurus*, pp. 343 ff.

[14] *Phys.* 203a21; *De Caelo* 303a16; *De Anima* 404a4.

[15] For example, Cornford and Peck. In his first paper ("Anaxagoras and the
Parts," p. 70), Peck went further to assume that even "parts" (which he takes
as equivalent in denotation with "seeds") refers only to the parts of organic
creatures.

term is employed with unrestricted generality. There are "seeds of *all things*" in all the products of the cosmogonic process; and wherever the expression "all things" occurs in the fragments it means just what it says;[16] it would be forcing the texts to take it in any other way. And this is confirmed by the reference to the earth in connection with the "infinite multitude of seeds." [17]

A departure of this magnitude could not have been made carelessly. Unlike "root" in Empedocles, it cannot be discounted as poetic license. Hesiod had spoken of the "roots" of the earth,[18] and Xenophanes had echoed the expression in a sense which is obviously metaphorical.[19] Empedocles borrows the term along with so many other turns of poetic diction to which he clearly attaches no literal significance. But An-

[16] B1, B4, B12. That *chrēmata* may denote either the qualities (hot-cold, etc.) or the seeds or both does not, of course, detract from the force of my contention.

[17] As Cherniss points out, καὶ γῆς πολλῆς ἐνεούσης καὶ σπερμάτων ἀπείρων πλῆθος, etc., "is a genitive absolute giving the cause for the preceding statement" (op. cit., p. 401); that is to say, the "mixture of all things, of the moist and the dry, etc." is explained by the presence of an infinite variety of seeds (each of which, as I shall argue in Section II, consists of the moist-dry, hot-cold, etc., in varying proportions). There is no satisfactory explanation of the mention of earth in this connection, unless earth were one variety of seed. This interpretation is supported by the immediately following sentence: "For neither did any of the others (τῶν ἄλλων) in any way resemble one another." τῶν ἄλλων here must refer to σπερμάτων in the preceding sentence; it cannot refer to the moist-dry, hot-cold, etc., of that sentence, because (a) these opposites are so obviously different that there is no sense in roundly affirming that they do not resemble each other, and (b) the parallel declaration in B12 ("for no other thing [scil., other than *nous*] is like any other") clearly refers to composite bodies (compounds of the moist-dry, hot-cold, etc.) which, as we shall see, can only be the seeds. Now if the reference of τῶν ἄλλων is to σπερμάτων, the sense can only be "neither did any of the seeds other than the earth resemble one another," which would clinch my contention that the earth is here spoken of as a seed. The only positive evidence to the contrary is Aristotle's round affirmation that the earth (as well as fire, air, water) were not Anaxagorean "elements," but only "seed-aggregates" (*De Gen. et Corr.* 314a25 ff.; cf. *De Caelo* 302a28 ff.). I believe that this is an Aristotelian misunderstanding; it will be fully discussed in Section III.

[18] *Op.* 19; *Theog.* 728.

[19] Arist. *De Caelo* 294a23, assuming that ἐπ' ἄπειρον ἐρριζῶσθαι is quoted from Xenophanes. The Pythagorean description of the *tetraktys* (B15) as "source and root of eternal nature" is also in metrical form.

axagoras is a prose writer, not a poet; and his prose is singularly sober, the spare idiom of logic and physical inquiry. When he used the term "seed" he would do so with due regard to the proper meaning of the word in its ordinary biological context. To find that meaning we must ask what it was that his own scientific contemporaries understood a seed to be.

The general view among philosophers and medical men alike is clear enough.[20] A seed is a compound of all the essential constituents of the parent body from which it comes and of the new organism into which it will grow. In its ovular or uterine environment (or, in the case of vegetable seeds, in the earth) the compound grows on the principle of "like to like," [21] each ingredient of the seed being "nourished" by bits of the same stuff supplied by its environment. That this is Anaxagoras' own notion of a "seed" is what we would expect; and the expectation is confirmed explicitly in B10:[22]

[20] See especially the Hippocratic treatises on *The Germ*, *Nature of the Child*, *Diseases* IV.32–34, and *Airs*, *Waters*, *Places* 14; Arist. *De Gen. An.* 721b7 ff., 763b30 ff.; Aetius 5.3.3 and 6; Censorinus 5.2 and 3.

[21] See *Nature of the Child* 17 and 22; *Diseases* IV.34.

[22] To this fragment we might add the unnamed view of the germ in Arist. *De Gen. An.* 769a28 ff. This is in all probability the theory of Anaxagoras, since it is given as an alternative to the view of Empedocles, Democritus, and others (769a7 ff.), while earlier (763b30 ff.) Anaxagoras had been named as the author of the theory of generation opposed to that of Empedocles, Democritus, and others. The present view is that "the semen, though a unity, is as it were a 'seed-aggregate' consisting of a large number of ingredients. It is as though someone were to mix together many humors in one fluid, and then could take thence (scil., some of the ingredients), not always an equal amount of each, but sometimes more of this one, sometimes more of that, and sometimes some of one and none of another. So, they say, it is with the semen, which is a mixture of many ingredients. And the offspring will resemble the form of that one of the parents from which the most (scil., of the several ingredients) is derived." Ἀφ' οὗ . . . πλεῖστον ἐγγένηται in the last sentence cannot mean "from which most of the semen is derived," since the coderivation of the semen from male and female is the theory of Empedocles and Democritus to which the present theory is contrasted. It can only mean "from which the most of each of the ingredients of the embryo is derived," i.e. that the kind of nourishment provided by the mother in the uterus will be a codeterminant of the constitution of the offspring equally with the kind of semen provided by the father. This is the only ground on which Anaxagoras, who held that the semen comes from the father alone, could account for cases where the offspring "takes after" the mother rather than the father. (Censorinus 6.4,

For in the same germ [he said] there are hair, nails, veins, arteries, sinews, bones, which are not manifest because of the smallness of [their] parts, but become distinct little by little as they grow. "For how," he says, "could hair come from not-hair, or flesh from not-flesh?"

Here we have, strictly speaking, only a theory of the generation of the offspring from the seed, scil., that the seed contains all the essential tissues of the offspring (the "pre-formation" theory). But the same reasoning would apply no less to the current theory of the generation of the seed from the parent-body, scil., that the seed contains all the essential tissues of the parent-body (the "pan-genesis" theory). The two are complementary, and Anaxagoras could justify both by the same general principle that "hair cannot come from not-hair, nor flesh from not-flesh." Anaxagoras' theory of nutrition[23] is similarly complementary to the theory of the seed, enabling him to explain the growth of the seed in egg, womb, or earth, and is similarly deducible from the same principle that "hair cannot come from not-hair"; if hair is nourished by the consumption of bread or flesh, hair must have pre-existed in bread and flesh. Thus when Anaxagoras speaks of "seeds" of all kinds of things, pre-existing in the primitive mixture and persisting in each of its products, he must mean that all these things are contained in their antecedents, just as all the parts of a man are contained in the sperm and all the parts of a plant are contained in its seed. Whatever is generated *from* a seed was *in* the seed. Biological generation is only the separating out of things which were mixed together in seed and nutriment; imperceptible in the mixture, they became "manifest" through a process of segregation and recomposition. When Anaxagoras through the concept of the *seed* generalizes this principle of germination from biology to cosmology, extending it to any process of generation whatever, he is seeking to convey a new idea for which none of the traditional terms offered a fitting vehicle. What is this new idea?

There is nothing new about the notion of a mixture whence things are generated by segregation and recomposition. This goes back to the beginnings of Ionian speculation. Anaximander's generation of the

---

Anaxagoras autem eius parentis faciem referre liberos iudicavit, qui seminis amplius contulisset, must be a misunderstanding.)

[23] Aet. 1.3.5; Simpl. *Phys.* 460.15–19; Lucr. I.861–67; Arist. *De Gen. An.* 723a11.

world from the *apeiron* was founded on this idea.[24] Parmenidean logic had necessitated its recasting in conformity with the requirements of the new concept of Being.[25] If whatever *is* is unalterably, then whatever *is* now must have *been* in the primitive mixture; whatever properties are part of its being it must possess eternally, in the original mixture as much as out of it ever after. Parmenides himself had pointed the way by which this idea could be applied to cosmology,[26] and Empedocles had followed it with unprecedented rigor and systematic completeness. The general formula that there is no absolute generation or destruction, that becoming and perishing are mere "names," that really there is only "mixture and interchange of things mixed" had been stated by Empedocles (B8). Was Anaxagoras then only parroting Empedocles when he asserted the same principle in almost exactly the same words in B17? It is at just this point, where he is closest to Empedocles, that we must look for the real difference and for the true originality of his physics.

To apply the concept of being to the world of becoming Parmenides and Empedocles had to make an ad hoc hypothesis. They were forced to assume that of all the vast variety of known substances, only a small number—two and four respectively—could claim the title of Being. They, and they alone, were truly self-identical, unalterably unmixed.[27] Bone, flesh, and everything else had no being; they were only mixtures, whose very birth carried with it the certainty of eventual death. As an imaginative transformation of both the popular world view and of its philosophical reconstruction this had the most far-reaching consequences. The abyss which traditional religion had fixed between gods and men now yawned within the visible world itself, dividing it up into two classes of things, the one original and everlasting, the other derivative and temporary,[28] the one immortal, the other mortal.[29] Empedocles

[24] See n. 11, above.

[25] See my "Equality and Justice in Early Greek Cosmologies," *CP*, 42 (1947), 171 [repr. in Furley and Allen, I, pp. 56–91].

[26] By his assumption of two opposite forms of being, each with its own self-identical powers, "in every way the same as itself, and not the same as the other" (B8.57–58).

[27] ἠνεκὲς αἰὲν ὁμοῖα (B17.35), like Parmenidean Being which was πᾶν ὁμοῖον (Parm. B8.22, Melissus B7). From *Ancient Medicine* we can get a good idea of what it was in Empedocles that struck (in this case, shocked) his contemporary audience: it was the doctrine that earth, fire, etc., have "pure," unmixed being. See below, Section II.

[28] The Ionians too had divided up nature into a divine original (Anaximander's *apeiron*, Anaximenes' air) and mortal creatures. But the division

was not ashamed of this conclusion. He proudly proclaimed the divinity of his roots, giving them the names of gods.[30] This was his challenge to the scientific world, no less than to common sense, and we can still gauge its power both from the violence of the opposition which it provoked[31] and from the enormous influence it exerted.[32] To this challenge Anaxagoras addresses himself in the first book of his treatise. When he asserts that "the contents of the one world"—whose unity had been shattered by the cosmological dualism of Parmenides and pluralism of Empedocles—"are not sundered from each other, the hot from the cold, or the cold from the hot" (B8), the butt of his attack is clear and has been noticed often enough. But it has not been sufficiently noticed[33] that the detailed account of the generation of aether, air,

---

had never been as sharp as in Empedocles, since the very substance of the divine original was transformed into its mortal creatures throughout the cosmogonic process. The trend in Ionia had been to bridge the gap. Heraclitus proclaimed that *this* world was everlasting (B30); the opposition between mortals and immortals is abolished (B62); all things are one (B50), and opposite things are "one and the same" (B60, B88).

[29] The expression "those things became mortal which had been immortal before, those things were mixed that had before been unmixed" (B35.14 ff.) does not, of course, mean that the four roots themselves became "mixed" and "mortal." In themselves they cannot become anything; they always are themselves (cf. the thrice repeated αὐτὰ ἔστιν ταῦτα, 17.34, 21.13, 26.3). It is their products which are mortal mixtures; mortality and mixture is predicated not of their being, but of their temporary conjunctions.

[30] These are the real gods of Empedoclean cosmology; the traditional gods are in the same boat with men and animals, products of the roots (B21), and they are spoken of as "long-lived" (δολιχαίωνες) not "everlasting" (αἰὲν ἐόντες); only the roots αἰὲν ἔασιν (B26.12). On δολιχαίωνες see W. Jaeger, *Theology of the Early Greek Philosophers* (Oxford, 1947), p. 33 and p. 206 n. 52.

[31] In the well-known instance of *Ancient Medicine*. The author is not tilting against speculative windmills, but is on the defensive against an aggressive opponent who has invaded his own (medical) home ground. See especially chapter 13 ad init., where he refers to those whose "researches in the art" (scil., medicine) and medical therapy are based on this newfangled hypothesis.

[32] For example, Philistion (4th century), who still conserved the four roots in his medical system, and the (probably earlier) *Nature of Man* whose four humors with hot, cold, dry, moist, as their respective properties, are doubtless adapted from the Empedoclean school.

[33] But see Tannery, p. 292.

water, earth is no less effective as anti-Empedoclean polemic. The dogma that earth, water, air, fire can never be transformed into one another is here disposed of: air is shown to turn into water, water into earth. It was on this very exemption from intermutation and mixture that their title to being had rested in Empedocles. Anaxagoras abolishes the exemption without impairing the title. Being is no longer the exclusive privilege of four divine things, but the common possession of all things. This is the revolutionary principle of his physics.[34] The meaning of the proposition that "things are [only] mixed together and separated out of things that have being" [35] has now changed, for the denotation of "things that have being" has changed. Flesh and bone, no less than earth and fire, have the property of being, though all are subject to mixture. Being and mixture are not incompatible as in Parmenides and Empedocles, but complementary. So they appear in the seed; and the two sentences in which the word "seed" is used in the surviving fragments are both expressions of this idea, both employing the new term to assert propositions never before asserted in Greek physics.

The mixture of the moist and the dry, the hot and the cold, and the rest, in the primordial matrix was an old story in Ionian speculation. But the further statement in the account of this mixture, "there being much earth in it and an infinite multitude of seeds in no way resembling one another" is new. No Ionian had ever said that earth had been "in" the original matrix. Empedocles had said just that, precisely because he had endowed earth with Parmenidean being. Anaxagoras takes a long step in the same direction. He holds that earth, air, aether, as well as hair, flesh, and every other substance are "in" the primitive mixture, for they all have Parmenidean being. Even if we had lost this particular text, we could have reconstructed the doctrine from his general principle

---

[34] And was properly appreciated as such by Aristotle, in spite of his other misunderstandings of the system: *Met.* 984a8 ff., in Empedocles only the four roots "persist eternally and do not become," while in Anaxagoras "nearly all the *homoiomerē*, like air and water [scil., in Empedocles], are thus generated and destroyed only by congregation and segregation, but otherwise are neither generated nor destroyed, but persist eternally." The weakening of the generality of the proposition by the initial "nearly" ($\sigma\chi\epsilon\delta\acute{o}\nu$) may be disregarded as both unwarranted and inconsistent with other passages in which Aristotle makes no qualifications to the statement that Anaxagoras' *homoiomerē* were "elements" (e.g. *De Caelo* 302a28 ff.); cf. Theophrastus, *ap.* Simplic., *Phys.* 27.5–6, "all the *homoiomerē* are ungenerated and incorruptible."

[35] Literally "out of things that are," $\grave{\alpha}\pi\grave{o}$ $\dot{\epsilon}\acute{o}\nu\tau\omega\nu$ $\chi\rho\eta\mu\acute{\alpha}\tau\omega\nu$.

that hair cannot come from that which is not-hair. What this text adds is the precious word "seeds." It tells us *how* Anaxagoras conceived of the pre-existence of all these substances in the cosmic matrix. They were there as seeds. The primitive mixture was a seed-aggregate, just as every ordinary seed is a seed-aggregate. A bit of human sperm is a mixture of flesh-seeds, hair-seeds, bone-seeds, etc. So the primordial matrix was a mixture of an "infinite multitude of seeds," earth-seeds, flesh-seeds, and the rest. The mixture was homogeneous, every part of it like every other part, since "nothing was manifest" in it.[36] Yet these homogeneous parts were full of seeds as different from each other as earth from aether and hair from flesh, just as the ordinary seed, visibly homogeneous, is none the less full of heterogeneous things, resembling one another as little as a hair-seed resembles a flesh-seed.

Consider now the second proposition that each of the things that arise in the cosmogonic process "contain many things of all sorts and seeds of all things having all sorts of forms and colors and savors." Here again we have something new. The things of this created world, it is asserted, are as full of "seeds of all things," as rich in creative potency, as was the primordial infinite. And here too we have a doctrine which, in the absence of this particular text, could have been reconstructed from another fragment. For we are told in B6 that "as it was in the beginning, so now, all things are together." The things which emerge from the original mixture are mixtures in precisely the same sense. Anaxagoras could not have declared this identity more emphatically than by repeating, as he does here, his favorite phrase, "all things together," which he uses no less than three times in the surviving portions of his treatise to describe the original mixture. The mention of the "seed" simply shows how this concept duly generalized ties together the first term of the cosmogonic series with all its subsequent terms. No one would have said that an ordinary seed is a seed-aggregate

[36] Fr. 1 has been persistently misunderstood (Tannery, p. 299; Burnet, p. 266; Bailey, p. 546; Peck, p. 118) to say that air and aether were manifest in the primitive mixture, while nothing else was. Nothing of the kind is said in the fragment, which states emphatically that "all things being together, nothing was manifest," and proceeds to mention the predominance ($\kappa\alpha\tau\epsilon\hat{\iota}\chi\epsilon\nu$) of air and aether not as an exception to the statement but as a *reason* for it ($\gamma\acute{\alpha}\rho$). (For my suggested explanation of this difficult statement, see n. 80, below.) The preceding statement that all things in the mixture were "infinite both in multitude and smallness" is also fully general, and would apply to air and aether as much as to everything else.

of *all* substances. But the cosmic matrix must be just such a seed-aggregate, since all substances emerge from it. Similarly every part of every subsequent phase of the world process must be a seed-aggregate in just this sense, containing "seeds of all things." [37] The infinite variety of being contained in the infinite matrix from which the world arose is also contained in any portion of that world.

Can the finite then contain the infinite? Here we are forced to take account of the second major innovation of Anaxagoras' physics, hitherto disregarded for the sake of expository simplicity: the principle that given any portion of being, however small, there always exist still smaller portions. [38] The idea of the seed was the imaginative searchlight which brought to light a whole new world of conceptual possibilities. The idea of continuity was the logical compass with which Anaxagoras was able to explore these new regions and show how they could be added to the chart of intelligible truth. If "of the small there is no smallest, but always a smaller" (B3), the new idea intuitively suggested by the "world-metaphor" of the seed need never run afoul of logical absurdity. Any portion of being, however small, may contain the infinite variety of being in portions sufficiently small. Any two things, however small, may now be shown to be both alike, since they contain "portions of everything," and unlike, if they contain these portions in unequal ratios. Fuller discussion of this part of the system must await clarification of the further question: What are these "portions" of the seed?

II. The Opposites

The correct answer, and therewith the most important step ever taken toward the true understanding of Anaxagoras, was made by Tannery's

---

[37] The similarity is borne out by the parallelism between the description of the germ in B10 and of the precosmic state in B1. In both cases we have a mixture of parts of which none is manifest (οὐδὲν ἔνδηλον, B1; ἀφανῆ, B10) because of their "smallness" (ὑπὸ σμικρότητος, B1; διὰ μικρομέρειαν, B10). Cornford has drawn attention (pp. 21 ff.) to the valuable passage where Simplicius (*Phys.* 460.28 ff.) even tells us that Anaxagoras "passed from the mixture in the individual thing to the mixture of all things." Anaxagoras would not have, of course, derived from the seed the general idea of the origin of the world from a primitive mixture, which was wholly traditional. What he may well have derived from it was, as I have suggested, the specific idea of the preformation of all things in the original mixture on the model of the preformation of all the tissues in the organic seed.

[38] B1, B3, B6.

suggestion that the ultimate ingredients of the seeds are the hot and the cold, the dry and the moist, and all the traditional "opposites" of Ionian cosmology.[39] These are conceived not as properties of Aristotelian substances, but as "quality-things" [40] or, better still, as forms of energy or "power" (*dynamis*). Long before Plato coined the technical term *poiotēs*,[41] the current term for "quality" was *dynamis*, power.[42] The hot is that which heats, the moist that which moistens; each is an active tendency to change other things after its own fashion, unless checked, or balanced, by its opposite.[43] Sensation itself is conceived as just such a change in the percipient. I perceive anything as hot so far, and only so far, as that thing heats me, the effect on the sensitive organism being exactly the same as that on all other bodies.[44]

As to the number of these powers, the general assumption seems to have been that it was indefinitely large.[45] The hot and the cold, the dry

---

[39] Tannery's account of the scientific scope of Anaxagoras' theory of matter, as a perfectly logical alternative to the atomic hypothesis, is still the best. There is only one major confusion in his reconstruction: he first assumes that Anaxagoras' qualities are "pure abstractions" (p. 295), but then (pp. 298 ff.) reverts to the (correct) view that the distinction between substance and qualities is not to be found in Anaxagoras. The uncertainty could have been cleared up and the historicity of the latter view firmly established against Zeller's objections by a study of the qualities as substantial "powers" in the Hippocratic literature.

[40] The term is Cornford's.

[41] *Theaetetus* 182a.

[42] So, e.g., in Alcmaeon B4, Parmenides B9.2 and 18.2–4, and generally in the Hippocratic treatises.

[43] I cannot understand what leads Peck to say "There is no notion here [scil., in the Hippocratic usage of *dynamis* in the sense of 'strong substance, of a particular character'] of the substance *having* power in the sense of power to affect an external body in a particular way" (Introduction to Aristotle's *Parts of Animals*, Loeb ed., p. 31). This is just the sense in the Hippocratics from the very start; see e.g. *Ancient Medicine* 15: the hot-astringent will produce exactly just such an effect, the cold-astringent the opposite effect, and this "not only in man, but in a leathern vessel and in wood and in many other things less sensitive than man." The whole theory of the administration of drugs or slops depends on just this assumption: that if *x* has a given set of powers, it will affect the patient in just these ways and in proportion to the intensity of its own powers. Peck's other remarks on *dynamis*, both here and in his Introduction to Aristotle's *Generation of Animals*, Loeb ed., pp. xlix ff., seem to me both accurate and illuminating.

[44] See e.g. *Sacred Disease* 16.

[45] *Anc. Med.* 17.10, where the mention of various properties, bitter, acid,

and the moist, the rare and the dense, the bright and the dark are, of course, more prominent than any others in cosmological inquiry. But these others would be no less real and substantial. The "sweet" and the "bitter" figure in Alcmaeon's list of opposites whose equipoise constitutes health. For the physiologist and the medical man such gustatory qualities would be extremely significant. "It is not the hot which possesses the great power," says the author of *Ancient Medicine* in his polemic against Empedocles, "but the astringent, the insipid, and the other [gustatory] qualities I have mentioned, both in man and out of man, whether eaten or drunk or externally applied as ointment or plaster." [46] Their importance may be gauged from the speedy dominance of the doctrine of the *chymoi*, or "humors," in medical theory, *chymos* denoting both the savor of a given substance and the substance which has that savor. In the first, formative stages of the doctrine we can see how a specific "humor" is identified primarily by its gustatory quality. Thus when the author of *Ancient Medicine* refers certain symptoms of "nausea, burning, and weakness" to a certain humor, he speaks of it as "a certain bitterness which we call yellow bile" (19.28), while "frenzy, gnawings, and distress of the bowels and chest" are explained by the presence of certain "pungent and acrid acidities" in the body (19.36).

That Anaxagoras shared the traditional view of the "powers" is a reasonable assumption, and this not in spite but because of the scantiness of our notices on this topic. Had he deviated in any significant way, some trace of the innovation would have been left in the record. His extant fragments speak of the hot-cold, dry-moist, rare-dense, bright-dark;[47] also of "all sorts of colors and savors." [48] Since our fragments are mainly preoccupied with cosmogony, they concentrate in the traditional fashion upon the former. The formation of the broad masses of earth, water, air, and the fire depends, as in all previous ac-

---

salty, is capped with the words καὶ ἄλλα μυρία. Aristotle (*Met.* 986a22 ff.) implies that Alcmaeon did not attempt to specify a limited set of "opposites"; cf. Alcmaeon B4, "moist, dry, cold, hot, bitter, sweet, *and the rest*." Neither apparently did Anaximander: Simpl. *Phys.* 150.24, "and the opposites are the hot, cold, dry, moist, *and the rest*."

[46] 15.27–30.

[47] B4, B8, B12, B15, B16.

[48] B4; cf. Diogenes B5, where after mentioning differences with respect to the hot, cold, etc., he adds "and there are many other differences of savor and color, an infinite number of them."

counts, on the separation of the hot, the dry, the rare, and the bright from their respective opposites. These are the dominant, but not exclusive, properties of earth, water, air, and fire. Thus the earth contains salty savors, manifest in deposits of mineral salt and in the saltiness of sea water which has been filtered through the earth; "and there are also sharp humors in many parts of the earth." [49] Similarly the air is full of savors, though these become manifest to our senses only when concentrated by condensation.[50] What colors and savors Anaxagoras considered important we do not know.[51] But it is safe to assume that he believed in an indefinite number of savors and colors. This is confirmed by his statement that "in neither word nor deed can we know the number of the things that are being separated off." [52]

That none of these qualities can exist apart or "by itself," but only in commixture with others, had been the traditional assumption. So obvious a truth would never have been asserted, except in the face of its denial. The author of *Ancient Medicine* does assert it against Empedocles, protesting the outrageous dogma that "pure" qualities could ever exist "by themselves" anywhere in the world.[53] His very words are reminiscent of Anaxagoras' denial that anything (except mind) could ever be "by itself." [54] The doctrine that "there is a portion of everything in everything" is thus rooted in common sense, though Anaxagoras' principle that "of the small there is no smallest" reads far more into the common sense view than common sense in its innocence had ever

[49] A90.

[50] Theophr. *De Sensibus* 30 (= A92); cf. *Airs, Waters, Places* 8.

[51] All we know of his medical theory is Aristotle's single reference to (and refutation of) the Anaxagorean doctrine that bile is the cause of acute diseases, *De Part. An.* 677a5 ff.

[52] B7. For the meaning of the expression "things that are being separated off" (τῶν ἀποκρινομένων) see B12, "and the rare is separated off [ἀποκρίνεται] from the dense and the hot from the cold and the bright from the dark and the dry from the moist"; thus it is the powers (of which only the usual four pairs are enumerated here) which are the "things that are being separated off." The meaning of τῶν ἀποκρινομένων in B6 must be the same: the powers, an equal set of which is contained in all things, great and small. We have also Aristotle's testimony (*Phys.* 187a25) that the "opposites" (powers) of Anaxagoras were infinite in number, as well as the *homoiomerē*.

[53] 15.6, 19.22. A *relative* degree of separation is, of course, admitted as the cause of disease (14.35 ff.).

[54] Compare Anaxagoras' expressions ἐφ᾽ ἑαυτοῦ γενέσθαι or εἶναι in B6 and B12 with αὐτό τι ἐφ᾽ ἑαυτοῦ in *Anc. Med.* 15.6.

suspected. Certainly it would have never occurred to the author of *Ancient Medicine* that *all* the opposites exist in everything; and if it had, he would have asked how the same qualities could make up things so manifestly different. Anaxagoras is ready with the answer: "Each thing is and was most manifestly those things of which it has most in it." [55]

The form of this answer is not original in the least. The idea that the observable properties of a given thing could be explained by the proportions in which its constituent "powers" were mixed together was a familiar one.[56] Thus Empedocles had accounted for the difference between bone and flesh by specifying the different proportions in which their ingredients, the same for both, were put together.[57] What is still more significant, Empedocles had appealed to variations in the "ratio of the mixture" [58] to explain not only differences between different substances, but also differences between different kinds of the same substance. Thus blood, the organ of thought, consists of earth, water, air, fire in equal proportions; "a little more" of one or "a little less" of another ingredient would account for differences in the intellectual powers of different persons.[59]

Anaxagoras could adapt the same general theory to his own concept of matter. All things, great or small, have the same set of powers;[60] but they manifest different properties because of differences in the ratio of the mixture of these same powers.[61] The principle that "there is no

[55] B12, ad fin.

[56] So, e.g., in Alcmaeon's doctrine of health as the equipoise of the powers (i.e. in 1:1 proportion).

[57] A78 (= *Aet.* 5.22.1), B96 and B98.

[58] λόγος τῆς μίξεως, Arist. *De Part. An.* 642a22.

[59] B98.3. Theophr. *De Sens.* 11 (= A86). That Empedocles himself spoke of the ratio of the mixture as a *logos* is not impossible; Heraclitus (B31) had used the term in the sense of "measure," and it was currently used for "proportion" both in geometry and in common speech (see LSJ s.v., II, 1 and 2). At B96 Empedocles speaks of allotted portions or shares (μερέων λάχε), which comes very close to Anaxagoras' term *moirai* (in fact, some of the manuscripts of Aristotle and Simplicius read μοιράων or μοιρῶν for μερέων). Democritus too used *moira:* see Theophr. *De Sens.* 77.

[60] Their "shares" or "allotments" (*moirai*), B6, B11, B12. Cf. Plato *Phil.* 53a7.

[61] Since the qualitative ingredients are indefinitely numerous, the ratio of the mixture would have to be expressed not as a ratio of part to whole but as a ratio of each power to its specific opposite, white to black, hot to cold, sweet to bitter, etc.; and only those ratios would be given which would be presumed to account for the "manifest" properties of a given substance.

smallest" would enable Anaxagoras to work with ratios far more complex than the simple proportions of Empedocles' formulae and thus account for the finest shadings of difference between any two individuals, including individuals of the same kind.[62] The "little more" and "little less" of Empedocles could now be treated not as haphazard deviations from a set formula, but as different combination-formulae, corresponding to different manifest properties. Anaxagoras could thus lay down the formal proposition that no two individuals are absolutely similar, which is exactly what he declares in the immediately preceding sentence of the present fragment: "For no other thing [scil., other than *nous*] is like anything else." [63] The general proposition that no two things are absolutely unlike (B8) is thus balanced by the no less general proposition that no two things are absolutely alike. Both propositions are conceived through the principle of continuity.

Through the same principle Anaxagoras could conceive a third idea: the absolute homogeneity of a given thing with any of its parts, however small. If we take, say, a bit of flesh which manifests such and such properties and proceed by mechanical division, each of the resulting sections could "manifest" exactly the same properties provided that the combination-formula characteristic of the whole were exactly the same for each of the parts; and even when we come down to parts too small to "manifest" any properties, they would still *have* the same qualities, if ordered in the same ratio. The principle of continuity would make possible just such a conception; for no matter how slight the predominance of, say, hot to cold might be in the whole, the same ratio could be maintained in any of its parts *ad infinitum*. Thus a given bone, however dissimilar to flesh, hair, and every other thing in the world, including other kinds of bone, could be internally homogeneous through and through, retaining its characteristic properties throughout any process of division instead of suddenly breaking apart at a terminal step in the division, as it would in Empedocles, into three other things, qualitatively heterogeneous with the next larger parts. *Homoiomereia*—

---

[62] This difficulty in Empedocles' physiology must have been obvious (see e.g. pseudo-Arist. *De Spiritu* 485b26 ff.).

[63] The same assertion in B12 ad fin., cited above, Section I, n. 3. Diogenes may have been influenced at this point by Anaxagoras when he insisted that "none of the things which are differentiated can become exactly alike one with another, unless they become the same thing" (B5). He applies the proposition universally, rejecting the single exception to the rule that Anaxagoras had made in the case of mind (Anaxagoras B12: "but mind is all alike, both the lesser and the greater").

similarity of parts—would be the perfect term for this principle.[64] Our fragments, of course, contain no mention of this term nor any statement of the principle. But the fact that "the homoeomereia of things" is so generally taken by our ancient authorities as the distinctive concept of Anaxagoras' physics[65] is, I believe, sufficient evidence of the genuineness of the principle, if not also of the term.[65a]

We may now restate the foregoing interpretation of Anaxagoras' theory of matter. It is based on a traditional concept of the "powers" and an original concept of the "seed." The two are combined through his own unique principle that there are no smallest quantities in nature, which enables him to conserve yet transform the traditional notion of

[64] Peck has a different interpretation, taking *homoiomereia* to refer to the fact that any two substances contain "similar parts," since each contains the same set of ingredients. But if this were the original meaning, how account for the fact that it is never adopted, or even considered, by any of the ancient commentators? How can we, in the absence of textual evidence, reject the interpretation which commended itself to those who did have access to the texts? Peck must rest his case entirely on the literal meaning of *homoiomereia;* but this agrees with the traditional interpretation much better than with his. When Anaxagoras compares different substances with respect to the same set of portions contained in each, he speaks of the *equality*, not similarity, of their portions: B3, the large thing is "equal to the small in respect of the multitude" (scil., of the portions contained in each); cf. B6.

[65] Lucr. I.834 *rerum quam dicit homoeomerian.* Aet. I.3.5. "ὁμοιομερείας" αὐτὰς ἐκάλεσε καὶ ἀρχὰς τῶν ὄντων ἀπεφήνατο; D.L. 2.8 ἀρχὰς δὲ τὰς ὁμοιο-μερείας; Plut. *Pericles* 4 νοῦν . . . ἀποκρίνοντα τὰς ὁμοιομερείας; Galen *De Natur. Facult.* 2.8 οἱ τὰς ὁμοιομερείας ὑποτιθέμενοι; Simpl. *Phys.* 460.4 et passim.

[65a] Cf. Simpl. *Phys.* 1123.23 τὰ εἴδη, ἅπερ "ὁμοιομερείας" καλεῖ,—a statement entitled to respect, coming as it does from Simplicius, who knew Anaxagoras' work at first hand and quoted extensively from his book. However, many scholars have long felt reluctant to believe that Anaxagoras himself had the word ὁμοιομέρεια or even ὁμοιομερές: cf. Eduard Zeller, *A History of Greek Philosophy in the Time of Socrates,* Eng. transl. by S. F. Alleyne (London, 1881), vol. 2, pp. 335–36 and notes; and, most recently, Mathewson, pp. 78–79. The objections are serious, but not conclusive. Ὁμοιομερές is, of course, one of Aristotle's favorite technical terms; but is there any reason to suppose that it is his own coinage? Epicurus uses ὁμοιομερές (*Ep.* 1.52), ὁμοιομέρεια (*Peri Physeōs* XIV) in a perfectly straightforward manner, without any suggestion that he is borrowing Aristotelian idiom. For objection to the idea that even the principle of ὁμοιομέρεια is automatically Anaxagorean, see Guthrie, pp. 282 ff.

mixture and propound a new, continuous view of nature. For expository convenience the two ideas of the powers and the seeds have been treated separately. No such disjunction is, of course, presumed in Anaxagoras' own account of his system, where the two are complementary and interdependent. Every seed has all the powers. Dissimilar seeds contain dissimilar ratios of the same powers. There is an infinite variety of seeds, since there is an infinite variety of ratios in which the powers may be combined. Every seed has *being;* no seed can be generated or destroyed. Hair can only come from hair; a specific type of hair (say, blond, soft, light, etc.) can only come from that specific type of hair pre-existing in sperm and nutriment and in all their causal antecedents, back to the original mixture. Any bit of matter, whether in the created world or in the primordial mixture, contains not only all the powers, but also all the seeds; and any substance can grow from any other by assimilating from it its own kind of seed. Thus, in principle, "anything can be generated from anything." [66]

III. Every Power and Seed in Every Seed

The foregoing account, based in all essentials on the original fragments, has all but ignored the interpretations of Aristotle and his successors. It has thus avoided the problems which arise from the particular turns and twists which the doctrine of Anaxagoras suffers in the doxographic tradition. It is now time to descend to this other level of inquiry. For no responsible interpretation can ignore what is, after all, a major part of the available evidence. If it departs from doxographic interpretations it must account for the deviation, and explain how ancient authors in full possession of the original texts could misconstrue their doctrine at any significant point. Misconstructions do occur, and most of them can be traced back to the distorting medium of the Aristotelian transmission. This has been amply established by modern scholarship. [67] The danger nowadays is that of overestimating the extent of the distortion and making the taint of Aristotelian influence a good excuse for dismissing any testimony that

[66] Arist. *Phys.* 203a24, ὁτιοῦν ἐξ ὁτουοῦν γιγνόμενον; Simpl. *Phys.* 164.20–21 and 461.7, καὶ πᾶν ἐκ παντὸς ἐκκρίνεται. Here, as above, Section I, n. 34, Aristotle reports correctly a fundamental doctrine of Anaxagoras.

[67] See especially Heidel's pioneering paper, "Qualitative Change in Pre-Socratic Philosophy," *AGP*, 19 (1906), 333 ff. [repr. above, pp. 86–95], and the definitive study by Cherniss, cited above, n. 9.

does not happen to fit our own particular preconception. Sober criticism, I believe, must approach our secondary sources with the respect
due to authors who, however unhistorical in their interpretations of
the evidence, had access to a vastly larger mass of it than we shall ever
have. As reports on that evidence their statements must be presumed
innocent unless proved guilty.

Let us begin with the account of Anaxagoras in Lucretius 1.830 ff.
This tells us that all things are formed out of tiny particles of their own
kind. Each is generated by the concrescence[68] or coming together[69] of
small bits of its own kind: bone out of bone, blood out of blood, earth
out of earth. This is what Lucretius understands by the "homoeomereia
of things." He then proceeds to say (859 ff.) that, according to Anaxagoras, any given substance contains particles not only of its own kind
but of other—indeed all other—kinds of matter. "All things are mixed
in hiding in all things"; and by the things so mixed in others he understands not the powers, but the various kinds of substance, blood in
wheat, milk in grass, etc., that one substance being "manifest (*apparere*)
whereof the most [scil., particles] are mingled in it." Thus a given bit of
flesh would consist of (i) flesh-particles, and (ii) particles of bone, hair,
and every other substance, the flesh-particles quantitatively predominating over the rest.

Now if we compare this account with the surviving fragments we
shall find it defective at a number of points. There is no mention of the
concept of the "seed," nor of the opposites. The one sentence which
is almost a verbatim quotation can be shown to involve a serious discrepancy with the original. When Anaxagoras says that "each thing is
most manifestly those things of which it has the most" (B12 sub. fin.)
the context strongly suggests that he is thinking of the variety of
opposites—rare, dense, etc.—not of the variety of seeds which it
contains;[69a] it is the predominance of hot-rare-light-bright over their

[68] *Concrescere*, 840, literally "growing together," but in this context probably the Latin rendering for Anaxagoras' συμπηγνύναι (B16, συμπήγνυται γῆ;
here *terram concrescere*). The same word in Cicero *Acad.* 2.31.100 (under
Anaxagoras A97 in DK) again as a translation of συμπηγνύναι; snow *concreta*
out of water; cf. the parallel in Sextus *Pyrrh. hypot.* 1.33, ἡ χιὼν ὕδωρ ἐστὶ
πεπηγός.

[69] *Coeuntibus*, 837, probably for συνιέναι. Cf. Leuc. A19, συνιόντα καὶ
πιλούμενα; Anaxag. A81, σύνοδος ἀστέρων; and σύνοδος, συνέρχεσθαι, of the
"coming together" of the roots in Empedocles B17.

[69a] Only opposites are mentioned.

opposites which makes the difference between aether and air, not the predominance of aether-seeds over all the other seeds contained by aether. Lucretius assumes the latter, ignoring the former, and in this he is pretty typical of our secondary sources.[70] The question then is why the prominence of the opposites in the fragments should be thus submerged in the account of Lucretius and others. We shall try to answer this question in due course. But let us now note that, when due allowance has been made for the deficiences that have just been noted, Lucretius' residual rendering of Anaxagoras is perfectly sound. Turning to Anaxagoras immediately after his encounter with Empedocles, Lucretius fastens, quite properly, on two cardinal points at which Anaxagoras differs from Empedocles as much as from the atomists:

(i) Flesh, bone, hair, and a vast variety of other qualitatively dissimilar substances (not just four of them, as in Empedocles, or none of them, as in the atomists) are all "primordial" (1.847 ff.), so that none of them could be generated from any of the rest, singly or in combination; each can only arise from particles of its own specific kind.

(ii) Each of these substances nevertheless contains every other kind of substance (contrary to both Empedocles and the atomists). On the present reconstruction both of these points appear as substantially correct statements of the unique challenge of the system to the atomists.

(i) is the eternity and (ii) the commixture of the Anaxagorean seeds. Both can be grounded in the fragments: (i) in B10, (ii) in B4. The omission of the term "seed" may be explained, if not excused, by its early importation into atomistic vocabulary which transposed it to an entirely different set of categories.[71]

But is this account of Anaxagoras' doctrine logically consistent? Cornford's study of Anaxagoras, one of the most thorough and

[70] So e.g. Theophr. *ap.* Simpl. *Phys.* 27.8 ff.: "For that thing appears as gold in which there is much gold, though all (scil., other substance) are present in it." See below, n. 75.

[71] See above, Section I, n. 13. The principle of the seed in the atomists carried with it the imputation that a certain thing can only arise from its own *specific* seeds, i.e., kind of atoms (cf. Aris. *Phys.* 195a31), in opposition to the Anaxagorean principle "anything can be generated from anything" (above, Section II, n. 66). Postulating that everything is a seed-aggregate of all things, Anaxagoras can hold that the two ideas listed as (i) and (ii) in the text above are complementary, while the atomists would appeal to the ordinary meaning of the seed (e.g. that wheat can grow only out of wheat-seeds) to argue that (i) and (ii) are incompatible.

thoughtful ever made, has pressed this question and answered it in the negative.[72] Cornford saw "flat contradiction" in the two propositions which we find in Lucretius' as well as in Aristotle's, Theophrastus', and Simplicius' account of Anaxagoras: (i) There are homoeomerous substances; (ii) Each of them contains portions of all the rest. If (ii) were true, Cornford argues, (i) would have to be false. For (ii) would mean that a given substance like flesh would not be homoeomerous, any of its parts having exactly the same properties as every other, but extremely heteromerous, since it would have to contain a vast number of heterogeneous parts. Moreover, Cornford argues, (ii) is intrinsically unsound, for it leads to an endless regress. It assumes that a given substance, x, consists of a collection of dissimilar particles, x, y, z, etc., with the x-particles predominating over the rest. On this assumption we would never have any x's at all (or, for that matter, y's, or z's); for any x, however small, is in turn composed of the motley collection of x's, y's, z's, etc. Unless at some point we could get hold of genuine x's— particles which are x and nothing but x—we could never begin the process of composition in which x's could be mixed with y's, z's, etc. in the required proportion. Cornford's solution would be to throw out this whole conception as a misconception fathered by Aristotle on the tradition. "A portion of everything in everything," Cornford holds, must mean only (a) "a portion of every opposite in every seed," not (b), as Lucretius assumed, "a portion of every seed in every seed," nor (a) *and* (b), as Aristotle (*Phys.* 187a25–26) and others assumed, "a portion of every opposite *and* every seed in every seed." For only (a) would vindicate the principle of homoeomereia and break the vicious regress involved in (b).

Of these two arguments, the second is inconclusive. Why should the infinite regress hold any terrors for Anaxagoras, who is committed to the principle of infinite divisibility?[72a] The same objection could have

---

[72] See the opening paragraph of his paper (p. 14) et passim.

[72a] In view of subsequent criticism (Strang, pp. 101 ff.) I should emphasize the fact that the infinite regress which, I contend, would cause Anaxagoras no logical trouble would be that generated by the principle stated in the middle of the preceding paragraph. A clearer statement of the principle might perhaps run as follows: Any portion of matter of sensible size belonging to a given natural kind, x, consists of a collection of particles in which all the natural kinds, x, y, z, etc., are represented, but particles of kind x predominate in bulk. The same is true *mutatis mutandis* of particles, sub-particles, sub-sub-particles, . . . belonging to natural kind x. I maintain that the sup-

been urged against his principle that "of the small there is no smallest, but always a smaller." As Zeno would have argued, how could there be any magnitude at all on this assumption, since there is no "smallest" magnitude with which to begin the process of composition? It is the first, and only the first, of Cornford's arguments which points to a serious difficulty to which an answer must be found. But Cornford's

position that this would remain true at infinitely many levels of subdivision would not of itself lead to any logical difficulty whatever: The regress generated by this principle is no more logically noxious than is that generated by the principle of the infinite divisibility of matter. In defending Cornford against my criticism of him on this point, Strang apparently fails to note that my criticism is directed exclusively to Cornford's assumption that a regress generated by the above principle would be vicious, and that the regress which he (Strang) thinks is vicious is generated by an entirely different principle, which he formulates as follows: "The predominant ingredients in a substance are responsible for its most distinctive features." Does *this* principle generate a vicious regress? I have no doubt that it might, if suitably explicated and fortified with the requisite ancillary premises. What I fail to see is that the quoted statement is a faithful transcript of the closing part of B12 ("each thing is and was most manifestly those things of which it has most in it"), which Strang supposes it to be. My own understanding of this text would be rather as follows: To belong to a given natural kind, x, a sensible thing does not need to consist exclusively of ingredients belonging to the same natural kind; it may—and, in fact, always does—contain ingredients belonging to innumerable other natural kinds; this does not prevent it from "manifesting" the properties characteristic of its own natural kind, provided only the ingredients belonging to its own kind greatly preponderate over those of its ingredients which belong to other natural kinds. I fail to see how this principle could generate any infinite regress whatever. In the first place, would the question of "manifest" properties (presumably, manifest to the senses) of the original datum recur with respect to its ingredients (presumably, of infra-sensible size)? Even if it did, and not only at this level, but at all of the infinitely many subsequent levels, there would still be no vicious regress, unless we were to suppose that Anaxagoras held that the properties "manifested" at the level of the original datum could not be identified, or explained, until the same thing had been done at each of the infinitely many subsequent levels—surely a gratuitous assumption. The fact that what happens at a given level *implies* that something happens at each of infinitely many lower levels would of itself be logically harmless; there would be trouble if, and only if, in order to characterize, identify, explain, etc. what happens at a given level we must have completed the process of characterizing, identifying, explaining, etc. what happens at all of the lower levels.

answer cannot possibly be the right one. Quite apart from the violence
it would do to a great mass of our ancient reports, it would founder on
the fragments themselves. First of all, we have the statement in B4,
already discussed in Section I, that "in all the things that are coming
together there must be many things of all sorts and seeds of all things
having all sorts of forms and colors and savors." The plain sense of
this statement is that *any* creature of the creative process will contain
"seeds of all things." On Cornford's view (pp. 28–29) this must be
explained away to mean that "seeds of all things" are contained not in
each emergent, but in all of them taken as a totality. But the statement
that "there are many things in all things" recurs in B6; and there it is
certain that "in all things" does not mean "in the whole totality of
things" but "in each and every thing." [73] In the second place, we have
the unambiguous and decisive implication of Anaxagoras' theory of
nutrition for the point at issue. Flesh, milk, wheat are homoeomerous
yet each of them must contain hair, bone, etc. If flesh will nourish hair,
then flesh must contain hair *somehow*.[74] The only question is, How?

We must agree with Cornford that Aristotle's answer to this question[75] cannot be the right answer. It is the idea that a given substance

[73] As is clear from the sequel, "and of the [scil., powers which are] separating out [scil., there is] an equal multitude both in the greater and the lesser
[scil., things]." Anaxagoras' expression for "the totality of things" is τὸ σύμπαν (B4), τὰ σύμπαντα (B1), and this is what he would have used here, had he
meant to say that seeds of all things were contained in the whole of creation
rather than in each and every creature.

[74] It is astonishing that a mind as acute as Cornford's should have missed
this very obvious implication. He ignored it by restricting his discussion of
Anaxagoras' theory of nutrition to the case of bread (mentioned by Sim-
plicius and Aetius): bread is made of wheat, which is a seed and therefore (on
Cornford's view) not a homoeomerous substance (p. 20). That seeds are non-
homoeomerous is an ad hoc hypothesis, without foundation in the evidence.
Anyhow, this particular loophole would be wholly lacking in the case of flesh.
If Anaxagoras believed in the existence of *any* homoeomerous substance, he
must certainly have held flesh to be such; it is Aristotle's star example of
Anaxagorean *homoiomerē*.

[75] Best expressed in his account of Anaxagoras in *Phys.* 187b4 ff.: "Nothing
is purely [εἰλικρινῶς] and entirely white or black or sweet or flesh or bone,
but the nature of a thing appears to be that of which it contains the most."
Thus a given thing will contain portions of both the powers (white, black,
sweet, etc.) *and* homoeomerous substances (flesh, bone, etc.); cf. 187a25,
"both the homoeomeries and the opposites [scil., the powers] are infinite in

is composed of the juxtaposition of two *separate* sets of ingredients, the powers, on one hand, the seeds, on the other, both sets being necessary, neither being sufficient, to account for its distinctive and characteristic properties. This idea need only be spelled out to reveal its inherent redundancy. Flesh has any number of qualities: it is red, soft, heavy, etc. Given these powers in the required ratio, the result would *be* flesh. Why then need we mix flesh-seeds (or any other seeds) *to* these powers to produce flesh? The powers of flesh are *sufficient* to constitute flesh-seeds; flesh contains flesh-seeds not because these have been added to its powers as an additional set of necessary ingredients, but simply because in possessing the powers of flesh in the proper ratio, it *is* a set of flesh-seeds.[76] The only reason for supposing the necessity of adding flesh-seeds to the powers of flesh to produce flesh would be the assumption that there is some simple quality, fleshiness, which flesh possesses in addition to all its other specifiable powers. What reason could there be for such an assumption, so foreign to Ionian thought? Peck refers us to Aristotle's "explicit" testimony that Anaxagoras held flesh, bone, etc., to be "simple" substances (pp. 31 ff.). Aristotle is explicit enough on

---

number." Lucretius' account disregards the powers as ingredients, and merely mentions the particles of other homoeomerous substances in any given substance. So does Simplicius in the main, though he has hints of the other view as at *Phys.* 27.1 (following Theophrastus?), where it is said that the infinity of Anaxagorean *archai* are "composite, heterogeneous, and opposite" (ἐναντίας, which must refer to the powers; cf. ἐναντίας [scil., τὰς ἀρχάς] in Arist. *Phys.* 184b22 and τἀναντία, 187a25).

[76] For this interpretation of Anaxagoras see Porphyry and Themistius *ap.* Simpl. *Phys.* 44.5 ff.: "for they (the school of Anaxagoras) suppose that hotnesses and coldnesses, drynesses and wetnesses, rarenesses and densities, and the other qualitative contrasts are in the *homoiomereiai*, which they regard as *archai*, and make the differences between the *homoiomereiai*." The translation is Cornford's (p. 92), who rightly calls attention to the importance of this passage. The closing sentence seems to me particularly significant as the only doxographic text which agrees unambiguously with the sense that Anaxagoras' phrase, "each thing is most manifestly those things [scil., powers] of which it contains the most," has in its own context in B12. The next best text in this respect is Galen's statement of Anaxagoras' doctrine that the qualities are "eternally unalterable and unchangeable," apparent alterations being due to their "segregation and congregation" (*De Natur. Facult.* 1.2.4; cited by Burnet, p. 263 n. 1), and Alexander's testimony (*ap.* Simpl., *Phys.* 155.4 ff.) that "the oppositions as well as all the [scil., qualitative] differences are in the *homoiomereiai*," and Simplicius' own comment ad loc.

this point; but his testimony here is worthless, for it is demonstrably contradictory and confused. For while he does tell us in *De Gen. et Corr.* 314a25 ff. (and by implication in *De Caelo* 308a28 ff.) that Anaxagoras held flesh, bone, etc., to be "simple substances" [77] he clearly implies at *Phys.* 187b24 that flesh is *not* simple, since water is "separated out of flesh" exactly as flesh is "separated out" of water. More generally, he tells us that flesh, bone, etc., are *seeds;*[78] but if seeds, they must be compounds: this, as I have argued in Section I, is of the essence of the contemporary concept of the seed, and is specifically borne out by Anaxagoras' own account of the seed. But even if, for any reason whatever, one should discount this argument from the composite nature of the seed, flesh would still not be "simple," since on this view (Aristotle's and Peck's) flesh would contain the powers *and* flesh-seeds (as well as other kinds of seeds), and so would any of its parts *ad infinitum.* Thus any flesh-seed, however small, would be a compound, and no argument whatever may be premised on its supposed "simplicity."

There is a simpler answer to our question, and one which is wholly free from the redundancy of the traditional view. It explains how a bit of flesh does contain both (a) the infinite variety of powers *and* (b) the infinite variety of seeds, without assuming that (b) is a separate set of ingredients over and above (a). Any seed is made up of the various powers in its own proper ratio; and since *all* the seeds are made up of

[77] And that they are "simpler" than earth, water, air, and fire, which he thought "composite." An impressive number of modern commentators have taken at face value Aristotle's statements in these passages. Among these are W. D. Ross (ad Arist. *Met.* 984a14), and even Cornford, who does not scruple to reject the fundamentals of the Aristotelian interpretation of Anaxagoras. Yet I cannot believe that Aristotle can possibly be right on this particular point. What possible motive could have led Anaxagoras to discriminate against fire, air, water, and earth, which are the basic constituents of Ionian cosmology (including his own), denying them the title of Being which he assigned to every other substance? A departure of this magnitude could not have been overlooked by the doxographic tradition; but there is no trace of it after Aristotle. It is universally ignored, and is contradicted by Lucretius, who takes fire, air, etc. to be *homoiomerē* on all fours with flesh, bone, etc., as well as by Simplicius (*Phys.* 27.5) and Philoponus (*De Gen. et Corr.* 13.26). As for the fragments, there is not a word to lend color to this Aristotelian view, while the mention of the earth among the seeds (above, Section I, n. 17) tells against it.

[78] *De Caelo* 308a28 ff.

the same set of powers, though in different ratios, it would follow that any seed contains any other, simply through the fact that it contains their necessary ingredients in portions which, however small, would still suffice to produce any of these other seeds in correspondingly minute form.[79] Thus any seed, x, contains any other seed, y, not because y-particles are to be found side by side with the x-particles in any portion of the substance x, but simply through the fact that any x-seed contains the powers which would produce y-seeds if sorted out of x in the ratio appropriate to y. Let the seed x be composed of the powers, a, b, c, d, etc., in the ratio of $10a$ for every b, c, d, etc.; and let the formula for a y-seed be $10b$ for every a, c, d, etc. Any x-seed would then contain a y-seed, since it is always possible to separate out of x appropriately smaller portions of a, b, c, d, etc., to make up a y in the required ratio. By the same token, an x-seed would also contain any other seed, z, since whatever may be the ratio of the powers in z, we would still be able to get a z out of x. Let the ratio of b to a, etc., in z be a million to one; we would still be able to say that every x contains a z, a z-seed being always (on this calculation) less than one-millionth the size of the x-seed in which it is contained.[80] Conversely, any z-seed would always contain an

---

[79] This idea is implicit in the Tannery-Burnet interpretation. But I have not seen it explicitly made in the literature, except in F. M. Cleve's recent *Philosophy of Anaxagoras* (New York, 1949), pp. 87–88. I am directly indebted to Mr. Cleve at this important point. See my review of this book, *Philosophical Review*, 59 (1960), 124–26.

[80] Since (i) all but the first two factors in the z-seed (i.e. c, d, etc.) would each be (by hypothesis) one-millionth of the b-factor in x; and (ii) the b-factor in the z-seed would have to be smaller than the b-factor in the x-seed: were it as large, the separation of the z-seed from the x-seed would leave the latter without any b-factors at all, which would be contrary to the "portion of everything in everything" principle. Incidentally, we can now explain the sense in which air and aether "prevailed" in B1 (see above, Section I, n. 36): the constitution of the primitive mixture would be such that any portion of it could be separated without remainder into equal portions of air and aether, while to separate any two other substances out of it (say, flesh and bone) would leave a (relatively large) remainder. In other words, the constitution of the matrix was of the form 1 a, 1 not-a, 1 b, 1 not-b, 1 c, 1 not-c, etc., where a, b, c, etc., stand for the various qualities, hot, dry, light, etc., and their respective opposites. (This on the general assumption of Pre-Socratic cosmologies—Anaximander, Parmenides, Empedocles—that opposite powers are contained in equal ratio in the totality of existence; see my "Equality and Justice".) If

x-seed correspondingly smaller than itself. There is no difficulty in such a conception that would trouble one who believes that "of the small there is no smallest, but always a smaller."

This explanation meets the logical difficulty which Cornford rightly saw in the traditional view; it accounts for the containment of heterogeneous substances in one another (and therefore for the generation of heterogeneous substances from one another) without destroying the homogeneity of each. Thus flesh is homoeomerous through and through; proceeding by division we would find that all its parts, however small, are always flesh, containing the powers of flesh in exactly the same ratio as the whole; we would never find hair-particles, bone-particles, etc., in a bit of flesh side by side with flesh-particles, as Lucretius and other commentators assumed. Any part of flesh *is* flesh; you can never reduce flesh to not-flesh, as in Empedocles, by the mere process of division and subdivision. Yet any part of flesh does contain hair, bone, and the rest, since it contains the powers of each in sufficient quantities to generate each in their characteristic ratios. Thus hair can arise out of flesh, since the ingredients of flesh are also the ingredients of hair, and will constitute hair if taken in the required proportion. Yet hair never arises "out of not-hair"; it arises out of the ingredients of hair which are in flesh (as well as in every other substance) and need only be taken out of flesh in the proportion proper to hair.

The logical elegance of this proposal need not seduce us into taking it for anything more than what it is: a purely hypothetical reconstruction. On just such a scheme (and on no other yet proposed), Anaxagoras *could* have consistently held those two ideas which, on the evidence of both the fragments and the overwhelming mass of our ancient reports, he *did* hold: that (i) a homogeneous substance like flesh has being, so that it can only be generated from its own kind, yet (ii) every such substance contains seeds of all others, so that (in principle) any substance can be generated from any other. To say that this particular scheme was developed in parts of the text which have since been lost to us would be a mere guess, and an implausible one, since Aristotle, Simplicius, and the rest were not so stupid or so dishonest as to disregard a plain statement in the text which ran counter to their own interpretations. All that we can, or need, do is to show that if this were

---

the formula for aether be, say, 9 *a*, 1 not-*a*, 9 *b*, 1 not-*b*, 9 *c*, 1 not-*c*, etc., that for air would be 1 *a*, 9 not-*a*, 1 *b*, 9 not-*b*, 1 *c*, 9 not-*c*, etc. Thus air and aether between them *exhaust* the actual distribution of powers in the matrix.

the implied structure of Anaxagoras' thought, it is not hard to account for those misconceptions which Aristotle's clumsy exegesis foisted on the tradition.

It is the leveling of the privileged status of the four Empedoclean elements that struck Aristotle as the main innovation of Anaxagoras;[81] and not without good reason, since this (as I have suggested in Section I) was the major polemical thesis of the first book of Anaxagoras' treatise. Here fire, air, water, earth were shown to be subject to mixture and transformation; and when Aristotle read (B4) that air, water, etc., arise through the successive transformation of a mixture that contained "an infinite variety of seeds," and that each of the successive products contained, like the original matrix, "seeds of all things," he concluded, quite rightly, that air, water, etc., are "composite substances" or "seed-aggregates." And he was equally right in observing that flesh, bone, hair, and all those other substances which Empedocles had degraded to purely derivative status are in this new system "elements," all equally primitive and underived, pre-existing eternally as seeds in the primordial matrix. And since Aristotle took it as axiomatic that only "simple" substances can be "elements," [82] he concluded without further ado that flesh, hair, bone, and the other homoeomerous substances must also be "simple" for Anaxagoras and must differ in this respect from fire, air, water, earth, which are "composite." [83] The slipshod logic of this conclusion should mislead no one: it did not even convince Aristotle himself, for, as we have seen, he knew perfectly well that in this system flesh was "composite" after all, his own flat assertions to the contrary notwithstanding. We have here just another instance of his constitu-

[81] See the contrast with Empedocles in *Met*. 984a8 ff., cited above, Section I, n. 34. Similarly at *Phys*. 187a22 ff. Much the same contrast at *De Caelo* 302a28 ff. and *De Gen. et Corr*. 314a25 ff., but exaggerated to the point of saying that the Empedoclean "elements," so far from being the only "elements" in Anaxagoras, were not "elements" at all, but mere "composites," while those (and *only* those) substances which Empedocles had construed as composites became *the* "simples" of Anaxagoras' physics.

[82] See, e.g., the formal definition of *stoicheion* at *Met*. 1014a26.

[83] This does not mean, of course, that Aristotle himself would concede the "simplicity" of the *homoiomerē* which he imputed to Anaxagoras. Clearly he could not, since in Aristotle's system flesh, bone, etc., are *not* simple and therefore not "elements." Anaxagoras is criticized on this ground at *De Caelo* 302b14 ff., immediately after he had been credited (or, as it now turns out, debited) with the view that "the *homoiomerē* are elements" (ibid., 302a31 and b11).

tional incapacity to respect the logic of a set of categories which cut across his own.

But once we allow for this particular blind spot and look to Aristotle not for exegesis of the system but for reports of what he read in the texts, we shall find that this residue is fully consistent with the reconstruction of the fragments that has been offered in this paper. In one important respect his account is closer to the original than that of Theophrastus[84] or Lucretius. He conserves, as they do not, a mention of the powers as determinative of the specific nature of a given seed, though he immediately reveals his confusion by adding the seeds themselves as codeterminative of that nature.[85] The statement that "each thing is most manifestly those things of which it has the most," which, in its original context, seems to have referred to a ratio of powers, is taken by Aristotle to refer to a ratio of powers and/or a ratio of seed-particles. As we trace the fortunes of this statement in Theophrastus, Lucretius, and Simplicius, we can see the powers dropping out in favor of the homoeomerous seed-particles.[86] This must have been the prevailing interpretation, else it could not have been asserted so baldly by Lucretius; those who preserved the original doctrine must have been a small, uninfluential minority.[87] And it is not hard to explain the change. How much truth there is in the Aristotelian summary that the *homoiomerē* were the "elements" of Anaxagoras we have already seen. Once this caption gained currency, Anaxagoras' doctrine could be confidently contrasted with that of his predecessors and contemporaries in the formula that his "elements" were not the air of Anaximenes or the fire of Heraclitus or the roots of Empedocles or the atoms of Leucippus, but the infinite variety of *homoiomereiai*. This was his innovation, and this would loom largest in the minds of most of his summarizers and critics, eclipsing the doctrine of the powers which he shared in traditional fashion with so many of his predecessors.

---

[84] On the assumption that the first few lines of Simpl. *Phys.* 27 are a paraphrase of the section on Anaxagoras in Theophrastus' *Phys. Opin.* Simplicius had Theophrastus' text before him, since he quotes it repeatedly in this page (see Diels, *Dox. Gr.*, pp. 478–79), and it is unlikely that he deviates here in any important respect from Theophrastus' account.

[85] See above, n. 75.

[86] Loc. cit.

[87] See above, n. 76.

20

ANAXAGORAS AND THE CONCEPT
OF MATTER BEFORE ARISTOTLE

G. B. Kerferd

The major difficulty which confronts us[1] in any attempt to reconstruct
Anaxagoras' views about the nature of the material world lies not so
much in the absence of information as in the problem of reconciling
the various doctrines attributed to him by ancient writers. In particular
it has been widely held during the present century that Anaxagoras
could not possibly have held all of the major views thus attributed to
him because their logical relationship to each other is such that the
result would be self-contradictory, and self-contradictory in a way that
would have been obvious to Anaxagoras himself and to everyone else
living at the same time as he did. Consequently it is sometimes concluded that it is impossible to recover the true nature of his thought, and
more often it has been felt that the problem is to decide which parts of
the ancient tradition must be rejected or modified in order to arrive at
a possible overall position which he could plausibly have chosen to
promulgate.[2] In what follows I wish to argue that these approaches are

From *Bulletin of the John Rylands Library*, 52 (1969), 129–43. Reprinted
with the permission of the Governors of the John Rylands Library and of the
author.

[1] This paper presents the substance of a lecture delivered in the John Rylands Library on Wednesday, March 12, 1969.

[2] The more important modern discussions are the following: A. L. Peck,
"Anaxagoras and the Parts," *CQ*, 20 (1926), 57–62, "Anaxagoras: Predica-
tion as a Problem in Physics," *CQ*, 25 (1931), 27–37, 112–20; F. M. Cornford,
"Anaxagoras' Theory of Matter," *CQ*, 24 (1930), 14–30, 83–95; Cyril Bailey,
The Greek Atomists and Epicurus (Oxford, 1928), Appendix I; Gregory
Vlastos, "The Physical Theory of Anaxagoras," *Philosophical Review*, 59
(1950), 31–57 [reprinted above, pp. 459–88]; J. E. Raven, "The Basis of
Anaxagoras' Cosmology," *CQ*, N.S. 4 (1954), 123–37, and in G. S. Kirk and
J. E. Raven, *The Presocratic Philosophers* (Cambridge, 1960), pp. 362–94;

unsatisfactory and unnecessary because they rest upon a mistake. There is no logical inconsistency between the major doctrines attributed to Anaxagoras in antiquity, and consequently as far as logic is concerned there is no reason why he should not have combined all of them in a single coherent theory. Of course it does not follow that he actually did so and what I am offering is perhaps rather prolegomena to the reconstruction of his views than an actual reconstruction. But as, if I am right, the major difficulty that has troubled modern attempts at reconstruction will have been removed, it will at least make it likely that he held the positions actually attributed to him by ancient writers.

The most significant statements about Anaxagoras' doctrines that survive come from Aristotle and from the commentary on Aristotle's *Physics* by Simplicius. Although the latter wrote in the sixth century A.D. there is every reason to believe that he had Anaxagoras' own book available to him when he was writing his commentary.[3] Both Aristotle and Simplicius appear to attribute the following basic positions to Anaxagoras:

> 1. Nothing comes into being out of nothing. (fr. 17 DK = Simplicius *In Ar. Phys.* 163.18 ff.; Ar. *Phys.* 187a26 = A52 DK) "The Greeks do not hold correct views about coming into existence and being destroyed. For nothing comes into existence nor is it destroyed, but it is compounded and dissolved from things that are. So they would be right to call coming into existence being compounded, and being destroyed being dissolved."

This, following Cornford (1930, p. 30), we may call the canon of No Becoming.

Charles Mugler, "Le Problème d'Anaxagore," *Revue des études grecques*, 69 (1956), 314–76; R. Mathewson, "Aristotle and Anaxagoras: An Examination of F. M. Cornford's Interpretation," *CQ*, N.S. 8 (1958), 67–81; Colin Strang, "The Physical Theory of Anaxagoras," *AGP*, 45 (1963), 101–18; Michael C. Stokes, "On Anaxagoras," *AGP*, 47 (1965), 1–19, 217–50. The fragments and testimonia in what follows are quoted from Diels-Kranz, *Die Fragmente der Vorsokratiker*, abbreviated to DK. Simplicius and Themistius are quoted from the Berlin edition of *Commentaria in Aristotelem Graeca*.

[3] See Simplicius *In Ar. Phys.* 461.14, which, when taken together with 153.23 ff., seems conclusive against the view of Daniel E. Gershenson and Daniel A. Greenberg, *Anaxagoras and the Birth of Physics* (New York, 1964), pp. 370–72.

2. There is no limit to the divisibility of a thing. (fr. 3 DK = Simplicius *In Ar. Phys.* 164.16, cf. fr. 6; Ar. *Phys.* 187b22 ff., 188a2–5) "Neither is there a smaller part of what is small, but there is always a smaller—for it is impossible that what is should cease to be." [4]

This may be called the principle of Infinite Divisibility.

3. In everything there is always a portion of everything else so that change can be explained by the *emerging* of what is already there, without the need for any coming into being. (fr. 11 DK = Simplicius *In* Ar. *Phys.* 164.22, cf. frr. 4, 6, 12; Ar. *Phys.* 187a36 ff.) "In everything there is a share of everything except of mind, and in some things mind also is present."

This may be called the principle of Universal Mixture.

4. Things are what they are despite the fact that they contain a share of everything else because in some sense they contain a predominance of what they are. (fr. 12. fin. DK = Simplicius *In Ar. Phys.* 157.4, cf. Ar. *Phys.* 187a36 ff.) "Each single thing is and was most plainly those things of which there are most in it." [5]

This may be called the principle of Predominance.

5. Things are made of parts which are like one another and are also like the whole. These parts are the elements out of which all things are made, and are what Aristotle calls *homoiomerē*. This doctrine does not seem to be referred to in any actual fragment from Anaxagoras' book, and it may be that he never used thé term *homoiomerē*, which is a technical Aristotelian expression. But the *doctrine* is attributed to him repeatedly and emphatically by both Aristotle and Simplicius. (Cf. Ar. *Phys.* 187a23 ff., *De Caelo* 302a28 ff., *Met.* 984a11; Simplicius *In Ar. Phys.* 460.4 ff.; Lucretius 1.830 ff.)

This may be called the principle of Homoeomereity.

It looks very much as if we have an actual example[6] of how Anaxag-

---

[4] The clever emendation of τὸ μὴ οὐκ εἶναι to τομῇ οὐκ εἶναι is in fact not necessary, cf. Diego Lanza, *Anassagora* (Florence, 1966), pp. 198–99.

[5] Or possibly "Those things of which there are most in something are and were most plainly the single individual thing."

[6] It is preserved by Aëtius A46 DK (and so was already in Theophrastus) and by Simplicius (A45 DK) and is referred to in what there is no reason to doubt is a genuine fragment (fr. 10 DK).

oras supposed these five principles might be applied, namely bread, which was regarded as actually containing within itself particles of flesh, bones, veins, sinews, hair, and all the other constituents of the body. These are extracted and assembled in the process of digestion, and it will be convenient to use the example in the discussion which follows. On this view, as all things seem to change into all things (if not immediately, at least by stages, cf. Simplicius *In Ar. Phys.* 460.11 ff.), it follows that there is a share of everything in everything else. The world would consist solely of a mixture of its perceivable ingredients, and there would be no need for any more ultimate substances or matter out of which it might be constructed. Differentiation would be explained by the principle of Predominance. Even when from bread, for example, various substances had been extracted, Universal Mixture would not be impaired because the residue of the bread might still contain a share of everything else—Universal Mixture—as long as it is remembered that one can always divide it up a little further by the principle of Infinite Divisibility.

Such a theory, however, has been widely labeled impossible, and impossible in such a way that Anaxagoras could not have held it. The classical formulation of the problem is due to Cornford and is best expressed in his own words:

> Anaxagoras' theory of matter . . . rests on two principles which seem flatly to contradict one another. One is the principle of Homoeomereity: A natural substance, such as a piece of gold, consists solely of parts which are like the whole and like one another—every one of them gold and nothing else. The other is: "There is a portion of everything in everything," understood to mean that a piece of gold (or any other substance), so far from containing nothing but gold, contains portions of every other substance in the world. Unless Anaxagoras was extremely muddleheaded, he cannot have propounded a theory which simply *consists* of this contradiction. One or the other proposition must be reinterpreted so as to bring them into harmony. Some critics attack one, some the other; some try to modify both.[7]

In our surviving sources a doctrine of Homoeomereity is first attributed to Anaxagoras by Aristotle. It is accordingly important to ask what it is that Aristotle attributes to Anaxagoras before trying to decide whether his evidence can be accepted or not. The neuter plural adjective

[7] Page 16.

homoiomerē, meaning "like-parted" or something similar, has a fairly frequent application within Aristotle's own system of thought. It is applied to various natural substances, intermediate in range between the four "simple" bodies, earth, air, fire, and water, and compound bodies and entities such as a face which are described as "anhomoeomerous." In this intermediate range come metals, wood and bark, bone, flesh, marrow, blood, and so on, all of which in turn are combined into composite bodies such as animals. These intermediate homoeomerous substances are mixtures of earth, air, fire, and water. Earth, air, fire, and water might seem to be themselves homoeomerous, and it is clear that Aristotle did so regard them when occurring in the visible world around us, as in fire or air (*Top.* 135a24; *Met.* 992a7). The term was less frequently applied to earth, air, fire, and water as elements,[8] possibly because they are further analyzable into opposite qualities, and it does seem to be the case that in general within Aristotle's own system the term "homoeomerous" has a restricted application only, and was not simply identical with "being like-parted."

Since the term *homoiomerē* has such an application within the system of Aristotle's own thought, it is natural and reasonable to suppose that when he uses the expression in connection with the theories of Anaxagoras he is not altering the sense of the word,[9] and it has been argued that he means us to understand that for Anaxagoras the term applied either to the same restricted range of substances or at least to a similarly restricted range of biological substances.[10] This is neither necessary nor likely. When a thinker applies one of his own technical terms to the system of another thinker in order to criticize his views it is usually the connotation rather than the denotation of the term that is in question. Fortunately Aristotle himself has explained clearly and precisely exactly what is the connotation in this case: *homoiomerē* are substances like bone, flesh, and marrow, and anything else of which the part bears the

---

[8] See *Met.* 1014a30–31 and *De Caelo* 302b10–20, and Gustav A. Seeck, *Über die Elemente in der Kosmologie des Aristoteles* (Munich, 1964), pp. 67–74, 82–86. The situation is complicated by the application of the term "simple" (*hapla*) to the *homoiomerē* as well as to the four elements, see *De Part. An.* 647a1, and by the apparent withdrawal of the term *hapla* from the elements in *De Gen. et Corr.* 330b21–30, on which see W. J. Verdenius and J. H. Waszink, *Aristotle on Coming-to-be and Passing Away*, 2d ed. (Leiden, 1966), pp. 54–55.

[9] See, e.g., KR p. 387.

[10] So Peck.

same name as the whole—ὧν ἑκάστου συνώνυμον τὸ μέρος ἐστίν (*De Gen. et Corr.* 314a20 = A46 DK). In other words, *homoiomerē are* things with parts like each other and like the whole. This is the meaning of the term for Aristotle, and this is its connotation. Naturally it will *denote* many different things and substances, all of which will exhibit the characteristic of having parts like one another and like the whole. Aristotle's own example is flesh contrasted with a face—divide flesh and the parts consist of flesh, divide a face and the parts do not consist of faces. But flesh is only an example of what is homoeomerous—it is one of the things denoted by the term but it does not express its connotation.

With this distinction in mind—the distinction between connotation and denotation—I would now like to turn to the passages where Aristotle attributes *homoiomerē* to Anaxagoras. In each case Aristotle attributes to Anaxagoras a doctrine of *homoiomerē* without restriction to any particular group of substances such as biological tissues. When Aristotle says that for Anaxagoras all things have *homoiomerē* as their elements he means that they are built up out of parts like one another and like the whole—so if it be diamonds these are constituted of diamond particles, gold of gold particles, bread of bread particles, and so on.

The first passage comes from the *De Caelo* (302a28–b5 = A43 DK) and may be translated as follows:

> Anaxagoras speaks about the elements in a way opposite to Empedocles. For Empedocles says that fire and earth and the rest of the list are the elements of bodies and all things are made from these. But Anaxagoras says the opposite. For he holds that the homoeomeries are the elements (I mean by homoeomeries things like flesh and bone and each and everything of that kind), and air and fire he maintains are mixtures of these and all the other seeds. For each of these two, air and fire, consists of the homoeomeries, being unseen, all massed together. So also all things come into existence from these. For he gives the same name to fire and to aether.

The main point made here is that for Empedocles all things come from the four Empedoclean elements, earth, air, fire, and water. For Anaxagoras these four are not elements but are mixtures like everything else. So he takes the opposite view from Empedocles by supposing that all things, including earth, air, fire, and water, come into being out of homoeomeries. This is clearly the point of the statements at the end—

"For each of these two, air and water, consists of the homoeomeries being unseen, all massed together. So also all things come into existence from these." Here "these" must be the things out of which air and fire are also made. But all things cannot be made merely out of the homoeomeries of air and fire as in that case they would simply be made out of air and fire[11] and there would be *no* opposition between Empedocles and Anaxagoras. No. Air and fire are made out of their own homoeomeries and other things are made out of parts homoeomerous with themselves.

There can thus be no justification for the attempt to interpret Aristotle as saying that all things are made of air and fire, still less for supposing that he means all things are made only from biological substances such as flesh and bone. These when mentioned earlier were given as examples of the application of the term *homoiomerē* and so they express its denotation, not its connotation. By the Universal Mixture principle it is true all homoeomeries do contain shares of everything else, and so of biological as well as other substances, but this is not *why* they are called homoeomeries. They are called homoeomeries in each case because they are like each other and are like the specific whole that they constitute. The passage was so understood by Simplicius (*In Ar. De Caelo* 603.26) and he must be right.[12]

The same comparison between Empedocles and Anaxagoras is found in a number of other Aristotelian passages. In *De Gen. et Corr.* 314a18 we are told that "Anaxagoras makes the homoeomeries elements, for example, bone, flesh, marrow, and the rest of which the part has the same name as the whole." Once again it is clear that Aristotle is giving illustrative examples of *homoiomerē* before proceeding, on this occasion only, to state the connotation of the term. A little further on he continues (a24 ff.): "Anaxagoras and his followers clearly speak in opposite terms to Empedocles and his followers. For Empedocles says that Fire,

---

[11] As, e.g., Guthrie (Loeb trans., 1939), *History of Greek Philosophy*, vol. 2 (Cambridge, 1965), p. 328; Lanza, pp. 67, 77; Raven in KR, p. 384; Peck, (1931), p. 115.

[12] Themistius *In Ar. De Caelo* 174.13 ff., seems to give a different interpretation from mine to the sentence "air and fire are mixtures of these and all the other seeds" by supposing that air and fire are mixtures of the homoeomeries and all the other seeds. But even this does not involve taking the homoeomeries in a restricted or specifically Aristotelian sense. His meaning is that air consists of its own homoeomeries, i.e. air-particles and also the whole infinite range of other particles.

Water, Air, and Earth are four elements and are simple, rather than flesh and bone and similar things among the *homoiomerē*, whereas Anaxagoras and his followers assert that these are simple and are elements, but that earth, fire, water, and air are composite; for each of them is, they say, a general seed-mixture (*panspermia*) of these, i.e. of *homoiomerē*." [13] Once again we must be dealing with the reduction of the Empedoclean elements to more fundamental *homoiomerē*. These *homoiomerē* are not a limited range of homoeomerous Aristotelian substances such as flesh and bone; these substances are only mentioned as examples—notice once again the added phrase "and similar things." Earth, fire, water, and air are themselves composed of the complete range of *homoiomerē*, and so contain not only *homoiomerē* of earth, fire, water, and air, i.e. of themselves, but also *homoiomerē* of everything else (the principle of Universal Mixture). It is in this sense that they are each of them a "general seed-mixture."

I turn next to a passage from the *Metaphysics* (984a11 = DK A43), where the central part can be translated and has been translated by different scholars in two rather different ways, either of which accords excellently with the overall meaning which I believe the passage must have:

> Anaxagoras of Clazomenae, who was earlier in age than Emped-
> ocles but was later than him in his works, declares that the princi-
> ples of things are infinite. For virtually all the *homoiomerē* come
> into existence and are destroyed, he says, in the same way as water
> or fire, that is by accretion and separation only, but otherwise do
> not come into existence nor are they destroyed but they continue
> for ever.

Here the majority of modern interpreters take the passage as I have translated it above. [14] This fits well with the Greek. But the occurrence

[13] For a demonstration of the correctness of this interpretation—as against Cherniss, *Aristotle's Criticism of Presocratic Philosophy* (Baltimore, 1935), p. 108 n. 444, and Forster's translation in the Loeb series—see Verdenius and Waszink, p. 1.

[14] So, e.g., Burnet, *EGP*, p. 265 n. 2; Cornford, p. 27 n. 2; Ross, Commentary, ad loc.; Guthrie, vol. 2, pp. 293 n. 2, 327. For the controversy about the meaning of the first sentence and a different view, which seems to me mistaken, see D. O'Brien, "The Relation of Anaxagoras and Empedocles," *JHS*, 88 (1968), 97–105.

of strikingly similar phraseology in the passages already discussed suggests that a different translation may be the right one,[15] namely:

> For virtually all the *homoiomerē* (such as water or fire) come into existence and are destroyed, he says, by accretion and separation only, but otherwise do not come into existence nor are they destroyed but they continue for ever.[16]

Whichever translation be preferred, it makes no difference—Aristotle is speaking not of a restricted range of things but of all things. All things are composed of *homoiomerē* by combination—the exception is probably *Nous* (Mind), which because it has to function as a cosmic prime mover is itself always in existence.

There is, however, one passage in Aristotle which at first sight may seem to suggest that Aristotle is attributing a rather different view to Anaxagoras from that so far described, namely *Physics*, 187a24–26. Once again we are concerned with the contrast between Empedocles and Anaxagoras, and Aristotle says that whereas Empedocles introduced only the standard elements, Anaxagoras introduced infinite elements (or an infinite number of elements), namely the *homoiomerē* and the Opposites. The addition of the phrase "*and* the Opposites" seems to suggest that the *homoiomerē* alone do not exhaust the list of Anaxagoras' elements, but that the Opposites functioned alongside them as some sort of additional elements out of which things are made. And if this were so it would suggest that perhaps after all the range of *homoiomerē* was more limited for Anaxagoras than I have been suggesting Aristotle supposed. Simplicius, in discussing this passage of Aristotle, tells us[17] that Alexander of Aphrodisias stated that the Opposites were included as well as all other properties *among* the homoeomeries, and that Alexander referred to an earlier passage in Aristotle's *Physics* (184b20–22), where Aristotle suggested that if there are an unlimited number of sources for things they must differ in shape and form, or even be of contrasted nature as well. In other words, somehow or other

[15] So Ross in the second edition of the Oxford translation of the *Metaphysics* (1928).

[16] It looks as if Simplicius, *In Ar. Phys.* 27.2 ff. = A41 DK, took the passage in this second way, although we cannot be certain that he is not speaking generally since he adds "gold" to the examples of water and fire.

[17] *In Ar. Phys.* 155.4 ff. Similarly Themistius *In Ar. Phys.* 2.30, 13.19 ff., 17.27.

opposite qualities must be actually *in* the *homoiomerē*. In fact Anaxagoras himself had clearly referred to such opposite qualities in fr. 4,
where we have an actual quotation preserved by Simplicius. According
to this, when all things were together before the initial separating out,
which was the first stage in the formation of our world, the mixture of
all things meant that there was no color at all. This mixture involved
the wet and the dry, the hot and the cold, the light and the dark,
abundance of earth, and an infinite number of seeds all dissimilar.

Now this passage is clearly concerned with the presence of all qualities
and all substances in the original universal mixture which preceded the
formation of the world. Among these qualities there must be included
the opposite qualities such as the hot and the cold and the wet and the
dry, because so many of the Pre-Socratics who preceded Anaxagoras
had treated these opposites as primary constituents of the universe.
Anaxagoras has got to have them in his mixture to make it clear that
they, like everything else, were already there and did not originate or
emerge from elsewhere. But he lists them as examples of "all the things"
which are present in the mixture, not as something additional to these
things. So we need not doubt that when Aristotle in the *Physics* speaks
of the homoeomeries and the Opposites he means "the homoeomeries
including the Opposites," or "the homoeomeries and in particular the
Opposites," especially as for Aristotle as well as for the earlier Pre-
Socratics the Opposites had a special position within his own system.
This is probably what Aristotle had in mind.

I have not attempted to deal with every detail and every problem
raised by the passages from Aristotle which I have been discussing.
But I hope one point is now sufficiently clear. Aristotle is attributing a
doctrine of *homoiomerē* as elements to Anaxagoras. Indeed he is saying
that for Anaxagoras these were the only elements. And he is not
suggesting any restricted meaning for *homoiomerē*, but is attributing to
Anaxagoras the general principle of Homoeomereity.

The post-Aristotelian tradition, above all the discussions in Simplicius, are even clearer. In fact the tradition that Anaxagoras held the
principle of Homoeomereity as part of his physical theory is just about
as clear as one could possibly ask for. Why then has it even been
doubted that Anaxagoras in fact held such a doctrine? The reason is
simple. It springs from the belief that Anaxagoras could not possibly
have held such a doctrine because if he had done so he would have
fallen into blatant and hopeless contradictions—contradictions so

obvious that he must have seen them and once he had seen them he must have abandoned the doctrine of *homoiomerē*.

If this were true it would be a serious objection indeed. But in fact this whole way of looking at the matter is mistaken. There is no logical contradiction involved in holding all five of the principles attributed to Anaxagoras—the principle of No Becoming, the principle of Infinite Divisibility, the principle of Universal Mixture, the principle of Predominance, and the principle of Homoeomereity. It is all a modern misunderstanding and once it is cleared away there is no difficulty in accepting the Aristotelian account of Anaxagoras' views as correct. It will be convenient to take the points one by one.

1. Cornford maintained that there was a flat contradiction between the principle of Homoeomereity and the principle of Universal Mixture. A natural substance cannot consist solely of parts like one another and like the whole and at the same time consist of portions of every other substance in the world. That Cornford was mistaken can be demonstrated by a homely example. Let us suppose that the contents of a cup of coffee consist of a combination of coffee-bean extracts and water. The contents are then a mixture. Yet the contents are homoeomerous in the sense that they can be divided into two half cups and these into still smaller portions all of which are like each other and like the whole contents. There is no logical inconsistency between the principle of Homoeomereity and the principle of mixture in this case. It is true that I have posited a mixture of two things—coffee essences and water—but there is no logical reason why the number of ingredients should not be increased indefinitely to produce Universal Mixture. It is true that *we* suppose that if the process of separation is carried far enough and we arrive at small enough parts the mixture will break down into its separate constituents. But this is not something which logic requires us to believe—we believe it on other grounds, and there is no logical objection to extending the combination of the principles of Homoeomereity and Universal Mixture down to the infinitesimal.

2. A second objection has taken the form of arguing that given Homoeomereity and Universal Mixture both would very soon break down as a result of extraction.[18] It is all very well to say that bread contains particles of blood, bone, hair, and skin, but the process of extraction will soon produce a residue that no longer exhibits Universal Mixture. Indeed very soon we will have numerous substances which as

[18] Bailey, p. 538.

the result of extraction would *not* contain a portion of everything else. So once again the analysis becomes untenable for what seem to be essentially logical reasons. But this objection also is unsound. It would have weight if substances consisted of a limited and so finite number of parts from which one could extract specific-substance parts until the supply of the specific substance was exhausted, e.g. by taking all the blood out of bread. But for Anaxagoras substances are infinitely divisible, so that they all have an infinite number of parts. Consequently no matter what quantity is extracted short of the whole there remains a substance with an infinite number of parts. Given an infinite number of parts there is no logical objection to the survival of Universal Mixture indefinitely.

3. A further objection might maintain that if you combine Universal Mixture with Homoeomereity you cannot also hold to the principle of Predominance. If gold is really a mixture of gold and everything else, you may still on the analogy of the contents of a cup of coffee be able to say that it is none the less homoeomerous. If you go on to maintain that it is gold because it contains a predominance of gold in it, and each of its parts is gold because they contain a predominance of gold, and each of their parts are gold because *they* contain a predominance of gold, then sooner or later, it is argued, something has to happen. Either you get to a stage when you reach a particle of pure gold and in that case the principle of Universal Mixture breaks down; or else you reach a stage when the proportion of gold to other parts must alter in order to make room for all the other parts needed to maintain universal mixture, and then your principle of Predominance will be threatened and eventually overthrown with the result that you lose the goldness of your gold parts and so lose homoeomereity of parts in relation to the original lump of gold. Now this objection in one or other of its forms would be true given a finite number of parts. But it is clear that Anaxagoras believed in infinite divisibility and so in an infinite number of parts. Once this is granted the objection evaporates. Moreover, as we would say, a set of numbers extending to infinity may contain within itself a number of other sets each also extending to infinity. Thus we can readily agree that the series of whole numbers can be extended to infinity and within that series the number of even numbers and the number of numbers divisible by ten will each also extend to infinity. But we must not say that one series extended to infinity is greater or lesser in relation to another such series extending to infinity and this might seem to involve the disappearance of the needed predominance of parts in, e.g.,

gold when subdivision is carried to infinity. The answer is that when two such series are compared, and the comparison is made at any finite stage in the process of subdivision, the original proportions between the two series will still obtain—it is only when subdivision is carried to infinity that the proportions cease to apply. It is not necessary to suppose that in any meaningful sense Anaxagoras anticipated the theory of sets—it is sufficient for the present argument simply to observe that there is in fact no logical objection to combining the three principles of Universal Mixture, Homoeomereity, and Predominance at any finite stage in the process of subdivision.[19]

4. A different version of the same objection, however, would maintain that the principle of Predominance itself requires the existence of pure parts and so requires us to suppose that in the process of subdivision we must come to a stage where Universal Mixture is excluded. Gold based on a predominance of gold implies of necessity constituent gold which is wholly gold and is not in turn based on a predominance of gold. The same argument would apply to the minority constituents of gold, e.g. blood, if these also are constituted only by a predominance of parts of themselves. The need to avoid an infinite regress of this kind has been the starting point for a long series of theories[20] all positing one kind or another of unmixed elemental substances or entities. Here the question we have to ask ourselves is whether a regress of this kind is logically vicious. It is true to say that we cannot give an account of substances such as gold by analyzing them into "a predominance of gold" and so on to infinity. In such a case we have failed to give either a satisfactory definition or a satisfactory account of gold because we have included the term gold in our attempts at definition and description. But it is not an objection to any position maintained by Anaxagoras, as he had no reason to attempt a definition or a description of

---

[19] Less satisfactory, I think, is the approach to this question by T. G. Sinnige, *Matter and Infinity in the Presocratic Schools and Plato* (Assen, 1968), pp. 126–37, in that he seems to suggest that one infinite quantity can be greater than another. But he points out that in B6 DK Anaxagoras was able to say "there are as many parts in number in the great and the small," so apparently recognizing with Zeno (B3 DK) that a set taken as a whole cannot be larger or smaller than itself. From this it would follow that the infinitely large or infinitely small are not unequal.

[20] Paul Tannery, *Pour l'Histoire de la science hellène*, 2d ed. (Paris, 1930), pp. 296 ff.; Burnet, p. 263; Vlastos (1950), pp. 52 ff. [reprinted here, pp. 459–88], and above all Strang (1963). Cf. KR, p. 378.

gold in this way. He is concerned with change and not with description or definition. Provided perceived gold can be recognized it can be treated as primary, not derivative, not as something to be built up from smaller particles, but as a starting point for analysis. The objection that you would never get gold without pure gold to start with would not be an objection to trouble Anaxagoras.

None the less from the point of view of logic the objection would seem to be sound. Predominance must be predominance of something over something else, of A over not-A, and A cannot itself consist of predominance and nothing more than mere predominance. It is this that has led to the widespread conclusion that Anaxagoras must have assumed the emergence of simple substances at some definite stage in the process of subdivision. But if we ask at what stage, and think of the example of coffee or of bread, or any other mixture, we realize that there is no point at which further subdivision cannot occur—there is no least part but always a lesser (fr. 3 DK)—and the results of subdivision can always be two further mixed parts just as was the case with the first subdivision of a cup of coffee into two half cupfuls. It follows that the point at which in logic pure substances must be reached in subdivision is nowhere short of the infinitesimal, in other words a point which is never reached by any finite series of subdivisions. Consequently the logical requirement for pure substances as a condition of predominance cannot be used as an argument to show that Anaxagoras must have posited such substances at a finite stage in the analysis of phenomenal objects.[21]

It follows that there are no fundamental objections based on any logical difficulties to the supposition that Anaxagoras' view of the material world rested upon all five of the principles attributed to him in the ancient tradition, the canon of No Becoming, the principles of Infinite Divisibility, Universal Mixture, Predominance, and Homoeomereity. To show that it actually did so would require a separate investigation, but the removal of supposed but unreal objections can at least clear the way. Whereas Aristotle contributed to the history of philosophy the concept of matter as a neutral quality-less substrate which can never actually exist apart, and which consequently we never perceive as such, what was probably Anaxagoras' way of looking at things had affinities rather with what would now be called phenomenalism. According to a phenomenalist approach to the world a material

[21] Nor is it correct to hold, as Stokes does, p. 15, that such a pure substance must occupy a *finite* portion of space.

object would be regarded not as a mysterious something "behind" the appearances which we experience in sensation but as simply the totality of all the actual and possible appearances occurring when the object is present to the senses. Both the earlier Pre-Socratics and Aristotle were attempting to explain the phenomenal world by referring it to entities and concepts which were not themselves visibly present in what was perceived. The most sustained and radical attempt to avoid doing this— to explain the perceived world as completely as possible without reference to anything beyond itself—would seem to be found in the phenomenal physics of Anaxagoras.

21

THE ATOMISTS' REPLY
TO THE ELEATICS

David J. Furley

Aristotle discusses the composition of material substance in his *De Generatione et Corruptione*. In chapter 8 of the first book, he studies the views of earlier philosophers on the subject of the interaction of such substances (τὸ ποιεῖν καὶ πάσχειν). He mentions first those who believed that all interaction takes place through "pores," and then compares the pore theory with that of Leucippus and Democritus:

> Some, then, like Empedocles, held this theory with regard to *some* substances—not only those which interact with each other, but also they say that substances mix with each other if and only if their pores are commensurate. Leucippus and Democritus, on the other hand, held a theory which was supremely methodical and which applied to all substances; they began at the starting point given by nature.[1]
>
> For some of the ancients had thought that what *is* must necessarily be one and motionless, since what is void is nonexistent, and there could be no motion without a separately existing void, and again there could be no plurality of existents without something to

[1] An alternative reading ᾗπερ ἔστιν, suggested by H. H. Joachim, *Aristotle: On Coming-to-be and Passing-away* (Oxford, 1922), ad loc., would mean beginning at the natural starting point, viz. that it-*is*." This would be a reference to the Eleatic doctrine reported in the next sentence. This is ingenious, but seems to me implausible. What Aristotle means by "the starting point given by nature" is not, I think, Eleatic monism, but the observed facts of change, motion, and plurality (cf. 325a25, below).

separate them. If someone thinks the universe is not continuous but consists of divided pieces in contact with each other, this is no different, they held, from saying that it is many, not one, and is void. For if it is divisible everywhere, there is no unit, and therefore no many, and the whole is void. If on the other hand it is divisible in one place and not another, this seems like a piece of fiction. For how far is it divisible, and why is one part of the whole like this— full—and another part divided? (*De Gen. et Corr.* I.8.324b32– 325a12)

"Some of the ancients" are clearly of the Eleatic school. The argument that the non-existence of void entails the impossibility of motion belongs to Melissus, certainly, and probably to Parmenides.[2] It was Parmenides who said there could be no plurality without something to separate the units (at least, this seems to be one of a number of possible paraphrases of B8.25). The argument against a universe "divisible everywhere" but containing no void is, I think, Zeno's "Argument A," which I have discussed in another context.[a] At least the argument that if the universe is divisible everywhere there is no unit and therefore no "many" appears to be Zeno's; the further conclusion put into Eleatic mouths by Aristotle, that such a universe must therefore be void, is not expressed anywhere else, so far as I know.

I have quoted rather more of Aristotle's summary of the Eleatic position than is usually done by those who wish to explain the Atomists. The reason is that abbreviated quotation has suggested that the Atomists answered only the first two of these Eleatic arguments; and I want to show that in all probability they also answered the third, about divisibility. However, it is possible to omit the rest of Aristotle's remarks on the Eleatics without distortion, and I continue with his report of the Atomists' answer:

But Leucippus thought he had arguments which would assert what is consistent with sense perception and not do away with coming-into-being and perishing and motion and the plurality of existents. He agrees with sensible appearances to this extent, but he concedes to those who maintain the One that there would be no motion without void, and says that what is void is not-being, and that no part of what *is* is not-being—for what *is* in the strict sense is

[2] See G. S. Kirk and M. C. Stokes, "Parmenides' Refutation of Motion," *Phronesis*, 5 (1960), 1–4. Melissus B7, §7.

[a] [See above, pp. 353–67.—Ed.]

wholly and fully being. But such being, he says, is not one; there is an infinite number of them, and they are invisible because of the smallness of their mass. They move in the void (for there *is* void), and when they come together they cause coming-to-be, and when they separate they cause perishing. (*De Gen. et Corr.* I.8.325a23–32)

The connection between the Eleatics and the Atomists, which John Burnet called "the most important point in the history of early Greek philosophy," [3] is made in these famous words of Aristotle's, and confirmed by other writers, some of whom indeed say that Leucippus was a pupil of Zeno. It is unlikely that Leucippus ever sat at the feet of Zeno or any other Eleatic, but there is no reason to doubt that both he and Democritus consciously sought to reply to the Eleatics. It is generally agreed that Aristotle's account of their relation to the Eleatics on the subject of void, motion, and plurality is correct. But Aristotle mentions an argument about divisibility when he summarizes the Eleatic position. In the present passage he does not say anything at all about the Atomists' answer, but the implication that they did have an answer is strong enough.

The implication is confirmed by something Aristotle says in the *Physics*:

Some gave in to both of these [scil. Eleatic] arguments—to the argument that all is one if "what is" means one, by saying that not-being exists, and to the argument from Dichotomy, by positing atomic magnitudes. (I.3.187a1–3)

The ancient commentators, Alexander and Porphyry, who are quoted by Simplicius in his note on this passage, seem to have gone off on the wrong track here. They apparently took Aristotle's "some" to refer to Plato and Xenocrates: it was Plato who said that not-being exists, and Xenocrates who posited atomic magnitudes. They can quote in support of this attribution *Metaphysics* 1089a2–6, where the Platonic theory of not-being is related to Parmenides. But it is much more likely that Aristotle was thinking of Leucippus and Democritus. The assertion that not-being (i.e. void) exists, and the relation of this assertion to the Eleatic One Being are mentioned in the passage of the *De Generatione et Corruptione* which we have just examined, and the assertion is there attributed to Leucippus by name. Admittedly in that passage the argument for One Being is expressed differently, but I think that is of

[3] *EGP*, p. 334.

no importance: "all is one if 'what is' means one," in the *Physics*, looks to me like a summary of a large part of the Eleatic philosophy, rather than one particular argument. If, then, the Atomists are said to have "given in" to the first argument, it is almost certainly they who are mentioned in connection with the second: the sentence, after all, has only one subject, and it is no surprise to hear that they "posited atomic magnitudes." [4]

But what is "the argument from Dichotomy"? It has not been mentioned earlier in the *Physics*; Aristotle evidently felt that the name itself was enough to identify it. I suppose the obvious candidate is the first of Zeno's four arguments about motion, listed by Aristotle in *Physics* VI.9.[b] Aristotle refers to this argument as "the Dichotomy" ($\tau\hat{\eta}$ $\delta\iota\chi o\tau o\mu\acute{\iota}\dot{a}$, 239b22; $\tau\hat{\omega}$ $\delta\iota\chi o\tau o\mu\epsilon\hat{\iota}\nu$, b19). It is not clear, however, whether he is using the expression as a technical name or merely as a convenient term for reference; his use of the word is certainly not confined to reports of Zeno. Alexander, quoted by Simplicius, did not think Aristotle meant this argument, but another—still Zeno's—which he gives in the following form: If what *is* has magnitude and is divided, what *is* would be many and not one; hence the one would be none of the things that *are*. This is a similar move to the one mentioned by Aristotle in *De Generatione et Corruptione* 325a8 (p. 505 above), which—as I have already pointed out—is derived from Zeno's Argument A.

In fact it does not matter much which of the two arguments Aristotle is supposed to have had in mind. Both arguments involve dichotomy, and both are invalidated if there are indivisible magnitudes. Argument A starts by supposing that what exists is divisible into ultimate units, and then claims that if such a division is completed, the resultant units have no magnitude and therefore cannot be parts of the original "what exists"; the argument called "Dichotomy" shows that if such a division can never be completed but goes on for ever, the whole can never be traversed. Both arguments are blocked if what exists is divisible into indivisible magnitudes.[5]

---

[4] I have the support of Sir David Ross on this point: see his edition of *Physics* (Oxford, 1936), p. 480.

[b] [See above, pp. 353–67.—Ed.]

[5] It is sometimes said that Zeno's arguments *proved* infinite divisibility. If so, then they could not be blocked merely by asserting finite divisibility; it would have been necessary to refute his proof first. But since his whole aim was to prove that "what exists" is indivisible, he can hardly have claimed to prove that it is infinitely divisible.

Further details of the Atomists' answer to the Eleatics can be recovered from another passage of Aristotle's *De Generatione et Corruptione*, where he gives at length what he describes as "the argument
which appears to prove that there are indivisible magnitudes." There
can be no doubt that Aristotle has Democritus and Leucippus in mind
when he reproduces this argument: his conclusion contains a phrase
which has been previously used in a summary of their theory,[6] and he
begins it by praising Democritus for "having been persuaded by proper,
physical arguments," as opposed to the abstract arguments used by the
Platonists to establish their "indivisible planes." With due caution
Harold Cherniss remarks:[7] "Aristotle outlines what he feels to be the
reasoning which makes men think atomic bodies necessary; he does not
say that it was the reasoning which led the Atomists to their theory, and
it is not mentioned in what purports to be the historical account of the
origin of Atomism." But in that historical account, which is of course
the passage quoted at the beginning of this chapter, none of the Atomists' arguments are described at all; it is just mentioned that Leucippus
thought he had some. So the absence of this particular argument from
that account does not signify that the argument is a construction of
Aristotle's and not a report of what the Atomists themselves wrote.
Philoponus certainly took it to be Democritus' own argument,[8] and
most commentators have followed him. Mau is one who has not.[9] He
finds the whole argument to be permeated with Aristotelian concepts,
and carefully tailored by Aristotle to suit the refutation which is to
follow. He contrasts the hesitant optative with which Aristotle speaks
here of Democritus with the confident indicative he uses elsewhere.[10]
All this is true: Aristotle has certainly expressed the argument in his
own terms. But I still think it probable that the logic of the argument
belongs to Democritus. I cannot see why else Aristotle should begin as
he does:

[6] 316b33; cf. 315b6.

[7] Harold Cherniss, *Aristotle's Criticism of Presocratic Philosophy* (Baltimore, 1935), p. 113.

[8] *In De Generatione et Corruptione*, ad loc.

[9] Jürgen Mau, *Zum Problem des Infinitesimalen bei den antiken Atomisten*
(Berlin, 1954), pp. 25–26.

[10] The potential optative is probably to be explained by connecting it with
the adjectives. Aristotle is qualifying his assertion that Democritus' arguments
were "proper, physical ones."

One group says that (otherwise) the Triangle-itself will be many, but Democritus would appear to have been persuaded by proper, physical arguments. What we mean will become clear as we proceed. (*De Gen. et Corr.* I.2.316a11–14)

The argument is unmistakably reminiscent of Zeno's argument against plurality (Argument A), as Luria observed.[11] Suppose that a body is stated to be everywhere divisible, and (I take this to be an Aristotelian refinement) that there is no impossibility involved in its being *actually* divided—

Suppose then that it *is* divided; now, what will be left? Magnitude? No, that cannot be, since there will then be something not divided, whereas it was everywhere divisible. But if there is to be no body or magnitude [left] and yet [this] division is to take place, then either the whole will be made of points and then the [parts] of which it is composed will have no size, or [that which is left will be] nothing at all. [In the latter case] it would come into being or be composed out of nothing and the whole would be nothing but an [illusory] appearance. Similarly if it is made out of points, it will not be a quantity. For when they were in contact and there was one magnitude and they were together, they did not increase the magnitude of the whole; for when it was divided into two or more, the whole was no larger or smaller than formerly. So if they are all put together, they will not make a magnitude. (*De Gen. et Corr.* I.2.316a24–34)

I have inserted some words in the translation to make the line of reasoning clearer.

Aristotle states two alternatives (a third possibility is dealt with later): either the products of this division must be points, or they must be nothing at all. In either case, such units cannot be the components of a magnitude. Zeno argued from "something having no size does not contribute to the size of the whole" to "something having no size is nothing." Aristotle's text distinguishes two cases: certainly a collection of "nothings" cannot be anything but an illusion; but also a collection of points (i.e. *things*—not "nothings"—having no magnitude) cannot be a magnitude. There is a close similarity between Zeno's argument and the second of these two given by Aristotle. The latter argues that if a given line is divided in two the sum of its two parts remains the same

[11] S. Luria, "Die Infinitesimallehre der antiken Atomisten," *Quellen und Studien zur Geschichte der Mathematik*, B 2 (1933), 130 ff.

as the length of the original whole; yet there are now two points, at the inner end of each of the two half-lines, where formerly there was only one; hence the extra point made no difference to the length—and so any number of points will make no difference to length. The distinction between "nothings" and points may be Aristotle's work; but because of its likeness to Zeno's argument we may confidently attribute to Democritus at least an argument that units having no magnitude cannot add up to a magnitude, and hence that no magnitude can be reduced to such units by division.

The argument reported by Aristotle then considers a third possibility: that the results of the division may be of no size, but the magnitude somehow disappears in the process of division, like sawdust. But if the sawdust is corporeal, then the problem of *its* divisibility arises, and we are faced with exactly the same dilemma as before. If it is not a body, but some kind of form or quality, then we are faced with the absurdity of a magnitude's being composed of elements without magnitude. After some further variations, which seem likely to be Aristotle's own,[12] the conclusion is stated: "there must be indivisible bodies and magnitudes."

So far I have concentrated on establishing the conclusion that in Aristotle's view the theory of indivisible magnitudes was advanced by Leucippus and Democritus as an answer to certain Eleatic arguments, including Zeno's Argument A. The next step is to consider what kind of a theory would be needed to answer these arguments. Having done this we may look for further evidence that will either refute or confirm the hypothesis that they held a theory of this kind.

The first part of the program should present no difficulty. Nobody, so far as I know, has argued that the Eleatics were trying to defend a One Being that was only physically unsplittable. Their arguments against the divisibility of what exists were aimed at *all* kinds of divisibility. Parmenides B4 is about theoretical divisibility.[c] Melissus believed in a Being that was incorporeal and indivisible—and this must be theoretical indivisibility. Zeno's arguments have usually been taken as

----

[12] Note the use of δυνάμει in 316b12.

[c] [See Furley, *Two Studies*, ch. 4. In the introduction, p. 4, Furley distinguishes between "physical division" and "theoretical division" as follows: "*physical division* . . . is the division of something in such a way that formerly contiguous parts are separated by a spatial interval. This is opposed to *theoretical division:* an object is theoretically divisible if parts can be distinguished within it by the mind, even if the parts can never be separated from each other by a spatial interval."—Ed.]

bearing on mathematical problems of divisibility; it may not indeed be the case that his attack was specifically directed against mathematical concepts, but it would be too much of a *volte-face* to say that the theoretical, as opposed to practical, divisibility of what exists was excluded from his target.

If this is so, a physically unsplittable atom which is still theoretically divisible will not meet the Eleatic arguments at all. Most English scholars have taken it almost for granted that Leucippus and Democritus were physical atomists only, perhaps following Sir Thomas Heath's question-begging dictum[13] that Democritus was "too good a mathematician" to believe in indivisible geometrical magnitudes. Thus Burnet remarked:[14] "We must observe that the atom is not mathematically indivisible, for it has magnitude." G. S. Kirk repeats this:[15] "They [scil. the atoms] were indivisible in fact, though not (since they had extension in space) in thought." But this will not do. A theoretically divisible atom would certainly not answer the argument from Dichotomy—whichever of Zeno's arguments Aristotle meant when he used the phrase. Argument A would show that an atom theoretically divisible to infinity must be infinite in magnitude; and the first of Zeno's "arguments about motion" would show that such an atom could never be traversed—that is, if one starts imagining it, one can never imagine the whole of it.

There is an *a priori* likelihood, then, that Leucippus and Democritus were more than physical atomists. We must now see whether this hypothesis will stand up to such tests as we can devise for it.

First, we can ask whether the Atomists' argument, as reported by Aristotle, tends to prove the existence of physically unsplittable bodies, or of theoretically indivisible ones; and this can perhaps be answered by studying Aristotle's criticism of the argument.

Having gone through the steps of the argument and stated its conclusion, "it follows that there are indivisible bodies and magnitudes," [16] Aristotle continues:

[13] T. L. Heath, *A History of Greek Mathematics* (Oxford, 1921), vol. 1, p. 181.

[14] *EGP*, p. 336.

[15] KR, p. 408.

[16] 316b15 ἀνάγκη εἶναι σώματα ἀδιαίρετα καὶ μεγέθη. It hardly needs pointing out that in Aristotle's usage σώματα καὶ μεγέθη does not necessarily mean two sets of objects, (a) physical solids, *and* (b) mathematical magnitudes.

However, those who assert this are involved in just as many impossibilities; these have been examined elsewhere. (*De Gen. et
Corr.* I.2.316b16–18)

The reference, as Philoponus saw, is to *De Caelo* III and *Physics* VI
(Philoponus also mentions *De Lineis Insecabilibus*, "which some
attribute to Theophrastus").

In *De Caelo* III.4, Aristotle lists a number of objections to the theory
of Leucippus and Democritus, including the following:

Moreover, they must be in conflict with mathematics when they
say there are indivisible bodies, and rule out many common opinions and sensible phenomena, which have already been discussed
in the works on Time and Motion. (*De Caelo* III.4.303a20–24)

This passage also refers to the *Physics*, then, for Aristotle habitually
calls the later books of the *Physics* "the books on Motion." But before
turning to what he says there, we must comment on this sentence of the
De Caelo. When Aristotle says that the Democritean theory of indivisible magnitudes is in conflict with mathematics, can he mean anything
other than theoretically indivisible magnitudes? How could physical
atoms be in conflict with mathematics? We can see more clearly what
Aristotle had in mind from something he says earlier in the same work,
to illustrate the point that a small divergence from truth early in an
argument is enormously multiplied as one proceeds:

For example, suppose one were to say that there is a smallest magnitude: by introducing this "smallest" one upsets the greatest
features of mathematics. (*De Caelo* I.5.271b9–11)

The conflict consists in the fact that the hypothesis of indivisible magnitudes denies one of the principles of mathematics, and so destroys the
structure built on these principles. Simplicius, commenting on these
two passages, fills in the detail: the Atomists' assumption means the
denial of the principle that any given line may be divided into two. And
this interpretation is confirmed by a scholium on Euclid Book 10:

That there is no smallest magnitude, as the Democriteans say, is
proved also by this theorem, that it is possible to obtain a magnitude smaller than any given magnitude. (DK 68A48a)

One more passage in the *De Caelo* is worth some attention. In III.7,
Aristotle groups together some criticisms of Empedocles, Democritus,
and the Platonists on the subject of the transformation of the simple

bodies (earth, air, fire, and water) into each other. At the relevant point, where he speaks of "indivisible bodies," it is chiefly Plato that he has in mind, since he argues against the theory that the simple bodies are reducible to planes; but then he generalizes his comment so as to combat any theory which distinguishes its simple bodies by shape:

> They are compelled to deny that every body is divisible, and so to be in conflict with the most exact sciences. For the mathematical sciences take even the intelligible to be divisible, whereas these philosophers do not even allow that every sensible body is divisible, in their anxiety to save their theory. For all those who allot a shape to each of the elements and distinguish their natures by shapes are compelled to say that they are indivisible, since when a pyramid or a sphere is divided in some way the remainder is not a sphere or pyramid. So either the part of fire will not be fire, and there will be something prior to the element (since everything is either an element or a product of elements), or not every body is divisible. (*De Caelo* III.7.306a26–b2)

There is one point here which should alert us at once to a difference between Aristotle's outlook and ours. He alters what seems to us the natural emphasis. His opponents, he says, do not *even* allow every sensible body to be divisible—as if the indivisibility of a sensible body were *more incredible* than that of a conceptual magnitude. We may contrast this Aristotelian viewpoint with that of Sir Thomas Heath, for example, who found it incredible that Democritus should believe in an indivisible mathematical magnitude, but saw no difficulty in the concept of a physical atom. Aristotle believed that every physical body was potentially divisible everywhere in exactly the same way as every mathematical body: matter, or the substratum of physical bodies, was continuous, and so all the laws of the mathematical continuum could be applied to it. It will be important to bear this in mind when we come back to the criticism of the Atomists' argument in *De Generatione et Corruptione* I.2.[17]

[17] Professor Vlastos kindly drew my attention to this passage of *De Caelo* III in a letter. He observed that the phrase μάχεσθαι ταῖς ἀκριβεστάταις ἐπιστήμαις is used here, and explained by Simplicius, to mean something like "holding a physical doctrine which is out of step with a mathematical doctrine," not "holding a mathematical doctrine which is inconsistent with mathematical principles."

Up to a point I can agree with this. But I do not think it carries any damag-

It is the *Physics* to which Aristotle refers, as we have seen, for a full discussion of the problem of "indivisible magnitudes." He referred to this book in connection with Leucippus and Democritus: the question before us is whether the discussion in the *Physics* concerns physically unsplittable atoms or theoretically indivisible magnitudes. Fortunately there is no need to take long about answering it. It is abundantly clear that Aristotle discusses theoretically indivisible magnitudes. There cannot be anything continuous, he says,[18] made of indivisibles, e.g. a line made of points. The reason is that things are continuous if and only if "their extremities are one," and an indivisible has no extremities. It is clear at once that this has nothing to do with physical atoms; for unless the object is theoretically indivisible there is no reason why it should not have extremities.

But this argument is the basis of the whole discussion in *Physics* VI. Aristotle begins chapter 2 with a summary, "since every magnitude is divisible into magnitudes (for we have shown that nothing continuous can be made of indivisibles, and all magnitude is continuous) . . . ," and proceeds to make some points about motion and change. He argues, for instance, that a "partless body" (i.e. an indivisible body) cannot move or change at all.[19] This is the kind of objection that is meant in the *De Caelo* 303a20 (p. 512 above), where Aristotle says that those who

---

ing implications for my argument about *De Caelo* 303a20 (above, p. 512). Aristotle seems to have believed that the infinite divisibility of the geometrical continuum entails the infinite divisibility of matter. Hence he was able to regard any denial of the infinite divisibility of matter as being contrary to mathematical principles (not merely "out of step with" them).

It must be admitted that this consideration weakens the force of Aristotle's evidence about Democritus. For it might be held that it was only Aristotle's own conviction that mathematical and physical divisibility must march in step which enabled him to accuse Democritus of being in conflict with mathematics. However, I should argue against this (1) that in any case the indivisible magnitudes required to meet the Eleatic arguments are still indivisible in the stronger sense; (2) that Aristotle must have been guilty of more than ordinary disingenuousness or ignorance if he had failed to mention or notice a distinction in Democritus' work between physical and conceptual divisibility; and (3) that there is no good reason for thinking that Democritus was clearer on the subject of this distinction than Aristotle was.

[18] 231a24.

[19] *Physics* VI.10.240b8 ff.

believe in indivisible bodies "have to rule out many sensible phenomena."

To sum up the argument of the last few pages, then: Aristotle begins his criticism of the "indivisible magnitudes" of Democritus, in *De Generatione et Corruptione*, by saying that the resultant impossibilities have been examined elsewhere. We have seen reason to believe that the reference must be to the *De Caelo* and *Physics*. In these two works, the "indivisible magnitudes" discussed are theoretically indivisible magnitudes, not merely physical atoms, and the alleged impossibilities result from this. It is perhaps worth saying at this point that the traditional Democritus, "too good a mathematician to believe in indivisible magnitudes," should have agreed with every word of Aristotle's criticisms of him.

I return now to *De Generatione et Corruptione* I.2:

We must try to solve these problems; so we must restate the case from the beginning.

That every sensible body should be divisible at any point and be indivisible is nothing out of the way—it will be the former in potentiality, the latter in actuality. But that it should be divisible everywhere *simultaneously* in potentiality would seem to be impossible. For if it were possible, it would happen; . . . so there will be nothing left, and the body will have been destroyed into what is not body, and would come into being either out of points or out of nothing at all. And how is this possible? (*De Gen. et Corr.* I.2.316b18–27)

This is a tricky passage. The difficulty is to know which clauses belong to Aristotle's stage directions, so to speak, and which to his formulation of the Atomists' argument.[20] The opening sentence of the second

[20] W. J. Verdenius and J. H. Waszink, *Aristotle: Coming-to-be and Passing-away: Some Comments*, Philosophia Antiqua, I (Leiden, 1946), ad loc., argue that the passage has been interpolated by "a zealous but not very intelligent Aristotelian." They would bracket: b20 καὶ ἀδιαίρετον; b21 τὸ μὲν γὰρ δυνάμει, τὸ δ' ἐντελεχείᾳ ὑπάρξει; b22 δυνάμει; and b23–5 οὐχ ὥστε . . . ὁτιοῦν σημεῖον. They may be right; I admit that I can make nothing of the last of these, even on Joachim's hypothesis that it was originally a marginal note. I have omitted it from my translation, but I have thought it best to try to make sense of the rest.

paragraph, I think, is introductory. Aristotle wishes to point out that the problem cannot be solved simply by introducing potentiality and actuality; so he begins by showing how far these concepts can go. "Divisible everywhere" and "indivisible" need not be incompatible predicates, if the former belongs potentially, the latter actually. So far as that goes, Democritus might agree with Aristotle. The trouble is that "divisible everywhere" seems an impossible predicate even in a potential sense—that is the first proposition in Aristotle's formulation of the Atomist argument. "For if it were possible, it would happen," and then the result would be exactly what Aristotle described in his first statement of the argument (text quoted above, p. 509).

> But it is clear that it is divided into separate magnitudes, and always into smaller ones, and into pieces which are distinct and separated. But when one divides step by step, neither would the process of breaking the thing up be infinite, nor could it be divided simultaneously at every point (since that is impossible); it would only go so far and no further. Hence there must be indivisible magnitudes in it, which cannot be seen—especially if generation and destruction take place through association and dissociation respectively.
>
> This then is the argument which seems to prove the existence of indivisible magnitudes. (*De Gen. et Corr.* I.2.316b28–317a1)

When an extended body is actually divided, it is divided into smaller parts which are in actual existence, separate from each other. But actual division like this cannot be continued infinitely, nor can the thing be actually divided simultaneously at every point in it. So far as I can see, Aristotle would accept the argument up to this point—even the statement that the process of division cannot be continued infinitely. For this statement seems to mean only that "division to infinity" cannot take place in actuality. Aristotle would agree to this, but he goes on to point out that the impossibility of infinite division *in this sense* does not entail indivisible magnitudes.

Having thus restated the argument, Aristotle proceeds with the refutation:

> Let us now explain that this argument contains a fallacy, and where the fallacy is. Since point is not next to point, there is a sense in which the predicate "divisible everywhere" belongs to magnitudes and a sense in which it does not. When this is asserted [scil. that

magnitudes are divisible everywhere], it seems that there is a point anywhere and everywhere, so that the magnitude must have been divided up into nothing—since there is a point everywhere, and so it will be made either of points or of contacts. Yet there is a sense in which there is a point everywhere, in that there is one point anywhere, and all of them are there if you take them one by one. But there is not more than one (since they are not consecutive to each other), and so they are not everywhere. (*De Gen. et Corr.* I.2.317a1–9)

The refutation of the Atomists' argument depends on Aristotle's analysis of the concepts of "point," "next to," "contact," etc., which he offers in full in *Physics* V.3. It is impossible to divide a magnitude "at every point," because points are not next to each other; between *any* two points there is a magnitude. But this does not entail that there are indivisible magnitudes; every magnitude has points on it, at which it may be divided.

It must be conceded that the whole of this discussion is about sensible magnitudes. Does that entail that it is about physical atoms? I. Hammer-Jensen, who was the first modern scholar, I think, to show that this was Aristotle's report of a genuine argument of the Atomists, thought it referred only to physical divisibility. "By way of introduction Aristotle strongly emphasizes that in the present context, which is one regarding the division of bodies (not of mathematical magnitudes), the concern is not with abstract possibility, but rather with the sort of possibility which at any moment can emerge as empirical actuality. It is for this reason that Aristotle reminds us that 'infinite' is more than ten thousand times ten thousand." [21]

Is this true? Certainly Aristotle does mention "ten thousand times ten thousand divisions," but his purpose is not quite what Hammer-Jensen takes it to be:

If [a body or magnitude] is divisible everywhere, and this is possible, then it might be simultaneously divided, even if the acts of dividing were not simultaneous; and if this happened, nothing impossible would result. So in the same way, if [a body] is divisible everywhere, whether by [progressive] bisection or in any other way, then nothing impossible will have taken place if it *is* divided. For even if it is divided into ten thousand times ten thousand divi-

[21] I. Hammer-Jensen, "Demokrit und Platon," *AGP*, 23 (1910), 104.

sions, this is nothing impossible, even though I suppose no one would actually do it. (*De Gen. et Corr.* I.2.316a17–23)

Aristotle's purpose here is to point out that the "impossibility" which is an essential element in the Atomists' argument is not merely a question of human limitations. If a body is everywhere divisible, then nothing impossible will have happened if it is everywhere divided; of course no one is likely to try, but nothing *logically* impossible will have happened.

Other details of Aristotle's language in this passage, like this one, leave it doubtful whether he is considering the physical or theoretical division of physical bodies. The only way in which we can make any progress is by taking the whole passage—the statement and restatement of the argument, and Aristotle's solution of the difficulty—and try to read it as applying only to atomism in the limited sense, physical but not theoretical. This is the traditional Democritean atomism. The Democritus of tradition understands that his physical atoms are theoretically divisible to infinity. He applies the Eleatic "argument from dichotomy" to physical divisibility, and cannot answer it except by positing indivisible magnitudes. But either he does not apply it at all to theoretical divisibility (although this was its original application), or else he applies it and *solves the problem differently*—solves it, in fact, in much the same way as Aristotle does. Aristotle, on this hypothesis, takes Democritus' argument for physical atomism, applies to it his own theory of continuity, and thus shows that the argument is not cogent; and he does so without ever mentioning that Democritus too did not think the argument cogent at the theoretical level. He does so, in fact, without apparently being conscious that any distinction is necessary or possible.

There are too many paradoxes here. It seems much simpler to believe that neither Democritus nor Aristotle made any distinction between physical and theoretical divisibility. Just as Aristotle thought his own theory of continuity held good at the physical level as well as the theoretical level, so Democritus thought of his indivisible magnitudes as being theoretically as well as physically indivisible.[22]

---

[22] I am tempted to quote an additional piece of Aristotelian evidence, *De Anima* I.4.409a10–16. Here Aristotle appears to draw a parallel between Xenocrates' theory that soul is a number, and therefore (according to Aristotle) made of monads, and Democritus' theory that soul is composed of "little corpuscles." This parallel might well suggest that Aristotle thought of

So much for the evidence of Aristotle. I turn now to other sources. The hypothesis that Democritus believed in theoretically indivisible magnitudes is confirmed by Simplicius:

> Leucippus and Democritus think that the cause of the indivisibility of the primary bodies is not merely their imperviousness (*apatheia*) but also their smallness and partlessness; Epicurus, later, does not think they are partless, but says they are atomic because of their imperviousness. (Simplicius *Physics* 925.13 ff. = DK 67A13)

In another context, Simplicius again refers to "the school of Leucippus and Democritus, who say that the atoms, atomic because of their smallness and hardness, are elements." [23]

A pause must be made here to refute a heresy. Cyril Bailey writes:[24] "It is certain that the Leucippean argument from size is nowhere attributed to Democritus and indeed cannot have been used by him." This is an unaccountable mistake, since this argument plainly *is* attributed to Democritus, at least twice, in these passages of Simplicius; and unfortunately it is an influential one.[25] Bailey built quite an edifice of theory on this alleged difference between Leucippus and Democritus.

Three pieces of evidence *for* the difference may be considered. First, Bailey quotes a statement of Galen[26] which distinguishes the Epicureans, who believed the atoms to be unbreakable because of their hardness, from "the school of Leucippus," who believed them to be unbreakable because of their smallness. But in the context of course Galen would include Democritus in "the school of Leucippus."

Secondly, Simplicius himself contradicts the statements I have quoted above. Commenting on Aristotle's use of the word "indivisible," he distinguishes three senses of "undivided." [27] There is (a) that which is

---

Democritean soul atoms as being partless, like monads. But unfortunately I do not fully understand Aristotle's argument here: "a very difficult passage," as Ross observes in his commentary.

Somewhat similar is *Metaphysics* XIII.8.1084b26. Here again Aristotle seems to compare the Atomists (ἕτεροί τινες, but the identification is fairly sure), who composed things out of "the minimum" (τὸ ἐλάχιστον), with the Pythagoreans who used "the one" or "the monad" in this way. See Cherniss, p. 130.

[23] Simplicius *De Caelo* 609.17.
[24] Cyril Bailey, *The Greek Atomists and Epicurus* (Oxford, 1928), p. 126.
[25] See Mau, pp. 19–20; KR, p. 408 n. 1.
[26] *De Elementis secundum Hippocratem* I.2 = DK 68A49.
[27] Simplicius *Physics* 82.1.

divisible but not yet divided, like any continuous quantity; (b) the absolutely indivisible, because it has no parts, like a point or monad; (c) that which has parts and magnitude, but is impervious through hardness and compactness, *like Democritus' atoms*. But it is clear, I think, that Simplicius is assuming here that magnitude entails "having parts," as it did to all good Aristotelians. His hasty reference here should not be preferred to what he says when he explicitly distinguishes two different positions held by the Atomists.

Thirdly, there is the undeniable fact that Democritus certainly said his atoms had magnitude, and there are texts which suggest that some atoms had quite considerable magnitude. For there is a report, of rather doubtful authority, that distinguishes between Epicurus, who held that "all the atoms are very small and therefore imperceptible," and Democritus, who said that some atoms are very large.[28] Could Democritus have suggested that atoms are indivisible because of their smallness, and yet that some of them are "very large"? Could he in fact have held (as he undoubtedly did) that atoms differed from each other in size, and claimed also that they had no distinguishable parts?

From this point on we may forget Bailey's erroneous distinction between Leucippus and Democritus, and treat the matter more generally. What could be the reasoning behind the assertion that smallness is a cause of indivisibility? Simplicius ties smallness to partlessness, and if the Atomists were answering the Eleatics, this must be correct. The most likely line of argument, then, is the one used by Epicurus—that is, from the analogy with perception.[d] There is a minimum perceptible quantity within which no parts can be distinguished by a perceiver. The mind's eye, as it were, functions as a microscope: it can distinguish much smaller parts than the senses can, but there is still a lower limit beyond which it cannot make any distinctions. I can find no proof that this was the reasoning of Leucippus and Democritus, but I think it is suggested by fragment 11 of Democritus. There he distinguishes between "genuine knowledge" and "darkling knowledge." The fragment breaks off in the middle, but it is virtually certain that it says that the former, which is a product of the mind, takes over when the latter, which is sense perception, "can no longer see into smaller detail nor hear nor taste," etc.[29] Since Democritus seems to have drawn a general analogy between sense perception and thought, and since the concept

[28] Dionysius, reported by Eusebius, DK 68A43.
[d] [See *Lett. to Hdt.* §§56.5–59, and cf. Furley, *Two Studies*, ch. I.—Ed.]
[29] DK 68B11.

of something too small to be seen was certainly familiar to him, it seems quite likely that he might have used the idea of something so small that no parts can be distinguished even by the mind.

But what are we to say about the "very large" atoms attributed to Democritus? The evidence for the attribution is not very good, and it may be that it can be explained away. Epicurus[30] disputed Democritus' assertion that the shapes of atoms are infinitely varied, on the ground that this would mean that some of them were infinitely large. It is very likely that later writers, contrasting Epicurus with Democritus, would carelessly write as though Democritus himself had spoken of infinitely large atoms. It seems to me that this would explain the testimony of Dionysius, quoted above, and also the single, unrelated mention of "world-sized" atoms by Aëtius.[31] Diogenes Laertius' statement that "the atoms are infinite in size and number" [32] seems too careless to be worth anything. On the other hand we have some reliable evidence from Aristotle's lost work *On Democritus*, quoted by Simplicius:

> Democritus thinks of his substances [i.e. the atoms] as being so small that they escape our senses; they have all sorts of shapes and figures and differences of magnitude. (Aristotle *On Democritus* Fr. 1 Ross = Simplicius *De Caelo* 295.5 ff.)

This makes much better sense, as well as having much better authority.[33]

The probability is, then, that Democritus' atoms were supposed to be so small that distinctions could not be made inside them. Yet they had some magnitude, and many variations in shape and size. There seems to be an inescapable contradiction here. If we take together a smaller atom and a larger one, we can always distinguish in the larger one that part which is covered by the smaller and that which is not. Even within the limits of a single atom, supposing it to be of a complex shape (say hook-shaped), we can always distinguish one part of the shape from another (say the hook from the shaft). S. Luria, in his learned and pioneering paper, accepted the evidence of Aristotle as proving that Democritus' theory included the idea of theoretically

[30] See Lucretius 2.481–521 and Epicurus *Lett. to Hdt.* §55.

[31] DK 68A47.

[32] DK 68A1.

[33] I note Jürgen Mau's ingenious argument, p. 24, that the size of atoms had something to do with the commensurability problem: astronomical calculations, having a large common measure, might admit "world-sized atoms." But I doubt if this ingenuity is necessary.

indivisible units: but he was so daunted by the thought of the magnitude of the atoms that he decided Democritus' theory was the same as Epicurus'; that is, that atoms are physically unsplittable, but divisible theoretically into smaller, absolutely indivisible parts. Against Luria, Jürgen Mau correctly insists on the evidence of Aristotle. Aristotle shows no signs whatever of distinguishing between two kinds of indivisible units in Democritean theory. To my mind this is nearly conclusive: but there is one piece of evidence which may be added to strengthen Mau's case. It is in fact used by Luria to support his thesis, but I think it can be turned against him.

In the *De Caelo*[34] Aristotle mentions that Leucippus and Democritus "did not define clearly what shape each of the elements had, except that they allotted the sphere to fire." Later he adds a remarkable criticism:

> Even according to their own assumptions, the elements would not seem to be infinite, if the bodies differ in shape and all shapes are composed of pyramids, straight-edged ones of straight-edged pyramids, and the sphere out of eight pieces. For there must be certain *archai* of the shapes. So if they (scil. the *archai*) are one or two or some larger number, the simple bodies also must come to the same number. (*De Caelo* III.4.303a29–b3)

At first sight this seems to tell in favor of Luria's position: Aristotle does indeed say "according to their own assumptions" and continues "if . . . all shapes are composed of pyramids," etc. I feel convinced, however, that this appearance is misleading. The Atomists' assumptions are that material substances differ in quality because of the differences in the shapes of their component atoms, and that such differences are innumerable. The second clause ("if all shapes are composed of pyramids," etc.) is not one of their assumptions; Aristotle gives this away by adding as a piece of justification "there *must* be certain *archai* of the shapes," not "they said these were the *archai*." Simplicius confirms this in his paraphrase: if the Atomists said the atoms are infinite because they differ in shape and shapes are infinite, then, "*if some argument shows* that the primary shapes are finite," then the elements will be finite too.[35] Aristotle himself, in the next chapter, reveals that the reduction of all shapes to elementary pyramids is a widespread assumption; for there he attributes it to some thinkers (Simplicius in his note says they were Pythagoreans) who believed that fire is characterized by

[34] III.4.303a12.
[35] Simplicius *De Caelo* 613.12–16. Note the indefinite ἐὰν δείξῃ τις λόγος.

a pyramidal shape.[36] The Atomists thought fire atoms were spherical.

I think, therefore, that this part of Luria's case can be turned against him. If Aristotle applied someone else's idea, that all shapes are composed of elementary pyramids, to the Atomists' doctrine with hostile intent, it must follow that the Atomists themselves had no idea that their atoms were not of elementary, irreducible shape, or at any rate that Aristotle did not know of such an idea of theirs. For he could have used their own theory against them much more effectively.

The most direct piece of evidence Luria can quote is from Alexander's commentary on *Metaphysics* I. Aristotle observes that Leucippus and Democritus neglected to say anything about the origin of motion.[37] Alexander says that they explained how atoms moved by collision, but not how they moved naturally:

> For they do not even explain how atoms get their weight. They say that the partless units which are conceptually present in the atoms and which are parts of them are without weight; and how could weight come about through the association of weightless units? (Alexander *Metaphysics* 36.25–27)

This says explicitly that Democritean atoms had parts which were themselves partless; in fact it identifies Democritean and Epicurean atoms. That is probably the explanation, though it is hard to prove it— and I am not sure that what Alexander reports is true even of Epicurean atoms. We have to strike a balance between conflicting evidence: against this statement of Alexander's we must set the contradictory statements of Simplicius (see above, pp. 519–20), and the (to my mind) overwhelming consideration that Aristotle does not distinguish between "partless units" and atoms. Theophrastus evidently knew nothing of the doctrine reported by Alexander; for he could hardly have failed to mention it in his account of the weight of Democritean atoms, which we possess.[38] Alexander's seems to be a unique testimony. The only possible conclusion is that it is mistaken.[39]

[36] III.5.304a10.

[37] *Metaphysics* I.4.985b19.

[38] Theophrastus *De Sensibus* 61 = DK 68A135: βαρὺ μὲν οὖν καὶ κοῦφον τῷ μεγέθει διαιρεῖ Δημόκριτος. εἰ γὰρ διακριθὲν ἓν ἕκαστον κατὰ σχῆμα διαφέρει σταθμῷ, τῷ μεγέθει διαφέρειν. That this or something like it is the true reading is cogently argued by John B. McDiarmid, "Theophrastus *De Sensibus* 61–62," *CP*, 55 (1960), 28–30.

[39] In rejecting this testimony I can claim the support of Diels and Kranz,

Luria quotes the text of Simplicius which we have examined above, p. 519, where it is said that Leucippus and Democritus gave two causes of the indivisibility of atoms—their imperviousness (*apatheia*) and their partlessness. Simplicius failed to understand, Luria maintains, that these causes apply to *two different kinds* of atom. This will hardly carry conviction—particularly as the Epicurean theory is contrasted explicitly with the Democritean in the same sentence. However, it might be as well to pursue the question: Why did Democritus stress the hardness and imperviousness of the atoms, and the fact that they contained no void, as causes of their indivisibility? He certainly did so; yet to meet the Eleatics' arguments it was a partless unit that was required, rather than a hard one. The answer can be found, I think, in the first passage of *De Generatione et Corruptione* quoted at the beginning of this chapter. The Eleatics, says Aristotle, objected to the pluralists that if the universe is divisible in one place and not in another, this seems like a piece of fiction. Why should it be so? We have the Atomists' answer in the hardness of the atoms. What *is*, they said, is indivisible (as the Eleatics claimed): each atom is absolutely solid, packed with being and nothing else. There is no void, or not-being, in an atom; hence nothing can penetrate it, so as to divide it.[40] The universe as a whole is divisible, however, in the sense that there is a plurality of existents separated by void.

All the evidence I have produced so far has been in second-hand reports. Clearly some attempt must be made to clinch the argument by means of the original fragments of Democritus. But they are unfortunately quite inconclusive. Only one of them, so far as I can see, says anything to the point at all; that is the fragment which discusses

---

Kirk and Raven, Burnet, and all those who believe that Democritus was only a physical atomist.

Luria also quotes Themistius *De Caelo* 186.26, which seems to suggest that there is found in the atoms something which admits division conceptually into seven (*sic*) parts. This is a Latin version of a Hebrew version of an Arabic version of the Greek; the text is also corrupt.

He claims also that there is support for his case in Simplicius *Physics* 82.1, *De Caelo* 648.26 and 649.2 ff. The first of these has been dealt with on p. 519; the last two explain Aristotle's criticism, and are not necessarily derived from Democritus at all.

[40] Cf. the similar argument in Lucretius 1.528–39, and Epicurus *Letter to Herodotus* §41.

the problem of slicing a cone in a plane parallel to the base. It is quoted by Plutarch, who was interested in Chrysippus' answer to the problem and did not think Democritus' solution was worth mentioning (supposing that he knew it in the first place).

> If a cone is cut along a plane parallel to its base, what must we think of the surfaces of the two segments—that they are equal or unequal? If they are unequal, they will make the cone uneven, with many step-like indentations and roughnesses: if they are equal, then the segments will be equal, and the cone will turn out to have the same properties as a cylinder, being composed of equal and not of unequal circles—which is quite absurd. (Plutarch *De Communibus Notitiis* 1079E = DK 68B155)

The cone fragment has sometimes been taken for proof that Democritus did not believe in indivisible magnitudes, but I do not see that it proves this at all. It could well be that he adopted the first of his alternatives: the two faces *are* unequal, and the cone does taper not smoothly but in steps. His theory of knowledge can perfectly well account for this: for "darkling knowledge" the cone is smooth, but for "genuine knowledge," which knows that if the cone is anything at all it must be made of indivisible magnitudes, it is stepped.

The only other direct evidence about Democritus on this subject is furnished by the titles of some of his books.[41] These show at least that he interested himself in geometry, and particularly in the problems of irrational proportions and others which involve the concept of a limit. But, as with the cone problem, the fact that he discussed the problem does not tell us how he attempted to solve it. We know that attempts were made in antiquity to handle the problems of irrationals by using approximations which could be made as near as you please.[42] If Democritus regarded geometry as the science of measuring bodies, then all his geometry could well have been adapted to an atomistic view of the composition of bodies; and there seems to be no evidence that he did not adapt it in this way. It is worth observing that in the title of his book *On Irrational Lines and Solids* (περὶ ἀλόγων γραμμῶν καὶ ναστῶν) there is a startling juxtaposition of mathematics and physics: "ναστός" is

[41] DK 68B11*l*: περὶ διαφορῆς γωνίης (for this reading, see Heath, vol. I, pp. 178–79) ἢ περὶ ψαύσιος κύκλου καὶ σφαίρης. IIρ περὶ ἀλόγων γραμμῶν καὶ ναστῶν.

[42] See Plato *Republic* 546c, and the many commentaries on this passage, along with Heath, vol. I, pp. 305 ff.

Democritus' own word for "solid," in the sense in which a physical atom is solid.

The balance of the evidence, then, supports the view that Leucippus and Democritus were more than physical atomists. They believed their atoms to be theoretically as well as physically indivisible. There is no evidence, so far as I have noticed, that they also regarded space as composed of indivisible minima. I think this was an innovation by Epicurus.[43]

[43] W. K. C. Guthrie, *A History of Greek Philosophy*, vol. 2 (Cambridge, 1965), pp. 503–07, has independently reached the same conclusion about the atoms of Democritus.

SELECTIVE BIBLIOGRAPHY

Like the anthology as a whole, this bibliography is geared to the level of English-speaking advanced undergraduate and beginning graduate students. References to works in languages other than English are made only for works of unusual importance, or if no similar study is available in English. For explanation of abbreviations used, see above, p. xv. The works listed under General Studies should also be consulted for discussions of each of the philosophers or schools (sections IX–XIX), including, of course, those (e.g. Thales, Anaximenes, Diogenes of Apollonia) for whom no section is specifically assigned. Where note of one of these general studies is explicitly taken in other sections, it indicates that the work referred to is especially helpful on that particular topic. The relevant articles in *The Encyclopedia of Philosophy*, ed. Paul Edwards, 8 vols. (New York: The Macmillan Company and Free Press, 1967) are of high quality and are especially recommended. The beginning student may consult with profit not only the *Encyclopedia*'s articles on individual Pre-Socratics but also articles listed in the *Encyclopedia*'s Index under "Pre-Socratic Philosophy," also those under "Greek Philosophy —Terms," and the articles "Orphism" and "Sophists."

I. SOURCES AND SOURCE BOOKS

Burnet, John. *Early Greek Philosophy*. 4th ed. (a reprint of the 3d ed.). London: Adam and Charles Black, 1930. Repr. Cleveland and New York: Meridian Books, 1957.

Diels, Hermann. *Die Fragmente der Vorsokratiker*. 6th ed. rev. W. Kranz. 3 vols. Berlin: Weidmann, 1952.

Freeman, Kathleen. *The Presocratic Philosophers: A Companion to Diels, Fragmente der Vorsokratiker*. Oxford: Basil Blackwell, 1946.

———. *Ancilla to the Pre-Socratic Philosophers: A Complete Translation of the Fragments in Diels*, Fragmente der Vorsokratiker. Oxford: Basil Black-well, 1956.

Kirk, G. S., and Raven, J. E. *The Presocratic Philosophers*. Cambridge: Cambridge University Press, 1957.

Robinson, John Mansley. *An Introduction to Early Greek Philosophy*. Boston: Houghton Mifflin Company, 1968.

(For the Ionians, Pythagoreans, Heraclitus, Xenophanes, Parmenides, Melissus, Zeno, and Anaxagoras, see also the individual volumes of "Testimonianze e frammenti" in the section *Filosofia antica* of the series *Biblioteca di studi superiori* [Florence: "La Nuova Italia" Editrice]. These volumes give the most complete presentation of the source materials available at this time.)

II. GENERAL STUDIES

Baldry, H. C. "Embryological Analogies in Pre-Socratic Cosmogony," *CQ*, 26 (1932), 27–34.

Beare, J. I. *Greek Theories of Elementary Cognition*. Oxford: Clarendon Press, 1906.

Burnet, John, *Early Greek Philosophy* (see I, above).

Cherniss, Harold F. "The Characteristics and Effects of Presocratic Philosophy," *Journal of the History of Ideas*, 12 (1951), 319–45. Repr. in Furley and Allen, I, pp. 1–28; also in the Bobbs-Merrill Reprint Series in Philosophy, PHIL-52.

Cornford, F. M. *From Religion to Philosophy*. London: Edward Arnold, 1912. Repr. New York: Harper Torchbooks, 1957.

———. "Mystery Religions and Pre-Socratic Philosophy." In J. B. Bury, S. A. Cook, F. E. Adcock, eds., *The Cambridge Ancient History, Vol. IV: The Persian Empire and the West* (Cambridge: Cambridge University Press, 1926), ch. 15, pp. 522–78.

———. "Was the Ionian Philosophy Scientific?" *JHS*, 62 (1942), 1–7. Repr. in Furley and Allen, I, pp. 29–41.

———. *The Unwritten Philosophy and Other Essays*. Cambridge: Cambridge University Press, 1950.

———. *Principium Sapientiae*. Cambridge: Cambridge University Press, 1952. Repr. as *Origins of Greek Philosophical Thought*. Philadelphia: University of Pennsylvania Press, 1973.

Dodds, E. R. *The Greeks and the Irrational*. Sather Classical Lectures, 25. Berkeley and Los Angeles: University of California Press, 1951.

Fränkel, Hermann. *Wege und Formen frühgriechischen Denkens*. 3d ed. Munich: C. H. Beck, 1968.

———. *Dichtung und Philosophie des frühen Griechentums*. 3d ed. Munich: C. H. Beck, 1969.

von Fritz, Kurt. *Grundprobleme der Geschichte der antiken Wissenschaft*, Berlin: Walter de Gruyter, 1971.

Gomperz, Heinrich. "Problems and Methods of Early Greek Science," *Journal of the History of Ideas*, 4 (1943), 161–76. Repr. in the Bobbs-Merrill Reprint Series in the History of Science, HS-21.

Guthrie, W. K. C. "The Presocratic World-Picture," *The Harvard Theological Review*, 45 (1952), 87–104.

———. *In the Beginning. Some Greek Views on the Origins of Life and the Early State of Man*. Ithaca, N.Y.: Cornell University Press, 1957.

———. *A History of Greek Philosophy. Vol. I: The Earlier Presocratics and the Pythagoreans*. Cambridge: Cambridge University Press, 1962. *Vol. II: The Presocratic Tradition from Parmenides to Democritus*. 1965. *Vol. III: The Fifth-Century Enlightenment*. 1969.

Heidel, W. A. "Qualitative Change in Pre-Socratic Philosophy," *AGP*, 19 (1906), 333–79. (Excerpt repr. above, pp. 86–95.)

Hölscher, Uvo. *Anfängliches Fragen: Studien zur frühen griechischen Philosophie*. Göttingen: Vandenhoeck u. Ruprecht, 1968.

Hussey, Edward. *The Presocratics*. London: Duckworth, 1972.

Jaeger, Werner. *The Theology of the Early Greek Philosophers*. Oxford: Clarendon Press, 1947.

Kirk, G. S. "Sense and Common-Sense in the Development of Greek Philosophy," *JHS*, 81 (1961), 105–17.

Lloyd, G. E. R. "Hot and Cold, Dry and Wet in Early Greek Thought," *JHS*, 84 (1964), 92–106. Repr. in Furley and Allen, I, pp. 255–80.

———. *Polarity and Analogy: Two Types of Argumentation in Early Greek Thought*. Cambridge: Cambridge University Press, 1966.

Mourelatos, Alexander P. D. "The Real, Appearances, and Human Error in Early Greek Philosophy," *The Review of Metaphysics*, 19 (1965), 346–65.

Nietzsche, Friedrich. *Philosophy in the Tragic Age of the Greeks*. Trans. by Marianne Cowan. Chicago: Henry Regnery Company, Gateway Edition, 1962.

Robinson, *Intro. to Early Greek Philosophy* (see above, I).

Stokes, Michael C. *One and Many in Presocratic Philosophy*. Washington, D.C.: Center for Hellenic Studies, 1971.

Stratton, G. M. *Theophrastus and the Greek Physiological Psychology before Aristotle*. London, 1917. Repr. Amsterdam, 1964.

Tannery, Paul. *Pour l'Histoire de la science hellène*. Paris: Alcan, 1887. Repr. Paris: Gauthier-Villars, 1930.

Vlastos, Gregory. "Equality and Justice in Early Greek Cosmologies," *CP*, 42 (1947), 156–78. Repr. in Furley and Allen, I, pp. 56–91.

———. "Theology and Philosophy in Early Greek Thought," *Philosophical Quarterly*, 2 (1952), 97–123. Repr. in Furley and Allen, I, pp. 92–129.

————. Review of Cornford, *Principium Sapientiae, Gnomon*, 27 (1955), 65–76. Repr. in Furley and Allen, I, pp. 42–55.

Zeller, Eduard. *A History of Greek Philosophy from the Earliest Period to the Time of Socrates.* 2 vols. Trans. by S. F. Alleyne. London: Longmans, Green and Co., 1881.

III. Collections of Critical Essays

Anton, John P., with Kustas, George L., eds. *Essays in Ancient Greek Philosophy.* Albany: State University of New York Press, 1971.

Furley, David J., and Allen, R. E., eds. *Studies in Presocratic Philosophy. Vol. I: The Beginnings of Philosophy.* London: Routledge and Kegan Paul, 1970. *Vol. II: The Eleatics and the Pluralists.* (forthcoming).

Gadamer, Hans-Georg, ed. *Um die Begriffswelt der Vorsokratiker.* Wege der Forschung, 9. Darmstadt: Wissenschaftliche Buchgesellschaft, 1968.

IV. Bibliographies

Kerferd, G. B. "Recent Work on Presocratic Philosophy," *American Philosophical Quarterly*, 2 (1965), 130–40. (Covers the period 1953–62.)

Minar, Edwin L., Jr. "A Survey of Recent Work in Pre-Socratic Philosophy," *The Classical Weekly*, 47 (1954), 161–70, 177–82. (Covers the period 1945–52.)

————. "Pre-Socratic Studies, 1953–1966, "*The Classical World*, 60 (1966), 143–63.

Sweeney, Leo. *Infinity in the Presocratics: A Bibliographical and Philosophical Study.* The Hague: Martinus Nijhof, 1972. (An exhaustive bibliographical essay, much ampler in scope than its title suggests.)

V. Assessment of Sources

Cherniss, Harold F. *Aristotle's Criticism of Presocratic Philosophy.* Baltimore: The Johns Hopkins Press, 1935. Repr. New York: Octagon Books, 1964.

Diels, Hermann. *Doxographi Graeci.* Berlin, 1879. Repr. 1958.

Guthrie, W. K. C. "Aristotle as a Historian of Philosophy: Some Preliminaries," JHS, 77 (1957), 35–41. Repr. in Furley and Allen, I, pp. 239–54.

McDiarmid, J. B. "Theophrastus on the Presocratic Causes," *Harvard Studies in Classical Philology*, 61 (1953), 85–156. Excerpt repr. in Furley and Allen, I, pp. 178–238.

Philip, J. A. "The Fragments of the Presocratic Philosophers," *Phoenix*, 10 (1956), 116–23.

VI. Philosophical vs. Philological Reconstruction:
the Popper-Kirk Controversy

Popper, Karl. "Back to the Presocratics, "*Proceedings of the Aristotelian Society*, 59 (1958–59), 1–24. Revised version repr. in Popper, *Conjectures and Refutations* (London: Routledge and Kegan Paul, 1963), pp. 136–53; also in Furley and Allen, I, pp. 130–53.

Kirk, G. S. "Popper on Science and the Presocratics," *Mind*, 69 (1960), 318–39. Repr. in Furley and Allen, I, pp. 154–77.

Popper, Karl. "Kirk on Heraclitus, and on Fire as the Cause of Balance," *Mind*, 72 (1963), 386–92. Repr. with revisions in *Conjectures and Refutations*, pp. 153–65.

Lloyd, G. E. R. "Popper versus Kirk: A Controversy in the Interpretation of Greek Science," *The British Journal for the Philosophy of Science*, 18 (1967), 21–38. Repr. in the Bobbs-Merrill Reprint Series in the History of Science, HS-45.

VII. CONCEPT STUDIES

A. *ALĒTHEIA*, "TRUTH"

Boeder, Heribert. "Der frühgriechische Wortgebrauch von *Logos* und *Aletheia*," *Archiv für Begriffsgeschichte*, 4 (1959), 82–112.

Heitsch, Ernst. "Die nicht-philosophische ΑΛΗΘΕΙΑ," *Hermes*, 90 (1962), 24–33.

Krischer, Tilman, "ΕΤΥΜΟΣ und ΑΛΗΘΗΣ," *Philologus*, 109 (1965), 161–74.

Starr, Chester G. "Ideas of Truth in Early Greece," *La parola del passato*, fasc. 122 (1968), 348–59.

B. COGNITION

von Fritz, Kurt. "Νόος and Νοεῖν in the Homeric Poems," *CP*, 38 (1943), 79–93.

———. "Νοῦς, Νοεῖν and Their Derivatives in Pre-Socratic Philosophy (Excluding Anaxagoras)," *CP*, 40 (1945), 223–42 and 41 (1946), 12–34. Repr. above, pp. 23–85.

Snell, Bruno. *Die Ausdrücke für den Begriff des Wissens in der vorplatonischen Philosophie*. Philologische Untersuchungen, 29. Berlin: Weidmannsche Buchhandlung, 1924.

C. *DOXA*

Mourelatos, *The Route* (see XIII, below), pp. 194–202.

D. *EINAI*, "To Be"

Kahn, Charles H. "The Greek Verb 'To Be' and the Concept of Being," *Foundations of Language*, 2 (1966), 245–65. Repr. in the Bobbs-Merrill Reprint Series in Philosophy, PHIL-114.

———. *The Verb 'Be' in Ancient Greek*. Foundations of Language Supplementary Series, 16. Dordrecht: Reidel, 1973.

E. *KOSMOS*

Diller, Hans. "Der vorphilosophische Gebrauch von ΚΟΣΜΟΣ und ΚΟ-ΣΜΕΙΝ," In *Festschrift Bruno Snell* (Munich: C. H. Beck, 1956), pp. 47–60.
Kerchensteiner, Jula. *Kosmos: Quellenkritische Untersuchungen zu den Vorsokratikern.* Zetemata, 30. Munich: C. H. Beck, 1962.

F. *LOGOS*

Boeder, "Logos und Aletheia" (see VIIA, above).

G. *PEITHŌ*, "Persuasion" and *PISTIS*, "Faith"

Mourelatos, *The Route* (see XIII, below), pp. 136–63.

H. *PHYSIS*

Heidel, W. A. "Περὶ Φύσεως: A Study of the Conception of Nature among the Pre-Socratics," *Proceedings of the American Academy of Arts and Sciences*, 45 (1910), 77–133.

I. INFINITY

Sweeney, Leo, *Infinity* (see IV, above).

J. OPPOSITES

Ferguson, John, "The Opposites," *Apeiron*, 3 (1969), 1–17.
Lloyd, "Hot and Cold, Dry and Wet" (see II, above).
———, *Polarity and Analogy* (see II, above).

K. GENERAL

Notopoulos, James A. "Parataxis in Homer," *TAPA*, 80 (1949), 1–23.
Perry, Ben Edwin. "The Early Greek Capacity for Viewing Things Separately," *TAPA*, 68 (1937), 403–27.
Snell, Bruno. *The Discovery of the Mind: The Greek Origins of European Thought*. Trans. from the 2d German ed. by T. G. Rosenmeyer. Cambridge, Mass.: Harvard University Press, 1953. Repr. New York: Harper Torchbooks, 1960.
Webster, T. B. L. "Language and Thought in Early Greece," *Memoirs and Proceedings of the Manchester Literary and Philosophical Society*, 94 (1952–53), 17–38.

VIII. MYTHICAL, RELIGIOUS, AND ORIENTAL ORIGINS

Conger, George P. "Did India Influence Early Greek Philosophies?" *Philosophy East and West*, 2 (1952), 102–28.
Frankfort, H. and H. A., Wilson, John A., and Jacobsen, Thorkild. *Before Philosophy*. Baltimore, Md.: Penguin Books, 1949.

Hölscher, Uvo. "Anaximander and the Beginnings of Greek Philosophy." In Furley and Allen, I, pp. 281–322.

Onians, Richard Broxton. *The Origins of European Thought*. 2d ed. Cambridge: Cambridge University Press, 1954.

Riezler, Kurt. "Das homerische Gleichnis und der Anfang der Philosophie," *Die Antike*, 12 (1936), 253–71. Repr. in Gadamer, *Begriffswelt*, pp. 1–20.

Stokes, Michael C. "Hesiodic and Milesian Cosmogonies," *Phronesis*, 7 (1962), 1–37, and 8 (1963), 1–34.

West, M. L. *Early Greek Philosophy and the Orient*. Oxford: Clarendon Press, 1971.

(See also the works by Cornford, Dodds, Jaeger, and Vlastos, in II, above.)

IX. ANAXIMANDER

Gottschalk, H. B. "Anaximander's *Apeiron*," *Phronesis*, 10 (1965), 37–53.

Hölscher, "Anaximander and the Beginnings" (see VIII, above).

Kahn, Charles H. "Anaximander and the Arguments Concerning the ἄπειρον at *Physics* 203b4–15." In *Festschrift Ernst Kapp* (Hamburg, 1958), pp. 19–29.

———. *Anaximander and the Origins of Greek Cosmology*. New York: Columbia University Press, 1960. Excerpt repr. above, pp. 99–117.

Kirk, G. S. "Some Problems in Anaximander," *CQ*, N.S. 5 (1955), 21–38. Repr. in Furley and Allen, I, pp. 323–49.

Rescher, Nicholas. "Cosmic Evolution in Anaximander," *Studium Generale*, 11 (1958), 718–31. Repr. in Rescher, *Essays in Philosophical Analysis* (Pittsburgh: University of Pittsburgh Press, 1969), pp. 3–32.

Robinson, John Mansley. "Anaximander and the Problem of the Earth's Immobility." In Anton and Kustas, pp. 111–18.

Seligman, Paul. *The "Apeiron" of Anaximander*. London: The Athlone Press, 1962.

Solmsen, Friedrich. "Anaximander's Infinite: Traces and Influences," *AGP*, 44 (1962), 109–31.

X. PYTHAGORAS AND THE PYTHAGOREANS

Burkert, Walter. *Lore and Science in Ancient Pythagoreanism*. Trans. by Edwin L. Minar, Jr. Cambridge, Mass.: Harvard University Press, 1972.

Cornford, F. M. "Mysticism and Science in the Pythagorean Tradition," *CQ*, 16 (1922), 137–50, and 17 (1923), 1–12. Excerpt repr. above, pp. 135–60.

———. "The Invention of Space." In *Essays in Honour of Gilbert Murray* (London: George Allen & Unwin, 1936), pp. 215–35.

———. *Plato and Parmenides*. London: Routledge & Kegan Paul, 1939.

Repr. New York: The Library of Liberal Arts, 1957. (See ch. 1, "The Earliest Pythagorean Cosmogony," pp. 1–27.)

von Fritz, Kurt. "The Discovery of Incommensurability by Hippasus of Metapontum," *Annals of Mathematics*, 46 (1945), 242–64. Repr. in Furley and Allen, I, pp. 382–412.

Guthrie, *History*, I, pp. 146–340.

Heath, T. L. *A History of Greek Mathematics*. Oxford: Clarendon Press, 1921. (See vol. I, pp. 65–117, 141–69.)

Heidel, W. A. "The Pythagoreans and Greek Mathematics," *AJP*, 61 (1940), 1–33. Repr. in Furley and Allen, I, pp. 350–81.

Helm, E. Eugene. "The Vibrating String of the Pythagoreans," *Scientific American*, vol. 27, 6 (Dec. 1967), 92–103.

Kahn, Charles H. "Pythagorean Philosophy before Plato," above, pp. 161–85.

Morrison, J. S. "Pythagoras of Samos," *CQ*, N.S. 6 (1956), 135–56.

Philip, J. A. *Pythagoras and Early Pythagoreanism*. *Phoenix* Suppl. Vol. 7. Toronto: University of Toronto Press, 1966.

Raven, J. E. *Pythagoreans and Eleatics*. Cambridge: Cambridge University Press, 1948. Repr. Amsterdam: Adolf M. Hakkert, 1966.

XI. Xenophanes

Bowra, C. M. "Xenophanes on Songs at Feasts," *CP*, 33 (1938), 353–67. Repr. in Bowra, *Problems in Greek Poetry* (Oxford: The Clarendon Press, 1953), pp. 1–14.

Fränkel, Hermann. "Xenophanesstudien." In Fränkel, *Wege und Formen*, pp. 335–49. Excerpt repr. above, pp. 118–31.

Guthrie, *History*, I, pp. 360–402.

Jaeger, *Theology*, pp. 38–54.

Marinone, Nino. *Lessico di Senofane*. Rome, 1967. Repr. Hildesheim: Georg Olms, 1972.

Reiche, H. A. T. "Empirical Aspects of Xenophanes' Theology." In Anton and Kustas, pp. 88–110.

XII. Heraclitus

Fränkel, Hermann. "A Thought Pattern in Heraclitus," *AJP*, 59 (1938), 309–37. Excerpt repr. above, pp. 214–28.

Guthrie, W. K. C. "Flux and *Logos* in Heraclitus," from Guthrie, *History*, I, pp. 446–53, 459–69. Repr. above, pp. 197–213.

Hölscher, Uvo. "Paradox, Simile, and Gnomic Utterance in Heraclitus," above, pp. 229–38.

Kahn, Charles H. "A New Look at Heraclitus," *American Philosophical Quarterly*, 1 (1964), 189–203. Repr. in the Bobbs-Merrill Reprint Series in Philosophy, PHIL-238.

Kirk, G. S. "Natural Change in Heraclitus," *Mind*, 60 (1951), 35–42. Repr. above, pp. 189–96.

———. *Heraclitus: The Cosmic Fragments*. Cambridge: Cambridge University Press, 1954. Repr. with corrections, 1962.

Marcovich, M. *Heraclitus: Greek Text with a Short Commentary*. Merida, Venezuela: Los Andes University Press, 1967.

Mourelatos, Alexander P. D. "Heraclitus, Parmenides, and the Naïve Metaphysics of Things." In *Exegesis and Argument: Studies in Greek Philosophy Presented to Gregory Vlastos*, ed. E. N. Lee, A. P. D. Mourelatos, and R. Rorty, *Phronesis* Suppl. Vol. I. (Assen: Van Gorcum, 1973), pp. 16–48.

Owens, Joseph. "The Interpretation of the Heraclitean Fragments." In *An Étienne Gilson Tribute*, ed. Charles J. O'Neil (Milwaukee: Marquette University Press, 1959), pp. 148–68.

Reinhardt, Karl. "Heraclitea," *Hermes*, 77 (1942), 225–48. Repr. in Reinhardt, *Vermächtnis der Antike* (Göttingen, 1960), pp. 72–97; also in Gadamer, *Begriffswelt*, pp. 177–208.

———. "Heraklits Lehre vom Feuer," *Hermes*, 77 (1942), 1–27. Repr. in *Vermächtnis der Antike*, pp. 41–71.

Roussos, Evangelos N. *Heraklit-Bibliographie*. Darmstadt: Wissenschaftliche Buchgesellschaft, 1971.

Vlastos, Gregory. "On Heraclitus," *AJP*, 76 (1955), 337–68. Excerpt repr. in Furley and Allen, I, pp. 413–29.

XIII. PARMENIDES

Anscombe, G. E. M. "Parmenides, Mystery and Contradiction," *Proceedings of the Aristotelian Society*, 69 (1968–69), 125–32.

Bowra, C. M. "The Proem of Parmenides," *CP*, 32 (1937), 97–112. Repr. in Bowra, *Problems in Greek Poetry*, pp. 38–53.

Burkert, Walter. "Das Proömium des Parmenides und die Katabasis des Pythagoras," *Phronesis*, 14 (1969), 1–30.

Calogero, Guido. *Studi sull' eleatismo*. Rome: Tipografia del senato, 1932. German trans., *Studien über den Eleatismus*. Darmstadt: Wissenschaftliche Buchgesellschaft, 1970.

Cornford, *Plato and Parmenides*. (See ch. 2, "Parmenides' *Way of Truth*," pp. 28–52.)

Cosgrove, Matthew R. "The *Kouros* Motif in Parmenides: B1.24," *Phronesis*, forthcoming.

Fränkel, Hermann. "Parmenidesstudien," *Nachrichten der Göttinger Gesellschaft der Wissenschaften*, 1930, 153–92. Repr. with revisions in Fränkel, *Wege und Formen*, pp. 157–97. In trans. in Furley and Allen, II.

Furley, David J. "Notes on Parmenides." In *Exegesis and Argument* (see XII, above), pp. 1–15.

Furth, Montgomery. "Elements of Eleatic Ontology," *Journal of the History of Philosophy*, 6 (1968), 111–32, Repr. above, pp. 241–70.

Hölscher, Uvo. *Parmenides: Vom Wesen des Seienden*. Theorie I. Frankfurt a.M.: Suhrkamp Verlag, 1969.

Jones, Barrington. "Parmenides' 'The Way of Truth,' " *Journal of the History of Philosophy*, 11 (1973), 287–98.

Kahn, Charles H. Review of Tarán, *Parmenides*, *Gnomon*, 40 (1968), 123–33.

———. "The Thesis of Parmenides," *The Review of Metaphysics*, 22 (1969), 700–24.

———. "More on Parmenides," *The Review of Metaphysics*, 23 (1969), 333–40.

———. Review of Mansfeld, *Die Offenbarung des Parmenides*, *Gnomon*, 42 (1970), 113–19.

Long, A. A. "The Principles of Parmenides' Cosmogony," *Phronesis*, 8 (1963), 90–107. Repr. in Furley and Allen, II.

Mansfeld, Jaap. *Die Offenbarung des Parmenides und die menschliche Welt*. Assen: Van Gorcum, 1964.

Mourelatos, Alexander P. D. "Comments on 'The Thesis of Parmenides,' " *The Review of Metaphysics*, 22 (1969), 735–44. (Discussion of Kahn, above.)

———. *The Route of Parmenides: A Study of Word, Image, and Argument in the Fragments*. New Haven and London: Yale University Press, 1970. Shorter version of ch. 7 repr. in Anton and Kustas, pp. 59–80; of ch. 9, above, pp. 312–49.

———. "Heraclitus, Parmenides, and the Naïve Metaphysics of Things" (see XII, above).

Merlan, Philip. "Neues Licht auf Parmenides," *AGP*, 48 (1966), 267–76

Owen, G. E. L. "Eleatic Questions," *CQ*, N.S. 10 (1960), 84–102. Repr. in Furley and Allen, II.

———. "Plato and Parmenides on the Timeless Present," *The Monist*, 50 (1966), 317–40. Repr. above, pp. 271–92.

Reinhardt, Karl. *Parmenides und die Geschichte der griechischen Philosophie*. Bonn: Friedrich Cohen, 1916. Repr. Frankfurt a.M.: Vittorio Klostermann, 1959. Excerpt in trans. repr. above, pp. 293–311.

Schofield, Malcolm. "Did Parmenides Discover Eternity?" *AGP*, 52 (1970), 113–35.

Schwabl, Hans. "Sein und Doxa bei Parmenides," *Wiener Studien*, 66 (1953), 50–75. Repr. in Gadamer, *Begriffswelt*, pp. 390–422.

Tarán, Leonardo. *Parmenides: A Text with Translation, Commentary, and Critical Essays*. Princeton, N.J.: Princeton University Press, 1965.

Tilghman, B. R. "Parmenides, Plato, and Logical Atomism," *Southern Journal of Philosophy*, 7 (1969), 151–60.

Tugendhat, Ernst. "Das Sein und das Nichts." In *Durchblicke: Martin Heidegger zum 80. Geburtstag* (Frankfurt a.M.: Vittorio Klostermann, 1970), pp. 132–61.

Vlastos, Gregory. "Parmenides' Theory of Knowledge," *TAPA*, 77 (1946), 66–77.

Woodbury, Leonard. "Parmenides on Names," *Harvard Studies in Classical Philology*, 63 (1958), 145–60. Repr. in Anton and Kustas, pp. 145–62.

XIV. ZENO

Booth, N. B. "Were Zeno's Arguments a Reply to Attacks upon Parmenides?" *Phronesis*, I (1957), I–9.

———. "Were Zeno's Arguments Directed against the Pythagoreans?" *Phronesis*, I (1957), 90–103.

———. "Zeno's Paradoxes," *JHS*, 78 (1957), 189–201.

Cornford, *Plato and Parmenides*. (See ch. 3, "Zeno and Pythagorean Atomism," pp. 53–62.)

Fränkel, Hermann. "Zeno of Elea's Attacks on Plurality," *AJP*, 63 (1942), 1–25 and 193–206. Repr. in Furley and Allen, II.

Furley, David J. *Two Studies in the Greek Atomists*. Princeton, N.J.: Princeton University Press, 1967. (See I, ch. 5, "Zeno," repr. above, pp. 353–67.)

Grünbaum, Adolf. *Modern Science and Zeno's Paradoxes*. Middletown, Conn.: Wesleyan University Press, 1967. Rev. ed. London: George Allen & Unwin Ltd., 1968.

Lee, H. D. P. *Zeno of Elea: A Text with Translation and Notes*. Cambridge: Cambridge University Press, 1936. Repr. Amsterdam: Hakkert, 1967.

Owen, G. E. L. "Zeno and the Mathematicians," *Proceedings of the Aristotelian Society*, 58 (1957–58), 199–222. Repr. in Salmon, pp. 139–63; also in Furley and Allen, II.

Raven. *Pythagoreans and Eleatics* (see above, X), pp. 66–77.

Ross, W. D. *Aristotle's* Physics. Oxford: Clarendon Press, 1936. (See pp. 71–85).

Salmon, Wesley C., ed. *Zeno's Paradoxes*. Indianapolis and New York: Bobbs-Merrill, 1970.

Solmsen, Friedrich. "The Tradition about Zeno of Elea Re-Examined," *Phronesis*, 16 (1971), 116–41. Repr. above, pp. 368–93.

Stokes, *One and Many* (see II, above), pp. 175–218.

Tannery, Paul. "Le Concept scientifique du continu: Zenon d' Élée et Georg Cantor," *Revue philosophique de la France et de l'étranger*, 20 (1885), 385–410.

———. *Science hellène* (see II, above), pp. 255–70.

Vlastos, Gregory. "A Note on Zeno's Arrow," *Phronesis*, II (1966), 3–18. Repr. in Furley and Allen, II.

———. "Zeno's Race Course," *Journal of the History of Philosophy*, 4(1966), 95–108. Repr. in Furley and Allen, II.

————. "Zeno of Elea," s.v. in *The Encyclopedia of Philosophy*, ed. by Paul Edwards. New York: The Macmillan Company and The Free Press, 1967.

(*Mind* has been an especially lively forum for articles on Zeno during the past ten years. See tables of contents for volumes 72 [1963]–74 [1965], 76 [1967]–78 [1969], 80 [1971].)

XV. MELISSUS

Booth, N. B. "Did Melissus Believe in Incorporeal Being?" *AJP*, 79 (1958), 61–65.

Raven, *Pythagoreans and Eleatics*, pp. 78–92.

Solmsen, Friedrich. "The 'Eleatic One' in Melissus," *Mededelingen der koninklijke nederlandse akademie van wetenschappen, Afd. Letterkunde*, nieuwe reeks, deel 32 No. 8 (1969), 221–33.

XVI. EMPEDOCLES

Bercovitch, Sacvan. "Empedocles in the English Renaissance," *Studies in Philology*, 65 (1968), 67–80.

Bollack, Jean. *Empédocle I: Introduction a l'ancienne physique*. Paris: Les Éditions de Minuit, 1965.

————. *Empédocle II: Les Origines: Édition critique et traduction des fragments et des témoignages*. Paris: Les Éditions de Minuit, 1969.

————. *Empédocle III: Les Origines: Commentaire des fragments et des témoignages*. 2 vols. Paris: Les Éditions de Minuit, 1969.

Furley, David J. "Empedocles and the Clepsydra," *JHS*, 77 (1957), 31–34. Repr. in Furley and Allen, II.

Hölscher, Uvo. "Weltzeiten und Lebenszyklus, eine Nachprüfung der Empedocles-Doxographie," *Hermes*, 93 (1965), 7–33. Repr. with additions in *Anfängliches Fragen*, pp. 173–212.

Kahn, Charles H. "Religion and Natural Philosophy in Empedocles' Doctrine of the Soul," *AGP*, 42 (1960), 3–35. Repr. with revisions and "Retractationes" in Anton and Kustas, pp. 3–38; also repr. above, pp. 426–56.

Long, A. A. "Thinking and Sense-Perception in Empedocles: Mysticism or Materialism," *CQ*, N.S. 16 (1966), 256–76.

————. "Empedocles' Cosmic Cycle in the 'Sixties," above, pp. 397–425.

Long, Herbert S. "The Unity of Empedocles' Thought," *AJP*, 70 (1949), 142–58.

Mansfeld, Jaap. "Ambiguity in Empedocles B17, 3–5: A Suggestion," *Phronesis*, 17 (1972), 17–39.

Minar, Edwin L., Jr. "Cosmic Periods in the Philosophy of Empedocles," *Phronesis*, 8 (1963), 127–45. Repr. in Anton and Kustas, pp. 39–58.

O'Brien, Denis. "Empedocles' Cosmic Cycle," *CQ*, N.S. 17 (1967), 29–40.

————. *Empedocles' Cosmic Cycle*. Cambridge: Cambridge University Press, 1969.

Reinhardt, Karl, "Empedokles, Orphiker und Physiker," *CP*, 45 (1950), 170–79. Repr. in Reinhardt, *Vermächtnis der Antike*, pp. 101–13; also in Gadamer, *Begriffswelt*, pp. 497–511.

Solmsen, Friedrich. "Love and Strife in Empedocles' Cosmology," *Phronesis*, 10 (1965), 109–48. Repr. in Furley and Allen, II.

Zuntz, Günther. *Persephone: Three Essays on Religion and Thought in Magna Graecia*. Oxford: Clarendon Press, 1971. (See esp. Book 2: "Empedocles' *Katharmoi*," pp. 181–274.)

XVII. ANAXAGORAS

Cornford, F. M. "Anaxagoras' Theory of Matter," *CQ*, 24 (1930), 14–30 and 83–95. Repr. in Furley and Allen, II.

von Fritz, Kurt. "Der ΝΟΤΣ des Anaxagoras," *Archiv für Begriffsgeschichte*, 9 (1964), 87-102. Repr. in von Fritz, *Grundprobleme* (see above, II), pp. 576–93.

Kerferd, G. B. "Anaxagoras and the Concept of Matter Before Aristotle," *Bulletin of the John Rylands Library*, 52 (1969), 129–43. Repr. above, pp. 489–503.

Mathewson, I. R. "Aristotle and Anaxagoras: An Examination of F. M. Cornford's Interpretation," *CQ*, N.S. 8 (1958), 67–81.

Peck, A. L. "Anaxagoras and the Parts," *CQ*, 20 (1926), 57–62.

————. "Anaxagoras: Predication as a Problem in Physics," *CQ*, 25 (1931), 27–37 and 112–20.

Raven, J. E. "The Basis of Anaxagoras' Cosmology," *CQ*, N.S. 4 (1954), 123–37.

————. "Anaxagoras of Clazomenae," ch. 15 in KR.

Reesor, Margaret E. "The Meaning of Anaxagoras," *CP*, 55 (1960), 1–8.

————. "The Problem of Anaxagoras," *CP*, 58 (1963), 29–33. Repr. in Anton and Kustas, pp. 81–87.

Stokes, Michael C. "On Anaxagoras," *AGP*, 47 (1965), 1–19 and 217–50.

Strang, Colin. "The Physical Theory of Anaxagoras," *AGP*, 45 (1963), 101–18. Repr. in Furley and Allen, II.

Vlastos, Gregory. "The Physical Theory of Anaxagoras," *The Philosophical Review*, 59 (1950), 31–57. Repr. in Furley and Allen, II; also above, pp. 459–88.

XVIII. THE ATOMISTS

Cole, A. T. *Democritus and the Sources of Greek Anthropology*. American Philological Association Monographs, No. 25. Cleveland: The Press of Case Western Reserve University, 1967.

von Fritz, *Philosophie und sprachlicher Ausdruck bei Demokrit, Plato und Aristoteles.* New York, 1938. Repr. Darmstadt: Wissenschaftliche Buchgesellschaft, 1966.

———. "Democritus' Theory of Vision." In *Science, Medicine, and History: Essays on the Evolution of Scientific Thought and Medical Practice Written in Honour of Charles Singer*, ed. E. Ashworth Underwood, 2 vols. (London: Oxford University Press, 1953), vol. 1, pp. 83–99. Repr. in German in *Grundprobleme* (see above, II), pp. 594–622.

Furley, *Two Studies*, I, ch. 6, "The Atomists' Reply to the Eleatics." Repr. above, pp. 504–26.

Furley, David J. "Aristotle and the Atomists on Infinity." In Ingemar Düring, ed. *Naturphilosophie bei Aristoteles und Theophrast* (Heidelberg: Lothar Stiehm, 1969), pp. 85–96.

Guthrie, *History*, II, pp. 382–507.

de Ley, H. "Democritus and Leucippus: Two Notes on Ancient Atomism," *L'Antiquité classique*, 37 (1968), 620–33.

Luria, Solomon. *Demokrit.* Leningrad, 1970. (The most complete critical edition of Democritean fragments and testimonia. Greek and Latin text with apparatus; translation and commentary in Russian.)

Stokes, *One and Many*, pp. 218–36.

Taylor, C. C. W. "Pleasure, Knowledge, and Sensation in Democritus," *Phronesis*, 12 (1967), 6–27.

Vlastos, Gregory. "Ethics and Physics in Democritus," *The Philosophical Review*, 54 (1945), 578–92, and 55 (1946), 53–64. Repr. in Furley and Allen, II.

Weiss, Helene, "Democritus' Theory of Cognition," *CQ*, 32 (1938), 47–56.

XIX. The Sophists

Guthrie, *History*, III, pp. 3–319. Repr. as paperback, *The Sophists*, Cambridge: Cambridge University Press, 1972.

Kerferd, G. B. "Gorgias on Nature or That Which Is Not," *Phronesis*, 1 (1955), 3–25.

Robinson, John Mansley. "On Gorgias." In *Exegesis and Argument* (above, XII), pp. 49–60.

Segal, Charles P. "Gorgias and the Psychology of the *Logos*," *Harvard Studies in Classical Philology*, 66 (1962), 99–155.

Sprague, Rosamond Kent, trans. "*Dissoi Logoi* or *Dialexeis*," *Mind*, 77 (1968), 155–67.

———, ed. *The Older Sophists. A Complete Translation by Several Hands.* Columbia, S.C.: University of South Carolina Press, 1972.

Vlastos, Gregory, ed. *Plato:* Protagoras. Indianapolis and New York: Bobbs-Merrill, Library of Liberal Arts, 1956. (See editor's introduction, pp. vii–lvi.)

XX. Pre-Socratic Philosophy and Early Greek Science

Becker, Oskar. *Das mathematische Denken der Antike.* 2d ed. Göttingen: Vandenhoeck & Ruprecht, 1966.

Dicks, D. R. *Early Greek Astronomy to Aristotle.* Ithaca, N.Y.: Cornell University Press, 1970.

von Fritz, *Grundprobleme* (see above, II).

Heath, T. L. *Aristarchus of Samos.* Oxford: Clarendon Press, 1913. (See pp. 1–133, on early Greek astronomy.)

Heidel, W. A. "Antecedents of Greek Corpuscular Theories," *Harvard Studies in Classical Philology,* 22 (1911), 111–72.

Jones, W. H. S. *Philosophy and Medicine in Ancient Greece. Bulletin of the History of Medicine,* Suppl. Vol. 8. Baltimore: Johns Hopkins Press, 1946.

Kahn, Charles H. "On Early Greek Astronomy," *JHS,* 90 (1970), 99–116.

Lloyd, G. E. R. *Early Greek Science: Thales to Aristotle.* London: Chatto & Windus, 1970.

Longrigg, James. "Philosophy and Medicine: Some Early Interactions," *Harvard Studies in Classical Philology,* 67 (1963), 147–75.

Neugebauer, O. *The Exact Sciences in Antiquity.* 2d ed. Providence, R.I.: Brown University Press, 1957.

Szabó, Árpád. "The Transformation of Mathematics into Deductive Science and the Beginnings of its Foundation on Definitions and Axioms," *Scripta Mathematica,* 27 (1964), 27–48a, 113–39. Repr. in the Bobbs-Merrill Reprint Series in the History of Science, HS-71.

van der Waerden, B. L. *Science Awakening.* Trans. by Arnold Dresden. New York: Oxford University Press, 1961.

XXI. Influences of the Pre-Socratics on Classical Philosophy

Cherniss, *Aristotle's Criticism of Presocratic Philosophy* (see V, above).

Cherniss, Harold F. "Parmenides and the *Parmenides* of Plato," *AJP,* 53 (1932), 122–38.

Classen, C. J. "The Creator in Greek Thought from Homer to Plato," *Classica et Mediaevalia,* 23 (1962), 1–22.

Cornford, *Plato and Parmenides* (see X, above).

von Fritz, Kurt. "Zeno of Elea in Plato's *Parmenides.*" In *Serta Turyniana. Essays Presented to Alexander Turyn on his Seventieth Birthday* (Urbana, Ill., forthcoming), pp. 346–58.

Furley, "Aristotle and the Atomists" (see XVIII, above).

Lacey, A. R. "The Eleatics and Aristotle on Some Problems of Change," *Journal of the History of Ideas,* 26 (1965), 451–68.

Owen, "Plato and Parmenides" (see XIII, above).

Rist, J. M. "Parmenides and Plato's *Parmenides,*" *CQ,* N.S. 20 (1970), 221–29.

Solmsen, Friedrich. "Aristotle and Presocratic Cosmology," *Harvard Studies in Classical Philology*, 63 (1958), 265–82.

———. *Aristotle's System of the Physical World: A Comparison with His Predecessors*. Cornell Studies in Classical Philology, 33. Ithaca, N.Y.: Cornell University Press, 1960.

———. "Anaximander's Infinite" (see above, IX).

XXII. HEIDEGGER ON THE PRE-SOCRATICS

Heidegger, Martin. "Der Spruch des Anaximander," *Holzwege*, 3d ed. (Frankfurt a.M.: Vittorio Klostermann, 1957), pp. 296–343.

———. *An Introduction to Metaphysics*. Trans. by Ralph Manheim. New Haven: Yale University Press, 1959.

———. "Logos (Heraklit, Fragment 50)," *Vorträge und Aufsätze*, Teil III, 3d ed. (Pfullingen: Neske, 1967), pp. 3–25.

———. "Moira (Parmenides, Fragment VIII, 34–41)," ibid., pp. 27–52.

———. "Aletheia (Heraklit, Fragment 16)," ibid., pp. 53–78.

———. *What Is Called Thinking?* Trans. by Fred D. Wieck and J. Glenn Gray. New York: Harper & Row, 1968.

Heidegger, Martin and Fink, Eugen. *Heraklit*. Frankfurt a.M.: Vittorio Klostermann, 1970.

Seidel, George J. *Martin Heidegger and the Pre-Socratics*. Lincoln, Neb.: University of Nebraska Press, 1964.

Vick, George R. "Heidegger's Linguistic Rehabilitation of Parmenides' 'Being,' " *American Philosophical Quarterly*, 8 (1971), 139–50.

INDEXES

References to names and subjects that can be located from the Table of Contents (in section headings or in the titles of individual essays) are not indexed. For topics of large scope and for general reference, the reader should also consult the Editor's Introduction, above pp. 1–19.

The four Indexes (I. Ancient Texts; II. Personal Names; III. Glossary and Index of Greek Words Discussed; IV. Subject Index) have been prepared with the assistance of Miss Olga Vorloou and of Messrs. Matthew R. Cosgrove, John Justice, Gary Schouborg, and Stephen Wear.

i. *ANCIENT TEXTS*

Passages are indexed only if the reference involves interpretation, or noteworthy translation, or significant comparison. The standard numerical passage reference (verses, lines, paragraph, fragment, or book section) is shown enclosed in parentheses.

Alcmaeon: (B1), 128 and n. 47
Alexander of Aphrodisias: *In Metaph.* (36.25–27), 523
Anaxagoras: (A41), 497 n. 16; (A43), 494, 496–97; (A45), 491 n. 6; (A46), 491 n. 6, 494; (A52), 490; (B1), 104, 110, 459 n., 469 n. 36, 470 n. 37, 485 n. 80; (B3), 110, 459 n., 470, 491, 502; (B4), 461 and n. 9, 479, 482, 487, 498; (B5), 110; (B6), 277 and n. 10, 459 n., 469, 473 n. 52, 482; (B7), 459 n., 473 and n. 52; (B8), 104, 466, 467, 475; (B10), 464, 470 n. 37, 479, 491 n. 6; (B11), 491; (B12), 114, 277, 463 n. 17, 473 n. 52, 474 and n. 55, 478, 481 n. 72a, 483 n. 76, 491; (B17), 466, 490; (B21a), 75 and nn. 166–67
Anaximander: (A9), 99 ff.; (A10), 305; (A26), 279; (B1), 191 and n. 8
Antiphon: (B9), 284
Archytas: (B1), 178
Aristotle: *Categ.* (10a16), 88
  —*De An.* (I.4), 145 and n. 18; (404a17), 175 and n. 29; (405a25),

207; (408a10–28), 450 n. 69; (409a10–16), 518 n. 22
  —*De Caelo*, 515; (271b9–11), 512; (298b29), 202; (300b25–31), 424; (303a20–24), 512; (303a29–b3), 522; (304a7), 158; (306a26–b2), 513 and n. 17; (308a28 ff.), 484
  —*De Gen. An.* (722b17–29), 424; (769a28 ff.), 464 n. 22
  —*De Gen. et Corr.*, 515; (314a15), 86 n. 1; (314a18), 495; (314a24 ff.), 495; (314a25 ff.), 484; (316a11–14), 509; (316a14–b34), 387 n. 55; (316a17–23), 518; (316a24–34), 509; (316b16–18), 512; (316b18–27), 515 and n. 20–516; (316b28–317a1), 516; (316b33), 508 and n. 6; (317a1–9), 517; (319b10), 87 and n. 4; (324b32–325a12), 505, 524; (325a23–32), 506; (330b4), 109 n. 22; (333a18 ff.), 110
  —*Metaph.* (983b6), 93 n. 20; (984a29–b1), 279; (985b23), 171; (986a15), 148 and n. 27; (986a19), 150 n. 34; (986a22 ff.), 171, 180;

ii. PERSONAL NAMES

iii. GLOSSARY AND INDEX
OF GREEK WORDS DISCUSSED (SELECTION)

Alphabetical order is in accordance with the Latin rather than the Greek alphabet, as required by the transliteration. Note, however, that words starting with χ (chi), η (eta), υ (ypsilon), φ (phi), ψ (psi), or θ (theta) are grouped separately, under the letter complexes CH, Ē, HY, PH, PS, and TH, respectively. Words with initial aspirated letter other than ὑ are grouped under H.

Translations furnish the prima facie or most widely applicable English equivalents. For precise translation, see the passages referred to. The abbreviation "q.v." indicates that there are relevant references in the Subject Index under the word here used for translation. The same abbreviation is also occasionally used for cross references within the Greek Word Index.

A (a)

ADAES (ἀδαές): "obscure/ignorant," 329–31
ADIKEIN (ἀδικεῖν): "to commit injustice against," 100

ADIKIA (ἀδικία): "injustice," 101, 105
AĒR (ἀήρ): "air, mist," 108 n. 22, 110
AGATHON (ἀγαθόν): "good," 376 n. 24
AĪDĒLOS, -A (ἀΐδηλος, pl. -α): "rendering unseen/ invisible," 325–26

AIŌN (αἰών): "lifetime," 111 and n. 28

AIŌNIOS (αἰώνιος): "eternal," 286

AISTHANESTHAI (αἰσθάνεσθαι): "to perceive," 53, 71, 437

AISTHĒSIS (αἴσθησις): "sensation," 41, 43, 67, 71, 72, 76, 78, 82–85

AITHERION (αἰθέριον): "heavenly," 329–31

AITHĒR (αἰθήρ): "ether, sky," 108 n. 22, 110, 211 and n. 39

AITION (αἴτιον): "cause," 116

AKOUSMATA (ἀκούσματα): "secret doctrines," 147

ALĒTHEIA (ἀλήθεια): "truth," 301. See also Real, the; Real(ity) vs. appearances; "What-is"

ALLOIŌSIS (ἀλλοίωσις): "qualitative change," 86–95

AMPHILLOGIAI (ἀμφιλλογίαι): "double talk," 316 and n. 16. See also Amphilogy

ANATHYMIASIS (ἀναθυμίασις): "evaporation" (q.v.), 91, 207 n. 26. See also Exhalation

ANHARMOSTIA (ἀναρμοστία): "absence of proper arrangement," 147

ANOĒMŌN (ἀνοήμων): "unintelligent," 80 n. 180

ANTIA, TA (ἀντία, τά) neuter pl. of ἀντίος, q.v. See also ENANTIOS

ANTIOS (ἀντίος): "contrary," 318. See also ENANTIOS

APATHEIA (ἀπάθεια): "imperviousness," 524

APEIRON (ἄπειρον): "boundless" (q.v.), 107 n. 21, 108, 142, 150, 199, 355, 358. See also Infinite, the; Infinite (adj.); Unlimited

ARCHĒ, -AI (ἀρχή, pl. -αί): "principle," 204–7, 522

ATHANASIA (ἀθανασία): "deathlessness," 436. See also Immortality

ATHREIN (ἀθρεῖν): "to gaze at," 58

CH (χ)

CHAUNOS (χαῦνος): "empty," 345

CHŌRA (χώρα): "field," 158

CHRĒMA, -TA (χρῆμα, pl. -τα): "thing," 463 n. 16

CHREŌN (χρεών): "required," 101

CHRĒSTON (χρηστόν): "useful," 121 and n. 9

CHROIA (χροιά): "colored surface," 94, 153

CHRONOS (χρόνος): "time" (q.v.), 111 n. 28

CHYMOS (χυμός): "humor" (q.v.), 472

D (δ)

DAIMŌN (δαίμων): See Daimon (Index IV)

DEILOS (δειλός): "miserable," 431

DIAKOSMEŌ (διακοσμέω): "divide and marshal," 318

DIAKOSMOS (διάκοσμος): "divided array," 297 n. b, 318

DIDONAI DIKĒN (διδόναι δίκην): "to give compensation," 105. See also TISIS; Reparation

DIKĒ (δίκη): "justice" (q.v.), 105, 116

DIZĒSIS (δίζησις): "quest," 338

DOKEI MOI (δοκεῖ μοι): "it seems to me," 128

DOKIMOS, -ON (δόκιμος, -ον): "acceptable," 128, 131

DOKOS (δόκος): "opinion," 34 n. 39, 128

DOXA (δόξα): "opinion, appearance," 53, 128, 246; Platonic, 128 n. 43, 246; in Parmenides, 293–311 passim. See also "Doxa" (part of Parmenides' poem); Appearance vs. reality

DOXASTON, TO (δοξαστόν, τό): "what is believed," 245, 247

DOXAZEIN (δοξάζειν): "to believe," 247

DYNAMIS (δύναμις): "power" (q.v.), 110, 471 and n. 43

E (ε)

EIDENAI (εἰδέναι): "to know," 123, 124 n. 20, 244–45. See also OIDA; GIGNŌSKEIN; EPISTASTHAI; NOEIN; Knowing, conception of

EIDOS (εἶδος): "form" (q.v.), 153. See also IDEA; MORPHĒ

EIDŌS (εἰδώς): "man who knows," 123, 124 and n. 20

EINAI (εἶναι): "to be," 45. See also EON; ESTI; ON; Being; Predication; Existence; "What-is"

EKPYRŌSIS (ἐκπύρωσις): "conflagration," 107 n. 19

ELAPHRON (ἐλαφρόν): "slight, nimble," 329–31

ELENCHOS (ἔλεγχος). See Elenchus (Index IV)

EMBRITHES (ἐμβριθές): "grave," 329–31

ENANTIA (ἐναντία): neuter pl. of ENANTIOS, q.v.

ENANTIOS (ἐναντίος): "contrary," 318, 383, 389

EOIKŌS, -TA (ἐοικώς, -ότα): "seeming," 297 n. b, 317–19

EON (ἐόν): Ionic form of ὄν (ON), "what-

son," in Heraclitus, 40–42, 110,
191–92, 194–95, 223–25; in Sextus
Empiricus, 42 n. 68, 43, 83; "proportion," 158, 209, 474 n. 59. *See
also* Logos, the (Heraclitus)

M (μ)

MALISTA (μάλιστα): "most, especially,"
126

MALLON (μᾶλλον): "more, rather," 126

MANIĒ (μανίη): "madness," 430. *See also*
Ecstasy

MATHEIN (μαθεῖν): "to learn," 36

-MATHIĒ (-μαθίη), "-learning," 36–37

MEGETHOS (μέγεθος): "bulk," 110, 386,
391 n. 63. *See also* Magnitude

MEIGMA (μεῖγμα): "mixture" (*q.v.*), 306

MELEA (μέλεα): "limbs," 342 and n. 69

MELEOS (μέλεος): "vain, idle," 342 n. 69

MERIMNA, -AI (μέριμνα, *pl.* -αι): "care(s),"
59, 60, 81

METABASIS (μετάβασις): "running over,"
361

METECHEIN (μετέχειν): "to participate in,"
95

METHEXIS (μέθεξις): "participation," 95,
141 and n. 9

METRON, -A (μέτρον, *pl.* -α): "measure(s)"
(*q.v.*), 191, 193–96, 210

MĒ ON (μὴ ὄν): "What-is-not" (*q.v.*), 73

MĒTIESTHAI (μητίεσθαι): "to ponder," 59,
81

MĒTIS (μῆτις): "wisdom," 59, 60, 81

MIMEISTHAI (μιμεῖσθαι): "to represent,"
136, 142, 153, 159

MIMĒSIS (μίμησις): "representation," 140–
41, 174 and n. 27. *See also* Imitation

MIXIS (μῖξις): "mixture" (*q.v.*), 89–91, 348

MOIRA, -AI (μοῖρα, *pl.* -αι): "portion(s),"
(*q.v.*), 474 nn. 59, 60

MONAS, -DES (μονάς, *pl.* -άδες): "unit(s),"
414. *See also* Monad, the; Unit,
the; Units

MORPHĒ, -AI (μορφή, *pl.* -αί): "form(s)"
(*q.v.*), 153, 329–31, 374. *See also*
EIDOS; IDEA

N (ν)

NASTOS (ναστός): "solid," 525

NOEIN (νοεῖν): "to know, to think," 437,
439 n. 34. *See also the derivatives*
NOĒMA; NOOS; NOUS; *also* GIGNŌS-
KEIN; EIDENAI; EPISTASTHAI; OIDA;
Knowing, conception of

NOĒMA (νόημα): "thought," 23–95 passim,
437, 439

NOMOS (νόμος): "law, custom," vs. physis,
75, 311, 296–97

NOMŌI (νόμῳ): *dative sing. of* nomos, *q.v.*

NOOS (νόος, *uncontracted form of* νοῦς):
"mind," 23–85 passim, 202. *See
also* NOUS; PHRĒN; Mind, conception of

NOUS (νοῦς, *contracted form of* νόος):
"mind," in Aristotle, 435; in Empedocles, 446

NYKTIPHAES (νυκτιφαές): "night-shining,"
314, 324

O (o)

OIDA (οἶδα): "I know," 125. *See also*
EIDENAI

ON, -TA (ὄν, *pl.* -τα): "being thing(s),"
102–4, 242–48. *See also* EON; Being;
Real, the; "What-is"

ONKOS (ὄγκος): "body," 363, 365, 383

OURANOS (οὐρανός): "heaven, universe,"
111

OUSIA (οὐσία): "substance," 70 n. 147

P (π)

PACHOS (πάχος): "bulk," 357, 383, 387 n.
53, 391 n. 63

PALAMĒ (παλάμη): "open hand," 58

PANSPERMIA (πανσπερμία): "general
seed-mixture," 496

PAREINAI (παρεῖναι): "to be present in,"
95

PARELKEIN (παρέλκειν): "to be redundant," 121 and n. 8

PARISTASTHAI (παρίστασθαι): "to occur to
one," 342

PEIRAS, -TA (πεῖρας, *pl.* -τα): "limit(s)"
(*q.v.*), 348

PERAINONTA (περαίνοντα): "limiting (*pl.*)"
(*q.v.*), 300 and n. 4. *See also* PERAS

PERAS (πέρας): "limit" (*q.v.*), 199. *See also*
PEIRAS

PERICHŌRĒSIS (περιχώρησις): "(cosmic)
revolution," 114

PERILAMBANEIN (περιλαμβάνειν): "to encompass," 57–58

PISTIS (πίστις): "faith," 339, 348, 428 and
n. 5

PLANKTOS (πλαγκτός): "wandering"
(*q.v.*), 48–49, 53–54. *See also* POLY-
PLANKTOS

PLEIONA, TA (πλείονα, τά): *variant form of*
PLEONA, TA, *q.v.*

PLEON (πλέον): "more, full," 341–42, 343
and n. 76, 344–45

PLEONA, TA (πλέονα, τά): "the many," 402, 409

PLĒ- (πλη-) words: *signify* "fulfillment," 345. *See also* Fullness

PLĒRĒS (πλήρης): "full," 345

PLEROŌ (πληρόω): "I fill full of," 344–45

PNEUMA (πνεῦμα): "breathed air," 172, 176, 183

POION (ποιόν): "such-like, quality," 69, 70 n. 147. *See also* POIOTĒS; Quality

POIOTĒS, -TĒTES (ποιότης, *pl.* -τητες): "quality" (*q.v.*), 69, 471

POLLA (πολλά): "many" (*q.v.*), 368–93 passim

POLYPLANKTOS (πολύπλαγκτος): "much led astray," 48, 307, 342 and n. 70. *See also* PLANKTOS; "Wandering"

POTE (ποτέ): "at some time," 274

PRAPIDES (πραπίδες): "organ of thought," 59, 60

PRĒSTĒR (πρηστήρ): "fiery waterspout," 208 n. 30, 225

PROSŌPON (πρόσωπον): "person," 436 n. 24

PYKINON (πυκινόν): "thick/wise," 329–31

PH (φ)

PHAINESTHAI (φαίνεσθαι): "to appear," 68, 389. *See also* PHIANOMENON; Appearance(s) vs. reality

PHAINOMENON, -A (φαινόμενον, *pl.* -a): "appearance(s)," 42 n. 68, 75–76, 78. *See also* PHAINESTHAI; Appearance(s) vs. reality

PHANTASIA (φαντασία): "appearance," 68

PHATIZEIN (φατίζειν): "to express," 47

PHILIA (φιλία): "friendship," 137–38, 152. *See also* PHILOTĒS; Love

PHILOTĒS (φιλότης): "love" (*q.v.*), 433, 445, 452 n. 70. *See also* PHILIA

PHORA (φορά): "motion," 87, 88 n. 8

PHRĒN, -ES (φρήν, *pl.* -ες): "mind," 33–34, 37, 60–61, 74–81 passim, 84–85, 439 n. 34, 450 n. 68, 453. *See also* NOOS; Mind, conception of

PHRONEEIN (φρονέειν): *uncontracted form of phronein, q.v.*

PHRONEIN (φρονεῖν): "to be of a mind to, be aware of," 34, 37, 50, 53, 81, 83–85, 344, 437, 439 n. 34

PHRONĒSIS (φρόνησις): "intent awareness," 32–34, 59

PHYESTHAI (φύεσθαι): "to grow," 402–3

PHYSEI (φύσει): *dative of* PHYSIS, *q.v.*

PHYSIKOS, -OI (φυσικός, *pl.* -οί): "natural philosopher(s)," 292–93, 305–6

PHYSIS (φύσις): "essence, nature," 232–33, 344, 438–39; vs. NOMOS, 75, 296–97, 311

PS (ψ)

PSYCHĒ (ψυχή): "soul" (*q.v.*), 175, 436, 439 n. 34, 452 n. 70, 456

S (σ)

SAPHES, TO (σαφές, τό): "truth," 123 and n. 18, 127 and n. 35, 130

SCHĒMA (σχῆμα): "form" (*q.v.*), 153. *See also* EIDOS; IDEA

SĒMA, -TA (σῆμα, *pl.* -τα): "sign(s)" (*q.v.*), 333, 337

SOPHIĒ (σοφίη): "skill, wisdom," 118 n.1

SŌMA (σῶμα): "body," 357

SPERMA, -TŌN (σπέρμα, *genitive* -των): "seed" (*q.v.*), 157, 463 n. 17

SPHAIROS (Σφαῖρος). *See* Sphere, the, in Empedocles

STOICHEION (στοιχεῖον): "element," 204–5

STYGEROS (στυγερός): "abominable," 338 and n. 56

SYMMIXIS (σύμμιξις): "co-mingling," 461 n. 10. *See also* MIXIS; Mixture

SYMPAN, TO (σύμπαν, τό): "the totality of things," 482 n. 73

SYMPHŌNIA (συμφωνία): "concord" (*q.v.*), 145–46, 158

SYNKRISIS (σύγκρισις): "compounding," 461 n. 10

SYNODOS (σύνοδος): "coming together," 403, 407, 408

T (τ)

TANTIA (τἀντία): "contrariwise," 303. *See also* ANTIA, TA; Opposites

TAXIS (τάξις): "array, assessment," 116. *See also* Order

TEL- (τελ-) words: *signify* "accomplishment," 340, 345

TETELESMENON (τετελεσμένον): "actual, perfect," 125–26, 345, 348

TETRAKTYS (τετρακτύς): Pythagorean symbol of the, 147–48, 150, 152, 156

TISIS (τίσις): "retribution," 116. *See also* Reparation

TYCHĒ (τύχη): "fortune," 126

TYNCHANŌ (τυγχάνω): "I happen to, succeed in," 126 and n. 28

TH (θ)

THANATOS (θάνατος): "Death," 295

THEOS (θεός): "god " (*q.v.*), 433

THEŌRIA (θεωρία): "intellectual contemplation," 137, 142

THIASOS (θίασος): "group," 141

THNĒTA, -ŌN (θνητά, *genitive* -ῶν): "mortal things," 403, 408–10

THYMOS (θυμός): "spirit," 34, 85

X (ξ)

XYNON (ξυνόν). *See* KOINON

iv. *SUBJECT INDEX*

NOTES ON CONTRIBUTORS

F. M. CORNFORD, 1874–1943, was Laurence Professor of Ancient Philosophy and Fellow of Trinity College in the University of Cambridge.

HERMANN FRÄNKEL is Emeritus Professor of Classics at Stanford University.

KURT VON FRITZ is Emeritus Professor of Classical Philology at the University of Munich. In the period 1937–54 he was Professor of Classics at Columbia University. He has also taught at the Free University of Berlin and at Reed College, Oregon.

DAVID J. FURLEY is Professor of Classics at Princeton University. He had previously taught at University College, London.

MONTGOMERY FURTH is Professor of Philosophy at the University of California, Los Angeles.

W. K. C. GUTHRIE has been Master of Downing College and Laurence Professor of Ancient Philosophy in the University of Cambridge.

W. A. HEIDEL, 1868–1941, was Research Professor of Greek at Wesleyan University, Middletown, Connecticut.

UVO HÖLSCHER is Professor of Classical Philology at the University of Munich. He had previously taught at the University of Heidelberg and at the Free University of Berlin.

CHARLES H. KAHN is Professor of Philosophy at the University of Pennsylvania. He had previously taught in Classics at Columbia University.

G. S. KIRK is Professor of Greek at the University of Bristol, and is Regius Professor of Greek elect in the University of Cambridge. He had also previously taught at Yale University.

G. B. KERFERD is Hulme Professor of Greek at the University of Manchester.

A. A. LONG is Gladstone Professor of Greek in the University of Liverpool.

ALEXANDER P. D. MOURELATOS is Professor of Philosophy at The University of Texas at Austin.

G. E. L. OWEN is Laurence Professor of Ancient Philosophy in the University of Cambridge. He had previously been Professor of Philosophy and the Classics at Harvard University, and Professor of Ancient Philosophy and Fellow of Corpus Christi College at Oxford University.

KARL REINHARDT, 1886–1958, was Professor of Classical Philology at the University of Frankfurt.

FRIEDRICH SOLMSEN is Moses Slaughter Professor at the Institute for Research in the Humanities and the Department of Classics at The University of Wisconsin, Madison. He had previously taught at Cornell University.

GREGORY VLASTOS is Stuart Professor of Philosophy at Princeton University. He had previously taught at Cornell University and at The Queen's University in Kingston, Ontario.